Catalog of
American Car
I D Numbers
1970-79

Compiled by the Staff of Cars & Parts Magazine

Published by
Amos Press Inc.
911 Vandemark Road
Sidney, Ohio 45365

Publishers of
Cars & Parts
The Magazine Serving the Car Hobbyist

Catalog of American ID Numbers 1960-69

Printed and bound in the United States of America

Library of Congress Cataloging-In-Publication Data
ISBN 0-87938-518-9

ACKNOWLEDGEMENTS

The staff of *Cars & Parts* Magazine devoted more than a year to the research and development of the Catalog of American Car ID Numbers 1970-79. It has been a labor-intensive project which required assistance from hundreds of car collectors, clubs, researchers, and a tremendous amount of interviewing and photography at car shows, swap meets and auctions.

This book wouldn't have been possible without very special help from the following:

Motor Vehicle Manufacturers Association
Dan Kirchner - Researcher
Tom Hinson - Computer Programmer
Chrysler Corporation
Automotive History Collection of the
    Detroit Public Library
Ford Motor Company

In addition, there were others who helped enormously in specific areas, including Greg Donahue, Chuck Kuhn, Jeff Kennedy, and others. Thank you for making this book possible.

Catalog of
American Car
I D Numbers
1970-79

Compiled by the Staff of Cars & Parts Magazine

The information contained in The Catalog of American ID Numbers 1970-79 was compiled from a variety of sources including original manufacturers' catalogs (when available) and official published shop manuals. The *Cars & Parts* staff and researchers made every attempt to verify the information contained herein. However, many manufacturers made changes from year-to-year and model-to-model, as well as during mid-year production. And, in some instances, conflicting information and reports surfaced during the course of our indepth research. As a result, *Cars & Parts* does not guarantee the absolute accuracy of all data presented in this ID catalog.

INTRODUCTION

Authentication has become such a critical issue within the old car hobby that the need for a comprehensive, accurate and dependable identification guide has become quite apparent to anyone involved in buying, selling, restoring, judging, owning, researching or appraising a collector car. With this indepth and detailed ID guide, the staff of *Cars & Parts* magazine has compiled as much data as possible on the years and makes covered to help take the fear out of buying a collector car.

Deciphering trim codes, verifying vehicle identification numbers (VIN), interpreting body codes and authenticating engine numbers will become a much easier process with this guide at your side. Putting this information at your fingertips has not been a simple task, but one worth the tremendous time and money spent on its production.

Each car manufacturer used a different system of identification and changed its system almost annually in the '70s. The *Cars & Parts* staff has developed the most consistent information possible from year to year for each manufacturer. Some data are not presented due to lack of availability, space, time considerations, and the researchers' inability to verify sources.

Each corporation, division, year, model, VIN, body plate and engine number required decisions about what to print. The staff of *Cars & Parts* is justifiably proud of this book and invites your comments. Additional information is especially welcome.

The information contained in the Catalog of American ID Numbers 1970-79 was compiled from a variety of sources including original manufacturers' catalogs (when available) and official published shop manuals. The *Cars & Parts* staff and researchers made every attempt to verify the information contained herein. However, many manufacturers made changes from year-to-year and model-to-model, as well as during mid-year production. And, in some instances, conflicting information and reports surfaced during the course of our indepth research. As a result, *Cars & Parts* does not guarantee the absolute accuracy of all data presented in this ID catalog.

HOW TO USE THIS CATALOG

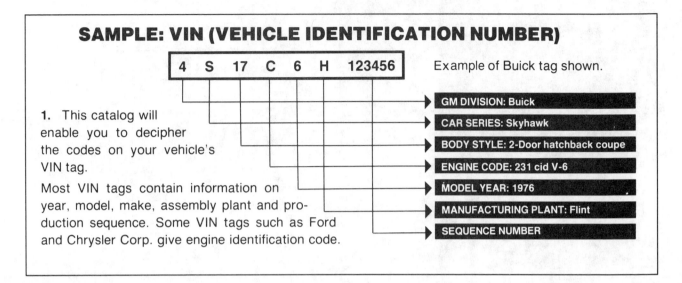

SAMPLE: VIN (VEHICLE IDENTIFICATION NUMBER)

| 4 | S | 17 | C | 6 | H | 123456 |

Example of Buick tag shown.

1. This catalog will enable you to decipher the codes on your vehicle's VIN tag.

Most VIN tags contain information on year, model, make, assembly plant and production sequence. Some VIN tags such as Ford and Chrysler Corp. give engine identification code.

- **GM DIVISION:** Buick
- **CAR SERIES:** Skyhawk
- **BODY STYLE:** 2-Door hatchback coupe
- **ENGINE CODE:** 231 cid V-6
- **MODEL YEAR:** 1976
- **MANUFACTURING PLANT:** Flint
- **SEQUENCE NUMBER**

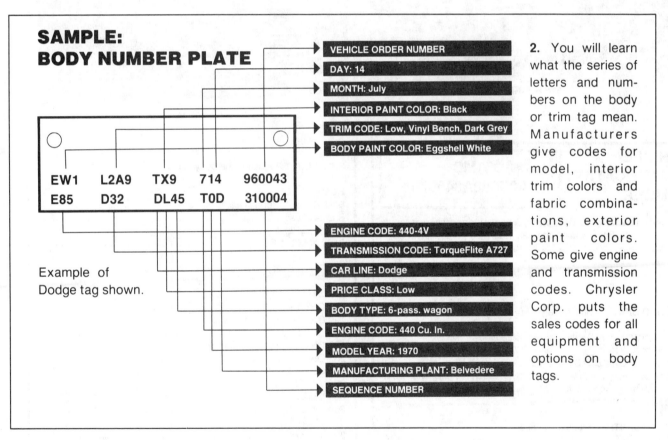

SAMPLE: BODY NUMBER PLATE

| EW1 | L2A9 | TX9 | 714 | 960043 |
| E85 | D32 | DL45 | T0D | 310004 |

- **VEHICLE ORDER NUMBER**
- **DAY:** 14
- **MONTH:** July
- **INTERIOR PAINT COLOR:** Black
- **TRIM CODE:** Low, Vinyl Bench, Dark Grey
- **BODY PAINT COLOR:** Eggshell White

- **ENGINE CODE:** 440-4V
- **TRANSMISSION CODE:** TorqueFlite A727
- **CAR LINE:** Dodge
- **PRICE CLASS:** Low
- **BODY TYPE:** 6-pass. wagon
- **ENGINE CODE:** 440 Cu. In.
- **MODEL YEAR:** 1970
- **MANUFACTURING PLANT:** Belvedere
- **SEQUENCE NUMBER**

Example of Dodge tag shown.

2. You will learn what the series of letters and numbers on the body or trim tag mean. Manufacturers give codes for model, interior trim colors and fabric combinations, exterior paint colors. Some give engine and transmission codes. Chrysler Corp. puts the sales codes for all equipment and options on body tags.

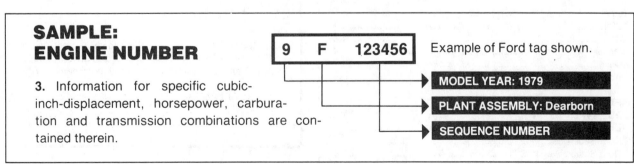

SAMPLE: ENGINE NUMBER

| 9 | F | 123456 |

Example of Ford tag shown.

3. Information for specific cubic-inch-displacement, horsepower, carburation and transmission combinations are contained therein.

- **MODEL YEAR:** 1979
- **PLANT ASSEMBLY:** Dearborn
- **SEQUENCE NUMBER**

1970 GREMLIN

1970 REBEL

1970 HORNET

1970 JAVELIN

VEHICLE IDENTIFICATION NUMBER

AMC
A0S050A345678

Located on the top of the dash on the driver's side and visible through the windshield from outside the car. It is also printed on a non-removable label affixed to the left front door adjacent to the door latch.

FIRST DIGIT: Identifies the Division (A=American Motors Corporation)

SECOND DIGIT: Identifies the year (0=1970)

THIRD DIGIT: Identifies the transmission type

TRANSMISSION	CODE
Standard Column Shift 3-Spd	S
Automatic Column Shift 3-Spd	A
Shift Command Console Mtd	C
4-Spd Floor Shift Floor Mtd	M

FOURTH DIGIT: Identifies the series

SERIES	CODE
Hornet	0
Rebel	1
AMX	3
Gremlin	4
Javelin	7
Ambassador	8

FIFTH DIGIT: Identifies the body type

BODY TYPE	CODE
4-Door Sedan	5
2-Door Sedan	6
4-Door Station Wagon	8
Hardtop	9

SIXTH DIGIT: Identifies the body class

BODY CLASS	CODE
Basic-Hornet, Rebel, Gremlin	0
Basic-Ambassador	2
Javelin, DPL, 4-Pass. Gremlin	5
SST, AMX (All SSTs)	7

SEVENTH DIGIT: Identifies the engine

ENGINE	CODE
199 OHV Six, 1V	A
199 OHV Six, 1V (Low Comp)	B
232 OHV Six, 1V	E
232 OHV Six, 1V (Low Comp)	F
232 OHV Six, 2V	G
232 OHV Six, 2V (Low Comp)	Q
304 V8, 2V	H
304 V8, 2V (Low Comp)	I
360 V8, 2V	N
360 V8, 4V	P
390 V8, 2V	S
390 V8, 4V, 325 HP	X
390 V8, 4V, 340 HP	Y

LAST SIX DIGITS: Represent the assembly plant and the basic production sequence. Kenosha-built bodies start with body number 000001. Brampton-built bodies start with body number 700001.

ASSEMBLY PLANT	CODE
Kenosha, WI	1-6
Brampton, Ont., CAN	7-9

1

BODY NUMBER PLATE

The body number plate is located on the left front door adjacent to the door latch. This plate identifies the model year, car division, series, body style, body assembly plant, body numbers, trim combination, paint code and build date code.

```
        AMERICAN MOTORS
          CORPORATION

   UNDER THE UNITED STATES NATIONAL
  TRAFFIC AND MOTOR VEHICLE SAFETY ACT
   OF 1966, CERTIFIES TO THE DEALER THAT
     THIS VEHICLE MEETS ALL FEDERAL MOTOR
    VEHICLE SAFETY STANDARDS APPLICABLE
       ON THE DATE OF MANUFACTURE.

   ADVANCED UNIT CONSTRUCTION COMBINES
     BODY AND FRAME INTO A SINGLE ALL
    WELDED STRUCTURAL UNIT DEEP-DIP
   PRIMER PAINT GALVANIZED STEEL SECTIONS.
   PLUS LUSTRE GARD BAKED ACRYLIC ENAMEL
      PROTECT AGAINST BODY RUST.


      BODY K        074332
      MODEL 70      06 5
      TRIM          043S
      PAINT         82A
```

Example:

Body
K ....Kenosha Assembly Plant
074332 ....Production Sequence

Model
70 ....Model Year (1970)
06 ....Body Type (2-Door Sedan)
5 ....Body Class

Trim
0 ....Model Year (1970)
4 ....Series (Gremlin)
3 ....Blue
S ....Split-Back Bench

Paint
82A ....Bayshore Blue Metallic

HORNET 01 SERIES	CODE
4-Door Sedan	7005-0
4-Door Sedan SST	7005-7
2-Door Sedan	7006-0
2-Door Sedan SST	7006-7

REBEL 10 SERIES	CODE
4-Door Sedan	7015-0
4-Door Sedan SST	7015-7
4-Door Station Wagon	7018-0
4-Door Station Wagon SST	7018-7
2-Door Hardtop	7019-0
2-Door Hardtop SST	7019-7

*The Machine option available

AMX 30 SERIES	CODE
2-Door Sports Coupe	7039-7

GREMLIN 40 SERIES	CODE
2-Passenger	7046-0
4-Passenger	7046-5

JAVELIN 70 SERIES	CODE
2-Door Hardtop	7079-5
2-Door Hardtop SST	7079-7

AMBASSADOR 80 SERIES	CODE
4-Door Sedan	7085-2
4-Door Sedan DPL	7085-5
4-Door Sedan SST	7085-7
4-Door Station Wagon DPL	7088-5
4-Door Station Wagon SST	7088-7
2-Door Hardtop DPL	7089-5
2-Door Hardtop SST	7089-7

THE TRIM CODE furnishes the key to the interior color and material scheme.

HORNET 2-DOOR/4-DOOR SEDAN TRIM

COLOR	CLOTH	VINYL	LEATHER	CODE
White		•		021
Black	•	•		041
Black/White	•			021
Blue	•	•		023
Blue		•		043
Green	•	•		024
Green		•		044
Red	•	•		025
Red	•			045

REBEL 4-DR SDN/4-DR WGN/2-DR HDTP TRIM

COLOR	CLOTH	VINYL	LEATHER	CODE
Blue	•	•		053
Green	•	•		054
Brown	•	•		056
Black		•		051

REBEL SST & MACHINE TRIM

COLOR	CLOTH	VINYL	LEATHER	CODE
Black	•	•		071/071*
Black		•		051*+
Blue	•	•		073/071*
Blue		•		053*+
Green	•	•		074
Brown	•	•		076
Brown		•		056*+
Red		•		075/075*

*Bucket seats
+Machine hardtop only

AMX SPORTS COUPE TRIM

COLOR	CLOTH	VINYL	LEATHER	CODE
Black		•	•	031*
Blue		•		033*
Red		•	•	035*
Brown		•		036*

*Bucket seats

GREMLIN 2-DOOR SEDAN TRIM

COLOR	CLOTH	VINYL	LEATHER	CODE
Black		•		001/011*
White		•		008
Blue		•		013/013*
Green		•		014/014*
Red		•		015/015*

*Bucket seats

JAVELIN 2-DOOR HARDTOP TRIM

COLOR	CLOTH	VINYL	LEATHER	CODE
Black		•		061*
Blue		•		063*
Green		•		064*
Red		•		065*
Brown		•		066*

*Bucket seats

JAVELIN SST TRIM

COLOR	CLOTH	VINYL	LEATHER	CODE
Black	•	•	•	061*
Blue	•	•		063*
Green	•	•		064*
Red	•		•	065*
Brown	•	•	•	066*

*Bucket seats

AMBASSADOR 4-DOOR SEDAN TRIM

COLOR	CLOTH	VINYL	LEATHER	CODE
Black		•		081
Blue	•	•		083
Green	•	•		084
Brown	•	•		086

AMBASSADOR SST TRIM

COLOR	CLOTH	VINYL	LEATHER	CODE
Black	•	•		091+
Blue	•	•		093+
Green	•	•		094
Red		•		095
Brown	•	•		096

+Optional velour fabric

AMBASSADOR DPL TRIM

COLOR	CLOTH	VINYL	LEATHER	CODE
Black	•	•		091
Blue	•	•		093
Green	•	•		094
Brown	•	•		096
Red		•		095

THE PAINT CODE furnishes the key to the paint colors used on the car. Two, two-digit codes indicate the bottom and top body colors respectively. NOTE: For two-tone bodies, first number designates lower body color, second number designates upper body color.

COLOR	CODE
Classic Black	1A
Big Bad Blue	2A
Big Bad Orange	3A
Big Bad Green	4A
Red, White and Blue	25A
Matador Red	39A
Hialeah Yellow	58A
Frost White	72A
Bittersweet Orange Metallic	79A
Bayshore Blue Metallic	82A
Commodore Blue Metallic	84A
Sea Foam Aqua Metallic	85A
Mosport Green Metallic	86A
Glen Green Metallic	87A
Golden Lime Metallic	90A
Tijuana Tan Metallic	91A
Moroccan Brown Metallic	94A
Sonic Silver Metallic	95A

ENGINE NUMBER

The engine code number is located on a tag which is attached to the right bank cylinder head cover. The cubic inch displacement is cast into the cylinder block on both banks between the first and second core plug location.

ENGINE CODE	NO CYL	CID	HORSE-POWER	COMP. RATIO	CARB
HORNET					
A	6	199	128	8.5:1	1 BC
B	6	199	N/A	N/A	1 BC
E	6	232	145	8.5:1	1 BC
F	6	232	N/A	N/A	1 BC
G	6	232	155	8.5:1	2 BC
Q	6	232	N/A	N/A	2 BC
HORNET SST					
E	6	232	145	8.5:1	1 BC
F	6	232	N/A	N/A	1 BC
G	6	232	155	8.5:1	2 BC
Q	6	232	N/A	N/A	2 BC
H	8	304	210	9.0:1	2 BC
I	8	304	N/A	N/A	2 BC
REBEL					
E	6	232	145	8.5:1	1 BC
F	6	232	N/A	N/A	1 BC
G	6	232	155	8.5:1	2 BC
Q	6	232	N/A	N/A	2 BC
H	8	304	210	9.0:1	2 BC
I	8	304	N/A	N/A	2 BC
N	8	360	245	9.0:1	2 BC
P	8	360	290	10.0:1	4 BC
X	8	390	325	10.0:1	4 BC
MACHINE					
Y	8	390	340	10.0:1	4 BC
AMX					
P	8	360	290	10.0:1	4 BC
X	8	390	325	10.0:1	4 BC
Y	8	390	340	10.0:1	4 BC
GREMLIN					
A	6	199	128	8.5:1	1 BC
B	6	199	N/A	N/A	1 BC
E	6	232	145	8.5:1	1 BC
F	6	232	N/A	N/A	1 BC
JAVELIN					
E	6	232	145	8.5:1	1 BC
F	6	232	N/A	N/A	1 BC
H	8	304	210	9.0:1	2 BC
I	8	304	N/A	N/A	2 BC
N	8	360	245	9.0:1	2 BC
P	8	360	290	10.0:1	4 BC
X	8	390	325	10.0:1	4 BC
Y	8	390	340	10.0:1	4 BC
AMBASSADOR					
G	6	232	155	8.5:1	2 BC
Q	6	232	N/A	N/A	2 BC
H	8	304	210	9.0:1	2 BC
I	8	304	N/A	N/A	2 BC
N	8	360	245	9.0:1	2 BC
P	8	360	290	10.0:1	4 BC
AMBASSADOR DPL/SST					
H	8	304	210	9.0:1	2 BC
I	8	304	N/A	N/A	2 BC
N	8	360	245	9.0:1	2 BC
P	8	360	290	10.0:1	4 BC
X	8	390	325	10.0:1	4 BC

1971 AMBASSADOR

1971 MATADOR

1971 HORNET

1971 JAVELIN AMX

1971 JAVELIN

1971 JAVELIN AMX

VEHICLE IDENTIFICATION NUMBER

AMC
A1S465E123456

Located on the top of the dash on the driver's side and visible through the windshield from outside the car. It is also printed on a non-removable label affixed to the left front door adjacent to the door latch.

FIRST DIGIT: Identifies the Division (A=American Motors Corporation)

SECOND DIGIT: Identifies the year (1=1971)

THIRD DIGIT: Identifies the transmission type

TRANSMISSION	CODE
Standard Column Shift, 3-Spd	S
Floor Shift, 3-Spd	F
Automatic Column Shift, 3-Spd	A
Automatic Floor Shift, Console	C
Floor Shift, 4-Spd	M

FOURTH DIGIT: Identifies the series

SERIES	CODE
Hornet	0
Matador	1
Gremlin	4
Javelin	7
Ambassador	8

FIFTH DIGIT: Identifies the body type

BODY TYPE	CODE
4-Door Sedan	5
2-Door Sedan	6
Station Wagon	8
2-Door Hardtop	9

SIXTH DIGIT: Identifies the body class

BODY CLASS	CODE
Hornet or Gremlin 2-Passenger	0
SC360 Hornet	1
Ambassador DPL	2
Gremlin 4-Passenger, Javelin, Ambassador SST	5
Hornet SST, Hornet Sportabout, Matador, Javelin SST, Ambassador Brougham	7
Javelin AMX	8

SEVENTH DIGIT: Identifies the engine

ENGINE	CODE
258 OHV 6	A
258 OHV 6 (Low Comp)	B
232 OHV 6	E
232 OHV 6 (Low Comp)	F
304 V8, 2 bbl	H
304 V8, 2 bbl (Low Comp)	I
360 V8, 2 bbl	N
360 V8, 4 bbl	P
401 V8, 4 bbl	Z

LAST SIX DIGITS: Represent the assembly plant and the basic production sequence. Kenosha-built bodies start with body number 000001. Brampton-built bodies start with body number 700001.

ASSEMBLY PLANT	CODE
Kenosha, WI	100,001 - 699,999
Brampton, Ont., CAN	700,000 - 1,000,000

BODY NUMBER PLATE

The body number plate is located on the left front door adjacent to the door latch. This plate identifies the model year, car division, series, body style, body assembly plant, body numbers, trim combination, paint code and build date code.

BODY K	023465
MODEL 71	06 5
TRIM	143S
PAINT	2A

Example:

Body

K	Kenosha Assembly Plant
023465	Production Sequence

Model

71	Model Year (1971)
06	Body Type (2-Door Sedan)
5	Body Class

Trim

1	Model Year (1971)
4	Series (Gremlin)
3	Blue
S	Split-Back Bench

Paint

A4	Skyline Blue

HORNET	CODE
4-Door Sedan	7105-0
4-Door Sedan SST	7105-7
2-Door Sedan	7106-0
2-Door Sedan SC360	7106-1
2-Door Sedan SST	7106-7
Station Wagon (Sportabout)	7108-7

MATADOR	CODE
4-Door Sedan	7115-7
Station Wagon	7118-7
2-Door Hardtop	7119-7

GREMLIN	CODE
2-Passenger	7146-0
4-Passenger	7146-5*

*Gremlin "X" Option Pakcge

JAVELIN	CODE
2-Door Hardtop	7179-5
2-Door Hardtop SST	7179-7
2-Door Hardtop AMX	7179-8

AMBASSADOR	CODE
4-Door Sedan DPL	7185-2
4-Door Sedan SST	7185-5
4-Door Sedan Brougham	7185-7
Station Wagon SST	7188-5
Station Wagon Brougham	7188-7
2-Door Hardtop SST	7189-5
2-Door Hardtop Brougham	7189-7

THE TRIM CODE furnishes the key to the interior color and material scheme.

HORNET 2-DOOR/4-DOOR TRIM

COLOR	CLOTH	VINYL	LEATHER	CODE
Black	•			21
Blue	•			23
Green	•			24
White		•		28

HORNET SST, SC/360/SPORTABOUT TRIM

COLOR	CLOTH	VINYL	LEATHER	CODE
Black	•	•		41
Blue	•	•		43
Green	•	•		44
Red	•	•		45

JAVELIN 2-DOOR HARDTOP TRIM

COLOR	CLOTH	VINYL	LEATHER	CODE
Black		•		61*
Blue		•		63*
Green		•		64*
Red		•		65*

*Bucket seats

JAVELIN SST AND AMX TRIM

COLOR	CLOTH	VINYL	LEATHER	CODE
Black	•	•	•	61*
Blue	•	•		63*
Green	•	•		64*
Red	•	•	•	65*
White		•		68*

*Bucket seats

GREMLIN 2-PASS/4-PASS TRIM

COLOR	CLOTH	VINYL	LEATHER	CODE
Black		•		01/11*
Blue		•		03/13*
White		•		08
Green		•		14*
Red		•		15*

*Bucket seats

MATADOR TRIM

COLOR	CLOTH	VINYL	LEATHER	CODE
Black	•	•		71
Blue	•	•		73
Green	•	•		74
Red	•	•		75

AMBASSADOR DPL TRIM

COLOR	CLOTH	VINYL	LEATHER	CODE
Black	•	•		81
Blue	•	•		83
Green	•	•		84

AMBASSADOR SST TRIM

COLOR	CLOTH	VINYL	LEATHER	CODE
Black	•	•		91
Blue	•	•		93
Green	•	•		94
Red	•	•		95

AMBASSADOR BROUGHAM TRIM

COLOR	CLOTH	VINYL	LEATHER	CODE
Black	•	•		91+
Blue	•	•		93+
Green	•	•		94
Red	•	•		95

+Fabric Harem available on 4-door sedan and 2-door hardtop only

THE PAINT CODE furnishes the key to the paint colors used on the car. Two, two-digit codes indicate the bottom and top body colors respectively. NOTE: For two-tone bodies, first number designates lower body color, second number designates upper body color.

COLOR	CODE
Snow White	A1
Canary Yellow	A2
Skyline Blue	A4
Midway Blue Metallic	A5
Midnight Blue Metallic	A6
Limelight Green Metallic	A7
Meadow Green Metallic	A8
Raven Green Metallic	A9
Burnish Brown Metallic	B2
Quick Silver Metallic	B3
Charcoal Gray Metallic	B4
Deep Maroon Metallic	B5
Electric Blue Metallic	B6
Brilliant Green Metallic	B7
Mustard Yellow	B8
Matador Red	B9
Golden Lime Metallic	C1
Surfside Turquoise	C6
Baja Bronze	D3
Wild Plum	D9
Classic Black	P1
Gray	P81

ENGINE NUMBER

The 6 cylinder engine code number is located on a machined surface of the block between number two and three cylinders. The V8 engine code number is located on a tag which is attached to the right bank cylinder head cover. The cubic inch displacement is cast into the cylinder block on both banks between the first and second core plug location.

ENGINE CODE	NO CYL	CID	HORSE-POWER	COMP. RATIO	CARB	OTHER
E	6	232	135	8.0:1	1 BC	
F	6	232	N/A	N/A	1 BC	Hornet & Gremlin
A	6	258	150	8.0:1	1 BC	
B	6	258	N/A	N/A	1 BC	
H	8	304	210	8.4:1	2 BC	Javelin
I	8	304	N/A	N/A	2 BC	
N	8	360	245	8.5:1	2 BC	Javelin & Hornet
P	8	360	285	8.5:1	4 BC	Hornet, Javelin & Matador
Z	8	401	330	9.5:1	4 BC	Matador, Javelin, AMX & Ambassador

1972 JAVELIN SST

1972 JAVELIN AMX

1972 MATADOR

1972 AMBASSADOR STATION WAGON

1972 GREMLIN

1972 MATADOR

1972 HORNET SPORTABOUT

VEHICLE IDENTIFICATION NUMBER

AMC
A2E465E134567

Located on the top of the dash on the driver's side and visible through the windshield from outside the car. It is also printed on a non-removable label affixed to the left front door adjacent to the door latch.

FIRST DIGIT: Identifies the Division (A=American Motors Corporation)

SECOND DIGIT: Identifies the year (2=1972)

THIRD DIGIT: Identifies the transmission type

TRANSMISSION	CODE
Automatic Column Shift	A
Automatic Console Shift	C
4-Spd. Manual Floor Shift	M
3-Spd. Manual Column Shift	S
3-Spd. Manual Floor Shift	F

FOURTH DIGIT: Identifies the series.

SERIES	CODE
Hornet	0
Matador	1
Gremlin	4
Javelin	7
Ambassador	8

FIFTH DIGIT: Identifies body type

BODY TYPE	CODE
4-Door Sedan	5
2-Door Sedan	6
4-Door Station Wagon	8
2-Door Hardtop	9

SIXTH DIGIT: Identifies the body class

BODY CLASS	CODE
Gremlin, Ambassador SST	5
Hornet SST, Javelin SST, Matador or Amb. Brougham	7
Javelin AMX	8

SEVENTH DIGIT: Identifies the engine

ENGINE	CODE
258 OHV 6	A
258 OHV 6 (Low Comp)	B
232 OHV 6	E
232 OHV 6 (Low Comp)	F
304 V8, 2 BC	H
304 V8 (Low Comp)	I
360 V8, 2 BC	N
360 V8, 4 BC	P
401 V8, 4 BC	Z

LAST SIX DIGITS: Represent the assembly plant and the basic production sequence. Kenosha-built bodies start with body number 000001. Brampton-built bodies start with body number 700001.

ASSEMBLY PLANT	CODE
Kenosha, WI	1-6
Brampton, Ont., CAN	7-9

BODY NUMBER PLATE

The body number plate is located on the left front door adjacent to the door latch. This plate identifies the model year, car division, series, body style, body assembly plant, body numbers, trim combination, paint code and build date code.

AMERICAN MOTORS CORPORATION

UNDER THE UNITED STATES NATIONAL TRAFFIC AND MOTOR VEHICLE SAFETY ACT OF 1966, CERTIFIES TO THE DEALER THAT THIS VEHICLE MEETS ALL FEDERAL MOTOR VEHICLE SAFETY STANDARDS APPLICABLE ON THE DATE OF MANUFACTURE.

ADVANCED UNIT CONSTRUCTION COMBINES BODY AND FRAME INTO A SINGLE ALL WELDED STRUCTURAL UNIT DEEP-DIP PRIMER PAINT GALVANIZED STEEL SECTIONS. PLUS LUSTRE GARD BAKED ACRYLIC ENAMEL PROTECT AGAINST BODY RUST.

BODY K	034567
MODEL 72	06 7
TRIM	243S
PAINT	C3

Example:

Body
K ... Kenosha Assembly Plant
034567 ... Production Sequence

Model
72 ... Model Year (1972)
06 ... Body Type (2-Door Sedan)
7 ... Body Class

Trim
2 ... Model Year (1972)
4 ... Series (Gremlin)
3 ... Blue
S ... Standard

Paint
C3 ... Skyway Blue

HORNET	CODE
4-Door Sedan SST	7205-7
2-Door Sedan SST	7206-7*#
Station Wagon (Sportabout)	7208-7*$+

*X option available
+DL option available
$Gucci option available
RALLYE

MATADOR	CODE
4-Door Sedan	7215-7
Station Wagon	7218-7
2-Door Hardtop	7219-7

GREMLIN

	CODE
2-Door 4-Passenger	7246-5

*X option available

JAVELIN

	CODE
2-Door Hardtop SST	7279-7*
2-Door Hardtop AMX	7279-8*

*Cardin option available

AMBASSADOR

	CODE
4-Door Sedan SST	7285-5
4-Door Sedan Brougham	7285-7
Station Wagon SST	7288-5
Station Wagon Brougham	7288-7
2-Door Hardtop SST	7289-5
2-Door Hardtop Brougham	7289-7

THE TRIM CODE furnishes the key to the interior color and material scheme.

HORNET SST/SPORTABOUT TRIM

COLOR	CLOTH	VINYL	LEATHER	CODE
Black	•	•		41
Blue	•	•		43
Green	•	•		44
Tan	•	•		46
White Sts w/Blk Int		•		48
Gucci	•			44W

GREMLIN TRIM

COLOR	CLOTH	VINYL	LEATHER	CODE
Black	•	•		01/11*
Blue	•	•		03/13*
Tan/Buff	•	•		06/16*
White Sts w/Blk Int		•		08/18*
Black/Red		•		15/15*

*Bucket seats

JAVELIN SST AND AMX TRIM

COLOR	CLOTH	VINYL	LEATHER	CODE
Black	•	•		61*
Blue	•	•		63*
Green	•	•		64*
Black/Red		•		65*
Tan/Buff	•	•		66*
White Sts. w/Blk Int		•		68*
Cardin		•		61W

*Bucket seats

MATADOR TRIM

COLOR	CLOTH	VINYL	LEATHER	CODE
Black	•	•		71
Blue	•	•		73
Green	•	•		74
Tan	•	•		76

AMBASSADOR TRIM

COLOR	CLOTH	VINYL	LEATHER	CODE
Black	•	•		91
Blue	•	•		93
Green	•	•		94
Tan	•	•		96

THE PAINT CODE furnishes the key to the paint colors used on the car. Two, two-digit codes indicate the bottom and top body colors respectively. NOTE: For two-tone bodies, first number designates lower body color, second number designates upper body color.

COLOR	CODE
Snow White	A1
Canary Yellow	A2
Charcoal Gray Metallic	B4
Stardust Silver Metallic	C2
Skyway Blue	C3
Jetset Blue Metallic	C4
Admiral Blue Metallic	C5
Surfside Turquoise	C6
Grasshopper Green Metallic	C8
Hunter Green Metallic	C9
Jolly Green Metallic	D1
Yaca Tan Metallic	D2
Baja Bronze Metallic	D3
Cordoba Brown Metallic	D4
Butterscotch Brown	D5
Trans-Am Red	D7
Sparkling Burgundy	D8
Wild Plum Metallic	D9
Classic Black	P1

ENGINE NUMBER

The 6 cylinder engine code number is located on a machined surface of the block between number two and three cylinders. The 8 cylinder engine code is located on a tag which is attached to the right bank cylinder head cover. The cubic inch displacement is cast into the cylinder block on both banks between the first and second core plug location.

ENGINE CODE	NO CYL	CID	HORSE-POWER	COMP. RATIO	CARB
E	6	232	100	8.0:1	1 BC
F	6	232	N/A	N/A	1 BC
A	6	258	110	8.0:1	1 BC
B	6	258	N/A	N/A	1 BC
H	8	304	150	8.4:1	2 BC
I	8	304	N/A	N/A	2 BC
N	8	360	175	8.5:1	2 BC
P	8	360	195	8.5:1	4 BC
P (Dual Exh.)	8	360	220	8.5:1	4 BC
Z	8	401	255	8.5:1	4 BC

Hornet Engines - E, F, A, B, H, I, N
Gremlin - E, F, A, B, H, I
AMX - H, I, N, P, Z
Matador - E, F, A, B, H, I, N, P, Z
Javelin - E, F, A, B, H, I, N, P, Z
Ambassador - A, B, H, I, N, P, Z

1973 MATADOR

1973 JAVELIN

1973 AMBASSADOR

1973 HORNET STATION WAGON

1973 AMBASSADOR STATION WAGON

1973 GREMLIN

1973 HORNET

1973 AMBASSADOR STATION WAGON

VEHICLE IDENTIFICATION NUMBER

AMC
A3S157H123455

Located on the top of the dash on the driver's side and visible through the windshield from outside the car. It is also printed on a non-removable label affixed to the left front door adjacent to the door latch.

FIRST DIGIT: Identifies the Division (A =American Motors Corporation)

SECOND DIGIT: Identifies the year (3=1973)

THIRD DIGIT: Identifies the transmission type

TRANSMISSION	CODE
Standard Column Shift, 3-Spd	S
3-Spd. Floor Shift, Floor Mounted (2-3 Synchromesh)	F
Automatic, Column Shift	A
Automatic, Floor Shift	C
4-Spd. Floor Shift, Floor Mtd	M

FOURTH DIGIT: Identifies the series

SERIES	CODE
Hornet	0
Matador	1
Gremlin	4
Javelin	7
Ambassador	8

FIFTH DIGIT: Identifies the body type

BODY TYPE	CODE
2-Door Hatchback	3
4-Door Sedan	5
2-Door Sedan	6
Station Wagon	8
2-Door Hardtop	9

SIXTH DIGIT: Identifies the body class

BODY CLASS	CODE
Gremlin	5
Hornet, Matador, Javelin, Ambassador Brougham	7
Javelin AMX	8

SEVENTH DIGIT: Identifies the engine

ENGINE	CODE
258 OHV 6	A
258 OHV 6 (Low Comp)	B
232 OHV 6	E
232 OHV 6 (Low Comp)	F
304 V8	H
304 V8 (Low Comp)	I
360 V8, 2 BC	N
360 V8, 4 BC	P
401 V8, 4 BC	Z

LAST SIX DIGITS: Represent the assembly plant and the basic production sequence. Kenosha-built bodies start with body number 000001. Brampton-built bodies start with body number 700001.

ASSEMBLY PLANT	CODE
WI	1-6
Ont., CAN	7-9

BODY NUMBER PLATE

The body number plate is located on the left front door adjacent to the door latch. This plate identifies the model year, car division, series, body style, body assembly plant, body numbers, trim combination, paint code and build date code.

AMERICAN MOTORS CORPORATION

UNDER THE UNITED STATES NATIONAL TRAFFIC AND MOTOR VEHICLE SAFETY ACT OF 1966, CERTIFIES TO THE DEALER THAT THIS VEHICLE MEETS ALL FEDERAL MOTOR VEHICLE SAFETY STANDARDS APPLICABLE ON THE DATE OF MANUFACTURE.

ADVANCED UNIT CONSTRUCTION COMBINES BODY AND FRAME INTO A SINGLE ALL WELDED STRUCTURAL UNIT DEEP-DIP PRIMER PAINT GALVANIZED STEEL SECTIONS. PLUS LUSTRE GARD BAKED ACRYLIC ENAMEL PROTECT AGAINST BODY RUST.

BODY K	034565
MODEL 73	03 5
TRIM	343S
PAINT	E1

Example:

Body
K	Kenosha Assembly Plant
034565	Production Sequence

Model
73	Model Year (1973)
03	Body Type (2-Door Hatchback)
5	Body Class

Trim
3	Model Year (1973)
4	Series (Gremlin)
3	Blue
S	Split-Back Bench

Paint
E1	Diamond Blue Metallic

HORNET	CODE
2-Door Hatchback	7303-7*
4-Door Sedan	7305-7
2-Door Sedan	7306-7
Station Wagon (Sportabout)	7308-7*

*X option available
*DL option available
*Gucci option available
*Levi option available

MATADOR	CODE
4-Door Sedan	7315-7
Station Wagon	7318-7
2-Door Hardtop	7319-7

GREMLIN — CODE
2-Door, 4-Passenger 7346-5
*X option available
*Levi option available

JAVELIN — CODE
2-Door Hardtop 7379-7
2-Door Hardtop AMX .... 7379-8*#
*Cardin option available
"GO" Package

AMBASSADOR — CODE
4-Door Sedan 7385-7
Station Wagon 7388-7
2-Door Hardtop 7389-7

THE TRIM CODE furnishes the key to the interior color and material scheme.

HORNET, SPORTABOUT AND HATCHBACK TRIM

COLOR	CLOTH	VINYL	LEATHER	CODE
Black	•	•		31
Blue	•	•		33
Green	•	•		34
Cinnamon	•	•		36
Black/Red		•		35
White		•		38
Gucci Green		•		34

*Bucket seats - Hatchback

GREMLIN TRIM

COLOR	CLOTH	VINYL	LEATHER	CODE
Black		•		01/11
Blue		•		03/13
Green		•		04/14
Cinn/Buff		•		06/16
White		•		18
Black/Red		•		15
Levi Blue		•		13

*Bucket seats - Gremlin X

MATADOR TRIM

COLOR	CLOTH	VINYL	LEATHER	CODE
Black	•	•		51
Blue	•	•		53
Green	•	•		54
Cinnamon	•	•		56

JAVELIN, AMX & CARDIN TRIM

COLOR	CLOTH	VINYL	LEATHER	CODE
Black	•	•		41
Blue	•	•		43
Green	•	•		44
Cinnamon	•	•		46
White		•		48
Cardin	•	•		41

AMBASSADOR BROUGHAM TRIM

COLOR	CLOTH	VINYL	LEATHER	CODE
Black	•	•		81
Blue	•	•		83
Green	•	•		84
Cinnamon	•	•		86

THE PAINT CODE furnishes the key to the paint colors used on the car. Two, two-digit codes indicate the bottom and top body colors respectively. NOTE: For two-tone bodies, first number designates lower body color, second number designates upper body color.

COLOR	CODE
Snow White	A1
Grasshopper Green Metallic	C8
Cordoba Brown Metallic	D4
Trans-Am Red	D7
Diamond Blue Metallic	E1
Olympic Blue Metallic	E2
Fairway Green Metallic	E3
Tallyho Green Metallic	E4
Pewter Silver Metallic	E5
Fawn Beige	E6
Copper Tan Metallic	E7
Mellow Yellow	E9
Blarney Green Metallic	F1
Maxi Blue	F2
Fresh Plum Metallic	F3
Daisy Yellow	F4
Vineyard Burgundy Metallic	F5
Dark Blue Metallic	F7
Harvest Gold Metallic	F8
Copper Metallic	F9
Silver Green Metallic	G1
Medium Green Metallic	G2
Dark Green Metallic	G3
Plum Metallic	G4
Sienna Orange	G6
Classic Black	P1

ENGINE NUMBER

The 6 cylinder engine number is located on a machined surface of the block between number two and three cylinders. The 8 cylinder engine code is located on a tag attached to the right bank cylinder head cover. The cubic inch displacement is cast into the cylinder block on both banks between the first and second core plug location.

ENGINE CODE	NO CYL	CID	HORSE-POWER	COMP. RATIO	CARB
E	6	232	100	8.0:1	1 BC
F	6	232	N/A	N/A	1 BC
A	6	258	110	8.0:1	1 BC
B	6	258	N/A	N/A	1 BC
H	8	304	150	8.4:1	2 BC
I	8	304	N/A	N/A	2 BC
N	8	360	175	8.5:1	2 BC
P	8	360	195	8.5:1	4 BC
P*	8	360	220	8.5:1	4 BC
Z	8	401	255	8.5:1	4 BC

*Dual exhaust

Engines available as indicated below:
Hornet - E, F, A, B, H, N, I
Gremlin - E, F, A, B, H, I
Matador - E, F, A, B, H, I, N, P, Z
Matador Wagon - A, B, H, I, N, P, Z
Javelin - E, F, A, B, H, I, N, P, Z
AMX - H, I, N, P, Z
Ambassador - A, B, N, H, I, P, Z

1974 HORNET

1974 HORNET STATION WAGON

1974 MATADOR 4-DOOR

1974 JAVELIN

1974 AMBASSADOR

1974 AMBASSADOR STATION WAGON

1974 GREMLIN

1974 MATADOR X

VEHICLE IDENTIFICATION NUMBER

AMC
A4S037A234567

Located on the top of the dash on the driver's side and visible through the windshield from outside the car. It is also printed on a non-removable label affixed to the left front door adjacent to the door latch.

FIRST DIGIT: Identifies the Division (A=American Motors Corporation)

SECOND DIGIT: Identifies the year (4=1974)

THIRD DIGIT: Identifies the transmission type

TRANSMISSION	CODE
Automatic (Column Shift)	A
Automatic (Floor Shift)	C
4-Spd. Manual (Floor Shift)	M
3-Spd. Manual (Column Shift)	S
3-Spd. Manual (Floor Shift)	E

FOURTH DIGIT: Identifies the series

SERIES	CODE
Hornet	0
Matador	1
Gremlin	4
Javelin	7
Ambassador	8

FIFTH DIGIT: Identifies the body type

BODY TYPE	CODE
2-Door Hatchback	3
4-Door Sedan	5
2-Door Sedan (Coupe)	6
4-Door Station Wagon	8
2-Door Hardtop	9

SIXTH DIGIT: Identifies the body class

BODY CLASS	CODE
Gremlin	5
Hornet, Javelin, Matador, Ambassador Brougham	7
Javelin AMX, Matador X	8
Matador Brougham	9
Police	P
Taxicab	T

SEVENTH DIGIT: Identifies the engine

ENGINE	CODE
258 OHV 6	A
232 OHV 6	E
304 V8	H
360 V8, 2 BC	N
360 V8, 4 BC	P
401 V8, 4 BC	Z

LAST SIX DIGITS: Represent the assembly plant and the basic production sequence. Kenosha-built bodies start with body number 000001. Brampton-built bodies start with body number 700001.

ASSEMBLY PLANT	CODE
Kenosha, WI	1-6
Brampton, Ont., CAN	7-9

BODY NUMBER PLATE

The body number is located on the left front door adjacent to the door latch. This plate identifies the model year, car division, series, body style, body assembly plant, body numbers, trim combination, paint code and build date code.

Example:

AMERICAN MOTORS CORPORATION

UNDER THE UNITED STATES NATIONAL TRAFFIC AND MOTOR VEHICLE SAFETY ACT OF 1966, CERTIFIES TO THE DEALER THAT THIS VEHICLE MEETS ALL FEDERAL MOTOR VEHICLE SAFETY STANDARDS APPLICABLE ON THE DATE OF MANUFACTURE.

ADVANCED UNIT CONSTRUCTION COMBINES BODY AND FRAME INTO A SINGLE ALL WELDED STRUCTURAL UNIT DEEP-DIP PRIMER PAINT GALVANIZED STEEL SECTIONS. PLUS LUSTRE GARD BAKED ACRYLIC ENAMEL PROTECT AGAINST BODY RUST.

BODY K	024356
MODEL 74	03 7
TRIM	443S
PAINT	F6

Body

K	Kenosha Assembly Plant
024356	Production Sequence

Model

74	Model Year (1974)
03	Body Type (2-Door Hatchback)
7	Body Class

Trim

4	Model Year (1974)
4	Series (Gremlin)
3	Blue
S	Split-Back Bench

Paint

F6	Medium Blue Metallic

HORNET	CODE
2-Door Hatchback	7403-7
4-Door Sedan	7405-7
2-Door Sedan	7406-7
Station Wagon (Sportabout)	7408-7

*X option available
*DL option available
*Levi option available

MATADOR	CODE
4-Door Sedan	7415-7
2-Door Coupe	7416-7
2-Door Coupe X	7416-8
2-Door Coupe Brougham	7416-9
Station Wagon	7418-7

*Cassini option available

GREMLIN   **CODE**
2-Door, 4-Passenger 7446-5
*X option available
*Levi option available

JAVELIN   **CODE**
2-Door Hardtop 7479-7
2-Door Hardtop AMX 7479-8

AMBASSADOR   **CODE**
4-Door Sedan 7485-7
Station Wagon 7488-7

THE TRIM CODE furnishes the key to the interior color and material scheme.

GREMLIN TRIM

COLOR	CLOTH	VINYL	LEATHER	CODE
Black		•		01
White		•		08
Blue		•		03*
Green		•		04
Black/Red		•		05
Cinn/Buff		•		06

*Levi's fabric & bucket seats optional

HORNET TRIM

COLOR	CLOTH	VINYL	LEATHER	CODE
Black	•	•		11
White		•		18
Blue	•	•		13
Green	•	•		14
Black/Red		•		15
Cinnamon	•	•		16

JAVELIN TRIM

COLOR	CLOTH	VINYL	LEATHER	CODE
Black	•	•		21*
White		•		28*
Blue	•	•		23*
Green	•	•		24*
Cinnamon	•	•		26*

*Bucket seats

MATADOR TRIM

COLOR	CLOTH	VINYL	LEATHER	CODE
Black	•	•		31
White		•		38
Blue	•	•		33
Green	•	•		34
Cinnamon	•	•		36

AMBASSADOR TRIM

COLOR	CLOTH	VINYL	LEATHER	CODE
Black	•	•		71
Blue	•	•		73
Green	•	•		74
Cinnamon	•	•		76

THE PAINT CODE furnishes the key to the paint colors used on the car. Two, two-digit codes indicate the bottom and top body colors respectively. NOTE: For two-tone bodies, first number designates lower body color, second number designates upper body color.

COLOR	CODE
Snow White	A1
Cordoba Brown Metallic	D4
Trans-Am Red	D7
Diamond Blue Metallic	E1
Fawn Beige	E6
Mellow Yellow	E9
Maxi Blue	F2
Daisy Yellow	F4
Vineyard Burgundy Metallic	F5
Medium Blue Metallic	F6
Dark Blue Metallic	F7
Harvest Gold Metallic	F8
Copper Metallic	F9
Silver Green Metallic	G1
Medium Green Metallic	G2
Dark Green Metallic	G3
Plum Metallic	G4
Pewter Mist Metallic	G5
Sienna Orange	G6
Ivory Green	J7
Caramel Tan	J8
Classic Black	P1

ENGINE NUMBER

The 6 cylinder engine code number is located on a machined surface of the block between number two and three cylinders. The 8 cylinder engine code is located on a tag attached to the right bank cylinder head cover. The cubic inch displacement is cast into the cylinder block on both banks between the first and second core plug location

ENGINE CODE	NO CYL	CID	HORSE-POWER	COMP. RATIO	CARB
E	6	232	100	8.0:1	1 BC
A	6	258	110	8.0:1	1 BC
H	8	304	150	8.4:1	2 BC
N	8	360	175	8.25:1	2 BC
P	8	360	195	8.25:1	4 BC
P*	8	360	220	8.25:1	4 BC
Z	8	401	255	8.25:1	4 BC

*Dual exhaust

Engines are available as indicated below:

Gremlin - E, A, H
Hornet - E, A, H, N
Javelin - E, A, H, N, P, Z
AMX - H, N, P, Z
Matador - E, A, H, N, P, Z
Matador X - H, N, P, Z
Matador Wagons - A, H, N, P, Z
Ambassador - H, N, P, Z

1975 AMC GREMLIN

1975 AMC PACER

1975 AMC MATADOR COUPE

1975 AMC GREMLIN

1975 AMC HORNET SPORTABOUT

1975 AMC HORNET SPORTABOUT

1975 AMC HORNET

1975 AMC MATADOR

1975 AMC MATADOR STATION WAGON

1975 AMC MATADOR STATION WAGON

VEHICLE IDENTIFICATION NUMBER

> AMC
> A5S037A234567

Located on the top of the dash on the driver's side and visible through the windshield from outside the car. It is also printed on a non-removable label affixed to the left front door adjacent to the door latch.

FIRST DIGIT: Identifies the Division (A=American Motors Corporation)

SECOND DIGIT: Identifies the year (5 =1975)

THIRD DIGIT: Identifies the transmission type

TRANSMISSION	CODE
Automatic Column Shift	A
Automatic Floor Shift	C
3-Spd. Floor Shift	E
3-Spd. Column Shift (W/Overdrive)	O
3-Spd. Column Shift	S

FOURTH DIGIT: Identifies the series

SERIES	CODE
Hornet	0
Matador 2-Door	1
Gremlin	4
Pacer	6
Matador 4-Door	8

FIFTH DIGIT: Identifies the body type

BODY TYPE	CODE
2-Door Hatchback	3
4-Door Sedan	5
2-Door Sedan (Coupe)	6
Station Wagon	8

SIXTH DIGIT: Identifies the body class

BODY CLASS	CODE
Gremlin	5
Hornet, Matador, Pacer	7
Police	P
Taxi	T

SEVENTH DIGIT: Identifies the engine

ENGINE	CODE
258 6, 1 BC	A
232 6	E
304 V8	H
360 V8, 2 BC	N
360 V8, 4 BC	P
401 V8, 4 BC	Z

LAST SIX DIGITS: Represent the assembly plant and the basic production sequence. Kenosha-built bodies start with body number 000001. Brampton-built bodies start with body number 700001.

ASSEMBLY PLANT	CODE
Kenosha, WI	0-6
Brampton, Ont., CAN	7-9

BODY NUMBER PLATE

The body number plate is located on the left front door adjacent to the door latch. This plate identifies the model year, car division, series, body style, body assembly plant, body numbers, trim combination, paint code and build date code.

> ## AMERICAN MOTORS CORPORATION
>
> UNDER THE UNITED STATES NATIONAL TRAFFIC AND MOTOR VEHICLE SAFETY ACT OF 1966, CERTIFIES TO THE DEALER THAT THIS VEHICLE MEETS ALL FEDERAL MOTOR VEHICLE SAFETY STANDARDS APPLICABLE ON THE DATE OF MANUFACTURE.
>
> ADVANCED UNIT CONSTRUCTION COMBINES BODY AND FRAME INTO A SINGLE ALL WELDED STRUCTURAL UNIT DEEP-DIP PRIMER PAINT GALVANIZED STEEL SECTIONS. PLUS LUSTRE GARD BAKED ACRYLIC ENAMEL PROTECT AGAINST BODY RUST.
>
> | | |
> | --- | --- |
> | BODY K | 024356 |
> | MODEL 75 | 03 7 |
> | TRIM | 543S |
> | PAINT | E9 |

Example:

Body
K	Kenosha Assembly Plant
023546	Production Sequence

Model
75	Model Year (1975)
03	Body Type (2-Door Hatchback)
7	Body Class

Trim
5	Model Year (1975)
4	Series (Gremlin)
3	Blue
S	Split-Back Bench

Paint
E9	Mellow Yellow

HORNET	CODE
2-Door Hatchback	7503-7
4-Door Sedan	7505-7
2-Door Sedan	7506-7
Station Wagon (Sportabout)	7508-7

*X option available
*DL option available
*Levi option available

MATADOR	CODE
2-Door Coupe	7516-7

*X option available
*Cassini option available

GREMLIN   CODE
2-Door Sedan 7546-5
*X option available
*Levi option available

PACER   CODE
2-Door Coupe 7566-7
*X option available
*DL option available

MATADOR   CODE
4-Door Sedan 7585-7
Station Wagon 7588-7
*Brougham option available

THE TRIM CODE furnishes the key to the interior color and material scheme.

PACER TRIM

COLOR	CLOTH	VINYL	LEATHER	CODE
Black	•	•		21
Black/White		•		28
Blue	•	•		23
Blue/White		•		83
Berry	•	•		25
Berry/White		•		85
Tan	•	•		26
Tan/White		•		86

MATADOR TRIM

COLOR	CLOTH	VINYL	LEATHER	CODE
Black	•	•		51/61
White		•		58
Blue	•	•		53/63
Green	•	•		54/64
Tan	•	•		56/66

HORNET TRIM

COLOR	CLOTH	VINYL	LEATHER	CODE
Black	•	•		11
White		•		18
Blue	•	•		13
Green	•	•		14
Tan	•	•		16

GREMLIN TRIM

COLOR	CLOTH	VINYL	LEATHER	CODE
Black		•		01
White		•		08
Blue		•		03*
Green		•		04
Tan/Buff		•		06

*Levi's fabric

THE PAINT CODE furnishes the key to the paint colors used on the car. Two, two-digit codes indicate the bottom and top body colors respectively. NOTE: For two-tone bodies, first number designates lower body color, second number designates upper body color.

COLOR	CODE
Trans-Am Red	D7
Fawn Beige	E6
Mellow Yellow	E9
Copper Metallic	F9
Dark Green Metallic	G3
Sienna Orange	G6
Alpine White	G7
Pastel Blue	G8
Medium Blue Metallic	G9
Deep Blue Metallic	H1
Dark Cocoa Metallic	H4
Green Apple	H5
Golden Jade Metallic	H6
Aztec Copper Metallic	H7
Autumn Red Metallic	H8
Silver Dawn Metallic	H9
Brandywine Metallic	J2
Ivory Green	J7
Caramel Tan	J8
Classic Black	P1

ENGINE NUMBER

The 6 cylinder engine code number is located on a machined surface of the block between number two and three cylinders. The 8 cylinder engine code is located on a tag attached to the right bank cylinder head cover. The cubic inch displacement is cast into the cylinder block on both banks between the first and second core plug location.

ENGINE CODE	NO CYL	CID	HORSE-POWER	COMP. RATIO	CARB
E	6	232	100	8.0:1	1 BC
A	6	258	110	8.0:1	1 BC
H	8	304	150	8.4:1	2 BC
N	8	360	175	8.25:1	2 BC
P	8	360	195	8.25:1	4 BC
P*	8	360	220	8.25:1	4 BC
Z	8	401	255	8.25:1	4 BC

*Dual exhaust

Engines are available as indicated below:

Gremlin - E, A, H
Hornet - E, A, H
Matador - A, H, N, P, Z
Pacer - E, A

1976 AMC PACER

1976 AMC GREMLIN

1976 AMC HORNET

1976 AMC HORNET

1976 AMC HORNET SPORTABOUT

1976 AMC MATADOR BARCELONA

1976 AMC MATADOR STATION WAGON

1976 AMC MATADOR

VEHICLE IDENTIFICATION NUMBER

AMC
• A6S037A234567 •

Located on the top of the dash on the driver's side and visible through the windshield from outside the car. It is also printed on a non-removable label affixed to the left front door adjacent to the door latch.

FIRST DIGIT: Identifies the Division (A=American Motors Corporation)

SECOND DIGIT: Identifies the year (6 = 1976)

THIRD DIGIT: Identifies the transmission type

TRANSMISSION	CODE
Automatic Column Shift	A
Automatic Floor Shift	C
3-Spd. Floor Shift (W/Overdrive)	D
3-Spd. Floor Shift	E
3-Spd. Column Shift (W/Overdrive)	O
3-Spd. Column Shift	S

FOURTH DIGIT: Identifies the series

SERIES	CODE
Hornet	0
Matador 2-Door	1
Gremlin	4
Pacer	6
Matador 4-Door	8

FIFTH DIGIT: Identifies the body type

BODY TYPE	CODE
2-Door Hatchback	3
4-Door Sedan	5
2-Door Sedan (Coupe)	6
Station Wagon	8

SIXTH DIGIT: Identifies the body class

BODY CLASS	CODE
Gremlin	3
Gremlin	5
Hornet, Matador, Pacer	7
Police	P
Taxi	T

SEVENTH DIGIT: Identifies the engine

ENGINE	CODE
258 6, 1 BC	A
258 6, 2 BC	C
232 6	E
304 V8	H
360 V8, 2 BC	N
360 V8, 4 BC	P
401 V8, 4 BC	Z

LAST SIX DIGITS: Represent the assembly plant and the basic production sequence. Kenosha-built bodies start with body number 000001. Brampton-built bodies start with body number 700001.

ASSEMBLY PLANT	CODE
Kenosha, WI	1-6
Brampton, Ont., CAN	7-9

BODY NUMBER PLATE

The body number plate is located on the left front door adjacent to the door latch. This plate identifies the model year, car division, series, body style, body assembly plant, body numbers, trim combination, paint code and build date code.

AMERICAN MOTORS CORPORATION

UNDER THE UNITED STATES NATIONAL TRAFFIC AND MOTOR VEHICLE SAFETY ACT OF 1966, CERTIFIES TO THE DEALER THAT THIS VEHICLE MEETS ALL FEDERAL MOTOR VEHICLE SAFETY STANDARDS APPLICABLE ON THE DATE OF MANUFACTURE.

ADVANCED UNIT CONSTRUCTION COMBINES BODY AND FRAME INTO A SINGLE ALL WELDED STRUCTURAL UNIT DEEP-DIP PRIMER PAINT GALVANIZED STEEL SECTIONS. PLUS LUSTRE GARD BAKED ACRYLIC ENAMEL PROTECT AGAINST BODY RUST.

BODY K	065432
MODEL 76	03 7
TRIM	603S
PAINT	6R

Example:

Body
K	Kenosha Assembly Plant
065432	Production Sequence

Model
76	Model Year (1976)
03	Body Type (2-Door Hatchback)
7	Body Class

Trim
6	Model Year (1976)
0	Series (Hornet)
3	Blue
S	Split-Back Bench

Paint
6R	Brilliant Blue

HORNET	CODE
2-Door Hatchback	7603-7
4-Door Sedan	7605-7
2-Door Sedan	7606-7
Station Wagon (Sportabout)	7608-7

*X option available
*DL option available

GREMLIN	CODE
2-Door Sedan	7656-5

*X option available
*Custom option available
*Levi option available

PACER

	CODE
2-Door Coupe	7666-7

*X option available
*DL option available

MATADOR

	CODE
2-Door Coupe	7616-7
4-Door Sedan	7685-7
Station Wagon	7688-7

*Barcelona option available
*Brougham option available

THE TRIM CODE furnishes the key to the interior color and material scheme.

GREMLIN STANDARD TRIM

COLOR	CLOTH	VINYL	LEATHER	CODE
Black		•		01
Tan/Buff		•		06

GREMLIN CUSTOM TRIM

COLOR	CLOTH	VINYL	LEATHER	CODE
Black	•	•		01
White		•		08
Blue	•	•		03
Green	•	•		04
Tan/Buff	•	•		06

PACER TRIM

COLOR	CLOTH	VINYL	LEATHER	CODE
Black	•	•		21
White/Black		•		28
Blue	•	•		23
White/Blue		•		83
Berry	•	•		25
White/Berry		•		85
Tan	•	•		26
White/Tan		•		86

HORNET TRIM

COLOR	CLOTH	VINYL	LEATHER	CODE
Black	•	•		11
White/Black		•		18
Blue	•	•		13
White/Blue		•		38
Green	•	•		14
White/Green		•		48
Tan	•	•		16
White/Tan		•		68

MATADOR COUPE TRIM

COLOR	CLOTH	VINYL	LEATHER	CODE
Black	•	•		51
Black	•			51+
White		•		58
Blue	•	•		53
Tan	•	•		56
Tan	•			56+

+Brougham package only

MATADOR SEDAN/WAGON TRIM

COLOR	CLOTH	VINYL	LEATHER	CODE
Black	•	•		61
Blue	•	•		63
Tan	•	•		66

*4-Door sedan hunter's plaid fabric only

THE PAINT CODE furnishes the key to the paint colors used on the car. Two, two-digit codes indicate the bottom and top body colors respectively. NOTE: For two-tone bodies, first number designates lower body color, second number designates upper body color.

COLOR	CODE
Black	P1
Sienna Orange	G6
Alpine Orange	G7
Medium Blue Metallic	G9
Dark Cocoa Metallic	H4
Autumn Red Metallic	H8
Seaspray Green	6B
Evergreen Metallic	6C
Sand Tan	6D
Burnished Bronze Metallic	6E
Silver Frost Metallic	6J
Limefire Metallic	6K
Firecracker Red	6P
Brilliant Blue	6R
Nautical Blue Metallic	6T
Sunshine Yellow	6V

ENGINE NUMBER

The 6 cylinder engine code number is located on a machined surface of the block between number two and three cylinders. The 8 cylinder engine code is located on a tag attached to the right bank cylinder head cover. The cubic inch displacement is cast into the cylinder block on both banks between the first and second core plug location.

ENGINE CODE	NO CYL	CID	HORSE-POWER	COMP. RATIO	CARB
E	6	232	90	8.0:1	1 BC
A	6	258	95	8.0:1	1 BC
C	6	258	120	8.0:1	2 BC
H	8	304	120	8.4:1	2 BC
N	8	360	140	8.25:1	2 BC
P	8	360	180	8.25:1	4 BC
Z*	8	401	255	8.25:1	4 BC

*Available in law enforcement vehicles only

Engines are available as indicated below:

Pacer - E, A, C
Gremlin - E, A, H
Hornet - E, A, H
Matador - A, H, N, P, Z
Matador Wagon - H, N, P, Z

1977 AMC HORNET

1977 AMC GREMLIN

1977 AMC MATADOR BARCELONA

1977 AMC HORNET SPORTABOUT

1977 AMC MATADOR

1977 AMC MATADOR STATION WAGON

1977 AMC PACER STATION WAGON

1977 AMC PACER

VEHICLE IDENTIFICATION NUMBER

AMC
A7M464G123654

Located on the top of the dash on the driver's side and visible through the windshield from outside the car. It is also printed on a non-removable label affixed to the left front door adjacent to the door latch.

FIRST DIGIT: Identifies the Division (A=American Motors Corporation)

SECOND DIGIT: Identifies the year (7 = 1977)

THIRD DIGIT: Identifies the transmission type

TRANSMISSION	CODE
Automatic Column Shift	A
Automatic Floor Shift	C
3-Spd. Manual Floor Shift	E
4-Spd. Manual Floor Shift	M

FOURTH DIGIT: Identifies the series

SERIES	CODE
Hornet	0
Matador 2-Door	1
Gremlin	4
Pacer	6
Matador 4-Door SW	8

FIFTH DIGIT: Identifies the body type

BODY TYPE	CODE
2-Door Hatchback	3
4-Door Sedan	5
2-Door Sedan	6
Station Wagon	8

SIXTH DIGIT: Identifies the body class

BODY CLASS	CODE
Gremlin (2 Litre)	4
Gremlin (Base)	5
Pacer, Hornet, Matador, Gremlin (Custom)	7

SEVENTH DIGIT: Identifies the engine

ENGINE	CODE
258 OHV 6, 1V	A
258 OHV 6, 2V	C
232 OHV 6, 1V	E
304 V8, 2V	H
360 V8, 2V	N
2 Litre, OHC 4, 2V	G

LAST SIX DIGITS: Represent the assembly plant and the basic production sequence. Kenosha-built bodies start with body number 000001. Brampton-built bodies start with body numer 700001.

ASSEMBLY PLANT	CODE
Kenosha, WI	1-6
Brampton, Ont., CAN	7-9

BODY NUMBER PLATE

The body number plate is located on the left front door adjacent to the door latch. This plate identifies the model year, car division, series, body style, body assembly plant, body numbers, trim combination, paint code and build date code.

AMERICAN MOTORS CORPORATION

UNDER THE UNITED STATES NATIONAL TRAFFIC AND MOTOR VEHICLE SAFETY ACT OF 1966, CERTIFIES TO THE DEALER THAT THIS VEHICLE MEETS ALL FEDERAL MOTOR VEHICLE SAFETY STANDARDS APPLICABLE ON THE DATE OF MANUFACTURE.

ADVANCED UNIT CONSTRUCTION COMBINES BODY AND FRAME INTO A SINGLE ALL WELDED STRUCTURAL UNIT DEEP-DIP PRIMER PAINT GALVANIZED STEEL SECTIONS. PLUS LUSTRE GARD BAKED ACRYLIC ENAMEL PROTECT AGAINST BODY RUST.

BODY K	023456
MODEL 77	03 7
TRIM	703S
PAINT	6P

Example:

Body
K	Kenosha Assembly Plant
023456	Production Sequence

Model
77	Model Year (1977)
03	Body Type (2-Door Hatchback)
7	Body Class

Trim
7	Model Year (1977)
0	Series (Hornet)
3	Blue
S	Split-Back Bench

Paint
6P	Firecracker Red

HORNET	CODE
2-Door Hatchback	7703-7
4-Door Sedan	7705-7
2-Door Sedan	7706-7
Station Wagon (Sportabout)	7708-7

*X option available
*DL option available
*AMX option available

GREMLIN

	CODE
2-Door Sedan (4-cyl)	7746-4
2-Door Sedan (Base)	7746-5
2-Door Sedan (Custom)	7746-7

*X option available
*Sundowner option available

PACER

	CODE
2-Door Coupe	7766-7
Station Wagon	7768-7

*X option available
*DL option available

MATADOR

	CODE
2-Door Coupe	7716-7
4-Door Sedan	7785-7
Station Wagon	7788-7

*Barcelona II option available

THE TRIM CODE furnishes the key to the interior color and material scheme.

GREMLIN TRIM

COLOR	CLOTH	VINYL	LEATHER	CODE
Black		•		701
White/Black		•		70A
Blue	•	•		703
White/Blue		•		70B
Berry		•		705
White/Berry		•		70D
Tan		•		706
White/Tan		•		70E
Black/Orange	•			70J
Black/Blue	•			70G
Black/Yellow	•			70K
Black/Green	•			70H

HORNET TRIM

COLOR	CLOTH	VINYL	LEATHER	CODE
Black	•	•		711
White		•		71A
Blue	•	•		713
Berry	•	•		715
Tan	•	•		716

PACER TRIM

COLOR	CLOTH	VINYL	LEATHER	CODE
Black	•	•		721
White/Black		•		72A
Blue	•	•		723
White/Blue		•		72B
Berry	•	•		725
White/Berry		•		72D
Tan	•	•		726
White/Tan		•		72E

MATADOR COUPE TRIM

COLOR	CLOTH	VINYL	LEATHER	CODE
Black	•	•		751
Blue	•	•		753
Berry	•	•		755
Tan	•	•		756

MATADOR SEDAN/WAGON TRIM

COLOR	CLOTH	VINYL	LEATHER	CODE
Black	•	•		761
Blue	•	•		763
Berry	•	•		765
Tan	•	•		766

THE PAINT CODE furnishes the key to the paint colors used on the car. Two, two-digit codes indicate the bottom and top body colors respectively. NOTE: For two-tone bodies, first number designates lower body color, second number designates upper body color.

COLOR	CODE
Black	P1
Alpine White	G7
Brandywine Metallic	J2
Sand Tan	6D
Silver Frost Metallic	6J
Firecracker Red	6P
Brilliant Blue	6R
Sunshine Yellow	6V
Misty Jade Metallic	7A
Mocha Brown Metallic	7B
Autumn Red Metallic	7C
Powder Blue	7D
Loden Green Metallic	7L
Golden Ginger Metallic	7M
Lime Green	7P
Captain Blue Metallic	7W
Tawny Orange	7Y
Sun Orange	7Z

ENGINE NUMBER

The 4 cylinder engine code is part of a number stamped on machined pad at left rear of cylinder block adjacent to engine oil dipstick. The 6 cylinder engine code number is located on a machined surface of the block between number two and three cylinders. The 8 cylinder engine code is located on a tag attached to the right bank cylinder head cover.

ENGINE CODE	NO CYL	CID	HORSE-POWER	COMP. RATIO	CARB	TRANS
G	4	121	80	8.1:1	2 BC	
E	6	232	90	8.0:1	1 BC	
A	6	258	95	8.0:1	1 BC	
C	6	258	120	8.0:1	2 BC	
H	8	304	120	8.4:1	2 BC	Auto
N	8	360	140	8.25:1	2 BC	Auto

Engines are available as indicated below:
Pacer - E, A; Gremlin - E, A, G; Hornet - E, A, H, C; Matador - A, H, N; Matador Wagon - H, N

1978 AMC AMX

1978 AMC CONCORD

1978 AMC CONCORD WAGON

1978 AMC GREMLIN

1978 AMC PACER WAGON

1978 AMC MATADOR

1978 AMC MATADOR COUPE

1978 AMC PACER

VEHICLE IDENTIFICATION NUMBER

AMC
A8A037A132435

Located on the top of the dash on the driver's side and visible through the windshield from outside the car. It is also printed on a non-removable label affixed to the left front door adjacent to the door latch.

FIRST DIGIT: Identifies the Division (A = American Motors Corporation)

SECOND DIGIT: Identifies the year (8 = 1978)

THIRD DIGIT: Identifies the transmission type

TRANSMISSION	CODE
Automatic Column Shift	A
Automatic Floor Shift	C
3-Spd. Manual Floor Shift	E
4-Spd. Manual Floor Shift	M

FOURTH DIGIT: Identifies the series

SERIES	CODE
Concord, AMX	0
Matador 2-Door	1
Gremlin	4
Pacer	6
Matador 4-Door Sedan/SW	8

FIFTH DIGIT: Identifies the body type

BODY TYPE	CODE
2-Door Hatchback	3
4-Door Sedan	5
2-Door Sedan	6
Station Wagon	8

SIXTH DIGIT: Identifies the body class

BODY CLASS	CODE
Gremlin (2-Liter)	4
Gremlin (Base)	5
Pacer, Gremlin (Custom), Concord, Matador	7
AMX	9

SEVENTH DIGIT: Identifies the engine

ENGINE	CODE
258 OHV 6, 1V	A
258 OHV 6, 2V	C
232 OHV 6, 1V	E
2-Liter 4, 2V	G
304 V8, 2V	H
360 V8, 2V	N

LAST SIX DIGITS: Represent the assembly plant and the basic production sequence. Kenosha-built bodies start with body number 000001. Brampton-built bodies start with body number 700001.

ASSEMBLY PLANT	CODE
Kenosha, WI	1-6
Brampton, Ont., CAN	7-9

BODY NUMBER PLATE

The body number plate is located on the left front door adjacent to the door latch. This plate identifies the model year, car division, series, body style, body assembly plant, body numbers, trim combination, paint code and build date code.

AMERICAN MOTORS CORPORATION

UNDER THE UNITED STATES NATIONAL TRAFFIC AND MOTOR VEHICLE SAFETY ACT OF 1966, CERTIFIES TO THE DEALER THAT THIS VEHICLE MEETS ALL FEDERAL MOTOR VEHICLE SAFETY STANDARDS APPLICABLE ON THE DATE OF MANUFACTURE.

ADVANCED UNIT CONSTRUCTION COMBINES BODY AND FRAME INTO A SINGLE ALL WELDED STRUCTURAL UNIT DEEP-DIP PRIMER PAINT GALVANIZED STEEL SECTIONS. PLUS LUSTRE GARD BAKED ACRYLIC ENAMEL PROTECT AGAINST BODY RUST.

BODY K	034576
MODEL 78	03 7
TRIM	803S
PAINT	6V

Example:

Body
K .... Kenosha Assembly Plant
034576 .... Production Sequence

Model
78 .... Model Year (1978)
03 .... Body Type (2-Door Hatchback)
7 .... Body Class

Trim
8 .... Model Year (1978)
0 .... Series (Concord)
3 .... Blue
S .... Split-Back Bench

Paint
6V .... Sunshine Yellow

AMX	CODE
2-Door Hatchback	7803-9

CONCORD	CODE
2-Door Hatchback	7803-7
4-Door Sedan	7805-7
2-Door Sedan	7806-7
Station Wagon	7808-7

*DL option available

GREMLIN	CODE
2-Door Sedan (4 cyl)	7846-4
2-Door Sedan (Base)	7846-5
2-Door Sedan (Custom)	7846-7

*X option available
*GT option available

PACER

	CODE
2-Door Coupe	7866-7
Station Wagon	7868-7

*DL & Sport options available

MATADOR

	CODE
2-Door Coupe	7816-7
4-Door Sedan	7885-7
Station Wagon	7888-7

*Barcelona option available

THE TRIM CODE furnishes the key to the interior color and material scheme.

CONCORD D/L PKG TRIM

COLOR	CLOTH	VINYL	LEATHER	CODE
Black	•	•		11
Blue	•	•		13
Berry	•	•		15
Beige	•	•		16
Flax	•	•		17

CONCORD BASE/SPORT TRIM

COLOR	CLOTH	VINYL	LEATHER	CODE
Black	•	•		11*
Flax/Black		•		1A*
Blue	•	•		13*
Flax/Blue		•		1B*
Berry	•	•		15*
Flax/Berry		•		1D*
Beige	•	•		16*
Flax	•	•		17*

*Bucket seats standard

AMX TRIM

COLOR	CLOTH	VINYL	LEATHER	CODE
Black	•	•		11
Flax/Black		•		1A
Blue	•	•		13
Flax/Blue		•		1B
Beige	•	•		16

PACER TRIM

COLOR	CLOTH	VINYL	LEATHER	CODE
Black	•	•		21
Flax/Black		•		2A
Blue	•	•		23
Flax/Blue		•		2B
Berry	•	•		25
Flax/Berry		•		2D
Beige	•	•		26
Flax	•	•		27

GREMLIN TRIM

COLOR	CLOTH	VINYL	LEATHER	CODE
Black		•		01*
Flax/Black		•		0A*
Blue		•		03*
Flax/Blue		•		0B*
Berry		•		05*
Flax/Berry		•		0D*
Beige		•		06*

*Bucket seats standard

GREMLIN X PKG TRIM

COLOR	CLOTH	VINYL	LEATHER	CODE
Black	•	•		01*
Flax/Black		•		0A*
Blue	•	•		03*
Flax/Blue		•		0B*
Berry	•	•		05*
Flax/Berry		•		0D*
Beige	•	•		06*

*Bucket seats standard

MATADOR TRIM

COLOR	CLOTH	VINYL	LEATHER	CODE
Black	•	•		51
Blue	•	•		53
Berry	•	•		55
Beige	•	•		56

THE PAINT CODE furnishes the key to the paint colors used on the car. Two, two-digit codes indicate the bottom and top body colors respectively. NOTE: For two-tone bodies, first number designates lower body color, second number designates upper body color.

COLOR	CODE
Black	P1
Alpine White	G7
Sand Tan	6D
Firecracker Red	6P
Sunshine Yellow	6V
Mocha Brown Metallic	7B
Powder Blue	7D
Midnight Blue Metallic	7K
Loden Green Metallic	7L
Golden Ginger Metallic	7M
Sun Orange	7Z
Khaki	8A
British Bronze Metallic	8B
Quick Silver Metallic	8C
Claret Metallic	8D

ENGINE NUMBER

The 4 cylinder engine code is part of a number stamped on a machined pad at the left rear of cylinder block adjacent to the engine oil dipstick. The 6 cylinder engine code number is located on a machined surface of the block between number two and three cylinders. The 8 cylinder engine code is located on a tag which is attached to the right bank cylinder head cover.

ENGINE CODE	NO CYL	CID	HORSE-POWER	COMP. RATIO	CARB
G	4	121	80	8.2:1	2 BC
E	6	232	90	8.0:1	1 BC
A	6	258	100	8.0:1	1 BC
C	6	258	120	8.0:1	2 BC
H	8	304	130	8.4:1	2 BC
N	8	360	140	8.25:1	2 BC

Engines available as indicated below:
Concord - E, C, H; AMX - C, H; Pacer - E, C, H; Pacer Sport - C, H; Gremlin - G, E, C; Matador - C, N; Matador Wagon - N

1979 AMC AMX

1979 AMC CONCORD

1979 AMC PACER

1979 AMC CONCORD WAGON

1979 AMC SPIRIT

1979 AMC PACER WAGON

1979 AMC AMX

1979 AMC SPIRIT LIFTBACK

VEHICLE IDENTIFICATION NUMBER

AMC A9A037C132435

Located on the top of the dash on the driver's side and visible through the windshield from outside the car. It is also printed on a non-removable label affixed to the left front door adjacent to the door latch.

FIRST DIGIT: Identifies the Division (A = American Motors Corporation)

SECOND DIGIT: Identifies the year (9 = 1979)

THIRD DIGIT: Identifies the transmission type

TRANSMISSION	CODE
Automatic Column Shift	A
Automatic Floor Shift	C
3-Spd. Manual Floor Shift	E
4-Spd. Manual Floor Shift	M

FOURTH DIGIT: Identifies the series

SERIES	CODE
Concord	0
Spirit, AMX	4
Pacer	6

FIFTH DIGIT: Identifies the body type

BODY TYPE	CODE
2-Door Hatchback or Liftback	3
4-Door Sedan	5
2-Door Sedan or Hatchback	6
Station Wagon	8

SIXTH DIGIT: Identifies the body class

BODY CLASS	CODE
Pacer, Spirit, Concord	7
AMX	9

SEVENTH DIGIT: Identifies the engine

ENGINE	CODE
258 OHV 6, 1V	A
258 OHV 6, 2V	C
232 OHV 6, 1V	E
2-Liter 4, 2V	G
304 V8, 2V	H

LAST SIX DIGITS: Represent the assembly plant and the basic production sequence. Kenosha-built bodies start with body number 000001. Brampton-built bodies start with body number 700001.

ASSEMBLY PLANT	CODE
Kenosha, WI	K
Brampton, Ont., CAN	B

BODY NUMBER PLATE

The body number plate is located on the left front door adjacent to the door latch. This plate identifies the model year, car division, series, body style, body assembly plant, body numbers, trim combination, paint code and build date code.

AMERICAN MOTORS CORPORATION

UNDER THE UNITED STATES NATIONAL TRAFFIC AND MOTOR VEHICLE SAFETY ACT OF 1966, CERTIFIES TO THE DEALER THAT THIS VEHICLE MEETS ALL FEDERAL MOTOR VEHICLE SAFETY STANDARDS APPLICABLE ON THE DATE OF MANUFACTURE.

ADVANCED UNIT CONSTRUCTION COMBINES BODY AND FRAME INTO A SINGLE ALL WELDED STRUCTURAL UNIT DEEP-DIP PRIMER PAINT GALVANIZED STEEL SECTIONS. PLUS LUSTRE GARD BAKED ACRYLIC ENAMEL PROTECT AGAINST BODY RUST.

BODY K	032546	
MODEL 79	03	7
TRIM	903S	
PAINT	9H	

Example:

Body

K	Kenosha Assembly Plant
032546	Production Sequence

Model

79	Model Year (1979)
03	2-Door Hatchback
7	Body Class

Trim

9	Model Year (1979)
0	Series (Concord)
3	Blue
S	Split-Back Bench

Paint

9H	Cumberland Green Metallic

CONCORD	CODE
2-Door Hatchback	7903-7
4-Door Sedan	7905-7
2-Door Sedan	7906-7
Station Wagon	7908-7

*Concord option available
*Limited option available

SPIRIT	CODE
2-Door Liftback	7943-7
2-Door Sedan	7946-7

*DL option available
*Limited option available
*GT option available

AMX	
2-Door Liftback	7943-9

PACER

	CODE
2-Door Hatchback	7966-7
Station Wagon	7968-7

*DL option available
*Limited option available

THE TRIM CODE furnishes the key to the interior color and material scheme.

SPIRIT TRIM

COLOR	CLOTH	VINYL	LEATHER	CODE
Black	•	•		BV1/BF1
Blue	•	•		BV3/BF3
Blue		•		NV3+
Beige	•	•		BV6/BF6
Beige			•	BL6
Beige		•		NV6+
Russet	•	•		BV5/BF5
Flax	•	•		BV7/BF7

+Base only

AMX TRIM

COLOR	CLOTH	VINYL	LEATHER	CODE
Black	•	•		BV1/BF1*
Blue	•	•		BV3/BF3*
Beige	•	•		BV6/BF6*

*Bucket Seats

PACER DL TRIM

COLOR	CLOTH	VINYL	LEATHER	CODE
Black	•	•		RV1/RF1/BF1
Blue	•	•		RV3/RF3/BF3
Russet	•	•		RV5/RF5/BF5
Beige	•	•		RV6/RF6/BF6
Beige			•	RL6
Flax	•	•		RV7/RF7/BF7

CONCORD BASE TRIM

COLOR	CLOTH	VINYL	LEATHER	CODE
Blue	•	•		NV3/NF3
Beige	•	•		NV6/NF6

CONCORD DL TRIM

COLOR	CLOTH	VINYL	LEATHER	CODE
Black	•	•		RV1/RF1
Blue	•	•		RV3/RF3
Russet	•	•		RV5/RF5
Beige	•	•		RV6/RF6
Beige			•	RL6+
Flax	•	•		RV7/RF7

+Not available on 2-Door Hatchback

THE PAINT CODE furnishes the key to the paint colors used on the car. Two, two-digit codes indicate the bottom and top body colors respectively. NOTE: For two-tone bodies, first number designates lower body color, second number designates upper body color.

COLOR	CODE
Classic Black	P1
Firecracker Red	6P
Khaki	8A
British Bronze Metallic	8B
Quick Silver Metallic	8C
Alpaca Brown Metallic	9A
Olympic White	9B
Russet Metallic	9C
Wedgwood Blue	9E
Cumberland Green Metallic	9H
Sable Brown Metallic	9K
Saxon Yellow	9L
Starboard Blue Metallic	9M
Morocco Buff	9N
Bordeaux Metallic	9P
Misty Beige Clearcoat	9Z

ENGINE NUMBER

The 4 cylinder engine code is part of a number stamped on a machined pad at left rear of the cylinder block adjacent to the engine oil dipstick. The 6 cylinder engine code number is located on a machined surface of the block between number two and three cylinders. The 8 cylinder engine code is located on a tag attached to the right bank cylinder head cover.

ENGINE CODE	NO CYL	CID	HORSE-POWER	COMP. RATIO	CARB
G	4	121	80	8.1:1	2 BC
E	6	232	90	8.0:1	1 BC
A	6	258	100	8.3:1	1 BC
C	6	258	110	8.3:1	2 BC
H	8	304	125	8.4:1	2 BC

Engines available as indicated below:
Spirit - G, E, C, H
AMX - C, H
Concord - G, E, C, H
Concord Wagon - E, C, H
Pacer - C, H

1970 BUICK RIVIERA

1970 BUICK LE SABRE

1970 BUICK SKYLARK

1970 BUICK WILDCAT

1970 BUICK ESTATE WAGON

1970 BUICK GS

VEHICLE IDENTIFICATION NUMBER

• BUICK 434270H000000 •

Located on the top of the dash on the driver's side and visible through the windshield from outside the car.

FIRST DIGIT: Identifies GM Division (4 = Buick)

SECOND AND THIRD DIGITS: Identify the series

SERIES	CODE
Skylark	33
Sport Wagon	34
GS	34
Skylark 350	35
Skylark Custom	44
GS 455	46
LeSabre	52
LeSabre Custom	54
Estate Wagon	60

SERIES	CODE
LeSabre Custom 455	64
Wildcat Custom	66
Electra 225	82
Electra 225 Custom	84
Riviera	94

FOURTH AND FIFTH DIGITS: Identify the body style

BODY STYLE	CODE
2-Door Coupe	27
4-Door 2-Seat Station Wagon	35
4-Door 2-Seat Wagon	36
2-Door Hardtop Coupe	37
4-Door Hardtop Sedan	39
4-Door 3-Seat Station Wagon	46
4-Door Hardtop	47
2-Door 2-Seat Sport Wagon	56
2-Door Hardtop Coupe	57
2-Door 3-Seat Sport Wagon	66
Convertible	67
4-Door Sedan	69
2-Door Hardtop	87

SIXTH DIGIT: Identifies the year (0 = 1970)

SEVENTH DIGIT: Identifies the assembly plant

ASSEMBLY PLANT	CODE
Flint, MI	H
Southgate, CA	C
Doraville, GA	D
Framingham, MA	G
Leeds, MO	K
Fairfax, KS	X
Wilmington, DE	Y
Fremont, CA	Z

LAST 6 DIGITS: Represent the basic production numbers

EXAMPLE:

4	52	69	0	H	000000
Buick Div	Series	Body Style	Year	Asm Plant	Prod Code

BODY NUMBER PLATE

The body number plate is located on the firewall, just below the rear edge of the hood. This plate identifies the model year, car division, series, body style, body assembly plant, body numbers, trim combination, paint code and build date code.

```
        BUICK DIV. GENERAL MOTORS
                  CORP.
              FLINT, MICHIGAN
     ST 70   45469      H 123456 BDY
     TR 428              19 19 PNT

       GENERAL MOTORS CORPORATION CERTIFIES
        TO THE DEALER THAT THIS VEHICLE
        CONFORMS TO ALL U.S., FEDERAL MOTOR
            VEHICLE SAFETY STANDARDS
         APPLICABLE AT TIME OF MANUFACTURE.
```

Example:

70	Model Year (1970)
4	Car Division (Buick)
54	Series (LeSabre Custom)
69	Style (4-Dr. Sdn Thin Pillar)
H	Body Assembly Plant (Flint, MI)
123456	Production Sequence
428	Black Vinyl Trim
19 19	Regal Black Paint

SKYLARK	CODE
2-Door Coupe Thin Pillar	43327
4-Door Sedan Thin Pillar	43369

SPORTWAGON	CODE
4-Door 2-Seat Wagon	43435
4-Door 2-Seat Wagon	43436

SKYLARK 350	CODE
2-Door Coupe Hardtop	43537
4-Door Sedan Thin Pillar	43569

GS	CODE
2-Door Coupe Hardtop	43437

SKYLARK CUSTOM	CODE
2-Door Coupe Hardtop	44437
4-Door Hardtop	44439
2-Door Convertible	44467
4-Door Sedan Thin Pillar	44469

GS 455	CODE
2-Door Coupe Hardtop	44637
2-Door Convertible	44667

*Stage 1 option available
*GSX option available

LESABRE	CODE
2-Door Coupe Hardtop	45237
4-Door Hardtop	45239
4-Door Sedan Thin Pillar	45269

LESABRE CUSTOM	CODE
2-Door Coupe Hardtop	45437
4-Door Hardtop	45439
2-Door Convertible	45467
4-Door Sedan Thin Pillar	45469

LESABRE CUSTOM 455	CODE
2-Door Coupe Hardtop	46437
4-Door Hardtop	46439
4-Door Sedan Thin Pillar	46469

ESTATE WAGON	CODE
4-Door 2-Seat Wagon	46036
4-Door 3-Seat Wagon	46046

WILDCAT CUSTOM	CODE
2-Door Coupe Hardtop	46637
4-Door Hardtop	46639
2-Door Convertible	46667

ELECTRA 225	CODE
2-Door Coupe Hardtop	48257
4-Door Hardtop	48239
4-Door Sdn Semi-Thin Pillar	48469

ELECTRA 225 CUSTOM	CODE
2-Door Coupe Hardtop	48457
4-Door Hardtop	48439
2-Door Convertible	48467
4-Door Sdn Semi-Thin Pillar	48469

*Limited option available

RIVIERA	CODE
2-Door Coupe Hardtop	49487

*GS option available

THE TRIM CODE furnishes the key to the interior color and material scheme.

SKYLARK COUPE

COLOR	CLOTH	VINYL	LEATHER	CODE
Black	•	•		108
Black		•		118
Blue		•		111
Sandalwood		•		104
Sandalwood		•		114

SKYLARK SEDAN

COLOR	CLOTH	VINYL	LEATHER	CODE
Black	•	•		108
Black		•		128
Blue	•	•		101
Blue		•		121
Sandalwood	•	•		104
Sandalwood		•		124

SPORT WAGON

COLOR	CLOTH	VINYL	LEATHER	CODE
Blue		•		121
Sandalwood		•		124
Burnished Saddle		•		129

GS

COLOR	CLOTH	VINYL	LEATHER	CODE
Black		•		128
Black		•		178#
Black		•		188*
Blue		•		121
Blue		•		181
Sandalwood		•		124
Green		•		170#
Pearl White		•		175#
Pearl White		•		185*
Saddle		•		176#
Burnished Saddle		•		179#
Burnished Saddle		•		189*

SKYLARK 350 COUPE

COLOR	CLOTH	VINYL	LEATHER	CODE
Black		•		128
Black		•		178#
Blue		•		121
Sandalwood		•		124
Green		•		170#
Pearl White		•		175#
Saddle		•		176#
Burnished Saddle		•		179#

SKYLARK 350 SEDAN

COLOR	CLOTH	VINYL	LEATHER	CODE
Black	•	•		138
Black		•		128
Blue		•		121
Sandalwood	•	•		134
Sandalwood		•		124
Green	•	•		130

SKYLARK CUSTOM 2-DOOR

COLOR	CLOTH	VINYL	LEATHER	CODE
Black	•	•		148#
Black		•		178#
Black		•		188*
Blue	•	•		141
Blue		•		181*
Sandalwood	•	•		249
Green		•		170#
Pearl White		•		175#
Pearl White		•		185*
Saddle		•		176#
Burnished Saddle		•		179#
Burnished Saddle		•		189*

SKYLARK CUSTOM 4-DOOR

COLOR	CLOTH	VINYL	LEATHER	CODE
Black	•	•		148
Black		•		178#
Blue	•	•		141
Sandalwood	•	•		144
Green	•	•		140
Green		•		170#
Saddle		•		176#
Burnished Saddle		•		179#

SKYLARK CONVERTIBLE

COLOR	CLOTH	VINYL	LEATHER	CODE
Black		•		158
Black		•		188*
Sandalwood		•		154
Pearl White		•		175#
Pearl White		•		185*
Burnished Saddle		•		179#
Burnished Saddle		•		189*

SKYLARK SEDAN 4-DOOR

COLOR	CLOTH	VINYL	LEATHER	CODE
Black	•	•		148
Black		•		158
Blue	•	•		141
Sandalwood	•	•		144
Green	•	•		140
Burnished Saddle		•		159

GS 455

COLOR	CLOTH	VINYL	LEATHER	CODE
Black		•		128
Black		•		178#
Black		•		188*
Blue		•		121
Blue		•		181*
Sandalwood		•		124
Green		•		170#
Pearl White		•		175#
Pearl White		•		185*
Saddle		•		176
Burnished Saddle		•		179#
Burnished Saddle		•		189*

GS 455 CONVERTIBLE

COLOR	CLOTH	VINYL	LEATHER	CODE
Black		•		158
Black		•		188*
Sandalwood		•		154
Pearl White		•		175#
Pearl White		•		185*
Burnished Saddle		•		179#
Burnished Saddle		•		189*

LESABRE

COLOR	CLOTH	VINYL	LEATHER	CODE
Black	•	•		408
Blue	•	•		401
Sandalwood	•	•		404
Green	•	•		400

LESABRE CUSTOM 2-DOOR

COLOR	CLOTH	VINYL	LEATHER	CODE
Black		•		428
Blue	•	•		411
Blue		•		421
Sandalwood	•	•		414
Green	•	•		410
Green		•		420
Saddle		•		426

LESABRE CUSTOM 4-DOOR HT

COLOR	CLOTH	VINYL	LEATHER	CODE
Black		•		428
Blue	•	•		411
Blue		•		421
Sandalwood	•	•		414
Green	•	•		410
Green		•		420
Saddle		•		426

LESABRE CUSTOM CONVERTIBLE

COLOR	CLOTH	VINYL	LEATHER	CODE
Black		•		428
Blue		•		421
Red		•		427
Saddle		•		426

LESABRE CUSTOM 4-DOOR SEDAN

COLOR	CLOTH	VINYL	LEATHER	CODE
Black		•		428
Blue	•	•		411
Blue		•		421
Sandalwood	•	•		414
Green	•	•		410
Green		•		420
Saddle		•		426

ESTATE WAGON 2-SEAT

COLOR	CLOTH	VINYL	LEATHER	CODE
Blue		•		441
Blue		•		451#
Sandalwood		•		444
Sandalwood		•		454#
Green		•		440
Green		•		450#
Burnished Saddle		•		449
Burnished Saddle		•		459#

ESTATE WAGON 3-SEAT

COLOR	CLOTH	VINYL	LEATHER	CODE
Blue		•		441
Blue		•		451#
Sandalwood		•		444
Sandalwood		•		454#
Green		•		440
Green		•		450#
Burnished Saddle		•		449
Burnished Saddle		•		459#

LESABRE 455 2-DOOR HT

COLOR	CLOTH	VINYL	LEATHER	CODE
Black		•		428
Blue	•	•		411
Blue		•		421
Sandalwood	•	•		414
Green	•	•		410
Green		•		420
Saddle		•		426

LESABRE 455 4-DOOR HT

COLOR	CLOTH	VINYL	LEATHER	CODE
Black		•		428
Blue	•	•		411
Blue		•		421
Sandalwood	•	•		414
Green	•	•		410
Green		•		420
Saddle		•		426

WILDCAT CUSTOM 2-DOOR HT

COLOR	CLOTH	VINYL	LEATHER	CODE
Black		•		468#
Black		•		478*
Green		•		460#
Pearl White		•		465#
Saddle		•		466#

WILDCAT CUSTOM 4-DOOR HT

COLOR	CLOTH	VINYL	LEATHER	CODE
Black	•	•		438#
Black		•		468#
Sandalwood	•	•		434#
Green		•		460#
Pearl White		•		465#
Red		•		466#

WILDCAT CUSTOM CONVERTIBLE

COLOR	CLOTH	VINYL	LEATHER	CODE
Black		•		468#
Pearl White		•		465#

ELECTRA

COLOR	CLOTH	VINYL	LEATHER	CODE
Black	•	•		488
Black		•		498
Blue	•	•		481
Sandalwood	•	•		484
Sandalwood		•		494

ELECTRA CUSTOM 4-DOOR HT/SEDAN

COLOR	CLOTH	VINYL	LEATHER	CODE
Black	•	•		608
Black	•	•		637
Black		•		618#
Black		•		628#
Black		•		638
Black		•		648#
Blue	•	•		601
Blue	•	•		632
Blue		•		631#
Sandalwood	•	•		604
Sandalwood	•	•		635
Sandalwood		•		614#
Sandalwood		•		624#
Sandalwood		•		634#
Green	•	•		600
Burnished Saddle		•		619#
Burnished Saddle		•		629#
Burnished Saddle		•		639#

ELECTRA CUSTOM 2-DOOR HT

COLOR	CLOTH	VINYL	LEATHER	CODE
Black		•		618#
Black		•		628#
Black		•		638#
Blue		•		631#
Sandalwood		•		614#
Sandalwood		•		624#
Sandalwood		•		634#
Burnished Saddle		•		619#
Burnished Saddle		•		629#
Burnished Saddle		•		649#

ELECTRA CUSTOM CONVERTIBLE

COLOR	CLOTH	VINYL	LEATHER	CODE
Black		•		618#
Sandalwood		•		614#
Red		•		617#
Burnished Saddle		•		619#

RIVIERA 2-DOOR HT

COLOR	CLOTH	VINYL	LEATHER	CODE
Black	•	•		678#
Black		•		688#
Black		•		668*
Black		•		698*
Blue		•		681#
Sandalwood	•	•		674#
Sandalwood		•		654#
Sandalwood		•		684#
Green		•		650#
Green		•		680#
Pearl White		•		695*
Saddle		•		686#
Saddle		•		666*
Burnished Saddle	•	•		679#
Burnished Saddle		•		659
Burnished Saddle		•		699*

* Bucket seats
# Notch back or 60-40 seats

THE PAINT CODE furnishes the key to the paint colors used on the car. Two, two-digit codes indicate the bottom and top body colors respectively. NOTE: Vinyl roof and convertible top codes appear in the second set of digits.

COLOR	CODE
Glacier White	10
Silver Mist	14
Tealmist Gray	16
Regal Black	19

COLOR	CODE
Azure Blue	20
Gulfstream Blue	25
Stratomist Blue	26
Diplomat Blue	28
Aqua Mist	34
Seamist Green	45
Emerald Mist	46
Sherwood Green	48
Bamboo Cream	50
Cornet Gold	55
Harvest Gold	58
Sand Piper Beige	61
Desert Gold	63
Burnished Saddle	68
Titan Red	74
Fire Red	75
Sunset Sage	76
Burgundy Mist	78

VINYL ROOF COLORS

COLOR	CODE
White	1
Black	2
Dark Gold	7
Dark Brown	8
Dark Green	9

CONVERTIBLE TOP COLORS

COLOR	CODE
White	1
Black	2
Sandalwood	5

ENGINE NUMBER

A Buick engine is stamped with two different identification codes. One is the engine production code which identifies the engine and its approximate production date. The other code is the engine serial number — it matches the VIN (vehicle identification number).

EXAMPLE:
F   12   07   SB
0   H   12   3456

Top row: F = Flint
    12 = Month
    07 = Day
    SB = Trans. or Option usage

Bottom row: 0 = Year (1970)
    H = Flint
    123456 = Production Code

The 250 CID OHV6 engine number and production code number are on the right side, to the rear of the distributor.
The 350 CID V8 engine number is on the front of the left bank of cylinders. The production code number is between the left exhaust manifold and the two front spark plugs.
The 455 CID V8 engine number is between the two front spark plugs and the exhaust manifold. The production code number is between the two rear spark plugs and the left exhaust manifold.

ENGINE CODE	NO CYL	CID	HORSE-POWER	COMP RATIO	CARB
SA	6	250	155	8.5:1	1 BC
SB	8	350	285	9.0:1	4 BC
SF	8	455	370	10.5:1	4-BC
SO	8	350	260	9.0:1	2 BC
SP	8	350	315	10.25:1	4-BC
SR	8	455	350	10.0:1	4-BC
SS	8	455	360	10.5:1	4-BC

Engines available as indicated below:
Skylark & 350 - SA, SO, SB, SP; Sportswagon & Skylark Custom - SO, SB, SP; Skylark GS - SP: Skylark GS 455 - SR, SS; Estate Wagon - SF; LeSabre & Custom - SO, SB, SP; LeSabre Custom 455 - SF; Wildcat Custom - SF; Electra 225 & 225 Custom - SF; Riviera - SF.

1971 BUICK CENTURION

1971 BUICK GS

1971 BUICK ELECTRA

1971 BUICK LE SABRE

1971 BUICK SKYLARK

1971 BUICK RIVIERA

VEHICLE IDENTIFICATION NUMBER

**BUICK
45269IH000000**

Located on the top of the dash on the driver's side and visible through the windshield from outside the car.

FIRST DIGIT: Identifies GM Division (4 = Buick)

SECOND AND THIRD DIGITS: Identify the series

SERIES	CODE
Skylark	33
Sport Wagon	34
GS	34
Skylark Custom	44
LeSabre	52
LeSabre Custom	54
Estate Wagon	60
Centurion	66
Electra 225	82
Electra Custom 225	84
Riviera	94

FOURTH AND FIFTH DIGITS: Identify the body style

BODY STYLE	CODE
2-Door Thin Pillar Sedan	27
Station Wagon, 2-Seat	35
Station Wagon, 2-Seat (Dual Action)	36
2-Door Hardtop	37
4-Door Hardtop	39
Station Wagon, 3-Seat	45
2-Door Hardtop	47
2-Door Hardtop Sport Coupe	57
Convertible	67
4-Door Sedan	69
2-Door Hardtop	87

SIXTH DIGIT: Identifies the year (1 = 1971)

SEVENTH DIGIT: Identifies the assembly plant

ASSEMBLY PLANT	CODE
Southgate, CA	C
Framingham, MA	G
Flint, MI	H
Oshawa, CAN	I
Fairfax, KS	X
Wilmington, DE	Y
Fremont, CA	Z

4 - 6

LAST SIX DIGITS: Represent the basic production numbers

EXAMPLE:

4	52	69	1	H	000000
Buick Div.	Series	Body Style	Year	Asm Plant	Prod Code

BODY NUMBER PLATE

The body number plate is located on the firewall, just below the rear edge of the hood. This plate identifies the model year, car division, series, body style, body assembly plant, body numbers, trim combination, paint code and build date code.

```
   BUICK DIV. GENERAL MOTORS
             CORP.
        FLINT, MICHIGAN
  ST 71  45469      H 123456 BDY
  TR 438              62 62 PNT
         11 A
  GENERAL MOTORS CORPORATION CERTIFIES
    TO THE DEALER THAT THIS VEHICLE
   CONFORMS TO ALL U.S., FEDERAL MOTOR
       VEHICLE SAFETY STANDARDS
     APPLICABLE AT TIME OF MANUFACTURE.
```

Example:

71	Model Year (1971)
4	Car Division (Buick)
54	Series (LeSabre Custom)
69	Style (4-Dr. Sedan Thin Pillar)
H	Body Assembly Plant (Flint, MI)
123456	Production Sequence
438	Black Vinyl Trim
62 62	Bittersweet Mist Paint
11	Eleventh Month (November)
A	First Week of Month

SKYLARK
	CODE
2-Door Coupe Thin Pillar	43327
2-Door Coupe Hardtop	43337
4-Door Sedan Thin Pillar	43369

SKYLARK CUSTOM
	CODE
2-Door Coupe Hardtop	44437
2-Door Convertible	44467
4-Door Hardtop	44439
4-Door Sedan Thin Pillar	44469

GS
	CODE
2-Door Coupe Hardtop	43437
2-Door Convertible	43467

*GS 455 option available
*Stage 1 option available
*GSX option available

SPORT WAGON
	CODE
4-Door 2-Seat Wagon	43436

LESABRE
	CODE
2-Door Coupe Hardtop	45257
4-Door Hardtop	45239
4-Door Sedan Thin Pillar	45269

LESABRE CUSTOM
	CODE
2-Door Coupe Hardtop	45457
2-Door Convertible	45467
4-Door Hardtop	45439
4-Door Sedan Thin Pillar	45469

ESTATE WAGON
	CODE
4-Door 2-Seat Wagon	46035
4-Door 3-Seat Wagon	46045

CENTURION
	CODE
2-Door Coupe Hardtop	46647
2-Door Convertible	46667
4-Door Hardtop	46639

ELECTRA 225
	CODE
2-Door Coupe Hardtop	48237
4-Door Hardtop	48239

ELECTRA 225 CUSTOM
	CODE
2-Door Coupe Hardtop	48437
4-Door Hardtop	48439

RIVIERA
	CODE
2-Door Coupe Hardtop	49487

*GS option available

THE TRIM CODE furnishes the key to the interior color and material scheme.

SKYLARK COUPE TRIM
COLOR	CLOTH	VINYL	LEATHER	CODE
Green	•			110
Green		•		100
Blue	•			111
Sandalwood	•			114
Sandalwood		•		104
Black		•		108

SKYLARK 2-DOOR HT TRIM
COLOR	CLOTH	VINYL	LEATHER	CODE
Green	•			110
Green		•		100
Green		•		150#
Blue	•			111
Sandalwood	•			114
Sandalwood		•		104
Sandalwood		•		154#
Black		•		108
Black		•		158#
Saddle		•		156#

SKYLARK 4-DOOR SEDAN TRIM
COLOR	CLOTH	VINYL	LEATHER	CODE
Green	•			110
Green		•		100
Blue	•			111
Sandalwood	•			114
Sandalwood		•		104
Black		•		108

SPORT WAGON TRIM

COLOR	CLOTH	VINYL	LEATHER	CODE
Green		•		100
Blue		•		101
Sandalwood		•		104

GS 2-DOOR HT TRIM

COLOR	CLOTH	VINYL	LEATHER	CODE
Green		•		100
Green		•		150#
Sandalwood		•		104
Sandalwood		•		154#
Black		•		108
Black		•		158#
Black		•		168*
Saddle		•		156#
Saddle		•		166*
Pearl White		•		165*

GS CONVERTIBLE TRIM

COLOR	CLOTH	VINYL	LEATHER	CODE
Sandalwood		•		134
Black		•		138
Green		•		150#
Pearl White		•		155#
Saddle		•		156#

SKYLARK CUSTOM 2-DOOR HT TRIM

COLOR	CLOTH	VINYL	LEATHER	CODE
Green	•			140
Green		•		150#
Blue	•			141
Sandalwood	•			144
Sandalwoody		•		154#
Black		•		158#
Black		•		168*
Saddle		•		156#
Saddle		•		166*
Pearl White		•		165*

SKYLARK CUSTOM 4-DOOR HT TRIM

COLOR	CLOTH	VINYL	LEATHER	CODE
Green	•			140
Green		•		150#
Blue	•			141
Sandalwood	•			144
Sandalwood		•		154#
Black		•		158#
Saddle		•		156#

SKYLARK CUSTOM CONVERTIBLE TRIM

COLOR	CLOTH	VINYL	LEATHER	CODE
Sandalwood		•		134
Black		•		138
Green		•		150#
Pearl White		•		155#
Saddle		•		156#

SKYLARK CUSTOM 4-DOOR SEDAN TRIM

COLOR	CLOTH	VINYL	LEATHER	CODE
Green	•			140
Blue	•			141
Sandalwood	•			144
Sandalwood		•		134
Black		•		138

LESABRE 4-DOOR HT TRIM

COLOR	CLOTH	VINYL	LEATHER	CODE
Green	•			400
Blue	•			401
Sandalwood	•			404
Black	•			408
Black		•		418
Saddle		•		416

LESABRE 2-DOOR HT TRIM

COLOR	CLOTH	VINYL	LEATHER	CODE
Green	•			400
Blue	•			401
Sandalwood	•			404
Black	•			408
Black		•		418
Saddle		•		416

LESABRE 4-DOOR SEDAN TRIM

COLOR	CLOTH	VINYL	LEATHER	CODE
Green	•			400
Blue	•			401
Sandalwood	•			404
Black	•			408
Black		•		418
Saddle		•		416

LESABRE CUSTOM 4-DOOR HT TRIM

COLOR	CLOTH	VINYL	LEATHER	CODE
Green	•			420
Green		•		430
Blue	•			421
Sandalwood	•			424
Sandalwood		•		434
Black		•		438
Saddle		•		436

LESABRE CUSTOM 2-DOOR HT TRIM

COLOR	CLOTH	VINYL	LEATHER	CODE
Green	•			420
Green		•		430
Blue	•			421
Sandalwood	•			424
Sandalwood		•		434
Black		•		438
Saddle		•		436

LESABRE CUSTOM CONVERTIBLE TRIM

COLOR	CLOTH	VINYL	LEATHER	CODE
Sandalwood		•		434
Black		•		438
Saddle		•		436

LESABRE CUSTOM 4-DOOR SEDAN TRIM

COLOR	CLOTH	VINYL	LEATHER	CODE
Green	•			420
Green		•		430
Blue	•			421
Sandalwood	•			424
Sandalwood		•		434
Black		•		438
Saddle		•		436

ESTATE WAGON 2-SEAT TRIM

COLOR	CLOTH	VINYL	LEATHER	CODE
Green		•		440
Green		•		450#
Blue		•		441
Sandalwood		•		444
Saddle		•		446
Saddle		•		456#

ESTATE WAGON 3-SEAT TRIM

COLOR	CLOTH	VINYL	LEATHER	CODE
Green		•		440
Green		•		450#
Blue		•		441
Sandalwood		•		444
Sandalwood		•		454#
Saddle		•		446
Saddle		•		456#•

CENTURION 4-DOOR HT TRIM

COLOR	CLOTH	VINYL	LEATHER	CODE
Green		•		460#
Sandalwood	•			462#
Sandalwood		•		464#
Black	•			463#
Black		•		468#
Saddle				466#

CENTURION 2-DOOR HT TRIM

COLOR	CLOTH	VINYL	LEATHER	CODE
Green		•		460#
Sandalwood		•		464#
Black		•		468#
Saddle		•		466#

CENTURION CONVERTIBLE TRIM

COLOR	CLOTH	VINYL	LEATHER	CODE
Blue		•		461#
Black		•		468#
Pearl White		•		465#
Saddle		•		466#

ELECTRA 2-DOOR HT TRIM

COLOR	CLOTH	VINYL	LEATHER	CODE
Green	•			480
Blue	•			481
Sandalwood	•			484
Sandalwood		•		494
Black		•		498

ELECTRA 4-DOOR HT TRIM

COLOR	CLOTH	VINYL	LEATHER	CODE
Green	•			480
Blue	•			481
Sandalwood	•			484
Sandalwood		•		494
Black		•		498

ELECTRA CUSTOM 2-DOOR HT TRIM

COLOR	CLOTH	VINYL	LEATHER	CODE
Green	•			610#
Green		•		620#
Blue	•			611#
Sandalwood	•			614#
Sandalwood		•		624#
Black		•		628#
Rosewood		•		627#

ELECTRA LIMITED 2-DOOR HT TRIM

COLOR	CLOTH	VINYL	LEATHER	CODE
Green	•			640#
Blue	•			641#
Sandalwood	•			644#
Black		•		642#

ELECTRA CUSTOM 4-DOOR HT TRIM

COLOR	CLOTH	VINYL	LEATHER	CODE
Green	•			600
Green		•		620#
Blue	•			601
Sandalwood	•			604
Sandalwood		•		624#
Black	•			608
Black		•		628#
Rosewood		•		627#

ELECTRA LIMITED 4-DOOR HT TRIM

COLOR	CLOTH	VINYL	LEATHER	CODE
Green	•			630
Green	•			640#
Blue	•			631
Blue	•			641#
Sandalwood	•			632
Sandalwood	•			644#
Black	•			633
Black		•		648
Black		•		642#

RIVIERA 2-DOOR HT TRIM

COLOR	CLOTH	VINYL	LEATHER	CODE
Green	•			670#
Green		•		680#
Blue	•			671#
Sandalwood	•			674
Sandalwood		•		654
Sandalwood		•		684#
Sandalwood		•		664*
Black	•			678#
Black		•		658
Black		•		688#
Black		•		668*
Black		•		698*
Saddle		•		686#
Rosewood		•		697*
Pearl White		•		695*

* Bucket seats
# Notch back or 60-40 seats

THE PAINT CODE furnishes the key to the paint colors used on the car. Two, two-digit codes indicate the bottom and top body colors respectively. NOTE: vinyl roof and convertible top codes appear in the second set of digits.

COLOR	CODE
Arctic White	11
Platinum Mist	13
Tealmist Gray	16
Regal Black	19
Cascade Blue	24
Stratomist Blue	26
Nocturne Blue	29
Twilight Turquoise	39
Silver Fern	41
Willomist Green	42
Lime Mist	43
Verdemist Green	49
Bamboo Cream	50
Cortez Gold	53
Cornet Gold	55
Sandpiper Beige	61
Bittersweet Mist	62

COLOR	CODE
Copper Mist	65
Burnished Cinnamon	67
Deep Chestnut	68
Pearl Beige	70
Sunset Mist	73
Vintage Red	74
Fire Red	75
Rosewood	78

VINYL ROOF COLORS

COLOR	CODE
White	1
Black	2
Sandalwood	5
Dark Brown	8
Dark Green	9

CONVERTIBLE TOP COLORS

COLOR	CODE
White	1
Black	2
Sandalwood	5
Dark Green	9

ENGINE NUMBER

A Buick engine is stamped with two different identification codes. One is the engine production code which identifies the engine and its approximate production date. The other code is the engine serial number — it matches the VIN (vehicle identification number).

The 250 CID OHV6 engine number and production code number are on the right side, to the rear of the distributor.

The 350 CID V8 engine number is on the front of the left bank of cylinders. The production code number is between the left exhaust manifold and the two front spark plugs.

The 455 CID V8 engine number is between the two front spark plugs and the exhaust manifold. The production code number is between the two rear spark plugs and the left exhaust manifold.

EXAMPLE:

```
F     12     07     SB
1     H      12     3456
```

Top row:
F = Flint
12 = Month
07 = Day
SB = Trans. or Option usage

Bottom row: 1 = Year (1971)
H = Flint
123456 = Production Code

ENGINE CODE	NO. CYL.	CID	HORSE-POWER	COMP. RATIO	CARB	TRANS
DF	6	250	145	8.5:1	1-BC	Man 3-spd
EA	6	250	155	8.5:1	1-BC	TH-350
TO	8	350	230	8.5:1	2-BC	Man 3-spd or TH 350
TD	8	350	260	8.5:1	4-BC	TH-350
TB	8	350	260	8.5:1	4-BC	Man 3-spd, TH 350, 4-spd
TC	8	350	230	8.5:1	2-BC	TH 350
TA	8	455	335	8.5:1	4-BC	TH 400
TR	8	455	310	8.5:1	4-BC	TH 400, 3-spd or Man 4-spd
TS	8	455*	345	8.5:1	4-BC	TH 400 or Man 4-spd

* Stage 1
Engines available as indicated below:
Skylark - DF, EA, TO, TD; Skylark Custom - TO, TD; GS - TB, TD, TR, TS; LeSabre & LeSabre Custom - TC, TO, TR; Centurion - TR, TA; Estate Wagon - TR; Electra 225 & Electra 225 Custom - TR; Riviera - TR; Riviera GS - TA; Sport Wagon - TO, TB

1972 BUICK LE SABRE

1972 BUICK SKYLARK

1972 BUICK RIVIERA

1972 BUICK RIVIERA

1972 BUICK CENTURION

1972 BUICK ELECTRA

VEHICLE IDENTIFICATION NUMBER

**BUICK
4L39H2H100001**

Located on the top of the dash on the driver's side and visible through the windshield from outside the car.

FIRST DIGIT: Identifies GM Division (4 = Buick)

SECOND DIGIT: Identifies the series

SERIES	CODE
Skylark	D
Sport Wagon	F
GS	G
Skylark Custom	H
LeSabre	L
LeSabre Custom	N
Centurion	P

SERIES	CODE
Estate Wagon	R
Electra 225	U
Electra 225 Custom	V
Riviera	Y

THIRD AND FOURTH DIGITS: Identify the body style

BODY STYLE	CODE
2-Door Coupe	27
Station Wagon, 2-Seat	35
Station Wagon, 2 Seat Sportwagon	36
2-Door Hardtop	37
4-Door Hardtop	39
Station Wagon, 3-Seat	45
2-Door Hardtop	47
2-Door Hardtop	57
Convertible	67
4-Door Sedan	69
2-Door Hardtop	87

FIFTH DIGIT: Identifies the engine

ENGINE	CODE
V8-350 2-BC Dual Exhaust	G
V8-350 2-BC	H
V8-350 4-BC	J
V8-350 4-BC Dual Exhaust	K
V8-455 4-BC	T
V8-455 4-BC Dual Exhaust	U
V8-455 4-BC Stage 1	V
V8-455 4-BC Stage 1	W

SIXTH DIGIT: Identifies the year 1972

SEVENTH DIGIT: Identifies the assembly plant

ASSEMBLY PLANT	CODE
Southgate, CA	C
Framingham, MA	G
Flint, MI	H
Fairfax, KS	X
Wilmington, DE	Y
Fremont, CA	Z

LAST SIX DIGITS: Represent the basic production numbers

EXAMPLE:

4	L	39	H	2	H	100001
Buick Div.	Series	Body Style	Engine Code	Year	Asm Plant	Prod Code

BODY NUMBER PLATE

The body number plate is located on the firewall, just below rear the edge of the hood. This plate identifies the model year, car division, series, body style, body assembly plant, body numbers, trim combination, paint code and build date code.

```
BUICK DIV. GENERAL MOTORS
           CORP.
       FLINT, MICHIGAN
 ST 72  4N69      123456 BDY
 TR 438            19 19 PNT
      11 A
GENERAL MOTORS CORPORATION CERTIFIES
  TO THE DEALER THAT THIS VEHICLE
 CONFORMS TO ALL U.S., FEDERAL MOTOR
     VEHICLE SAFETY STANDARDS
 APPLICABLE AT TIME OF MANUFACTURE.
```

Example:

72	Model Year (1972)
4	Car Division (Buick)
N	Series (LeSabre Custom)
69	Style (4-Dr. Sdn. Thin Pillar)
H	Body Assembly Plant (Flint, MI)
123456	Production Sequence
438	Black Vinyl Trim
19 19	Regal Black
11	Eleventh Month (November)
A	First week of month

SKYLARK	CODE
2-Door Coupe Thin Pillar	4D27
2-Door Coupe Hardtop	4D37
4-Door Sedan Thin Pillar	4D69

*Skylark 350 Option
*Sun Coupe option available

SKYLARK CUSTOM	CODE
2-Door Coupe Hardtop	4H37
2-Door Convertible	4H67
4-Door Hardtop	4H39
4-Door Sedan Thin Pillar	4H69

GS	CODE
2-Door Coupe Hardtop	4G37
2-Door Convertible	4G67

SPORT WAGON	CODE
4-Door 2-Seat Wagon	4F36

LESABRE	CODE
2-Door Coupe Hardtop	4L57
4-Door Hardtop	4L39
4-Door Sedan Thin Pillar	4L69

LESABRE CUSTOM	CODE
2-Door Coupe Hardtop	4N57
2-Door Convertible	4N67
4-Door Hardtop	4N39
4-Door Sedan Thin Pillar	4N69

ESTATE WAGON	CODE
4-Door 2-Seat Wagon	4R35
4-Door 3-Seat Wagon	4R45

CENTURION	CODE
2-Door Coupe Hardtop	4P47
2-Door Convertible	4P67
4-Door Hardtop	4P39

ELECTRA 225	CODE
2-Door Coupe Hardtop	4U37
4-Door Hardtop	4U39

ELECTRA 225 CUSTOM	CODE
2-Door Coupe Hardtop	4V37
4-Door Hardtop	4V39

*Limited option available

RIVIERA	CODE
2-Door Coupe Hardtop	4Y87

*GS option available

THE TRIM CODE furnishes the key to the interior color and material scheme.

SKYLARK 2-DOOR COUPE THIN PILLAR

COLOR	CLOTH	VINYL	LEATHER	CODE
Green	•			110
Green		•		100
Blue	•			111
Covert				114
Saddle		•		106
Black		•		108

4 - 12

SKYLARK 2-DOOR COUPE HT

COLOR	CLOTH	VINYL	LEATHER	CODE
Green	•			110
Green		•		100
Blue	•			111
Covert	•			114
Covert		•		133#
Saddle		•		106
Saddle		•		136#
Black		•		108
Black		•		138#
Black		•		139*
White		•		135#
White		•		135*
Tan Black		•		138*

SKYLARK 4-DOOR SEDAN THIN PILLAR

COLOR	CLOTH	VINYL	LEATHER	CODE
Green	•			110
Green		•		100
Blue	•			111
Covert	•			114
Saddle		•		106
Saddle		•		136#
Black		•		108
Black		•		138#

SKYLARK CUSTOM 2-DOOR COUPE HT

COLOR	CLOTH	VINYL	LEATHER	CODE
Green	•			140
Blue	•			141
Covert	•			144
Covert		•		133#
White		•		135#
White		•		135*
Saddle		•		136#
Black		•		138#
Black		•		138*
Tan Black		•		137*

SKYLARK CUSTOM 4-DOOR HT

COLOR	CLOTH	VINYL	LEATHER	CODE
Green	•			140
Green		•		130#
Blue	•			141
Covert	•			144
Saddle		•		136#
Black		•		138#

SKYLARK CUSTOM CONVERTIBLE

COLOR	CLOTH	VINYL	LEATHER	CODE
Green		•		130#
White		•		135#
Saddle		•		136#
Black		•		138#

SKYLARK CUSTOM 4-DOOR SEDAN THIN PILLAR

COLOR	CLOTH	VINYL	LEATHER	CODE
Green	•			140
Blue	•			141
Covert	•			144
Saddle		•		136#
Black		•		137#

SPORT WAGON

COLOR	CLOTH	VINYL	LEATHER	CODE
Green		•		100
Blue		•		101
Covert		•		104
Saddle		•		106

GS 2-DOOR HT

COLOR	CLOTH	VINYL	LEATHER	CODE
Green		•		100
Saddle		•		106
Saddle		•		136#
Black		•		108
Black		•		138#
Black		•		138*
White		•		135#
White		•		135*
Tan Black		•		137*

GS CONVERTIBLE

COLOR	CLOTH	VINYL	LEATHER	CODE
Green		•		130#
White		•		135#
Saddle		•		136#
Black		•		138#

LESABRE 2-DOOR COUPE HT

COLOR	CLOTH	VINYL	LEATHER	CODE
Green	•			400
Blue	•			401
Covert	•			404
Black	•			408
Black		•		418
Saddle		•		416

LESABRE 4-DOOR HT

COLOR	CLOTH	VINYL	LEATHER	CODE
Green	•			400
Blue	•			401
Covert	•			404
Black	•			408
Black		•		418
Saddle		•		416

LESABRE 4-DOOR SEDAN THIN PILLAR

COLOR	CLOTH	VINYL	LEATHER	CODE
Green	•			400
Blue	•			401
Covert	•			404
Black	•			408
Black		•		418
Saddle		•		416

LESABRE CUSTOM 2-DOOR HT

COLOR	CLOTH	VINYL	LEATHER	CODE
Green	•			420
Green		•		430
Blue	•			421
Covert	•			424
Covert		•		434
Saddle		•		436
Black		•		438

LESABRE CUSTOM 4-DOOR HT

COLOR	CLOTH	VINYL	LEATHER	CODE
Green	•			420
Green		•		430
Blue	•			421
Covert	•			424
Covert		•		434
Saddle		•		436
Black		•		438

LESABRE CUSTOM CONVERTIBLE

COLOR	CLOTH	VINYL	LEATHER	CODE
White		•		435
Saddle		•		436
Black		•		438

LESABRE CUSTOM 4-DOOR SEDAN THIN PILLAR

COLOR	CLOTH	VINYL	LEATHER	CODE
Green	•			420
Green		•		430
Blue	•			421
Covert	•			424
Covert		•		434
Saddle		•		436
Black		•		438

ESTATE WAGON 2-SEAT

COLOR	CLOTH	VINYL	LEATHER	CODE
Green		•		440
Green		•		450#
Blue		•		441
Covert		•		444
Saddle		•		446
Saddle		•		456#

ESTATE WAGON 3-SEAT

COLOR	CLOTH	VINYL	LEATHER	CODE
Green		•		440
Green		•		450#
Blue		•		441
Covert		•		444
Covert		•		454#
Saddle		•		446
Saddle		•		456#

CENTURION 2-DOOR HT

COLOR	CLOTH	VINYL	LEATHER	CODE
Covert	•			464#
Covert		•		474#
Green		•		470#
Saddle		•		476#
Black		•		478#

CENTURION 4-DOOR HT

COLOR	CLOTH	VINYL	LEATHER	CODE
Covert	•			464#
Covert		•		474#
Black	•			468#
Black		•		478#
Green		•		470#
Saddle		•		476#

CENTURION CONVERTIBLE

COLOR	CLOTH	VINYL	LEATHER	CODE
Green		•		470#
White		•		475#
Saddle		•		476#
Black		•		478#

ELECTRA 225 2-DOOR HT

COLOR	CLOTH	VINYL	LEATHER	CODE
Green	•			480
Blue	•			481
Covert	•			484
Covert		•		494
Black		•		498

ELECTRA 225 4-DOOR HT

COLOR	CLOTH	VINYL	LEATHER	CODE
Green	•			480
Blue	•			481
Covert	•			484
Covert		•		494
Black		•		498

ELECTRA 225 CUSTOM 2-DOOR HT

COLOR	CLOTH	VINYL	LEATHER	CODE
Green		•		600
Green		•		620#
Blue		•		601
Covert		•		604
Covert		•		624#
Saddle		•		626#
Black		•		628#

ELECTRA 225 LIMITED 2-DOOR HT

COLOR	CLOTH	VINYL	LEATHER	CODE
Green	•			630#
Blue	•			631#
Covert	•			634#
Saddle		•		646#

ELECTRA 225 CUSTOM 4-DOOR HT

COLOR	CLOTH	VINYL	LEATHER	CODE
Green	•			600
Green		•		620#
Blue	•			601
Covert	•			604
Covert		•		624#
Black	•			608
Black		•		628#
Saddle		•		626#

ELECTRA 225 LIMITED 4-DOOR HT

COLOR	CLOTH	VINYL	LEATHER	CODE
Green	•			630
Green	•			630#
Blue	•			631
Blue	•			631#
Covert	•			634
Covert	•			634#
Black	•			638
Saddle		•		646#

RIVIERA 2-DOOR HT

COLOR	CLOTH	VINYL	LEATHER	CODE
Green	•			670#
Green		•		680#
Blue	•			671#
Covert	•			674#
Covert		•		654
Covert		•		684#
Covert		•		654*
Saddle	•			676#
Saddle		•		684#
Saddle		•		686*
Black		•		658
Black		•		688#
Black		•		658*
Black		•		688*
White		•		685*

* Bucket seats
\# Notch back or 60-40 seat

THE PAINT CODE furnishes the key to the paint colors used on the car. A one letter code indicates the bottom and top colors respectively. NOTE: vinyl roof and convertible top codes appear in the second set of digits.

COLOR	CODE
Arctic White	11
Silver Mist	14
Charcoal Mist	18
Regal Black	19
Crystal Blue	21
Cascade Blue	24
Stratomist Blue	26
Royal Blue	28
Heritage Green	36
Seamist Green	43
Emerald Mist	45
Hunter Green	48
Sandalwood	50
Cortez Gold	53
Champagne Gold	54
Sunburst Yellow	56
Antique Gold	57

COLOR	CODE
Sierra Tan	62
Burnished Copper	63
Flame Orange	65
Deep Chestnut	67
Nutmeg	69
Vintage Red	73
Fire Red	75
Burnished Bronze	77

VINYL ROOF COLORS

COLOR	CODE
White	A
Black	B
Covert	T
Tan	F
Green	G
Blue	D
Silver	H

CONVERTIBLE TOP COLORS

COLOR	CODE
White	A
Black	B
Covert	T
Green	G

ENGINE NUMBER

A Buick engine is stamped with two different identification code production code which identifies the engine and its approximate production date. The other code is the engine serial number — it matches the VIN (vehicle identification number).

The 350 CID V8 engine number is on the front of the right cylinder bank. The production code number is between the left exhaust manifold and the two front spark plugs.

The 455 CID engine number is on the front of the right cylinder bank. The production code number is between the left exhaust manifold and the two rear spark plugs.

ENGINE CODE	NO. CYL.	CID	HORSE- POWER	COMP. RATIO	CARB
WC	8	350	155	8.5:1	2-BC
WB	8	350	175	8.5:1	4-BC
WF	8	455	225	8.5:1	4-BC
WS	8	455*	270	8.5:1	4-BC
WA	8	455**	260	8.5:1	4-BC
WC (1)	8	350	150	8.5:1	2-BC
WB (1)	8	350	180	8.5:1	4-BC
WB (2)	8 (Dual Exhaust)	350	190	8.5:1	4-BC
WF (1)	8 (Dual Exhaust)	455	250	8.5:1	4-BC

*Stage 1
**GS Riviera

Engines are available as indicated below:
Skylark, Skylark Custom & Sportwagon - WC Auto, WC (1) Man & Calif Auto, WB Man & Calif Auto, WB (1) auto; GS - WB (2), WF (1), WS; LeSabre & LeSabre Custom - WC, WC(1), WB, WB(1), WF; Centurion - WF, WF(1); Estate Wagon - WF; Electra 225 & Electra 225 Custom - WF; Riviera - WF, WA.

1973 BUICK CENTURY

1973 BUICK REGAL COUPE

1973 BUICK CENTURION

1973 BUICK ELECTRA LIMITED

1973 BUICK LE SABRE

1973 BUICK RIVIERA

VEHICLE IDENTIFICATION NUMBER

**BUICK
4V57J3H446727**

Located on the top of the dash on the driver's siisible through the windshield from outside the car.

FIRST DIGIT: Identifies GM Division (4 = Buick)

SECOND DIGIT: Identifies the series

SERIES	CODE
Apollo	B
Century	D
Century Luxus	H
Regal	J
Century Wagon	F
Century Luxus Wagon	K
LeSabre	L
LeSabre Custom	N
Estate Wagon	R
Centurion	P
Electra 225	T
Electra 225 Custom	V
Riviera	Y

THIRD AND FOURTH DIGITS: Identify the body style

BODY STYLE	CODE
2-Door Hatchback	17
2-Door Coupe	27
4-Door Sedan	29
Station Wagon, 2-Seat	35
2-Door Coupe	37
4-Door Hardtop	39
Station Wagon, 3-Seat	45
2-Door Hardtop or Coupe	57
Convertible	67
4-Door Sedan	69
2-Door Hardtop	87

FIFTH DIGIT: Identifies the engine

ENGINE	CODE
6-250	D
V8-350 2-BC	H
V8-350 4-BC	J
V8-350 4-BC Dual Exhaust	K
V8-455 4-BC	T
V8-455 4-BC Dual Exhaust	U
V8-455 4-BC Stage 1	V
V8-455 4-BC Stage 1	W

SIXTH DIGIT: Identifies the year (3 = 1973)

SEVENTH DIGIT: Identifies the assembly plant

ASSEMBLY PLANT	CODE
Southgate, CA	C
Framingham, MA	G
Flint, MI	H
Van Nuys, CA	L
Fairfax, KS	X
Wilmington, DE	Y
Fremont, CA	Z

LAST SIX DIGITS: Represent the basic production numbers

EXAMPLE:

4	V	57	J	3	H	123456
Buick Div.	Series	Body Style	Engine Code	Model Year	Asm Plant	Prod Code

BODY NUMBER PLATE

The body number plate is located on the firewall, just below the rear edge of the hood. This plate identifies the model year, car division, series, body style, body assembly plant, body numbers, trim combination, paint code and build date code.

```
BUICK DIV. GENERAL MOTORS
           CORP.
      FLINT, MICHIGAN
ST 73  4AD29   H  123456 BDY
TR 100              11 11 PNT
       11 A
GENERAL MOTORS CORPORATION CERTIFIES
TO THE DEALER THAT THIS VEHICLE
CONFORMS TO ALL U.S., FEDERAL MOTOR
VEHICLE SAFETY STANDARDS
APPLICABLE AT TIME OF MANUFACTURE.
```

Example:

73	Model Year (1973)
4	Car Division (Buick)
AD	Series (Century)
29	Style (4-Door Sedan)
H	Body Assembly Plant (Flint, MI)
123456	Production Sequence
100	Green Trim
11 11	Arctic White Paint
11	Eleventh Month (Nov.)
A	First Week of month

CENTURY	CODE
4-Door Sedan	4AD29
2-Door Coupe	4AD37
Station Wagon	4AF35

*GS option available

CENTURY LUXUS	CODE
4-Door Sedan	4AH29
2-Door Coupe	4AH57
Station Wagon	4AK35

REGAL	CODE
2-Door	4AJ57

LESABRE	CODE
4-Door Hardtop	4BL39
2-Door Hardtop	4BL57
4-Door Sedan	4BL69

LESABRE CUSTOM	CODE
4-Door Hardtop	4BN39
2-Door Hardtop	4BN57
4-Door Sedan	4BN69

CENTURION	CODE
4-Door Hardtop	4BP39
2-Door Hardtop	4BP57
Convertible	4BP67

ESTATE WAGON	CODE
2-Seat	4BR35
3-Seat	4BR45

ELECTRA	CODE
2-Door Hardtop	4CT37
4-Door Hardtop	4CT39

ELECTRA CUSTOM	CODE
2-Door Hardtop	4CV37
4-Door Hardtop	4CV39

*Limited option available

RIVIERA	CODE
2-Door Hardtop	4EY87

*GS option available

APOLLO	CODE
2-Door Hatchback	4XB17
2-Door Coupe	4XB27
4-Door Sedan	4XB69

THE BODY NUMBER is the production serial number of the body. The prefix letter denotes the plant in which the body was built (refer to the assembly plant codes on the VIN plate).

THE TRIM CODE furnishes the key to the interior color and material scheme.

CENTURY 4-DOOR SEDAN

COLOR	CODE
Green	100/120
Green	130
Blue	111
Neutral	114/104
Neutral	124/134
Black	108/128
Black	138
Saddle	126/136

CENTURY 2-DOOR COUPE

COLOR	CODE
Green	100/120
Green	130
Blue	111
Neutral	114/104
Neutral	124/134
Black	108/128
Black	138
Saddle	126/136
White	135
Oxblood	139

CENTURY STATION WAGON

COLOR	CODE
Green	120
Blue	121
Saddle	126

CENTURY LUXUS STATION WAGON

COLOR	CODE
Green	130
Blue	131
Saddle	136
Oxblood	139

CENTURY LUXUS 4-DOOR SEDAN

COLOR	CODE
Green	140/130
Blue	141
Neutral	144/134
Saddle	136
Black	138

CENTURY LUXUS 2-DOOR SEDAN

COLOR	CODE
Green	140/130
Blue	141
Neutral	144/134
White	135
Saddle	136
Black	138
Oxblood	139

REGAL 2-DOOR

COLOR	CODE
Green	160
Green	150/350
Blue	151/351
Neutral	164
Neutral	154/354
White	165
Saddle	166
Black	168
Black	158/358
Oxblood	139

LESABRE 4-DOOR HT

COLOR	CODE
Green	400
Blue	401
Neutral	404
Black	418
Saddle	416

LESABRE 2-DOOR HT

COLOR	CODE
Green	400
Blue	401
Neutral	404
Black	418
Saddle	416

LESABRE 4-DOOR SEDAN

COLOR	CODE
Green	400
Blue	401
Neutral	404
Black	418
Saddle	416

LESABRE CUSTOM 4-DOOR HT

COLOR	CODE
Green	420/430
Green	440
Blue	421/451
Neutral	424/434
Neutral	444/454
Saddle	436/446
Black	438/448

LESABRE CUSTOM 2-DOOR HT

COLOR	CODE
Green	420/430
Green	440
Blue	421/451
Neutral	424/434
Neutral	444/454
Black	438/448
Saddle	436/446

LESABRE CUSTOM 4-DOOR SEDAN

COLOR	CODE
Green	420/430
Blue	421
Neutral	424/434
Black	438
Saddle	436

CENTURION 4-DOOR HT

COLOR	CODE
Green	440
Blue	451
Blue	(151)
Neutral	444/454
Neutral	(154)
Saddle	446
Black	448

CENTURION 2-DOOR HT

COLOR	CODE
Green	440
Neutral	444/454
Saddle	446
Black	448
Blue	451

CENTURION CONVERTIBLE

COLOR	CODE
Green	440
Neutral	444
Black	448
Saddle	446

ESTATE WAGON, 2-SEAT

COLOR	CODE
Green	410/440
Blue	411
Saddle	416/446
Neutral	444

ESTATE WAGON, 3-SEAT

COLOR	CODE
Green	410/440
Blue	411
Saddle	416/446
Saddle	456
Neutral	444

ELECTRA 2-DOOR HT

COLOR	CODE
Green	600
Blue	601
Neutral	604/614
Black	618

ELECTRA 4-DOOR HT

COLOR	CODE
Green	600
Blue	601
Neutral	604/614
Black	618

ELECTRA CUSTOM 2-DOOR HT

COLOR	CODE
Green	630/620
Blue	621
Neutral	635/624
White	635
Saddle	636/656
Black	638/648

ELECTRA CUSTOM 4-DOOR HT

COLOR	CODE
Green	620/640
Green	460/650
Green	470
Blue	621/641
Blue	461/651
Blue	471
Neutral	624/644
Neutral	464/654
Neutral	474
Black	648/658
Black	668/478
Black	638
Saddle	656/476
Saddle	636
White	635

RIVIERA 2-DOOR HT

COLOR	CODE
Green	690
Blue	681
Neutral	684/694
Neutral	674
Black	698/678
Saddle	686/696
Oxblood	699
White	695

APOLLO 2-DOOR HATCHBACK

COLOR	CODE
Green	190
Blue	191
Neutral	174/194
Black	178
Saddle	176

APOLLO 2-DOOR COUPE

COLOR	CODE
Green	180/190
Green	176
Blue	181/191
Neutral	184/174
Neutral	194
Black	178
Saddle	176

APOLLO 4-DOOR SEDAN

COLOR	CODE
Green	180/190
Blue	181/191
Neutral	184/194
Black	178
Saddle	176

THE PAINT CODE furnishes the key to the paint colors used on the car. A one letter code indicates the bottom and top colors respectively.

COLOR	CODE
Arctic White	11
Regal Black	19
Medium Blue Metallic	24
Mediterranean Blue	26
Midnight Blue	29
Jade Green	42
Willow Green	44
Green-Gold Metallic	46
Dark Green	48
Apollo Yellow	51
Autumn Gold	54
Colonial Yellow	56
Harvest Gold	60
Silver Cloud	64
Burnt Coral	65
Taupe Metallic	66
Midnight Gray	67
Brown Metallic	68
Burgundy	74
Apollo Red	75
Yellow Beige	81
Apollo Orange	97

CONVERTIBLE TOP COLOR

COLOR	CODE
White	A
Black	B
Green	G
Sandalwood	T

VINYL TOP COLOR

COLOR	CODE
White	A
Black	B
Blue	D
Green	G
Burgundy	H
Dark Brown	R
Sandalwood	T

ENGINE NUMBER

A Buick engine is stamped with two different identification codes. One is an engine production code which identifies the engine and its approximate production date. The other code is the engine serial number — it matches the VIN (vehicle identification number).

The V6 engine production code number is between the front and middle branches of the right exhaust manifold. The engine serial number is just below the front of the left cylinder head.

The 350 CID V8 engine number is on the front of the right cylinder bank. The production code number is between the left exhaust manifold and the two front spark plugs.

The 455 CID V8 engine serial number is on the front of the right cylinder bank. The production code number is between the left exhaust manifold and the two rear spark plugs.

ENGINE CODE	NO. CYL.	CID	HORSE-POWER	COMP. RATIO	CARB	TRANS
CCC,CCD	6	250	100	8.2:1	1-BC	Man
CCA,CCB	6	250	100	8.2:1	1-BC	Auto
XC	8	350	150	8.5:1	2-BC	3-spd Man
XB (Single Exh.)	8	350	175	8.5:1	4-BC	3-spd Auto
XB (Dual Exh.)	8	350	190	8.5:1	4-BC	
XF (Single Exh.)	8	455	225	8.5:1	4-BC	
XF (Dual Exh.)	8	455	250	8.5:1	4-BC	3-spd Auto
XS	8	455	260	8.5:1	4-BC	3-spd Auto
XA Stage 1	8	455	270	8.5:1	4-BC	3-spd Auto

Engines are available as indicated below:

Apollo - CCC, CCD, CCA, CCB, XC, XB (Single); Century, Century Luxus & Regal - XC, XB (Single), XF (Dual, Coupe Only); GS - XC, XB (Single), XB (Dual), XF (Dual), XA; LeSabre & LeSabre Custom - XC, XB (Single), XF (Single), XF (Dual); Centurion - XB (Single), XF (Single) XF (Dual), XS; Electra - XF (Single), XF (Dual); Estate Wagon - XF (Single); Riviera - XF (Dual), XS.

1974 BUICK ELECTRA LIMITED

1974 BUICK LE SABRE

1974 BUICK ELECTRA LIMITED

1974 BUICK CENTURY

1974 BUICK RIVIERA

VEHICLE IDENTIFICATION NUMBER

• BUICK
4N39T4X100000 •

Located on the top of the dash on the driver's side and visible through the windshield from outside the car.

FIRST DIGIT: Identifies GM Division (4 = Buick)

SECOND DIGIT: Identifies the series

SERIES	CODE
Apollo	B
Century	D
Century Luxus	H
Regal	J
Century Wagon	F
Century Luxus Wagon	K
LeSabre	N
LeSabre Luxus	P
Estate Wagon	R
Electra 225	T
Electra 225 Custom	V
Electra Limited	X
Riviera	Y

THIRD AND FOURTH DIGITS: Identify the body style

BODY STYLE	CODE
2-Door Hatchback	17
2-Door Coupe	27
4-Door Sedan	29
Station Wagon, 2-Seat	35
2-Door Coupe	37
4-Door Hardtop	39
Station Wagon, 3-Seat	45
2-Door Hardtop or Coupe	57
Convertible	67
4-Door Sedan	69
2-Door Hardtop	87

FIFTH DIGIT: Identifies the engine

ENGINE	CODE
6-250	D
V8-350 2-BC Dual Exhaust	G
V8-350 2-BC	H
V8-350 4-BC	J
V8-350 4-BC Dual Exhaust	K
V8-455 2-BC	P
V8-455 2-BC Dual Exhaust	R
V8-455 4-BC	T
V8-455 4-BC Dual Exhaust	U
V8-455 4-BC Stage 1	V
V8-455 4-BC Stage 1	W

SIXTH DIGIT: Identifies the year (4 = 1974)

SEVENTH DIGIT: Identifies the assembly plant

ASSEMBLY PLANT	CODE
Southgate, CA	C
Framingham, MA	G
Flint, MI	H
Van Nuys, CA	L
Norwood, OH	N
Fairfax, KS	X
Wilmington, DE	Y
Fremont, CA	Z

LAST SIX DIGITS: Represent the basic production numbers

EXAMPLE:

4	V	39	J	4	H	445346
Buick Div.	Series	Body Style	Engine Code	Model Year	Asm Plant	Prod Code

BODY NUMBER PLATE

The body number plate is located on the firewall, just below the rear edge of the hood. This plate identifies the model year, car division, series, body style, body assembly plant, body numbers, trim combination, paint code and build date code.

```
BUICK DIV. GENERAL MOTORS
            CORP.
       FLINT, MICHIGAN
ST 74   4AH57    H 123456 BDY
TR 620               11 11 PNT
     11A   A51

GENERAL MOTORS CORPORATION CERTIFIES
  TO THE DEALER THAT THIS VEHICLE
 CONFORMS TO ALL U.S., FEDERAL MOTOR
      VEHICLE SAFETY STANDARDS
   APPLICABLE AT TIME OF MANUFACTURE.
```

Example:
74	Model Year (1974)
4	Car Division (Buick)
AH	Series (Century)
57	Style (2-Door Coupe)
H	Body Assembly Plant (Flint, MI)
123456	Production Sequence
160	Green Trim
11	Arctic White Paint
11	Eleventh Month (Nov.)
A	1st Week of month
A51	Modular Seat Code

CENTURY	CODE
350 4-Door Sedan	4AD29
2-Door Coupe	4AD37
Station Wagon	4AF35

CENTURY LUXUS	CODE
4-Door Sedan	4AH29
2-Door Coupe	4AH57
Station Wagon	4AK35

REGAL	CODE
4-Door Sedan	4AJ29
2-Door Coupe	4AJ57

LESABRE	CODE
4-Door Hardtop	4BN39
2-Door Hardtop	4BN57
4-Door Sedan	4BN69

LESABRE LUXUS	CODE
4-Door Hardtop	4BP39
2-Door Hardtop	4BP57
Convertible	4BP67
4-Door Sedan	4BP69

ESTATE WAGON	CODE
2-Seat	4BR35
3-Seat	4BR45

ELECTRA	CODE
2-Door Hardtop	4CT37
4-Door Hardtop	4CT39

ELECTRA CUSTOM	CODE
2-Door Hardtop	4CV37
4-Door Hardtop	4CV39

ELECTRA LIMITED	CODE
2-Door Hardtop	4CX37
4-Door Hardtop	4CX39

RIVIERA	CODE
2-Door Hardtop	4EY87
*GS option available	

APOLLO	CODE
2-Door Hatchback	4XB17
2-Door Coupe	4XB27
4-Door Sedan	4XB69

THE TRIM CODE furnishes the key to the interior color and material scheme.

APOLLO 2-DR HATCHBACK TRIM

COLOR	CODE
Green	100
Green	120
Blue	101
Blue	121
Neutral	103
Neutral	124
Saddle	124
Saddle	114
Red	107
Black	118
White/Green	112
White/Blue	116
White/Red	117
White/Saddle	115
White/Black	119

APOLLO 2-DR COUPE TRIM

COLOR	CODE
Green	100
Green	120
Blue	101
Blue	121
Neutral	103
Neutral	124
Saddle	124
Saddle	114
Red	107
Black	118
White/Green	112
White/Blue	116
White/Red	117
White/Saddle	115
White/Black	119

APOLLO 4-DR SEDAN

COLOR	CODE
Green	100
Green	120
Blue	101
Blue	121
Neutral	103
Neutral	124
Neutral	113
Saddle	124
Saddle	114
Black	118

CENTURY 2-DOOR COUPE TRIM

COLOR	CODE
Green	140
Green	160
Green	150
Green	170
Blue	141
Blue	161
Blue	151
Saddle	144
Saddle	164
Saddle	154
Saddle	174
Black	168
Black	178
Oxblood	177
White/Green	172
White/Blue	176
White/Saddle	175
White/Oxblood	167
White/Black	179

CENTURY 350 4-DOOR SEDAN TRIM

COLOR	CODE
Green	140
Green	160
Green	150
Green	170
Blue	141
Blue	161
Blue	151
Saddle	144
Saddle	164
Saddle	154
Saddle	174
Black	168
Black	178
Oxblood	177
White/Green	172
White/Blue	176
White/Saddle	175

CENTURY 350 4-DOOR SEDAN TRIM

COLOR	CODE
White/Oxblood	167
White/Black	179

CENTURY 350 STATION WAGON TRIM

COLOR	CODE
Green	150
Green	170
Blue	161
Blue	151
Blue	171
Saddle	164
Saddle	154
Saddle	174
Oxblood	177

CENTURY LUXUS STATION WAGON TRIM

COLOR	CODE
Green	150
Green	170
Blue	161
Blue	151
Blue	171
Saddle	164
Saddle	154
Saddle	174
Oxblood	177

CENTURY LUXUS 4-DOOR SEDAN TRIM

COLOR	CODE
Green	160
Green	170
Blue	161
Blue	171
Saddle	164
Saddle	174
Black	168
Black	178
Oxblood	177
White/Green	172
White/Blue	176
White/Saddle	175
White/Oxblood	167
White/Black	179

CENTURY LUXUS 2-DOOR COUPE TRIM

COLOR	CODE
Green	160
Green	170
Blue	161
Saddle	164
Saddle	174
Black	168
Black	178
Oxblood	177
White/Green	172
White/Blue	176
White/Saddle	175
White/Oxblood	167
White/Black	179

REGAL 2-DOOR COUPE TRIM

COLOR	CODE
Green	180
Green	188
Blue	181
Neutral	183
Oxblood	187
Oxblood	197
Saddle	194
Black	198
Black/White	188
White/Green	192
White/Blue	196
White/Neutral	182
White/Saddle	195
White/Oxblood	185
White/Black	199

REGAL 4-DOOR SEDAN TRIM

COLOR	CODE
Green	180
Blue	181
Neutral	183
Neutral	193
Saddle	194
Oxblood	187
Oxblood	197
Black	198
Black/White	188

LESABRE 2-DOOR HARDTOP TRIM

COLOR	CODE
Green	400
Green	410
Blue	401
Blue	411
Saddle	404
Saddle	414

LESABRE 4-DOOR HARDTOP TRIM

COLOR	CODE
Green	400
Green	410
Blue	401
Blue	411
Saddle	404
Saddle	414

LESABRE 4-DOOR SEDAN TRIM

COLOR	CODE
Green	400
Green	410
Blue	401
Blue	411
Saddle	404
Saddle	414

LESABRE LUXUS 2-DOOR HARDTOP TRIM

COLOR	CODE
Green	420
Blue	421
Blue	431
Saddle	424
Saddle	434
Oxblood	427
Oxblood	437
Black	438
White/Green	432
White/Blue	436
White/Saddle	435
White/Oxblood	433
White/Black	439

LESABRE LUXUS 4-DOOR HARDTOP TRIM

COLOR	CODE
Green	420
Blue	421
Blue	431
Saddle	424
Saddle	434
Oxblood	427
Oxblood	437
Black	438
White/Green	432
White/Blue	436
White/Saddle	435
White/Oxblood	433
White/Black	439

LESABRE CONVERTIBLE TRIM

COLOR	CODE
Blue	431
Saddle	434
Oxblood	437
White/Blue	436
White/Saddle	435
White/Oxblood	433

LESABRE 4-DOOR SEDAN TRIM

COLOR	CODE
Green	420
Blue	421
Blue	431
Saddle	424
Saddle	434
Oxblood	427
Oxblood	437
Black	438
White/Green	432
White/Blue	436
White/Saddle	435
White/Oxblood	433
White/Black	439

ESTATE WAGON 2-SEAT TRIM

COLOR	CODE
Green	410
Green	430
Blue	411
Blue	421
Blue	431
Saddle	424
Saddle	414
Saddle	434
Oxblood	437

ESTATE WAGON 3-SEAT TRIM

COLOR	CODE
Green	410
Green	430
Blue	421
Blue	411
Blue	431
Saddle	424
Saddle	414
Saddle	434
Oxblood	437

ELECTRA 2-DOOR HARDTOP TRIM

COLOR	CODE
Blue	601
Neutral	603
Neutral	613
Black	608
Black	618

ELECTRA 4-DOOR HARDTOP TRIM

COLOR	CODE
Blue	601
Neutral	603
Neutral	613
Black	608
Black	618

ELECTRA CUSTOM 2-DOOR HT TRIM

COLOR	CODE
Green	620
Green	630
Blue	621
Neutral	623
Saddle	634
Oxblood	627
Black	638
White/Green	632
White/Blue	636
White/Neutral	633
White/Saddle	635
White/Oxblood	625
White/Black	639

ELECTRA CUSTOM 4-DOOR HT TRIM

COLOR	CODE
Green	620
Green	630
Blue	621
Neutral	623
Saddle	634
Oxblood	627
Black	638
White/Green	632
White/Blue	636
White/Neutral	633
White/Saddle	635
White/Oxblood	625
White/Black	639

ELECTRA LIMITED 4-DOOR HT TRIM

COLOR	CODE
Green	640
Blue	641
Blue	651
Neutral	643
Saddle	644
Oxblood	647
Black	648

RIVIERA 2-DOOR HT TRIM

COLOR	CODE
Green	660
Blue	661
Neutral	663
Black	668

THE PAINT CODE furnishes the key to the paint colors used on the car. Two, two-digit codes indicate the bottom and top body colors respectively. NOTE: vinyl roof and convertible top codes appear in the second set of digits.

COLOR	CODE
Arctic White	11
Regal Black	19
Medium Blue Metallic	24
Mediterranean Blue	26
Midnight Blue	29
Crystal Lake Blue	36
Mint Green	40
Ranch Green	44
Leaf Green Metallic	46
Forest Green Metallic	49
Sand Beige	50
Canary Yellow	51
Ginger Metallic	53
Gold Mist	54
Nugget Gold	55
Nutmeg Metallic	59
Silver Cloud	64
Cinnamon Metallic	66
Dark Brown Metallic	69
Ruby Red	72
Burgundy Metallic	74
Apple Red	75
Plum Metallic	79

VINYL TOP COLORS

COLOR	CODE
Black	A
White	C
Blue	D
Green	I
Beige	L
Dark Brown	U
Burgundy	H

CONVERTIBLE TOP COLORS

COLOR	CODE
Black	A
White	C
Beige	L
Burgundy	H

ENGINE NUMBER

A Buick engine is stamped with two different identification codes. One is the engine production code which identifies the engine and its approximate production date. The other code is the engine serial number — it matches the VIN (vehicle identification number).

The 250 CID V6 production code number is between the front and he right exhaust manifold. The engine serial number is just below the front of the left cylinder head.

The 350 CID V8 engine serial number is on the front of the right cylinder bank. The production code number is between the left exhaust manifold and the two front spark plugs.

The 455 CID V8 engine serial number is on the front of the right cylinder bank. The production code number is between the left exhaust manifold and the two rear spark plugs.

ENGINE CODE	NO. CYL.	CID	HORSE-POWER	COMP. RATIO	CARB	OTHER
CCW	6	250	100	8.2:1	1-BC	California
CCX	6	250	100	8.2:1	1-BC	
CCR	6	250	100	8.2:1	1-BC	
ZC	8	350	150	8.5:1	2-BC	
ZP	8	350	150	8.5:1	2-BC	California
ZB	8	350	175	8.5:1	4-BC	
ZM	8	350	175	8.5:1	4-BC	California
ZI	8	455	175	8.5:1	2-BC	
ZH	8	455	190	8.5:1	2-BC	Dual Exhaust
ZF	8	455	210	8.5:1	4-BC	
ZK	8	455	230	8.5:1	4-BC	Dual Exhaust
ZS	8	455	245	8.5:1	4-BC	Stage 1
ZA	8	455	255	8.5:1	4-BC	Riviera GS

Engines are available as indicated below:

Apollo - CCW, CCX, CCR, ZC, ZP, ZB, ZM; Century, Century Luxus, Regal - ZC, ZP, ZB, ZM, ZI, ZH, ZF, ZK; GS - ZC, ZP, ZB, ZM, ZI, ZH, ZF, ZK, ZA; LeSabre & LeSabre Luxus - ZC, ZB, ZM, ZI, ZH, ZF, ZK, ZS; Electra 225, Custom, Limited & Estate Wagon - ZF, ZK, ZS; Riviera - ZF, ZK, ZS.

1975 BUICK CENTURY

1975 BUICK SKYLARK / APOLLO

1975 BUICK SKYHAWK

1975 BUICK ESTATE STATION WAGON

1975 BUICK LE SABRE

1975 BUICK RIVIERA

VEHICLE IDENTIFICATION NUMBER

BUICK 4N39T5100000

Located on the top of the dash on the driver's side and visible through the windshield from outside the car.

FIRST DIGIT: Identifies GM Division (4 = Buick)

SECOND DIGIT: Identifies the series

SERIES	CODE
Apollo or Skylark	B
Apollo or Skylark SR	C
Century	D
Century Special	E
Century Wagon	F
Century Custom	H
Regal	J
Century Custom Wagon	K
LeSabre	N
LeSabre Custom	P
Estate Wagon	R
Skyhawk	S
Electra 225	V
Electra Limited	X
Riviera	Z

THIRD AND FOURTH DIGITS: Identify the body style

BODY STYLE	CODE
2-Door Hatchback	07
2-Door Hatchback	17
2-Door Coupe	27
4-Door Sedan	29
Station Wagon, 2-Seat	35
2-Door Coupe	37
4-Door Hardtop	39
Station Wagon, 3-Seat	45
2-Door Hardtop or Coupe	57
Convertible	67
4-Door Sedan	69
2-Door Hardtop	87

FIFTH DIGIT: Identifies the engine

ENGINE	CODE
V6-231 2-BC	C
L6, 250 1-BC	D
V8-260 2-BC	F
V8-350 2-BC	H
V8-350 4-BC	J
V8-455 4-BC	T

SIXTH DIGIT: Identifies the year (5 = 1975)

SEVENTH DIGIT: Identifies the assembly plant

ASSEMBLY PLANT	CODE
St. Therese, CAN	2
Framingham, MA	G
Flint, MI	H
Leeds, MO	K
Van Nuys, CA	L
Fairfax, KS	X
Wilmington, DE	Y
Fremont, CA	Z

LAST SIX DIGITS: Represent the basic production numbers

EXAMPLE:

4	N	39	5	H	H	123456
Buick Div.	Series	Body Style	Year	Engine	Asm Plant	Prod Code

BODY NUMBER PLATE

The body number plate is located on the firewall, just below the rear edge of the hood. This plate identifies the model year, car division, series, body style, body assembly plant, body numbers, trim combination, paint code and build date code.

BUICK DIV. GENERAL MOTORS CORP.
FLINT, MICHIGAN
ST 75 4BN57   H 123456 BDY
TR 26C 11A   29 29 PNT
000   000

GENERAL MOTORS CORPORATION CERTIFIES TO THE DEALER THAT THIS VEHICLE CONFORMS TO ALL U.S., FEDERAL MOTOR VEHICLE SAFETY STANDARDS APPLICABLE AT TIME OF MANUFACTURE.

Example:

75	Model (1975)
4	Car Division (Buick)
BN	Series (LeSabre)
57	Style (4-Dr. Hardtop)
H	Body Assembly Plant (Flint, MI)
123456	Production Sequence
26C	Blue Trim
29	Indigo Paint
11	Eleventh Month (Nov.)
A	1st Week of month

CENTURY	CODE
4-Door Sedan	4AD29
2-Door Coupe	4AD37*
Station Wagon 2 Seat	4AF35
Station Wagon 3 Seat	4AF45
*Grand Sport Option available	

CENTURY CUSTOM	CODE
4-Door Sedan	4AH29
2-Door Coupe	4AH57
Station Wagon 2 Seat	4AK35
Station Wagon 3 Seat	4AK45

CENTURY SPECIAL	CODE
2-Door Coupe	4AE37

REGAL	CODE
4-Door Sedan	4AJ29
2-Door Coupe	4AJ57
*Landau option available	

LESABRE	CODE
4-Door Hardtop	4BN39
2-Door Hardtop	4BN57
4-Door Sedan	4BN69

LESABRE CUSTOM	CODE
4-Door Hardtop	4BP39
2-Door Hardtop	4BP57
Convertible	4BP67
4-Door Sedan	4BP69

ESTATE WAGON	CODE
2-Seat	4BR35
3-Seat	4BR45

ELECTRA 225	CODE
2-Door Hardtop	4CV37
4-Door Hardtop	4CV39

ELECTRA LIMITED	CODE
2-Door Hardtop	4CX37
4-Door Hardtop	4CX39
*Park Avenue option available	
*Landau option available	

RIVIERA	CODE
2-Door Hardtop	4EZ87
*GS option available	

SKYHAWK	CODE
2-Door Hatchback	4HS07
*S option available	

SKYLARK	CODE
2-Door Hatchback	4XB17
2-Door Coupe	4XB27
*S option available	

APOLLO	CODE
4-Door Sedan	4XB69

SKYLARK SR	CODE
2-Door Hatchback	4XC17
2-Door Coupe	4XC27

APOLLO SR	CODE
4-Door Sedan	4XC69

THE TRIM CODE furnishes the key to the interior color and material scheme.

CENTURY 4-DOOR SEDAN TRIM

COLOR	CODE
Blue	26B/26V
Blue	26C/29D
Blue	26D/21D
Black	19D/19W
Burgundy	73W#*
Green	44C/44V
Green	44D#
Saddle	63V/63C
Saddle	63W#*
Saddle	63D#
Black/Saddle	63B

CENTURY 2-DOOR COUPE TRIM

COLOR	CODE
Blue	26C/26V
Blue	29D#
Blue	26D#
Blue	21D#
Black	19D#
Black	19W#
Burgundy	73W#*
Green	44D#
Saddle	63C/63V
Saddle	63W#*
Saddle	63D#
Sandstone	55D#
White/Black	91W#*
White/Blue	92W#*
White/Green	94W#*
White/Burgundy	97W#*
White/Saddle	96W#*

CENTURY STATION WAGON TRIM

COLOR	CODE
Blue	26V
Green	44V
Saddle	63V

CENTURY CUSTOM 4-DOOR SEDAN TRIM

COLOR	CODE
Black	19D#
Black	19W#
Blue	29D#
Blue	26D#
Blue	21D#
Burgundy	73W#*
Green	44D#
Saddle	63W#*
Saddle	63D#
Sandstone	55D#

CENTURY CUSTOM 2-DOOR COUPE TRIM

COLOR	CODE
Black	19D#
Black	19W#
Blue	29D#
Blue	26D#
Blue	21D#
Burgundy	73W#*
Green	44D#
Saddle	63W#*
Saddle	63D#
Sandstone	55D#
White/Black	91W#*
White/Blue	92W#*
White/Green	94W#*
White/Burgundy	97W#*
White/Saddle	96W#*

REGAL 4-DOOR SEDAN TRIM

COLOR	CODE
Black	19G#
Black	19Y#
Blue	26G#
Blue	26E#
Burgundy	73Y#
Burgundy	73E#
Green	44E#
Graystone	16E#
Saddle	63Y#
Sandstone	55G#
Sandstone	55E#
White/Black	91Y#
White/Blue	92Y#
White/Burgundy	97Y#
White/Sandstone	95Y#
White/Saddle	96W#
White/Saddle	96Y#

REGAL 2-DOOR COUPE TRIM

COLOR	CODE
Black	19G#
Black	19Y#
Blue	26G#
Blue	26E#
Burgundy	73Y#
Burgundy	73E#
Green	44E#
Graystone	16E#
Saddle	63Y#
Sandstone	55G#
Sandstone	55E#
White/Black	91Y#
White/Blue	92Y#
White/Burgundy	97Y#
White/Sandstone	95Y#
White/Saddle	96W#
White/Saddle	96Y#

CENTURY CUSTOM STATION WAGON TRIM

COLOR	CODE
Blue	26W#
Burgundy	73W#*
Green	44W#
Saddle	63D#
Saddle	63W#*

LESABRE 4-DOOR HT TRIM

COLOR	CODE
Blue	26C/26V
Green	44V
Saddle	63C/63V

LESABRE 2-DOOR HT TRIM

COLOR	CODE
Blue	26C/26V
Green	44V
Saddle	63C/63V

LESABRE 4-DOOR SEDAN TRIM

COLOR	CODE
Blue	26C/26V
Green	44V
Saddle	63C/63V

LESABRE CUSTOM 4-DOOR HT TRIM

COLOR	CODE
Black	19G#
Black	19W#
Blue	26G#
Blue	26D#
Burgundy	73D#
Burgundy	73W#
Green	44D#
Saddle	63D#
Saddle	63W#
Sandstone	55G#
White/Black	91W#
White/Blue	92W#
White/Green	94W#
White/Burgundy	97W#
White/Saddle	96W#

LESABRE CUSTOM 2-DOOR HT TRIM

COLOR	CODE
Black	19G#
Black	19W#
Blue	26G#
Blue	26D#
Burgundy	73D#
Burgundy	73W#
Green	44D#
Saddle	63D#
Saddle	63W#
Sandstone	55G#
White/Black	91W#
White/Blue	92W#
White/Green	94W#
White/Burgundy	97W#
White/Saddle	96W#

LESABRE CONVERTIBLE TRIM

COLOR	CODE
Burgundy	73W#
Saddle	63W#
White/Blue	92W#
White/Burgundy	97W#
White/Saddle	96W#

LESABRE CUSTOM 4-DOOR SEDAN TRIM

COLOR	CODE
Black	19G#
Black	19W#
Blue	26G#
Blue	26D#
Burgundy	73D#
Burgundy	73W#
Green	44D#
Saddle	63D#
Saddle	63W#
Sandstone	55G#
White/Black	91W#
White/Blue	92W#
White/Green	94W#
White/Burgundy	97W#
White/Saddle	96W#

ESTATE WAGON 2-SEAT TRIM

COLOR	CODE
Blue	26E#
Blue	26W#
Burgundy	73W#
Green	44V
Green	44W#
Saddle	63V
Saddle	63E#
Saddle	63W#

ESTATE WAGON 3-SEAT TRIM

COLOR	CODE
Blue	26E#
Blue	26W#
Burgundy	73W#
Green	44V
Green	44W#
Saddle	63V
Saddle	63E#
Saddle	63W#

ELECTRA 2-DOOR HT TRIM

COLOR	CODE
Black	19W#
Blue	26C#
Blue	26D#
Burgundy	73C#
Burgundy	73W#
Burgundy	73D#
Green	44D#
Sandstone	55C#
Sandstone	55W#
Sandstone	55D#
White/Black	91W#
White/Blue	92W#
White/Green	94W#
White/Burgundy	97W#
White/Sandstone	95W#

ELECTRA 4-DOOR HT TRIM

COLOR	CODE
Black	19W#
Blue	26C/26D
Blue	26C#
Blue	26D#
Burgundy	73C/73D
Burgundy	73C#
Burgundy	73W#
Burgundy	73D#
Green	44C/44D
Sandstone	55C/55D
Sandstone	55C#
Sandstone	55W#
Sandstone	55D#
White/Black	91W#
White/Blue	92W#
White/Green	94W#
White/Burgundy	97W#
White/Sandstone	95W#

ELECTRA LIMITED 2-DOOR HT TRIM

COLOR	CODE
Black	194#
Black	19W#
Blue	26C#
Blue	26D#
Blue	26E#
Burgundy	73C#
Burgundy	73W#
Burgundy	73D#
Burgundy	73E#
Green	44C#
Green	44D#
Green	44E#
Graystone	16E#
Saddle	634#
Sandstone	55C#
Sandstone	55W#
Sandstone	55D#
Sandstone	55E#
White	114#
White/Black	91W#
White/Blue	92W#
White/Green	94W#
White/Burgundy	97W#
White/Sandstone	95W#

ELECTRA LIMITED 4-DOOR HT TRIM

COLOR	CODE
Black	19W#
Black	194#
Black	19G#
Blue	26C#
Blue	26D#
Blue	26E#
Burgundy	73C#
Burgundy	73W#
Burgundy	73D#
Burgundy	73E#
Burgundy	73G#
Green	44C#
Green	44D#
Green	44E#
Graystone	16E#
Saddle	634#
Saddle	63G#
Sandstone	55C#
Sandstone	55W#
Sandstone	55D#
Sandstone	55E#
White	114#
White/Black	91W#
White/Blue	92W#
White/Green	94W#
White/Burgundy	97W#
White/Sandstone	95W#

RIVIERA 2-DOOR HT TRIM

COLOR	CODE
Black	194#
Blue	26D#
Burgundy	73D#
Burgundy	73E#
Burgundy	73W#
Green	44D#
Saddle	634#
Sandstone	55D#
Sandstone	55W#
Silver	14D#
Silver	14W#
White/Black	91W#
White/Blue	92W#
White/Green	94W#
White/Burgundy	97W#
White/Sandstone	95W#
White/Saddle	96W#

SKYHAWK 2-DOOR HATCHBACK TRIM

COLOR	CODE
Black	19Z*
Black	192*
Blue	29C*
Blue	26C*
Burgundy	73Z*
Burgundy	732*
Saddle	63Z*
Saddle	632*
Sandstone	35C*
White	11Z*
Black/Green	49C*
White/Black	11C*

SKYLARK 2-DOOR HATCHBACK TRIM

COLOR	CODE
Black	19V
Blue	26B/26G
Blue	26C/26D
Burgundy	73V/73G
Burgundy	73C/73D
Burgundy	72Y#
Sandstone	53B/55Y
Sandstone	55G/55C
Sandstone	55D
Sandstone	55Y#
White/Black	91V
White/Black	91Y#
White/Blue	92V
White/Blue	92Y#
White/Green	94V
White/Green	94Y#
White/Burgundy	97V
White/Burgundy	97Y#
White/Sandstone	95V
White/Sandstone	95Y#

SKYLARK 2-DOOR COUPE TRIM

COLOR	CODE
Black	19V
Blue	26B/26C
Blue	26G/26D
Burgundy	73V/73G
Burgundy	73C/73D
Burgundy	72Y#
Green	44B/44G
Green	44C/44D
Sandstone	53B/55Y
Sandstone	55G/55C
Sandstone	55D
Sandstone	55Y#
White/Black	91V
White/Black	91Y#
White/Blue	92V
White/Blue	92Y#
White/Green	94V
White/Green	94Y#
White/Burgundy	97V
White/Burgundy	97Y#
White/Sandstone	95V
White/Sandstone	95Y#

APOLLO 4-DOOR SEDAN TRIM

COLOR	CODE
Black	19V
Blue	26B/26G
Blue	26C/26D
Burgundy	73V/73G
Burgundy	73C/73D
Burgundy	73Y#
Green	44B/44G
Green	44C/44D
Sandstone	55B/55V
Sandstone	55G/55C
Sandstone	55D
Sandstone	55Y#

SKYLARK SR 2-DOOR HATCHBACK TRIM

COLOR	CODE
Blue	26E*
Burgundy	73E*
Sandstone	55E*

SKYLARK SR 2-DOOR COUPE TRIM

COLOR	CODE
Blue	26E*
Burgundy	73E*
Sandstone	55E*

APOLLO SR 4-DOOR SEDAN TRIM

COLOR	CODE
Blue	26E*
Burgundy	73E*
Sandstone	55E*

* Bucket seats
\# Notch back or 60-40 seats

THE PAINT CODE furnishes the key to the paint colors used on the car. Two, two-digit codes indicate the bottom and top body colors respectively. NOTE: vinyl roof and convertible top codes appear in the second set of digits.

COLOR	CODE
Arctic White	11
Silver Mist	13
Dove Gray	15
Pewter	16
Antique Silver	18
Regal Black	19
Horizon Blue	21
Glacier Blue	24
Majestic Blue	26
Blue Haze	28
Indigo	29
Ranch Green	44
Verde Mist	49
Sand Beige	50
Canary Yellow	51
Sandstone	55
Honey Gold	57
Almond Mist	58
Walnut Mist	59
Golden Tan	63
Bittersweet	64
Ruby Red	72
Burgundy	74
Apple Red	75
Rhone Red	79
Pumpkin	80

VINYL TOP COLORS

COLOR	CODE
White	1
Black	2
Sandalwood	5
Dark Brown	8
Dark Green	9

CONVERTIBLE TOP COLORS

COLOR	CODE
White	1
Black	2
Sandalwood	5
Dark Green	9

4 - 32

ENGINE NUMBER

A Buick engine is stamped with two different identification codes. One is the engine production code which identifies the engine and its approximate production date. The other code is the engine serial number — it matches the VIN (vehicle identification number).

The 250 CID V6 engine production code number is between the front and middle branches of the right exhaust manifold. The engine serial number is just below the front of the left cylinder head.

The 260 CID V8 engine serial number is on the front of the right cylinder bank. The production code number is between the left exhaust manifold and the two front spark plugs.

The 455 CID V8 engine serial number is on the front of the right cylinder bank. The production code number is between the left exhaust manifold and the two rear spark plugs.

On most 1975 models the production code can be found with the serial number.

ENGINE CODE	NO. CYL.	CID	HORSE-POWER	COMP. RATIO	CARB	TRANS
AD	6	231	110	8.0:1	2-BC	4-spd Man
D	6	250	105	8.25:1	1-BC	3-spd Man
QE,QJ*	8	260	110	8.5:1	2-BC	
TE,TJ**	8	260	110	8.5:1	2-BC	
AB	8	350	145	8.0:1	2-BC	3-spd Auto
AM	8	350	165	8.0:1	4-BC	3-spd Auto
AF	8	455	205	7.9:1	4-BC	3-spd Auto

* Federal
** California

Engines are available as indicated below:

Skyhawk - AD; Skylark - AD, D, QE, QJ, TE, TJ, AB, AM; Apollo - D, QE, QJ, TE, TJ, AB, AM; Century Special - AD; Century & Century Custom, Regal - AD, AB, AM; LeSabre & LeSabre Custom - AM, AF; Electra & Electra Limited, Riviera - AF.

1976 BUICK SKYHAWK

1976 BUICK SKYLARK

1976 BUICK SPECIAL

1976 BUICK ELECTRA

1976 BUICK CENTURY STATION WAGON

1976 BUICK REGAL

1976 BUICK LE SABRE

1976 BUICK RIVIERA

VEHICLE IDENTIFICATION NUMBER

BUICK
4V39J6H446727

Located on the top of the dash on the driver's side and visible through the windshield from outside the car.

FIRST DIGIT: Identifies GM Division (4 = Buick)

SECOND DIGIT: Identifies the series

SERIES	CODE
Century	D
Century Special	E
Century Custom	H
Skylark	B
Skylark SR	C
Skylark S	W
Regal	J
Century Custom Wagon	K
LeSabre	N

SERIES	CODE
LeSabre Custom	P
Estate Wagon	R
Electra 225	V
Electra Limited	X
Riviera	Z
Skyhawk	S
Skyhawk S	T

THIRD AND FOURTH DIGITS: Identify the body style

BODY STYLE	CODE
2-Door Hatchback Coupe	07
2-Door Hatchback Coupe	17
2-Door Coupe	27
4-Door Sedan	29
Station Wagon 2-Seat	35
2-Door Coupe	37
4-Door Sedan Hardtop	39
Station Wagon 3-Seat	45
2-Door Coupe Hardtop	57
4-Door Sedan	69
2-Door Sport Coupe Hardtop	87

FIFTH DIGIT: Identifies the engine

ENGINE	CODE
V6-231	C
V8-260	F
V8-350	H
V8-350	J
V8-455	T

SIXTH DIGIT: Identifies the year (6 = 1976)

SEVENTH DIGIT: Identifies the assembly plant

ASSEMBLY PLANT	CODE
St. Therese, CAN	2
Southgate, CA	C
Linden, NJ	E
Framingham, MA	G
Flint, MI	H
Leeds, MO	K
Van Nuys, CA	L
Tarrytown, NY	T
Fairfax, KS	X
Fremont, CA	Z

LAST SIX DIGITS: Represent the basic production numbers

EXAMPLE:

4	P	39	J	6	X	123456
Buick Div.	Series	Body Style	Engine Code	Model Year	Asm Plant	Prod Code

BODY NUMBER PLATE

The body number plate is located on the firewall, just below the rear edge of the hood. This plate identifies the model year, car division, series, body style, body assembly plant, body numbers, trim combination, paint code and build date code.

```
BUICK DIV. GENERAL MOTORS
            CORP.
        FLINT, MICHIGAN
 ST 76   4XB17     H 123456 BDY
 TR 64N                  78 PNT

GENERAL MOTORS CORPORATION CERTIFIES
   TO THE DEALER THAT THIS VEHICLE
 CONFORMS TO ALL U.S., FEDERAL MOTOR
        VEHICLE SAFETY STANDARDS
    APPLICABLE AT TIME OF MANUFACTURE.
```

Example:

76	Model Year (1976)
4	Car Division (Buick)
XB	Series (Skylark)
17	Style (2-Door Hatchback)
H	Body Assembly Plant (Flint, MI)
123456	Production Sequence
64N	Buckskin Trim
78	Firecracker Orange

CENTURY	CODE
4-Door Hardtop	4AD29
2-Door Hardtop	4AD37

CENTURY SPECIAL	CODE
2-Door	4AE37

CENTURY CUSTOM	CODE
4-Door Hardtop	4AH29
2-Door Hardtop	4AH57
4-Door Station Wagon 2-Seat	4AK35
4-Door Station Wagon 3-Seat	4AK45

REGAL	CODE
2-Door Hardtop	4AJ57
4-Door Custom Hardtop	4AJ29

*S/R option available

LESABRE	CODE
4-Door Hardtop	4BN39
2-Door Hardtop	4BN57
4-Door Sedan	4BN69

LESABRE CUSTOM	CODE
4-Door Hardtop	4BP39
2-Door Hardtop	4BP57
4-Door Sedan	4BP69

ESTATE WAGON	CODE
4-Door 2-Seat	4BR35
4-Door 3-Seat	4BR45

ELECTRA 225	CODE
2-Door Hardtop	4CV37
4-Door Hardtop	4CV39

ELECTRA LIMITED	CODE
2-Door Hardtop	4CX37
4-Door Hardtop	4CX39

*Park Avenue option available

RIVIERA	CODE
2-Door Hardtop	4EZ87

*S/R option available

SKYHAWK	CODE
2-Door Hatchback	4HS07

SKYHAWK S	CODE
2-Door Hatchback	4HT07

SKYLARK	CODE
2-Door Hatchback	4XB17
2-Door Coupe	4XB27
4-Door Sedan	4XB69

SKYLARK SR	CODE
2-Door Hatchback	4XC17
2-Door Coupe	4XC27
4-Door Sedan	4XC69

SKYLARK S	CODE
2-Door Pillar Coupe	4XW27

THE TRIM CODE furnishes the key to the interior color and material scheme.

CENTURY TRIM

COLOR	CODE
White	11M/11B
White	110
Black	19E/19C
Blue	92N/26N
Blue	26C/020
Blue	26E
Lime	030
Buckskin	64M/96M
Buckskin	64B/64N
Buckskin	96N/64C
Buckskin	060/64E
Buckskin	64G
Firethorn	71B/97M
Firethorn	71B/71N
Firethorn	97N/71C
Mahogany	080
Mahogany	740/74E
Mahogany	74G

LESABRE TRIM

COLOR	CODE
Black	19N/91N
Black	19C
Blue	26N/92N
Blue	26C
Buckskin	64M/64N
Buckskin	96N/64C
Mahogany	74N/98N
Mahogany	74C

ELECTRA TRIM

COLOR	CODE
White	112
Black	19M/91M
Black	192/19D
Black	19E
Blue	92M/26B
Blue	022/26D
Blue	26E
Lime	032
Buckskin	64M/96M
Buckskin	64B/642
Buckskin	062/64D
Buckskin	64E
Mahogany	74M/98M
Mahogany	74B/742
Mahogany	082/74D
Mahogany	74E

RIVIERA TRIM

COLOR	CODE
White	11M/112
Blue	02M/26B
Blue	022
Lime	03M/032
Buckskin	64M/06M
Buckskin	64B/642
Buckskin	062/64C
Firethorn	71M/07M
Firethorn	71B/712
Firethorn	072/71C

SKYHAWK TRIM

COLOR	CODE
White	11N/11B
Black	19N
Blue	02N/26B
Lime	03N
Buckskin	64N/06N
Firethorn	71N/07N
Firethorn	71B

SKYLARK TRIM

COLOR	CODE
Black	19M/91M
Black	19B/91V
Blue	92V/26C
Buckskin	64M/96M
Buckskin	64B/64N
Buckskin	64V/96V
Buckskin	64C/64D
Firethorn	71M/97M
Firethorn	71B/71N
Firethorn	71V/97V
Firethorn	71C/71D

THE PAINT CODE furnishes the key to the paint colors used on the car. Two, two-digit codes indicate the bottom and top body colors respectively. NOTE: vinyl roof codes appear in the second set of digits.

COLOR	CODE
Liberty White	11
Pewter Gray	13
Medium Gray	16
Judical Black	19
Potomac Blue	28
Continental Blue	35
Boston Red	0
Dark Green	49
Mt. Vernon Cream	50
Colonial Yellow	51
Cream Gold	57
Buckskin	65
Musket Brown	67
Red	72
Firecracker Orange	78

VINYL ROOF COLORS

COLOR	CODE
Black	A
White	C
Silver	D
Blue	H
Buckskin	Q
Red	V
Dark Red	W

ENGINE NUMBER

A Buick engine is stamped with two different identification codes. One is the engine production code which identifies the engine and its approximate production date. The other code is the engine serial number — it matches the VIN (vehicle identification number).

ENGINE SERIAL NUMBER LOCATIONS

BUICK ENGINES

ENGINE CODE	NO. CYL.	CID	HORSE-POWER	COMP. RATIO	CARB	TRANS
FA	6	231	105	8.0:1	2-BC	Man
FB,FC,FF*	6	231	105	8.0:1	2-BC	Auto
FD,FE,FG*	6	231	105	8.0:1	2-BC	Auto
FP,FR	6	231	105	8.0:1	2-BC	Auto
FO*,FH	6	231	105	8.0:1	2-BC	Std
FJ*,FI	6	231	105	8.0:1	2-BC	Auto
QA,QD	8	260	110	8.5:1	2-BC	Man
QB,QC	8	260	110	8.5:1	2-BC	Auto
TE*,TJ*	8	260	110	8.5:1	2-BC	Auto
PA,PB	8	350	140	8.0:1	2-BC	Auto
PC,PD	8	350	140	8.0:1	2-BC	Auto
PE,PF	8	350	155	8.0:1	4-BC	Auto
PK*,PL*	8	350	155	8.0:1	4-BC	Auto
PM*,PN*	8	350	155	8.0:1	4-BC	Auto
PR*,PS*	8	350	155	8.0:1	4-BC	Auto
PT,PU	8	350	155	8.0:1	4-BC	Auto
SA	8	455	205	7.9:1	4-BC	Auto
SB*	8	455	205	7.9:1	4-BC	Auto

* California

Engines are available as indicated below:

Skyhawk & Skyhawk S - FH, FI, FJ, FO; Skylark - FA, QB, FP, PM, QA, QC, FF, PN, QD, TE, FG, PA, TJ, PE, PB, FR, PF; Skylark S & Skylark SR - FR, FP, FF, FG, QA, QB, QC, QD, TE, TJ, PA, PB, PE, PF, PM, PN; Century Coupe - FA, PC, PD, PT,PU, PK, PL; Century Custom Sedan, Century Sedan, Regal - FA, FD, FE, PC, PD, PT, PU, PK, PL; Century Coupe - FA, FB, FC, FF, FG, PC, PD, PT, PU, PK, PL; Century Custom Coupe - FA, FB, FC, PC, PD, PT, PU, PK, PL; Century Wagon - PC, PD, PT, PU, PR, PS; LeSabre - FA, FB, FC, FD, FE, FF, FG, SA, SB; LeSabre Custom - PT, PU, PR, PS, SA, SB; Riviera & Estate Wagon - SA, SB; Electra & Electra Limited - SA, SB, PR, PS, PT, PU.

1977 BUICK PARK AVENUE

1977 BUICK REGAL

1977 BUICK SKYHAWK

1977 BUICK RIVIERA

1977 BUICK ESTATE WAGON

1977 BUICK SKYLARK

1977 BUICK ELECTRA

1977 BUICK CENTURY

VEHICLE IDENTIFICATION NUMBER

• **BUICK**
4N37C7X100001 •

Located on the top of the dash on the driver's side and visible through the windshield from outside the car.

FIRST DIGIT: Identifies GM Division (4 = Buick)

SECOND DIGIT: Identifies the Series

SERIES	CODE
Skylark	B
Skylark SR	C
Century	D
Century Special	E
LeSabre	F
Century Custom	H
Regal	J
Century Custom Wagon	K
LeSabre Sport Coupe	N

SERIES	CODE
LeSabre Custom	P
Estate Wagon	R
Skyhawk	S
Skyhawk S	T
Electra 225	V
Skylark S	W
Electra Limited	X
Riviera	Z

THIRD AND FOURTH DIGITS: Identify the body style

BODY STYLE	CODE
2-Door Hatchback Coupe	07
2-Door Hatchback Coupe	17
2-Door Coupe	27
4-Door Sedan	29
4-Door Station Wagon 2-Seat	35
2-Door Coupe	37
2-Door Coupe	57
4-Door Sedan	69

FIFTH DIGIT: Identifies the engine

ENGINE	CODE
V6-231 2 BC	C
V8-350 2 BC	H
V8-350 4 BC	J
V8-403 4 BC	K
V8-350 4 BC	L
V8-350 4 BC	R
V8-305 2 BC	U
V8-301 2 BC	Y

SIXTH DIGIT: Identifies the year (7 = 1977)

SEVENTH DIGIT: Identifies the assembly plant

ASSEMBLY PLANT	CODE
St. Therese, Que., CAN	2
Baltimore, MD	B
Southgate, CA	C
Linden, NJ	E
Framingham, MA	G
Flint, MI	H
Leeds, MO	K
Van Nuys, CA	L
Tarrytown, NY	T
Fairfax, KS	X
Fremont, CA	Z

LAST 6 DIGITS: Represent the basic production numbers

EXAMPLE:

4	N	37	C	7	X	123456
Buick Div.	Series	Body Style	Engine Code	Year	Asm Plant	Prod Code

BODY NUMBER PLATE

The body number plate is located on the firewall, just below the rear edge of the hood. This plate identifies the model year, car division, series, body style, body assembly plant, body numbers, trim combination, paint code and build date code.

```
BUICK DIV. GENERAL MOTORS
          CORP.
      FLINT, MICHIGAN
ST 77  4AK35      H 123456 BDY
TR 19D                75  75 PNT
       11A
 GENERAL MOTORS CORPORATION CERTIFIES
   TO THE DEALER THAT THIS VEHICLE
   CONFORMS TO ALL U.S., FEDERAL MOTOR
      VEHICLE SAFETY STANDARDS
   APPLICABLE AT TIME OF MANUFACTURE.
```

Example:

77	Model Year (1977)
4	Car Division (Buick)
AK	Series (Century)
35	Style (4-Dr. Wagon)
H	Body Assembly Plant (Flint, MI)
123456	Production Sequence
19D	Black Trim
75	Bright Red Paint
11	Eleventh Month (Nov.)
A	1st Week of month

CENTURY	CODE
4-Door Hardtop Sedan	4AD29
2-Door Hardtop Coupe	4AD37

CENTURY SPECIAL	CODE
2-Door Hardtop Coupe	4AE37

CENTURY CUSTOM	CODE
4-Door Hardtop Sedan	4AH29
2-Door Hardtop Coupe	4AH57
4-Door Station Wagon	4AK35

REGAL	CODE
4-Door Custom HT Sedan	4AJ29
2-Door Hardtop Coupe	4AJ57

LESABRE	CODE
2-Door Hardtop Coupe	4BN37
4-Door Sedan	4BN69

LESABRE CUSTOM	CODE
2-Door Hardtop Coupe	4BP37
4-Door Custom Sedan	4BP69

LESABRE SPORT COUPE	CODE
2-Door Hardtop	4BF37

ESTATE WAGON	CODE
4-Door 2-Seat	4BR35

RIVIERA	CODE
2-Door Hardtop Coupe	4BZ37

ELECTRA 225	CODE
2-Door Hardtop Coupe	4CV37
4-Door Sedan	4CV69

ELECTRA LIMITED	CODE
2-Door Hardtop Coupe	4CX37
4-Door Sedan	4CX69

SKYHAWK	CODE
2-Door Hatchback Coupe	4HS07

SKYLARK	CODE
2-Door Hatchback Coupe	4XB17
2-Door Coupe	4XB27

SKYLARK S	CODE
2-Door Coupe	4XW27
4-Door Sedan	4XB69

SKYLARK SR	CODE
2-Door Hatchback Coupe	4XC17
2-Door Coupe	4XC27
4-Door Sedan	4XC69

THE TRIM CODE furnishes the key to the interior color and material scheme.

CENTURY 4-DOOR TRIM

COLOR	CLOTH	VINYL	LEATHER	CODE
White	•	•		11B
White		•		11N#
Blue		•		24R
Blue	•	•		24B
Blue	•	•		24C#
Buckskin		•		64R
Buckskin	•	•		64B
Buckskin		•		64N#
Buckskin	•	•		64C#
Firethorn		•		71N#
Firethorn	•	•		71C#
Green		•		44R
Green		•		44N#

CENTURY 2-DOOR TRIM

COLOR	CLOTH	VINYL	LEATHER	CODE
White		•		11R
White	•	•		11B
White		•		11N#
White		•		11N*
Blue		•		24R
Blue	•	•		24B
Blue	•	•		24C#
Buckskin		•		64R
Buckskin	•	•		64B
Buckskin		•		64N#
Buckskin		•		64N*
Buckskin	•	•		64C#
Firethorn		•		71N#
Firethorn		•		71N*
Firethorn	•	•		71C#
Green		•		44R
Green		•		44N#

CENTURY CUSTOM 4-DOOR TRIM

COLOR	CLOTH	VINYL	LEATHER	CODE
White		•		11N#
Blue	•	•		24C#
Buckskin		•		64N#
Buckskin	•	•		64C#
Firethorn		•		71N#
Firethorn	•	•		71C#
Green		•		71C#

CENTURY CUSTOM 2-DOOR COUPE TRIM

COLOR	CLOTH	VINYL	LEATHER	CODE
White		•		11N#
White		•		11N*
White		•		11V#
Black	•	•		19D#
Blue	•	•		24C#
Blue	•	•		24D#
Blue	•	•		24G*
Buckskin		•		64N#
Buckskin		•		64N*
Buckskin	•	•		64C#
Buckskin		•		64V#
Buckskin	•	•		64D#
Buckskin	•	•		64G*
Firethorn		•		71N#
Firethorn		•		71N*
Firethorn	•	•		71C#
Firethorn		•		71V#
Firethorn	•	•		71D#
Firethorn	•	•		71G*

REGAL 4-DOOR TRIM

COLOR	CLOTH	VINYL	LEATHER	CODE
White		•		11N#
Black	•	•		19D#
Blue	•	•		24C#
Blue	•	•		24D#

REGAL 2-DOOR TRIM

COLOR	CLOTH	VINYL	LEATHER	CODE
White		•		11N#
White		•		11N*
White		•		11V#
Black	•	•		19D#
Blue	•	•		24C#
Blue	•	•		24D#
Blue	•	•		24G*
Buckskin		•		64N#
Buckskin		•		64N*
Buckskin	•	•		64C#
Buckskin		•		64V#
Buckskin	•	•		64D#
Buckskin	•	•		64G*

CENTURY CUSTOM STATION WAGON TRIM

COLOR	CLOTH	VINYL	LEATHER	CODE
Blue		•		24N#
Buckskin		•		64N#
Firethorn		•		71N#

LESABRE 2-DOOR COUPE TRIM

COLOR	CLOTH	VINYL	LEATHER	CODE
Blue		•		24R
Blue	•	•		24B
Blue	•	•		24D
Blue		•		24W
Buckskin		•		64R
Buckskin	•	•		64B
Buckskin	•	•		64D
Buckskin		•		64W
Firethorn		•		71R
Firethorn		•		71W
Green		•		44R
Green		•		44W

LESABRE 4-DOOR SEDAN TRIM

COLOR	CLOTH	VINYL	LEATHER	CODE
Blue		•		24R
Blue	•	•		24B
Blue	•	•		24D
Blue		•		24W
Buckskin		•		64R
Buckskin	•	•		64B
Buckskin	•	•		64D
Buckskin		•		64W
Firethorn		•		71R
Firethorn		•		71W
Green		•		44R
Green		•		44W

LESABRE CUSTOM 2-DOOR COUPE TRIM

COLOR	CLOTH	VINYL	LEATHER	CODE
White		•		11N#
Black		•		19N#
Blue	•	•		24C#
Blue	•	•		24E#
Buckskin		•		64N#
Buckskin	•	•		64C#
Buckskin	•	•		64E#
Firethorn	•	•		71C#
Firethorn	•	•		71E#
Green		•		44N#

LESABRE CUSTOM 4-DOOR SEDAN TRIM

COLOR	CLOTH	VINYL	LEATHER	CODE
White		•		11N#
Black		•		19N#
Blue	•	•		24C#
Blue	•	•		24E#
Buckskin		•		64N#
Buckskin	•	•		64C#
Buckskin	•	•		64E#
Firethorn	•	•		71C#
Firethorn	•	•		71E#
Green		•		44N#

ESTATE WAGON TRIM

COLOR	CLOTH	VINYL	LEATHER	CODE
Blue		•		24N#
Buckskin		•		64N#
Buckskin	•	•		64C#
Buckskin	•	•		64E#
Firethorn		•		71N#

RIVIERA 2-DOOR COUPE TRIM

COLOR	CLOTH	VINYL	LEATHER	CODE
White		•		11V
Black	•	•		19G
Blue	•	•		24G
Buckskin		•		64V
Buckskin	•	•		64C
Firethorn	•	•		71G
Green		•		44V

ELECTRA 225 TRIM

COLOR	CLOTH	VINYL	LEATHER	CODE
White		•		11R#
Blue	•	•		24B#
Blue	•	•		24G#
Buckskin		•		64R#
Buckskin	•	•		64B#
Buckskin	•	•		64G#
Firethorn		•		71R#
Firethorn	•	•		71B#
Firethorn	•	•		71G#

ELECTRA LIMITED 2-DOOR COUPE TRIM

COLOR	CLOTH	VINYL	LEATHER	CODE
White		•		11N#
Black	•	•		19D#
Black	•	•		19H#
Blue	•	•		24D#
Blue	•	•		24H#
Buckskin		•		64N#
Buckskin	•	•		64D#
Buckskin	•	•		64H#
Firethorn	•	•		71D#
Firethorn	•	•		71H#
Green	•	•		44D#
Green	•	•		44H#

ELECTRA LIMITED 4-DOOR SEDAN TRIM

COLOR	CLOTH	VINYL	LEATHER	CODE
White		•		11N#
Black	•	•		19D#
Black	•	•		19H#
Black	•	•		19E
Blue	•	•		24D#
Blue	•	•		24H#
Blue	•	•		24E
Buckskin		•		64N#
Buckskin	•	•		64D#
Buckskin	•	•		64H#
Buckskin	•	•		64E

ELECTRA LIMITED 4-DOOR SEDAN TRIM

COLOR	CLOTH	VINYL	LEATHER	CODE
Firethorn	•	•		71D#
Firethorn	•	•		71H#
Firethorn	•	•		71E
Green	•	•		44D#
Green	•	•		44H#
Green	•	•		44E

SKYHAWK TRIM

COLOR	CLOTH	VINYL	LEATHER	CODE
White		•		11N*
White	•	•		11B*
Black		•		19N*
Blue		•		02N*
Blue	•	•		24B*
Aqua		•		03N*
Buckskin		•		64N*
Buckskin		•		06N*
Firethorn		•		71N*
Firethorn		•		07N*
Firethorn	•	•		71B*
Mandarin		•		08N*

SKYLARK 2-DOOR HATCHBACK TRIM

COLOR	CLOTH	VINYL	LEATHER	CODE
White		•		11R
White		•		11R*
White		•		11V
Black		•		19R
Blue		•		24R
Blue	•	•		24B
Blue	•	•		24C
Buckskin		•		64R
Buckskin		•		64B
Buckskin		•		64V
Buckskin	•	•		64C
Firethorn		•		71V
Firethorn	•	•		71C

SKYLARK 2-DOOR COUPE TRIM

COLOR	CLOTH	VINYL	LEATHER	CODE
White		•		11R
White		•		11R*
White		•		11V
Black		•		19R
Blue		•		24R
Blue	•	•		24B
Blue	•	•		24C
Buckskin		•		64N
Buckskin		•		64R
Buckskin	•	•		64B
Buckskin		•		64V
Buckskin	•	•		64C
Firethorn		•		71V
Firethorn	•	•		71C

SKYLARK 4-DOOR SEDAN TRIM

COLOR	CLOTH	VINYL	LEATHER	CODE
White		•		11R
White		•		11R*
White		•		11V
Black		•		19R
Blue		•		24R
Blue	•	•		24B
Blue	•	•		24C
Buckskin		•		64R
Buckskin	•	•		64B
Buckskin		•		64V
Buckskin	•	•		64C
Firethorn		•		71V
Firethorn	•	•		71C

SKYLARK SR TRIM

COLOR	CLOTH	VINYL	LEATHER	CODE
Blue	•	•		24D*
Buckskin	•	•		64D*
Firethorn	•	•		71D*

* Bucket seats
\# Notch back or 60-40 seats

THE PAINT CODE furnishes the key to the paint colors used on the car. Two, two-digit codes indicate the bottom and top body colors respectively. NOTE: vinyl roof codes appear in the second set of digits.

COLOR	CODE
White	11
Silver	13
Gray	15
Medium Gray	16
Black	19
Light Blue	22
Dark Blue	29
Firethorn	36
Dark Aqua	38

COLOR	CODE
Medium Green	44
Dark Green	48
Cream	50
Yellow	51
Buckskin	61
Gold	63
Brown	69
Red	72
Bright Red	75
Orange	78
Medium Blue	85
Blue Firemist	91
Amber Firemist	92
Red Firemist	93

VINYL TOP COLORS

COLOR	CODE
White	11T
Silver	13T
Black	19T
Light Blue	22T
Firethorn	36T
Medium Green	44T
Light Buckskin	61T

ENGINE NUMBER

A Buick engine is stamped with two different identification codes. One is the engine production code which identifies the engine and its approximate production date. The other code is the engine serial number — it matches the VIN (vehicle identification number).

ENGINE CODE	NO. CYL.	CID	HORSE- POWER	COMP. RATIO	CARB
RA,RB,SG	6	231	105	8.0:1	2-BC
SI,ST,SM	6	231	105	8.0:1	2-BC
SK,SU,SN	6	231	105	8.0:1	2-BC
SL,SJ,SA	6	231	105	8.0:1	2-BC
SB,SD,SO	6	231	105	8.0:1	2-BC
SX,SY	6	231	105	8.0:1	2-BC
FA,FB,FK	8	350	140	8.0:1	2-BC
FC,FD,FG	8	350	155	8.0:1	4-BC
FH,FL	8	350	155	8.0:1	4-BC
U2,U3,UA	8	403	185	7.9:1	4-BC
UB,VA,VB	8	403	185	7.9:1	4-BC
VJ,VK	8	403	185	7.9:1	4-BC
CKR,CKM	8	350	170	8.5:1	4-BC
TK,TL,TN	8	350	170	8.5:1	4-BC
TO,Q3,Q2	8	350	170	8.5:1	4-BC
QP,QQ,QK	8	350	170	8.5:1	4-BC
QL,Q7,Q6	8	350	170	8.5:1	4-BC
TX,TY,Q8	8	350	170	8.5:1	4-BC
Q9	8	350	170	8.5:1	4-BC
CPA,CPY	8	305	145	8.5:1	2-BC
YW,YX,YF	8	301	135	8.2:1	2-BC
YJ	8	301	135	8.2:1	2-BC

Engines are available as indicated below:
Skyhawk & Skyhawk S - SA, SB, SD, SO, SX, SY; Skylark, Skylark S & Skylark SR - SG, SI, SJ, SM, RA, SK, SL, RB, SN, ST, SU, YF, YJ, CPA, CPY, TX, TY, Q8, Q9, CKR, CKM; Century Special - SG, SI, ST, SM, SK, SU; Century, Century Custom & Regal - SG, SI, ST, SM, SK, SU, YW, YX, FA, FB, FK, FC, FD, FG, FH, FL, TK, TL, Q2, Q3, TN, TO, CKR, CKM; Regal Sedan - YW, YX, FA, FB, FK, FC, FD, FG, FH, FL, TK, TL, Q2, Q3, TN, TO, CKR, CKM; Century Wagon - FC, FD, FG, FH, FL, TK, TL, Q2, Q3, TN, TO, CKR, CKM, U2, U3; LeSabre & LeSabre Custom - SI, SK, SM, SN, ST, SL, SJ, RA, RB, YW, YX, FC, FD, QP, QQ, QK, QL, TL, Q6, Q7, TK, UA, UB, U2, U3, VA, VB, VJ, VK; LeSabre Sport Coupe - YW, YX, FC, FD, FL, QP, QQ, QK, QL, TL, Q6, Q7, KK, UA, UB, U2, U3, VA, VB, VJ, VK; Estate Wagon, Riviera, Electra 225 & Electra Limited - FC, FD, FL, QP, QQ, QK, QL, TL, Q6, Q7, TK, UA, UB, U2, U3, VA, VB, VJ, VK.

1978 BUICK CENTURY WAGON

1978 BUICK SKYLARK

1978 BUICK ESTATE WAGON

1978 BUICK CENTURY

1978 BUICK RIVIERA

1978 BUICK PARK AVENUE

1978 BUICK LE SABRE

1978 BUICK REGAL

VEHICLE IDENTIFICATION NUMBER

**BUICK
4L09K8H100001**

Located on the top of the dash on the driver's side and visible through the windshield from outside the car.

FIRST DIGIT: Identifies GM Division (4 = Buick)

SECOND DIGIT: Identifies the series

SERIES	CODE
Skylark	B
Skylark Custom	C
Century Special	E
LeSabre Sport Coupe	F
Century Sport Coupe	G
Century Custom	H
Regal	J
Regal Sport Coupe	K
Century Limited	L

SERIES	CODE
Regal Limited	M
LeSabre	N
LeSabre Custom	P
Estate Wagon	R
Skyhawk	S
Skyhawk S	T
Electra Park Ave	U
Electra 225	V
Skylark S	W
Electra Limited	X
Riviera	Z

THIRD AND FOURTH DIGITS: Identify the body style

BODY STYLE	CODE
2-Door Hatchback Coupe	07
4-Door Sedan	09
2-Door Hatchback Coupe	17
2-Door Coupe	27
4-Door Station Wagon	35
2-Door Coupe	37
2-Door Coupe	47
4-Door Sedan	69
2-Door Coupe	87

FIFTH DIGIT: Identifies the engine

ENGINE	CODE
V6-231 2-BC	2
V6-231 4-BC Turbo	3
V6-231 2-BC	A
V6-231 2-BC Turbo	G
V6-196 2-BC	C
V8-305 4-BC	H
V8-403 4-BC	K
V8-350 4-BC	L
V8-350 4-BC	R
V8-305 2-BC	U
V8-350 4-BC	X
V8-301 2-BC	Y

SIXTH DIGIT: Identifies the year 1978

SEVENTH DIGIT: Identifies the assembly plant

ASSEMBLY PLANT	CODE
Southgate, CA	C
Linden, NJ	E
Framingham, MA	G
Flint, MI	H
Tarrytown, NY	T
Lordstown, OH	U
Willow Run, MI	W
Fairfax, KS	X
Fremont, CA	Z

LAST SIX DIGITS: Represent the basic production numbers

EXAMPLE:

4	L	09	K	8	H	123456
Buick Div.	Series	Body Style	Engine Code	Year	Asm Plant	Prod Code

BODY NUMBER PLATE

The body number plate is located on the firewall, just below the rear edge of the hood. This plate identifies the model year, car division, series, body style, body assembly plant, body numbers, trim combination, paint code and build date code.

```
BUICK DIV. GENERAL MOTORS
            CORP.
       FLINT, MICHIGAN
ST 78   4BP37     H 123456 BDY
TR 62N  A51          56 56 PNT
       11A
GENERAL MOTORS CORPORATION CERTIFIES
   TO THE DEALER THAT THIS VEHICLE
 CONFORMS TO ALL U.S., FEDERAL MOTOR
       VEHICLE SAFETY STANDARDS
  APPLICABLE AT TIME OF MANUFACTURE.
```

Example:

78	Model Year (1978)
4	Car Division (Buick)
BP	Series (LeSabre Custom)
37	Style (2-Door Coupe)
H	Body Assembly Plant (Flint, MI)
123456	Production Sequence
62N	Dk/Camel Tan Cloth & Vinyl Trim
56	Gold Poly Paint
11	Eleventh Month (Nov.)
A	1st Week of month

CENTURY SPECIAL	CODE
4-Door Sedan	4AE09
Station Wagon	4AE35
2-Door Coupe	4AE87

CENTURY SPORT COUPE	CODE
Sport Coupe	4AG87

CENTURY CUSTOM	CODE
4-Door Sedan	4AH09
Station Wagon	4AH35
2-Door Coupe	4AH87

REGAL	CODE
2-Door Coupe	4AJ47
Sport Coupe	4AK47

CENTURY LIMITED	CODE
4-Door Sedan	4AL09
2-Door Coupe	4AL87

REGAL LIMITED	CODE
2-Door Coupe	4AM47

LESABRE SPORT COUPE	CODE
Sport Coupe	4BF37

LESABRE	CODE
2-Door Coupe	4BN37
4-Door Sedan	4BN69

LESABRE CUSTOM   **CODE**
2-Door Coupe 4BP37
4-Door Sedan 4BP69

ESTATE WAGON   **CODE**
4-Door 2-Seat 4BR35
*Limited option available

RIVIERA   **CODE**
2-Door Coupe 4BZ37

ELECTRA PARK AVENUE   **CODE**
2-Door 4CU37
4-Door 4CU69

ELECTRA 225   **CODE**
2-Door 4CV37
4-Door 4CV69

ELECTRA LIMITED   **CODE**
2-Door 4CX37
4-Door 4CX69

SKYHAWK   **CODE**
2-Door 4HS07

SKYHAWK S   **CODE**
2-Door 4HT07

SKYLARK   **CODE**
2-Door Hatchback Coupe 4XB17
2-Door Coupe 4XB27
4-Door Sedan 4XB69

SKYLARK S   **CODE**
2-Door Coupe 4XW27

SKYLARK CUSTOM   **CODE**
2-Door Hatchback Coupe 4XC17
2-Door Coupe 4XC27
4-Door Sedan 4XC69

THE TRIM CODE furnishes the key to the interior color and material scheme.

CENTURY SPECIAL 4-DOOR TRIM

COLOR	CLOTH	VINYL	LEATHER	CODE
Lt. Blue		•		24R
Lt. Blue	•	•		24B
Dk/Sage Grn.		•		44R
Dk/Camel Tan		•		62R
Dk/Camel Tan	•	•		62B
Dk/Carmine		•		74B
Dk/Carmine	•	•		74B

CENTURY SPECIAL STATION WAGON TRIM

COLOR	CLOTH	VINYL	LEATHER	CODE
Dk/Camel Tan		•		62R

CENTURY SPECIAL 2-DOOR TRIM

COLOR	CLOTH	VINYL	LEATHER	CODE
White		•		11R
Lt. Blue		•		24R
Lt. Blue	•	•		24B
Dk/Sage Grn.		•		44R
Dk/Carmine		•		74R
Dk/Carmine	•	•		74B

CENTURY CUSTOM 4-DOOR SEDAN TRIM

COLOR	CLOTH	VINYL	LEATHER	CODE
White		•		11V#
Black	•	•		19D#
Lt. Blue	•	•		24C#
Lt. Blue	•	•		24D#
Dk/Sage Grn.		•		44N#
Dk/Sage Grn.	•	•		44D#
Dk/Camel Tan		•		62N#
Dk/Camel Tan		•		62N*
Dk/Camel Tan	•	•		62C#
Dk/Camel Tan	•	•		62D#
Dk/Carmine		•		74N*
Dk/Carmine	•	•		74C#
Dk/Carmine	•	•		74D#

CENTURY CUSTOM STATION WAGON TRIM

COLOR	CLOTH	VINYL	LEATHER	CODE
Dk/Camel Tan		•		62N*
Dk/Carmine		•		74N*

CENTURY CUSTOM 2-DOOR COUPE TRIM

COLOR	CLOTH	VINYL	LEATHER	CODE
White		•		11N#
White		•		11N*
White		•		11V#
Black	•	•		19D#
Lt. Blue	•	•		24C#
Lt. Blue	•	•		24D#
Dk/Sage Grn.		•		44N#
Dk/Sage Grn.	•	•		44D#
Dk/Camel Tan		•		62N#
Dk/Camel Tan		•		62N*
Dk/Camel Tan		•		62C#
Dk/Camel Tan	•	•		62D#
Dk/Carmine		•		74N#
Dk/Carmine		•		74N*
Dk/Carmine	•	•		74C#
Dk/Carmine	•	•		74D#

REGAL 2-DOOR COUPE TRIM

COLOR	CLOTH	VINYL	LEATHER	CODE
White		•		11N#
White		•		11N*
White		•		11V#
Black	•	•		19D#
Lt. Blue	•			24C#
Lt. Blue	•			24D#
Dk/Sage Grn.		•		44N#
Dk/Sage Grn.	•			44D#
Dk/Camel Tan		•		62N#
Dk/Camel Tan		•		62N*
Dk/Camel Tan	•	•		62C#
Dk/Camel Tan	•	•		62D#
Dk/Carmine		•		74N#
Dk/Carmine		•		74N*
Dk/Carmine	•	•		74C#
Dk/Carmine	•	•		74D#

LESABRE 2-DOOR COUPE TRIM

COLOR	CLOTH	VINYL	LEATHER	CODE
Lt. Blue		•		24W
Lt. Blue	•	•		24D
Dk/Sage Grn.		•		44W
Dk/Camel Tan		•		62W
Dk/Camel Tan	•	•		62D
Dk/Carmine		•		74W

LESABRE 4-DOOR SEDAN TRIM

COLOR	CLOTH	VINYL	LEATHER	CODE
White		•		11N#
Black		•		19N#
Lt. Blue		•		24W
Lt. Blue	•	•		24D
Dk/Sage Grn.		•		44W
Dk/Camel Tan		•		62W
Dk/Camel Tan	•	•		62D
DK/Carmine		•		74W

LESABRE CUSTOM 2-DOOR COUPE TRIM

COLOR	CLOTH	VINYL	LEATHER	CODE
White		•		11N#
Black		•		19N#
Lt. Blue		•		24W
Lt. Blue	•	•		24D
Lt. Blue	•		•	24E#
Dk/Sage Grn.		•		44W
Dk/Sage Grn	•	•		44E#
Dk/Camel Tan		•		62W
Dk/Camel Tan	•	•		62D
Dk/Camel Tan		•		62N#
Dk/Camel Tan	•	•		62E#
Dk/Carmine		•		74W
Dk/Carmine		•		74N#
Dk/Carmine	•	•		74E#

LESABRE CUSTOM 4-DOOR SEDAN TRIM

COLOR	CLOTH	VINYL	LEATHER	CODE
White		•		11N#
Black		•		19N#
Lt. Blue	•	•		24E#
Dk/Sage Grn.	•	•		44E#
Dk/Camel Tan		•		62N#
Dk/Camel Tan	•	•		62E#
Dk/Carmine		•		74N#
Dk/Carmine	•	•		74E#

ESTATE WAGON TRIM

COLOR	CLOTH	VINYL	LEATHER	CODE
Lt. Blue	•	•		24J#
Dk/Sage Grn.	•	•		44J#
Dk/Camel Tan	•	•		62E#
Dk/Camel Tan	•	•		62J#
Dk/Carmine	•	•		74J#

RIVIERA 2-DOOR COUPE TRIM

COLOR	CLOTH	VINYL	LEATHER	CODE
White		•		11V#
Black	•	•		19G#
Lt. Blue	•	•		24G#
Dk/Sage Grn.	•	•		44V#
Dk/Camel Tan	•	•		62V#
Dk/Camel Tan	•	•		62G#
Dk/Carmine	•	•		74G#
Lt. Gray			•	152#

ELECTRA 225 TRIM

COLOR	CLOTH	VINYL	LEATHER	CODE
White		•		11R#
Lt. Blue	•	•		24G#
Dk/Sage Grn.	•	•		44G#
Dk/Camel Tan		•		62R#
Dk/Camel Tan	•	•		62G#
Dk/Carmine		•		74R#
Dk/Carmine	•	•		74G#

ELECTRA LIMITED TRIM

COLOR	CLOTH	VINYL	LEATHER	CODE
White		•		11N#
Black	•	•		19H#
Black	•	•		19E#
Lt. Blue	•	•		24H#
Lt. Blue	•	•		24E#
Dk/Sage Grn.	•	•		44H#
Dk/Sage Grn.	•	•		44E#
Dk/Camel Tan		•		62N#
Dk/Camel Tan	•	•		62H#
Dk/Camel Tan	•	•		62E#
Dk/Carmine	•	•		74H#
Dk/Carmine	•	•		74E#

SKYHAWK TRIM

COLOR	CLOTH	VINYL	LEATHER	CODE
White		•		11R*
Black		•		19N*
Lt. Blue		•		24R*
Lt. Blue	•	•		24C*
Dk/Camel Tan		•		62N*
DK/Camel Tan	•	•		62C*
Dk/Carmine		•		74R*
Dk/Carmine	•	•		74C*

SKYLARK 2-DOOR HATCHBACK COUPE TRIM

COLOR	CLOTH	VINYL	LEATHER	CODE
White		•		11R*
Black		•		19R
Lt. Blue	•	•		24B
Dk/Sage Grn.		•		44R
Dk/Camel Tan		•		62R
Dk/Camel Tan		•		62B

SKYLARK 2-DOOR COUPE TRIM

COLOR	CLOTH	VINYL	LEATHER	CODE
White		•		11R*
Black		•		19R
Lt. Blue	•	•		24B
Dk/Sage Grn.		•		44R
Dk/Camel Tan		•		62N
Dk/Camel Tan		•		62R
Dk/Camel Tan	•	•		62B

SKYLARK 4-DOOR SEDAN TRIM

COLOR	CLOTH	VINYL	LEATHER	CODE
White		•		11R
Black		•		19R
Lt. Blue	•	•		24B
Dk/Sage Grn.		•		44R
Dk/Camel Tan		•		62R
Dk/Camel Tan	•	•		62B

SKYLARK CUSTOM TRIM

COLOR	CLOTH	VINYL	LEATHER	CODE
White		•		11V
Lt. Blue	•	•		24D
Lt. Blue	•	•		24D*
Dk/Sage Grn.	•	•		44D
Dk/Sage Grn.	•	•		44D*
Dk/Camel Tan	•	•		62D
Dk/Camel Tan	•	•		62D*
Dk/Carmine	•	•		74D
Dk/Carmine	•	•		74D*

*Bucket seats
#Notch back or 60-40 seat

THE PAINT CODE furnishes the key to the paint colors used on the car. Two, two-digit codes indicate the bottom and top body colors respectively. NOTE: vinyl roof codes appear in the second set of digits.

COLOR	CODE
White	11
Silver Poly	15
Gray Poly	16*
Black	19
Pastel Blue	21
Medium Blue Poly	22
Ultramarine Blue Poly	24
Dark Blue Poly	29
Light Green Poly	44
Dark Green Poly	48
Yellow	51
Gold Poly	56*
Tan	61
Dark Gold Poly	63
Saffron Poly	67
Brown	69

COLOR	CODE
Bright Red	75
Red	77
Dark Red	79
Blue Firemist Poly	91
Amber Firemist Poly	92
Red Firemist Poly	93
Medium Blue Irid	85*

*Two-Tone

VINYL TOP COLORS

COLOR	CODE
White	11T
Silver Poly	15T
Black	19T
Light Blue Poly	22T
Medium Green Poly	44T
Camel Beige	61T
Dark Carmine	79T

ENGINE NUMBER

A Buick engine is stamped with two different identification codes. One is the engine production code which identifies the engine and its approximate production date. The other code is the engine serial number.

ENGINE CODE	NO. CYL.	CID	HORSE-POWER	COMP. RATIO	CARB	OTHER
OG	6	231	105	8.0:1	2-BC	
PA,PB	6	196	95	8.0:1	2-BC	
EA,EG,OH	6	231	105	8.0:1	2-BC	
OK,EJ,EG	6	231	105	8.0:1	2-BC	
EI,EK,EL	6	231	105	8.0:1	2-BC	
OA,OB,OC	6	231	105	8.0:1	2-BC	
OD,OE,OF	6	231	105	8.0:1	2-BC	
EC	6	231	105	8.0:1	2-BC	
EE,OR	6	231	105	8.0:1	2-BC	
OL,EO	6	231	150	8.0:1	2-BC	Turbo
ES,EP,ER	6	231	165	8.0:1	4-BC	Turbo
XA,XC	8	301	140	8.2:1	2-BC	
	8	305	160	8.5:1	4-BC	
CEK,CPZ	8	305	145	8.5:1	2-BC	
CRU,CRX	8	305	145	8.5:1	2-BC	
CRY,CRZ	8	305	145	8.5:1	2-BC	
CTM,CTW	8	305	145	8.5:1	2-BC	
CTR,CTX	8	305	145	8.5:1	2-BC	
C3P,CTJ	8	305	145	8.5:1	2-BC	
CTH,CPJ	8	305	145	8.5:1	2-BC	
C3N,CTK	8	305	145	8.5:1	2-BC	
CPM	8	305	145	8.5:1	2-BC	
CMC,CHM	8	350	170	8.5:1	4-BC	
CKM,CUS	8	350	170	8.5:1	4-BC	
CUR,CHL	8	350	170	8.5:1	4-BC	
CUM	8	350	170	8.5:1	4-BC	
Q2,TP,TO	8	350	170	8.0:1	4-BC	
Q3,TQ,TS	8	350	170	8.0:1	4-BC	
MA,MB	8	350	155	8.0:1	4-BC	
UA,UB,U2	8	403	185	8.0:1	4-BC	
VA,VB,U3	8	403	185	8.0:1	4-BC	

Engines available as indicated below:
Skyhawk & Skyhawk S - OA, OB, OC, OD, OE, OF, OG; Skylark, Skylark S & Skylark Custom - EA, EC, EG, EE, OR, CTJ, CUR, CTH, CPJ, C3N, CHL, CTK, CPM, CUS, CUM; Regal, Regal Limited, Century Special, Century Custom, Century Sport Coupe & Century Limited - PA, PB, EA, EG, OH, OK, CRU, CRX, CRY, CRZ, CTM, CTW, CTR, CTX, C3P; Regal Sport Coupe - OL, ES, EP, ER; Century Special Wagon & Custom Wagon - EA, EG, OH, OK, CRU, CRX, CRY, CRZ, CPZ, CTM, CTW, CTR, CTX, C3P, CMC; LeSabre & LeSabre Custom - EJ, EG, EI, EK, EL, XA, XC, MA, MB, VA, VB, U2, UA, UB,U3, CEK, Q2, TQ, Q3, TS, CHM, CKM; LeSabre Sport Coupe - EO, ES, ER, EP; Riviera , Estate Wagon, Electra 225, Electra Limited, Electra Park Avenue - MA, MB, Q2, TQ, Q3, TS, UA, UB, U2, VA, VB, U3.

1979 BUICK SKYHAWK

1979 BUICK CENTURY

1979 BUICK CENTURY WAGON

1979 BUICK REGAL

1979 BUICK ELECTRA PARK AVENUE

1979 BUICK RIVIERA

1979 BUICK ELECTRA

1979 BUICK SKYLARK

1979 BUICK LE SABRE

1979 BUICK ROAD HAWK

VEHICLE IDENTIFICATION NUMBER

> **BUICK**
> **4N37H9H100001**

Located on the top of the dash on the driver's side and visible through the windshield from outside the car.

FIRST DIGIT: Identifies GM Division (4 = Buick)

SECOND DIGIT: Identifies the series

SERIES	CODE
Skylark	B
Skylark Custom	C
Century Special	E
LeSabre Custom Sport Coupe	F
Century Sport Coupe	G
Century Custom	H
Regal	J
Regal Sport Coupe	K
Century Limited	L
Regal Limited	M
LeSabre	N
LeSabre Custom	P
Estate Wagon	R
Skyhawk	S
Skyhawk S	T
Electra Park Ave	U
Electra 225	V
Skylark S	W
Electra Limited	X
Riviera S	Y
Riviera	Z

THIRD AND FOURTH DIGITS: Identify the body style

BODY STYLE	CODE
2-Door Hatchback Coupe	07
4-Door Sedan	09
2-Door Hatchback Coupe	17
2-Door Coupe	27
4-Door Station Wagon	35
2-Door Coupe	37
2-Door Coupe	47
2-Door Notchback Coupe	57
4-Door Sedan	69
2-Door Coupe	87

FIFTH DIGIT: Identifies the engine

ENGINE	CODE
V6-231 2-BC	2
V6-231 4-BC Turbo	3
V6-231 2-BC	A
V6-196 2-BC	C
V8-305 2-BC	G
V8-305 4-BC	H
V8-403 4-BC	K
V8-350 4-BC	L
V8-350 4-BC	R
V8-301 4-BC	W
V8-350 4-BC	X
V8-301 2-BC	Y

SIXTH DIGIT: Identifies the year (9 = 1979)

SEVENTH DIGIT: Identifies the assembly plant

ASSEMBLY PLANT	CODE
Southgate, CA	C
Linden, NJ	E
Framingham, MA	G
Flint, MI	H
Tarrytown, NY	T
Lordstown, OH	7
Willow Run, MI	W
Fairfax, KS	X
Fremont, CA	Z

EXAMPLE:

4	N	37	H	9	X	100001
Buick Div.	Series	Body Style	Engine Code	Year	Asm Plant	Prod Code

BODY NUMBER PLATE

The body number plate is located on the firewall, just below the rear edge of the hood. This plate identifies the model year, car division, series, body style, body assembly plant, body numbers, trim combination, paint code and build date code.

> **BUICK DIV. GENERAL MOTORS CORP.**
> **FLINT, MICHIGAN**
> ST 79 4BF37   X 123456 BDY
> TR 24D   29 PNT
>   000   000
> GENERAL MOTORS CORPORATION CERTIFIES TO THE DEALER THAT THIS VEHICLE CONFORMS TO ALL U.S., FEDERAL MOTOR VEHICLE SAFETY STANDARDS APPLICABLE AT TIME OF MANUFACTURE.

Example:

79	Model Year (1979)
4	Car Division (Buick)
BF	Series (LeSabre Custom)
37	Style (2-Door Sport Coupe)
H	Body Assembly Plant (Flint, MI)
123456	Production Sequence
24D	Light Blue Cloth Trim
29	Dark Blue Irid Paint
11	Eleventh Month (Nov.)
A	1st Week of month

CENTURY SPECIAL	CODE
4-Door Sedan	4AE09
Station Wagon	4AE35
2-Door Coupe	4AE87

CENTURY	CODE
Sport Coupe	4AG87

*Turbo Coupe option available

CENTURY CUSTOM	CODE
4-Door Sedan	4AH09
Station Wagon	4AH35
2-Door Coupe	4AH87

REGAL

	CODE
2-Door Coupe	4AJ47
Sport Coupe	4AK47

CENTURY LIMITED

	CODE
4-Door Sedan	4AL09

REGAL LIMITED

	CODE
2-Door Coupe	4AM47

LESABRE

	CODE
Sport Coupe	4BF37
2-Door Coupe	4BN37
4-Door Sedan	4BN69

LESABRE LIMITED

	CODE
2-Door Coupe	4BP37
4-Door Sedan	4BP69

*Palm Beach option available

ESTATE WAGON

	CODE
4-Door 2-Seat	4BR35

*Limited option available

RIVIERA

	CODE
2-Door, 6 cyl	4EY57
2-Door, 8 cyl	4EZ57

ELECTRA PARK AVENUE

	CODE
2-Door	4CU37
4-Door	4CU69

ELECTRA 225

	CODE
2-Door	4CV37
4-Door	4CV69

ELECTRA LIMITED

	CODE
2-Door	4CX37
4-Door	4CX69

SKYHAWK

	CODE
2-Door	4HS07
S-2-Door	4HT07

*Road Hawk option available
*Designers Accent Edition option available

SKYLARK

	CODE
2-Door Hatchback	4XB17
2-Door Coupe	4XB27
4-Door Sedan	4XB69
S-2-Door	4XW27

SKYLARK CUSTOM

	CODE
2-Door Coupe	4XC27
4-Door Sedan	4XC69

THE TRIM CODE furnishes the key to the interior color and material scheme.

SKYLARK 2-DOOR HATCHBACK TRIM

COLOR	CLOTH	VINYL	LEATHER	CODE
White		•		11R
White		•		11R*
Black		•		19R
Lt. Blue	•	•		24B
Dk/Camel Tan		•		62N
Dk/Camel Tan		•		62R
Dk/Camel Tan	•	•		62B

SKYLARK 2-DOOR COUPE TRIM

COLOR	CLOTH	VINYL	LEATHER	CODE
White		•		11R
White		•		11R*
Black		•		19R
Lt. Blue	•	•		24B
Dk/Camel Tan		•		62N
Dk/Camel Tan		•		62R
Dk/Camel Tan	•	•		62B

SKYLARK 4-DOOR SEDAN TRIM

COLOR	CLOTH	VINYL	LEATHER	CODE
White		•		11R
White		•		11R*
Black		•		19R
Lt. Blue	•	•		24B
Dk/Camel Tan		•		62R
Dk/Camel Tan	•	•		62B

SKYLARK CUSTOM TRIM

COLOR	CLOTH	VINYL	LEATHER	CODE
White		•		11V
Black	•	•		19D
Lt. Blue	•	•		24D
Dk/Camel Tan	•	•		62D
Dk/Carmine	•	•		74D

CENTURY SPECIAL 4-DOOR SEDAN TRIM

COLOR	CLOTH	VINYL	LEATHER	CODE
Lt. Blue		•		24R
Lt. Blue	•	•		24B
Dk/Camel Tan		•		62R
Dk/Camel Tan	•	•		62B
Dk/Carmine	•	•		74B

CENTURY SPECIAL STATION WAGON TRIM

COLOR	CLOTH	VINYL	LEATHER	CODE
Lt. Blue	•	•		24E#
Lt. Blue		•		24N#
Lt. Blue		•		24N*
Dk/Willow Grn		•		44N#
Dk/Camel Tan		•		62R
Dk/Camel Tan	•	•		62E#
Dk/Camel Tan	•	•		62E*
Dk/Camel Tan		•		62N#
Dk/Camel Tan		•		62N*
Dk/Carmine	•	•		74E#
Dk/Carmine		•		74N#
Dk/Carmine		•		74N*

CENTURY SPECIAL 2-DOOR COUPE TRIM

COLOR	CLOTH	VINYL	LEATHER	CODE
Lt. Blue		•		24R
Lt. Blue	•	•		24B
Lt. Blue		•		24N#
Lt. Blue		•		24N*
Lt. Blue	•	•		24C#
Dk/Willow Grn.		•		44R
Dk/Willow Grn.		•		44N#
Dk/Camel Tan		•		62R
Dk/Camel Tan	•	•		62B
Dk/Camel Tan		•		62N#
Dk/Camel Tan		•		62N*
Dk/Camel Tan	•	•		62C#
Dk/Camel Tan	•	•		62C*
Dk/Carmine	•	•		74B
Dk/Carmine		•		74N#
Dk/Carmine		•		74N*
Dk/Carmine	•	•		74C#
Dk/Oyster		•		12R
Dk/Oyster		•		12N#
Dk/Oyster		•		12N*

CENTURY CUSTOM 4-DOOR SEDAN TRIM

COLOR	CLOTH	VINYL	LEATHER	CODE
Black	•	•		19D#
Lt. Blue		•		24N#
Lt. Blue		•		24N*
Lt. Blue	•	•		24C#
Lt. Blue	•	•		24D#
Dk/Willow Grn.		•		44N#
Dk/Willow Grn.	•	•		44D#
Dk/Camel Tan		•		62N#
Dk/Camel Tan		•		62N*
Dk/Camel Tan	•	•		62C#
Dk/Camel Tan	•	•		62C*
Dk/Camel Tan	•	•		62D#
Dk/Carmine		•		74N#
Dk/Carmine		•		74N*
Dk/Carmine	•	•		74C#
Dk/Carmine	•	•		74D#
Dk/Oyster	•	•		12G#

CENTURY CUSTOM STATION WAGON TRIM

COLOR	CLOTH	VINYL	LEATHER	CODE
Lt. Blue		•		24N#
Lt. Blue		•		24N*
Lt. Blue	•	•		24E#
Dk/Willow Grn.		•		44N#
Dk/Camel Tan		•		62N#
Dk/Camel Tan		•		62N*
Dk/Camel Tan	•	•		62E#
Dk/Camel Tan	•	•		62E*
Dk/Carmine		•		74N#
Dk/Carmine		•		74N*
Dk/Carmine	•	•		74E#

CENTURY CUSTOM 2-DOOR COUPE TRIM

COLOR	CLOTH	VINYL	LEATHER	CODE
Lt. Blue		•		24N#
Lt. Blue		•		24N*
Lt. Blue	•	•		24C#
Dk/Willow Grn.		•		44N#
Dk/Camel Tan		•		62N#
Dk/Camel Tan		•		62N*
Dk/Camel Tan	•	•		62C#
Dk/Camel Tan	•	•		62C*
Dk/Carmine		•		74N#
Dk/Carmine		•		74N*
Dk/Carmine	•	•		74C#
Dk/Oyster		•		12N#
Dk/Oyster		•		12N*

REGAL TRIM

COLOR	CLOTH	VINYL	LEATHER	CODE
Black	•	•		19D#
Lt. Blue		•		24N#
Lt. Blue		•		24N*
Lt. Blue	•	•		24C#
Lt. Blue	•	•		24D#
Dk/Willow Grn.		•		44N#
Dk/Willow Grn.	•	•		44D#
Dk/Camel Tan		•		62N#
Dk/Camel Tan		•		62N*
Dk/Camel Tan	•	•		62C#
Dk/Camel Tan	•	•		62D#
Dk/Carmine		•		74N#
Dk/Carmine		•		74N*
Dk/Carmine	•	•		74C#
Dk/Carmine	•	•		74C*
Dk/Carmine	•	•		74D#
Dk/Oyster		•		12N#
Dk/Oyster		•		12N*
Dk/Oyster		•		12V#
Dk/Oyster	•	•		12G#

LESABRE 2-DOOR COUPE TRIM

COLOR	CLOTH	VINYL	LEATHER	CODE
Lt. Blue	•	•		24D
Dk/Willow Grn.		•		44W
Dk/Camel Tan		•		62W
Dk/Camel Tan	•	•		62D
Dk/Camel Tan	•	•		62D*
Dk/Carmine		•		74W

LESABRE 4-DOOR SEDAN TRIM

COLOR	CLOTH	VINYL	LEATHER	CODE
Lt. Blue	•	•		24D
Dk/Willow Grn.		•		44W
Dk/Camel Tan		•		62W
Dk/Camel Tan	•	•		62D

LESABRE LIMITED 2-DOOR TRIM

COLOR	CLOTH	VINYL	LEATHER	CODE
Black	•	•		19E#
Lt. Blue	•	•		24D
Lt. Blue	•	•		24E#
Dk/Willow Grn.		•		44W
Dk/Willow Grn.	•	•		44E#
Dk/Camel Tan	•	•		62D*
Dk/Camel Tan		•		62W
Dk/Camel Tan	•	•		62D
Dk/Camel Tan		•		62N#
Dk/Camel Tan	•	•		62E#
Dk/Carmine		•		74W
Dk/Carmine		•		74N#
Dk/Carmine	•	•		74E#
Dk/Oyster		•		12N#
Dk/Oyster	•	•		12H#
Lt. Yellow	•	•		52G#

LESABRE LIMITED 4-DOOR SEDAN TRIM

COLOR	CLOTH	VINYL	LEATHER	CODE
Black	•	•		19E#
Lt. Blue	•	•		24E#
Dk/Willow Grn.	•	•		44E#
Dk/Camel Tan		•		62N#
Dk/Camel Tan	•	•		162E#
Dk/Carmine	•	•		74E#
Dk/Oyster		•		12N#
Dk/Oyster	•	•		12H#

ESTATE WAGON TRIM

COLOR	CLOTH	VINYL	LEATHER	CODE
Lt. Blue		•		24N#
Lt. Blue	•	•		24J#
Dk/Willow Grn.		•		44N#
Dk/Willow Grn.	•	•		44J#
Dk/Camel Tan		•		62N#
Dk/Camel Tan	•	•		62E#
Dk/Camel Tan	•	•		162J#
Dk/Carmine		•		74N#
Dk/Carmine		•		74J#

RIVIERA TRIM

COLOR	CLOTH	VINYL	LEATHER	CODE
Black	•	•		19B#
Black	•	•		19C*
Lt. Blue	•	•		24B#
Lt. Blue	•	•		24C*
Dk/Willow Grn.	•	•		44B#
Dk/Willow Grn.	•	•		44C*
Dk/Camel Tan		•		62R#
Dk/Camel Tan			•	622#
Dk/Camel Tan	•	•		62B#
Dk/Camel Tan		•		62N*
Dk/Camel Tan	•	•		62C*
Dk/Camel Tan			•	623*
Dk/Carmine		•		74R#
Dk/Carmine	•	•		74B#
Dk/Carmine		•		74N*
Dk/Carmine	•	•		74C*
Dk/Oyster	•	•		12D#
Dk/Oyster		•		122#
Dk/Oyster			•	123*

ELECTRA 225 TRIM

COLOR	CLOTH	VINYL	LEATHER	CODE
Lt. Blue	•	•		24G#
Dk/Willow Grn.	•	•		44G#
Dk/Camel Tan		•		62R#
Dk/Camel Tan	•	•		62G#
Dk/Carmine	•	•		74G#
Dk/Oyster		•		12R#

ELECTRA LIMITED TRIM

COLOR	CLOTH	VINYL	LEATHER	CODE
Black	•	•		19J#
Black	•	•		19E#
Black	•	•		19D#
Lt. Blue	•	•		24G#
Lt. Blue	•	•		24J#
Lt. Blue	•	•		24E#
Lt. Blue	•	•		24D#
Dk/Willow Grn.	•	•		44G#
Dk/Willow Grn.	•	•		44J#
Dk/Willow Grn.	•	•		44E#
Dk/Willow Grn.	•	•		44D#
Dk/Camel Tan	•	•		62G#
Dk/Camel Tan		•		62N#
Dk/Camel Tan	•	•		62J#
Dk/Camel Tan	•	•		62E#
Dk/Camel Tan	•	•		62D#
Dk/Carmine	•	•		74J#
Dk/Carmine	•	•		74D
Oyster		•		12N#
Dk/Oyster	•	•		12E#
Dk/Oyster	•	•		12D#

SKYHAWK TRIM

COLOR	CLOTH	VINYL	LEATHER	CODE
Black		•		19N*
Lt. Blue	•	•		24C*
Dk/Camel Tan		•		62N*
Dk/Camel Tan		•		62R*
Dk/Camel Tan	•	•		62C*
Dk/Carmine		•		74R*
Dk/Carmine	•	•		74C*
Dk/Oyster		•		12R*
Dk/Oyster		•		12V*

*Bucket seats
#Notch back or 60-40 seats

THE PAINT CODE furnishes the key to the paint colors used on the car. Two, two-digit codes indicate the bottom and top body colors respectively. NOTE: vinyl roof codes appear as a second set of digits.

COLOR	CODE
White	11
Silver Irid	15
Gray Irid	16*
Pastel Blue	21
Light Blue Irid	22
Bright Blue Irid	24
Dark Blue Irid	29
Caramel Firemist	33
Pastel Green	40
Medium Green Irid	44
Bright Yellow	51
Light Yellow	54
Medium Beige	61
Camel Irid	63
Dark Brown Irid	69
Bright Red	75
Carmine Irid	77
Dark Carmine Irid	79
Medium Blue Irid	85*
Charcoal Irid	98
Saffron Firemist	99
Black	19
Beige Met	38#
Yellow Beige	84#

* Two-Tone only
# Special order colors

VINYL TOP COLORS

COLOR	CODE
White	11T
Silver Poly	15T
Black	19T
Light Blue Poly	22T
Pastel Green	40T
Medium Beige	61T
Dark Carmine Poly	79T

ENGINE NUMBER

A Buick engine is stamped with two different identification codes. One is the engine production code which identifies the engine and its approximate production date. The other code is the engine serial number — it matches the VIN (vehicle identification number).

BUICK ENGINES

ENGINE CODE	NO. CYL.	CID	HORSE-POWER	COMP. RATIO	CARB
FA,FE,FG	6	106	105	8.0:1	2-BC
FH,FB	6	106	105	8.0:1	2-BC
RA,RW,RJ	6	231	115	8.0:1	2-BC
NJ,RB,RC	6	231	115	8.0:1	2-BC
RG,NA,NB	6	231	115	8.0:1	2-BC
NC,NE,NG	6	231	115	8.0:1	2-BC
NH,NM,NL	6	231	115	8.0:1	2-BC
RX	6	231	115	8.0:1	2-BC
RY	6	231	115	8.0:1	2-BC
RM,RN	6	231	115	8.0:1	2-BC
RR,RU,RV	6	231	165	8.0:1	4-BC
RO,RS,RP	6	231	165	8.0:1	4-BC
RT	6	231	165	8.0:1	4-BC
XP,XR	8	301	140	8.2:1	2-BC
PXL,PXN	8	301	150	8.2:1	4-BC
DNJ	8	305	140	8.5:1	2-BC
DNX,DNY	8	305	160	8.5:1	4-BC
DTA	8	305	160	8.5:1	4-BC
DRY,DRJ	8	350	160	8.5:1	4-BC
U9,VK,VA	8	350	170	8.0:1	4-BC
UZ	8	350	170	8.0:1	4-BC
SA,SB	8	350	155	8.0:1	4-BC
GB,G3,TB	8	403	185	8.0:1	4-BC
QB,Q3	8	403	185	8.0:1	4-BC

Engines are available as indicated below:
Skyhawk & Skyhawk S - NA, NB, NC, NE, NG, NH, NM; Skylark, Skylark Custom & Skylark S - NL, RX, RY, DNJ, DRJ, DRY; Century Special, Century Custom & Century Sport Coupe - FA, FB, FE, FG, FH, RA, RJ, RB, RW, NJ, RM, RN, RR, RU, RV, DNX, DNY, DTA, XP, XR, PXL, PXN; Century Wagon - RA, RJ, RB, RW, NJ, RM, RN, XP, XR, DXL, DXN, DNY, DTA, DRY, DRJ; Regal, Regal Limited - FA, FB, FE, FG, FH, RA, RJ, RB, RW, NJ, RM, RN, XP, XR, PXL, PXN, DNX, DNY, DTA; Regal Sport Coupe - RR, RU, RV; LeSabre & LeSabre Custom - RC, XP, U9, SA, RG, XR, VK, SB; LeSabre Sport Coupe - RO, RS; Estate Wagon - U9, SA, GB, TB, VK, SB, G3; Electra 225, Electra Limited & Electra Park Avenue - U9, SA, QB, TB, VK, SB, Q3; Riviera & Riviera S - RP, RT, VA, UZ.

1970 CADILLAC COUPE DE VILLE

1970 CADILLAC SEDAN DE VILLE

1970 CADILLAC ELDORADO

1970 CADILLAC ELDORADO

1970 CADILLAC FLEETWOOD

1970 CADILLAC SEDAN DE VILLE

1970 CADILLAC LIMOUSINE

1970 CADILLAC CALAIS COUPE

VEHICLE IDENTIFICATION NUMBER

CADILLAC M0100001

Located on the top of the dash on the driver's side and visible through the windshield from outside the car. Also stamped on a pad on the rear upper portion of the cylinder block behind the intake manifold.

FIRST DIGIT: Identifies the series

SERIES	CODE
Calais Coupe	G
Calais Hardtop Sedan	N
Coupe DeVille	J
Hardtop Sedan DeVille	B
DeVille Convertible	F
Sedan DeVille	L
Fleetwood Sixty Special Sedan	M
Fleetwood Brougham	P
Eldorado Coupe	H
Fleetwood Seventy-Five Sedan	R
Fleetwood Seventy-Five Limo	S
Commercial Chassis	Z

SECOND DIGIT: Identifies the year (0 = 1970)

LAST SIX DIGITS: Represent the basic production numbers

BODY NUMBER PLATE

Complete identification of each body is provided by a plate attached to the top surface of the cowl, under the hood.

BODY BY FISHER

ST 70 68069   Q 123456 BDY
TR 016   11 11 PNT
A51

GENERAL MOTORS CORPORATION CERTIFIES TO THE DEALER THAT THIS VEHICLE CONFORMS TO ALL U.S., FEDERAL MOTOR VEHICLE SAFETY STANDARDS APPLICABLE AT TIME OF MANUFACTURE.

Example:

70	Model Year (1970)
6	Car Division (Cadillac)
80	Series (Fleetwood)
69	Style (4-Door Pillar Sedan)
Q	Assembly Plant (Detroit, MI)
123456	Production Sequence
016	Light Gray Cloth
11 11	Cotillion White
A51	Modular Seat Code

CALAIS	CODE
2-Door HT Coupe	68247
4-Door HT Sedan	68249

DEVILLE	CODE
2-Door HT Coupe	68347
4-Door HT Sedan	68349
2-Door Convertible	68367
4-Door Pillar Sedan	68369

FLEETWOOD	CODE
2-Door Notchback HT Coupe	69347

FLEETWOOD SIXTY SPECIAL	CODE
4-Door Pillar Sedan	68069

FLEETWOOD BROUGHAM	CODE
4-Door Pillar Sedan	68169

FLEETWOOD SEVENTY-FIVE	CODE
4-Door Limo/Aux. Seat	69723
4-Door Limo w/Center Window	69733

COMMERCIAL	CODE
Commercial Chassis	69890

THE TRIM CODE furnishes the key to the interior color and material scheme.

FLEETWOOD 60 SPECIAL & BROUGHAM TRIM

COLOR	CLOTH	VINYL	LEATHER	CODE
Black	•			011,011S
Lt. Gray	•			016,016S
Med. Blue	•			021,021S
Med. Turq.	•			028,028S
Dk. Green	•			031,031S
Med. Beige	•			043,043S
Med. Gold	•			044,044S
Dk. Mauve	•			047,047S
Black			•	051,051S
White			•	052,052S
Dk. Blue			•	066,066S
Ant. Med. Beige			•	083,083S
Ant. Med. Gold			•	084,084S
Ant. Dk. Brown			•	086,086S
Med. Red			•	088,088S

CALAIS TRIM

COLOR	CLOTH	VINYL	LEATHER	CODE
Black	•			211
Med. Blue	•			220
Med. Turquoise	•			228
Dk. Green	•			231
Med. Beige	•			243
Med. Gold	•			244
Black	•			251
Ant. Med. Beige	•			283

DEVILLE HARDTOP/SEDAN TRIM

COLOR	CLOTH	VINYL	LEATHER	CODE
Black	•			311,311S
Med. Blue	•			320,320S
Med. Turquoise	•			328,328S
Dk. Green	•			331,331S
Med. Beige	•			343,343S
Med. Gold	•			344,344S
Dk. Mauve	•			347,347S
Black			•	351,351S
White			•	352,352S
White			•	353,353S*
White			•	357,357S**
Dk. Blue			•	366,366S
Ant. Med. Beige			•	383,383S
Ant. Med. Gold			•	384,384S
Ant. Dk. Brown			•	386,386S
Med. Red			•	388,388S**

*Exc. styles 68349,69
**Exc. styles 68369

DEVILLE CONVERTIBLE TRIM

COLOR	CLOTH	VINYL	LEATHER	CODE
Black			•	351,351S
White			•	352,352S
White			•	353,353S
White			•	354,354S
White			•	357,357S
Dk. Blue			•	366,366S
Ant. Med. Beige			•	383,383S
Ant. Med. Gold			•	384,384S
Ant. Dk. Brown			•	386,386S
Med. Red			•	388,388S

ELDORADO COUPE TRIM

COLOR	CLOTH	VINYL	LEATHER	CODE
Black	•			411
Med.Blue	•			420
Med. Turquoise	•			428
Dk. Green	•			431
Med. Beige	•			443
Med. Gold	•			444
Dk. Mauve	•			447
Black			•	451,451B
White			•	452
White			•	457
Dk. Blue			•	466
Ant. Med. Beige			•	483
Ant. Med. Gold			•	484
Ant. Dk. Brown			•	486
Med. Red			•	488

FLEETWOOD 75 SEDAN TRIM

COLOR	CLOTH	VINYL	LEATHER	CODE
Black			•	711
Lt. Gray	•			716
Med. Gray	•			719
Med. Blue	•			721
Med. Beige	•			743

FLEETWOOD 75 LIMOUSINE TRIM

COLOR	CLOTH	VINYL	LEATHER	CODE
Black			•	711
Black			•	716
Black			•	719
Black			•	721
Black			•	743

S 60/40 front seat

THE PAINT CODE furnishes the key to the paint colors used on the car. A two number code indicates the color of the car. Two, two-digit codes indicate the bottom and top body colors respectively. NOTE: vinyl roof and convertible top codes appear in the second set of digits.

COLOR	CODE
Cotillion White	11
Patina Silver	14
Phantom Gray	18
Sable Black	19
Corinthian Blue	24
Condor Blue	29
Adriatic Turquoise	34
Lanai Green	42
Glenmore Green	49
Byzantine Gold	54
Bayberry	59
Sauterne	64
Dark Walnut	69
San Mateo Red	74
Monarch Burgundy	79
Spartacus Blue Firemist	90
Lucerne Aqua Firemist	93
Regency Bronze Firemist	94
Cinnamon Firemist	95
Nottingham Green Firemist	96
Briarwood Firemist	97
Chateau Mauve Firemist	99

ROOF TOP COLORS

White	J
Black	K
Blue	L
Beige	M
Bayberry	N
Mauve	P
Brown	R

CONVERTIBLE TOP COLORS

Black	B
Blue	C
White	J
Beige	M
Bayberry	N

ENGINE NUMBER

The serial number of all 1970 Cadillac engines is stamped on the lower left hand side of the cylinder block, just above the edge of the oil pan.

ENGINE CODE	NO. CYL.	CID	HORSE-POWER	COMP. RATIO	CARB
	8	472	375	10.0:1	4-BC
	8	500	400	10.0:1	4-BC

1971 CADILLAC COUPE DE VILLE

1971 CADILLAC CALAIS SEDAN

1971 CADILLAC SIXTY SPECIAL BROUGHAM

1971 CADILLAC FLEETWOOD SIXTY SPECIAL BROUGHAM

1971 CADILLAC FLEETWOOD ELDORADO

1971 CADILLAC SEDAN DE VILLE

1971 CADILLAC SEDAN DE VILLE

1971 CADILLAC FLEETWOOD ELDORADO

VEHICLE IDENTIFICATION NUMBER

• CADILLAC 683471Q100001 •

Located on the top of the dash on the driver's side and visible through the windshield from outside the car. Also stamped on a pad on the rear upper portion of the cylinder block behind the intake manifold.

FIRST DIGIT: Identifies GM Division (6 is Cadillac)

SECOND THRU FIFTH DIGITS: Identify the series and model

SERIES	CODE
Calais 4-Door Sedan	8249
Calais 2-Door Coupe	8247
DeVille 4-Door Sedan	8349
DeVille 2-Door Coupe	8347
Fleetwood 60 Special Brougham	8169
Fleetwood 75 4-Door Sedan	9723
Fleetwood Limousine	9733
Fleetwood Eldo 2-Dr HT Coupe	9347
Fleetwood 2-Dr Convertible	9367
Commercial Chassis	9890

SIXTH DIGIT: Identifies the year (1 = 1971)

SEVENTH DIGIT: Identifies the assembly plant

ASSEMBLY PLANT	CODE
Detroit, MI	Q
Linden, NJ	E

LAST SIX DIGITS: Identify the basic production code

BODY NUMBER PLATE

Complete identification of each body is provided by a plate attached to the top surface of cowl, under the hood.

```
          BODY BY FISHER
ST 71-68347          E  123456 BDY
TR 351                    11-K PNT
A51
   •                              •

GENERAL MOTORS CORPORATION CERTIFIES
  TO THE DEALER THAT THIS VEHICLE
CONFORMS TO ALL U.S., FEDERAL MOTOR
      VEHICLE SAFETY STANDARDS
  APPLICABLE AT TIME OF MANUFACTURE.
```

Example:

71	Model Year (1971)
6	Car Division (Cadillac)
83	Series (DeVille)
47	Style (2-Door Coupe)
E	Assembly Plant (Linden, NJ)
123456	Production Sequence
351	Black Leather
11-K	Cotillion White/Black Vinyl Top
A51	Modular Seat Code

5 - 5

THE TRIM CODE furnishes the key to the interior color and material scheme.

FLEETWOOD 60 SPECIAL BROUGHAM TRIM

COLOR	CLOTH	VINYL	LEATHER	CODE
Black	•			011
Med. Gray	•			016
Med. Blue	•			021
Dk. Blue	•			026
Med. Aqua	•			028
Dk. Jade	•			031
Med. Beige	•			043
Med. Maize	•			044
Med. Heather	•			047
Black			•	051
White			•	052/053
Ant. Med. Pewter			•	059
Dk. Blue			•	066
Med. Aqua			•	068
Ant. Dk. Jade			•	071
Ant. Lt. Sandalwood			•	082
Med. Maize			•	084
Ant. Dk. Saddle			•	085
Dk. Carmine			•	088

CALAIS TRIM

COLOR	CLOTH	VINYL	LEATHER	CODE
Black	•			211
Dk. Blue	•			226
Med. Aqua	•			228
Dk. Jade	•			231
Med. Beige	•			243
Med. Maize	•			244
Black	•			251
Dk. Saddle	•			285

DEVILLE TRIM

COLOR	CLOTH	VINYL	LEATHER	CODE
Black	•			311,611
Med. Blue	•			320,620
Dk. Blue	•			326,626
Med. Aqua	•			328,628
Dk. Jade	•			331,631
Med. Beige	•			343,643
Med. Maize	•			344,644
Med. Heather	•			347,647
Black			•	351,651
White			•	352,652
White			•	353,653
White			•	354,654
Ant. Med. Pewter			•	359,659
Dk. Blue			•	366,666
Med. Aqua			•	368,668
Dk. Jade			•	371,671
Ant. Lt. Sandalwood			•	382,682
Med. Maize			•	384,684
Ant. Dk. Saddle			•	385,685
Dk. Carmine			•	388,688

600 Series trim combination number designates the 60-40 seat.

ELDORADO COUPE TRIM

COLOR	CLOTH	VINYL	LEATHER	CODE
Black	•			411
Med. Blue	•			420
Dk. Blue	•			426
Med. Aqua	•			428
Dk. Jade	•			431
Med. Beige	•			443
Med. Maize	•			444
Med. Heather	•			447

ELDORADO COUPE/CONVERTIBLE TRIM

COLOR	CLOTH	VINYL	LEATHER	CODE
Black			•	451
White			•	452
White			•	453
White			•	454
Ant. Med. Pewter			•	459
Dk. Blue			•	466
Med. Aqua			•	468
Dk. Jade			•	471
Ant. Lt. Sandalwood			•	482
Med. Maize			•	484
Ant. Dk. Saddle			•	485
Dk. Carmine			•	488

FLEETWOOD 75 SEDAN TRIM

COLOR	CLOTH	VINYL	LEATHER	CODE
Black	•			711
Med. Gray	•			716
Dk. Blue	•			726
Med. Beige	•			743

FLEETWOOD 75 LIMO TRIM

COLOR	CLOTH	VINYL	LEATHER	CODE
Black w/Black			•	711
Black w/Med. Gray			•	716
Black w/Dk. Blue			•	726
Black w/Med. Beige			•	743

THE PAINT CODE furnishes the key to the paint colors used on the car. A two number code indicates the color of the car. Two, two-digit codes indicate the bottom and top body colors respectively. NOTE: vinyl roof and convertible top codes appear in the second set of digits.

COLOR	CODE
Cotillion White	11
Grenoble Silver	13
Oxford Gray	16
Sable Black	19
Zodiac Blue	24
Brittany Blue	29
Adriatic Turquoise	34
Cypress Green	44
Sylvan Green	49
Casablanca Yellow	50
Duchess Gold	55
Desert Beige	64
Clove	69
Cambridge Red	74
Empire Maroon Firemist	89
Bavarian Blue Firemist	90
Pewter Firemist	92
Chalice Gold Firemist	94
Almond Firemist	95
Sausalito Green Firemist	96
Primrose Firemist	99

VINYL ROOF TOP COLORS

COLOR	CODE
White	J
Black	K
Blue	L
Aqua	M
Green	N
Gold	P
Brown	R
Lt. Beige	S

ELDORADO CONVERTIBLE TOP COLORS

White	A
Black	B
Blue	C
Lt. Beige	E
Green	N
Brown	R

ENGINE NUMBER

The engine number is located on the rear of the cylinder block, behind the intake manifold.

ENGINE CODE	NO. CYL.	CID	HORSE-POWER	COMP. RATIO	CARB
	8	472	345	8.5:1	4-BC
	8	500	365	8.5:1	4-BC

1972 CADILLAC COUPE DE VILLE

1972 CADILLAC SEDAN DE VILLE

1972 CADILLAC ELDORADO

1972 CADILLAC ELDORADO

1972 CADILLAC FLEETWOOD

1972 CADILLAC FLEETWOOD

VEHICLE IDENTIFICATION NUMBER

CADILLAC
6C47R2Q100001

Commonly referred to as the VIN NUMBER, this series of letters and numbers is stamped on a steel plate and riveted to the cowl bar at the lower left corner of the windshield. Also stamped on a pad on the rear upper portion of the cylinder block behind the intake manifold, and on the left side of the transmission case. (Minus Model Identity Symbol).

FIRST DIGIT: Identifies GM Division (6 is Cadillac)

SECOND DIGIT: Identifies the series

SERIES	CODE
Fleetwood 60 Special Brougham	B
Calais Coupe/Sedan	C
Coupe DeVille/Sedan DeVille	D
Fleetwood 75 Sedan	F
Eldorado	L
Commercial Chassis	Z

THIRD AND FOURTH DIGITS: Identify the body style

BODY STYLE	CODE
4-Door Limo w/Aux. Seat	23
4-Door Limo w/Center Window	33
2-Door Hardtop Coupe	47
4-Door Hardtop (4 Window) Sedan	49
2-Door Convertible Coupe	67
4-Door Pillar Sedan	69
Commercial Chassis	90

FIFTH DIGIT: Identifies the engine

ENGINE	CODE
V8-472	R
V8-500	S

SIXTH DIGIT: Identifies the year (2 = 1972)

SEVENTH DIGIT: Identifies the assembly plant

ASSEMBLY PLANT	CODE
Detroit, MI	Q
Linden, NJ	E

LAST SIX DIGITS: Represent the basic production numbers

BODY NUMBER PLATE

Complete identification of each body is provided by a plate attached to the top surface of the cowl, under the hood.

BODY BY FISHER

ST 72 68347   E 123456 BDY
TR 351   11-K PNT
A51

GENERAL MOTORS CORPORATION CERTIFIES TO THE DEALER THAT THIS VEHICLE CONFORMS TO ALL U.S., FEDERAL MOTOR VEHICLE SAFETY STANDARDS APPLICABLE AT TIME OF MANUFACTURE.

Example:

72	Model Year (1972)
6	Car Division (Cadillac)
83	Series (DeVille)
47	Style (2-Door Hardtop Coupe)
E	Assembly Plant (Linden, NJ)
123456	Production Sequence
351	Black Leather
11-K	Cotillion White/Black Vinyl Top
A51	Modular Seat Code

CALAIS	CODE
2-Door Hardtop	68247
4-Door Hardtop	68249

FLEETWOOD 60 SPECIAL BROUGHAM	CODE
4-Door Pillar Sedan	68169

FLEETWOOD 75 LIMO	CODE
4-Door w/Aux. Seat	69723
4-Door w/Center Window	69733

DEVILLE	CODE
2-Door Hardtop	68347
4-Door Hardtop	68349

ELDORADO	CODE
2-Door Hardtop Coupe	69347
Convertible Coupe	69367

COMMERCIAL	CODE
Commercial Chassis	69890

THE TRIM CODE furnishes the key to the interior color and material scheme.

FLEETWOOD 60 SPECIAL BROUGHAM TRIM

COLOR	CLOTH	VINYL	LEATHER	CODE
Black	•			011
Med. Pewter	•			019
Dk. Blue	•			026
Med. Aqua	•			028
Dk. Jade	•			031
Med. Beige	•			043
Med. Maize	•			044
Dk. Covert	•			046
Black		•		051
White w/Black		•		052
White w/Dk. Blue		•		053
White w/Dk. Oxblood		•		054
White w/Dk. Jade		•		057
Dk. Blue		•		066
Dk. Jade		•		071
Lt. Covert		•		083
Med. Maize		•		084
Dk. Saddle		•		085
Dk. Covert		•		086
Dk. Oxblood		•		089

CALAIS TRIM

COLOR	CLOTH	VINYL	LEATHER	CODE
Black	•			211
Dk. Blue	•			226
Med. Aqua	•			228
Dk. Jade	•			231
Med. Beige	•			242
Med. Maize	•			244
Black	•			251
Dk. Saddle	•			285

DEVILLE TRIM

COLOR	CLOTH	VINYL	LEATHER	CODE
Black	•			311
Dk. Blue	•			326
Med. Aqua	•			328
Dk. Jade	•			331
Med. Beige	•			342
Med. Maize	•			344
Dk. Covert	•			346
Black		•		351
White w/Black		•		352
White w/Dk. Blue		•		353
White w/Dk. Oxblood		•		354
White w/Jade		•		357
Dk. Blue		•		366
Dk. Jade		•		371
Lt. Covert		•		383
Med. Maize		•		384
Dk. Saddle		•		385
Dk. Covert		•		386
Dk. Oxblood		•		389

ELDORADO COUPE TRIM

COLOR	CLOTH	VINYL	LEATHER	CODE
Black Mor.	•			411
Dk. Blue Mor.	•			426
Med. Aqua	•			428
Dk. Jade	•			431
Med. Beige	•			442
Med. Maize	•			444
Dk. Covert	•			446
Black			•	451
White w/Black			•	452
White w/Dk. Blue			•	453
White w/Dk. Oxblood			•	454
White w/Jade			•	457
Dk. Blue			•	466
Dk. Jade			•	471
Lt. Covert			•	483
Med. Maize			•	484
Dk. Saddle			•	485
Dk. Covert			•	486
Dk. Oxblood			•	489

ELDORADO CONVERTIBLE TRIM

COLOR	CLOTH	VINYL	LEATHER	CODE
Black			•	451
White w/Black			•	452
White w/Dk. Blue			•	453
White w/Dk. Oxblood			•	454
White w/Jade			•	457
Dk. Blue			•	466
Dk. Jade			•	471
Lt. Covert			•	483
Med. Maize			•	484
Dk. Saddle			•	485
Dk. Covert			•	486
Dk. Oxblood			•	489

FLEETWOOD 75 SEDAN TRIM

COLOR	CLOTH	VINYL	LEATHER	CODE
Black	•			711
Med. Pewter	•			719
Dk. Blue	•			726
Med. Beige	•			742

FLEETWOOD 75 LIMO TRIM

COLOR	CLOTH	VINYL	LEATHER	CODE
Black w/Black			•	711
Black w/Med. Pewter			•	719
Black w/Dk. Blue			•	726
Black w/Med. Beige			•	742

THE PAINT CODE furnishes the key to the paint colors used on the car. A two number code indicates the color of the car. Two, two-digit codes indicate the bottom and top body colors respectively. NOTE: vinyl roof and convertible top codes appear in the second set of digits.

COLOR	CODE
Cotillion White	11
Contessa Pewter	14
Mayfair Gray	18
Sable Black	19
Zodiac Blue	24
Brittany Blue	29
Adriatic Turquoise	34
Sumatra Green	44
Brewster Green	49
Willow	50
Promenade Gold	54
Stratford Covert	59
Tawny Beige	64
Cognac	69
Cambridge Red	73
Ice Blue Firemist	90
St. Moritz Blue Firemist	92
Palomino Firemist	93
Patrician Covert Firemist	94
Balmoral Green Firemist	96
Russet Firemist	99

ELDORADO CONVERTIBLE TOP COLORS

White	A
Black	B
Blue	C
Lt. Beige	E
Covert	M

ROOF TOP COVER COLORS

White	J
Black	K
Blue	L
Covert	M
Green	N
Brown	R
Beige	S

ENGINE NUMBER

The engine number is located on the rear of the block behind the intake manifold.

ENGINE CODE	NO. CYL.	CID	HORSE-POWER	COMP. RATIO	CARB
R	8	472	220	8.5:1	4-BC
S	8	500	235	8.5:1	4-BC

1973 CADILLAC COUPE DE VILLE

1973 CADILLAC SEDAN DE VILLE

1973 CADILLAC FLEETWOOD ELDORADO CONVERTIBLE

1973 CADILLAC FLEETWOOD ELDORADO COUPE

1973 CADILLAC FLEETWOOD SIXTY SPECIAL BROUGHAM

1973 CADILLAC FLEETWOOD SIXTY SPECIAL BROUGHAM

VEHICLE IDENTIFICATION NUMBER

CADILLAC
6C47R3Q100001

Located on the top of the dash on the driver's side and visible through the windshield from outside the car. Also stamped on a pad on the rear upper portion of the cylinder block beind the intake manifold.

FIRST DIGIT: Identifies GM Division (6 is Cadillac)

SECOND DIGIT: Identifies the series

SERIES	CODE
Fleetwood 60 Special Brougham	B
Calais Coupe/Sedan	C
DeVille Coupe/Sedan	D
Fleetwood 75 Sedan	F
Eldorado	L
Commercial Chassis	Z

THIRD AND FOURTH DIGITS: Identify the body style.

BODY STYLE	CODE
4-Door Limo w/Aux. Seat	23
4-Door Limo w/Center Window	33
2-Door Hardtop Coupe	47
4-Door Hardtop (4-Window) Sedan	49
2-Door Convertible Coupe	67
4-Door Pillar (4-Window) Sedan	69
Commercial Chassis	90

FIFTH DIGIT: Identifies the engine

ENGINE	CODE
V8-472	R
V8-500	S

SIXTH DIGIT: Identifies the year (3 = 1973)

SEVENTH DIGIT: Identifies the assembly plant

ASSEMBLY PLANT	CODE
Detroit, MI	Q
Linden, NJ	E

LAST SIX DIGITS: Represent the basic production numbers

BODY NUMBER PLATE

Complete identification of each body is provided by a plate attached to the top surface of the cowl, under the hood.

```
           BODY BY FISHER
ST 73  6CD47      E   123456 BDY
TR 351                11-K PNT
A51
   •                          •

   GENERAL MOTORS CORPORATION CERTIFIES
     TO THE DEALER THAT THIS VEHICLE
   CONFORMS TO ALL U.S., FEDERAL MOTOR
        VEHICLE SAFETY STANDARDS
    APPLICABLE AT TIME OF MANUFACTURE.
```

Example:

73	Model Year (1973)
6	Car Division (Cadillac)
CD	Series (DeVille)
47	Style (2-Door Hardtop Coupe)
E	Assembly Plant (Linden, NJ)
123456	Production Sequence
351	Black Leather
11-K	Cotillion White/Black Vinyl Top
A51	Modular Seat Code

FLEETWOOD 60 SPECIAL BROUGHAM	CODE
4-Door Pillar (4-Window)	6CB69

FLEETWOOD 75 LIMO	CODE
4-Door w/Aux. Seat	6DF23
4-Door w/Center Window	6DF33

CALAIS	CODE
2-Door Hardtop Coupe	6CC47
4-Door Hardtop Sedan	6CC49

DEVILLE	CODE
2-Door Hardtop Coupe	6CD47
4-Door Hardtop Sedan	6CD49

ELDORADO	CODE
2-Door Hardtop Coupe	6EL47
Convertible	6EL67

COMMERCIAL	CODE
Commercial Chassis	6ZZ90

THE TRIM CODE furnishes the key to the interior color and material scheme.

FLEETWOOD 60 SPECIAL BROUGHAM TRIM

COLOR	CLOTH	VINYL	LEATHER	CODE
Black	•			011
Dk. Blue	•			025
Dk. Blue	•			026
Dk. Teal	•			029
Dk. Jade	•			031
Med. Beige	•			042
Med. Maize	•			044
Dk. Taupe	•			047
Black			•	051
White w/Black			•	052
White w/Blue			•	053
Ant. Dk. Blue			•	066
Ant. Dk. Jade			•	071
Ant. Lt. Sandalwood			•	082
Ant. Med. Maize			•	084
Ant. Dk. Saddle			•	085
Ant. Dk. Taupe			•	087
Ant. Med. Scarlet			•	088
Dk. Blue		•		125
Med. Beige		•		142
Med. Maize		•		144
Dk. Taupe		•		147
White w/Blue			•	153
White w/Beige			•	155
White w/Maize			•	158
White w/Taupe			•	159
Ant. Dk. Blue			•	166
Ant. Lt. Sandalwood			•	182
Ant. Med. Maize			•	184
Ant. Dk. Saddle			•	185
Ant. Dk. Taupe			•	187

CALAIS TRIM

COLOR	CLOTH	VINYL	LEATHER	CODE
Black	•			211
Dk. Blue	•			226
Dk. Teal	•			229
Dk. Jade		•		231
Med. Beige	•			242
Med. Maize	•			244
Black		•		251
Dk. Saddle		•		285

DEVILLE TRIM

COLOR	CLOTH	VINYL	LEATHER	CODE
Black	•			311
Dk. Blue	•			326
Dk. Teal	•			329
Dk. Jade	•			331
Med. Beige	•			342
Med. Maize	•			344
Dk. Taupe	•			347
Black			•	351
White w/Black			•	352
White w/Blue			•	353
White w/Scarlet			•	354
White w/Jade			•	357
Ant. Dk. Blue			•	366
Ant. Dk. Jade			•	371
Ant. Lt. Sandalwood			•	382
Ant. Med. Maize			•	384
Ant. Dk. Saddle			•	385
Ant. Dk. Taupe			•	387
Med. Scarlet			•	388

ELDORADO COUPE TRIM

COLOR	CLOTH	VINYL	LEATHER	CODE
Black/White	•			411
Dk. Blue	•			426
Dk. Teal	•			429
Dk. Jade	•			431
Med. Beige	•			442
Med. Maize	•			444
Dk. Taupe	•			447
Black			•	451
White w/Black			•	452
White w/Blue			•	453
White w/Scarlet			•	454
White w/Jade			•	457
Ant. Dk. Blue			•	466
Ant. Dk. Jade			•	471
Ant. Lt. Sandalwood			•	482
Ant. Med. Maize			•	484
Ant. Dk. Saddle			•	485
Ant. Dk. Taupe			•	487
Med. Scarlet			•	488

ELDORADO CONVERTIBLE TRIM

COLOR	CLOTH	VINYL	LEATHER	CODE
Black			•	451
White w/Black			•	452
White w/Blue			•	453
White w/Scarlet			•	454
White w/Jade			•	457
Ant. Dk. Blue			•	466
Ant. Dk. Jade			•	471
Ant. Lt. Sandalwood			•	482
Ant. Med. Maize			•	484
Ant. Dk. Saddle			•	485
Ant. Dk. Taupe			•	487
Med. Scarlet			•	488

FLEETWOOD 75 SEDAN TRIM

COLOR	CLOTH	VINYL	LEATHER	CODE
Black	•			711
Med. Gray	•			719
Dk. Blue	•			726
Med. Beige	•			742

FLEETWOOD 75 LIMO TRIM

COLOR	CLOTH	VINYL	LEATHER	CODE
Black w/Black			•	711
Black w/Med. Gray			•	719
Black w/Blue			•	726
Black w/Med. Beige			•	742

THE PAINT CODE furnishes the key to the paint colors used on the car. A two number code indicates the color of the car. Two, two-digit codes indicate the bottom and top body colors respectively. NOTE: vinyl roof and convertible top codes appear in the second set of digits.

COLOR	CODE
Cotillion White	11
Georgian Silver	13
Park Avenue Gray	18
Sable Black	19
Antigua Blue	24
Diplomat Blue	29
Garganey Teal	39
Sage	44
Forest Green	49
Renaissance Gold	54
Laredo Tan	63
Mirage Taupe	64
Burnt Sienna	68
Dynasty Red	72
Harvest Yellow	81
Shadow Taupe Firemist	90
St. Tropez Blue Firemist	92
Phoenix Gold Firemist	94
Oceanic Teal Firemist	95
Viridian Green Firemist	96
Saturn Bronze Firemist	99

ELDORADO CONVERTIBLE TOP COLORS

White	A
Black	B
Blue	C
Lt. Beige	E
Med. Maize	M

VINYL ROOF COVERING COLORS

White	J
Black	K
Blue	L
Med. Maize	M
Green	N
Taupe	P
Lt. Beige	S
Brown	X

ENGINE NUMBER

The engine number is located on the rear of the block behind the intake manifold.

ENGINE CODE	NO CYL.	CID	HORSE-POWER	COMP. RATIO	CARB
R	8	472	220	8.5:1	4-BC
S	8	500	235	8.5:1	4-BC

1974 CADILLAC FLEETWOOD ELDORADO CONVERTIBLE

1974 CADILLAC FLEETWOOD ELDORADO COUPE

1974 CADILLAC COUPE DE VILLE

1974 CADILLAC COUPE DE VILLE

1974 CADILLAC FLEETWOOD SIXTY SPECIAL BROUGHAM

1974 CADILLAC SEDAN DE VILLE

VEHICLE IDENTIFICATION NUMBER

```
┌─────────────────────────┐
│ •  CADILLAC             •│
│    6C47R4Q100001         │
└─────────────────────────┘
```

Located on the top of the dash on the driver's side and visible through the windshield from outside the car. Also stamped on a pad on the rear upper portion of the cylinder block, behind the intake manifold.

FIRST DIGIT: Identifies GM Division (6 is Cadillac)

SECOND DIGIT: Identifies the series

SERIES	CODE
Fleetwood 60 Special Brougham	B
Calais Coupe/Sedan	C
DeVille Coupe/Sedan	D
Fleetwood 75 Sedan	F
Eldorado	L
Commercial Chassis	Z

THIRD AND FOURTH DIGITS: Identify the body style

BODY STYLE	CODE
4-Door Limo w/Aux. Seat	23
4-Door Limo w/Center Window	33
2-Door Hardtop Coupe	47
4-Door Hardtop (4-Window) Sedan	49
2-Door Convertible Coupe	67
4-Door Pillar (4-Window) Sedan	69
Commercial Chassis	90

FIFTH DIGIT: Identifies the engine

ENGINE	CODE
V8-472	R
V8-500	S

SIXTH DIGIT: Identifies the year (4 = 1974)

SEVENTH DIGIT: Identifies the assembly plant

ASSEMBLY PLANT	CODE
Detroit, MI	Q
Linden, NJ	E

LAST SIX DIGITS: Represent the basic production number

BODY NUMBER PLATE

Complete identification of each body is provided by a plate attached to the top surface of the cowl, under the hood.

```
┌──────────────────────────────────────┐
│        BODY BY FISHER                  │
│  ST 74 6CD47      E   123456 BDY       │
│  TR 351               11-K PNT         │
│  A51                                   │
│  •                                  •  │
│  GENERAL MOTORS CORPORATION CERTIFIES  │
│     TO THE DEALER THAT THIS VEHICLE    │
│   CONFORMS TO ALL U.S., FEDERAL MOTOR  │
│        VEHICLE SAFETY STANDARDS        │
│        APPLICABLE AT TIME OF MANUFACTURE. │
└──────────────────────────────────────┘
```

Example:

74	Model Year (1974)
6	Car Division (Cadillac)
CD	Series (DeVille)
47	Style (2-Door Hardtop)
E	Assembly Plant (Linden, NJ)
123456	Production Sequence
351	Black Leather
11-K	Cotillion White/Black Vinyl Top
A51	Modular Seat Code

FLEETWOOD 60 SPECIAL BROUGHAM	CODE
4-Door Pillar Sedan	6CB69

CALAIS	CODE
2-Door Hardtop Coupe	6CC47
4-Door Hardtop Sedan	6CC49

DEVILLE	CODE
2-Door Hardtop Coupe	6CD47
4-Door Hardtop Sedan	6CD49

FLEETWOOD 75 LIMO	CODE
4-Door w/Aux. Seat	6DF23
4-Door w/Center Window	6DF33

ELDORADO	CODE
2-Door Hardtop Coupe	6EL47
Convertible Coupe	6EL67

COMMERCIAL	CODE
Commercial Chassis	6ZZ90

THE TRIM CODE furnishes the key to the interior color and material scheme.

FLEETWOOD 60 SPECIAL BROUGHAM TRIM

COLOR	CLOTH	VINYL	LEATHER	CODE
Black Medici	•			010
Black	•			011
Dk. Blue	•			025
Dk. Blue	•			026
Med. Green	•			030
Med. Saddle	•			043
Med. Maize	•			044
Med. Amber	•			046
Terra Cotta	•			047
Terra Cotta	•			048
Black		•		051
White w/Black		•		052
White w/Dk. Blue		•		053
Ant. Dk. Blue		•		066
Ant. Med. Green		•		070
Ant. Lt. Sandalwood		•		082
Ant. Med. Saddle		•		083
Med. Maize		•		084
Ant. Terra Cotta		•		087
Med. Red		•		088
Black	•			110*
Dk. Blue	•			125*
Dk. Blue	•			126*
Med. Amber	•			146*
Terra Cotta	•			148*
Black	•			510#
Dk. Blue	•			525#
Med. Amber	•			546#
Terra Cotta	•			548#
Dk. Blue			•	565#
Med. Saddle			•	585#

* d'Elegance option
\# Talisman option

CALAIS HARDTOP TRIM

COLOR	CLOTH	VINYL	LEATHER	CODE
Black	•			211
Dk. Blue	•			226
Med. Green	•			230
Med. Maize	•			244
Black	•			251
Med. Saddle	•			283

DEVILLE HARDTOP TRIM

COLOR	CLOTH	VINYL	LEATHER	CODE
Black	•			311
Dk. Blue	•			325
Dk. Blue	•			326
Med. Green	•			330
Med. Green	•			332
Med. Saddle	•			342
Med. Saddle	•			343
Med. Maize	•			344
Med. Mandarin	•			345
Med. Amber	•			346
Terra Cotta	•			347
Terra Cotta	•			348
Black			•	351
White w/Black			•	352
White w/Dk. Blue			•	353
White w/Med. Red			•	354
White w/Med. Lime			•	356
White w/Med. Green			•	357
White w/Dk. Cranberry			•	359
Ant. Dk. Blue			•	366
Ant. Med. Green			•	370
Ant. Lt. Sandalwood			•	382
Ant. Med. Saddle			•	383
Med. Maize			•	384
Ant. Terra Cotta			•	387
Med. Red			•	388
Black Mardi	•			811*
Dk. Blue	•			825*
Med. Amber	•			846*
Terra Cotta	•			848*

* d'Elegance option

ELDORADO COUPE TRIM

COLOR	CLOTH	VINYL	LEATHER	CODE
Black	•			411
Dk. Blue	•			425
Dk. Blue	•			426
Med. Green	•			430
Med. Green	•			432
Med. Saddle	•			442
Med. Saddle	•			443
Med. Maize	•			444
Med. Mandarin	•			445
Med. Amber	•			446
Terra Cotta	•			447
Terra Cotta	•			448
Black			•	451
White w/Black			•	452
White w/Blue			•	453
White w/Med. Red			•	454
White w/Dk. Lime			•	456
White w/Med. Green			•	457
White w/Dk. Cranberry			•	459
Ant. Dk. Blue			•	466
Ant. Med. Green			•	470
Ant. Lt. Sandalwood			•	482
Ant. Med. Saddle			•	483
Med. Maize			•	484
Ant. Terra Cotta			•	487
Med. Red			•	488

ELDORADO CONVERTIBLE TRIM

COLOR	CLOTH	VINYL	LEATHER	CODE
Black			•	451
White w/Black			•	452
White w/Dk. Blue			•	453
White w/Med. Red			•	454
White w/Dk. Lime			•	456
White w/Med. Green			•	457
White w/Dk. Cranberry			•	459
Ant. Dk. Blue			•	466
Ant. Med. Green			•	470
Ant. Lt. Sandalwood			•	482
Ant. Med. Saddle			•	483
Med. Maize			•	484
Ant. Terra Cotta			•	487
Med. Red			•	488

FLEETWOOD 75 SEDAN TRIM

COLOR	CLOTH	VINYL	LEATHRE	CODE
Black	•			711
Med. Gray	•			719
Dk. Blue	•			725
Med. Saddle	•			743

FLEETWOOD 75 LIMO TRIM

COLOR	CLOTH	VINYL	LEATHER	CODE
Black w/Black			•	711
Black w/Med. Gray			•	719
Black w/Dk. Blue			•	725
Black w/Med. Saddle			•	743

THE PAINT CODE furnishes the key to the paint colors used on the car. A two number code indicates the color of the car. Two, two-digit codes indicate the bottom and top body colors respectively. NOTE: vinyl roof and convertible top codes appear in the second set of digits.

COLOR	CODE
Cotillion White	11
Georgian Silver	13
Deauville Gray	18
Sable Black	19
Antiqua Blue	24
Diplomat Blue	29
Lido Green	30
Mandarin Orange	34
Pueblo Beige	38
Jasper Green	44
Pinehurst Green	49
Promenade Green	54
Apollo Yellow	57
Canyon Amber	59
Conestoga Tan	63
Chesterfield Brown	69
Andes Copper	71
Dynasty Red	72
Regal Blue Firemist	92
Victorian Amber Firemist	94
Pharoah Gold Firemist	95
Persian Lime Firemist	96
Terra Cotta Firemist	98
Cranberry Firemist	99

CONVERTIBLE TOP COLORS

	CODE
White	A
Black	B
Blue	C
Maize (Gold)	M
Amber	Q
Sandalwood	S
Terra Cotta	T

ROOF TOP COVER COLORS

Dark Blue C
White ....J
Black ....K
Maize (Gold) ....M
Green ....N
Amber ....Q
Sandalwood ....S
Terra Cotta ....T
Beige ....U
Light Green V
Brown X
Orange ....Y
Medium Blue ....Z

ENGINE NUMBER

The engine number is located on the rear of the block, behind the intake manifold.

ENGINE CODE	NO CYL.	CID	HORSE-POWER	COMP. RATIO	CARB
R	8	472	205	8.25:1	4-BC
S	8	500	210	8.25:1	4-BC

1975 CADILLAC SEDAN DE VILLE

1975 CADILLAC COUPE DE VILLE

1975 CADILLAC CALAIS SEDAN

1975 CADILLAC FLEETWOOD

1975 CADILLAC FLEETWOOD ELDORADO

1975 CADILLAC FLEETWOOD ELDORADO CONVERTIBLE

VEHICLE IDENTIFICATION NUMBER

• ☐ **CADILLAC 6C47S5Q100001** ☐ •

Located on the top of the dash on the driver's side and visible through the windshield from outside the car. Also stamped on a pad on the rear upper portion of the cylinder block, behind the intake manifold.

FIRST DIGIT: Identifies GM Division (6 is Cadillac)

SECOND DIGIT: Identifies the series

SERIES	CODE
Fleetwood 60 Special Brougham	B
Calais Coupe/Sedan	C
Coupe/Sedan DeVille	D
Fleetwood 75 Sedan	F
Eldorado	L
Commercial Chassis	Z

THIRD AND FOURTH DIGITS: Identify the body style

BODY STYLE	CODE
4-Door Limo w/Aux. Seat	23
4-Door Limo w/Center Window	33
2-Door Hardtop Coupe	47
4-Door Hardtop (4-Window) Sedan	49
2-Door Convertible Coupe	67
4-Door Pillar (4-Window)	69
Commercial Chassis	90

FIFTH DIGIT: Identifies the engine

ENGINE	CODE
V8-500	S

SIXTH DIGIT: Identifies the year (5 = 1975)

SEVENTH DIGIT: Identifies the assembly plant

ASSEMBLY PLANT	CODE
Detroit, MI	Q
Linden, NJ	E

LAST SIX DIGITS: Identify the basic production number

BODY NUMBER PLATE

Complete identification of each body is provided by a plate attached to the top surface of the cowl, under the hood.

```
          BODY BY FISHER
  ST 75 6CD47          E 123456 BDY
  TR 193               11-K PNT
  A51
```

GENERAL MOTORS CORPORATION CERTIFIES TO THE DEALER THAT THIS VEHICLE CONFORMS TO ALL U.S., FEDERAL MOTOR VEHICLE SAFETY STANDARDS APPLICABLE AT TIME OF MANUFACTURE.

Example:

75	Model Year (1975)
6	Car Division (Cadillac)
CD	Series (DeVille)
47	Style (2-Door Hardtop Coupe)
E	Assembly Plant (Linden, NJ)
123456	Production Sequence
193	Black Leather
11-K	Cotillion White/Black Vinyl Top
A51	Modular Seat Code

CALAIS — **CODE**
2-Door Hardtop Coupe 6CC47
4-Door Hardtop Sedan 6CC49

DEVILLE — **CODE**
2-Door Hardtop Coupe 6CD47
4-Door Hardtop Sedan 6CD49

FLEETWOOD 60 SPECIAL BROUGHAM — **CODE**
4-Door Pillar (4-Window) 6CB69

FLEETWOOD 75 LIMO — **CODE**
4-Door w/Aux. Seat Sedan 6DF23
4-Door w/Center Window 6DF33

ELDORADO — **CODE**
2-Door Hardtop Coupe 6EL47
2-Door Convertible 6EL67

COMMERCIAL — **CODE**
Commercial Chassis 6ZZ90

THE TRIM CODE furnishes the key to the interior color and material scheme.

FLEETWOOD 60 SPECIAL BROUGHAM TRIM

COLOR	CLOTH	VINYL	LEATHER	CODE
Med. Graystone	•			16D
Black	•			19E
Dk. Blue	•			26D
Med. Jasper	•			44C
Med. Gold	•			51D
Med. Saddle	•			65C
Dk. Crimson	•			73D
Dk. Rosewood	•			79D

COLOR	CLOTH	VINYL	LEATHER	CODE
White w/Dk. Blue			•	022
White w/Black			•	112
Black			•	192
Ant. Dk. Blue			•	262
Ant. Med. Jasper			•	442
Ant. Lt. Sandalwood			•	602
Ant. Dk. Brown			•	692
Ant. Dk. Crimson			•	732
Ant. Dk. Rosewood			•	792
Black	•			19G*
Dk. Blue	•			29G*
Med. Maize	•			51G*
Dk. Rosewood	•			79G*
Black	•			19B#
Midnght. Blue	•			29B#
Med. Maize	•			51B#
Dk. Rosewood	•			79B#

CALAIS HARDTOP TRIM

COLOR	CLOTH	VINYL	LEATHER	CODE
Blk./Gray/Red	•			19D
Blue/Gray/Blk.	•			26D
Saddle Morocco	•			65C
Red/Gray/Blk.	•			73D
Black		•		19V
Ant. Brown		•		69V

DEVILLE HARDTOP TRIM

COLOR	CLOTH	VINYL	LEATHER	CODE
Med. Orange	•			06M
Black	•			19G
Black	•			19J
Dk. Blue	•			26E
Blue/Green	•			32N
Med. Jasper	•			44E
Med. Jasper	•			44M
Med. Gold	•			51T
Med. Saddle	•			65E
Med. Saddle	•			65M
Dk. Firethorn	•			71N
Dk. Crimson	•			73G
Dk. Rosewood	•			79G
White w/Dk. Blue			•	023
White w/Dk. Crimson			•	073
White w/Black			•	113
Black			•	193
Ant. Dk. Blue			•	263
Ant. Med. Jasper			•	443
Ant. Lt. Sandalwood			•	603
Ant. Dk. Brown			•	693
Ant. Dk. Crimson			•	733
Ant. Dk. Rosewood			•	793
Dk. Blue	•			26B*
Med. Saddle	•			65B*
Dk. Crimson	•			73B*
Dk. Rosewood	•			79B*

ELDORADO COUPE TRIM

COLOR	CLOTH	VINYL	LEATHER	CODE
Med. Orange	•			06G
Black/White	•			11D
Dk. Blue	•			26E
Blue/Green	•			32N
Med. Jasper	•			44E
Med. Jasper	•			44G
Med. Gold	•			51E
Med. Saddle	•			65E
Med. Saddle	•			65G
Firethorn	•			71N
Dk. Crimson	•			73E
Dk. Rosewood	•			79E

COLOR	CLOTH	VINYL	LEATHER	CODE
White w/Blue			•	022
White w/Dk. Crimson			•	072
White w/Black			•	112
Black			•	192
Ant. Lt. Blue			•	242
Ant. Dk. Blue			•	262
Ant. Med. Jasper			•	442
Ant. Lt. Sandalwood			•	602
Ant. Med. Orange			•	672
Ant. Dk. Brown			•	692
Ant. Dk. Crimson			•	732
Ant. Dk. Rosewood			•	792

ELDORADO CONVERTIBLE TRIM

COLOR	CLOTH	VINYL	LEATHER	CODE
White w/Dk. Blue			•	022
White w/Dk. Crimson			•	072
White w/Black			•	112
Black			•	192
Lt. Blue w/Dk. Blue			•	242
Ant. Dk. Blue			•	262
Ant. Med. Jasper			•	442
Ant. Lt. Sandalwood			•	602
Ant. Med. Orange			•	672
Ant. Dk. Brown			•	692
Ant. Dk. Crimson			•	732
Ant. Dk. Rosewood			•	792

FLEETWOOD 75 SEDAN TRIM

COLOR	CLOTH	VINYL	LEATHER	CODE
Graystone	•			16D
Black	•			19C
Dk. Blue	•			29E

FLEETWOOD 75 LIMO TRIM

COLOR	CLOTH	VINYL	LEATHER	CODE
Black w/Graystone			•	16D
Black w/Black			•	19C
Black w/Dk. Blue			•	29E

* d'Elegance option
\# Talisman option

THE PAINT CODE furnishes the key to the paint colors used on the car. A two number code indicates the color of the car. Two, two-digit codes indicate the bottom and top body colors respectively. NOTE: vinyl roof and convertible top codes appear in the second set of digits.

COLOR	CODE
Cotillion White	11
Georgian Silver	13
Vapour Gray	15
Sable Black	19
Jennifer Blue	24
Monarch Blue	29
Lido Green	30
Med. Blue Green Firemist	32
Mandarin Orange	34
Firethorn Metallic Firemist	36
Pueblo Beige	38

COLOR	CODE
Jasper Green	44
Inverarary Green	49
Bombay Yellow	52
Tarragon Gold	54
Knickerbocker Tan	65
Roan Brown	69
Roxena Red	77
Rosewood	78
Gossamer Blue Firemist	92
Lt. Blue Green Firemist	94
Cameo Rosewood Firemist	97
Emberust Firemist	98
Cerise Firemist	99

CONVERTIBLE TOP COLORS

COLOR	CODE
White	A
Black	B
Dark Blue	C
Yellow	E
Graystone	G
Dark Red	H
Sandalwood	S
Orange	Y

ROOF COVERING COLORS

COLOR	CODE
Dark Blue	C
Silver Blue Metallic	D
Yellow	E
Firethorn	F
Graystone	G
Dark Red	H
Black	K
Lt. Rosewood Metallic	L
Med. Green	N
Silver Metallic	P
Dk. Blue Green	R
Sandalwood	S
Beige Metallic	U
Silver Green Metallic	V
Dark Brown	X
Orange Metallic	Y

ENGINE NUMBER

The engine number is located on the left hand side of the cylinder block, just above the edge of the oil pan.

ENGINE CODE	NO. CYL.	CID	HORSE-POWER	COMP RATIO	CARB
S	8	500	190	8.5:1	4-BC

1976 CADILLAC COUPE DE VILLE

1976 CADILLAC SEDAN DE VILLE

1976 CADILLAC FLEETWOOD

1976 CADILLAC CALAIS SEDAN

1976 CADILLAC ELDORADO

1976 CADILLAC ELDORADO

1976 CADILLAC CALAIS COUPE

1976 CADILLAC SEVILLE

VEHICLE IDENTIFICATION NUMBER

CADILLAC
6S69R6Q100001

Located on the top of the dash on the driver's side and visible through the windshield from outside the car. Also stamped on a pad on the rear upper portion of the cylinder block, behind the intake manifold.

FIRST DIGIT: Identifies GM Division (6 is Cadillac)

SECOND DIGIT: Identifies the series

SERIES	CODE
Fleetwood 60 Special Brougham	B
Calais Coupe/Sedan	C
Coupe/Sedan DeVille	D
Fleetwood 75 Sedan	F
Eldorado	L
Seville	S
Commercial Chassis	Z

THIRD AND FOURTH DIGITS: Identify the body style

BODY STYLE	CODE
4-Door Limo w/Aux. Seat	23
4-Door Limo w/Center Window	33
2-Door Hardtop Coupe	47
4-Door Hardtop (4-Window)	49
2-Door Convertible Coupe	67
4-Door Pillar (4-Window)	69
Commercial Chassis	90

FIFTH DIGIT: Identifies the engine

ENGINE	CODE
V8-350	R
V8-500	S

SIXTH DIGIT: Identifies the year (6 = 1976)

SEVENTH DIGIT: Identifies the assembly plant

ASSEMBLY PLANT	CODE
Detroit, MI	Q
Linden, NJ	E

LAST SIX DIGITS: Represent the production number

BODY NUMBER PLATE

Complete identification of each body is provided by a plate attached to the top surface of the cowl, under the hood.

```
            BODY BY FISHER
ST 76  6KS69        E 123456 BDY
TR 112              19 11T  PNT
A51
```

GENERAL MOTORS CORPORATION CERTIFIES TO THE DEALER THAT THIS VEHICLE CONFORMS TO ALL U.S., FEDERAL MOTOR VEHICLE SAFETY STANDARDS APPLICABLE AT TIME OF MANUFACTURE.

Example:

76	Model Year (1976)
6	Car Division (Cadillac)
KS	Series (Seville)
69	Style (4-Door Pillar Sedan)
E	Assembly Plant (Linden, NJ)
123456	Production Sequence
112	White Leather
19 11	Sable Black/Cotillion White
A51	Modular Seat Code

FLEETWOOD BROUGHAM	CODE
4-Door Pillar (4-Window)	6CB69

CALAIS	CODE
2-Door Hardtop Coupe	6CC47
4-Door Hardtop (4-Window)	6CC49

DEVILLE	CODE
2-Door Hardtop Coupe	6CD47
4-Door Hardtop (4-Window)	6CD49

FLEETWOOD 75 LIMO	CODE
4-Door w/Aux. Seat	6DF23
4-Door w/Center Window	6DF33

ELDORADO	CODE
2-Door Hardtop Coupe	6EL47
2-Door Convertible	6EL67

SEVILLE	CODE
4-Door Pillar (4-Window)	6KS69

COMMERCIAL	CODE
Commercial Chassis	6ZZ90

THE TRIM CODE furnishes the key to the interior color and material scheme.

FLEETWOOD BROUGHAM TRIM

COLOR	CLOTH	VINYL	LEATHER	CODE
White w/Dk. Blue			•	022
White w/Dk. Firethorn			•	072
White w/Dk. Blue/Green			•	112
Black	•			19B
Black			•	192
Black	•			19D
Black	•			19E
Dk. Blue	•			26B
Dk. Blue	•			26C
Dk. Blue/Grn.	•			32B
Ant. Lt. Blue			•	242
Ant. Dk. Blue/Grn.			•	322
Dk. Blue	•			26E
Dk. Blue/Grn.	•			32D
Dk. Blue	•			26D
Lt. Buckskin	•			64B
Lt. Buckskin			•	642
Lt. Buckskin	•			64D
Dk. Firethorn			•	712
Lt. Smoke Gray	•			16B
Lt. Smoke Gray	•			15C
Ant. Lt. Smoke Gray			•	152
Lt. Smoke Gray	•			15D
Lt. Ivory/Gold	•			53C
Lt. Ivory/Gold			•	532

CALAIS TRIM

COLOR	CLOTH	VINYL	LEATHER	CODE
Black/Gray/Red	•			19B
Black/Gray/Blue	•			26B
Blk./Gray/Bl.-Grn.	•			32B
Black/Gray/Red	•			71B
Black	•			19M
Lt. Buckskin	•			64M

DEVILLE TRIM

COLOR	CLOTH	VINYL	LEATHER	CODE
White w/Dk. Blue			•	022
White w/Dk. Firethorn			•	072
White w/Black			•	112
White w/Dk. Blue-Grn.			•	312
Black	•			19C
Black	•			192
Black		•		19E
Dk. Blue	•			26G
Dk. Blue	•			26C
Dk. Blue-Grn.	•			32C
Dk. Blue-Grn.	•			32D
Ant. Lt. Blue			•	242
Ant. Dk. Blue-Grn.			•	322
Dk. Blue		•		26E
Dk. Blue-Grn.		•		32E
Med. Saddle		•		64G
Lt. Buckskin		•		64C
Ant. Lt. Buckskin			•	642
Lt. Buckskin		•		64E
Dk. Firethorn		•		71D
Dk. Firethorn		•		71C
Ant. Dk. Firethorn			•	712
Lt. Ivory-Gold	•			53C
Lt. Ivory-Gold			•	532
Ant. Lt. Smoke-Gray			•	152

FLEETWOOD TRIM

COLOR	CLOTH	VINYL	LEATHER	CODE
Black	•			19D
Black			•	15C
Black			•	26D
Dk. Blue	•			26D
Smoke Gray	•			15C
Black			•	19D

ELDORADO TRIM

COLOR	CLOTH	VINYL	LEATHER	CODE
White w/Dk. Blue-Green			•	312
White w/Dk. Blue			•	022
White w/Dk. Firethorn			•	072
White w/Black			•	112
Black	•			19C
Black	•			192
Dk. Blue	•			26C
Dk. Blue-Grn.	•			32B
Ant. Lt. Blue			•	242
Ant. Dk. Blue-Green			•	322
Lt. Buckskin	•			64C
Ant. Lt. Buckskin			•	642
Dk. Firethorn	•			71B
Ant. Dk. Firethorn			•	712
Ivory-Gold	•			53C
Lt. Ivory-Gold			•	532
Ant. Lt. Smoke Gray			•	152

SEVILLE TRIM

COLOR	CLOTH	VINYL	LEATHER	CODE
White			•	112
Black	•			19C
Black			•	192
Dk. Blue	•			26C
Dklue-Grn.	•			32C
Ant. Lt. Blue			•	242
Ant. Dk. Blue-Green			•	322

COLOR	CLOTH	VINYL	LEATHER	CODE
Lt. Buckskin	•			164C
Lt. Buckskin			•	642
Dk. Firethorn	•			71C
Dk. Firethorn			•	712
Smoke Gray	•			15C
Lt. Smoke Gray			•	152
Lt. Ivory-Gold	•			53C
Lt. Ivory-Gold			•	532

THE PAINT CODE furnishes the key to the paint colors used on the car. A two number code indicates the color of the car. Two, two-digit codes indicate the bottom and top body colors respectively. NOTE: vinyl roof and convertible top codes appear in the second set of digits.

COLOR	CODE
Cotillion White	11
Georgian Silver	13
Academy Gray	16
Sable Black	19
Innsbruck Blue	28
Commodore Blue	29
Dunbarton Green	32
Firethorn	36
Claret Red	37
Pueblo Beige	38
Kingswood Green	39
Calumet Cream	50
Phoenician Ivory	52
Brentwood Brown	67
Chesterfield Brown	69
Crystal Blue Firemist	90
Amberlite Firemist	91
Greenbriar Firemist	93
Gallaway Green Firemist	94
Florentine Gold Firemist	95
Emberglow Firemist	96

VINYL ROOF COVERS

COLOR	CODE
Dk. Blue Metallic	C
Silver Blue Metallic	D
Firethorn Metallic	F
White	J
Black	K
Mahogany Metallic	
Silver Metallic	P
Dk. Blue-Green	R
Buckskin	T
Ivory	V
Dk. Brown Metallic	X

CONVERTIBLE TOP COLORS

COLOR	CODE
White	A
Black	B
Dk. Blue	C
Firethorn	F
Dk. Blue-Green	R
Buckskin	T
Ivory	V

ENGINE NUMBER

The engine number is located on the lower left hand side of the cylinder block, just above the edge of the oil pan.

ENGINE CODE	NO. CYL.	CID	HORSE-POWER	COMP RATIO	CARB
	8	500	190	8.5:1	4-BC
R	8	350	170	8.25:1	Fuel Inj.
S	8	500	215	8.5:1	Fuel Inj.

1977 CADILLAC FLEETWOOD BROUGHAM

1977 CADILLAC FLEETWOOD BROUGHAM

1977 CADILLAC FLEETWOOD ELDORADO

1977 CADILLAC FLEETWOOD ELDORADO

1977 CADILLAC SEVILLE

1977 CADILLAC SEVILLE

1977 CADILLAC SEDAN DE VILLE

1977 CADILLAC COUPE DE VILLE

VEHICLE IDENTIFICATION NUMBER

CADILLAC
6B69S7Q100001

Located on the top of the dash on the driver's side and visible through the windshield from outside the car. Also stamped on a pad on the rear upper portion of the cylinder block, behind the intake manifold.

FIRST DIGIT: Identifies GM Division (6 is Cadillac)

SECOND DIGIT: Identifies the series

SERIES	CODE
Fleetwood Brougham	B
DeVille	D
Fleetwood Limo	F
Eldorado	L
Seville	S
Commercial Chassis	Z

THIRD AND FOURTH DIGITS: Identify the body style

BODY STYLE	CODE
4-Door w/Aux. Seat Sedan	23
4-Door w/Center Window	33
2-Door Coupe	47
4-Door Pillar Sedan	69
Commercial Chassis	90

FIFTH DIGIT: Identifies the engine

ENGINE	CODE
V8-350	R
V8-425	S
V8-425	T

SIXTH DIGIT: Identifies the year (7 = 1977)

SEVENTH DIGIT: Identifies the assembly plant

ASSEMBLY PLANT	CODE
Detroit, MI	Q
Linden, NJ	E

LAST SIX DIGITS: Identify the basic production number

BODY NUMBER PLATE

Complete identification of each body is provided by a plate attached to the top surface of the cowl, under the hood.

BODY BY FISHER	
ST 77 6CD47	E 123456 BDY
TR 193	11 PNT
A51	

GENERAL MOTORS CORPORATION CERTIFIES TO THE DEALER THAT THIS VEHICLE CONFORMS TO ALL U.S., FEDERAL MOTOR VEHICLE SAFETY STANDARDS APPLICABLE AT TIME OF MANUFACTURE.

Example:

77	Model Year (1977)
6	Car Division (Cadillac)
CD	Series (DeVille)
47	Style (2-Door Hardtop Coupe)
E	Assembly Plant (Linden, NJ)
123456	Production Sequence
193	Black Leather
11	Cotillion White
A51	Modular Seat Code

FLEETWOOD BROUGHAM	CODE
4-Door Pillar Sedan	6CB69

DEVILLE	CODE
2-Door Hardtop Coupe	6CD47
4-Door Pillar Sedan	6CD69

FLEETWOOD 75 LIMO	CODE
4-Door w/Aux. Seat	6DF23
4-Door w/Center Window	6DF33

ELDORADO	CODE
2-Door Hardtop Coupe	6EL47

SEVILLE	CODE
4-Door Pillar Sedan	6KS69

COMMERCIAL	
Commercial Chassis	6ZZ90

THE TRIM CODE furnishes the key to the interior color and material scheme.

FLEETWOOD BROUGHAM TRIM

COLOR	CLOTH	VINYL	LEATHER	CODE
Black	•	•	•	19B#
Black			•	192#
White			•	112#
Smoke Gray	•	•	•	15C#/15G#
Smoke Gray			•	152#
Lt. Blue			•	242#
Dk. Blue	•	•	•	26B#/26C#
Dk. Blue			•	022#
Dk. Blue	•	•		26G#
Sage Green	•			44C#
Sage Green			•	442#
Yellow Gold	•	•		54C#
Yellow Gold			•	542#
Buckskin	•	•	•	64B#/64C#
Buckskin			•	642#
Buckskin	•	•		64G#
Saffron	•	•		67C#
Saffron			•	672#
Crimson			•	732#
Claret	•	•	•	79B#/79C#
Claret			•	792#
Claret	•	•		79G#

DEVILLE TRIM

COLOR	CLOTH	VINYL	LEATHER	CODE
Black	•			19E#
Black			•	193#
White			•	113#
Lt. Blue			•	243#
Dk. Blue	•	•	•	26D#/26E#
Dk. Blue			•	023#
Dk. Blue	•	•		26H#

COLOR	CLOTH	VINYL	LEATHER	TRIM
Sage Green			•	44E#
Sage Green		•		443#
Yellow Gold		•		543#
Buckskin	•	•	•	64E#
Buckskin		•		643#
Buckskin	•	•	•	64H#
Saffron		•	•	67D#/67E#
Saffron		•		673#
Saffron	•		•	67H#
Crimson			•	733#/013#
Claret	•	•	•	79D#/79E#
Claret		•		793#
Claret	•	•	•	79H#

FLEETWOOD 75 TRIM

COLOR	CLOTH	VINYL	LEATHER	TRIM
Black	•	•	•	19C
Smoke Gray	•	•	•	15C
Dk. Blue	•	•		26D

FLEETWOOD 75 LIMO TRIM

COLOR	CLOTH	VINYL	LEATHER	TRIM
Black	•	•	•	19C#
Smoke Gray	•	•	•	15C#
Dk. Blue	•	•	•	26D#

ELDORADO TRIM

COLOR	CLOTH	VINYL	LEATHER	TRIM
Black	•	•	•	19B#
Black			•	192#/164#
White			•	112#
Lt. Blue			•	242#/243#
Lt. Blue			•	244#/022#
Dk. Blue	•	•	•	26B#
Sage Green	•	•	•	44B#
Sage Green			•	442#/443#
Yellow Gold	•	•	•	54B#
Yellow Gold			•	542#
Buckskin	•	•	•	64B#
Buckskin			•	642#/643#
Buckskin			•	644#
Saffron	•	•	•	67B#
Saffron			•	672#/673#
Saffron			•	674#
Crimson			•	732#/012#
Crimson			•	014#
Claret	•	•	•	79B#
Claret			•	792#

SEVILLE TRIM

COLOR	CLOTH	VINYL	LEATHER	CODE
Black	•	•	•	19C#
Black			•	192#
White			•	112#
Smoke Gray	•	•	•	15C#
Smoke Gray			•	152#
Lt. Blue			•	242#
Dk. Blue	•	•	•	26C#
Sage Green	•	•	•	44C#
Sage Green			•	442#
Yellow Gold	•	•	•	54C#
Yellow Gold			•	542#
Buckskin	•	•	•	64C#
Buckskin			•	642#
Saffron	•	•	•	67C#
Saffron			•	672#
Crimson			•	732#
Claret	•	•	•	79C#
Claret			•	792#

Notch back or 60-40 seat

THE PAINT CODE furnishes the key to the paint colors used on the car. A two number code indicates the color of the car. Two, two-digit codes indicate the bottom and top body colors respectively. NOTE: vinyl roof and convertible top codes appear in the second set of digits.

COLOR	CODE
Cotillion White	11
Georgian Silver	13
Sable Black	19
Jennifer Blue	24
Hudson Bay Blue	29
Seamist Green	40
Edinburgh Green	49
Naples Yellow	50
Sovereign Gold	54
Sonora Tan	61
Saffron	67
Demitasse Brown	69
Bimini Beige	74
Crimson	77
Maderia Maroon	79
Cerulean Blue Firemist	90
Thyme Green Firemist	94
Buckskin Firemist	95
Frost Orange Firemist	96
Damson Plum Firemist	98
Desert Rose Firemist	99

ROOF COLORS

	CODE
White	11T
Silver	13T
Black	19T
Dark Blue	28T
Med. Green	44T
Dark Green	49T
Yellow	50T
Gold	54T
Lt. Buckskin	61T
Dark Brown	69T
Pastel Red Beige	74T
Claret	79T
Silver Blue	90T
Buckskin	95T
Lt. Orange	96T
Dark Red	98T

ENGINE NUMBER

The engine number is located on the lower left hand side of the cylinder block, just above the edge of the oil pan.

ENGINE CODE	NO. CYL.	CID	HORSE-POWER	COMP RATIO	CARB
R	8	350	180	8.5:1	Fuel Inj.
S	8	425	180	8.2:1	4-BC
T	8	425	195	8.2:1	Fuel Inj.

1978 CADILLAC COUPE DE VILLE

1978 CADILLAC COUPE DE VILLE

1978 CADILLAC SEDAN DE VILLE

1978 CADILLAC SEDAN DE VILLE

1978 CADILLAC FLEETWOOD BROUGHAM

1978 CADILLAC FLEETWOOD LIMOUSINE

1978 CADILLAC ELDORADO

1978 CADILLAC SEVILLE ELEGANTE

1978 CADILLAC SEVILLE

1978 CADILLAC SEVILLE

VEHICLE IDENTIFICATION NUMBER

• CADILLAC 6B69T8Q100001 •

Located on the top of the dash on the driver's side and visible through the windshield from outside the car. Also stamped on a pad on the rear upper portion of the cylinder block behind the intake manifold.

FIRST DIGIT: Identifies GM Division (6 is Cadillac)

SECOND DIGIT: Identifies the series

SERIES	CODE
Brougham	B
DeVille	D
Fleetwood Limo	F
Eldorado	L
Seville	S
Commercial Chassis	Z

THIRD AND FOURTH DIGITS: Identify the body style

BODY STYLE	CODE
4-Door w/Aux. Seat	23
4-Door w/Center Window	33
2-Door Hardtop Coupe	47
4-Door Pillar Sedan	69
Commercial Chassis	90

FIFTH DIGIT: Identifies the engine

ENGINE	CODE
V8-350 Elec. Fuel Inj.	B
V8-350 Diesel	N
V8-425 4-BC	S
V8-425 Elec. Fuel Inj.	T

SIXTH DIGIT: Identifies the year (8 = 1978)

SEVENTH DIGIT: Identifies the assembly plant

ASSEMBLY PLANT	CODE
Detroit, MI	Q
Linden, NJ	E

LAST SIX DIGITS: Identify the basic production number

BODY NUMBER PLATE

Complete identification of each body is provided by a plate attached to the top surface of the cowl, under the hood.

BODY BY FISHER

ST 77 6CD47   E 123456 BDY
TR 193   11 PNT
A51

● GENERAL MOTORS CORPORATION CERTIFIES ●
TO THE DEALER THAT THIS VEHICLE
CONFORMS TO ALL U.S., FEDERAL MOTOR
VEHICLE SAFETY STANDARDS
APPLICABLE AT TIME OF MANUFACTURE.

Example:

77	Model Year (1977)
6	Car Division (Cadillac)
CD	Series (DeVille)
47	Style (2-Door Hardtop Coupe)
E	Assembly Plant (Linden, NJ)
123456	Production Sequence
193	Black Leather
11	Cotillion White
A51	Modular Seat Code

FLEETWOOD BROUGHAM	CODE
4-Door Pillar Sedan	6CB69

DEVILLE	CODE
2-Door Hardtop Coupe	6CD47
4-Door Pillar Sedan	6CD69

FLEETWOOD LIMO	CODE
4-Door w/Aux. Seat	6DF23
4-Door w/Center Window	6DF33

ELDORADO	CODE
2-Door Hardtop Coupe	6EL47

SEVILLE	CODE
4-Door Pillar Sedan	6KS69

COMMERCIAL	CODE
Commercial Chassis	6ZZ90

THE TRIM CODE furnishes the key to the interior color and material scheme.

FLEETWOOD BROUGHAM TRIM

COLOR	CLOTH	VINYL	LEATHER	CODE
White			•	112
Lt. Gray	•	•		16C
Lt. Gray			•	162
Lt. Gray	•	•		16G
Black	•	•		19C
Black			•	192
Lt. Blue	•	•		24C
Lt. Blue			•	242
Lt. Blue	•	•		24G
Dk. Green	•	•		49C
Dk. Green			•	492
Dk. Green	•	•		49G
Lt. Yellow	•	•		50C
Lt. Yellow			•	502
Dk. Saddle			•	602
Dk. Saddle			•	603
Lt. Beige	•	•		61C
Lt. Beige			•	612
Lt. Beige	•	•		61G
Dk. Carmine			•	742
Dk. Mulberry	•	•		78C
Dk. Mulberry			•	782
Dk. Mulberry	•	•		78G

DEVILLE TRIM

COLOR	CLOTH	VINYL	LEATHER	CODE
White			•	113
Lt. Gray	•	•		16E
Lt. Gray			•	163
Black	•	•		19E
Black			•	193
Lt. Blue	•	•		24E
Lt. Blue	•	•		24D

COLOR	CLOTH	VINYL	LEATHER	CODE
Lt. Blue			•	243
Lt. Blue	•	•		24H
Dk. Green	•	•		49E
Dk. Green			•	493
Dk. Green	•	•		49H
Lt. Yellow	•	•		50E
Lt. Yellow			•	503
Dk. Saddle			•	603
Lt. Beige	•	•		61E
Lt. Beige			•	613
Lt. Beige	•	•		61H
Dk. Carmine			•	743
Dk. Mulberry	•	•		78E
Dk. Mulberry	•	•		78D
Dk. Mulberry			•	783
Dk. Mulberry	•	•		78H

FLEETWOOD SEDAN TRIM

COLOR	CLOTH	VINYL	LEATHER	CODE
Lt. Gray	•	•		16D
Black	•	•		19D
Dk. Blue	•	•		26D

FLEETWOOD LIMO TRIM

COLOR	CLOTH	VINYL	LEATHER	CODE
Lt. Gray	•	•		16D
Black	•	•		19D
Dk. Blue	•	•		26D

ELDORADO TRIM

COLOR	CLOTH	VINYL	LEATHER	CODE
White			•	112
White			•	114
Lt. Gray	•	•		16C
Lt. Gray			•	162
Black	•	•		19B
Black			•	192
Lt. Blue	•	•		24C
Lt. Blue			•	242
Lt. Blue			•	243
Lt. Blue			•	244
Dk. Green	•	•		49B
Dk. Green			•	492
Lt. Yellow	•	•		50B
Lt. Yellow			•	502
Lt. Yellow			•	504
Dk. Saddle			•	602
Dk. Saddle			•	603
Dk. Saddle			•	604
Lt. Beige	•	•		61C
Lt. Beige			•	612
Lt. Beige			•	644
Dk. Carmine			•	742
Dk. Carmine			•	744
Dk. Mulberry	•	•		78B
Dk. Mulberry			•	782
Dk. Mulberry			•	783

SEVILLE TRIM

COLOR	CLOTH	VINYL	LEATHER	CODE
White			•	112
Lt. Gray	•	•		16C
Lt. Gray			•	162
Lt. Gray			•	163
Black	•	•		19C
Black			•	192
Lt. Blue	•	•		24C
Lt. Blue			•	242
Dk. Green	•	•		49C
Dk. Green			•	492
Lt. Yellow				50C

COLOR	CLOTH	VINYL	LEATHER	CODE
Lt. Yellow			•	502
Dk. Saddle			•	602
Dk. Saddle			•	603
Lt. Beige	•	•		61C
Lt. Beige			•	612
Dk. Carmine			•	742
Dk. Mulberry	•	•		78C
Dk. Mulberry	•		•	782

THE PAINT CODE furnishes the key to the paint colors used on the car. A two number code indicates the color of the car. Two, two-digit codes indicate the bottom and top body colors respectively. NOTE: vinyl roof and cortible top codes appear in the second set of digits.

COLOR	CODE
Cotillion White	11
Platinum Poly	15
Pewter Poly	16
Sable Black	19
Columbia Blue	21
Sterling Blue Poly	22
Commodore Blue Poly	28
Seamist Green	40
Blackwatch Green Poly	49
Colonial Yellow	54
Arizona Beige	62
Demitasse Brown Poly	64
Ruidoso Saddle Poly	69
Mulberry Poly	74
Carmine Red	80
Med. Blue Firemist Poly	90
Basil Green Firemist Poly	94
Aztec Gold Firemist Poly	95
Western Saddle Firemist Poly	96
Autumn Haze Firemist Poly	98
Canyon Copper Firemist Poly	99

VINYL ROOF COLORS

	CODE
Medium Blue Metallic	A
Dark Blue Metallic	C
Light Blue Metallic	D
Light Yellow	E
Medium Gold Metallic	G
White	J
Black	K
Dark Camel Metallic	L
Medium Green Metallic	N
Silver Metallic	P
Dark Green Metallic	R
Light Beige	T
Medium Saddle Metallic	U
Medium Beige Metallic	W
Dark Brown Metallic	X
Dark Mulberry Metallic	Y

ENGINE NUMBER

The engine number is located on the lower left hand side of the cylinder block, just above the edge of the oil pan.

ENGINE CODE	NO. CYL.	CID	HORSE-POWER	COMP. RATIO	CARB
B	8	350	120	22.0:1	Diesel
N	8	350	180	8.0:1	Fuel Inj.
S	8	425	180	8.2:1	4-BC
T	8	425	195	8.2:1	Fuel Inj.

1979 CADILLAC DE VILLE

1979 CADILLAC DE VILLE

1979 CADILLAC ELDORADO

1979 CADILLAC ELDORADO

1979 CADILLAC FLEETWOOD

1979 CADILLAC FLEETWOOD

1979 CADILLAC PHAETON

1979 CADILLAC LIMOUSINE

1979 CADILLAC SEVILLE

1979 CADILLAC SEVILLE

VEHICLE IDENTIFICATION NUMBER

CADILLAC
6D47S99100001

Located on the top of the dash on the driver's side and visible through the windshield from outside the car. Also stamped on a pad on the rear upper portion of the cylinder block behind the intake manifold.

FIRST DIGIT: Identifies GM Division (6 is Cadillac)

SECOND DIGIT: Identifies the series

SERIES	CODE
Fleetwood Brougham	B
DeVille	D
Fleetwood Limo	F
Eldorado	L
Seville	S
Commercial Chassis	Z

THIRD AND FOURTH DIGITS: Identify the body style

BODY STYLE	CODE
4-Door w/Aux. Seat	23
4-Door w/Center Window	33
2-Door Hardtop Coupe	47
2-Door Coupe	57
4-Door Sedan	69
Commercial Chassis	90

FIFTH DIGIT: Identifies the engine

ENGINE	CODE
V8-350 Elec. Fuel Inj.	B
V8-350 Diesel	N
V8-425 Carb	S
V8-425 Fuel Inj.	T

SIXTH DIGIT: Identifies the year (9 = 1979)

SEVENTH DIGIT: Identifies the assembly plant

ASSEMBLY PLANT	CODE
Detroit, MI	9
Linden, NJ	E
South Gate, CA	C

LAST SIX DIGITS: Represent the basic production numbers

BODY NUMBER PLATE

Complete identification of each body is provided by a plate attached to the top surface of the cowl, under the hood.

BODY BY FISHER
ST 79 6CD47   9 123456 BDY
TR 193   11 22 PNT
A65

GENERAL MOTORS CORPORATION CERTIFIES TO THE DEALER THAT THIS VEHICLE CONFORMS TO ALL U.S., FEDERAL MOTOR VEHICLE SAFETY STANDARDS APPLICABLE AT TIME OF MANUFACTURE.

Example:

79	Model Year (1979)
6	Car Division (Cadillac)
CD	Series (DeVille)
47	Style (2-Door Hardtop Coupe)
9	Assembly Plant (Detroit, MI)
123456	Production Sequence
193	Black Leather
11 22	Cotillion White/Sterling Blue Irid
A65	Notch Back Bench

FLEETWOOD BROUGHAM	CODE
4 Door Sedan	6CB69

DEVILLE	CODE
2-Door Coupe	6CD47
4-Door Sedan	6CD69

FLEETWOOD LIMO	CODE
4-Door w/Aux. Seat	6DF23
4-door w/Center Window	6DF33

ELDORADO	CODE
2-Door Coupe	6EL57

SEVILLE	CODE
4-Door Sedan	6KS69

COMMERCIAL	CODE
Commercial Chassis	6ZZ90

THE TRIM CODE furnishes the key to the interior color and material scheme.

FLEETWOOD BROUGHAM TRIM

COLOR	CLOTH	VINYL	LEATHER	CODE
White			•	112#
Slate Gray	•	•		13B#
Slate Gray			•	132#
Slate Gray	•	•		13G#
Slate Gray			•	133#
Black			•	192#
Lt. Blue	•	•		24B#
Lt. Blue			•	242#
Lt. Blue	•	•		24G#
Lt. Blue			•	243#
Dk. Aqua	•	•		31B#
Dk. Aqua			•	312#
Dk. Green	•	•		49B#
Dk. Green			•	492#
Dk. Green	•	•		49G#
Lt. Yellow			•	502#
Dk. Gold	•	•		51B#
Dk. Gold			•	512#
Dk. Gold	•	•		51G#
Dk. Saddle			•	602#
Dk. Saddle			•	603#
Dk. Cedar	•	•		70B#
Dk. Cedar			•	702#
Dk. Cedar	•	•		70T#
Dk. Carmine			•	742#

DEVILLE TRIM

COLOR	CLOTH	VINYL	LEATHER	CODE
White			•	113#
Slate Gray	•	•		13D#
Slate Gray			•	133#
Slate Gray			•	103#
Black			•	193#
Lt. Blue	•	•		24D#
Lt. Blue			•	243#
Lt. Blue	•	•		24H#
Dk. Aqua	•	•		31D#
Dk. Aqua			•	313#
Dk. Green	•	•		49D#
Dk. Green			•	493#
Dk. Green	•	•		49H#
Lt. Yellow			•	503#
Dk. Gold	•	•		51D#
Dk. Gold			•	513#
Dk. Gold	•	•		51H#
Dk. Saddle			•	603#
Dk. Cedar	•	•		70D#
Dk. Cedar			•	703#
Dk. Cedar	•	•		70H#
Dk. Carmine			•	743#

FLEETWOOD SEDAN TRIM

COLOR	CLOTH	VINYL	LEATHER	CODE
Slate Gray	•	•		13C
Black	•	•		19C
Dk. Blue	•	•		26C

FLEETWOOD LIMO TRIM

COLOR	CLOTH	VINYL	LEATHER	CODE
Slate Gray	•	•		13C#
Black	•	•		19C#
Dk. Blue	•	•		26C#

ELDORADO COUPE TRIM

COLOR	CLOTH	VINYL	LEATHER	CODE
White			•	112#
White			•	113#
Slate Gray	•	•		13B#
Slate Gray			•	132#
Black			•	192#
Lt. Blue	•	•		24B#
Lt. Blue			•	242#
Lt. Blue			•	243#
Lt. Blue	•	•		24C#
Dk. Aqua	•	•		31B#
Dk. Aqua			•	312#
Dk. Green	•	•		49B#
Dk. Green			•	492#
Lt. Yellow			•	502#
Lt. Yellow			•	503#
Dk. Gold	•	•		51B#
Dk. Gold			•	512#
Dk. Saddle			•	602#
Dk. Saddle			•	603#
Dk. Cedar	•	•		70B#
Dk. Cedar			•	702#
Dk. Carmine			•	742#
Dk. Carmine			•	743#

SEVILLE SEDAN TRIM

COLOR	CLOTH	VINYL	LEATHER	CODE
White			•	112#
Slate Gray	•	•		13C#
Slate Gray			•	132#
Slate Gray			•	133#
Black			•	192#
Lt. Blue	•	•		24C#
Lt. Blue			•	242#
Dk. Aqua	•	•		31C#
Dk. Aqua			•	312#
Dk. Green	•	•		49C#
Dk. Green			•	492#
Lt. Yellow			•	502#
Dk. Gold	•	•		51C#
Dk. Gold			•	512#
Dk. Saddle			•	602#
Dk. Cedar	•	•		70C#
Dk. Cedar			•	702#
Dk. Cedar			•	703#
Dk. Carmine			•	742#

Notch back or 60-40 seats

THE PAINT CODE furnishes the key to the paint colors used on the car. A two number code indicates the color of the car. Two, two-digit codes indicate the bottom and top body colors respectively. NOTE: vinyl roof codes appear in the second set of digits.

COLOR	CODE
Cotillion White	11
Platinum Irid	15
Sterling Blue Irid	22
Crater Lake Blue Irid	29
Atlantis Aqua Irid	41
Blackwatch Green Irid	49
Colonial Yellow	54
Laramie Beige	62
Burnished Gold	68
Post Road Brown Irid	69
Red Cedar Irid	76
Saxony Red	78
Norfolk Gray	89
Slate Firemist	90
Pottery Gold Firemist	91
Biscayne Aqua Firemist	92
Cedar Firemist	93
Basil Green Firemist	94
Cerulean Blue Firemist	95
Western Saddle Firemist	96
Sable Black	19

VINYL ROOF COLORS

Silver Blue Metallic	B
Dark Blue Metallic	C
Light Blue Metallic	D
Light Yellow	E
Light Gold Metallic	G
Light Gray	H
White	J
Black	K
Dark Aqua Metallic	M
Medium Green Metallic	N
Silver Metallic	P
Dark Green Metallic	R
Slate Gray Metallic	S
Light Beige	T
Saddle Metallic	U
Dark Brown Metallic	X
Light Cedar Metallic	Y

ENGINE NUMBER

The engine number is located on the lower left hand side of the cylinder block, just above the edge of the oil pan.

ENGINE CODE	NO. CYL.	CID	HORSE-POWER	COMP. RATIO	CARB
B	8	350	170	8.0:1	Fuel Inj.
N	8	350	125	22.5:1	Diesel
S	8	425	180	8.2:1	4-BC
T	8	425	195	8.2:1	Fuel Inj.

1970 CHEVROLET CAMARO

1970 CHEVROLET MONTE CARLO

1970 CHEVROLET CAPRICE

1970 CHEVROLET CHEVELLE

1970 CHEVROLET NOVA

1970 CHEVROLET IMPALA

1970 CHEVROLET CHEVELLE

1970 CHEVROLET CORVETTE STINGRAY

VEHICLE IDENTIFICATION NUMBER

CHEVROLET
136370B123456

On top left side of instrument panel, visible through the windshield.

Corvette VIN on left windshield pillar, visible through the windshield.

FIRST DIGIT: Indicates GM division (1 is Chevrolet)

SECOND DIGIT: Indicates series

SERIES	CODE
Nova	1
Camaro	2
Chevelle & Monte Carlo	3
Chevrolet Biscayne or Bel Air	5
Chevrolet Impala or Caprice	6
Corvette	9

THIRD DIGIT: Indicates engine
Odd Number - 4 or 6 cylinder
Even Number - 8 cylinder

FOURTH & FIFTH DIGITS: Indicate body style

DESCRIPTION	CODE
4-Dr. Station Wagon - 2-Seat - Dual Acting Tail Gate	36
2-Dr. Notch Back - Hardtop Coupe	37
4-Dr. Notch Back - Hardtop (4 Window) Sedan	39
4-Dr. Station Wagon - 3-Seat - Dual Acting Tail Gate	46
2-Dr. Notch Back - Hardtop Coupe	47
2-Dr. Notch Back - Hardtop Coupe	57
2-Dr. - Convertible Coupe	67
4-Dr. Notch Back - Pillar (4 Window) Sedan	69
2-Dr. Plain Back - Hardtop Coupe	87

SIXTH DIGIT: Indicates the year (0 is 1970)

SEVENTH DIGIT: (A letter) Indicates the assembly plant

ASSEMBLY PLANT	CODE
Atlanta	A
Baltimore	B
South Gate	C
Flint	F
Framingham	G
Oshawa, Canada	I
Janesville	J
Kansas City	K
Los Angeles	L
Norwood	N
Arlington	R
St. Louis	S
Tarrytown	T
Lordstown	U
Willow Run	W
Wilmington	Y
Fremont	Z

REMAINING LAST SIX DIGITS: Indicate production sequence number

EXAMPLE:

1	3	6	37	0	B	123456
Chevrolet Div	Series	Engine	Body Style	Year	Asm Plant	Prod Code

BODY NUMBER PLATE

Located on right or left side of firewall below rear edge of hood of all models, except Corvette. Corvette plate is located on upper left hand door hinge pillar.

THE BODY NUMBER PLATE identifies the model year, car division, series, style, body assembly plant, body number, trim combination, paint code and date build code.

```
            BODY BY FISHER
ST 70  12487  NOR        123456 BDY
TR 711                        19 PNT
11A

  GENERAL MOTORS CORPORATION CERTIFIES
      TO THE DEALER THAT THIS VEHICLE
        CONFORMS TO ALL U.S., FEDERAL MOTOR
           VEHICLE SAFETY STANDARDS
        APPLICABLE AT TIME OF MANUFACTURE.
```

EXAMPLE:

In the example above,

70	Model year (1970)
1	Car division (Chevrolet)
24	Series (Camaro V-8)
87	Style (2 Dr. Coupe)
NOR	Body assembly plant (Norwood, Ohio)
123456	Production sequence in that plant
711	Black vinyl trim
19	Tuxedo Black paint
11	Eleventh month (November)
A	First week of month

NOTE: Occassionally a code will appear below the paint code. It is a notation to assemlby line workers that this vehicle is not a standard issue item. An example would be a light-weight bodied car with radio delete, heater delete, etc. WE DO NOT HAVE BREAKDOWNS FOR THOSE CODES.

CHEVELLE	6-CYL CODE	V-8 CODE
4-Dr Sedan 6-Pass	13369	13469
2-Dr Sport Cpe 5-Pass	13337	13437
NOMAD		
4-Dr. SW 2 Seat	13136	13236
GREENBRIAR		
4-Dr SW 2-Seat	13336	13436
4-Dr SW 3-Seat		13446
CONCOURS		
4-Dr SW 2-Seat	13536	13636
4-Dr SW 3-Seat		13646
4-Dr Estate Wagon 3 Seat		13846
Malibu	**6 Cyl CODE**	**v-8 CODE**
4-Dr Sedan 6-Pass	13569	13669
4-Dr Sport Sedan 6-Pass	13539	13639
2-Dr Sport Cpe 5-Pass	13537	13637
2-Dr Conv 5-Pass	13567	13667

*SS-396 option available
*SS-454 option available

MONTE CARLO   **6 CYL CODE**   **V-8 CODE**
2-Dr Custom Cpe 5-Pass*   13857
*SS-454 option available

NOVA   **4-CYL CODE**   **6-CYL CODE**   **V-8 CODE**
2-Dr Sport Cpe 5-Pass   11127   11327   11427
4-Dr Sedan 6-Pass   11169   11369   11469
*SS option available
*Custom option available

CAMARO   **6-CYL CODE**   **V-8 CODE**
2-Dr Sport Cpe 4-Pass   12387   12487
*SS option available
*RS option available
*Z-28 option available

CORVETTE   **V-8 CODE**
2-Dr Sport Coupe 2-Pass   19437
2-Dr Convertible 2-Pass   19467

CHEVROLET   **6-CYL CODE**   **V-8 CODE**
Biscayne
4-Dr Sedan 6-Pass   15369   15469

Brookwood
                  15436

Bel Air
4-Dr Sedan 6-Pass   15569   15669

Townsman
4-Dr SW 2-Seat   15636
4-Dr SW 3-Seat   15646

Impala
4-Dr Sedan 6-Pass   16369   16469
4-Dr Sport Sedan 6-Pass   16339   16439
2-Dr Sport Cpe 5-Pass   16337   16437
2-Dr Conv 5-Pass   16467

Impala Custom
2-Dr Sport Cpe 5-Pass   16447

Kingswood
4-Dr SW 2-Seat   16436
4-Dr SW 3-Seat   16446

Kingswood Estate
4-Dr SW 2-Seat   16636
4-Dr SW 3-Seat   16646

Caprice
4-Dr Sport Sedan 6-Pass   16639
2-Dr Sport Cpe 5-Pass   16647

THE TRIM NUMBER furnishes the key to trim color and material for each model series.

CHEVELLE TRIM

Color	Cloth	Vinyl	Leather	Code
Black	•			753
Black		•		755
Black**		•		756
Blue	•			762
Blue		•		764
Blue**		•		765
Gold	•			776
Gold		•		777
Green	•			782
Green		•		795
Green**		•		796
Ivory		•		790
Ivory**		•		791
Red		•		787
Red**		•		788
Saddle		•		770
Saddle**		•		771
Turquoise	•			779

* Conventional seat with custom interior
** Strato-bucket seats with custom interior

MONTE CARLO TRIM

Color	Cloth	Vinyl	Leather	Code
Black	•			748
Black**	•			749
Black**		•		757
Blue	•			758
Blue	•			767
Gold	•			774
Green	•			780
Green**		•		784
Saddle		•		769
Sandalwood	•			792

* Conventional seat with custom interior
** Strato-bucket seats with custom interior

CHEVROLET WAGON TRIM

Color	Cloth	Vinyl	Leather	Code
Black		•		806
Black		•		804
Black		•		802
Black		•		755
Black		•		752
Black		•		750
Blue		•		821
Blue		•		819
Blue		•		815
Blue		•		764
Blue		•		761
Blue		•		759
Gold		•		841
Gold		•		839
Green		•		861
Saddle		•		830
Saddle		•		838
Saddle		•		831
Saddle		•		770
Saddle		•		773
Saddle		•		772

NOVA TRIM

Color	Cloth	Vinyl	Leather	Code
Black		•		731
Black*		•		732
Black**		•		733
Blue	•			735
Blue*	•			736
Gold	•			740
Gold*	•			741
Gold**		•		742
Green	•			745
Green*	•			744
Sandalwood*		•		747
Sandalwood**		•		746

* Conventional seat with custom interior
** Strato-bucket seats with custom interior

CAMARO TRIM

Color	Cloth	Vinyl	Leather	Code
Black		•		711
Black**	•			725
Black**		•		712
Blue		•		715
Blue**		•		716
Green		•		723
Green**		•		724
Saddle		•		726
Saddle**		•		727
Sandalwood		•		710
Sandalwood**		•		730
Blk/Blue**	•			714
Blk/Green**	•			720
Blk/Wht**	•			713

** Strato-bucket seats with custom interior

CORVETTE TRIM

Color	Cloth	Vinyl	Leather	Code
Black		•		400
Black			•	403
Blue		•		411
Brown		•		414
Green		•		422
Red		•		407
Saddle		•		418
Saddle			•	424

CHEVROLET TRIM

Color	Cloth	Vinyl	Leather	Code
Black	•			803
Black	•			805
Black		•		802
Black		•		804
Black		•		806
Blue	•			818
Blue	•			820
Blue	•			822
Blue		•		815
Blue		•		819
Blue		•		821
Blue	•			826
Gold	•			836
Gold	•			837
Gold	•			840
Gold		•		841
Gold		•		843
Green	•			848
Green	•			855
Green	•			860
Green		•		861
Red		•		866
Saddle		•		830
Sandalwood	•			870
Sandalwood		•		828
Turquoise	•			844
Turquoise	•			845

THE PAINT CODE furnishes the key to the paint colors used on the car.

COLOR	CODE
Classic White*	10
Cortez Silver*	14
Laguna Gray*	15
Shadow Gray	17
Tuxedo Black	19
Astro Turquoise	25
Mulsanna Blue*	26
Bridgehampton Blue*	27
Fathom Blue	28
Misty Turquoise	34
Donnybrook Green *	44
Green Mist	45
Forest Green	48
Gobi Beige	50
Daytona Yellow*	51
Champagne Gold	55
Autumn Gold	58
Ontario Orange*	62
Desert Sand	63
Monza Red*	72
Cranberry Red	75
Marlboro Maroon*	77
Black Cherry	78

*Corvette only available with one of these colors

TWO-TONE COMBINATIONS

LOWER COLOR	CODE	UPPER COLOR	CODE
Astro Blue	25	Fathom Blue	28
Astro Blue	25	Classic White	10
Fathom Blue	28	Astro Blue	25
Champagne Gold	55	Classic White	10
Autumn Gold	58	Classic White	10
Desert Sand	63	Classic White	10
Misty Turquoise	34	Classic White	10

VINYL ROOF COLORS

COLOR	CODE
White	AA
Black	BB
Dk Blue	CC
Dk Green	GG
Dk Gold	HH

CONVERTIBLE TOP COLORS

	COLOR	CODE
Corvette	White	AA
	Black	BB
	Sandalwood	

	COLOR	CODE
Chevelle & Impala	White	AA
	Black	BB

ENGINE NUMBER

THE ENGINE IDENTIFICATION NUMBER includes a letter code for the engine plant, followed by numbers which date the manufacture of the engine, then followed by a letter code to indicate the engine size and makeup.

THE ENGINE IDENTIFICATION NUMBER for V-8s is stamped on a pad located at the right-hand side of cylinder block, and stamped on a pad on the right-hand side of the block behind the distributor on 4-cylinder and 6-cylinder engines.

NOTE:

1. To properly identify Chevrolet Division engines, it will be necessary to identify the car model in which the engine is used. The same engine type may have a different code when used in different car models.

2. All 396 engines were 402 CID.

EXAMPLE

T	01	01	CCM
PLANT	MONTH	DAY	CODE

CHEVELLE ENGINES

Engine Code	No. Cyl.	CID	Horse Power	Comp. Ratio	Carb	Trans
CRG	6	250		Low Comp.	1 BC	Manual
CCH	6	250		Low Comp.	1 BC	PG
CCG	6	250	155	8.5:1	1 BC	PG or TH 350
CCF	6	250	155	8.5:1	1 BC	PG or TH 350
CCM	6	250	155	8.5:1	1 BC	PG
CCK	6	250	155	8.5:1	1 BC	TH 350
CCL	6	250	155	8.5:1	1 BC	Manual
CNC	8	307	200	9.0:1	2 BC	Manual
CND	8	307	200	9.0:1	2 BC	Man 4-spd.
CNE	8	307	200	9.0:1	2 BC	PG
CNF	8	307	200	9.0:1	2 BC	TH 350
CNI	8	350	250	9.0:1	2 BC	Manual
CRF	6	250	155	8.5:1	1 BC	Manual
CNG	8	307		Low Comp.	2 BC	Manual
CNH	8	307		Low Comp.	2 BC	PG
CNN	8	350	250	9.0:1	2 BC	TH 350
CNJ	8	350	300	10.25:1	4 BC	Manual
CNK	8	350	300	10.25:1	4 BC	PG
CRE	8	350	300	10.25:1	4 BC	TH 350
CNM	8	350	250	9.0:1	2 BC	PG
CTW	8	396	350	10.25:1	4 BC	TH 400
CTX	8	396	350	10.25:1	4 BC	Man 4-spd.
CTY	8	396	375	11.0:1	4 BC	TH 400
CTZ	8	396	350	10.25:1	4 BC	Man 4-spd*
CKN	8	396	375	11.0:1	4 BC	TH 400
CKO	8	396	375	11.0:1	4 BC	Man 4-spd
CKD	8	396	375	11.0:1	4 BC	Man 4-spd
CKP	8	396**	375	11.0:1	4 BC	TH 400
CKQ	8	396	375	11.0:1	4 BC	Man 4-spd*
CKT	8	396	375	11.0:1	4 BC	Man 4-spd
CKU	8	396	375	11.0:1	4 BC	Man 4-spd*
CZX	8	400	265	9.0:1	2 BC	Manual
CRH	8	400	265	9.0:1	2 BC	TH 350
CKN	8	400	330	10.25:1	4 BC	TH 400
CKR	8	400	330	10.25:1	4 BC	Man 4-spd
CKS	8	400	330	10.25:1	4 BC	Man 4-spd*
CRN	8	454	360	10.25:1	4 BC	Man 4-spd
CGT	8	454	360	10.25:1	4 Bc	TH 400
CRQ	8	454	360	10.25:1	4 BC	TH 400
CRR	8	454	450	11.0:1	4 BC	TH 400
CRM	8	454	360	10.25:1	4 Bc	TH 400
CRS	8	454**	450	11.0:1	4 BC	TH 400
CRT	8	454	360	10.25:1	4 BC	Man 4-spd
CRY	8	454**	450	11.0:1	4 BC	Man 4-spd*
CRV	8	454	450	11.0:1	4 BC	Man 4-spd
CGU	8	454	360	10.25:1	4 BC	Man 4-spd
CRU	8	454	360	10.25:1	4 BC	Man 4-spd
CRW	8	454**	450	11.0:1	4 BC	Man 4-spd
CRX	8	454	450	11.0:1	4 BC	Man 4-spd

*Heavy-Duty Clutch
**Aluminum Heads

MONTE CARLO ENGINES

Engine Code	No Cyl.	CID	Horse Power	Comp. Ratio	Carb	Trans
CNJ	8	350	300	10.25:1	4 BC	Manual
CNK	8	350	300	10.25:1	4 BC	PG
CRE	8	350	300	10.25:1	4 BC	TH 350
CZX	8	400	265	9.0:1	2 BC	Manual
CRH	8	400	265	9.0:1	2 BC	TH 350
CKR	8	400	330	10.25:1	4 BC	Manual
CKN	8	400	330	10.25:1	4 BC	TH 400
CKS	8	400*	330	10.25:1	4 BC	Manual
CRU	8	454	360	10.25:1	4 BC	TH 400
CRN	8	454	360	10.25:1	4 BC	Manual
CRT	8	454	360	10.25:1	4 BC	Manual
CRQ	8	454	360	10.25:1	4 BC	TH 400
CNI	8	350	250	9.0:1	2 BC	Manual
CNM	8	350	250	9.0:1	2 bc	PG
CNN	8	350	250	9.0:1	2 BC	TH 350
CGW	8	454	360	10.25:1	4 BC	
CGT	8	454	360	10.25:1	4 BC	

*Heavy-Duty Clutch
**Aluminum Heads

NOVA ENGINES

Engine Code	No Cyl.	CID	Horse Power	Comp. Ratio	Carb	Trans
CCR	6	230	140	Low Comp.	1 BC	Manual
CCF	6	230	140	Low Comp.	1 BC	PG
CCE	6	230	140	Low Comp.	1 BC	Manual
CCA	4	153	90	8.50:1	1 BC	Manual
CCB	4	153	90	8.50:1	1 BC	Torque
CCC	6	230	140	8.50:1	1 BC	Manual
CCD	6	230	140	8.50:1	1 BC	Torque
CCM	6	250	155	8.50:1	1 BC	PG
COM	6	250	155	8.50:1	1 BC	
CCG	6	250	155	8.50:1	1 BC	Manual
CCK	6	250	155	8.50:1	1 BC	TH 350
CCZ	6	250	155	8.50:1	1 BC	Manual
CCI	6	250	155	8.50:1	1 BC	Manual
CCL	6	250	155	8.50:1	1 BC	Manual
CCH	6	250	155	Low Comp.	1 Bc	PG
CRF	6	250	155	8.50:1	1 BC	Manual
CRG	6	250	155	Low Comp.	1 BC	Manual
CNC	8	307	200	9.0:1	2 BC	Manual
CNG	8	307	200	Low Comp.	2 Bc	Manual
CND	8	307	200	9.0:1	2 BC	Man 4-spd
CNH	8	307	200	Low Comp.	2 Bc	PG
CNE	8	307	200	9.0:1	2 BC	PG
CNF	8	307	200	9.0:1	2 BC	TH 350
CNI	8	350	250	9.0:1	2 BC	Manual
CNJ	8	350	300	10.25:1	4 BC	Manual
CNK	8	350	300	10.25:1	4 BC	PG
CRE	8	350	300	10.25:1	4 BC	TH 350
CNM	8	350	250	9.0:1	2 BC	PG
CNN	8	350	250	9.0:1	2 BC	TH 350
CTW	8	396	350	11.0:1	4 BC	TH 400
CTX	8	396	350	11.0:1	4 BC	Manual
CTY	8	396	375	11.0:1	4 BC	TH 400
CTZ	8	396	350	10.25:1	4 BC	Manual*
CKO	8	396	375	11.0:1	4 BC	Manual
CKP	8	396	375	11.0:1	4 BC	TH 400
CTY	8	396	375	11.0:1	4 Bc	TH 400
CKQ	8	396	375	11.0:1	4 BC	Manual
CKT	8	396	375	11.00:1	4 BC	Manual
CKU	8	396	375	11.00:1	4 BC	Manual

*Heavy-Duty Clutch

CAMARO ENGINES

Engine Code	No Cyl.	CID	Horse Power	Comp. Ratio	Carb	Trans
CCH	6	250	155	Low Comp.	1 BC	PG
CCM	6	250	155	8.5:1	1 BC	PG
CCG	6	250	155	8.5:1	1 BC	Manual
CCK	6	250	155	8.5:1	1 BC	TH 350
CCZ	6	250	155	8.5:1	1 BC	Manual
CCL	6	250	155	8.5:1	1 BC	Manual
CRF	6	250	155	8.5:1	1 BC	Manual
CRG	6	250	155	Low Comp.	1 BC	Manual
CNC	8	307	200	9.0:1	2 BC	Manual
CND	8	307	200	9.0:1	2 BC	Man 4-spd
CNG	8	307	200	Low Comp.	2 Bc	Manual
CNE	8	307	200	9.0:1	2 BC	PG
CNH	8	307	200	Low Comp.	2 BC	PG
CNF	8	307	200	9.0:1	2 BC	TH 350
CNI	8	350	250	9.0:1	2 BC	Manual
CNJ	8	350	300	10.25:1	2 BC	Manual
CNK	8	350	300	10.25:1	2 BC	PG
CRE	8	350	300	10.25:1	2 BC	TH 350
CNM	8	350	250	9.0:1	2 BC	PG
CNN	8	350	250	9.0:1	2 BC	TH 350
CTB	8	350	360	11.0:1	Z-28 4 BC	Manual
CTC	8	350	360	11.0:1	Z-28 4 BC	TH 400
CJL	8	396	375	11.0:1	4 BC	TH 400
CJF	8	396	350	10.25:1	4 BC	Manual
CJH	8	396	375	11.0"1	4 BC	Manual
CJI	8	396	350	10.25:1	4 BC	TH 400
CTW	8	396	350	10.25:1	4 BC	TH 400
CTX	8	396	350	10.25:1	4 BC	Manual
CTY	8	396	375	11.0:1	4 BC	TH 400
CKO	8	396	375	11.0:1	4 BC	Manual

CORVETTE ENGINES

Engine Code	No Cyl.	CID	Horse Power	Comp. Ratio	Carb	Trans
CTG	8	350	300	10.25:1	4 BC	TH 400
CTD	8	350	300	10.25:1	4 BC	Manual
CTL	8	350	300	10.25:1	4 BC	Manual
CTM	8	350	300	10.25:1	4 BC	TH 400
CTN	8	350	350	11.0:1	4 BC	Manual
CTO	8	350	350	11.0:1	4 BC	Manual
CTP	8	350*	350	11.0:1	4 BC	Manual
CTQ	8	350*	350	11.0:1	4 BC	Manual
CTR	8	350*	370	11.0:1	4 BC	Spc High Perf.
CTU	8	350*	370	11.0:1	4 BC	Spc High Perf.
CTV	8	350*	370	11.0:1	ZR1 4 BC	Manual 4-spd
CGW	8	454	390	10.25:1	4 BC	TH 400
CZU	8	454	390	10.25:1	4 BC	Manual
CZL	8	454**	465*	11.25:1	4 BC	Manual
CZN	8	454**	465*	11.25:1	4 BC	TH 400
CRI	8	454*	390	10:25:1	4 BC	Manual
CTH	8	350	350	11.0:1	4 BC	Manual
CTJ	8	350	350	11.0:1	4 BC	Manual
CTK	8	350	370	11.0:1	4 BC	Manual
CRJ	8	454*	390	10.25:1	4 BC	TH 400

*Transistor Ignition
**Aluminum heads

CHEVROLET ENGINES

Engine Code	No. Cyl.	CID	Horse Power	Comp. Ratio	Carb	Trans
CCM	6	250	155	8.5:1	1 BC	PG
CCG	6	250	155	8.5:1	1 BC	Manual
CCH	6	250		Low Comp.	1 BC	Manual
CCK	6	250	155	8.5:1	1 BC	TH 350
CCZ	6	250	155	8.5:1	1 BC	Manual
CCL	6	250	155	8.5:1	1 BC	Manual
CRF	6	250	155	8.5:1	1 BC	Manual
CRG	6	250	155	8.5:1	1 BC	Manual
CND	8	350	250	9.0:1	2 BC	Manual
CNP	8	350	250	9.0:1	2 BC	Manual
CNQ	8	350	300	10.25:1	2 BC	Manual

Engine Code	No. Cyl.	CID	Horse Power	Comp. Ratio	Carb	Trans
CNR	8	350	300	10.25:1	2 BC	TH 350
CNS	8	350	300	10.25:1	2 BC	PG
CNT	8	350	300	10.25:1	2 BC	TH 350
CNU	8	350	250	9.0:1	2 BC	PG
CNV	8	350	250	9.0:1	2 BC	TH 350
CNW	8	350	250	9.0:1	2 BC	PG
CNX	8	350	250	9.0:1	2 BC	TH 350
CGR	8	400	265	9.0:1	2 BC	Manual
CGV	8	454	345	10.25:1	4 BC	Manual
CGS	8	454	345	10.25:1	4 BC	Manual
CGT	8	454	390	10.25:1	4 BC	Manual
CGU	8	454	390	10.25:1	4 BC	Manual
CCJ	6	250		Low Comp.	1 BC	Manual
CCI	6	250	155	8.5:1	1 BC	Manual
CNO	8	350	250	9.0:1	2 BC	Manual
CNY	8	350		Low Comp.	2 BC	Manual
CNZ	8	350		Low Comp.	2 Bc	PG

1971 CHEVROLET CAPRICE

1971 CHEVROLET VEGA 2300 KAMMBACK WAGON

1971 CHEVROLET CAMARO SS

1971 CHEVROLET CORVETTE STINGRAY

1971 CHEVROLET IMPALA

1971 CHEVROLET NOVA

1971 CHEVROLET VEGA 2300

1971 CHEVROLET KINGSWOOD ESTATE STATION WAGON

1971 CHEVROLET MONTE CARLO

1971 CHEVROLET MALIBU

VEHICLE IDENTIFICATION NUMBER

CHEVROLET
136371K123456

On top left side of instrument panel, visible through the windshield.

Corvette VIN on left windshield pillar, visible through the windshield.

FIRST DIGIT: Indicates GM division (1 is Chevrolet)

SECOND DIGIT: Indicates series

CODE	SERIES
1	Nova
2	Camaro
3	Chevelle & Monte Carlo
4	Vega
5	Chevrolet Impala or Caprice
9	Corvette

THIRD DIGIT: Indicates engine
Odd number - 4 or 6 cylinder
Even Number - 8 cylinder

FOURTH & FIFTH DIGITS: Indicate body style

STYLE	DESCRIPTION
27	2-Dr. Notch Back - Pillar Coupe
36	4-Dr. Station Wagon - 2-Seat - Dual Acting Tail Gate
37	2-Dr. Notch Back - Hardtop Coupe
39	4-Dr. Notch Back - Hardtop (4 Window) Sedan
46	4-Dr. Station Wagon - 3-Seat - Dual Acting Tail Gate
57	2-Dr. Notch Back - Hardtop Coupe
67	2-Dr. Convertible Coupe
69	4-Dr. Notch Back - Pillar (4 Window) Sedan
77	2-Dr. Plain Back Pillar Coupe
80	2-Dr. Pick-Up Delivery
87	2-Dr. Plain Back - Hardtop Coupe
11	2-Dr. Sedan - Notch Back
15	2-Dr. Station Wagon - 2-Seat

SIXTH DIGIT: Indicates the year (1 is 1971)

SEVENTH DIGIT: (A letter) Indicates the assembly plant

ASSEMBLY PLANT	CODE
Atlanta	A
Baltimore	B
South Gate	C
Flint	F
Framingham	G
Oshawa, Canada	I
Janesville	J
Kansas City	K
Los Angeles	L
Norwood	N
Arlington	R
St. Louis	S
Tarrytown	T
Lordstown	U
Willow Run	W
Wilmington	Y
Fremont	Z

REMAINING LAST SIX DIGITS: Indicate production sequence number

EXAMPLE

1	3	6	37	1	K	123456
Chevrolet Div.	Series	Engine	Body Style	Year	Asm Plant	Prod Code

BODY NUMBER PLATE

Located on right or left side of firewall below rear edge of hood of all models, except Corvette. Corvette plate is located on upper left-hand door hinge pillar.

THE BODY NUMBER PLATE identifies the model year, car division, series, style, body assembly plant, body number, trim combination, paint code and date build code.

```
          BODY BY FISHER
ST 71  12487  NOR        123456 BDY
TR 775                       19 PNT
11A

GENERAL MOTORS CORPORATION CERTIFIES
   TO THE DEALER THAT THIS VEHICLE
  CONFORMS TO ALL U.S., FEDERAL MOTOR
        VEHICLE SAFETY STANDARDS
   APPLICABLE AT TIME OF MANUFACTURE.
```

EXAMPLE:

In the example above,

71	Model year (1971)
1	Car division (Chevrolet)
24	Series (Camaro V-8)
87	Style (2-Dr Coupe)
NOR	Body assembly plant (Norwood, Ohio)
123456	Production sequence in that plant
775	Black vinyl trim
19	Tuxedo Black paint
11	Eleventh month (November)
A	First week of month

NOTE: Occcassionally a code will appear below the paint code. It is a notation to the assembly line workers that this vehicle is not a standard issue item. An example would be a light weight bodied car with radio delete, heater delete, etc. WE DO NOT HAVE BREAK-DOWNS FOR THOSE CODES.

CHEVELLE	6-CYL CODE	V-8 CODE
Nomad		
Station Wagon	13136	13236
Greenbrier		
Wagon, 2-seat	13336	13436
Wagon, 3-seat		13446
Concours		
Wagon, 2-seat	13536	13636
Wagon, 3-seat		13646
Estate Wagon, 2-seat		13836
Estate Wagon, 3-seat		13846
Malibu		
2 Dr Hard Top	13537	13637
4 Dr Hard top	13539	13639
Convertible	13567	13667
4 Dr Sedan	13569	13669

*SS-350 option available
*SS-454 option available
*Heavy Chevy option available

MONTE CARLO **6-CYL CODE**   **V-8 CODE**
2 Dr Hard Top   13857
*SS-454 option available

NOVA   **6-CYL CODE**   **V-8 CODE**
2-Dr. Coupe   11327   11427
4 Dr Sedan   11369   11469
*SS option available
*Rally Nova option available

CAMARO   **6-CYL CODE**   **V-8 CODE**
2 Dr Hard Top   12387   12487
*Z-28 option available
*RS (Rally Sport) option available
*SS option available

CORVETTE   **V-8 CODE**
Sport Coupe   19437
Convertible   19467

VEGA   **4-CYL CODE**
Sedan   14111
Kammback Station Wagon   14115
Hatchback Coupe   14177
*GT option available

CHEVROLET   **6-CYL CODE**   **V-8 CODE**
Brookwood Wagon
2 Seat   15435

Biscayne
4-Dr Sedan   15369   15469

Bel Air
4-Dr Sedan   15569   15669

Townsman
Wagon, 2 Seat   15635
Wagon, 3 Seat   15645

Kingswood
Wagon, 2 Seat   16435
Wagon, 3 Seat   16445
Estate Wagon, 2 Seat   16635
Estate Wagon, 3 Seat   16645

Impala
4-Dr Hard Top   16439
Custom 2-Dr Hard Top   16447
2-Dr Hard Top   16357   16457
Convertible   16467
4-Dr Sedan   16369   16469

Caprice
4-Dr Hard Top   16639
2-Dr Hard Top   16647

THE TRIM NUMBER furnishes the key to trim color and material for each model series.

CHEVELLE TRIM

Color	Cloth	Vinyl	Leather	Code
Black	•			704
Black		•		705
Black**		•		706
Black	•			701
Black**	•			703
Blue	•			725
Blue		•		726
Blue	•			724
Jade	•			730
Jade		•		731
Jade**		•		732

Color	Cloth	Vinyl	Leather	Code
Jade	•			736
Saddle		•		721
Saddle**		•		722
Sandalwood	•			718
Sandalwood		•		714
Sandalwood**		•		715

* Conventional seat with custom interior
** Strato-bucket seats with custom interior

CHEVELLE WAGON TRIM

Color	Cloth	Vinyl	Leather	Code
Black		•		705
Black		•		703
Black		•		702
Jade		•		731
Saddle		•		720
Saddle		•		719
Saddle		•		721
Sandalwood		•		720
Sandalwood		•		719

MONTE CARLO TRIM

Color	Cloth	Vinyl	Leather	Code
Black	•			708
Black**				707
Black		•		710
Blue	•			728
Blue**	•			727
Jade	•			734
Jade**	•			733
Jade**		•		729
Saddle**		•		723
Sandalwood	•			717
Sandalwood**	•			716

* Conventional seat with custom interior
** Strato-bucket seats with custom interior

NOVA TRIM

Color	Cloth	Vinyl	Leather	Code
Black	•			750
Black		•		751
Black*	•			752
Black*		•		753
Black**		•		754
Blue	•			756
Blue		•		757
Jade	•			759
Jade		•		760
Jade*	•			761
Saddle**		•		767
Sandalwood		•		763
Sandalwood*		•		764

* Conventional seat with custom interior
** Strato-bucket seats with custom interior

CAMARO TRIM

Color	Cloth	Vinyl	Leather	Code
Black**		•		775
Black**	•			785
Blue**		•		776
Jade**		•		778
Saddle**		•		779
Sandalwood**		•		777
Blk/Blue**	•			786
Blk/Jade**	•			787
Blk/Sdl**	•			792
Blk/Wht**	•			789

* Conventional seat with custom interior
** Strato-bucket seats with custom interior

CORVETTE TRIM

Color	Cloth	Vinyl	Leather	Code
Black**	•			400
Black**			•	403
Blue**		•		412
Green**		•		423
Red**		•		407
Saddle**		•		407
Saddle**			•	420

* Conventional seat with custom interior
** Strato-bucket seats with custom interior

VEGA TRIM

Color	Cloth	Vinyl	Leather	Code
Black		•		873
Black		•		874
Green		•		878
Green		•		879
Saddle		•		883
Saddle		•		884
Sandalwood		•		888
Blue		•		892

CHEVROLET TRIM

Color	Cloth	Vinyl	Leather	Code
Black	•			807
Black	•			805
Black	•			803
Black		•		806
Black		•		804
Black		•		802
Blue	•			805
Blue	•			803
Blue	•			811
Blue		•		814
Blue		•		812
Blue		•		810
Jade	•			836
Jade	•			834
Jade	•			832
Jade		•		835
Maize	•			828
Maize	•			830
Maize	•			829
Maize		•		827
Saddle		•		825
Sandalwood	•			821
Sandalwood		•		820
Sandalwood		•		819
Sandalwood		•		818

CHEVROLET WAGON TRIM

Color	Cloth	Vinyl	Leather	Code
Black		•		806
Black		•		804
Black		•		802
Blue		•		814
Blue		•		812
Blue		•		810
Jade		•		835
Maize		•		827
Saddle		•		824
Saddle		•		823
Saddle		•		825

THE PAINT CODE furnishes the key to the paint colors used on the car.

COLOR	CODE
Classic White*	10
Antique White	11
Nevada Silver*	13
Silver Steel	16
Tuxedo Black	19
Ascot Blue	24
Mediterranean Blue	25
Mulsanne Blue*	26
Bridgehampton Blue*	27
Command Blue	29
Sea Aqua	39
Cottonwood Green	42
Lime Green	43
Brands Hatch Green*	48
Antique Green	49
Sunflower Yellow*	52
Placer Gold	53
Champagne Gold	55
Sandlewood	61
Burnt Orange	62
Mesa Sand	63
Classic Copper	67
Cranberry Red	75
Mille Miglia Red*	76
Rosewood	78
War Bonnet Yellow*	91
Ontario Orange*	97
Steel Cities Gray*	98

* Corvette only available with one of these colors.

TWO TONE COMBINATIONS

LOWER COLOR	CODE	UPPER COLOR	CODE
Mulsanne Blue	26	Antique White	11
Placer Gold	53	Antique White	11
Antique Green	49	Antique White	11
Lime Green	43	Antique White	11
Burnt Orange	62	Antique White	11
Sandalwood	61	Antique White	11
Sea Aqua	39	Antique White	11
Command Blue	29	Antique White	11
Ascot Blue	24	Antique White	11
Champagne Gold	55	Antique White	11
Cottonwood Green	42	Antique White	11
Command Blue	29	Antique White	11

VINYL ROOF CODES

COLOR	CODE
Black	BB
Dk Blue	CC
Dk Brown	FF
Dk Green	GG
White	AA

CONVERTIBLE TOP COLORS: Choice of white or black top available with all exterior colors.

ENGINE NUMBER

THE ENGINE IDENTIFICATION NUMBER includes a letter code for the engine plant, followed by numbers which date the manufacture of the engine, then followed by a letter code to indicate the engine size and makeup.

THE ENGINE IDENTIFICATION NUMBER for V-8s is stamped on a pad located at the right-hand side of the cylinder block, and stamped on a pad on the right-hand side of the block behind the distributor on 4-cylinder and 6-cylinder engines.

NOTE:

1. To properly identify Chevrolet Division engines, it will be necessary to identify the car model in which the engine is used. The same engine type may have a different code when used in different car models.

2. All 396 engines are 402 CID.

EXAMPLE

1	01	01	CCM
PLANT	MONTH	DAY	CODE

CHEVELLE ENGINES

Engine Code	No Cyl.	CID	Horse-power	Comp. Ratio	Carb	Trans
CAG	6	250	145	Low Comp.	1 BC	Manual
CAB	6	250	145	8.5:1	1 BC	PG
CAA	6	250	145	8.5:1	1 BC	Manual
CCA	8	307	200	8.5:1	2 BC	PG or TH 350
CCA	8	307	200	8.5:1	2 BC	Manual
CGA	8	350	245	8.5:1	2 BC	Manual
CGB	8	350	245	8.5:1	2 BC	PG
CGK	8	350	270	8.5:1	4 BC	Manual
CGL	8	350	270	8.5:1	4 BC	TH 350
CJD	8	350	270	8.5:1	4 BC	TH 350
CJJ	8	350	270	8.6:1	4 BC	Manual
CGC	8	350	245	8.5:1	2 BC	TH 350
CLP	8	396	300	8.5:1	4 BC	TH 350
CLB	8	396	300	8.5:1	4 BC	TH 400
CLL	8	396	300	8.5:1	4 BC	4-spd
CLR	8	396	300	8.5:1	4 BC	Manual
CLS	8	396	300	8.5:1	4 BC	Manual
CPA	8	454	365	8.5:1	4 BC	Manual
CPG	8	454	365	8.5:1	4 BC	Manual
CPD	8	454	365	8.5:1	4 BC	Manual
CPP	8	454	425	9.1:1	4 BC	Manual
CPR	8	454	425	9.1:1	4 BC	TH 400
CPZ	8	454	425	9.1:1	4 BC	Manual or TH 400

MONTE CARLO ENGINES

Engine Code	No Cyl.	CID	Horse-power	Comp. Ratio	Carb	Trans
CGA	8	350	245	8.5:1	2 BC	Manual
CGB	8	350	245	8.5:1	2 BC	PG
CGK	8	350	270	8.5:1	4 BC	Manual
CGL	8	350	270	8.5:1	4 BC	TH
CGC	8	350	245	8.5:1	2 BC	PG or TH 350
CJG	8	350	270	8.5:1	4 BC	Manual or TH 350
CLA	8	400	300	8.5:1	2 BC	Manual
CLB	8	400	300	8.5:1	4 BC	TH
CLJ	8	400	300	8.5:1	2 BC	Manual
CLK	8	400	300	8.5:1	2 BC	TH
CLL	8	400	300	8.5:1	4 BC	Manual
CLP	8	400	300	8.5:1	4 BC	TH
CPA	8	454	365	8.5:1	4 BC	Manual
CPG	8	454	365	8.5:1	4 BC	Manual
CPP	8	454	365	8.5:1	4 BC	Manual
CPR	8	454	365	8.5:1	4 BC	TH
CPD	8	454	365	8.5:1	4 BC	Manual or TH 400

NOVA ENGINES

Engine Code	No Cyl.	CID	Horse-power	Comp. Ratio	Carb	Manual
CAG	6	250	145	Low Comp.	1 Bc	Manual
CAA	6	250	145	8.5:1	1 BC	Manual
CAB	6	250	145	8.5:1	1 BC	PG
CCA	8	307	200	8.5:1	2 BC	Manual
CCC	8	307	200	8.5:1	2 BC	PG or TH 350
CGA	8	350	245	8.5:1	2 BC	Manual
CGB	8	350	245	8.5:1	2 BC	PG
CGC	8	350	245	8.5:1	2 BC	TH 350
CGK	8	350	270	8.5:1	4 BC	Manual
CGL	8	350	270	8.5:1	4 BC	TH 350
CJD	8	350	270	8.5:1	4 BC	TH 350
CJG	8	350	270	8.5:1	4 BC	Manual

CAMARO ENGINES

Engine Code	No Cyl.	CID	Horse-power	Comp. Ratio	Carb	Trans
CAA	6	250	145	8.5:1	1 BC	Manual
CAB	6	250	145	8.5:1	1 BC	PG
CCA	8	307	200	8.5:1	2 BC	Manual
CCC	8	307	200	8.5:1	2 BC	PG or TH 350
CGB	8	350	245	8.5:1	2 BC	PG
CGA	8	350	245	8.5:1	2 BC	Manual
CGC	8	350	245	8.5:1	2 BC	TH 350
CGR	8	350	330	9.0:1	Z-28 4 BC	TH 400
CGK	8	350	270	8.5:1	4 BC	Manual
CGL	8	350	270	8.5:1	4 BC	TH 350
CGP	8	350	330	9.0:1	Z-28 4 BC	Manual
CJD	8	350	270	8.5:1	4 BC	TH 350
CJG	8	350	270	8.5:1	4 BC	Manual
CLD	8	396	300	8.5:1	4 BC	TH 400
CLC	8	396	300	8.5:1	4 BC	Manual
CLA	8	396	300	8.5:1	4 BC	Manual
CLB	8	396	300	8.5:1	4 BC	TH 400

CORVETTE ENGINES

Engine Code	No Cyl.	CID	Horse-power	Comp. Ratio	Carb	Trans
CJL	8	350	270	8.5:1	4 BC	4-spd
CGT	8	350	270	8.5:1	4 BC	TH 400
CJK	8	350	270	8.5:1	4 BC	TH 400
CGZ	8	350	330	9.0:1	4 BC	4-spd
CGY	8	350	330	9.0:1	4 BC	4-spd
CJK	8	350	330	9.0:1	4 BC	TH 400
CPH	8	454	365	8.5:1	4 BC	4-spd
CPJ	8	454	365	8.5:1	4 BC	TH 400
CPW	8	454	425	9.0:1	4 BC	4-spd
CPX	8	454	425	9.0:1	4 BC	TH 400

VEGA ENGINES

Engine Code	No Cyl.	CID	Horse-power	Comp. Ratio	Carb	Trans
CHA	4	140	90	8.5:1	1 BC	PG or Torque
CHC	4	140	90	8.5:1	1 BC	Manual
CHB	4	140	110	8.5:1	2 BC	PG or Torque
CHD	4	140	110	8.5:1	2 BC	Manual

CHEVROLET ENGINES

Engine Code	No Cyl.	CID	Horse-power	Comp. Ratio	Carb	Trans
CAG	6	250		Low Comp.	2 BC	Manual
CAA	6	250	145	8.5:1	2 BC	Manual
CAB	6	250	145	8.5:1	2 BC	PG
CAC	6	250	145	8.5:1	2 BC	Manual
CAD	6	250	145	8.5:1	2 BC	PG
CGA	8	350	245	8.5:1	2 BC	Manual
CGB	8	350	245	8.5:1	2 BC	PG
CGC	8	350	245	8.5:1	2 BC	Manual
CGJ	8	350	245	8.5:1	2 BC	TH 350
CJB	8	350	245	8.5:1	4 BC	Manual
CJH	8	350	270	8.5:1	4 BC	Manual
CLP	8	400	300	8.5:1	4 BC	TH 350
CLK	8	400	300	8.5:1	2 BC	TH 350
CLR	8	400	300	8.5:1	2 BC	Manual
CLT	8	350	245	8.5:1	2 Bc	Manual
CJD	8	350	270	8.5:1	4 BC	Manual or TH 350
CJA	8	350		Low Comp.	4 BC	Manual
CLB	8	400	300	8.5:1	4 BC	TH 350
CPG	8	454	365	8.5:1	4 BC	Manual
CPD	8	454	365	8.5:1	4 BC	Manual

1972 CHEVROLET CAMARO

1972 CHEVROLET CAPRICE

1972 CHEVROLET CHEVELLE MALIBU

1972 CHEVROLET KINGSWOOD ESTATE WAGON

1972 CHEVROLET MONTE CARLO

1972 CHEVROLET NOVA

1972 CHEVROLET CORVETTE STINGRAY

1972 CHEVROLET VEGA

VEHICLE IDENTIFICATION NUMBER

CHEVROLET
1M57H2F123456

On top left side of instrument panel, visible through the windshield

Corvette VIN on left windshield pillar, visible through the windshield.

FIRST DIGIT: Indicates GM division (1 is Chevrolet)

SECOND DIGIT: Indicates series

CODE	SERIES
B	Nomad
C	Chevelle, El Camino, Greenbrier
D	Malibu, Custom El Camino, Concours
H	Monte Carlo, Concours Estate
K	Biscayne, Brookwood
L	Bel Air, Townsman
M	Impala, Kingswood
N	Caprice, Kingswood Estate
Q	Camaro
V	Vega
X	Nova
Z	Corvette

THIRD & FOURTH DIGITS: Indicate body style

STYLE	DESCRIPTION
23	4-Dr. Limousine with Auxiliary Seat
27	2-Dr. Notch Back - Pillar Coupe
33	4-Dr. Limo with Auxiliary Seat and Center Partition Window
35	4-Dr. Station Wagon 2-Seat
36	4-Dr. Station Wagon 2-Seat - Dual Acting Tail Gate
37	2-Dr. Notch Back - Hardtop Coupe
39	4-Dr. Notch Back - Hardtop (4 Window) Sedan
45	4-Dr. Station Wagon 3-Seat
46	4-Dr. Station Wagon 3-Seat - Dual Acting Tail Gate
47	2-Dr. Notch Back - Hardtop Coupe
49	4-Dr. Notch Back - Hardtop (4 Window) Sedan
56	4-Dr. Station Wagon 2-Seat - Dual Acting Tail Gate
57	2-Dr. Notch Back - Hardtop Coupe
66	4-Dr. Station Wagon 3-Seat - Dual Acting Tail Gate
67	2-Dr. Convertible Coupe
69	4-Dr. Notch Back - Pillar (4 Window) Sedan
77	2-Dr. Plain Back Pillar Coupe
80	2-Dr. Pick-up Delivery
87	2-Dr. Plain Back - Hardtop Coupe

FIFTH DIGIT: Indicates engine

CODE	CID	TYPE	CARB
B	140	L-4	1 & 2 BC
D	250	L-6	1 BC
F	307	V8	2 BC
H	350	V8	2 BC
J	350	V8	4 BC RPO L48
K	350	V8	4 BC Base Corvette
L	350	V8	4 BC RPO Z-28
R	400	V8	2 BC RPO LF6
S	402	V8	4 BC RPO LS 3 Single Exhaust
U	402	V8	4 BC RPO LS3 Dual Exhaust
V	454	V8	4 BC RPO LS5 Single Exhaust
W	454	V8	4 BC RPO LS5 Dual Exhaust

SIXTH DIGIT: Indicates the year (2 is 1972)

SEVENTH DIGIT: Indicates the asssembly plant

ASSEMBLY PLANT	CODE
Lakewood	A
Baltimore	B
Southgate	C
Doraville	D
Flint	F
Janesville	J

ASSEMBLY PLANT	CODE
Leeds	K
Van Nuys	L
Norwood	N
Arlington	R
St. Louis	S
Tarrytown	T
Lordstown	U
Pontiac	V
Willow Run	W
Wilmington	Y
Fremont	Z
Oshawa, Canada	1
St. Therese, Canada	2

LAST SIX DIGITS: Indicate production sequence number.

EXAMPLE

1	M	57	H	2	F	123456
Chev Div.	Series Style	Body Plant	Engine Code	Year	Asm	Prod

BODY NUMBER PLATE

Located on right or left side of firewall below rear edge of hood of all models, except Corvette. Corvette plate is located on upper left-hand door hinge pillar.

THE BODY NUMBER PLATE identifies the model year, car division, series, style, body assembly plant, body number, trim combination, paint code and date build code.

```
            BODY BY FISHER
  ST 72  12487  NOR        123456 BDY
  TR 775                      19 PNT
  11A

     GENERAL MOTORS CORPORATION CERTIFIES
         TO THE DEALER THAT THIS VEHICLE
        CONFORMS TO ALL U.S., FEDERAL MOTOR
               VEHICLE SAFETY STANDARDS
          APPLICABLE AT TIME OF MANUFACTURE.
```

EXAMPLE

In the example above,

ST 72	Model year (1972)
1	Car division (Chevrolet)
24	Series (Camaro V-8)
87	Style (2-Dr Coupe)
NOR	Body assembly plant (Norwood, Ohio)
123456	Production sequence in that plant
775	Black vinyl trim
19	Tuxedo Black paint
11	Eleventh month (November)
A	First week of month

NOTE: Occasionally a code will appear below the paint body. It is a notation to the assembly line workers that this vehicle is not a standard issue item. An example would be a light weight bodied car with radio delete, heater delete, etc. WE DO NOT HAVE BREAKDOWNS FOR THOSE CODES.

CHEVELLE

	6-CYL CODE	V-8 CODE
Nomad		
Station Wagon	13136	13236
Greenbrier		
Station Wagon, 2-seat		13436
Station Wagon, 3-seat		13446
Chevelle		
4-Dr. Sedan	13369	13469
2-Dr. Sport Coupe	13337	13437
Concours		
Wagon, 2-seat		13636
Wagon, 3-seat		13646
Estate Wagon, 2-seat		13836
Estate Wagon, 3-seat		13846
Malibu		
2-Dr Sport Coupe	13537	13637
2-Dr Convertible		13667
4-Dr Sedan	13569	13669
4-Dr Sport Sedan		13639

*SS option available
*Heavy Chevy option available

MONTE CARLO

	6-CYL CODE	V-8 CODE
2-Dr Coupe		13857

*Custom option available

NOVA

	6-CYL CODE	V-8 CODE
2-Dr Sport Coupe	11327	11427
4-Dr Sedan	11369	11469

*SS option available
*Rally option available

CAMARO

	6-CYL CODE	V-8 CODE
2-Dr Sport Coupe	12387	12487

*SS option available
*RS (Rally Sport) option available
*Z-28 option available

CORVETTE

	V-8 CODE
2-Dr Sport Coupe	19437
2-Dr Convertible	19467

VEGA

	4-CYL CODE
2-Dr Sedan	14111
2-Dr Hatchback Coupe	14177
2-Dr Kammback Sta Wgn	14115

*GT option available
*GT option available

CHEVROLET

	6-CYL CODE	V-8 CODE
Brookwood Wagon		
2-Seat		15435
Biscayne		
4-Dr Sedan	15369	15469
Bel Air		
4-Dr Sedan	15569	15669
Townsman		
Station Wagon, 2-seat		15635
Station Wagon, 3-seat		15645
Kingswood		
Station Wagon, 2-seat		16435
Station Wagon, 3-seat		16445
Kingswood Estate		
Station Wagon 2-seat		16635
Station Wagon 3-seat		16645

Impala	6 CYL CODE	V-8 CODE
2-Dr Sport Coupe	16357	16457
2-Dr Convertible		16467
4-Dr Sedan	16369	16469
4-Dr Sport Sedan		16439
Impala Custom		16447
Caprice		
2-Dr Sport Coupe		16647
4-Dr Sport Sedan		16639

THE TRIM NUMBER furnishes the key to trim color and material for each model series.

CHEVELLE & MALIBU TRIM

Color	Cloth	Vinyl	Leather	Code
Black		•		701
Black	•			702
Black	•			703
Black		•		704
Black**		•		704
Blue	•			724
Blue	•			723
Covert	•			730
Covert		•		732
Covert**		•		732
Green		•		710
Green	•			711
Green		•		713
Green**		•		713
Tan		•		719
Tan		•		720
Tan**		•		720
White		•		743
White**		•		743

* Conventional seat with custom interior
** Strato-bucket seats with custom interior

CHEVELLE WAGON TRIM

Color	Cloth	Vinyl	Leather	Code
Black		•		701
Black		•		704
Black		•		705
Green		•		710
Green		•		713
Tan		•		719
Tan		•		720
Tan		•		721

MONTE CARLO TRIM

Color	Cloth	Vinyl	Leather	Code
Black	•			706
Black**	•			706
Black		•		708
Black**		•		708
Blue	•			725
Covert	•			731
Covert		•		734
Green	•			715
Green**		•		717
Pewter	•			740
Pewter**	•			740
Saddle		•		735
Saddle**		•		735

* Conventional seat with custom interior
** Strato-bucket seats with custom interior

NOVA TRIM

Color	Cloth	Vinyl	Leather	Code
Black	•			750
Black		•		751
Black**		•		751
Black*	•			752
Black*		•		753
Black**		•		753
Blue	•			756
Covert	•			765
Covert		•		763
Covert*		•		764
Green	•			759
Green		•		760
Green*	•			761
Tan**		•		766
White**		•		767

* Conventional seat with custom interior
** Strato-bucket seats with custom interior

CAMARO TRIM

Color	Cloth	Vinyl	Leather	Code
Black		•		775
Black**	•			785
Blue		•		776
Blue**	•			786
Covert		•		779
Covert**	•			788
Green		•		777
Green**	•			787
Tan		•		778
White		•		780

* Conventional seat with custom interior
** Strato-bucket seats with custom interior

CORVETTE TRIM

Color	Cloth	Vinyl	Leather	Code
Black**		•		400
Black**			•	404
Blue**		•		412
Red**		•		407
Saddle**		•		407
Saddle**			•	421

* Conventional seat with custom interior
** Strato-bucket seats with custom interior

VEGA TRIM

Color	Cloth	Vinyl	Leather	Code
Black*		•		860
Black**	•			862
Black**		•		861
Covert*		•		868
Covert**	•			869
Covert**		•		874
Green*		•		863
Tan*		•		866
Tan**		•		867

* Bucket seats with standard interior
** Bucket seats with custom interior

CHEVROLET TRIM

Color	Cloth	Vinyl	Nylon	Code
Black	•			803
Black	•			805
Black	•			807
Black			•	838
Black		•		802

CHEVROLET

Color	Cloth	Vinyl	Nylon	Code
Black		•		804
Black		•		806
Blue	•			810
Blue	•			812
Blue	•			814
Blue		•		809
Blue		•		811
Blue		•		813
Covert	•			815
Covert	•			819
Covert		•		816
Covert		•		817
Covert		•		818
Green	•			828
Green	•			829
Green	•			831
Green			•	833
Green		•		830
Pewter	•			834
Pewter	•			836
Pewter		•		835
Saddle		•		826

CHEVROLET WAGON TRIM

Color	Cloth	Vinyl	Leather	Code
Black	•			808
Black		•		802
Black		•		804
Black		•		806
Blue		•		809
Blue		•		811
Blue		•		813
Covert		•		818
Green		•		830
Saddle		•		824
Saddle		•		825
Saddle		•		826

THE PAINT CODE furnishes the key to the paint colors used on the car.

COLOR	CODE
Classic White*	10
Antique White	11
Pewter Silver*	14
Dusk Gray	18
Tuxedo Black	19
Ascot Blue	24
Mediterranean Blue	25
Mulsanne Blue	26
Targa Blue*	27
Fathom Blue	28
Spring Green	36
Bryar Blue*	37
Gulf Green	43
Oasis Green	46
Elkhart Green *	47
Sequoia Green	48
Covert Tan	50
Sunflower Yellow*	52
Placer Gold	53
Desert Gold	54
Cream Yellow	56
Golden Brown	57
Turin Tan	58
Driftwoood	62
Mohave Gold	63

COLOR	CODE
Orange Flame	65
Midnight Bronze	68
Aegean Brown	69
Cranberry Red	75
Mille Miglia Red*	76
War Bonnet Yellow*	91
Ontario Orange*	97
Steel Cities Gray*	98

* Corvette only available with one of these colors

TWO-TONE COMBINATIONS

LOWER COLOR	CODE	UPPER COLOR	CODE
Ascot Blue	24	Antique White	11
Fathom Blue	28	Antique White	11
Golden Brown	57	Antique White	11
Desert Gold	54	Antique White	11
Gulf Green	43	Antique White	11
Sequoia Green	48	Antique White	11
Mulsanne Blue	26	Antique White	11
Mohave Gold	63	Antique White	11

VINYL ROOF CODES

COLOR	CODE
Black	BB
Blue	DD
Covert	TT
Green	GG
White	AA
Tan	TT

CONVERTIBLE TOP COLORS: Choice of white or black convertible top available with all exterior colors.

ENGINE NUMBER

THE ENGINE IDENTIFICATION NUMBER includes a letter code for the engine plant, followed by numbers which date the manufacture of the engine, then followed by a letter code to indicate the engine size and makeup.

THE ENGINE IDENTIFICATION NUMBER for V-8s is stamped on a pad located at the right hand side of the cylinder block, and stamped on a pad on the right hand side of the block behind the distributor on 4-cylinder and 6-cylinder engines.

NOTE:

1. To properly identify Chevrolet Division engines, it will be necessary to identify the car model in which the engine is used. The same engine type may have a different code when used in different car models.

2. The 396 engine is actually 402 CID.

EXAMPLE

1	01	01	CCM
PLANT	MONTH	DAY	CODE

CHEVELLE ENGINES

Engine Code	No Cyl.	CID	Horse-power	Comp. Ratio	Carb	Trans
CDM	6	250	110	8.5:1	1 BC	K-19
CDL	6	250	110	8.5:1	1 BC	K-19 & Auto
CBJ	6	250	110	8.5:1	1 BC	PG
CBG	6	250	110	8.5:1	1 BC	Manual
CSD	6	250	110	8.5:1	1 BC	PG w/NB2
CBA	6	250	110	8.5:1	1 BC	Manual w/NB2
CBK	6	250	110	8.5:1	1 BC	PG
CBD	6	250	110	8.5:1	1 BC	Manual w/NB2

Engine Code	No Cyl.	CID	Horse-power	Comp. Ratio	Carb	Trans
CAH	6	250	110	8.5:1	1 BC	
CKG	8	307	130	8.5:1	2 BC	Manual
CKH	8	307	130	8.5:1	2 BC	PG
CAY	8	307	130	8.5:1	2 BC	Manual w/NB2
CAZ	8	307	130	8.5:1	2 BC	PG w/NB2
CTK	8	307	130	8.5:1	2 BC	TH
CMA	8	307	130	8.5:1	2 BC	TH w/NB2
CKK	8	350	175	8.5:1	4 BC	Manual
CKA	8	350	165	8.5:1	2 BC	Manual
CTL	8	350	165	8.5:1	2 BC	TH
CKD	8	350	175	8.5:1	4 BC	TH
CSH	8	350	165	8.5:1	2 BC	TH
CDA	8	350	165	8.5:1	2 BC	Manual w/NB2
CDG	8	350	175	8.5:1	4 BC	Manual w/NB2
CMD	8	350	165	8.5:1	2 BC	TH w/NB2
CDD	8	350	175	8.5:1	4 BC	TH w/NB2
CAR	8	350	165	8.5:1	2 BC	PG
CDB	8	350	165	8.5:1	2 BC	PGw/NB2
CKB	8	350	175	8.5:1	4 BC	Manual
CLA	8	396	240	8.5:1	4 BC	Manual
CLB	8	396	240	8.5:1	4 BC	TH
CTA	8	396	240	8.5:1	4 BC	Manual w/AIR
CTB	8	396	240	8.5:1	4 BC	TH w/AIR
CLS	8	400	240	8.5:1	4 BC	Manual
CTJ	8	400	240	8.5:1	4 BC	TH w/AIR
CTH	8	400	240	8.5:1	4 BC	HD 3-spd
CPA	8	454	270	8.5:1	4 BC	Manual
CPD	8	454	270	8.5:1	4 BC	TH
CRX	8	454	270	8.5:1	4 BC	Manual w/AIR
CRW	8	454	270	8.5:1	4 BC	TH w/AIR

NOTES: 1. Horsepower figures given for 1972 are NET.
　　　　2. AIR means Air Injection Reactor system.

MONTE CARLO ENGINES

Engine Code	No Cyl.	CID	Horse-power	Comp. Ratio	Carb	Trans
CKA	8	350	165	8.5:1	2 BC	Manual
CTL	8	350	165	8.5:1	2 BC	TH
CKD	8	350	175	8.5:1	4 BC	TH
CDA	8	350	165	8.5:1	2 BC	Manual w/NB2
CMD	8	350	165	8.5:1	2 BC	TH w/NB2
CDD	8	350	175	8.5:1	4 BC	TH w/NB2
CKB	8	350	165	8.5:1	2 BC	PG
CDB	8	350	165	8.5:1	2 BX	PG
CLB	8	396	240	8.5:1	4 BC	TH
CTJ	8	396	240	8.5:1	4 BC	HD 3-spd
CTB	8	396	240	8.5:1	4 BC	K-19 Auto
CPD	8	454	270	8.5:1	4 BC	TH
CRX	8	454	270	8.5:1	4 BC	Manual w/AIR
CRW	8	454	270	8.5:1	4 BC	K-19 Auto

NOTES: 1. Horsepower figures given for 1972 are NET.
　　　　2. AIR means Air Injection Reactor system.

NOVA ENGINES

Engine Code	No Cyl.	CID	Horse-power	Comp. Ratio	Carb	Trans
CBG	6	250	110	8.5:1	1 BC	Manual
CBJ	6	250	110	8.5:1	1 BC	PG
CAL	6	250	110	8.5:1	1 BC	Manual
CBK	6	250	110	8.5:1	1 BC	PG
CDM	6	250	110	8.5:1	1 BC	Manual w/AIR
CDL	6	250	110	8.5:1	1 BC	PG w/AIR
CBA	6	250	110	8.5:1	1 BC	Manual w/NB2
CSD	6	250	110	8.5:1	1 BC	PG w/NB2

Engine Code	No Cyl.	CID	Horse-power	Comp. Ratio	Carb	Trans
CAH	6	250	110	8.5:1	1 BC	
CKG	8	307	130	8.5:1	2 BC	Manual
CKH	8	307	130	8.5:1	2 BC	PG
CTK	8	307	130	8.5:1	2 BC	TH
CAY	8	307	130	8.5:1	2 BC	Manual w/NB2
CAZ	8	307	130	8.5:1	2 BC	PG w/NB2
CMA	8	307	130	8.5:1	2 BC	TH w/NB2
CKA	8	350	165	8.5:1	2 BC	Manual
CTL	8	350	165	8.5:1	2 BC	TH
CKK	8	350	200	8.5:1	4 BC	Manual
CKD	8	350	200	8.5:1	4 BC	TH
CRL	8	350	200	8.5:1	4 BC	Manual w/AIR
CRK	8	350	200	8.5:1	4 BC	TH w/AIR
CDA	8	350	165	8.5:1	2 BC	Manual w/NB2
CMD	8	350	165	8.5:1	2 BC	TH w/NB2
CDG	8	350	200	8.5:1	4 BC	Manual w/NB2
CDD	8	350	200	8.5:1	4 BC	TH w/NB2

NOTES: 1. Horsepower figures given for 1972 are NET.
2. AIR means Air Injection Reactor system.

CAMARO ENGINES

Engine Code	No Cyl.	CID	Horse-power	Comp. Ratio	Carb	Trans
CBG	6	250	110	8.5:1	1 BC	Manual
CBJ	6	250	110	8.5:1	1 BC	PG
CDM	6	250	110	8.5:1	1 BC	Manual w/AIR
CDL	6	250	110	8.5:1	1 BC	PG w/AIR
CBA	6	250	110	8.5:1	1 BC	Manual w/NB2
CSD	6	250	110	8.5:1	1 BC	PG w/NB2
CKG	8	307	130	8.5:1	2 BC	Manual
CKH	8	307	130	8.5:1	2 BC	PG
CTK	8	307	130	8.5:1	2 BC	TH
CAY	8	307	130	8.5:1	2 BC	Manual w/NB2
CAZ	8	307	130	8.5:1	2 BC	PG w/NB2
CAZ	8	307	130	8.5:1	2 BC	TH w/NB2
CMA	8	307	130	8.5:1	2 BC	TH w/NB2
CKA	8	350	165	8.5:1	2 BC	Manual
CTL	8	350	165	8.5:1	2 BC	TH
CRG	8	350	165	8.5:1	2 BC	Manual w/AIR
CRD	8	350	165	8.5:1	2 BC	TH w/AIR
CKK	8	350	200	8.5:1	4 BC	Manual
CKD	8	350	200	8.5:1	4 BC	TH
CMH	8	350	165	8.5:1	2 BC	Manual w/NB2
CMB	8	350	165	8.5:1	2 BC	TH w/NB2
CDG	8	350	200	8.5:1	4 BC	Manual w/NB2
CDD	8	350	200	8.5:1	4 BC	TH w/NB2
CKS	8	350	255	9.0:1	4 BC	Manual
CKT	8	350	255	9.0:1	4 BC	TH
CLA	8	396	240	8.5:1	4 BC	Manual
CLB	8	396	240	8.5:1	4 BC	TH
CTA	8	396	240	8.5:1	4 BC	Manual w/AIR
CTB	8	396	240	8.5:1	4 BC	TH w/AIR

NOTES: 1. Horsepower figures given for 1972 are NET.
2. AIR means Air Injection Reactor system.

CORVETTE ENGINES

Engine Code	No Cyl.	CID	Horsepower	Comp. Ratio	Carb	Trans
CRS	8	350	200	8.5:1	4 BC	K-19 Auto
CKW	8	350	200	8.5:1	4 BC	4-spd
CDH	8	350	200	8.5:1	4 BC	NB2 4-spd
CKX	8	350	200	8.5:1	4 BC	THM*
CDJ	8	350	200	8.5:1	4 BC	NB2 THM*
CKY	8	350	255	9.0:1	4 BC	4-spd
CRT	8	350	255	9.0:1	4 BC	4-spd w/AIR
CKZ	8	350	255	9.0:1	4 BC	HD 4-spd
CPH	8	454	270	8.5:1	4 BC	4-spd
CPJ	8	454	270	8.5:1	4 BC	THM*
CSR	8	454	270	8.5:1	4 BC	4-spd w/AIR
CSS	8	454	270	8.5:1	4 BC	THM* w/AIR

* Turbo Hydra-Matic Transmission

NOTE: NB2 equipment was required on California bound 1972 Corvettes and consisted of an Air Injection Reactor (AIR) system and different camshaft with longer valve overlap. Horsepower figures given for 1972 are NET.

VEGA ENGINES

Engine Code	No Cyl.	CID	Horsepower	Comp. Ratio	Carb	Trans
CND	4	140	80	8.0:1	1 BC	Auto
CNA	4	140	80	8.0:1	1 BC	Manual
CGD	4	140	80	8.0:1	1 BC	Auto
CGB	4	140	80	8.0:1	1 BC	Manual
CSK	4	140	90	8.0:1	2 BC	Auto
CNB	4	140	90	8.0:1	2 BC	Manual
CBM	4	140	90	8.0:1	2 BC	Auto

CHEVROLET ENGINES

Engine Code	No Cyl.	CID	Horsepower	Comp. Ratio	Carb	Trans
CNJ	6	250	110	8.5:1	1 BC	Manual
CBJ	6	250	110	8.5:1	1 BC	PG
CBH	6	250	110	8.5:1	1 BC	Manual
CBK	6	250	110	8.5:1	1 BC	PG
CDL	6	250	110	8.5:1	1 BC	PG w/AIR
CAH	6	250	110	8.5:1	1 BC	
CBL	8	350	165	8.5:1	2 BC	
CSJ	8	350	165	8.5:1	4 BC	Manual
CKB	8	350	165	8.5:1	2 BC	TH
CAR	8	350	165	8.5:1	2 BC	TH w/NB2
CSH	8	350	165	8.5:1	2 BC	TH
CDB	8	350	165	8.5:1	2 BC	TH w/NB2
CLB	8	396	210	8.5:1	4 BC	Manual
CKP	8	400	170	8.5:1	2 BC	TH
CLR	8	396	210	8.5:1	4 BC	Manual
CAT	8	400	170	8.5:1	2 BC	TH w/NB2
CTB	8	396	210	8.5:1	4 BC	Manual w/AIR
CTJ	8	396	210	8.5:1	4 BC	Manual w/AIR
CDL	8	400	170	8.5:1	2 BC	TH
CDM	8	400	170	8.5:1	2 BC	TH w/NB2
CPD	8	454	270	8.5:1	4 BC	TH
CPG	8	454	270	8.5:1	4 BC	TH
CRW	8	454	270	8.5:1	4 BC	TH w/AIR
CRY	8	454	270	8.5:1	4 BC	TH w/AIR

NOTES: 1. Horsepower figures given for 1972 are NET.
2. AIR means Air Injection Reactor system.
3. Chevrolet Station Wagons 454 - 230 HP

1973 CHEVROLET CAPRICE

1973 CHEVROLET CAPRICE ESTATE WAGON

1973 CHEVROLET CAMARO

1973 CHEVROLET CORVETTE STINGRAY

1973 CHEVROLET HATCHBACK NOVA

1973 CHEVROLET VEGA

1973 CHEVROLET CHEVELLE LAGUNA

1973 CHEVROLET MONTE CARLO

VEHICLE IDENTIFICATION NUMBER

CHEVROLET
1L57H3S123456

On top left side of instrument panel, visible through the windshield.

Corvette VIN on left windshield pillar, visible through the windshield.

FIRST DIGIT: Indicates GM division (1 is Chevrolet)

SECOND DIGIT: Indicates series

CODE	SERIES
C	Chevelle Deluxe & El Camino
D	Chevelle Malibu & El Camino Custom
E	Chevelle Laguna
G	Chevelle Malibu Estate
H	Chevelle Monte Carlo & Laguna Estate
K	Bel Air
L	Impala
N	Caprice
Q	Camaro
S	Camaro LT
V	Vega
X	Nova
Y	Nova Custom
Z	Corvette

THIRD & FOURTH DIGITS: Indicate body style

CODE	STYLE
39	Sport Sedan (Chevrolet)
47	Coupe (Chevrolet)
57	Sport Coupe (Chevrolet/Monte Carlo)
57/Z03	Landau Coupe (Monte Carlo)
57/Z76	S Coupe (Monte Carlo)
67	Convertible (Chevrolet/Corvette)
69	4-Dr. Sedan (Chevrolet/Nova)
29	4-Dr. Sedan (Chevelle)
37	Sport Coupe (Chevelle/Corvette)
35	2-Seat Wagon (Chevrolet/Chevelle)
35/AQ4	3-Seat Wagon (Chevelle)
45	3-Seat Wagon (Chevrolet)
87	Sport Coupe (Camaro)
17	Hatchback Coupe (Nova)
27	Coupe (Nova)
05	Panel Express (Vega)
11	Panel Express (Vega)
15	Kammback Wagon (Vega)
77	Hatchback Coupe (Vega)

FIFTH DIGIT: Indicates engine

CODE	CID	TYPE	CARB
A	140	L-4	1 BC
B	140	L-4	2 BC
D	250	L-6	1 BC
F	307	V8	2 BC
H	350	V8	2 BC
K	350	V8	4 BC
R	400	V8	2 BC
T	350	V8	4 BC (Z-28 or L-82)
X	454	V8	4 BC (L54)
Y	454	V8	4 BC (L54)

SIXTH DIGIT: Indicates the year (3 is 1973)

SEVENTH DIGIT: Indicates the assembly plant

ASSEMBLY PLANT	CODE
Lakewood	A
Baltimore	B
Southgate	C
Doraville	D

ASSEMBLY PLANT	CODE
Flint	F
Janesville	J
Leeds	K
Van Nuys	L
Norwood	N
Arlington	R
St. Louis	S
Tarrytown	T
Lordstown	U
Pontiac	V
Willow Run	W
Wilmington	Y
Fremont	Z
Oshawa, Canada	1
St. Therese, Canada	2

REMAINING SIX DIGITS: Indicate production sequence number

EXAMPLE

1	L	57	H	3	S	123456
Chev Div.	Series	Body Style	Engine	Year	Asm Plant	Prod Code

BODY NUMBER PLATE

Located on right or left side of firewall below rear edge of hood of all models, except Corvette. Corvette plate is located on upper left hand door hinge pillar.

THE BODY NUMBER PLATE identifies the model year, car division, series, style, body assembly plant, body number, trim combination, paint code and date build code.

BODY BY FISHER
ST 73 1FQ87 N　　　　123456 BDY
TR 775　　　　　　　　　19 PNT
●11A　　　　　　　　　　　　　　●

GENERAL MOTORS CORPORATION CERTIFIES TO THE DEALER THAT THIS VEHICLE CONFORMS TO ALL U.S., FEDERAL MOTOR VEHICLE SAFETY STANDARDS APPLICABLE AT TIME OF MANUFACTURE.

EXAMPLE

In the example above,

73	Model year (1973)
1	Car division (Chevrolet)
FQ	Series (Camaro V-8)
87	Style (2-Dr Sport Coupe)
N	Body assembly plant (Norwood, Ohio)
123456	Production sequence in that plant
775	Black vinyl trim
19	Tuxedo Black paint
11	Eleventh month (November)
A	First week of month

NOTE: An option code will appear below the paint code. It is a notation to the assembly line workers that this vehicle is not a standard issue item. An example would be a radio delete, heater delete, etc. WE DO NOT HAVE BREAKDOWNS FOR THOSE CODES.

CHEVELLE	MODEL CODES
Deluxe	
Sport Sedan 4-Dr	1AC29
Sport Coupe 2-Dr	1AC37
Station Wagon 4-Dr*	1AC35
Malibu	
Sport Sedan 4-Dr	1AD29
Sport Coupe 2-Dr	1AD37
Station Wagon 4-Dr	1AD35
*SS option available	
Malibu Estate	
Station Wagon 4-Dr*	1AG35
Laguna	
Sport Sedan 4-Dr	1AE29
Sport Coupe 2-Dr	1AE37
Station Wagon 4-Dr*	1AE35
Laguna Estate	
Station Wagon 4-Dr*	1AH35

* Third seat available as RPO (Regular Production Option/Order) on V-8 equipped station wagons.

MONTE CARLO	MODEL CODES
Sport Coupe 2-Dr	1AH57
*S option available	
*Landau option available	

NOVA	MODEL CODES
Sedan 4-Dr	1XX69
Coupe 2-Dr	1XX27
Hatchback Coupe 2-Dr	1XX17
*SS option available	
Nova Custom	
Sedan 4-Dr	1XY69
Coupe 2-Dr	1XY27
Hatchback Coupe 2-Dr	1XY17

CAMARO	MODEL CODES
Sport Coupe 2-Dr	1FQ87
Camaro Type LT	1FS87
*Z-28 option available	

CORVETTE	MODEL CODES
Sport Coupe 2-Dr	1YZ37
Convertible 2-Dr	1YZ67

CHEVROLET	MODEL CODES
Bel Air	
Sedan 4-Dr	1BK69
Station Wagon 2-seat	1BK35
Station Wagon 3-seat	1BK45
Impala	
Sedan 4-Dr	1BL69
Sport Sedan 4-Dr	1BL39
Sport Coupe 2-Dr	1BL57
Custom Coupe 2-Dr	1BL47
Station Wagon 2-seat	1BL35
Station Wagon 3-seat	1BL45
Caprice Classic	
Sedan 4-Dr	1BN69
Sport Coupe 2-Dr	1BN47
Convertible 2-Dr	1BN67
Sport Sedan 4-Dr	1BN39

CHEVROLET	MODEL CODES
Caprice Estate	
Station Wagon 2-seat	1BN35
Station Wagon 3-seat	1BN45

VEGA	MODEL CODES
Sedan 2-Dr	1HV11
Hatchback Coupe 2-Dr	1HV77
Kammback Stn. Wagon 2-Dr	1HV15
*GT option available	

THE TRIM NUMBER furnishes the key to trim color and material for each model series.

CHEVELLE TRIM

Color	Cloth	Vinyl	Leather	Code
Black	•			702
Black	•			703
Black	•			712
Black		•		701
Black		•		704
Black		•		707
Blue	•			723
Blue	•			724
Blue	•			732
Blue		•		705
Blue		•		719
Chamo	•			716
Chamo		•		721
Green	•			711
Green	•			726
Green	•			730
Green		•		727
Green		•		713
Green		•		710
Neutral		•		734
Neutral		•		732
Neutral		•		733
Red	•			714
Red		•		709
Saddle		•		717
Saddle		•		720

CHEVELLE WAGON TRIM

Color	Cloth	Vinyl	Leather	Code
Black		•		806
Black		•		707
Black		•		704
Black		•		701
Blue		•		813
Blue		•		719
Blue		•		705
Green		•		830
Green		•		727
Green		•		713
Neutral		•		818
Neutral		•		817
Neutral		•		734
Neutral		•		732
Red		•		709
Saddle		•		826
Saddle		•		825
Saddle		•		720
Saddle		•		722

MONTE CARLO TRIM

Color	Cloth	Vinyl	Leather	Code
Black	•			706
Black		•		708
Blue	•			725
Green	•			715
Green		•		728
Neutral	•			731
Neutral		•		735
Red	•			740

NOVA TRIM

Color	Cloth	Vinyl	Leather	Code
Black	•			752
Black	•			750
Black	•			755
Black		•		754
Black		•		751
Black		•		753
Blue	•			756
Blue	•			772
Chamois		•		767
Green	•			761
Green	•			770
Green	•			759
Green	•			758
Green		•		760
Green		•		757
Neutral	•			764
Neutral	•			769
Neutral		•		771
Neutral		•		763

CAMARO TRIM

Color	Cloth	Vinyl	Leather	Code
Black	•			785
Black	•			776
Black	•			786
Black	•			774
Black		•		773
Black		•		775
Chamois		•		780
Green	•			781
Green		•		777
Neutral		•		788
Neutral		•		779
Saddle		•		778

CORVETTE TRIM

Color	Cloth	Vinyl	Leather	Code
Black		•		400
Black			•	404
Blue		•		413
Red		•		425
Saddle		•		418
Saddle			•	422
Saddle		•		415
Saddle			•	416

VEGA TRIM

Color	Cloth	Vinyl	Leather	Code
Black		•		860
Black		•		861
Black	•			871
Blue	•			872
Chamois		•		859
Chamois		•		876
Green		•		863
Green		•		864
Neutral		•		868
Neutral		•		874
Red		•		858
Red		•		875
Saddle		•		866
Saddle		•		867

CHEVROLET TRIM

Color	Cloth	Vinyl	Leather	Code
Black	•			805
Black	•			803
Black	•			802
Black	•			840
Black		•		806
Black		•		804
Blue	•			810
Blue	•			843
Blue	•			812
Blue		•		813
Green	•			829
Green	•			828
Green	•			842
Green		•		830
Green		•		827
Neutral	•			841
Neutral	•			815
Neutral		•		818
Red	•			836
White		•		816

CHEVROLET WAGON TRIM

Color	Cloth	Vinyl	Leather	Code
Black		•		806
Black		•		707
Black		•		704
Black		•		701
Blue		•		813
Blue		•		719
Blue		•		705
Green		•		830
Green		•		727
Green		•		713
Neutral		•		818
Neutral		•		817
Neutral		•		734
Neutral		•		732
Red		•		709
Saddle		•		826
Saddle		•		825
Saddle		•		720
Saddle		•		722

THE PAINT CODE furnishes the key to the paint colors used on the car.

COLOR	CODE
Classic White*	10
Antique White	11
Silver Metallic*	14
Tuxedo Black	19
Medium Blue Metallic*	22
Medium Blue	23
Light Blue Metallic	24
Dark Blue Metallic	26
Dark Blue Metallic*	27
Midnight Blue Metallic	29
Oasis Green	41
Dark Green Metallic	42
Light Green Metallic	44
Blue-Green Metallic*	45
Green-Gold Metallic	46
Elkhart Green Metallic*	47
Midnight Green	48
Light Yellow	51
Yellow*	52
Yellow Metallic*	53
Chamois	56
Light Copper Metallic	60
Light Orange	61
Medium Bronze Metallic	62
Silver Metallic	64
Taupe Metallic	66
Dark Brown Metallic	68
Dark Red Metallic	74
Medium Red	75

COLOR	CODE
Mille Miglia Red*	76
Orange Metallic*	80
Beige	81
Medium Orange Metallic	97

* Corvette only available with one of these colors

TWO-TONE COMBINATIONS

LOWER COLOR	CODE	UPPER COLOR	CODE
Light Blue	24	Antique White	11
Midnight Blue	29	Antique White	11
Chamois	56	Antique White	11
Green-Gold	46	Antique White	11
Light Green	44	Antique White	11
Midnight Green	48	Antique White	11

VINYL ROOF CODES

COLOR	CODE
Black	BB
Medium Blue	DD
Chamois	FF
Dark Red	HH
Light Neutral	TT
Medium Green	GG
White	AA

CONVERTIBLE TOP COLORS: Choice of white or black top available with all exterior colors.

ENGINE NUMBER

THE ENGINE IDENTIFICATION NUMBER includes a letter code for the engine plant, followed by numbers which date the manufacture of the engine, then followed by a letter code to indicate the engine size and makeup.

THE ENGINE IDENTIFICATION NUMBER for V-8s is stamped on a pad located at the right-hand side of the cylinder block, and stamped on a pad on the right-hand side of the block behind the distributor on 4-cylinder and 6-cylinder engines.

NOTE:

1. To properly identify Chevrolet Division engines, it will be necessary to identify the car model in which the engine is used. The same engine type may have a different code when used in different car models.

2. NB2 is California emission

EXAMPLE

1	01	01	CCM
PLANT	MONTH	DAY	CODE

CHEVELLE ENGINES

Engine Code	No Cyl.	CID	Horse-power	Comp. Ratio	Carb	Trans
CCK	6	250	100	8.25:1	1 BC	Export
CBD	6	250	100	8.25:1	1 BC	Taxi
CCA	6	250	100	8.25:1	1 BC	TH
CCB	6	250	100	8.25:1	1 BC	TH w/NB2
CCC	6	250	100	8.25:1	1 BC	Manual
CCD	6	250	100	8.25:1	1 BC	Manual w/NB2
CHD	8	307	115	8.5:1	2 BC	Manual w/NB2
CHA	8	307	115	8.5:1	2 BC	TH
CHB	8	307	115	8.5:1	2 BC	Manual
CHC	8	307	115	8.5:1	2 BC	TH w/NB2
CMA	8	307	115	8.5:1	2 BC	TH
CKM	8	350	175	8.5:1	4 BC	Police
CKR	8	350	175	8.5:1	4 BC	Police w/NB2
CKA	8	350	145	8.5:1	2 BC	Manual

CHEVELLE ENGINES

Engine Code	No Cyl.	CID	Horsepower	Comp. Ratio	Carb	Trans
CKL	8	350	145	8.5:1	2 BC	TH
CKB	8	350	145	8.5:1	2 BC	Manual 4-spd
CKC	8	350	145	8.5:1	2 BC	Manual w/NB2
CKK	8	350	145	8.5:1	2 BC	TH w/NB2
CKH	8	350	175	8.5:1	4 BC	Mnl 4-spd w/NB2
CKD	8	350	175	8.5:1	4 BC	TH w/NB2
CKJ	8	350	175	8.5:1	4 BC	TH
CWC	8	454	245	8.5:1	4 BC	Mnl 4-spd w/NB2
CWD	8	454	245	8.5:1	4 BC	TH w/NB2
CWR	8	454	245	8.5:1	4 BC	Manual
CWA	8	454	245	8.5:1	4 BC	Manual 4-spd
CWB	8	454	245	8.5:1	4 BC	TH

MONTE CARLO ENGINES

Engine Code	No Cyl.	CID	Horsepower	Comp. Ratio	Carb	Trans
CKA	8	350	145	8.5:1	2 BC	Manual
CKL	8	350	145	8.5:1	2 BC	TH
CKB	8	350	145	8.5:1	2 BC	Manual 4-spd
CKC	8	350	145	8.5:1	2 BC	Manual w/NB2
CKK	8	350	145	8.5:1	2 BC	TH w/NB2
CKH	8	350	175	8.5:1	4 BC	Mnl 4-spd w/NB2
CKD	8	350	175	8.5:1	4 BC	TH w/NB2
CKJ	8	350	175	8.5:1	4 BC	TH
CWC	8	454	245	8.5:1	4 BC	Mnl 4-spd w/NB2
CWD	8	454	245	8.5:1	4 BC	TH w/NB2
CWA	8	454	245	8.5:1	4 BC	Manual 4-spd
CWB	8	454	245	8.5:1	4 BC	TH

NOVA ENGINES

Engine Code	No Cyl.	CID	Horsepower	Comp. Ratio	Carb	Trans
CCA	6	250	100	8.25:1	1 BC	PG
CCB	6	250	100	8.25:1	1 BC	PG w/NB2
CCC	6	250	100	8.25:1	1 BC	Manual
CCD	6	250	100	8.25:1	1 BC	Manual w/NB2
CHB	8	307	115	8.5:1	2 BC	Manual
CHH	8	307	115	8.5:1	2 BC	TH
CHC	8	307	115	8.5:1	2 BC	TH w/NB2
CHD	8	307	115	8.5:1	2 BC	Manual w/NB2
CKA	8	350	145	8.5:1	2 BC	Manual
CKU	8	350	175	8.5:1	4 BC	TH
CKB	8	350	175	8.5:1	4 BC	Manual
CKW	8	350	145	8.5:1	2 BC	TH
CKC	8	350	145	8.5:1	2 BC	Manual w/NB2
CKK	8	350	145	8.5:1	2 BC	TH w/NB2
CKD	8	350	175	8.5:1	4 BC	TH w/NB2
CKH	8	350	175	8.5:1	4 BC	Manual w/NB2
CKV	8	350	175	8.5:1	4 BC	TH

CAMARO ENGINES

Engine Code	No Cyl.	CID	Horsepower	Comp. Ratio	Carb	Manual
CCA	6	250	100	8.25:1	1 BC	TH
CCB	6	250	100	8.25:1	1 BC	TH w/NB2
CCC	6	250	100	8.25:1	1 BC	Manual
CCD	6	250	100	8.25:1	1 BC	Manual w/NB2
CHB	8	307	115	8.5:1	2 BC	Manual
CHH	8	307	115	8.5:1	2 BC	TH
CHJ	8	307	115	8.5:1	2 BC	Manual w/NB2
CHK	8	307	115	8.5:1	2 BC	TH w/NB2
CLJ	8	350	245	9.0:1	4 BC	Manual 4-spd
CLK	8	350	245	9.0:1	4 BC	TH 400
CKA	8	350	145	8.5:1	2 BC	Manual 4-spd
CKU	8	350	175	8.5:1	4 BC	TH
CKB	8	350	175	8.5:1	4 BC	Manual
CKW	8	350	145	8.5:1	2 BC	TH
CLL	8	350	245	9.0:1	4 BC	TH 400 w/NB2
CLM	8	350	245	9.0:1	4 BC	Mnl 4-spd w/NB2
CKX	8	350	145	8.5:1	2 BC	TH w/NB2
CKY	8	350	145	8.5:1	2 BC	Mnl 4-spd w/NB2
CKD	8	350	175	8.5:1	4 BC	TH w/NB2
CKH	8	350	175	8.5:1	4 BC	Mnl 4-spd 2/NB2

CORVETTE ENGINES

Engine Code	No Cyl.	CID	Horsepower	Comp. Ratio	Carb	Trans
CKZ	8	350	190	8.5:1	4 BC	Manual
CLB	8	350	190	8.5:1	4 BC	Manual w/NB2
CLA	8	350	190	8.5:1	4 BC	TH
CLC	8	350	190	8.5:1	4 BC	TH w/NB2
CLR	8	350	250	9.0:1	4 BC	Manual
CLS	8	350	250	9.0:1	4 BC	Manual w/NB2
CLD	8	350	250	9.0:1	4 BC	TH
CLH	8	350	250	9.0:1	4 BC	TH w/NB2
CWS	8	454	275	8.5:1	4 BC	TH w/NB2
CWT	8	454	275	8.5:1	4 BC	Manual w/NB2
CWM	8	454	275	8.5:1	4 BC	Manual
CWR	8	454	275	8.5:1	4 BC	TH

VEGA ENGINES

Engine Code	No Cyl.	CID	Horsepower	Comp. Ratio	Carb	Trans
CAA	4	140	72	8.0:1	1 BC	Manual
CAB	4	140	72	8.0:1	1 BC	PG TH350
CAH	4	140	72	8.0:1	1 BC	PG TH350 w/NB2
CAJ	4	140	72	8.0:1	1 BC	Manual w/NB2
CAC	4	140	85	8.0:1	2 BC	PG TH350
CAD	4	140	85	8.0:1	2 BC	Manual
CAK	4	140	85	8.0:1	2 BC	PG TH350 w/NB2
CAL	4	140	85	8.0:1	2 BC	Manual w/NB2

CHEVROLET ENGINES

Engine Code	No Cyl.	CID	Horsepower	Comp. Ratio	Carb	Trans
CCK	8	250	100	8.25:1	1 BC	Export
CCL	6	250	100	8.25:1	1 BC	Manual
CCM	6	250	100	8.25:1	1 BC	Manual w/NB2
CKL	8	350	145	8.5:1	2 BC	TH
CKS	8	350	145	8.5:1	2 BC	TH
CKK	8	350	145	8.5:1	2 BC	TH w/NB2
CLT	8	350	145	8.5:1	2 BC	TH w/NB2
CLU	8	350	145	8.5:1	2 BC	TH
CLW	8	350	145	8.5:1	2 BC	TH w/NB2
CLX	8	350	145	8.5:1	2 BC	TH
CKR	8	350	175	8.5:1	4 BC	TH w/NB2
CKD	8	350	175	8.5:1	4 BC	TH w/NB2
CKJ	8	350	175	8.5:1	4 BC	TH
CKM	8	350	175	8.5:1	4 BC	Police
CSJ	8	400	150	8.5:1	2 BC	TH w/NB2
CSA	8	400	150	8.5:1	2 BC	TH
CSB	8	400	150	8.5:1	2 BC	TH
CSC	8	400	150	8.5:1	2 BC	TH w/NB2
CSD	8	400	150	8.5:1	2 BC	TH w/NB2
CSK	8	400	150	8.5:1	2 BC	TH
CSL	8	400	150	8.5:1	2 BC	Police TH w/NB2
CSM	8	400	150	8.5:1	2 BC	Police TH
CWD	8	454	245	8.5:1	4 BC	TH w/NB2
CWJ	8	454	245	8.5:1	4 BC	TH w/NB2
CWL	8	454	245	8.5:1	4 BC	TH
CWK	8	454	245	8.5:1	4 BC	TH

*454 station wagons 215 HP; other specs the same

1974 CHEVROLET CAPRICE

1974 CHEVROLET IMPALA

1974 CHEVROLET MONTE CARLO

1974 CHEVROLET NOVA

1974 CHEVROLET CORVETTE STINGRAY

1974 CHEVROLET CHEVELLE LAGUNA

1974 CHEVROLET VEGA ESTATE WAGON

1974 CHEVROLET CAMARO

VEHICLE IDENTIFICATION NUMBER

**CHEVROLET
1L57H4S123456**

On top left side of instrument panel, visible through the windshield.

Corvette VIN on left windshield, visible through the windshield.

FIRST DIGIT: Indicates GM division (1 is Chevrolet)

SECOND DIGIT: Indicates series

CODE	SERIES
C	Chevelle & Malibu
D	Malibu Classic
E	Laguna
G	Malibu Estate
H	Monte Carlo
K	Bel Air
L	Impala
N	Caprice Classic & Caprice Estate
Q	Camaro
S	Camaro LT
V	Vega
X	Nova
Y	Nova Custom
Z	Corvette

THIRD & FOURTH DIGITS: Indicate body style

STYLE	DESCRIPTION
39	Sport Sedan (Chevrolet)
47	Coupe (Chevrolet)
57	Sport Coupe (Chevrolet/Monte Carlo)
57/Z03	Landau Coupe (Monte Carlo)
57/Z76	S Coupe (Monte Carlo)
67	Convertible (Chevrolet/Corvette)
69	4-Dr. Sedan (Chevrolet/Nova)
29	4-Dr. Sedan (Chevelle)
37	Sport Coupe (Chevelle/Corvette)
35	2-Seat Wagon (Chevrolet/Chevelle)
35/AQ4	3-Seat Wagon (Chevelle)
45	3-Seat Wagon (Chevrolet)
87	Sport Coupe (Camaro)
17	Hatchback Coupe (Nova)
27	Coupe (Nova)
05	Panel Express (Vega)
11	Panel Express (Vega)
15	Kammback Wagon (Vega)
77	Hatchback Coupe (Vega)

FIFTH DIGIT: Indicates engine

CODE	CID	TYPE	CARB
A	140	L-4	1 BC
B	140	L-4	2 BC
D	250	L-6	1 BC
F	307	V8	2 BC
H	350	V8	2 BC
K	350	V8	4 BC
R	400	V8	2 BC
T	350	V8	4 BC
X	454	V8	4 BC
Y	454	V8	4 BC

SIXTH DIGIT: Indicates the year (4 is 1974)

SEVENTH DIGIT: Indicates the assembly plant

ASSEMBLY PLANT	CODE
Lakewood	A
Baltimore	B
Southgate	C
Doraville	D
Flint	F

ASSEMBLY PLANT	CODE
Janesville	J
Leeds	K
Van Nuys	L
Norwood	N
Arlington	R
St. Louis	S
Tarrytown	T
Lordstown	U
Pontiac	V
Willow Run	W
Wilmington	Y
Fremont	Z
Oshawa, Canada	1
St. Therese, Canada	2

REMAINING SIX DIGITS: Indicate production sequence number

EXAMPLE

1	L	57	H	4	S	123456
Chev Div.	Series	Body Style	Engine	Year	Asm Plant	Prod Code

FISHER BODY NUMBER PLATE

All models except Corvette, located on right or left side of firewall below rear edge of hood. Corvette plate is located on upper left-hand door hinge pillar.

THE BODY NUMBER PLATE identifies the model year, car division, series, style, body assembly plant, body number, trim combination, paint code and date build code.

BODY BY FISHER
ST 74 1FQ87 N   123456 BDY
TR 775   19 PNT
11A

GENERAL MOTORS CORPORATION CERTIFIES TO THE DEALER THAT THIS VEHICLE CONFORMS TO ALL U.S., FEDERAL MOTOR VEHICLE SAFETY STANDARDS APPLICABLE AT TIME OF MANUFACTURE.

EXAMPLE:

74	Model year (1974)
1	Car division (Chevrolet)
FQ	Series Camaro
87	Sytle (2-Door Sport Coupe)
N	Body assembly plant (Norwood, Ohio)
123456	Production sequence in that plant
775	Black vinyl trim
19	Tuxedo black paint
11	Eleventh month (November)
A	First week of month

CHEVELLE — MODEL CODES
Deluxe Malibu

4-Dr Sport Sedan	1AC29
2-Dr Sport Coupe	1AC37
Station Wagon 2-seat	1AC35

Malibu Classic

4-Dr Sport Sedan	1AD29
2-Dr Sport Coupe	1AD37
Station Wagon 2-seat	1AD35
Estate Wagon 2-seat	1AG35

*Landau option available

CHEVELLE MODEL CODES
Laguna Type S-3
2-Dr Sport Coupe 1AE37
Estate Wagon 2-seat 1AH35

MONTE CARLO MODEL CODES
2-Dr Sport Coupe 1AH57
*S option available
*Landau option available

NOVA MODEL CODES
4-Dr Sedan 1XX69
2-Dr Coupe 1XX27
2-Dr Hatchback 1XX17
4-Dr Custom Sedan 1XY69
2-Dr Custom Sedan 1XY27
2-Dr Custom Hatchback Coupe 1XY17
*SS option available
*Spirit of America option available

CAMARO MODEL CODES
2-Dr Sport Coupe 1FQ87
Type LT 2-Dr Sport Coupe 1FS87
*Z-28 option available

CORVETTE MODEL CODES
Sport Coupe 1YZ37
Convertible 1YZ67

VEGA MODEL CODES
2-Dr Sedan 1HV11
2-Dr Hatchback Coupe 1HV77
2-Dr Station Wagon 1HV15
*LX option available
*GT option available
*Spirit of America option available
*Estate Wagon option available

CHEVROLET MODEL CODES
Bel Air
4-Dr Sedan 1BK69
Station Wagon 2-seat 1BK35
Station Wagon 3-seat 1BK45

Impala
4-Dr Sedan 1BL69
Sport Sedan 1BL39
Sport Coupe 1BL57
Custom Coupe 1BL47
Station Wagon 2-seat 1BL35
Station Wagon 3-seat 1BL45
*Spirit of America option available

Caprice
Classic 4-Dr Sedan 1BN69
Classic 2-Dr Sport Coupe 1BN47
Classic 2-Dr Convertible 1BN67
Classic 4-Dr Sport Sedan 1BN39
Estate Wagon 2-seat 1BN35
Estate Wagon 3-seat 1BN45

THE TRIM NUMBER furnishes the key to trim color and material for each model series.

CHEVELLE TRIM

Color	Cloth	Vinyl	Leather	Code
Black	•	•		701, 702, 703, 705
Black/White	•	•		704
Black		•		706, 707, 708, 709
Lt. Neutral	•	•		711, 722
Lt. Neutral		•		713
Ant. Lt. Neatral		•		714, 715
Med. Green	•	•		723, 724, 725
Med. Green		•		727
Ant. Med. Green	•	•		728, 729
Midnight Blue	•	•		732, 733
Ant. Midnight Blue		•		735, 736
Ant. Medium Saddle		•		740, 741
Dark Oxblood	•	•		743

MONTE CARLO TRIM

Color	Cloth	Vinyl	Leather	Code
Black	•	•		705
Black		•		709
Ant. Light Neutral		•		715, 716
Med. Green	•	•		726
Med, Green		•		729, 730
Midnight Blue	•	•		734
Ant. Midnight Blue		•		735, 736
Ant. Midnight Blue		•		737
Ant. Medium Saddle		•		741, 742
Dark Oxblood	•	•		744

NOVA TRIM

Color	Cloth	Vinyl	Leather	Code
Black/White	•	•		750
Black	•	•		751, 752
Black		•		753, 754
Green/Black	•	•		756
Med. Green	•	•		757
Med. Green		•		758, 759
Neutral/Black	•	•		764
Lt. Neutral		•		765, 766
Midnight Blue	•	•		771
Midnight Blue		•		772, 773

CAMARO TRIM

Color	Cloth	Vinyl	Leather	Code
Black/White	•	•		775
Black	•	•		776
Black		•		777, 778
Black/Red		•		779
Lt. Neutral	•	•		780
Ant. Lt. Neutral		•		781
Med Taupe	•	•		783
Ant. Med. Taupe		•		784
Green/Black	•	•		786
Ant. Med. Green		•		787
Med Red		•		792
Saddle/Black	•	•		796
Med. Saddle	•	•		797
Ant. Med. Saddle		•		798, 799

CORVETTE TRIM

Color	Cloth	Vinyl	Leather	Code
Black		•		400
Black			•	404
Silver		•		406
Silver			•	407
Neutral		•		408
Blue		•		413
Saddle		•		415
Saddle			•	416
Red		•		425

VEGA TRIM

Color	Cloth	Vinyl	Leather	Code
Black		•		861
Black/White/Red		•		862, 884
Ant. Lt. Neutral		•		863
Black		•		869
Lt. Neutral		•		870
Black/White	•	•		871, 873
Med. Green		•		879
Ant. Med. Green		•		880
Lt. Neutral		•		881
Green/Black	•	•		883, 887
Med. Saddle		•		888
Ant. Med. Saddle		•		890

CHEVROLET TRIM

Color	Cloth	Vinyl	Leather	Code
Black/White	•	•		802
Black	•	•		803, 805, 840
Black		•		807, 807, 808
Ant. Midnight Blue		•		813
Lt. Neutral	•	•		815, 821, 822
Lt. Neutral		•		817
Ant. Lt, Neutral		•		819, 841
Midnight Blue	•	•		843, 847, 848
Med. Green	•	•		850, 852, 853, 854
Med. Green		•		851, 855
Dark Oxblood	•	•		856, 857
Med. Taupe	•	•		896

THE PAINT CODE furnishes the key to the paint colors used on the car.

COLOR	CODE
Classic White*	10
Antique White	11
Cosworth Silver Metallic	13
Corvette Slvr Mist Metallic*	14
Corvette Gray Metallic*	17
Tuxedo Black	19
Corvette Med Blue Metallic*	22
Light Blue Metallic	24
Medium Blue	25
Bright Blue Metallic	26
Midnight Blue Metallic	29
Aqua Blue Metallic	36
Lime-Yellow	40
Medium Green	44
Bright Green Metallic	46
Medium Green Metallic	47
Dark Green Metallic*	48
Medium Dark Green Metallic	49
Cream-Beige	50
Bright Yellow	51
Light Gold Metallic	53
Sandstone	55
Bright Corvette Yellow*	56
Golden Brown Metallic	59
Silver Metallic	64
Bronze Metallic	66
Bright Orange	67
Dark Brown Metallic*	68
Dark Taupe Metallic	69
Medium Red Metallic*	74
Medium Red	75
Mille Miglia Red*	76
Corvette Orange Metallic*	80

* Corvette only available with one of these colors

TWO-TONE COMBINATIONS

LOWER COLOR	CODE	UPPER COLOR	CODE
Aqua Blue Metallic	36	Antique White	11
Light Blue Metallic	24	Antique White	11
Midnight Blue Metallic	29	Antique White	11
Bronze Metallic	66	Antique White	11
Medium Green	44	Antique White	11
Med Dark Green Met.	49	Antique White	11
Medium Red Metallic	74	Antique White	11
Sandstone	55	Antique White	11
Aqua Blue Metallic	36	Antique White	11
Bronze Metallic	66	Antique White	11
Light Gold Metallic	53	Antique White	11

VINYL ROOF CODES

COLOR	CODE
Black	BB
Medium Blue	DD
Brown	FF
Cream-Beige	EE
Medium Green	GG
Dark Red	HH
Russet	LL
Medium Saddle	RR
Silver Taupe	WW
White	AA

ENGINE NUMBER

THE ENGINE IDENTIFICATION NUMBER includes a letter code for the engine plant, followed by numbers which date the manufacture of the engine, then followed by a letter code to indicate the engine size and makeup.

THE ENGINE IDENTIFICATION NUMBER for V-8s is stamped on a pad located at the right-hand side of the cylinder block, and stamped on a pad on the right-hand side of the block behind the distributor on 4-cylinder and 6-cylinder engines.

NOTE:

1. To properly identify Chevrolet Division engines, it will be necessary to identify the car model in which the engine is used. The same engine type may have a different code when used in different car models.

2. NB2 is California emission controls

EXAMPLE

1	01	01	CCR
PLANT	MONTH	DAY	CODE

CHEVELLE ENGINES

Engine Code	No Cyl.	CID	Horse-power	Comp. Ratio	Carb	Trans
CCR	6	250	100	8.25:1	1 BC	3-spd
CCW	6	250	100	8.25:1	1 BC	TH w/NB2
CCX	6	250	100	8.25:1	1 BC	TH
CCK	6	250	100	8.25:1	1 BC	
CMC	8	350	145	8.5:1	2 BC	3-spd
CMA	8	350	145	8.5:1	2 BC	TH
CMR	8	350	145	8.5:1	2 BC	TH
CKH	8	350	160	8.5:1	4 BC	3-spd w/NB2
CKD	8	350	160	8.5:1	4 BC	TH w/NB2
CTC	8	400	180	8.5:1	4 BC	TH w/NB2
CSU	8	400	180	8.5:1	4 Bc	TH w/NB2
CSX	8	400	180	8.5:1	4 BC	TH w/NB2
CTA	8	400	150	8.5:1	2 BC	TH
CWA	8	454	235	8.5:1	4 BC	Manual
CWX	8	454	235	8.5:1	4 BC	TH
CWD	8	454	235	8.5:1	4 BC	TH w/NB2
CXM	8	454	235	8.5:1	4 BC	Manual
CXR	8	454	235	8.5:1	4 BC	TH
CXS	8	454	235	8.5:1	4 BC	TH

MONTE CARLO ENGINES

Engine Code	No Cyl.	CID	Horse-power	Comp. Ratio	Carb	Trans
CMC	8	350	145	8.5:1	2 BC	3-spd
CMA	8	350	145	8.5:1	2 BC	TH
CMR	8	350	145	8.5:1	2 BC	TH
CKH	8	350	160	8.5:1	4 BC	3-spd w/NB2
CKD	8	350	160	8.5:1	4 BC	TH w/NB2
CTC	8	400	180	8.5:1	4 BC	TH w/NB2
CSU	8	400	180	8.5:1	4 BC	TH w/NB2
CSX	8	400	180	8.5:1	4 BC	TH w/NB2
CTA	8	400	150	8.5:1	2 BC	TH w/NB2
CWA	8	454	235	8.5:1	4 BC	Manual
CWX	8	454	235	8.5:1	4 BC	TH
CWD	8	454	235	8.5:1	4 BC	TH w/NB2

NOVA ENGINES

Engine Code	No Cyl.	CID	Horsepower	Comp. Ratio	Carb	Trans
CCR	6	250	100	8.25:1	1 BC	Manual
CCW	6	250	100	8.25:1	1 BC	TH w/NB2
CCX	6	250	100	8.25:1	1 BC	TH
CCK	6	250	100	8.25:1	1 BC	
CMC	8	350	145	8.25:1	2 BC	Manual
CMA	8	350	145	8.25:1	2 BC	TH
CKB	8	350	185	8.5:1	4 BC	Manual
CKH	8	350	185	8.5:1	4 BC	Manual
CKH	8	350	185	8.5:1	4 BC	Manual w/NB2
CKU	8	350	185	8.5:1	4 BC	TH
CKD	8	350	160	8.5:1	4 BC	TH w/NB2

CAMARO ENGINES

Engine Code	No Cyl.	CID	Horsepower	Comp. Ratio	Carb	Trans
CCR	6	250	100	8.25:1	1 BC	Manual
CCW	6	250	100	8.25:1	1 BC	TH w/NB2
CCX	6	250	100	8.25:1	1 BC	TH
CMA	8	350	145	8.25:1	2 BC	TH
CMC	8	350	145	8.25:1	2 BC	Manual
CKB	8	350	185	8.5:1	4 BC	Manual
CKH	8	350	160	8.5:1	4 BC	Manual w/NB2
CKH	8	350	185	8.5:1	4 BC	Manual w/NB2
CLJ	8	350	245	9.0:1	4 BC (Z-28)	Manual
CKU	8	350	185	8.5:1	4 BC	TH
CKD	8	350	160	8.5:1	4 BC	TH w/NB2
CKD	8	350	185	8.5:1	4 BC	TH w/NB2
CLK	8	350	185	8.5:1	4 BC	TH
CMT	8	350	245	9.0:1	4 BC (Z-28)	TH
CMS	8	350	245	9.0:1	4 BC (Z-28)	Manual

CORVETTE ENGINES

Engine Code	No Cyl.	CID	Horsepower	Comp. Ratio	Carb	Trans
CKZ	8	350	195	9.0:1	4 BC	Manual
CLB	8	350	195	9.0:1	4 BC	Manual w/NB2
CLR	8	350	250	9.0:1	4 BC	Manual
CLA	8	350	195	9.0:1	4 BC	TH
CLC	8	350	195	9.0:1	4 BC	TH w/NB2
CLD	8	350	250	9.0:1	4 BC	TH
CWM	8	454	270	8.25:1	4 BC	Manual
CWR	8	454	270	8.25:1	4 BC	TH
CWS	8	454	270	8.25:1	4 BC	TH w/NB2

VEGA ENGINES

Engine Code	No Cyl.	CID	Horsepower	Comp. Ratio	Carb	Trans
CAA	4	140	75	8.0:1	1 BC	Manual
CAB	4	140	75	8.0:1	1 BC	PG TH350
CAH	4	140	75	8.0:1	1 BC	PG TH 350 w/NB2
CAJ	4	140	75	8.0:1	1 BC	Manual w/NB2
ZCR	4	140	75	8.0:1	1 BC	4-spd
CAC	4	140	85	8.0:1	2 BC	PG TH350
CAD	4	140	85	8.0:1	2 BC	Manual
CAK	4	140	85	8.0:1	2 BC	PG TH 350 w/NB2
CAL	4	145	85	8.0:1	2 BC	Manual w/NB2

CHEVROLET ENGINES

Engine Code	No Cyl.	CID	Horse- power	Comp. Ratio	Carb	Trans
CMK	8	350	160	8.5:1	4 BC	TH w/NB2
CMA	8	350	145	8.5:1	2 BC	TH
CMD	8	350	145	8.5:1	2 BC	TH
CMH	8	350	160	8.5:1	4 BC	TH w/NB2
CMH	8	350	160	8.5:1	4 BC	TH w/NB2
CMJ	8	350	160	8.5:1	4 BC	TH w/NB2
CKD	8	350	160	8.5:1	4 BC	TH w/NB2
CTC	8	400	180	8.5:1	4 BC	TH w/NB2
CTD	8	400	180	8.5:1	4 BC	TH w/NB2
CTK	8	400	180	8.5:1	4 BC	TH w/NB2
CTJ	8	400	180	8.5:1	4 BC	TH w/NB2
CTA	8	400	150	8.5:1	2 BC	TH
CTB	8	400	150	8.5:1	2 BC	TH
CSU	8	400	150	8.5:1	2 BC	TH w/NB2
CSW	8	400	150	8.5:1	2 BC	TH
CWU	8	454	235	8.5:1	4 BC	TH
CWW	8	454	235	8.5:1	4 BC	TH w/NB2
CWY	8	454	235	8.5:1	4 BC	TH w/NB2
CXA	8	454	235	8.5:1	4 BC	TH w/NB2
CXB	8	454	235	8.5:1	4 BC	TH w/NB2
CXC	8	454	235	8.5:1	4 BC	TH w/NB2
CXT	8	454	235	8.5:1	4 BC	TH
CXU	8	454	235	8.5:1	4 BC	TH

1975 CHEVROLET CAMARO

1975 CHEVROLET MONZA

1975 CHEVROLET CAPRICE

1975 CHEVROLET NOVA

1975 CHEVROLET CAPRICE ESTATE WAGON

1975 CHEVROLET CHEVELLE MALIBU

1975 CHEVROLET MONTE CARLO

1975 CHEVROLET CORVETTE

1975 CHEVROLET VEGA KAMMBACK

1975 CHEVROLET IMPALA

VEHICLE IDENTIFICATION NUMBER

CHEVROLET
1L57H5S123456

On top left side of instrument panel, visible through the windshield. Corvette VIN on left windshield pillar, visible through the windshield.

FIRST DIGIT: Indicates GM division (1 is Chevrolet)

SECOND DIGIT: Indicates series

CODE	SERIES
C	Malibu
D	Malibu Classic
E	Laguna
G	Malibu Estate
H	Monte Carlo & Laguna Estate
K	Bel Air
L	Impala
M	Monza Coupe
N	Caprice Classic & Caprice Estate
Q	Camaro
R	Monza 2 + 2
S	Camaro LT
V	Vega
X	Nova
Y	Nova Custom
Z	Corvette

THIRD & FOURTH DIGITS: Indicate body style

STYLE	DESCRIPTION
07	2-Dr. Monza Hatchback
39	Sport Sedan (Chevrolet)
47	Coupe (Chevrolet)
57	Sport Coupe (Chevrolet/Monte Carlo)
57/Z03	Landau Coupe (Monte Carlo)
57/Z76	S Coupe (Monte Carlo
67	Convertible (Chevrolet/Corvette)
69	4-Dr. Sedan (Chevrolet/Nova)
29	4-Dr. Sedan (Chevelle)
37	Sport Coupe (Chevelle/Corvette)
35	2-Seat Wagon (Chevrolet/Chevelle)
35/AQ4	3-Seat Wagon (Chevelle)
45	3-Seat Wagon (Chevrolet)
87	Sport Coupe (Camaro)
17	Hatchback Coupe (Nova)
27	Coupe (Nova)
05	Panel Express (Vega)
11	Panel Express (Vega)
15	Kammback Wagon (Vega)
77	Hatchback Coupe (Vega)

FIFTH DIGIT: Indicates engine

CODE	CID	TYPE	CARB
A	140	L-4	1 BC
B	140	L-4	2 BC
D	250	L-6	1 BC
F	307	V8	2 BC
G	262	V8	2 BC
H	350	V8	2 BC
K	350	V8	4 BC
R	400	V8	2 BC
T	350	V8	4 BC
X	454	V8	4 BC
Y	454	V8	4 BC

SIXTH DIGIT: Indicates the year (5 = 1975)

SEVENTH DIGIT: Indicates the assembly plant

ASSEMBLY PLANT	CODE
Lakewood	A

ASSEMBLY PLANT	CODE
Baltimore	B
Southgate	C
Doraville	D
Flint	F
Janesville	J
Leeds	K
Van Nuys	L
Norwood	N
Arlington	R
St. Louis	S
Tarrytown	T
Lordstown	U
Pontiac	V
Willow Run	W
Wilmington	Y
Fremont	Z
Oshawa, Canada	1
St. Therese, Canada	2

REMAINING SIX DIGITS: Indicate production sequence number

EXAMPLE

1	L	57	H	5	S	123456
Chev Div.	Series	Engine	Body Style	Year	Asm Plant	Prod Code

BODY NUMBER PLATE

Located on right or left side of firewall below rear edge of hood of all models, except Corvette. Corvette plate is located on upper left-hand door hinge pillar.

THE BODY NUMBER PLATE identifies the model year, car division, series, style, body assembly plant, body number, trim combination, paint code and date build code.

```
            BODY BY FISHER
  ST 75  1FQ87  N          123456 BDY
  TR 19V                       19  PNT
  11A


  GENERAL MOTORS CORPORATION CERTIFIES
    TO THE DEALER THAT THIS VEHICLE
  CONFORMS TO ALL U.S., FEDERAL MOTOR
       VEHICLE SAFETY STANDARDS
    APPLICABLE AT TIME OF MANUFACTURE.
```

In the example above,

75	Model year (1975)
1	Car division (Chevrolet)
FQ	Series (Camaro V-8)
87	Style (2-Dr Sport Coupe)
N	Body assembly plant (Norwood, Ohio)
123456	Production sequence in that plant
19V	Black vinyl trim
19	Tuxedo Black paint
11	Eleventh month (November)
A	First week of month

NOTE: An option code will appear below the paint code. It is a notation to the assembly line workers that this vehicle is not a standard issue item. An example would be a radio delete, heater delete, etc. WE DO NOT HAVE BREAKDOWNS FOR THOSE CODES.

CHEVELLE — MODEL CODES
Malibu
4-Dr Sport Sedan 1AC29
2-Dr Sport Coupe 1AC37
4-Dr Station Wagon* 1AC35
*Landau option available

Malibu Classic
4-Dr Sport Sedan 1AD29
2-Dr Sport Coupe 1AD37
4-Dr Station Wagon* 1AD35

Malibu Classic Estate
4-Dr Station Wagon* 1AG35

Laguna
2-Dr. Sport Coupe 1AE37
*Third seat available as RPO (Regular Production Option/Order) on
V-8-equipped station wagon.

MONTE CARLO — MODEL CODES
Monte Carlo S
2-Dr Sport Coupe 1AH57
*Landau option available

Nova — MODEL CODES
4-Dr Sedan 1XX69
2-Dr Coupe 1XX27
2-Dr Hatchback Coupe 1XX17
*SS option available
*S option available

Nova Custom
4-Dr Sedan 1XY69
2-Dr Coupe 1XY27
2-Dr Hatchback Coupe 1XY17
*LN option available

CAMARO — MODEL CODES
Camaro
2-Dr Sport Coupe 1FQ87
*Rally Sport option available
Camaro "Type LT"
2-Dr Sport Coupe 1FS87

CORVETTE — MODEL CODES
2-Dr Sport Coupe 1YZ37
2-Dr Convertible 1YZ67

VEGA — MODEL CODES
2-Dr Sedan 1HV11
2-Dr Hatchback Coupe 1HV77
2-Dr Station Wagon 1HV15
*LX option available
*Cosworth option available
*GT option available
*Estate option available

MONZA — MODEL CODES
2-Dr Hatchback Coupe Monza 1HR07
2-Dr. Coupe Monza 1HM27
*S option available

CHEVROLET — MODEL CODES
Bel Air
4-Dr Sedan 1BK69
4-Dr Station Wagon 2-Seat 1BK35
4-Dr Station Wagon 3-Seat 1BK45

Impala — MODEL CODES
4-Dr Sedan 1BL69
4-Dr Sport Sedan 1BL39
2-Dr Sport Coupe 1BL57
2-Dr Custom Coupe 1BL47
4-Dr Station Wagon 2-Seat 1BL35
4-Dr Station Wagon 3-Seat 1BL45

Caprice Classic
4-Dr Sedan 1BN69
2-Dr Sport Coupe 1BN47
4-Dr Sport Sedan 1BN39
2-Dr Convertible 1BN67

Caprice Estate
4-Dr Station Wagon 2-Seat 1BN35
4-Dr Station Wagon 3-Seat 1BN45

THE TRIM NUMBER furnishes the key to trim color and material for each model series.

PASSENGER TRIM
Color	Cloth	Vinyl	Leather	Code
White		•		02W
White		•		04W
White		•		07W
White		•		11W
Black	•			19B
Black	•			19C
Black	•			19D
Black		•		19H
Black		•		19W
Blue	•			26B
Blue	•			26C
Blue	•			26D
Blue		•		26V
Blue		•		26W
Green	•			44B
Green	•			44D
Green		•		44W
Sandstone	•			55B
Sandstone	•			55C
Sandstone	•			55D
Sandstone		•		55H
Sandstone		•		55V
Sandstone		•		55W
Saddle	•			63E
Saddle		•		63W
Oxblood	•			73B

CHEVELLE TRIM
Color	Cloth	Vinyl	Leather	Code
White		•		02H
White		•		04H
Black		•		07E
White		•		07H
White		•		07Z
Black		•		11E
White		•		11H
White		•		11Z
Graystone	•			16D
Black	•			19B
Black	•			19C
Black	•			19D
Black		•		19E
Black		•		19H
Black		•		19N
Black		•		19V
Black		•		19W
Black		•		19Z
Blue	•			26B
Blue	•			26C
Blue		•		26D
Blue	•			26H

CHEVELLE TRIM

Color	Cloth	Vinyl	Leather	Code
Blue		•		26N
Blue		•		26V
Blue	•			26W
Green	•			44D
Green	•			44N
Green		•		44V
Sandstone	•			55B
Sandstone		•		55H
Sandstone	•			55N
Sandstone		•		55V
Sandstone		•		55W
Saddle		•		63E
Saddle		•		63W
Oxblood	•			77B
Saddle		•		63Z
Oxblood	•			73D
Oxblood		•		73E
Oxblood	•			73N
Oxblood		•		73Z

NOVA TRIM

Color	Cloth	Vinyl	Leather	Code
White		•		92W
White		•		04W
White		•		07W
White		•		11W
Graystone	•			16G
Black	•			19G
Black	•			19E
Black		•		19V
Black		•		19W
Blue	•			26C
Blue	•			26D
Blue	•			26G
Blue		•		26V
Green	•			44D
Sandstone	•			55C
Sandstone	•			55D
Sandstone	•			55G
Sandstone		•		55W
Sandstone		•		55V
Saddle	•			63E
Saddle		•		63V
Saddle		•		63W
Oxblood	•			73G
Oxblood		•		73W

CAMARO TRIM

Color	Cloth	Vinyl	Leather	Code
Graystone	•			16D
Black	•			19C
Black		•		19V
Sandstone	•			55C
Sandstone	•			55D
Sandstone		•		55V
Sandstone		•		55W
Saddle	•			63D
Saddle		•		63V
Saddle		•		63W
Oxblood	•			73D
White		•		91V
Saddle			•	632
Oxblood			•	732

VEGA & MONZA TRIM

Color	Cloth	Vinyl	Leather	Code
White		•		02Y
White		•		11Y
Cloth	•			16G
Graystone		•		16Z
Black	•			19D
Black	•			19E
Black	•			19G
Blk/Grystn		•		19V

VEGA & MONZA TRIM

Color	Cloth	Vinyl	Leather	Code
Black		•		19W
Black	•			19Y
Black		•		19Z
Blue	•			26B
Blue	•			26G
Blue		•		26V
Blue		•		26W
Blue		•		26Z
Sandstone	•			55B
Sandstone	•			55D
Sandstone	•			55E
Sandstone		•		55G
Sandstone		•		55W
Sandstone		•		55Y
Sandstone		•		55Z
Saddle	•			63G
Saddle		•		63V
Saddle		•		63W
Saddle		•		63Y
Saddle		•		63Z
Oxblood	•			73B
Oxblood		•		73G
Oxblood		•		73Y
Oxblood		•		73Z
Black			•	192
Saddle			•	632
Oxblood			•	732

THE PAINT CODE furnishes the key to the paint colors used on the car.

COLOR	CODE
White	10
Classic White*	10
White	11
Silver	13
Silver*	13
Light Graystone	15
Medium Graystone	16
Black	19
Silver Blue	21
Medium Blue	22
Bright Blue Metallic*	22
Medium Blue	24
Bright Blue	26
Dark Steel Blue	27
Steel Blue Metallic*	27
Dark Blue Metallic	29
Bright Green	42
Bright Green Metallic*	42
Medium Green	44
Light Green	45
Dark Green	49
Cream Beige	50
Bright Yellow	51
Sandstone	55
Bright Yellow	56
Bright Yellow*	56
Dark Brown	59
Light Saddle	63
Persimmon	64
Bronze	66
Medium Saddle	67
Medium Saddle Metallic*	67
Flame Red	70
Orange Flame*	70
Red	72
Dark Red	74
Dark Red Metallic*	74

COLOR

COLOR	CODE
Light Red	75
Red	76
Mille Miglia Red*	76
Burgundy	79
Orange	80

*Corvette only available with one of these colors

TWO-TONE COMBINATIONS

LOWER COLOR	CODE	UPPER COLOR	CODE
Bright Blue Metallic	26	Antique White	11
Medium Blue	24	Antique White	11
Midnight Metallic Blue	29	Antique White	11
Dark Metallic Brown	59	Antique White	11
Dark Metallic Green	49	Antique White	11
Medium Green	44	Antique White	11
Medium Met Orange	64	Antique White	11
Dark Metallic Red	74	Antique White	11
Light Red	75	Antique White	11
Sandstone	55	Antique White	11
Sandstone	55	Cream Beige	50
Dark Met Sandstone	58	Cream Beige	50
Black	19	Black	19
Black	19	Dark Red	HH
Black	19	Silver	WW
Black	19	White	AA
Bright Metallic Blue	26	Black	BB
Bright Metallic Blue	26	Bright Metallic Blue	26
Bright Metallic Blue	26	White	AA

LOWER COLOR	CODE	UPPER COLOR	CODE
Medium Met Orange	64	Black	BB
Medium Met Orange	64	Medium Met Orange	64
Medium Met Orange	64	White	AA
Dark Metallic Red	74	Black	BB
Dark Metallic Red	74	Dark Metallic Red	74
Dark Metallic Red	74	Silver Metallic	WW
Dark Metallic Red	74	White	AA
Silver	13	Black	BB
Silver	13	Dark Red	HH
Silver	13	Silver	13
Antique White	11	Black	BB
Antique White	11	Dark Red	HH
Antique White	11	Antique White	11

VINYL ROOF CODES

COLOR	CODE
Black	BB
Dark Blue	DD
Dark Brown	FF
Medium Green	GG
Dark Red	HH
Red	RR
Sandstone	TT
Metallic Silver	WW
White	AA

CONVERTIBLE TOP COLORS: Choice of white (AA) or black (BB) top available with all exterior colors.

ENGINE NUMBER

THE ENGINE IDENTIFICATION NUMBER includes a letter code for the engine plant, followed by numbers which date the manufacture of the engine, then followed by a letter code to indicate the engine size and makeup.

THE ENGINE IDENTIFICATION NUMBER for V-8s is stamped on a pad located at the right-hand side of the cylinder block, and stamped on a pad on the right-hand side of the block behind the distributor on 4-cylinder and 6-cylinder engines.

NOTE:

1. To properly identify Chevrolet Division engines, it will be necessary to identify the car model in which the engine is used. The same engine type may have a different code when used in different car models.

EXAMPLE

1	01	01	CJM
PLANT	MONTH	DAY	CODE

CHEVELLE ENGINES

Engine Code	No Cyl.	CID	Horse-power	Comp. Ratio	Carb
CJL	6	250	105	8.25:1	1 BC
CLM	6	250	105	8.25:1	1 BC
CJR	6	250	105	8.25:1	1 BC
CJS	6	250	105	8.25:1	1 BC
CJT	6	250	105	8.25:1	1 BC
CJU	6	250	105	8.25:1	1 BC
CJF	6	250	105	8.25:1	1 BC
CJZ	6	250	105	8.25:1	1 BC
CMF	8	350	145	8.5:1	2 BC
CMH	8	350	145	8.5:1	2 BC
CMJ	8	350	145	8.5:1	2 BC
CMM	8	350	145	8.5:1	2 BC
CMU	8	350	145	8.5:1	2 BC
CMY	8	350	145	8.5:1	2 BC
CRT	8	350	145	8.5:1	2 BC
CRU	8	350	145	8.5:1	2 BC

CHEVELLE ENGINES

Engine Code	No Cyl.	CID	Horse-power	Comp. Ratio	Carb
CRX	8	350	145	8.5:1	2 BC
CRY	8	350	145	8.5:1	2 BC
CRZ	8	350	145	8.5:1	2 BC
CTB	8	350	145	8.5:1	2 BC
CUS	8	350	145	8.5:1	2 BC
CSM	8	400	175	8.5:1	4 BC
CHS	8	400	175	8.5:1	4 BC
CTL	8	400	175	8.5:1	4 BC
CTR	8	400	175	8.5:1	4 BC
CTU	8	400	175	8.5:1	4 BC
CTX	8	400	175	8.5:1	4 BC
CXW	8	454	215	8.15:1	4 BC
CXK	8	454	215	8.15:1	4 BC

MONTE CARLO ENGINES

Engine Code	No Cyl.	CID	Horse-power	Comp. Ratio	Carb
CMF	8	350	145	8.5:1	2 BC
CMH	8	350	145	8.5:1	2 BC
CMJ	8	350	145	8.5:1	2 BC
CMU	8	350	145	8.5:1	2 BC
CRT	8	350	145	8.5:1	2 BC
CRU	8	350	145	8.5:1	2 BC
CTL	8	400	175	8.5:1	4 BC
CTU	8	400	175	8.5:1	4 BC
CTX	8	400	175	8.5:1	4 BC
CXW	8	454	215	8.15:1	4 BC

NOVA ENGINES

Engine Code	No Cyl.	CID	Horse-power	Comp. Ratio	Carb
CCS	6	250	105	8.25:1	1 BC
CCT	6	250	105	8.25:1	1 BC
CCU	6	250	105	8.25:1	1 BC
CCW	6	250	105	8.25:1	1 BC
CJF	6	250	105	8.25:1	1 BC
CJL	6	250	105	8.25:1	1 BC
CJM	6	250	105	8.25:1	1 BC
CJR	6	250	105	8.25:1	1 BC
CJS	6	250	105	8.25:1	1 BC
CJT	6	250	105	8.25:1	1 BC
CJU	6	250	105	8.25:1	1 BC
CJW	6	250	105	8.25:1	1 BC
CJX	6	250	105	8.25:1	1 BC
CJZ	6	250	105	8.25:1	1 BC
CGC	8	262	110	8.5:1	2 BC
CGD	8	262	110	8.5:1	2 BC
CGF	8	262	110	8.5:1	2 BC
CGH	8	262	110	8.5:1	2 BC
CZF	8	262	110	8.5:1	2 BC
CZH	8	262	110	8.5:1	2 BC
CZJ	8	262	110	8.5:1	2 BC
CZK	8	262	110	8.5:1	2 BC
CZL	8	262	110	8.5:1	2 BC
CZM	8	262	110	8.5:1	2 BC
CZY	8	262	110	8.5:1	2 BC
CZZ	8	262	110	8.5:1	2 BC
CHW	8	350	145	8.5:1	2 BC
CMF	8	350	145	8.5:1	2 BC
CMH	8	350	145	8.5:1	2 BC
CMU	8	350	145	8.5:1	2 BC
CMY	8	350	145	8.5:1	2 BC
CRC	8	350	145	8.5:1	2 BC
CRD	8	350	145	8.5:1	2 BC
CRT	8	350	145	8.5:1	2 BC
CRU	8	350	145	8.5:1	2 BC
CRX	8	350	145	8.5:1	2 BC
CRZ	8	350	145	8.5:1	2 BC
CUJ	8	350	145	8.5:1	2 BC
CUH	8	350	145	8.5:1	2 BC
CUM	8	350	145	8.5:1	2 BC
CUS	8	350	145	8.5:1	2 BC

CAMARO ENGINES

Engine Code	No Cyl.	CID	Horse-power	Comp. Ratio	Carb
CJF	6	250	105	8.25:1	1 BC
CJL	8	250	105	8.25:1	1 BC
CJM	6	250	105	8.25:1	1 BC
CJR	6	250	105	8.25:1	1 BC
CJT	6	250	105	8.25:1	1 BC
CJU	6	250	105	8.25:1	1 BC
CJY	6	250	105	8.25:1	1 BC
CJZ	6	250	105	8.25:1	1 BC
CHS	8	350	145	8.5:1	2 BC
CHT	8	350	145	8.5:1	2 BC
CHW	8	350	145	8.5:1	2 BC
CMB	8	350	145	8.5:1	2 BC
CMF	8	350	145	8.5:1	2 BC
CMH	8	350	145	8.5:1	2 BC
CML	8	350	145	8.5:1	2 BC
CMU	8	350	145	8.5:1	2 BC
CMY	8	350	145	8.5:1	2 BC
CRC	8	350	145	8.5:1	2 BC
CRD	8	350	145	8.5:1	2 BC
CRK	8	350	145	8.5:1	2 BC
CRR	8	350	145	8.5:1	2 BC
CRS	8	350	145	8.5:1	2 BC
CRT	8	350	145	8.5:1	2 BC
CRU	8	350	145	8.5:1	2 BC
CRX	8	350	145	8.5:1	2 BC
CRZ	8	350	145	8.5:1	2 BC
CUC	8	350	145	8.5:1	2 BC
CUH	8	350	145	8.5:1	2 BC
CUJ	8	350	145	8.5:1	2 BC
CUL	8	350	145	8.5:1	2 BC
CUM	8	350	145	8.5:1	2 BC
CUS	8	350	145	8.5:1	2 BC

CORVETTE ENGINES

Engine Code	No Cyl.	CID	Horse-power	Comp. Ratio	Carb	Trans
CUB	8	350	165	8.5:1	4 BC (L-48)	Manual
CUD	8	350	210	9.0:1	4 BC (L-82)	Manual
CRJ	8	350			4 BC	Manual
CRK	8	350			4 BC	Auto
CRL	8	350			4 BC	Manual
CRM	8	350			4 BC	Auto
CUT	8	350			4 BC	Manual
CUA	8	350			4 BC	Manual

VEGA & MONZA ENGINES

Engine Code	No Cyl.	CID	Horse-power	Comp. Ratio	Carb
ZCA	4	122	110	8.0:1	Cosworth F.I.
CAA	4	140	110	8.0:1	1 BC
CAB	4	140	110	8.0:1	1 BC
CAC	4	140	110	8.0:1	1 BC
CAD	4	140	110	8.0:1	1 BC
CAF	4	140	110	8.0:1	1 BC
CAH	4	140	110	8.0:1	1 BC
CAJ	4	140	110	8.0:1	1 BC
CAK	4	140	110	8.0:1	1 BC
CAM	4	140	110	8.0:1	1 BC
CAR	4	140	110	8.0:1	1 BC
CAS	4	140	110	8.0:1	1 BC
CAT	4	140	110	8.0:1	1 BC
CAU	4	140	110	8.0:1	1 BC
CAW	4	140	110	8.0:1	1 BC
CBB	4	140	110	8.0:1	1 BC
CBC	4	140	110	8.0:1	1 BC
CBD	4	140	110	8.0:1	1 BC
CBF	4	140	110	8.0:1	1 BC
CZA	8	262	110	8.5:1	2 BC
CZB	8	262	110	8.5:1	2 BC
CZC	8	262	110	8.5:1	2 BC
CZD	8	262	110	8.5:1	2 BC
CZT	8	262	110	8.5:1	2 BC
CZU	8	262	110	8.5:1	2 BC
CZW	8	262	110	8.5:1	2 BC
CHY	8	350	145	8.5:1	2 BC

CHEVROLET ENGINES

Engine Code	No Cyl.	CID	Horse-power	Comp. Ratio	Carb
CMJ	8	350	160	8.5:1	2 BC
CMX	8	350	160	8.5:1	2 BC
CMY	8	350	160	8.5:1	2 BC
CRF	8	350	160	8.5:1	2 BC
CRS	8	350	160	8.5:1	2 BC
CRU	8	350	160	8.5:1	2 BC
CRW	8	350	160	8.5:1	2 BC
CRY	8	350	160	8.5:1	2 BC
CRZ	8	350	160	8.5:1	2 BC
CSA	8	400	175	8.5:1	4 BC
CSH	8	400	175	8.5:1	4 BC
CSR	8	400	175	8.5:1	4 BC
CSS	8	400	175	8.5:1	4 BC
CST	8	400	175	8.5:1	4 BC
CTL	8	400	175	8.5:1	4 BC
CTM	8	400	175	8.5:1	4 BC
CTR	8	400	175	8.5:1	4 BC
CTS	8	400	175	8.5:1	4 BC
CTU	8	400	175	8.5:1	4 BC
CTW	8	400	175	8.5:1	4 BC
CTY	8	400	175	8.5:1	4 BC
CTZ	8	400	175	8.5:1	4 BC
CXK	8	454	215	8.15:1	4 BC
CXL	8	454	215	8.15:1	4 BC
CXX	8	454	215	8.15:1	4 BC
CXY	8	454	215	8.15:1	4 BC

1976 CHEVROLET MONZA 2+2

1976 CHEVROLET MONTE CARLO

1976 CHEVROLET NOVA

1976 CHEVROLET MONZA TOWNE COUPE

1976 CHEVROLET CHEVELLE

1976 CHEVROLET CHEVETTE

1976 CHEVROLET CORVETTE

1976 CHEVROLET IMPALA

1976 CHEVROLET VEGA

1976 CHEVROLET CAMARO

VEHICLE IDENTIFICATION NUMBER

CHEVROLET
1L57J6S123456

On top left side of instrument panel, visible through the windshield.

Corvette VIN on left windshield pillar, visible through the windshield.

FIRST DIGIT: Indicates GM division (1 is Chevrolet)

SECOND DIGIT: Indicates series

CODE	SERIES
V	Vega
X	Nova
Y	Nova Concours
Q	Camaro
S	Camaro Type LT
C	Malibu
D	Malibu Classic
G	Malibu Estate Station Wagon
E	Laguna
H	Monte Carlo
L	Chevrolet Impala
N	Chevrolet Caprice Classic
	Caprice Estate Station Wagon
Z	Corvette
B&J	Chevette
R	Monza 2 plus 2
M	Monza

THIRD & FOURTH DIGITS: Indicate body style

CODE	STYLE
11	2-Dr. Notch Back - Pillar Coupe
15	2-Dr. Station Wagon 2-Seat
17	2-Dr. Notch Back Coupe
23	4-Dr. Limousine with Auxiliary Seat
27	2-Dr. Notch Back - Pillar Coupe
29	4-Dr. Notch Back - Hardtop Sedan
35	4-Dr. Station Wagon - 2-Seat
37	2-Dr. Notch Back - Hardtop Coupe
39	4-Dr. Notch Back - Hardtop (4 Window) Sedan
45	4-Dr. Station Wagon 3-Seat
47	2-Dr. Notch Back - Hardtop Coupe
49	4-Dr. Notch Back - Hardtop (4 Window) Sedan
57	2-Dr. Notch Back - Hardtop Coupe
67	2-Dr. Convertible Coupe
69	4-Dr. Notch Back - Pillar (4 Window) Sedan
77	2-Dr. Plain Back - Pillar Coupe
87	2-Dr. Plain Back - Hardtop Coupe
08	2-Dr. Hatch Back Chevette
07	Hatch Back 2+2

FIFTH DIGIT: Indicates engine

CODE	CID	TYPE	CARB
I	85	I-4	1 BC
E	97.6	L-4	1 BC
O	122	L-4	E.F.I.
A	140	L-4	1 BC
B	140	L-4	2 BC
D	250	L-6	1 BC
G	262	V8	2 BC
Q	262	V8	2 BC
V	350	V8	2 BC
L	350	V8	4 BC
X	350	V8	4 BC
U	400	V8	4 BC
S	454	V8	4 BC

SIXTH DIGIT: Indicates the year (6 is 1976)

SEVENTH DIGIT: Indicates the assembly plant

ASSEMBLY PLANT	CODE
Lakewood	A
Baltimore	B
Southgate	C
Doraville	D
Flint (Trucks only)	F
Janesville	J
Leeds	K
Lordstown	U
Van Nuys	L
Norwood	N
Arlington	R
St. Louis	S
Tarrytown	T
Willow Run	W
Wilmington	Y
Fremont	Z
Oshawa, Ont., Canada	1
St. Therese, Que., Can	2
Detroit	3
Scarborough, Can	4
Fujisawa, Japan	8

REMAINING SIX DIGITS: Indicate production sequence number.

EXAMPLE

1	L	47	V	6	W	123456
Chev Div.	Series	Body Style	Engine	Year	Asm Plant	Prod Code

BODY NUMBER PLATE

Located on firewall below rear edge of hood of all models, except Corvette. Corvette plate is located on upper left-hand door hinge pillar.

THE BODY NUMBER PLATE identifies the model year, car division, series, style, body assembly plant, body number, trim combination, paint code and date build code.

BODY BY FISHER

ST 76 1FQ87 N   123456 BDY

TR 19C   19 PNT

11A

● GENERAL MOTORS CORPORATION CERTIFIES ●
TO THE DEALER THAT THIS VEHICLE
CONFORMS TO ALL U.S., FEDERAL MOTOR
VEHICLE SAFETY STANDARDS
APPLICABLE AT TIME OF MANUFACTURE.

In the example above,

76	Model year (1976)
1	Car division (Chevrolet)
FQ	Series (Camaro V-8)
87	Style (2-Dr Sport Coupe)
N	Body assembly plant (Norwood, Ohio)
123456	Production sequence in that plant
19C	Black Vinyl Trim
19	Tuxedo Black Paint
11	Eleventh month (November)
A	First week of month

NOTE: An option code will appear below the paint code. It is a notation to the assembly line workers that this vehicle is not a standard issue item. An example would be a radio delete, heater delete, etc. WE DO NOT HAVE BREAKDOWNS FOR THOSE CODES.

CHEVELLE	MODEL CODES
Malibu	
4-Dr Sport Sedan	1AC29
2-Dr Sport Coupe	1AC37
4-Dr Station Wagon*	1AC35

Malibu Classic	
4-Dr Sport Sedan	1AD29
2-Dr. Sport Coupe	1AD37
4-Dr. Station Wagon*	1AD35

Malibu Classic Estate
4-Dr Station Wagon* 1AG35

Laguna Type S-3
2-Dr Sport Coupe 1AE37
*Third seat available as RPO (Regular Production Option/Order) on V-8 equipped station wagons.

MONTE CARLO	MODEL CODES
Monte Carlo "S"	
2-Dr Sport Coupe	1AH57

*Landau option available

NOVA	MODEL CODES
Nova	
4-Dr Sedan	1XX69
2-Dr Coupe	1XX27
2-Dr Hatchback Coupe	1XX17

*SS option available

Nova Concours	
4-Dr Sedan	1XY69
2-Dr Coupe	1XY27
2-Dr Hatchback Coupe	1XY17

CAMARO	MODEL CODES
Camaro	
2-Dr Sport Coupe	1FQ87

*Rally Sport option available

Camaro "Type LT"
2-Dr Sport Coupe 1FS87

CORVETTE	MODEL CODES
2-Dr Sport Coupe	1YZ37

CHEVROLET	MODEL CODES
Impala	
4-Dr Sedan	1BL69
4-Dr Sport Sedan	1BL39
2-Dr Custom Coupe	1BL47
4-Dr Station Wagon 2-seat	1BL35
4-Dr Station Wagon 3-seat	1BL45

*S option available

Caprice Classic	
4-Dr Sedan	1BN69
2-Dr Sport Coupe	1BN47
4-Dr Sport Sedan	1BN39

Caprice Estate	
4-Dr Station Wagon 2-Seat	1BN35
4-Dr Station Wagon 3-Seat	1BN45

VEGA	MODEL CODES
Notchback Coupe	1HV11
Station Wagon	1HV15
Hatchback Coupe	1HV77

*GT option available
*Cosworth option available
*Estate option available

MONZA	MODEL CODES
Town Coupe	1HM27
2 Plus 2 Coupe	1HR07

CHEVETTE	MODEL CODES
2-Dr Hatchback Coupe	1TB08
2-Dr Hatchback Coupe Scooter	1TJ08

*Rally option available
*Estate option available

THE TRIM NUMBER furnishes the key to trim color and material for each model series.

PASSENGER TRIM

Color	Cloth	Vinyl	Leather	Code
White		•		11N
White		•		110
Black		•		19B
Black		•		19N
Black		•		19D
Blue		•		26B
Blue		•		O2N
Blue		•		26N
Blue		•		26D
Blue		•		O20
Lime		•		O3N
Lime		•		O30
Buckskin		•		64C
Buckskin		•		64N
Buckskin		•		640
Firethorn		•		71B
Firethorn		•		71C
Firethorn		•		O7N
Firethorn		•		71N
Mahogany		•		74D
Mahogany		•		740
Mahogany		•		O80

CHEVELLE WAGON TRIM

Color	Cloth	Vinyl	Leather	Code
White		•		11Y
White		•		11N
White		•		11V
White		•		11W
Black		•		19Y
Black		•		19B
Black		•		19C
Black		•		19H
Black		•		19N
Black		•		19E
Black		•		19V
Black	•			19G
Black	•			19J*
Black		•		19W
Blue		•		26Y
Blue		•		26C
Blue		•		26N
Blue		•		O2N
Blue		•		26E
Blue		•		02V
Blue	•			26G
Blue		•		O2W
Lime		•		O3Y
Lime		•		O3N
Lime		•		O3V
Lime		•		O3W

CHEVELLE WAGON TRIM

Color	Cloth	Vinyl	Leather	Code
Buckskin		•		64Y
Buckskin		•		64B
Buckskin		•		64C
Buckskin		•		64H
Buckskin		•		64N
Buckskin		•		64V
Buckskin		•		64W
Mahogany		•		O8Y
Mahogany		•		74Y
Mahogany		•		74C
Mahogany		•		74N
Mahogany		•		O8N
Mahogany		•		74E
Mahogany		•		74V
Mahogany		•		O8V
Mahogany	•			74G
Mahogany	•			74J*
Mahogany			•	O8W

*These combinations are for limited usage in order to use surplus cloth or leather.

CAMARO TRIM

Color	Cloth	Vinyl	Leather	Code
White		•		11M
White		•		11N
Black		•		19C
Black		•		19N
Black		•		19B
Black		•		19M
Blue		•		O2M
Blue		•		26C
Blue		•		O2N
Lime		•		O3M
Lime		•		O3N
Buckskin		•		64M
Buckskin		•		64N
Firethorn		•		71B
Firethorn		•		71M
Firethorn		•		O7M
Firethorn		•		71C
Firethorn		•		O7N

VEGA TRIM

Color	Cloth	Vinyl	Leather	Code
White		•		11W
Black		•		19B
Black		•		19M
Black		•		19D
Black		•		19W
Blue		•		O2W
Lime		•		O3W
Buckskin		•		64M
Buckskin		•		64D
Buckskin		•		64W
Firethorn		•		71B
Firethorn		•		71M
Firethorn		•		71D
Firethorn		•		71W
Firethorn		•		O7W
Firethorn		•		O7H

MONZA TRIM

Color	Cloth	Vinyl	Leather	Code
White		•		11N
White		•		11V
Black		•		19C
Black		•		19N
Black		•		19J
Black		•		19V
Black			•	193*
Blue		•		O2N
Blue		•		O2V
Lime		•		O3N

MONZA TRIM

Color	Cloth	Vinyl	Leather	Code
Lime		•		O3V
Buckskin		•		64C
Buckskin		•		64N
Buckskin		•		64J
Buckskin		•		64V
Buckskin			•	643*
Buckskin	•			64E
Firethorn		•		71C
Firethorn		•		71N
Firethorn		•		O7N
Firethorn		•		71J
Firethorn		•		71V
Firethorn		•		O7V
Firethorn	•			71E
Mahogany		•		OBN
Mahogany		•		O8V

*These combinations are for limited usage in order to use surplus cloth or leather.

CHEVETTE TRIM

Color	Cloth	Vinyl	Leather	Code
White		•		11N
Black		•		19V
Black		•		19M
Black		•		19C
Black		•		19N
Blue		•		26M
Blue		•		26C
Blue		•		26N
Blue		•		O2N
Lime		•		O3N
Buckskin		•		64G**
Buckskin		•		64B**
Buckskin		•		64V
Buckskin		•		64E**
Buckskin		•		62E**
Buckskin		•		62J**
Buckskin		•		64J**
Buckskin		•		64M
Buckskin		•		62M
Buckskin		•		64C
Buckskin		•		62C
Buckskin		•		64N
Buckskin		•		62N
Firethorn		•		71E**
Firethorn		•		72E**
Firethorn		•		72J**
Firethorn		•		71J**
Firethorn		•		71M
Firethorn		•		72M
Firethorn		•		71C
Firethorn		•		72C
Firethorn		•		71N
Firethorn		•		72N
Firethorn		•		O7N

**These combinations for limited usage in order to use surplus cloth with the "G & E" combinations being produced first and the "B & J" combinations second.

NOVA TRIM

Color	Cloth	Vinyl	Leather	Code
White		•		11N
White		•		11V
Black		•		19B
Black		•		19N
Black		•		19Z
Black	•			19E
Blue		•		26M
Blue		•		26C
Blue		•		O2N
Blue		•		O2V
Lime		•		O3N
Lime		•		O3V
Buckskin		•		64B

NOVA TRIM

Color	Cloth	Vinyl	Leather	Code
Buckskin		•		64M
Buckskin		•		64D
Buckskin		•		64Z
Buckskin	•			64E
Buckskin		•		64V
Firethorn		•		71B
Firethorn		•		71M
Firethorn		•		71C
Firethorn		•		71N
Firethorn		•		O7N
Firethorn	•			71E
Firethorn		•		71V
Firethorn		•		O7N

THE PAINT CODE furnishes the key to the paint colors used on the car.

COLOR	CODE
Classic White	10
Antique White	11
Silver	13
Medium Gray	16
Black	19
Light Blue	21
Corvette Bright Blue	22
Light Blue	28
Corvette Dark Green	33
Dark Blue	35
Firethorn	36
Mahogany	37
Lime	40
Lime Green	45
Dark Green	49
Cream	50

COLOR	CODE
Bright Yellow	51
Corvette Bright Yellow	56
Cream Gold	57
Corvette Lt. Buckskin	64
Buckskin	65
Burnt Orange	66
Medium Saddle	67
Corvette Dark Brown	69
Corvette Orange Flame	70
Medium Red	72
Light Red	75
Medium Orange	78

TWO-TONE COMBINATIONS

LOWER COLOR	CODE	UPPER COLOR	CODE
Black	19	Silver	13
Dark Blue	35	Light Blue	28
Firethorn	36	Mahogany	37
Mahogany	37	Firethorn	36
Lime	40	Antique White	11
Dark Green	49	Antique White	11
Cream Gold	57	Antique White	11
Buckskin	65	Cream	50
Medium Saddle	67	Cream	50
Medium Red	72	Antique White	11

VINYL ROOF CODES

COLOR	CODE
White	11T
Silver	13T
Black	19T
Dark Blue	35T
Firethorn	36T
Mahogany	37T
Light Buckskin	65T

ENGINE NUMBER

THE ENGINE IDENTIFICATION NUMBER includes a letter code for the engine plant, followed by numbers which date the manufacture of the engine, then followed by a letter code to indicate the engine size and makeup.

THE ENGINE IDENTIFICATION NUMBER for V-8s is stamped on a pad located at the right-hand side of the cylinder block, and stamped on a pad on the right-hand side of the block behind the distributor on 4-cylinder and 6-cylinder engines.

NOTE:

1. To properly identify Chevrolet Division engines, it will be necessary to identify the car model in which the engine is used. The same engine type may have a different code when used in different car models.

2. NB2 is California emission
EXAMPLE

1	01	01	CCC
PLANT	MONTH	DAY	CODE

CHEVELLE ENGINES

Engine Code	No Cyl.	CID	Horse-power	Comp. Ratio	Carb
CCC	6	250	105	8.25:1	1 BC
CCD	6	250	105	8.25:1	1 BC
CCF	6	250	105	8.25:1	1 BC
9W	8	305	140	8.5:1	2 BC
CPB	8	305	140	8.5:1	2 BC
9R	8	350	140	8.5:1	2 BC
CLF	8	350	145	8.5:1	2 BC
CMH	8	350	155	8.5:1	4 BC

CHEVELLE ENGINES

Engine Code	No Cyl.	CID	Horse-power	Comp. Ratio	Carb
CMJ	8	350	145	8.5:1	2 BC
CMM	8	350	155	8.5:1	4 BC
CUF	8	350	155	8.5:1	4 BC
CSA	8	400	155	8.5:1	4 BC
CSB	8	400	175	8.5:1	4 BC
CSF	8	400	175	8.5:1	4 BC
CSW	8	400	175	8.5:1	4 BC
CSX	8	400	175	8.5:1	4 BC
CTU	8	400	175	8.5:1	4 BC
CTX	8	400	175	8.5:1	4 BC

MONTE CARLO ENGINES

Engine Code	No Cyl.	CID	Horse-power	Comp. Ratio	Carb
CCC	6	250	105	8.25:1	1 BC
CCD	6	250	105	8.25:1	1 BC
CCF	6	250	105	8.25:1	1 BC
9W	8	305	140	8.5:1	2 BC
CPB	8	305	140	8.5:1	2 BC
9R	8	350	140	8.5:1	2 BC
CMH	8	350	155	8.5:1	4 BC
CMJ	8	350	145	8.5:1	2 BC
CMM	8	350	155	8.5:1	4 BC
CSB	8	400	175	8.5:1	4 BC
CSF	8	400	175	8.5:1	4 BC
CSX	8	400	175	8.5:1	4 BC
CTU	8	400	175	8.5:1	4 BC
CTX	8	400	175	8.5:1	4 BC
9R	8	350			
9W	8	305	140	8.5:1	2 BC

NOVA ENGINES

Engine Code	No Cyl.	CID	Horse-power	Comp. Ratio	Carb
CCB	6	250	105	8.25:1	1 BC
CCC	6	250	105	8.25:1	1 BC
CCD	6	250	105	8.25:1	1 BC
CCF	6	250	105	8.25:1	1 BC
CZL	8	262	110	8.5:1	2 BC
CZM	8	262	110	8.5:1	2 BC
9W	8	305	140	8.5:1	2 BC
CPA	8	305	140	8.5:1	2 BC
CPC	8	305	140	8.5:1	2 BC
CPJ	8	305	140	8.5:1	2 BC
CHW	8	350	140	8.5:1	4 BC
CKJ	8	350	140	8.5:1	4 BC
CKK	8	350	140	8.5:1	4 BC
CKY	8	350	140	8.5:1	4 BC
CMB	8	350	140	8.5:1	4 BC
CPB	8	350	140	8.5:1	4 BC
CPE	8	350	140	8.5:1	4 BC
CPF	8	350	140	8.5:1	4 BC
CPM	8	350	140	8.5:1	4 BC
CPN	8	350	165	8.5:1	4 BC
CPO	8	350	165	8.5:1	4 BC
CPP	8	350	165	8.5:1	4 BC
CHT	8	350	165	8.5:1	4 BC
CHU	8	350	165	8.5:1	4 BC
CML	8	350	165	8.5:1	4 BC
9M	8	350	165	8.5:1	4 BC

CAMARO ENGINES

Engine Code	No Cyl.	CID	Horse-power	Comp. Ratio	Carb
CCC	6	250	105	8.25:1	1 BC
CCD	6	250	105	8.25:1	1 BC
CCF	6	250	105	8.25:1	1 BC
9W	8	305	140	8.5:1	2 BC
CPA	8	305	140	8.5:1	2 BC
CPB	8	305	140	8.5:1	2 BC
CPC	8	305	140	8.5:1	2 BC
CPJ	8	305	140	8.5:1	2 BC
7X	8	350	165	8.5:1	4 BC
CHT	8	350	165	8.5:1	4 BC

CAMARO ENGINES

Engine Code	No Cyl.	CID	Horsepower	Comp. Ratio	Carb
CHU	8	350	165	8.5:1	4 BC
CHW	8	350	165	8.5:1	4 BC
CMB	8	350	165	8.5:1	4 BC
CML	8	350	165	8.5:1	4 BC
9M	8	350	165	8.5:1	4 BC

CORVETTE ENGINES

Engine Code	No Cyl.	CID	Horsepower	Comp. Ratio	Carb
CLS	8	350	180	8.5:1	4 BC (L-48)
CHC	8	350	210	9.0:1	4 BC (L-82)
CKC	8	350	210	9.0:1	4 BC (L-82)
CKW	8	350	180	8.5:1	4 BC (L-48)
CKX	8	350	180	8.5:1	4 BC (L-48)

CHEVROLET ENGINES

Engine Code	No Cyl.	CID	Horsepower	Comp. Ratio	Carb
CHS	8	350	145	8.5:1	2 BC
CKU	8	350	155	8.5:1	2 BC
CLF	8	350	145	8.5:1	2 BC
CLH	8	350	155	8.5:1	4 BC
CMJ	8	350	145	8.5:1	2 BC
CMM	8	350	155	8.5:1	4 BC
CSF	8	400	175	8.5:1	4 BC
CSJ	8	400	175	8.5:1	4 BC
CSW	8	400	170	8.5:1	4 BC
CSX	8	400	175	8.5:1	4 BC
CTL	8	400	175	8.5:1	4 BC
CXX	8	454	235	8.5:1	4 BC
CXY	8	454	235	8.5:1	4 BC

CHEVETTE ENGINES

Engine Code	No Cyl.	CID	Horsepower	Comp. Ratio	Carb
CDA	4	85	52	8.5:1	1 BC
CDB	4	85	52	8.5:1	1 BC
CDC	4	85	52	8.5:1	1 BC
CDD	4	85	52	8.5:1	1 BC
CDF	4	85	52	8.5:1	1 BC
CDH	4	85	52	8.5:1	1 BC
CDJ	4	85	52	8.5:1	1 BC
CDK	4	85	52	8.5:1	1 BC
CDL	4	85	52	8.5:1	1 BC
CDM	4	85	52	8.5:1	1 BC
CDN	4	85	52	8.5:1	1 BC
CDR	4	85	52	8.5:1	1 BC
CDS	4	85	52	8.5:1	1 BC
CDT	4	85	52	8.5:1	1 BC
CDU	4	85	52	8.5:1	1 BC
CDW	4	85	52	8.5:1	1 BC
CDX	4	85	52	8.5:1	1 BC
CDY	4	85	52	8.5:1	1 BC
CVA	4	85	52	8.5:1	1 BC
CVB	4	85	52	8.5:1	1 BC
CNA	4	97	60	8.5:1	1 BC
CNB	4	97	60	8.5:1	1 BC
CYA	4	97	60	8.5:1	1 BC
CYB	4	97	60	8.5:1	1 BC
CYC	4	97	60	8.5:1	1 BC
CYD	4	97	60	8.5:1	1 BC
CYE	4	97	60	8.5:1	1 BC
CYH	4	97	60	8.5:1	1 BC
CYJ	4	97	60	8.5:1	1 BC
CYK	4	97	60	8.5:1	1 BC
CYL	4	97	60	8.5:1	1 BC
CYM	4	97	60	8.5:1	1 BC
CYR	4	97	60	8.5:1	1 BC
CYS	4	97	60	8.5:1	1 BC
CYT	4	97	60	8.5:1	1 BC
CYU	4	97	60	8.5:1	1 BC
CYW	4	97	60	8.5:1	1 BC

CHEVETTE ENGINES

Engine Code	No Cyl.	CID	Horse-power	Comp. Ratio	Carb
CYX	4	97	60	8.5:1	1 BC
CYY	4	97	60	8.5:1	1 BC
CYZ	4	97	60	8.5:1	1 BC

MONZA & VEGA ENGINES

Engine Code	No Cyl.	CID	Horse-power	Comp. Ratio	Carb
ZCA	4	122	110	8.5:1	F.I.
ZCB	4	122	110	8.5:1	F.I.
CAY	4	140	70	8.0:1	1 BC
CAZ	4	140	70	8.0:1	1 BC
CBK	4	140	70	8.0:1	1 BC
CBL	4	140	70	8.0:1	1 BC
CBS	4	140	70	8.0:1	1 BC
CBT	4	140	70	8.0:1	1 BC
CBU	4	140	84	8.0:1	2 BC
CBW	4	140	84	8.0:1	2 BC
CBX	4	140	84	8.0:1	2 BC
CBY	4	140	84	8.0:1	2 BC
CBZ	4	140	70	8.0:1	1 BC
CGA	8	262	110	8.5:1	2 BC
CGB	8	262	110	8.5:1	2 BC
CGL	8	262	110	8.5:1	2 BC
CZU	8	262	110	8.5:1	2 BC
CZT	8	262	110	8.5:1	2 BC
CAA	8	305	140	8.5:1	2 BC
CAB	8	305	140	8.5:1	2 BC
CPK	8	305	140	8.5:1	2 BC
CPL	8	305	140	8.5:1	2 BC

1977 CHEVROLET MONTE CARLO

1977 CHEVROLET CAMARO

1977 CHEVROLET CAPRICE

1977 CHEVROLET CONCOURS

1977 CHEVROLET MONZA 2+2

1977 CHEVROLET CORVETTE

1977 CHEVROLET NOVA

1977 CHEVROLET IMPALA

1977 CHEVROLET VEGA

1977 CHEVROLET CHEVELLE

VEHICLE IDENTIFICATION NUMBER

• CHEVROLET •
1L57L7S123456

On top left side of instrument panel, visible through the windshield.

Corvette VIN on left windshield pillar, visible through the windshield.

FIRST DIGIT: Indicates GM Divison (1 is Chevrolet)

SECOND DIGIT: Indicates series

CODE	SERIES
B	Chevette
C	Malibu
D	Malibu Classic
H	Monte Carlo
J	Chevette "Scooter"
L	Impala
M	Monza Towne Coupe
N	Caprice Classic
Q	Camaro
R	Monza Hatchback
S	Camaro LT
V	Vega
X	Nova
Y	Nova Concours
Z	Corvette

THIRD & FOURTH DIGITS: Indicate body style

STYLE	DESCRIPTION
07	2-Dr. Coupe - Hatch Back
08	2-Dr. Sedan - Hatch Back
11	2-Dr. Sedan - Notch Back
15	2-Dr. Station Wagon - 2-Seat
17	2-Dr. Coupe - Hatch Back
27	2-Dr. Coupe - Notch Back
29	4-Dr. Sedan - 6 Window Notch Back
35	4-Dr. Station Wagon - 2-Seat
37	2-Dr. Coupe - Notch Back
47	2-Dr. Coupe - Notch Back
57	2-Dr. Coupe - Notch Back
69	4-Dr. Sedan - 4 Window Notch Back
77	2-Dr. Hatch Back
80	2-Dr. Pick-up Delivery
87	2-Dr. Coupe - Plain Back

FIFTH DIGIT: Indicates engine

CODE	CID	TYPE	CARB
B	140	L-4	2 BC
D	250	L-6	1 BC
I	85	L-4	1 BC
E	97.6	L-4	1 BC
U	305	V8	2 BC
L	350	V8	4 BC
X	350	V8	4 BC

SIXTH DIGIT: Indicates the year (7 is 1977)

SEVENTH DIGIT: Indicates the assembly plant

ASSEMBLY PLANT	CODE
Lakewood	A
Baltimore	B
Southgate	C
Doraville	D
Flint (Trucks only)	F
Janesville	J
Leeds	K
Lordstown	U
Van Nuys	L
Norwood	N
Arlington	R

ASSEMBLY PLANT	CODE
St. Louis	S
Tarrytown	T
Willow Run	W
Wilmington	Y
Fremont	Z
Oshawa, Ont., Can.	1
St. Therese, Que., Can	2
Detroit	3
Scarborough, Can.	4
Fujisawa, Japan	8

REMAINING SIX DIGITS: Indicate production sequence number

EXAMPLE

1	L	47	V	7	W	123456
Chev Div.	Series	Body Style	Engine	Year	Asm Plant	Prod Code

BODY NUMBER PLATE

Located on upper horizontal surface of shroud except models "X" (Nova) and "Y" (Nova Concours). On "X" models, plate is located on vertical surface of shroud. On "Y" models, it is located on the upper left-hand door hinge pillar.

THE BODY NUMBER PLATE identifies the model year, car division, series, style, body assembly plant, body number, trim combination, modular seat code, paint code and date build code.

```
           BODY BY FISHER
  ST 77  1FQ87  N           123456 BDY
  TR 19R                        19 PNT
 •11A                                   •

      GENERAL MOTORS CORPORATION CERTIFIES
         TO THE DEALER THAT THIS VEHICLE
        CONFORMS TO ALL U.S., FEDERAL MOTOR
               VEHICLE SAFETY STANDARDS
        APPLICABLE AT TIME OF MANUFACTURE.
```

EXAMPLE

In the example above,

77	Model year (1977)
1	Car division (Chevrolet)
FQ	Series Camaro
87	Style (2-Dr Sport Coupe)
N	Body assembly plant (Norwood, Ohio)
123456	Production sequence in that plant
19R	Black Vinyl Trim
19	Tuxedo Black Paint
11	Eleventh month (November)
A	First week of month

NOTE: An option code will appear below the paint code. It is a notation to the assembly line workers that this vehicle is not a standard issue item. An example would be a radio delete, heater delete, etc. WE DO NOT HAVE BREAKDOWNS FOR THOSE CODES.

CHEVELLE
Malibu

	MODEL CODES
4-Dr Sport Sedan	1AC29
2-Dr. Sport Coupe	1AC37
4-Dr Station Wagon*	1AC35

Malibu Classic — **MODEL CODES**
4-Dr Sport Sedan 1AD29
2-Dr Sport Coupe 1AD37
4-Dr Station Wagon* 1AD35
*Third seat available as RPO (Regular Production Option/Order) on station wagon.

MONTE CARLO — **MODEL CODES**
Monte Carlo "S"
2-Dr Sport Coupe 1AH57
*Landau option available

NOVA — **MODEL CODES**
Nova
4-Dr Sedan 1XX69
2-Dr Coupe 1XX27
2-Dr Hatchback Coupe 1XX17
*Rally option available

Nova Concours
4-Dr Sedan 1XY69
2-Dr Coupe 1XY27
2-Dr Hatchback Coupe 1XY17

CAMARO — **MODEL CODES**
Camaro
2-Dr Sport Coupe 1FQ87
*Z-28 option available

Camaro "Type LT"
2-Dr Sport Coupe 1FS87

CORVETTE — **MODEL CODES**
Corvette
2-Dr Sport Coupe 1YZ37

CHEVROLET — **MODEL CODES**
Impala
4-Dr Sedan 1BL69
2-Dr Coupe 1BL47
4-Dr Station Wagon* 1BL35

Caprice Classic
4-Dr Sedan 1BN69
2-Dr Coupe 1BN47
4-Dr Station Wagon* 1BN35
*Third seat available as RPO (Regular Production Option/Order) on station wagon.

VEGA — **MODEL CODES**
2-Dr Notchback Coupe (Sedan) 1HV11
2-Dr Hatchback Coupe 1HV77
2-Dr Station Wagon 1HV15
*GT option available
*Estate option available

MONZA — **MODEL CODES**
2-Dr 2 Plus 2 Coupe 1HR07
2-Dr Town Coupe 1HM27
*Spyder option available

CHEVETTE — **MODEL CODES**
2-Dr Hatchback Coupe 1TB08
2-Dr Hatchback Coupe Scooter 1TJ08
*Sandpiper option available

THE TRIM NUMBER furnishes the key to trim color and material for each model series.

CHEVELLE TRIM

Color	Cloth	Vinyl	Leather	Code
Black		•		19Y
Black	•	•		19B
Black		•		19N
Buckskin		•		64Y
Buckskin	•	•		64B
Buckskin	•	•		64C
Buckskin	•	•		64H
Buckskin		•		64N
White		•		11Y
White		•		11N
Blue	•	•		24B
Blue	•	•		02Y
Blue	•	•		24C
Blue		•		24N
Blue		•		02N
Firethorn	•	•		07Y
Firethorn	•	•		71C
Firethorn		•		71N
Firethorn		•		07N
Green	•	•		04Y
Green	•	•		44C
Green		•		04N

MONTE CARLO TRIM

Color	Cloth	Vinyl	Leather	Code
Black	•	•		19E
Black		•		19V
Blue	•	•		24E
Blue		•		02W
Blue		•		02V
Blue	•	•		24G
Firethorn	•	•		71E
Firethorn		•		71V
Firethorn		•		07V
Firethorn	•	•		71G
Firethorn		•		07W
Green		•		44V
Green		•		04V
Green		•		04W
Buckskin		•		64V
Buckskin	•	•		64G
Buckskin		•		64W
White		•		11V
White		•		11W

CHEVROLET TRIM

Color	Cloth	Vinyl	Leather	Code
White		•		11N
White		•		11V
Black	•	•		19B
Black		•		19N
Black	•	•		19D
Black		•		19V
Blue	•	•		24B
Blue		•		24N
Blue		•		02N
Blue	•	•		24D
Blue		•		02V
Blue	•	•		24E
Buckskin	•	•		64B
Buckskin	•	•		64C
Buckskin	•	•		64N
Buckskin	•	•		64D
Buckskin	•	•		64G
Buckskin	•	•		64V
Buckskin	•	•		64E
Firethorn	•	•		71B
Firethorn	•	•		71C
Firethorn		•		71N
Firethorn		•		07N
Firethorn	•	•		71D

CHEVROLET TRIM

Color	Cloth	Vinyl	Leather	Code
Firethorn	•	•		71V
Firethorn		•		07V
Firethorn	•	•		71E
Green		•		04N
Green		•		44N
Green	•	•		44D
Green		•		04V

CAMARO TRIM

Color	Cloth	Vinyl	Leather	Code
White		•		11R
White		•		11N
Black		•		19R
Black		•		19N
Blue		•		02R
Blue	•	•		24C
Blue		•		24N
Blue		•		02N
Buckskin	•	•		62B
Buckskin	•	•		64B
Buckskin		•		64R
Buckskin		•		62R
Buckskin		•		06R
Buckskin	•	•		64C
Buckskin	•	•		62C
Buckskin		•		64N
Buckskin		•		62N
Buckskin		•		06N
Firethorn	•	•		72B
Firethorn	•	•		71B
Firethorn		•		71R
Firethorn		•		72R
Firethorn		•		07R
Firethorn	•	•		71C
Firethorn	•	•		72C
Firethorn		•		07N
Green		•		03R
Green		•		03N

VEGA TRIM

Color	Cloth	Vinyl	Leather	Code
White		•		11W
Black	•	•		19B
Black		•		19R
Black		•		19W
Blue		•		24W
Blue		•		02W
Buckskin	•	•		64B
Buckskin		•		64R
Buckskin	•	•		64D
Buckskin		•		64W
Buckskin		•		06W
Firethorn		•		71R
Firethorn	•	•		71D
Firethorn		•		71W
Firethorn		•		07W
Green		•		03W

MONZA TRIM

Color	Cloth	Vinyl	Leather	Code
White		•		11V
Black	•	•		19G
Black	•	•		17G
Black	•	•		19J
Black		•		19V
Black			•	193
Blue		•		02V
Buckskin	•	•		64G
Buckskin	•	•		62G
Buckskin	•	•		64J
Buckskin		•		64V
Buckskin		•		06V
Buckskin	•	•		64E
Buckskin			•	643

MONZA TRIM

Color	Cloth	Vinyl	Leather	Code
Firethorn	•	•		71J
Firethorn		•		71V
Firethorn		•		07V
Firethorn	•	•		71E
Aqua		•		03V

CHEVETTE TRIM

Color	Cloth	Vinyl	Leather	Code
White		•		11N
Black		•		19V
Black		•		19R
Black		•		18R
Black		•		19N
Blue		•		24N
Blue		•		24R
Blue	•	•		24C
Blue	•	•		24G
Ylw/Gold	•	•		54D
Buckskin		•		62V
Buckskin	•	•		62B
Buckskin	•	•		64E
Buckskin		•		64R
Buckskin	•	•		64C
Buckskin		•		64N
Buckskin		•		06N
Firethorn	•	•		71E
Firethorn		•		71E
Firethorn	•	•		71C
Firethorn		•		71N
Firethorn		•		07N
Aqua		•		03N

NOVA TRIM

Color	Cloth	Vinyl	Leather	Code
White		•		11N
White		•		11V
Black	•	•		19B
Black		•		19N
Black		•		19Z
Black	•	•		19E
Blue		•		24R
Blue		•		02N
Blue	•	•		24C
Blue		•		02V
Buckskin	•	•		64B
Buckskin		•		64R
Buckskin	•	•		64D
Buckskin		•		64Z
Buckskin	•	•		64E
Buckskin		•		64V
Firethorn		•		71V
Firethorn	•	•		71E
Firethorn	•	•		71B
Firethorn		•		71R
Firethorn	•	•		71C
Firethorn		•		71N
Firethorn		•		07N
Firethorn		•		07V
Firethorn		•		71V
Aqua		•		03N
Aqua		•		03V

THE PAINT CODE furnishes the key to the paint colors used on the car.

COLOR	CODE
Corvette Classic White	10
Antique White	11
Silver	13
Medium Gray	16
Black	19
Light Blue	21

COLOR

COLOR	CODE
Light Blue	22
Corvette Light Blue	26
Corvette Dark Blue	28
Dark Blue	29
Light Lime	32
Firethorn	36
Dark Aqua	38
Medium Green	44
Dark Blue Green	48
Cream Gold	50
Bright Yellow	51
Corvette Yellow	52
Light Buckskin	61
Buckskin	63
Bright Orange	64
Corvette Orange	66
Brown	69
Red	72
Light Red	75
Orange	78
Corvette Tan Buckskin	80
Corvette Dark Red	83
Medium Blue	85

TWO-TONE COMBINATIONS

LOWER COLOR	CODE	UPPER COLOR	CODE
Dark Blue Metallic	29	Light Blue Metallic	22
Light Blue Metallic	22	Antique White	11
Blue-Green Met.	48	Medium Green Met	44
Brown Metallic	69	Light Buckskin	61
Medium Green Met	44	Antique White	11
Orange Metallic	78	Antique White	11
Medium Red	72	Antique White	11
Aqua Metallic	38	Antique White	11
Light Red	75	Antique White	11
Aqua(Met), White	38	Antique White	11
Dk Blue (Met)/Lt Blue	29	Light Blue (Met)	22

VINYL ROOF CODES

COLOR	CODE
White	11T
Silver	13T
Black	19T
Light Blue	22T
Firethorn	36T
Medium Green	44T
Light Buckskin	61T

ENGINE NUMBER

THE ENGINE IDENTIFICATION NUMBER includes a letter code for the engine plant, followed by numbers which date the manufacture of the engine, then followed by a letter code to indicate the engine size and makeup.

THE ENGINE IDENTIFICATION NUMBER for V-8s is stamped on a pad located at the right-hand side of the cylinder block, and stamped on a pad on the right-hand side of the block behind the distributor on 4-cylinder and 6-cylinder engines.

NOTE:

1. To properly identify Chevrolet Division engines, it will be necessary to identify the car model in which the engine is used. The same engine type may have a different code when used in different car models.

2. NB-2 is California emission

EXAMPLE

1	01	01	CCC
PLANT	MONTH	DAY	CODE

CHEVELLE ENGINES

Engine Code	No Cyl.	CID	Horse-power	Comp. Ratio	Carb
7SB	6	250	110	8.25:1	1 BC
CCA	6	250	110	8.25:1	1 BC
CCC	6	250	110	8.25:1	1 BC
CCD	6	250	110	8.25:1	1 BC
CCF	6	250	110	8.25:1	1 BC
CJA	6	250	110	8.25:1	1 BC
CRA	8	305	145	8.5:1	2 BC
CRF	8	305	145	8.5:1	2 BC
CPY	8	305	145	8.5:1	2 BC
CHA	8	350	170	8.5:1	4 BC
CHB	8	350	170	8.5:1	4 BC
CHX	8	350	170	8.5:1	4 BC
CKH	8	350	170	8.5:1	4 BC
CKJ	8	350	170	8.5:1	4 BC
CKK	8	350	170	8.5:1	4 BC
CKM	8	350	170	8.5:1	4 BC
CKR	8	350	170	8.5:1	4 BC
CMF	8	350	170	8.5:1	4 BC

MONTE CARLO ENGINES

Engine Code	No Cyl.	CID	Horsepower	Comp. Ratio	Carb
CPY	8	305	145	8.5:1	2 BC
CRA	8	305	145	8.5:1	2 BC
CRF	8	305	145	8.5:1	2 BC
CHA	8	350	170	8.5:1	4 BC
CHX	8	350	170	8.5:1	4 BC
CKH	8	350	170	8.5:1	4 BC
CKJ	8	350	170	8.5:1	4 BC
CKK	8	350	170	8.5:1	4 BC
CKM	8	350	170	8.5:1	4 BC
CKR	8	350	170	8.5:1	4 BC
CMF	8	350	170	8.5:1	4 BC

NOVA ENGINES

Engine Code	No Cyl.	CID	Horsepower	Comp. Ratio	Carb
7SB	6	250	110	8.25:1	1 BC
C2D	6	250	110	8.25:1	1 BC
C3C	6	250	110	8.25:1	1 BC
C8Y	6	250	110	8.25:1	1 BC
CCC	6	250	110	8.25:1	1 BC
CCD	6	250	110	8.25:1	1 BC
CCF	6	250	110	8.25:1	1 BC
CCT	6	250	110	8.25:1	1 BC
CCU	6	250	110	8.25:1	1 BC
CCW	6	250	110	8.25:1	1 BC
CJA	6	250	110	8.25:1	1 BC
C2M	8	305	145	8.5:1	2 BC
CPA	8	305	145	8.5:1	2 BC
CPC	8	305	145	8.5:1	2 BC
CPS	8	305	145	8.5:1	2 BC
CPT	8	305	145	8.5:1	2 BC
CPY	8	305	145	8.5:1	2 BC
C2K	8	305	145	8.5:1	2 BC
C2L	8	305	145	8.5:1	2 BC
CHA	8	350	170	8.5:1	4 BC
CHB	8	350	170	8.5:1	4 BC
CHX	8	350	170	8.5:1	4 BC
CKH	8	350	170	8.5:1	4 BC
CKM	8	350	170	8.5:1	4 BC
CKR	8	350	170	8.5:1	4 BC
CKS	8	350	170	8.5:1	4 BC

CAMARO ENGINES

Engine Code	No Cyl.	CID	Horsepower	Comp. Ratio	Carb
C3Y	6	250	110	8.25:1	1 BC
C8Y	6	250	110	8.25:1	1 BC
CCC	6	250	110	8.25:1	1 BC
CCD	6	250	110	8.25:1	1 BC
CCF	6	250	110	8.25:1	1 BC
CCW	6	250	110	8.25:1	1 BC
CJA	6	250	110	8.25:1	1 BC
CKH	6	250	110	8.25:1	1 BC
C2M	8	305	145	8.5:1	2 BC
CPA	8	305	145	8.5:1	2 BC
CPC	8	305	145	8.5:1	2 BC
CPY	8	305	145	8.5:1	2 BC
C2K	8	305	145	8.5:1	2 BC
C2L	8	305	145	8.5:1	2 BC
CHZ	8	350	170	8.5:1	2 BC
CKM	8	350	170	8.5:1	4 BC
CKR	8	350	170	8.5:1	4 BC
CKS	8	350	170	8.5:1	4 BC
CLU	8	350	170	8.5:1	4 BC
CLX	8	350	170	8.5:1	4 BC

CORVETTE ENGINES

Engine Code	No Cyl.	CID	Horse-power	Comp. Ratio	Carb
CKZ	8	350	180	8.5:1	4 BC
CLA	8	350	180	8.5:1	4 BC
CLB	8	350	180	8.5:1	4 BC
CLC	8	350	180	8.5:1	4 BC
CLD	8	350	210	9.0:1	4 BC
CLF	8	350	210	9.0:1	4 BC
CLH	8	350	210	9.0:1	4 BC
CHD	8	350	210	9.0:1	4 BC
CKD	8	350	210	9.0:1	4 BC

CHEVETTE ENGINES

Engine Code	No Cyl.	CID	Horse-power	Comp. Ratio	Carb
CDS	4	85	52	8.5:1	1 BC
CVA	4	85	52	8.5:1	1 BC
CVB	4	85	52	8.5:1	1 BC
CNA	4	97	60	8.5:1	1 BC
CNB	4	97	60	8.5:1	1 BC
CNC	4	97	60	8.5:1	1 BC
CND	4	97	60	8.5:1	1 BC
CNF	4	97	60	8.5:1	1 BC
CNH	4	97	60	8.5:1	1 BC
CNL	4	97	60	8.5:1	1 BC
CNN	4	97	60	8.5:1	1 BC
CNR	4	97	60	8.5:1	1 BC
CNS	4	97	60	8.5:1	1 BC
CNT	4	97	60	8.5:1	1 BC
CNU	4	97	60	8.5:1	1 BC
CYC	4	97	60	8.5:1	1 BC
CYD	4	97	60	8.5:1	1 BC
CYF	4	97	60	8.5:1	1 BC
CYH	4	97	60	8.5:1	1 BC
CYY	4	97	60	8.5:1	1 BC
CYZ	4	97	60	8.5:1	1 BC

CHEVROLET ENGINES

Engine Code	No Cyl.	CID	Horse-power	Comp. Ratio	Carb
CCA	6	250	110	8.25:1	1 BC
CCC	6	250	110	8.25:1	1 BC
CCF	6	250	110	8.25:1	1 BC
CCR	6	250	110	8.25:1	1 BC
CCS	6	250	110	8.25:1	1 BC
CCY	6	250	110	8.25:1	1 BC
CCZ	6	250	110	8.25:1	1 BC
CJA	6	250	110	8.25:1	1 BC
CJB	6	250	110	8.25:1	1 BC
CJF	6	250	110	8.25:1	1 BC
CPM	8	305	145	8.5:1	2 BC
CPR	8	305	145	8.5:1	2 BC
CRB	8	305	145	8.5:1	2 BC
CCK	8	350	170	8.5:1	4 BC
CHY	8	350	170	8.5:1	4 BC
CKA	8	350	170	8.5:1	4 BC
CKB	8	350	170	8.5:1	4 BC
CKC	8	350	170	8.5:1	4 BC
CLL	8	350	170	8.5:1	4 BC
CLT	8	350	170	8.5:1	4 BC
CMM	8	350	170	8.5:1	4 BC
CUB	8	350	170	8.5:1	4 BC
CUC	8	350	170	8.5:1	4 BC
CUD	8	350	170	8.5:1	4 BC

MONZA & VEGA ENGINES

Engine Code	No Cyl.	CID	Horse-power	Comp. Ratio	Carb
CAA	4	140	84	8.0:1	2 BC
CAB	4	140	84	8.0:1	2 BC
CAC	4	140	84	8.0:1	2 BC
CAY	4	140	84	8.0:1	2 BC
CAZ	4	140	84	8.0:1	2 BC
CBK	4	140	84	8.0:1	2 BC
CBL	4	140	84	8.0:1	2 BC
CBS	4	140	84	8.0:1	2 BC
CBT	4	140	84	8.0:1	2 BC
CBU	4	140	84	8.0:1	2 BC
CBW	4	140	84	8.0:1	2 BC
CBX	4	140	84	8.0:1	2 BC
CBY	4	140	84	8.0:1	2 BC
CBZ	4	140	84	8.0:1	2 BC
CPK	8	305	145	8.5:1	2 BC
CPL	8	305	145	8.5:1	2 BC
CPU	8	305	145	8.5:1	2 BC
CPX	8	305	145	8.5:1	2 BC
CRC	8	305	145	8.5:1	2 BC
CRD	8	305	145	8.5:1	2 BC

1978 CHEVROLET IMPALA

1978 CHEVROLET MONZA 2+2

1978 CHEVROLET MALIBU

1978 CHEVROLET CAMARO

1978 CHEVROLET MONTE CARLO

1978 CHEVROLET CHEVETTE

1978 CHEVROLET MONZA

1978 CHEVROLET CORVETTE

1978 CHEVROLET NOVA

1978 CHEVROLET CAPRICE

VEHICLE IDENTIFICATION NUMBER

CHEVROLET
1L47L8S123456

On top left side of instrument panel, visible through the windsheild.

Corvette VIN on left windshield pillar, visible through the windshield.

FIRST DIGIT: Indicates GM division (1 is Chevrolet)

SECOND DIGIT: Indicates series.

CODE	SERIES
B	Chevette
J	Chevette "Scooter"
L	Impala
M	Monza, Monza S
N	Caprice Classic
Q	Camaro
R	Monza 2 plus 2, Monza Sport
S	Camaro LT
T	Malibu
W	Malibu Classic
X	Nova
Y	Nova Custom
Z	Corvette
Z	Monte Carlo

THIRD & FOURTH DIGITS: Indicate body style

STYLE	DESCRIPTION
07	2-Dr. Hatch Back Monza 2+2
08	2-Dr. Hatch Back Coupe, 4-Passenger
15	2-Dr. Station Wagon
17	2-Dr. Hatch Back Coupe, 6-Passenger
19	4-Dr. Sedan, 6-Passenger
27	2-Dr. Coupe or Notch Back Coupe 4 or 6-Passenger
35	4-Dr. Station Wagon
37	2-Dr. Sport Coupe, 6-Passenger
47	2-Dr. Coupe, 6-Passenger
68	4-Dr. Hatchback Sedan, 4-Passenger
69	4-Dr. Sedan, 6-Passenger
77	2-Dr. Hatch Back Monza
87	2-Dr. Sport Coupe, 4-Passenger Camaro,
87	2-Passenger Corvette

FIFTH DIGIT: Indicates engine

CODE	CID	TYPE	CARB
E&J	97.6	L-4	1 BC
V	151	L-4	2 BC
C	196	L-6	2 BC
M	200	L-6	2 BC
A	231	L-6	2 BC
D	250	L-6	1 BC
U	305	V8	2 BC
L	350	V8	4 BC
H	350	V8	4 BC
4	350	V8	4 BC (L-82)

SIXTH DIGIT: Indicates the year (8 is 1978)

SEVENTH DIGIT: Indicates the assembly plant

ASSEMBLY PLANT	CODE
Lakewood	A
Baltimore	B
Southgate	C
Doraville	D
Janesville	J
Leeds	K
Lordstown	U
Van Nuys	L
Norwood	N

ASSEMBLY PLANT	CODE
Arlington	R
St. Louis	S
Tarrytown	T
Willow Run	W
Wilmington	Y
Fremont	Z
Oshawa, Ont., Can.	1
St. Therese, Que., Can.	2
Detroit	3
Scarborough, Can	4
Fujisawa, Japan	8

REMAINING SIX DIGITS: Indicate production sequence number

EXAMPLE

1	L	47	L	8	W	123456
Chev Div.	Series	Body Style	Engine	Year	Asm Plant	Prod Code

BODY NUMBER PLATE

Located on the firewall below the rear edge of the hood of all models, except Corvette. Corvette plate is located on the upper left-hand door hinge pillar.

THE BODY NUMBER PLATE identifies the model year, car division, series, style, body assembly plant, body number, trim combination, paint code and date build code.

BODY BY FISHER
ST 78 1FQ87 N   123456 BDY
TR 19R   19 PNT
● 11A   ●

GENERAL MOTORS CORPORATION CERTIFIES TO THE DEALER THAT THIS VEHICLE CONFORMS TO ALL U.S., FEDERAL MOTOR VEHICLE SAFETY STANDARDS APPLICABLE AT TIME OF MANUFACTURE.

EXAMPLE

In the example above,

78	Model year (1978)
1	Car division (Chevrolet)
FQ	Series (Camaro V-8)
87	Style (2-Dr Sport Coupe)
N	Body Assembly Plant (Norwood, Ohio)
123456	Production sequence in that plant
19R	Black Vinyl Trim
19	Tuxedo Black Paint
11	Eleventh month (November)
A	First week of month

NOTE: An option code will appear below the paint code. It is a notation to the assembly line workers that this vehicle is not a standard issue item. An example would be a radio delete, heater delete, etc. WE DO NOT HAVE BREAKDOWNS FOR THOSE CODES.

CHEVELLE Malibu	MODEL CODES
2-Dr Notchback Coupe	1AT27
4-Dr Sedan	1AT19
4-Dr Station Wagon	1AT35

Malibu Classic — MODEL CODES
2-Dr Notchback Coupe 1AW27
4-Dr Sedan 1AW19
4-Dr Station Wagon 1AW35
*Landau option available

MONTE CARLO — MODEL CODES
2-Dr Sport Coupe 1AZ37
*Landau option available

NOVA — MODEL CODES
Nova
4-Dr Sedan 1XX69
2-Dr Coupe 1XX27
2-Dr Hatchback Coupe 1XX17

Nova Custom
4-Dr Sedan 1XY69
2-Dr Coupe 1XY27
*Rally option available

CAMARO — MODEL CODES
Camaro
2-Dr Sport Coupe 1FQ87
*Z-28 option available
*Rally Sport option available

Camaro "Type LT"
2-Dr Sport Coupe 1FS87
*Rally Sport option available

CORVETTE — MODEL CODES
2-Dr Sport Coupe 1YZ87
*Silver Anniversary Pace Car option available

CHEVROLET — MODEL CODES
Impala
4-Dr Sedan 1BL69
2-Dr Coupe 1BL47
4-Dr Station Wagon 1BL35
*Landau option available

Caprice Classic
4-Dr Sedan 1BN69
2-Dr Coupe 1BN47
4-Dr Station Wagon 1BN35
*Landau option available

MONZA — MODEL CODES
2-Dr Hatchback Coupe 1HM77
2-Dr 2 plus 2 Hatchback Coupe 1HM07
2-Dr Notchback Coupe 1HM27
2-Dr Station Wagon 1HM15
2-Dr 2 plus 2 Hatchback Coupe 1HR07
2-Dr Notchback Coupe 1HR27
*Estate option available
*Spyder option available

CHEVETTE — MODEL CODES
Chevette Scooter 1TJ08
2-Dr Hatchback 1TB08
4-Dr Hatchback 1TB68

THE TRIM NUMBER furnishes the key to trim color and material for each model series.

CHEVELLE TRIM

Color	Cloth	Vinyl	Leather	Code
White		•		11N
White		•		11V
Black	•	•		19C
Black	•	•		19D
Black		•		19V
Black	•	•		19E

CHEVELLE TRIM

Color	Cloth	Vinyl	Leather	Code
Blue	•	•		24C
Blue		•		24N
Blue	•	•		24D
Blue		•		24V
Blue	•	•		24E
Green	•	•		44C
Green	•	•		44D
Tan	•	•		62C
Tan		•		62N
Tan	•	•		62D
Tan		•		62V
Tan	•	•		62E
Carmine		•		74N
Carmine	•	•		74D
Carmine		•		74V
Carmine	•	•		74E

MONTE CARLO TRIM

Color	Cloth	Vinyl	Leather	Code
White		•		11W
White		•		11Y
Black	•	•		19G
Blue	•	•		24G
Blue		•		24W
Blue	•	•		24H
Green	•	•		44G
Tan	•	•		62G
Tan		•		62W
Tan	•	•		62H
Tan		•		62Y
Carmine	•	•		74G
Carmine		•		74W
Carmine	•	•		74H
Carmine		•		74Y

CHEVROLET TRIM

Color	Cloth	Vinyl	Leather	Code
White		•		11N
White		•		11V
Black		•		19N
Black	•	•		19D
Blue	•	•		24B
Blue		•		24N
Blue	•	•		24D
Blue		•		24V
Blue	•	•		24G
Blue	•	•		24E
Green	•	•		44B
Green	•	•		44D
Green		•		44V
Green	•	•		44E

CAMARO TRIM

Color	Cloth	Vinyl	Leather	Code
White		•		11N
White		•		11R
White		•		11N
Black		•		19N
Black		•		19R
Black		•		19N
Blue	•	•		24C
Blue	•	•		24B
Green		•		44N
Green		•		44R
Tan	•	•		62C
Tan		•		62N
Tan	•	•		62B
Tan		•		62R
Carmine		•		74N
Carmine		•		74R
Carmine	•	•		74C
Carmine	•	•		74B

MONZA TRIM

Color	Cloth	Vinyl	Leather	Code
White		•		11V
White		•		11W
Black	•	•		19G
Black		•		19Y
Black	•	•		19B
Black		•		19R
Black		•		19V
Black		•		19W
Black	•	•		19J
Black	•	•		19D
Blue		•		24Y
Blue		•		24R
Blue	•	•		24J
Blue		•		24V
Blue		•		24W
Green		•		44V
Tan	•	•		62G
Tan		•		62Y
Tan		•		62B
Tan		•		62R
Tan	•	•		62J
Tan		•		62V
Tan	•	•		62D
Tan		•		62W
Carmine		•		74Y
Carmine		•		74R
Carmine		•		74V
Carmine		•		74W
Carmine	•	•		74J
Carmine	•	•		74D

NOVA TRIM

Color	Cloth	Vinyl	Leather	Code
White		•		11N
Black		•		19Z
Black		•		19R
Blue	•	•		24B
Blue		•		24R
Blue	•	•		24D
Green		•		44N
Tan		•		62Z
Tan	•	•		62B
Tan		•		62R
Tan	•	•		62D
Tan		•		62N
Carmine		•		74R
Carmine	•	•		74D
Carmine		•		74N

CHEVETTE TRIM

Color	Cloth	Vinyl	Leather	Code
White		•		11N
White		•		11Y
Black	•	•		17B
Black		•		17V
Black	•	•		19B
Black		•		19V
Black		•		17R
Black		•		19R
Black	•	•		19E
Black		•		17W
Black		•		19W
Black	•	•		19D
Black	•	•		19C
Black	•	•		19G
Black	•	•		17E
Black	•	•		17D
Blue		•		24R
Blue		•		24W
Blue	•	•		24C
Blue		•		24N
Blue	•	•		24G
Blue		•		24Y
Green		•		44G

CHEVETTE TRIM

Color	Cloth	Vinyl	Leather	Code
Green		•		44W
Green		•		44N
Green		•		44Y
Tan	•	•		62B
Tan		•		62V
Tan		•		62R
Tan	•	•		62E
Tan		•		62W
Tan	•	•		62D
Tan	•	•		62C
Tan		•		62N
Tan	•	•		62G
Tan		•		62Y
Carmine		•		74R
Carmine	•	•		74E
Carmine		•		74W
Carmine	•	•		74D
Carmine	•	•		74C
Carmine		•		74N
Carmine	•	•		74G
Carmine		•		74Y

THE PAINT CODE furnishes the key to the paint colors used on the car.

COLOR	CODE
Corvette Dk Gray Poly (Two-Tone)	7
Corvette Clasic White	10
Antique White	11
Corvette Silver Poly	13
Silver Poly	15
Gray Poly (Two-Tone)	16
Black	19
Pastel Blue	21
Lt. Blue Poly	22
Ultramarine Blue Poly	24
Corvette Frost Blue	26
Dark Blue Poly	29
Orange	34
Medium Green Poly	44
Dark Green Poly	45
Dark Blue Green Poly	48
Bright Yellow	51
Corvette Yellow	52
Gold Poly (Two-Tone)	56
Corvette Frost Beige	59
Camel Beige	61
Camel Tan Poly	63
Saffron Poly	67
Dark Camel Poly	69
Corvette Red	72
Red	75
Carmine Poly	77
Dark Carmine Poly	79
Corvette Mahogany Poly	82
Corvette Dark Blue Poly	83
Corvette Brown Poly	89

TWO-TONE COMBINATIONS

LOWER COLOR	CODE	UPPER COLOR	CODE
Dark Blue Met	29	Light Blue Metallic	22
Light Blue Met	22	Antique White	11
Camel Metallic	63	Antique White	11
Dark Camel Met	69	Light Camel	61
Carmine Metallic	77	Antique White	11
Light Green Met	44	Antique White	11
Med Green Met	45	Antique White	11
Blue Met/White	24	Antique White	11
Lt Blue Met/White	22	Antique White	11
Camel Met/Lt Camel	63	Light Camel	61
Dark Camel Metallic	69	Camel Metallic/Lt Camel	63
Light Red/White	75	Antique White	11

VINYL ROOF CODES

COLOR	CODE
White	11T
Silver Poly	15T
Black	19T
Light Blue Poly	22T
Medium Green Poly	44T
Camel Beige	61T
Dark Carmine Poly	79T

ENGINE NUMBER

THE ENGINE IDENTIFICATION NUMBER includes a letter code for the engine plant, followed by numbers which date the manufacture of the engine, then followed by a letter code to indicate the engine size and makeup.

THE ENGINE IDENTIFICATION NUMBER for V-8s is stamped on a pad located on the right-hand side of the cylinder block, and stamped on a pad on the right-hand side of the block behind the distributor on 4-cylinder and 6-cylinder engines.

NOTE:

1. To properly identify Chevrolet Division engines, it will be necessary to identify the car model in which the engine is used. The same engine type may have a different code when used in different car models.

2. NB-2 is California emission

EXAMPLE

1	01	01	CCC
PLANT	MONTH	DAY	CODE

MALIBU ENGINES

Engine Code	No Cyl.	CID	Horse-power	Comp. Ratio	Carb
CWA	6	200	95	8.2:1	2 BC
CWB	6	200	95	8.2:1	2 BC
CWC	6	200	95	8.2:1	2 BC
CWD	6	200	95	8.2:1	2 BC
D4	6	231	105	8.0:1	2 BC
EA	6	231	105	8.0:1	2 BC
OH	6	231	105	8.0:1	2 BC
OK	6	231	105	8.0:1	2 BC
C4D	8	305	145	8.4:1	2 BC
CER	8	305	145	8.4:1	2 BC
CPZ	8	305	145	8.4:1	2 BC
CRH	8	305	145	8.4:1	2 BC
CRU	8	305	145	8.4:1	2 BC
CRW	8	305	145	8.4:1	2 BC
CRX	8	305	145	8.4:1	2 BC
CRY	8	305	135	8.4:1	2 BC
CRZ	8	305	145	8.4:1	2 BC
DAF	8	305	145	8.4:1	2 BC
CMA	8	350	170	8.2:1	4 BC
CMB	8	350	160	8.2:1	4 BC
CMC	8	350	170	8.2:1	4 BC
CMD	8	350	170	8.2:1	4 BC

MONTE CARLO ENGINES

Engine Code	No Cyl.	CID	Horse-power	Comp. Ratio	Carb
DH	6	231	105	8.0:1	2 BC
EA	6	231	105	8.0:1	2 BC
OH	6	231	105	8.0:1	2 BC
OK	6	231	105	8.0:1	2 BC
C4D	8	305	145	8.4:1	2 BC
CER	8	305	145	8.4:1	2 BC
CPZ	8	305	145	8.4:1	2 BC

MONTE CARLO ENGINES

Engine Code	No Cyl.	CID	Horse-power	Comp. Ratio	Carb
CRH	8	305	145	8.4:1	2 BC
CRU	8	305	145	8.4:1	2 BC
CRW	8	305	145	8.4:1	2 BC
CRX	8	305	145	8.4:1	2 BC
CRY	8	305	135	8.4:1	2 BC
CRZ	8	305	145	8.4:1	2 BC
DAF	8	305	145	8.4:1	2 BC

NOVA ENGINES

Engine Code	No Cyl.	CID	Horse-power	Comp. Ratio	Carb
C2D	6	250	90	8.1:1	1 BC
CCH	6	250	110	8.1:1	1 BC
CCK	6	250	110	8.1:1	1 BC
CCJ	6	250	110	8.1:1	1 BC
CJM	6	250	110	8.1:1	1 BC
CJR	6	250	90	8.1:1	1 BC
CPJ	8	305	145	8.4:1	2 BC
CRM	8	305	145	8.4:1	2 BC
CTH	8	305	145	8.4:1	2 BC
CTJ	8	305	145	8.4:1	2 BC
CTK	8	305	145	8.4:1	2 BC
C2K	8	305	145	8.4:1	2 BC
CHJ	8	350	160	8.2:1	4 BC
CHL	8	350	170	8.2:1	4 BC
CUM	8	350	170	8.2:1	4 BC
CUR	8	350	170	8.2:1	4 BC
CUS	8	350	170	8.2:1	4 BC

CAMARO ENGINES

Engine Code	No Cyl.	CID	Horse-power	Comp. Ratio	Carb
CCH	6	250	90	8.1:1	1 BC
CCJ	6	250	110	8.1:1	1 BC
CCK	6	250	110	8.1:1	1 BC
C3Y	6	250	110	8.1:1	1 BC
CEM	8	305	145	8.4:1	2 BC
CTH	8	305	145	8.4:1	2 BC
CTJ	8	305	145	8.4:1	2 BC
CTK	8	305	145	8.4:1	2 BC
C3N	8	305	145	8.4:1	2 BC
CHF	8	350	170	8.2:1	4 BC
CHJ	8	350	160	8.2:1	4 BC
CHL	8	350	170	8.2:1	4 BC
CHR	8	350	170	8.2:1	4 BC
CHS	8	350	170	8.2:1	4 BC
CHT	8	350	160	8.2:1	4 BC
CHU	8	350	170	8.2:1	4 BC
C3T	8	350	170	8.2:1	4 BC

CORVETTE ENGINES

Engine Code	No Cyl.	CID	Horse-power	Comp. Ratio	Carb
CHW	8	350	185	8.2:1	4 BC (L-48)
CLM	8	350	185	8.2:1	4 BC (L-48)
CLR	8	350	175	8.2:1	4 BC (L-48)
CLS	8	350	185	8.2:1	4 BC (L-48)
CMR	8	350	220	8.9:1	4 BC (L-48)
CMS	8	350	220	8.9:1	4 BC (L-48)

CHEVROLET ENGINES

Engine Code	No Cyl.	CID	Horse-power	Comp. Ratio	Carb
CCH	6	250	90	8.1:1	1 BC
CCK	6	250	110	8.1:1	1 BC
CCL	6	250	110	8.1:1	1 BC
CCM	6	250	90	8.1:1	1 BC
CJJ	6	250	90	8.1:1	1 BC
CJK	6	250	110	8.1:1	1 BC
DAD	6	250	110	8.1:1	1 BC
CEJ	8	305	145	8.4:1	2 BC

CHEVROLET ENGINES

Engine Code	No Cyl.	CID	Horse-power	Comp. Ratio	Carb
CEK	8	305	135	8.4:1	2 BC
CTL	8	305	145	8.4:1	2 BC
DAA	8	305	145	8.4:1	2 BC
DAB	8	305	145	8.4:1	2 BC
CHF	8	350	170	8.2:1	4 BC
CHH	8	350	170	8.2:1	4 BC
CHJ	8	350	160	8.2:1	4 BC
CHK	8	350	170	8.2:1	4 BC
CHL	8	350	170	8.2:1	4 BC
CHM	8	350	170	8.2:1	4 BC
CHY	8	350	170	8.2:1	4 BC
CLK	8	350	170	8.2:1	4 BC
CLT	8	350	170	8.2:1	4 BC
CMT	8	350	170	8.2:1	4 BC
CNT	8	350	170	8.2:1	4 BC
CUF	8	350	170	8.2:1	4 BC
CUM	8	350	170	8.2:1	4 BC
CUR	8	350	170	8.2:1	4 BC
CUS	8	350	170	8.2:1	4 BC

MONZA ENGINES

Engine Code	No Cyl.	CID	Horse-power	Comp. Ratio	Carb
WB	4	151	85	8.3:1	2 BC
WD	4	151	85	8.3:1	2 BC
WH	4	151	85	8.3:1	2 BC
XL	4	151	85	8.3:1	2 BC
XN	4	151	85	8.3:1	2 BC
AC	4	151	85	8.3:1	2 BC
AD	4	151	85	8.3:1	2 BC
ZA	4	151	85	8.3:1	2 BC
ZB	4	151	85	8.3:1	2 BC
ZC	4	151	85	8.3:1	2 BC
ZD	4	151	85	8.3:1	2 BC
ZF	4	151	85	8.3:1	2 BC
ZH	4	151	85	8.3:1	2 BC
ZJ	4	151	85	8.3:1	2 BC
ZK	4	151	85	8.3:1	2 BC
ZL	4	151	85	8.3:1	2 BC
ZN	4	151	85	8.3:1	2 BC
PC	6	196	86	8.0:1	2 BC
PD	6	196	86	8.0:1	2 BC
OC	6	231	105	8.0:1	2 BC
OD	6	231	105	8.0:1	2 BC
OE	6	231	105	8.0:1	2 BC
OF	6	231	105	8.0:1	2 BC
CTA	8	305	145	8.5:1	2 BC
CTB	8	305	145	8.5:1	2 BC
CTC	8	305	135	8.5:1	2 BC
CTD	8	305	145	8.5:1	2 BC
CTF	8	305	135	8.5:1	2 BC

CHEVETTE ENGINES

Engine Code	No Cyl.	CID	Horse-power	Comp. Ratio	Carb
CYA	4	97	63	8.6:1	1 BC
CYB	4	97	63	8.6:1	1 BC
CYJ	4	97	63	8.6:1	1 BC
CYK	4	97	63	8.6:1	1 BC
CYL	4	97	63	8.6:1	1 BC
CYM	4	97	63	8.6:1	1 BC
CYR	4	97	63	8.6:1	1 BC
CYS	4	97	63	8.6:1	1 BC
CYT	4	97	63	8.6:1	1 BC
CYU	4	97	63	8.6:1	1 BC
CYW	4	97	63	8.6:1	1 BC
CYX	4	97	63	8.6:1	1 BC
ZTT	4	97	68	8.6:1	1 BC
ZTU	4	97	68	8.6:1	1 BC
ZTW	4	97	68	8.6:1	1 BC
ZTX	4	97	68	8.6:1	1 BC

1979 CHEVROLET CHEVETTE

1979 CHEVROLET CAMARO

1979 CHEVROLET CORVETTE

1979 CHEVROLET MONTE CARLO

1979 CHEVROLET IMPALA WAGON

1979 CHEVROLET MONZA

1979 CHEVROLET MALIBU WAGON

1979 CHEVROLET MONZA 2+2

1979 CHEVROLET CAPRICE

1979 CHEVROLET NOVA

VEHICLE IDENTIFICATION NUMBER

CHEVROLET
1L47L9S123456

On top left side of instrument panel, visible through the windshield.

Corvette VIN on left windshield pillar, visible through the windshield.

FIRST DIGIT: Indicates GM division (1 = Chevrolet)

SECOND DIGIT: Indicates series

CODE	SERIES
B	Chevette
J	Chevette "Scooter"
L	Impala
M	Monza, Monza S
N	Caprice Classic
Q	Camaro
R	Monza 2 plus 2, Monza Sport
S	Berlinetta
T	Malibu
W	Malibu Classic
X	Nova
Y	Nova Custom
Z	Corvette
Z	Monte Carlo

THIRD & FOURTH DIGITS: Indicate body style

CODE	STYLE
07	2-Dr. Hatch Back Coupe, 4-Passenger
08	2-Dr. Hatch Back Coupe, 4-Passenger
15	2-Dr. Station Wagon, 4-Passenger
17	2-Dr. Hatch Back Coupe, 6-Passenger
19	4-Dr. Sedan, 6-Passenger
27	2-Dr. Coupe or Notch Back Coupe, 4 or 6-Passenger
35	4-Dr. Station Wagon
37	2-Dr. Sport Coupe, 6-Passenger
47	2-Dr. Coupe, 6-Passenger
68	4-Dr. Hatch Back Sedan, 4-Passenger
69	4-Dr. Sedan, 6-Passenger
87	2-Dr. Sport Coupe, 4-Passenger Camaro

FIFTH DIGIT: Indicates engine

CID	CODE	TYPE	CARB
1	151	L-4	2 BC*
9	151	L-4	2 BC*
E & O	1.6L	L-4	2 BC
V	151	L-4	2 BC
C	196	V6	2 BC
M	200	V6	2 BC
2	231	V6	2 BC
A	231	V6	2 BC
D	250	V6	1 BC
J	267	V8	2 BC
G	305	V8	2 BC
H	305	V8	4 BC
4	350	V8	4 BC (L-82)
L	350	V8	4 BC
8	350	V8	4 BC

* (California w/Crossflow head)

SIXTH DIGIT: Indicates the year (9 = 1979)

SEVENTH DIGIT: Indicates the assembly plant

ASSEMBLY PLANT	CODE
Baltimore	B
Southgate	C
Doraville	D
Janesville	J
Leeds	K

ASSEMBLY PLANT	CODE
Van Nuys	L
Norwood	N
Arlington	R
St. Louis	S
Tarrytown	T
Willow Run	W
Wilmington	Y
Fremont	Z
Oshawa, Ont., Can.	1
Lordstone	U

REMAINING SIX DIGITS: Indicate production sequence number.

EXAMPLE

1	L	47	V	9	W	123456
Chev Div.	Series	Body Style	Engine	Year	Asm Plant	Prod Code

BODY NUMBER PLATE

Located on firewall below rear edge of hood of all models, except Corvette. Corvette plate is located on upper left-hand door hinge pillar.

THE BODY NUMBER PLATE identifies the model year, car division, series, style, body assembly plant, body number, trim combination, paint code and date build code.

BODY BY FISHER
ST 79 1FQ87 N   123456 BDY
TR 19R   19 PNT
11A

GENERAL MOTORS CORPORATION CERTIFIES TO THE DEALER THAT THIS VEHICLE CONFORMS TO ALL U.S., FEDERAL MOTOR VEHICLE SAFETY STANDARDS APPLICABLE AT TIME OF MANUFACTURE.

EXAMPLE

In the example above,

79	Model year (1979)
1	Car division (Chevrolet)
FQ	Series (Camaro V-8)
87	Style (2-Dr Coupe)
N	Body assembly plant (Norwood, Ohio)
123456	Production sequence in that plant
19R	Black vinyl trim
19	Tuxedo Black paint
11	Eleventh month (November)
A	First week of month

NOTE: An option code will appear below the paint code. It is a notation to the assembly line workers that this vehicle is not a standard issue item. An example would be a radio delete, heater delete, etc. WE DO NOT HAVE BREAKDOWNS FOR THOSE CODES.

CHEVELLE
Malibu MODEL CODES

4-Dr Sedan	1AT19
2-Dr Notchback Coupe	1AT27
4-Dr Station Wagon	1AT35

Malibu Classic
4-Dr Sedan 1AW19
2-Dr Notchback Coupe 1AW27
4-Dr Station Wagon 1AW35
*Landau option available

MONTE CARLO	**MODEL CODES**
2-Dr Coupe 1AW37	

*Landau option available

CHEVROLET	**MODEL CODES**

Impala
4-Dr Station Wagon 1BL35
2-Dr Coupe N/B Special 1BL47
4-Dr Sedan 1BL69
*Landau option available

Caprice Classic
4-Dr Station Wagon 1BN35
2-Dr Coupe 1BN47
4-Dr Sedan N/B Special 1BN69
*Landau option available

CAMARO	**MODEL CODES**

Camaro
2-Dr Sport Coupe 1FQ87
*Z-28 option available
*Rally Sport option available

Camaro Berlinetta
2-Dr Sport Coupe 1FS87

MONZA	**MODEL CODES**

Monza Coupe
2-Dr Notchback Coupe 1HM27

Monza 2 Plus 2 Hatch Coupe
2-Dr Hatchback Coupe 1HM07

Monza Station Wagon
2-Dr Station Wagon 1HM15

Monza 2 Plus 2 Sport Hatch
2-Dr Hatchback Coupe 1HR07
*Spyder option available

CHEVETTE	**MODEL CODES**

Chevette "Scooter"
2-Dr Hatchback Coupe 1TJ08

Chevette
2-Dr Hatchback Coupe 1TB08
4-Dr Hatchback Sedan 1TB68

NOVA	**MODEL CODES**

Nova
2-Dr Coupe 1XX27
4-Dr Sedan 1XX69
2-Dr Hatchback Coupe 1XX17

Nova Custom
2-Dr Coupe 1XY27
4-Dr Sedan 1XY69

CORVETTE	**MODEL CODES**

Corvette "Fastback"
2-Dr Sport Coupe 1YZ87

THE TRIM NUMBER furnishes the key to trim color and material for each model series.

CHEVELLE TRIM

Color	Cloth	Vinyl	Leather	Code
Oyster	•	•		12D
Black		•		19N
Black		•		19V
Blue		•		24N
Blue	•	•		24C
Blue	•	•		24D
Blue		•		24V
Green		•		44N
Green	•	•		44D
Tan		•		62N
Tan	•	•		62C
Tan	•	•		62D
Tan		•		62V
Carmine	•	•		74C
Carmine	•	•		74D
Carmine		•		74V

MONTE CARLO TRIM

Color	Cloth	Vinyl	Leather	Code
Oyster		•		12W
Oyster	•	•		12H
Black	•	•		19G
Black	•	•		19H
Blue	•	•		24G
Blue		•		24W
Blue	•	•		24H
Green	•	•		44G
Green		•		44W
Green	•	•		44H
Tan	•	•		62G
Tan		•		62W
Tan	•	•		62H
Carmine		•		74G
Carmine		•		74W
Carmine	•	•		74H

CHEVROLET TRIM

Color	Cloth	Vinyl	Leather	Code
Oyster		•		12V
Oyster	•	•		12E
Black		•		19N
Black	•	•		19D
Black		•		19V
Blue	•	•		24B
Blue		•		24N
Blue	•	•		24D
Blue		•		24V
Blue	•	•		24E
Green	•	•		44B
Green	•	•		44D
Green		•		44V
Tan	•	•		62C
Tan	•	•		62B
Tan	•	•		62N
Tan		•		62D
Tan		•		62V
Tan	•	•		62E
Carmine	•	•		74C
Carmine	•	•		74B
Carmine	•	•		74N
Carmine		•		74D
Carmine		•		74V
Carmine	•	•		74E

CAMARO TRIM

Color	Cloth	Vinyl	Leather	Code
Oyster	•	•		12C
Black	•			19B
Black		•		19R
Black	•	•		19C
Black		•		19N
Blue	•	•		24B
Blue		•		24R
Blue	•	•		24C
Blue		•		24N
Green		•		44R
Green	•	•		44C
Tan	•	•		62B
Tan		•		62R
Tan	•	•		62C
Tan		•		62N
Tan	•	•		62C
Carmine	•	•		74B
Carmine		•		74R
Carmine	•	•		74C
Carmine		•		74N

MONZA TRIM

Color	Cloth	Vinyl	Leather	Code
Oyster		•		14W
Oyster		•		12V
Black	•	•		19B
Black		•		19R
Black	•	•		19D
Black		•		19W
Black	•	•		19G
Black		•		19Y
Black	•	•		19C
Black		•		19N
Black	•	•		19J
Black		•		19V
Blue		•		24R
Blue	•	•		24D
Blue		•		24W
Blue		•		24Y
Blue		•		24N
Blue	•	•		24J
Blue		•		24V
Green	•	•		44G
Green	•	•		44C
Green	•	•		44J
Tan	•	•		62B
Tan	•	•		62R
Tan	•	•		62D
Tan		•		62W
Tan		•		62G
Tan		•		62Y
Tan	•	•		62C
Tan		•		62N
Tan	•	•		62J
Tan		•		62V
Carmine		•		74R
Carmine	•	•		74D
Carmine		•		74W
Carmine		•		74Y
Carmine		•		74N
Carmine	•	•		74J
Carmine		•		74V

CHEVETTE TRIM

Color	Cloth	Vinyl	Leather	Code
Oyster	•	•		12C
Oyster	•	•		12G
Black	•			19B
Black		•		19V
Black	•	•		17B
Black		•		17V
Black	•	•		19E
Black		•		19R
Black	•	•		17E
Black		•		17R
Black	•	•		19C
Black	•	•		19D
Black		•		19W
Black	•	•		17D
Black		•		17W
Black		•		19G
Blue	•	•		24E
Blue		•		24R
Blue	•	•		24C
Blue		•		24N
Blue		•		24D
Blue		•		24W
Blue	•	•		24G
Blue		•		24Y
Green		•		44N
Green		•		44Y
Tan	•	•		62B
Tan		•		62V
Tan	•	•		62E
Tan		•		62R
Tan	•	•		62C
Tan		•		62N
Tan		•		62D
Tan		•		62W
Tan	•	•		62G
Tan		•		62Y
Carmine		•		74R
Carmine	•	•		74C
Carmine		•		74N
Carmine		•		74W
Carmine	•	•		74G
Carmine		•		74Y

NOVA TRIM

Color	Cloth	Vinyl	Leather	Code
Black		•		19R
Blue	•	•		24B
Blue		•		24R
Blue	•	•		24D
Tan	•	•		62B
Tan		•		62R
Tan	•	•		62D
Tan		•		62N
Carmine		•		74R
Carmine	•	•		74D
Carmine		•		74N
White		•		11N

THE PAINT CODE furnishes the key to the paint colors used on the car.

COLOR	CODE
White*	10
White	11
Silver Irid*	13
Silver Irid	15
Gray Irid**	16
Pastel Blue	21
Light Blue Irid	22
Bright Blue Irid	24
Frost Blue*	28
Dark Blue Irid	29
Dark Red***	35
Medium Blue***	36
Medium Beige***	37
Oyster White***	39
Pastel Green	40
Medium Green Irid	44
Indy Silver Irid*	47
Bright Yellow	51
Corvette Yellow*	52
Light Yellow	54
Dark Green Irid*	58
Frost Beige*	59
Medium Beige	61
Camel Irid	63
Dark Brown Irid*	67
Dark Brown Irid	69
Red*	72
Red	75
Carmine Irid	77
Dark Carmine Irid	79

COLOR	CODE
Dark Blue Irid*	83
Medium Blue Irid**	85
Black (No Chip)	19
Red****	80
Gold***	50

*Corvette only
**Chevrolet Two-Tone only
***Corvette Two-Tone only
****Special Order Colors

TWO-TONE COMBINATIONS

LOWER COLOR	CODE	UPPER COLOR	CODE
Dark Blue Metallic	29	Light Blue Met	11
Light Blue Metallic	22	White	11
Dark Brown Metallic	69	Beige	61
Camel Metallic	63	Beige	61
Carmine Metallic	77	Beige	11
Light Green	40	Beige	11
Medium Green Metallic	44	Light Green	40
Bright Blue Metallic	24	White	11
Medium Green Metallic	24	White	11
Red	75	White	11

VINYL ROOF CODES

COLOR	CODE
White	11T
Silver Poly	15T
Black	19T
Light Blue Poly	22T
Pastel Green	40T
Medium Beige	61T
Dark Carmine Poly	79T

ENGINE NUMBER

THE ENGINE IDENTIFICATION NUMBER includes a letter code for the engine plant, followed by numbers which date the manufacture of the engine, then followed by a letter code to indicate the engine size and makeup.

THE ENGINE IDENTIFICATION NUMBER for V-8s is stamped on a pad located at the right-hand side of the cylinder block, and stamped on a pad on the right side of the block behind the distributor on 4-cylinder and 6-cylinder engines.

NOTE:

1. To properly identify Chevrolet Division engines, it will be necessary to identify the car model in which the engine is used. The same engine type may have a different code when used in different car models.

EXAMPLE

1	01	01	DCC
PLANT	MONTH	DAY	CODE

MALIBU ENGINES

Engine Code	No Cyl.	CID	Horse-power	Comp. Ratio	Carb
DHA	6	200	94	8.2:1	2 BC
DHB	6	200	94	8.2:1	2 BC
DHC	6	200	94	8.5:1	2 BC
NJ	6	231	115	8.0:1	2 BC
NT	6	231	115	8.0:1	2 BC
NU	6	231	115	8.0:1	2 BC
RA	6	231	115	8.0:1	2 BC
RB	6	231	115	8.0:1	2 BC
RJ	6	231	115	8.0:1	2 BC
RM	6	231	115	8.0:1	2 BC
RW	6	231	115	8.0:1	2 BC
SJ	6	231	115	8.0:1	2 BC
SO	6	231	115	8.0:1	2 BC
DMA	8	267	125	8.2:1	2 BC

MALIBU ENGINES

Engine Code	No Cyl.	CID	Horse-power	Comp. Ratio	Carb
DMB	8	267	125	8.2:1	2 BC
DMC	8	267	125	8.2:1	2 BC
DMD	8	267	125	8.2:1	2 BC
DMF	8	267	125	8.2:1	2 BC
DMH	8	267	125	8.2:1	2 BC
DMM	8	267	125	8.2:1	2 BC
DMR	8	267	125	8.2:1	2 BC
DNS	8	305	160	8.5:1	4 BC
DNT	8	305	160	8.5:1	4 BC
DNU	8	305	160	8.5:1	4 BC
DNW	8	305	160	8.5:1	4 BC
DNX	8	305	160	8.5:1	4 BC
DNY	8	305	160	8.5:1	4 BC
DWA	8	305	160	8.5:1	4 BC
DWB	8	305	160	8.5:1	4 BC
DRX	8	350	165	8.5:1	4 BC
DTA	8	305	160	8.5:1	4 BC
DTB	8	305	160	8.5:1	4 BC
DTF	8	305	160	8.5:1	4 BC
DTH	8	305	160	8.5:1	4 BC
DTJ	8	305	160	8.5:1	4 BC
DTS	8	305	160	8.5:1	4 BC
DTU	8	305	160	8.5:1	4 BC
DTW	8	305	160	8.5:1	4 BC
DTX	8	305	160	8.5:1	4 BC
DUF	8	350	165	8.5:1	4 BC
DUH	8	350	165	8.5:1	4 BC
DUJ	8	350	165	8.5:1	4 BC

*305 CID in California is 155 HP

MONTE CARLO ENGINES

Engine Code	No Cyl.	CID	Horse-power	Comp. Ratio	Carb
NJ	6	231	115	8.0:1	2 BC
NT	6	231	115	8.0:1	2 BC
NU	6	231	115	8.0:1	2 BC
RA	6	231	115	8.0:1	2 BC
RB	6	231	115	8.0:1	2 BC
RJ	6	231	115	8.0:1	2 BC
RM	6	231	115	8.0:1	2 BC
RW	6	231	115	8.0:1	2 BC
SJ	6	231	115	8.0:1	2 BC
SO	6	231	115	8.0:1	2 BC
DHA	6	200	94	8.2:1	2 BC
DHB	6	200	94	8.2:1	2 BC
DHC	6	200	94	8.2:1	2 BC
DMA	8	267	125	8.5:1	2 BC
DMB	8	267	125	8.5:1	2 BC
DMC	8	267	125	8.5:1	2 BC
DMD	8	267	125	8.5:1	2 BC
DMF	8	267	125	8.5:1	2 BC
DMH	8	267	125	8.5:1	2 BC
DMM	8	267	125	8.5:1	2 BC
DMR	8	267	125	8.5:1	2 BC
DNS	8	305	160	8.5:1	4 BC
DNT	8	305	160	8.5:1	4 BC
DNU	8	305	160	8.5:1	4 BC
DNW	8	305	160	8.5:1	4 BC
DNX	8	305	160	8.5:1	4 BC
DNY	8	305	160	8.5:1	4 BC
DTA	8	305	160	8.5:1	4 BC
DTB	8	305	160	8.5:1	4 BC
DTF	8	305	160	8.5:1	4 BC
DTH	8	305	160	8.5:1	4 BC
DTJ	8	305	160	8.5:1	4 BC
DTS	8	305	160	8.5:1	4 BC
DTU	8	305	160	8.5:1	4 BC
DTW	8	305	160	8.5:1	4 BC
DTX	8	305	160	8.5:1	4 BC
DWA	8	305	160	8.5:1	4 BC
DWB	8	305	160	8.5:1	4 BC

*305 CID in California is 155 HP

NOVA ENGINES

Engine Code	No Cyl.	CID	Horse-power	Comp. Ratio	Carb
DKA	6	250	115	8.1:1	1 BC
DKB	6	250	115	8.5:1	1 BC
DKD	6	250	115	8.5:1	1 BC
C8B	8	305	130	8.5:1	2 BC
DNF	8	305	130	8.5:1	2 BC
DNJ	8	305	130	8.5:1	2 BC
DNK	8	305	130	8.5:1	2 BC
DTM	8	305	130	8.5:1	2 BC
DRJ	8	350	165	8.5:1	4 BC
DRY	8	350	165	8.5:1	4 BC

*231 CID in California is 90 HP
*305 CID in California is 125 HP

CAMARO ENGINES

Engine Code	No Cyl.	CID	Horse-power	Comp. Ratio	Carb
DKA	6	250	115	8.1:1	1 BC
DKB	6	250	115	8.1:1	1 BC
DKD	6	250	115	8.1:1	1 BC
C8B	8	305	130	8.5:1	2 BC
DNF	8	305	130	8.5:1	2 BC
DNH	8	305	130	8.5:1	2 BC
DNK	8	305	130	8.5:1	2 BC
DTM	8	305	130	8.5:1	2 BC
DTR	8	305	130	8.5:1	2 BC
DRC	8	350	165	8.5:1	4 BC
DRD	8	350	165	8.5:1	4 BC
DRF	8	350	165	8.5:1	4 BC
DRH	8	350	165	8.5:1	4 BC
DRL	8	350	165	8.5:1	4 BC
DRY	8	350	165	8.5:1	4 BC
C8C	8	350	165	8.5:1	4 BC

*250 CID in California is 90 HP
*305 CID in California is 125 HP
*350 CID in California is same
*Z-28 350 CID in California is 175 HP
*Z-28 350 CID Federal is 180 HP

CORVETTE ENGINES

Engine Code	No Cyl.	CID	Horse-power	Comp. Ratio	Carb
ZAA	8	350	195	8.5:1	4 BC (L-48)
ZAB	8	350	195	8.5:1	4 BC
ZAC	8	350	195	8.5:1	4 BC
ZAD	8	350	195	8.5:1	4 BC
ZBA	8	350	225	9.0:1	4 BC (L-82)
ZBB	8	350	225	9.0:1	4 BC (L-82)

CHEVROLET ENGINES

Engine Code	No Cyl.	CID	Horse-power	Comp. Ratio	Carb
DCA	6	250	115	8.1:1	1 BC
DCB	6	250	115	8.1:1	1 BC
DCC	6	250	115	8.1:1	1 BC
DCD	6	250	115	8.1:1	1 BC
DKB	6	250	115	8.1:1	1 BC
DKC	6	250	115	8.1:1	1 BC
DKD	6	250	115	8.1:1	1 BC
DKF	6	250	115	8.1:1	1 BC
DNL	8	305	130	8.5:1	2 BC
DNM	8	305	130	8.5:1	2 BC
DNR	8	305	130	8.5:1	2 BC
DTC	8	305	170	8.5:1	2 BC
DTD	8	305	170	8.5:1	2 BC
DTY	8	305	130	8.5:1	2 BC
DTZ	8	305	130	8.5:1	2 BC
DXA	8	305	130	8.5:1	2 BC
DRA	8	350	130	8.5:1	4 BC
DRB	8	350	170	8.5:1	4 BC
DRH	8	350	170	8.5:1	4 BC
DRJ	8	350	170	8.5:1	4 BC
DRK	8	350	170	8.5:1	4 BC
DRL	8	350	170	8.5:1	4 BC

CHEVROLET ENGINES

Engine Code	No Cyl.	CID	Horse-power	Comp. Ratio	Carb
DRY	8	350	170	8.5:1	4 BC
DRZ	8	350	170	8.5:1	4 BC
DUB	8	350	170	8.5:1	4 BC
DUC	8	350	170	8.5:1	4 BC
DUD	8	350	170	8.5:1	4 BC

*250 CID 6-Cyl. Federal is 115 HP   *250 CID 6-Cyl. California is 90 HP
*305 CID 8-Cyl. Federal is 130 HP   *305 CID 8-Cyl. California is 125 HP
*350 CID 8-Cyl. Federal is 170 HP   *350 CID 8-Cyl. California is 160 HP

CHEVETTE ENGINES

Engine Code	No Cyl.	CID	Horse-power	Comp. Ratio	Carb
DBA	4	97	70/74	8.5:1	2 BC
DBB	4	97	70/74	8.5:1	2 BC
DBC	4	97	70/74	8.5:1	2 BC
DBD	4	97	70/74	8.5:1	2 BC
DBF	4	97	70/74	8.5:1	2 BC
DBH	4	97	70/74	8.5:1	2 BC
DBJ	4	97	70/74	8.5:1	2 BC
DBK	4	97	70/74	8.5:1	2 BC
DBL	4	97	70/74	8.5:1	2 BC
DBM	4	97	70/74	8.5:1	2 BC
DBR	4	97	70/74	8.5:1	2 BC
DBS	4	97	70/74	8.5:1	2 BC
DBT	4	97	70/74	8.5:1	2 BC
DBU	4	97	70/74	8.5:1	2 BC
DBW	4	97	70/74	8.5:1	2 BC
DBX	4	97	70/74	8.5:1	2 BC
DBY	4	97	70/74	8.5:1	2 BC
DBZ	4	97	70/74	8.5:1	2 BC
DSA	4	97	70/74	8.5:1	2 BC
DSB	4	97	70/74	8.5:1	2 BC

MONZA ENGINES

Engine Code	No Cyl.	CID	Horse-power	Comp. Ratio	Carb
AB	4	151	90	8.3:1	2 BC
AC	4	151	90	8.3:1	2 BC
AD	4	151	90	8.3:1	2 BC
AF	4	151	90	8.3:1	2 BC
AH	4	151	90	8.3:1	2 BC
AJ	4	151	90	8.3:1	2 BC
AM	4	151	90	8.3:1	2 BC
WD	4	151	90	8.3:1	2 BC
WJ	4	151	90	8.3:1	2 BC
WM	4	151	90	8.3:1	2 BC
XJ	4	151	90	8.3:1	2 BC
XK	4	151	90	8.3:1	2 BC
ZA	4	151	90	8.3:1	2 BC
ZB	4	151	90	8.3:1	2 BC
ZP	4	151	90	8.3:1	2 BC
ZR	4	151	90	8.3:1	2 BC
PWN	4	151	90	8.3:1	2 BC
PWP	4	151	90	8.3:1	2 BC
FC	6	196	105	8.0:1	2 BC
FD	6	196	105	8.0:1	2 BC
FF	6	196	105	8.0:1	2 BC
NA	6	231	115	8.0:1	2 BC
NB	6	231	115	8.0:1	2 BC
NC	6	231	115	8.0:1	2 BC
NE	6	231	115	8.0:1	2 BC
NF	6	231	115	8.0:1	2 BC
NH	6	231	115	8.0:1	2 BC
NR	6	231	115	8.0:1	2 BC
NS	6	231	115	8.0:1	2 BC
SM	6	231	115	8.0:1	2 BC
SS	6	231	115	8.0;1	2 BC
DNA	8	305	130	8.4:1	2 BC
DNB	8	305	130	8.4:1	2 BC
DNC	8	305	130	8.4:1	2 BC
DND	8	305	130	8.4:1	2 BC
DTK	8	305	130	8.4:1	2 BC
DTL	8	305	130	8.4:1	2 BC

*305 CID in California is 125 HP

1970 OLDSMOBILE CUTLASS SUPREME

1970 OLDSMOBILE CUTLASS SUPREME

1970 OLDSMOBILE 98

1970 OLDSMOBILE 98

1970 OLDSMOBILE TORONADO

1970 OLDSMOBILE TORONADO

1970 OLDSMOBILE DELTA 88

1970 OLDSMOBILE DELTA 88

1970 OLDSMOBILE DELTA ROYALE

1970 OLDSMOBILE DELTA ROYALE

VEHICLE IDENTIFICATION NUMBER

> OLDSMOBILE
> 336870M103133

Located on the top of the dash on the driver's side and visible through the windshield from outside the car.

FIRST DIGIT: Identifies GM Division (3 is Oldsmobile)

SECOND AND THIRD DIGITS: Identify the series, odd number is a 6-cylinder and even number is an 8-cylinder.

SERIES	6 CYL	CODE V8
F-85 Standard	31	32
Cutlass, Cutlass S	35	36
Cutlass Supreme		42
442		44
Vista Cruiser		48
Delta 88		54
Delta 88 Custom		64
Delta 88 Royale		66
Ninety-Eight Series		84
Ninety-Eight Luxury		86
Toronado Custom		94

FOURTH AND FIFTH DIGITS: Identify the body style

BODY STYLE	CODE
4-Dr. SW, 2-Seat	35
4-Dr. SW, 2-Seat	36
2-Door Hardtop Coupe	37
4-Door Hardtop (4-Window)	39
2-Door Hardtop Coupe	47
4-Dr. SW, 2-Seat	55
4-Dr. SW, 2-Seat	56
2-Door Hardtop Coupe	57
4-Dr. SW, 3-Seat	65
4-Dr. SW, 3-Seat	66
2-Door Convertible Coupe	67
4-Door Pillar (4-Window)	69
2-Door Plain Back Pillar Coupe	77
2-Door Plain Back HT Coupe	87

SIXTH DIGIT: Identifies the year 1970

SEVENTH DIGIT: Identifies the assembly plant

ASSEMBLY PLANT	CODE
South Gate, CA	C
Doraville, GA	D
Linden, NJ	E
Framingham, MA	G
Lansing, MI	M
Fairfax, KS	X
Fremont, CA	Z

LAST SIX DIGITS: Represent the basic production numbers

BODY NUMBER PLATE

The body number plate is located on the firewall, just below the rear edge of the hood. This plate identifies the model year, car division, series, body style, body assembly plant, body numbers, trim combination, paint code and build date code.

> BODY BY FISHER
> ST 70   33227   LAN 123456 BDY
> TR 10   19 19 PNT
> 000
>
> GENERAL MOTORS CORPORATION CERTIFIES TO THE DEALER THAT THIS VEHICLE CONFORMS TO ALL U.S., FEDERAL MOTOR VEHICLE SAFETY STANDARDS APPLICABLE AT TIME OF MANUFACTURE.

Example:

70	Model Year (1970)
3	Car Division (Oldsmobile)
32	Series (F-85)
27	Style (2-Door Coupe)
LAN	Body Assembly Plant (Lansing, MI)
123456	Production Sequence
10	Black Trim
19	Ebony Black Lower Body Color
19	Ebony Black Upper Body Color
000	Time Built Date

F-85	CODE
2-Door Coupe, L-6	3177
2-Door Coupe, V-8	3277

CUTLASS	CODE
2-Seat SW, 1-Way, L-6	3535
2-Seat SW, 1-Way, V-8	3635
4-Dr. Hardtop, L-6	3539
4-Dr. Hardtop, V-8	3639
4-Dr. Sedan, L-6	3569
4-Dr. Sedan, V-8	3669
Sports Coupe, L-6	3577
Sports Coupe, V-8	3677
2-Dr. Hardtop, L-6	3587
2-Dr. Hardtop, V-8	3687

*W-31 option available
*Rallye 350 option available

CUTLASS SUPREME	CODE
4-Dr. Hardtop	4239
2-Dr. Hardtop	4257
Convertible	4267

*SX option available

442	CODE
2-Door HT Coupe	4487
2-Door Sport Coupe	4477
Convertible	4467

*W-30 option available
*Indy Pace Car option available

VISTA CRUISER	CODE
2-Seat, 1-Way Gate	4855
3-Seat, 1-Way Gate	4865

DELTA 88   CODE
2-Dr. Hardtop 5437
4-Dr. Hardtop 5439
Convertible 5467
4-Dr. Sedan 6569

DELTA 88 CUSTOM   CODE
2-Dr. Hardtop 6437
4-Dr. Hardtop 6439
4-Dr. Sedan 6469

DELTA 88 ROYALE   CODE
2-Dr. Hardtop 6647

NINETY-EIGHT   CODE
4-Dr. Hardtop 8439
2-Dr. Hardtop 8457
Convertible 8467
4-Dr. Sedan 8469
4-Dr. Luxury Hardtop Sedan 8639
4-Dr. Luxury Sedan 8669

TORONADO   CODE
2-Door Hardtop Coupe 9487
2-Dr. Custom Interior HT Cpe. 9687

THE TRIM CODE furnishes the key to the interior color and material scheme.

TORONADO TRIM

COLOR	CLOTH	VINYL	LEATHER	CODE
Ivory				17
Ivory				37*
Ivory				57
Saddle				59
Saddle				79*
Black				10
Black				30*
Black				60
Black				70*
Blue				63
Gold				64
Green				62

*Bucket seats

NINETY-EIGHT LUXURY TRIM

COLOR	CLOTH	VINYL	LEATHER	CODE
Black			•	20
Black			•	90#
Black	•			40
Black	•			60#
Black				10
Green	•			42
Green	•			62#
Blue	•			43
Blue	•			63#
Gold	•			44
Gold	•			64#
Sandalwood	•			48
Sandalwood	•			68#

#Notch back or 60-40 seats

NINETY-EIGHT HOLIDAY COUPE TRIM

COLOR	CLOTH	VINYL	LEATHER	CODE
Black			•	20#
Black			•	90#
Black	•			40
Black				10
Green	•			42
Sandalwood	•			48

#Notch back or 60-40 seats

NINETY-EIGHT HOLIDAY SEDAN TRIM

COLOR	CLOTH	VINYL	LEATHER	CODE
Black	•			40
Black				10
Blue	•			43
Green	•			42
Gold	•			44
Sandalwood	•			48

NINETY-EIGHT CONVERTIBLE TRIM

COLOR	CLOTH	VINYL	LEATHER	CODE
Black	•			10
Blue			•	13
Gold			•	14
Ivory			•	17

DELTA 88 ROYALE HOLIDAY COUPE TRIM

COLOR	CLOTH	VINYL	LEATHER	CODE
Black				30*
Black				40
Ivory				17
Ivory				37*
Green				42
Blue				43
Gold				44

*Bucket seats

DELTA 88 CUSTOM SEDAN, HOLIDAY SEDAN/COUPE TRIM

COLOR	CLOTH	VINYL	LEATHER	CODE
Green				12
Green				42
Blue		•		43
Gold		•		44
Black				10
Black	•			40
Sandalwood				18

DELTA CONVERTIBLE TRIM

COLOR	CLOTH	VINYL	LEATHER	CODE
Black				10
Gold				14
Ivory				17
Green				12
Blue				13

DELTA 88 CUSTOM TRIM

COLOR	CLOTH	VINYL	LEATHER	CODE
Green	•			52
Black	•			60
Sandalwood				58
Blue	•			63
Gold	•			64

VISTA-CRUISER TRIM

COLOR	CLOTH	VINYL	LEATHER	CODE
Black				10
Saddle				19
Green				12
Gold	•			44
Blue				13

4-4-2 SPORT COUPE/HOLIDAY COUPE TRIM

COLOR	CLOTH	VINYL	LEATHER	CODE
Black				10
Black				30*
Green				12
Green				32*
Ivory				17
Ivory				37*
Gold				34*
Gold				44
Blue				33*
Blue				43

*Bucket seats

4-4-2 CONVERTIBLE TRIM

COLOR	CLOTH	VINYL	LEATHER	CODE
Black				10
Black				30*
Gold				14
Gold				34*
Ivory				17
Ivory				37*
Green				12
Green				32*
Blue				13
Blue				33*
Saddle				19
Saddle				39*

*Bucket seats

CUTLASS SUPREME HOLIDAY SEDAN TRIM

COLOR	CLOTH	VINYL	LEATHER	CODE
Green				12
Black	•			40
Sandalwood				18
Blue	•			43
Gold	•			44

CUTLASS SUPREME HOLIDAY COUPE, CONVERTIBLE TRIM

COLOR	CLOTH	VINYL	LEATHER	CODE
Black				10+
Black				30*
Black				40**
Saddle				19
Saddle				39*
Green				12+
Green				32*
Green				42**
Blue				13+
Blue				33*
Blue				43**
Gold				14+
Gold				34*
Gold				44**
Ivory				17
Ivory				37*

+Convertible only
*Bucket seats
** Holiday Coupe only

CUTLASS S SPORTS COUPE/HOLIDAY COUPE TRIM

COLOR	CLOTH	VINYL	LEATHER	CODE
Black				10
Black				30*
Gold				34*
Gold				44
Green				12
Green				32*
Ivory				17
Ivory				37*
Blue				43
Blue				33*

*Bucket seats

CUTLASS TWN SEDAN/HOLIDAY SEDAN/STA WAG TRIM

COLOR	CLOTH	VINYL	LEATHER	CODE
Black				10
Sandalwood				18***
Saddle				19**
Green				12**
Green				42***
Blue				13
Gold				44

**Station Wagon only
***Sedans only

F-85 SPORTS COUPE TRIM

COLOR	CLOTH	VINYL	LEATHER	CODE
Black				10
Blue				13
Green				12
Gold				14
Sandalwood				18

THE PAINT CODE furnishes the key to the paint colors used on the car. Two, two-digit codes indicate the bottom and top body colors respectively. NOTE: vinyl roof codes appear as a second set of digits.

COLOR	CODE
Porcelain White	10
Platinum	14
Oxford Gray	16
Ebony Black	19
Azure Blue	20
Astro Blue	25
Viking Blue	26
Twilight Blue	28
Reef Turquoise	34
Aegean Aqua	38
Aspen Green	45
Ming Jade	46
Sherwood Green	48
Bamboo	50
Sebring Yellow	51
Nugget Gold	53
Galleon Gold	55
Burnished Gold	58
Sandalwood	61
Copper	63
Cinnamon Bronze	68
Grenadier Red	74
Matador Red	75
Regency Rose	76
Burgundy Mist	78

VINYL ROOF COLOR	CODE
White	A
Black	B
Gold	D
Brown	F
Green	G
Gold	H

CONVERTIBLE TOP COLORS	CODE
White	A
Black	B
Blue	C
Gold	H

ENGINE NUMBER

An Oldsmobile engine is stamped with two different identification codes. One is the engine production code which identifies the engine and its approximate production date. The other code is the engine serial number — it matches the VIN (vehicle identification number).

OLDSMOBILE ENGINES

ENGINE CODE	NO. CYL.	CID	HORSE-POWER	COMP. RATIO	CARB	TRANS
VB,VF	6	250	155	8.5:1	1 BC	Auto
QI,QA,QJ	8	350	250	9.0:1	2 BC	Auto
TC,TD,TL	8	350	250	9.0:1	2 BC	Auto
QN,QP,QV	8	350	310	10.25:1	4 BC	Auto
QD,QX	8	350	325	10.5:1	4 BC	Auto
UC,UD,UJ	8	455	310	9.0:1	2 BC	Auto
TX,TY	8	455	320	10.25:1	2 BC	Auto
TP,TQ	8	455	365	10.5:1	4 BC	Auto
TU,TV,TW	8	455	365	10.5:1	4 BC	Auto
UN,UO	8	455	365	10.5:1	4 BC	Auto
TS,TT	8	455	370	10.5:1	4 BC	Auto
UL	8	455	390	10.25:1	4 BC	Auto
US,UT	8	455	375	10.25:1	4 BC	Auto
UV,UW	8	455	400	10.25:1	4 BC	Auto

1971 OLDSMOBILE TORONADO

1971 OLDSMOBILE TORONADO

1971 OLDSMOBILE DELTA 88 ROYALE

1971 OLDSMOBILE VISTA CRUISER

1971 OLDSMOBILE DELTA 88 CUSTOM

1971 OLDSMOBILE 4-4-2

1971 OLDSMOBILE 98 HARDTOP COUPE

1971 OLDSMOBILE 98 LUXURY SEDAN

1971 OLDSMOBILE CUTLASS SUPREME

1971 OLDSMOBILE CUTLASS S

VEHICLE IDENTIFICATION NUMBER

OLDSMOBILE
336871R103133

Located on the top of the dash on the driver's side and visible through the windshield from outside the car.

FIRST DIGIT: Identifies GM Division (3 is Oldsmobile)

SECOND AND THIRD DIGIT: Identify the series, odd number is a 6-cylinder and even number is an 8-cylinder

SERIES		CODE
	6 CYL	V8
F-85 Standard	31	32
Cutlass, Cutlass S	35	36
Cutlass Supreme		42
442		44
Vista Cruiser		48
Delta 88		54
Delta 88 Custom		64
Delta 88 Royale		66
Custom Cruiser		68
Ninety-Eight Series		84
Ninety-Eight Luxury		86
Toronado		96
Toronado Brougham		98

FOURTH AND FIFTH DIGITS: Identify the body style

BODY STYLE	CODE
4-Door SW, 2-Seat	35
4-Door SW, 2-Seat	36
2-Door Hardtop coupe	37
4-Door Hardtop (4-Window)	39
2-Door Hardtop Coupe	47
4-Door SW, 2-Seat	55
4-Door SW, 2-Seat	56
2-Door Hardtop Coupe	57
4-Door SW, 3-Seat	65
4-Door SW, 3-Seat	66
2-Door Convertible Coupe	67
4-Door Pillar (4-Window)	69
2-Door Plain Back Pillar Coupe	77
2-Door Plain Back HT Coupe	87

SIXTH DIGIT: Identifies the year 1971

SEVENTH DIGIT: Identifies the assembly plant

ASSEMBLY PLANT	CODE
Lansing, MI	M
Fremont, CA	Z
Fairfax, KS	X
Linden, NJ	E
Framingham, MA	G
Arlington, TX	R

LAST SIX DIGITS: Represent the basic production numbers

BODY NUMBER PLATE

The body number plate is located on the firewall, just below the rear edge of the hood. This plate identifies the model year, car division, series, body style, body assembly plant, body numbers, trim combination, paint code and build date code.

```
            BODY BY FISHER
ST 71   38437   LAN 123456 BDY
TR 10                   19 19 PNT
000

GENERAL MOTORS CORPORATION CERTIFIES
    TO THE DEALER THAT THIS VEHICLE
   CONFORMS TO ALL U.S., FEDERAL MOTOR
        VEHICLE SAFETY STANDARDS
    APPLICABLE AT TIME OF MANUFACTURE.
```

Example:

71	Model Year (1971)
3	Car Division (Oldsmobile)
84	Series (Ninety-Eight)
37	Style (2-Door Hardtop Coupe)
LAN	Body Assembly Plant (Lansing, MI)
123456	Production Sequence
10	Black Cloth Trim
19	Ebony Black Lower Body Color
19	Ebony Black Upper Body Color
000	Time Built Date

BODY STYLE		CODE
	6-CYL	8-CYL
F-85 STANDARD		
2-Door Cutlass HT Cpe	3187	3287
4-Door Sedan	3169	3269
CUTLASS S		
2-Door Sport Coupe	3577	3677
2-Door Hardtop	3587	3687
CUTLASS		
4-Door Sedan	3569	3669
4-Door SW, 2-Seat	3536	3636
CUTLASS SUPREME		
2-Door Notchback	——	4257
4-Door Hardtop	——	4239
Convertible	——	4267
4-4-2		
2-Door Hardtop Coupe	——	4487
Convertible	——	4467
*W-30 option available		
VISTA CRUISER		
4-Door SW, 2-Seat	——	4856
4-Door SW, 3-Seat	——	4866
DELTA 88		
2-Door Hardtop	——	5457
4-Door Hardtop	——	5439
4-Door Sedan	——	5469

CUSTOM CRUISER
4-Door SW, 2-Seat	—	6835
4-Door SW, 3-Seat	—	6845

DELTA 88 CUSTOM
2-Door Hardtop	—	6457
4-Door Hardtop	—	6439
4-Door Sedan	—	6469

DELTA 88 ROYALE
2-Door Hardtop Coupe	—	6647
Convertible	—	6667

NINETY-EIGHT SERIES
2-Door Hardtop	—	8437
4-Door Hardtop	—	8439

NINETY-EIGHT LUXURY
2-Door Hardtop Coupe	—	8637
4-Door Hardtop Sedan	—	8639

TORONADO CUSTOM
2-Door Hardtop	—	9657
2-Door Brougham	—	9857

THE TRIM CODE furnishes the key to the interior color and material scheme.

TORONADO TRIM
COLOR	CLOTH	VINYL	LEATHER	CODE
Black				50
Black	•			60
Jade Green	•			62
Blue	•			63
Maize	•			64
Briar	•			65

TORONADO CUSTOM TRIM
COLOR	CLOTH	VINYL	LEATHER	CODE
Black	•			40
Black				10
White				17
Jade Green	•			42
Blue	•			43
Maize	•			44
Briar	•			45

NINETY-EIGHT TRIM
COLOR	CLOTH	VINYL	LEATHER	CODE
Black				10
Black	•			40
Black				50#
Black	•			60#
Briar				15
White				17
Sandalwood				18
Jade Green	•			42
Blue	•			43
Briar	•			45

Divided bench seat

CUSTOM CRUISER TRIM
COLOR	CLOTH	VINYL	LEATHER	CODE
Black				10
Jade Green				12
Blue				13
Briar				15
Sandalwood				18

DELTA 88 TRIM
COLOR	CLOTH	VINYL	LEATHER	CODE
Blue	•			43
Black				10
Black	•			40
White				17*
Briar				15
Sandalwood				18**
Jade Green	•			42

*Except Town Sedan
**Town Sedan only

DELTA 88 ROYALE TRIM
COLOR	CLOTH	VINYL	LEATHER	CODE
Black				10*
Black	•			40**
Jade Green				12*
Jade Green	•			42**
Blue				13*
Blue	•			43**
Briar				15*
Briar	•			45**
White				17

*Convertible only
**Coupe only

DELTA 88 CUSTOM TRIM
COLOR	CLOTH	VINYL	LEATHER	CODE
Black				10
White				17*
Sandalwood				18**
Jade Green	•			42
Blue	•			43
Briar	•			45

*Except Town Sedan
**Town Sedan only

VISTA CRUISER TRIM
COLOR	CLOTH	VINYL	LEATHER	CODE
Black				10
Jade Green				12
Blue				13
Sienna				19

CUTLASS SUPREME TRIM
COLOR	CLOTH	VINYL	LEATHER	CODE
Black				10
Blue				13
Sienna				19
Jade Green	•			42

CUTLASS SUPREME 4-4-2 TRIM
COLOR	CLOTH	VINYL	LEATHER	CODE
Black				10
Black				30**
Black	•			40*
Blue				13#
Blue				33##
Blue	•			43*
White				17
White				37**
Jade Green				32**
Jade Green	•			42*
Sienna				19
Sienna				39**

*Coupe only
**Bucket seats
#Convertible, bench seat only
##Coupe, bucket seats only

CUTLASS 4-4-2 TRIM

COLOR	CLOTH	VINYL	LEATHER	CODE
Black				10
Black				30*
Blue				13
Blue				33*
White				17
White				37*
Sienna				19
Sienna				39*
Jade Green				32*
Jade Green				42#

*Bucket seats
#Bench seat

CUTLASS TOWN SEDAN TRIM

COLOR	CLOTH	VINYL	LEATHER	CODE
Black				10
Jade Green				12**
Jade Green	•			42*
Blue				13
White				17*
Sienna				19

*Town Sedan only
**Cutlass Cruiser only

CUTLASS S TRIM

COLOR	CLOTH	VINYL	LEATHER	CODE
Black				10
Black				30*
Blue				13
Blue				33**
White				17
White				37*
Sienna				19
Sienna				39**
Jade Green				32**
Jade Green	•			42#

*Bucket seats
**Hardtop, bucket seats
#Bench seat

CUTLASS HARDTOP COUPE TRIM

COLOR	CLOTH	VINYL	LEATHER	CODE
Black				10
Jade Green				12
White				17
Sienna				19

F-85 TRIM

COLOR	CLOTH	VINYL	LEATHER	CODE
Black				10
Jade Green				12
Sienna				19

THE PAINT CODE furnishes the key to the paint colors used on the car. Two, two-digit codes indicate the bottom and top body colors respectively. NOTE: vinyl roof codes appear as a second set of digits.

COLOR	CODE
Cameo White	11
Sterling Silver	13
Oxford Gray	16
Ebony Black	19
Nordic Blue	24
Viking Blue	26
Monarch Blue	29
Capri Aqua	39
Silver Mint	41
Palm Green	42
Lime Green	43
Antique Jade	49
Bamboo	50
Saturn Gold	53
Galleon Gold	55
Sandalwood	61
Bittersweet	62
Kashmir Copper	65
Sienna	67
Sable Brown	68
Doeskin	70
Briar	73
Venetian Red	74
Matador Red	75
Antique Briar	78

VINYL ROOF COLOR*

	CODE
White	AA
Black	BB
Blue	CC
Sandalwood	EE
Green	GG

* All except Toronado

VINYL ROOF COLOR (Toronado)

	CODE
White	AA
Black	BB
Gold	DD
Brown	FF
Green	GG

CONVERTIBLE TOP COLORS

	CODE
White	AA
Black	BB
Sandalwood	EE
Green	GG

ENGINE NUMBER

An Oldsmobile engine is stamped with two different identification codes. One is the engine production code which identifies the engine and its approximate production date. The other code is the engine serial number — it matches the VIN (vehicle identification number).

OLDSMOBILE ENGINES

ENGINE CODE	NO. CYL.	CID	HORSE- POWER	COMP. RATIO	CARB	TRANS
ZB,ZG	6	250	145	8.5:1	1 BC	
VB,VF	6	250	145	8.0:1	1 BC	
QA,QJ	8	350	240	8.5:1	2 BC	Auto
QI	8	350	240	8.5:1	2 BC	4-spd SM
TC,TD	8	350	240	8.5:1	2 BC	Auto
TE	8	350	240	8.5:1	2 BC	4-spd SM
QN,QP	8	350	260	8.5:1	4 BC	Auto
QB,QO	8	350	260	8.5:1	4 BC	4-spd SM
UC,UD	8	455	280	8.5:1	2 BC	Auto
UE	8	455	280	8.5:1	2 BC	4-spd SM
TY,TX	8	455	280	8.5:1	2 BC	Auto
TQ,TP	8	455	320	8.5:1	4 BC	Auto
TW,TV,TA	8	455	320	8.5:1	4 BC	Auto
TU,TN	8	455	320	8.5:1	4 BC	4-spd SM
UN,UO	8	455	320	8.5:1	4 BC	Auto
US,UT	8	455	350	8.5:1	4 BC	Auto
TT,TL	8	455	340	8.5:1	4 BC	Auto
TS,TB	8	455	340	8.5:1	4 BC	4-spd SM

1972 OLDSMOBILE DELTA 88 ROYALE

1972 OLDSMOBILE DELTA 88 ROYALE

1972 OLDSMOBILE 98

1972 OLDSMOBILE TORONADO CUSTOM

1972 OLDSMOBILE CUTLASS SUPREME

1972 OLDSMOBILE TORONADO CUSTOM

1972 OLDSMOBILE CUTLASS SUPREME

1972 OLDSMOBILE VISTA CRUISER

VEHICLE IDENTIFICATION NUMBER

OLDSMOBILE 3K35M2M103133

Located on the top of the dash on the driver's side and visible through the windshield from outside the car.

FIRST DIGIT: Identifies GM Division (3 is Oldsmobile)

SECOND DIGIT: Identifies the series

SERIES	CODE
F-85	D
Cutlass (Standard)	F
Cutlass	G
Cutlass Supreme	J
Vista Cruiser	K
Delta 88	L
Delta 88 Royale	N
Custom Cruiser	R
Ninety-Eight	U
Ninety-Eight Luxury	V
Toronado	Y
Special Sill Cowl Chassis	T
Toronado CKD Chassis	X

THIRD AND FOURTH DIGITS: Identify the body style

BODY STYLE	CODE
Station Wagon 2-Seat (CC)	35
Station Wagon 2-Seat	36
Hardtop Coupe	37
Hardtop Sedan	39
Station Wagon 3-Seat (CC)	45
Short Sill Cowl	51
Station Wagon 2-Seat	56
Hardtop Coupe	57
Station Wagon 3-Seat	66
Convertible	67
Town Sedan	69
Sports Coupe	77
Hardtop Coupe	87

FIFTH DIGIT: Identifies the engine

ENGINE	CODE
V8-350 2 BC	H
V8-350 2 BC	J
V8-350 2 BC (Dual Ex.)	K
V8-350 4 BC	K
V8-350 4 BC (Dual Ex.)	M
V8-455 4 BC	T
V8-455 4 BC (Dual Ex.)	U
V8-455 4 BC (Dual Ex.)	V
V8-455 4 BC	W
V8-455 4 BC	X

SIXTH DIGIT: Identifies the year 1972

SEVENTH DIGIT: Identifies the assembly plant

ASSEMBLY PLANT	CODE
Linden, NJ	E
Framingham, MA	G
Lansing, MI	M
Arlington, TX	R
Fairfax, KS	X
Fremont, CA	Z

LAST SIX DIGITS: Represent the basic production numbers

BODY NUMBER PLATE

The body number plate is located on the firewall, just below the rear edge of the hood. This plate identifies the model year, car division, series, body style, body assembly plant, body numbers, trim combination, paint code and build date code.

```
BODY BY FISHER
ST 72   33687   LAN 123456 BDY
TR 10                19 19 PNT
000
```

GENERAL MOTORS CORPORATION CERTIFIES TO THE DEALER THAT THIS VEHICLE CONFORMS TO ALL U.S., FEDERAL MOTOR VEHICLE SAFETY STANDARDS APPLICABLE AT TIME OF MANUFACTURE.

Example:

72	Model Year (1972)
3	Car Division (Oldsmobile)
36	Series (Cutlass "S")
87	Style (2-Door Hardtop Coupe)
LAN	Body Assembly Plant (Lansing, MI)
123456	Production Sequence
10	Black Trim
19	Ebony Black Lower Body Color
19	Ebony Black Upper Body Color
000	Time Built Date

F-85	CODE
4-Door Sedan	3269
2-Door Hardtop	3287

CUTLASS	CODE
Station Wagon	3636
4-Door Sedan	3669
S Coupe	3677
S 2-Door Hardtop	3687

CUTLASS SUPREME	CODE
4-Door Hardtop	4239
2-Door Hardtop	4257
Convertible	4267

*442 option packages W-29, W-25, W-30 available

VISTA CRUISER	CODE
4-Door SW, 2-Seat	4856
4-Door SW, 3-Seat	4866

DELTA 88 ROYALE	CODE
4-Door Hardtop	6439
2-Door Hardtop	6457
Convertible	6467
4-Door Sedan	6469

CUSTOM CRUISER	CODE
4-Door SW, 2-Seat	6835
4-Door SW, 3-Seat	6845

NINETY-EIGHT CODE

2-Door Hardtop 8437
4-Door Hardtop 8439
Luxury 2-Door Hardtop 8637
Luxury 4-Door Hardtop 8639
*Regency option available

TORONADO   **CODE**

CKD 9251
2-Door Hardtop 9657
2-Door Hardtop Brougham 9857

THE TRIM CODE furnishes the key to the interior color and material scheme.

F-85 TOWN SEDAN TRIM

COLOR	CLOTH	VINYL	LEATHER	CODE
Black				10
Green				12
Covert Gold		•		44

CUTLASS HARDTOP COUPE TRIM

COLOR	CLOTH	VINYL	LEATHER	CODE
Black				10
Green				12
White				17
Saddle				19
Covert Gold		•		44

CUTLASS TOWN SEDAN TRIM

COLOR	CLOTH	VINYL	LEATHER	CODE
Black				10
Green				12
White				17
Saddle				19
Blue		•		43
Covert Gold		•		44

CUTLASS S SPORTS COUPE TRIM

COLOR	CLOTH	VINYL	LEATHER	CODE
Black				10
Green				12
White				17
Blue		•		43
Covert Gold		•		44

CUTLASS S HARDTOP COUPE

COLOR	CLOTH	VINYL	LEATHER	CODE
Black				10
Black				30*
Green				12
Green				32*
Blue		•		43
Blue				33*
White				17
White				37*
Saddle				19
Saddle				39*
Covert Gold		•		44

*Bucket seats

CUTLASS SUPREME CONVERTIBLE TRIM

COLOR	CLOTH	VINYL	LEATHER	CODE
Black				10
Black				30*
White				17
White				37*
Saddle				19
Saddle				39*

*Bucket seats

CUTLASS SUPREME HARDTOP SEDAN TRIM

COLOR	CLOTH	VINYL	LEATHER	CODE
Black				10
Saddle				19
Green		•		42
Blue		•		43
Covert Gold		•		44

CUTLASS SUPREME HARDTOP COUPE TRIM

COLOR	CLOTH	VINYL	LEATHER	CODE
Black				10
Black				30*
White				17
White				37*
Saddle				19
Green		•		42
Green				32*
Blue		•		43
Blue				33*
Covert Gold		•		44

*Bucket seats

CUTLASS CRUISER TRIM

COLOR	CLOTH	VINYL	LEATHER	CODE
Green				12
Blue				13
Saddle				19

VISTA CRUISER TRIM

COLOR	CLOTH	VINYL	LEATHER	CODE
Green				12
Blue				13
Covert Gold				14
Covert Gold		•		44
Saddle				19

DELTA 88 TOWN SEDAN TRIM

COLOR	CLOTH	VINYL	LEATHER	CODE
Black				10
Covert Gold				14
Covert Gold		•		44
Green		•		42
Blue		•		43

DELTA 88 HARDTOP SEDAN/HT COUPE TRIM

COLOR	CLOTH	VINYL	LEATHER	CODE
Black				10
Covert Gold				14
Covert Gold		•		44
Saddle				19
Green		•		42
Blue		•		43

DELTA 88 ROYALE CONVERTIBLE TRIM

COLOR	CLOTH	VINYL	LEATHER	CODE
Black				10
Green				12
White				17
Saddle				19

DELTA 88 ROYALE TOWN SEDAN TRIM

COLOR	CLOTH	VINYL	LEATHER	CODE
Covert Gold				14
Covert Gold		•		44
Black		•		40
Green		•		42
Blue		•		43

DELTA 88 ROYALE HT SEDAN/HDT COUPE TRIM

COLOR	CLOTH	VINYL	LEATHER	CODE
Covert Gold				14
Covert Gold	•			44
Saddle				19
Black		•		40
Green		•		42
Blue		•		43

CUSTOM CRUISER TRIM

COLOR	CLOTH	VINYL	LEATHER	CODE
Green				12
Blue				13
Covert Gold				14
Covert Gold	•			44
Saddle				19

NINETY-EIGHT HT SEDAN/HT COUPE TRIM

COLOR	CLOTH	VINYL	LEATHER	CODE
Black				10
Black	•			40
Covert Gold				14
Covert Gold	•			44
Pewter		•		41
Green		•		42
Blue		•		43

NINETY-EIGHT LUXURY SEDAN/COUPE TRIM

COLOR	CLOTH	VINYL	LEATHER	CODE
Black	•			60
Pewter	•			61
Covert Gold	•			64

TORONADO CUSTOM TRIM

COLOR	CLOTH	VINYL	LEATHER	CODE
Black				10
Black	•			40
Black	•			60#
Covert Gold				14
Covert Gold	•			44
Covert Gold	•			64#
Saddle				19
Saddle				59#
Pewter		•		41
Pewter		•		61#
Green		•		42
Green		•		62#
Blue		•		43
Blue		•		63#

#Notch back or 60-40 seats

THE PAINT CODE furnishes the key to the paint colors used on the car. Two, two-digit codes indicate the bottom and top body colors respectively. NOTE: vinyl roof codes appear as a second set of digits.

COLOR	CODE
Cameo White	11
Silver Pewter	14
Antique Pewter	18
Ebony Black	19
Nordic Blue	24
Viking Blue	26
Royal Blue	28
Radiant Green	36
Pinehurst Green	43
Sequoia Green	48
Covert Beige	50
Saturn Gold	53
Sovereign Gold	54
Sunfire Yellow	56
Baroque Gold	57
Saddle Tan	62
Saddle Bronze	63
Flame Orange	65
Nutmeg	69
Matador Red	75
Bamboo	81

VINYL ROOF COVER COLORS

White	AA
Black	BB
Saddle Tan	FF
Green	GG
Covert Beige	TT

CONVERTIBLE TOP COLORS

White	AA
Black	BB
Green	GG
Covert Beige	TT

ENGINE NUMBER

An Oldsmobile engine is stamped with two different identification codes. One is the engine production code which identifies the engine and its approximate production date. The other code is the engine serial number — it matches the VIN (vehicle identification number).

OLDSMOBILE ENGINES

ENGINE CODE	NO. CYL.	CID	HORSE-POWER	COMP. RATIO	CARB	TRANS
QA	8	350	160	8.5:1	2 BC	Synchro-Mesh
QB,QC,QN	8	350	175	8.5:1	2 BC	Auto
QD,QE	8	350	180	8.5:1	4 BC	Synchro-Mesh
QJ,QK,QP	8	350	180	8.5:1	4 BC	Auto
	8	350	200	8.5:1	4 BC	
	8	455	250	8.5:1	4 BC	
UD,UE	8	455	270	8.5:1	4 BC	Synchro-Mesh
UA,UB	8	455	270	8.5:1	4 BC	Auto
US,UT,	8	455	225	8.5:1	4 BC	Auto
UU,UV	8	455	265	8.5:1	4 BC	Auto
UL,UN	8	455	300	8.5:1	4 BC	Synchro-Mesh
UO	8	455	300	8.5:1	4 BC	Auto

1973 OLDSMOBILE CUTLASS COLONNADE

1973 OLDSMOBILE TORONADO

1973 OLDSMOBILE OMEGA

1973 OLDSMOBILE 98

1973 OLDSMOBILE DELTA 88 ROYALE

1973 OLDSMOBILE DELTA 88 ROYALE

1973 OLDSMOBILE 98

1973 OLDSMOBILE OMEGA

VEHICLE IDENTIFICATION NUMBER

OLDSMOBILE 3G37M3R100001

Located on the top of the dash on the driver's side and visible through the windshield from outside the car.

FIRST DIGIT: Identifies GM Division (3 is Oldsmobile)

SECOND DIGIT: Identifies the series

SERIES	CODE
Omega	B
Cutlass	F
Cutlass	G
Cutlass Supreme	J
Vista Cruiser	J
Delta 88	L
Delta 88 Royale	N
Custom Cruiser	Q
Custom Cruiser	R
Ninety-Eight	T
Ninety-Eight Luxury	V
Ninety-Eight Regency	X
Toronado	Y

THIRD AND FOURTH DIGITS: Identify the body style

BODY STYLE	CODE
2-Door Hatchback Coupe	17
2-Door Pillar Coupe	27
Colonnade HT Sedan	29
Custom Cruiser 2-Seat	35
Colonnade HT Coupe	37
Hardtop Sedan	39
Custom Cruiser 3-Seat	45
Short Sill Cowl	51
2-Door Hardtop Coupe	57
Toronado CKD	60
Convertible	67
Town Sedan	69

FIFTH DIGIT: Identifies the engine

ENGINE	CODE
6-250 1 BC	D
8-350 2 BC	H
8-350 4 BC	K
8-350 4 BC (Dual Ex.)	M
8-455 4 BC	T
8-455 4 BC (Dual Ex.)	U
8-455 4 BC (Dual Ex.)	V
8-455 4 BC	W

SIXTH DIGIT: Identifies the year 1973

SEVENTH DIGIT: Identifies the assembly plant

ASSEMBLY PLANT	CODE
Linden, NJ	E
Framingham, MA	G
Van Nuys, CA	L
Lansing, MI	M
Arlington, TX	R
Willow Run, MI	W
Fairfax, KS	X

LAST SIX DIGITS: Represent the basic production numbers

BODY NUMBER PLATE

The body number plate is located on the firewall, just below the rear edge of the hood. This plate identifies the model year, car division, series, body style, body assembly plant, body numbers, trim combination, paint code and build date code.

```
          BODY BY FISHER
ST 73   3CV37  LAN 123456 BDY
TR 10                  19 19 PNT
000

GENERAL MOTORS CORPORATION CERTIFIES
     TO THE DEALER THAT THIS VEHICLE
  CONFORMS TO ALL U.S., FEDERAL MOTOR
        VEHICLE SAFETY STANDARDS
   APPLICABLE AT TIME OF MANUFACTURE.
```

Example:

73	Model Year (1973)
3	Car Division (Oldsmobile)
CV	Series (Ninety-Eight Luxury)
37	Style (2-Door Hardtop)
LAN	Body Assembly Plant (Lansing, MI)
123456	Production Sequence
10	Black Vinyl Trim
19	Ebony Black Lower Body Color
19	Ebony Black Upper Body Color
000	Time Built Date

CUTLASS	CODE
2-Door	AF37
4-Door	AG29

*442 option available

CUTLASS S	CODE
2-Door	AG37

*Hurst/Olds option available

CUTLASS SUPREME	CODE
4-Door	AJ29
2-Door	AJ57

*Salon option available

VISTA CRUISER	CODE
4-Door SW, 2-Seat	AJ35
4-Door SW, 3-Seat	AJ45

DELTA 88	CODE
4-Door Hardtop	BL39
2-Door Hardtop	BL57
4-Door Sedan	BL69

DELTA 88 ROYALE	CODE
4-Door Hardtop	BN39
2-Door Hardtop	BN57
Convertible	BN67
4-Door Sedan	BN69

CUSTOM CRUISER	CODE
4-Door SW, 2-Seat	BQ35
4-Door SW, 2-Seat	BR35
4-Door SW, 3-Seat	BQ45
4-Door SW, 3-Seat	BR45

NINETY-EIGHT	CODE
2-Door Hardtop	CT37
4-Door Hardtop	CT39

NINETY-EIGHT LUXURY	MODEL CODE
2-Door Hardtop	3CV37
4-Door Hardtop	3CV39

NINETY-EIGHT REGENCY	MODEL CODE
4-Door Hardtop	3CX39

TORONADO	MODEL CODE
Toronado	3EY57
Brougham	3EZ57

OMEGA	MODEL CODE
Hatchback	3XB17
Coupe	3XB27
Sedan	3XB69

THE TRIM CODE furnishes the key to the interior color and material scheme.

OMEGA HATCHBACK TRIM

COLOR	CLOTH	VINYL	LEATHER	CODE
Black		•		30*
Black	•			40
Green		•		12
Blue		•		13
White	•			47
Saddle		•		19
Saddle		•		39*

*Bucket seats

OMEGA PILLAR COUPE TRIM

COLOR	CLOTH	VINYL	LEATHER	CODE
Black		•		30*
Black	•			40
Green		•		12
Blue		•		13
White	•			47
Saddle		•		19
Saddle		•		39*

*Bucket seats

OMEGA PILLAR SEDAN TRIM

COLOR	CLOTH	VINYL	LEATHER	CODE
Black	•			40
Green		•		12
Blue		•		13
White	•			47
Saddle		•		19

CUTLASS COUPE/SEDAN TRIM

COLOR	CLOTH	VINYL	LEATHER	CODE
Black		•		10
Green		•		12
Blue	•			43
Oxblood		•		15**
Neutral	•			46
White		•		17
Saddle		•		19

**S Hardtop only

CUTLASS S HARDTOP COUPE TRIM

COLOR	CLOTH	VINYL	LEATHER	CODE
Black		•		30*
Green		•		32*
Oxblood		•		35*
White		•		37*
Saddle		•		39*

*Bucket seats

CUTLASS SUPREME PILLAR SEDAN TRIM

COLOR	CLOTH	VINYL	LEATHER	CODE
Black		•		10
Black		•		30*
Green	•			42
Blue	•			43
Oxblood	•			25*
Neutral	•			46
Saddle		•		19
Saddle	•			29*

*Bucket seats

CUTLASS SUPREME VISTA CRUISER TRIM

COLOR	CLOTH	VINYL	LEATHER	CODE
Green		•		12
Blue		•		13
Oxblood		•		15
Neutral		•		16
Neutral	•			46
Saddle		•		19

CUTLASS SUPREME HARDTOP COUPE TRIM

COLOR	CLOTH	VINYL	LEATHER	CODE
Black		•		30*
Black		•		10
Green		•		32*
Green	•			42
Blue	•			43
Oxblood		•		35*
Oxblood		•		15
Neutral	•			46
White		•		37*
White		•		17
Saddle		•		39*
Saddle		•		19

*Bucket seats

DELTA 88 TRIM

COLOR	CLOTH	VINYL	LEATHER	CODE
Black		•		10
Green	•			42
Blue	•			43
Chamois	•			44
Neutral		•		16
Saddle		•		19

DELTA ROYALE TRIM

COLOR	CLOTH	VINYL	LEATHER	CODE
Black	•			40
Green	•			42
Blue	•			43
Chamois	•			44
Neutral		•		16
Saddle		•		19

DELTA ROYALE CONVERTIBLE TRIM

COLOR	CLOTH	VINYL	LEATHER	CODE
Black		•		10
Oxblood		•		15
White		•		17
Saddle		•		19

CUSTOM CRUISER TRIM

COLOR	CLOTH	VINYL	LEATHER	CODE
Green		•		12
Blue		•		13
Oxblood		•		15
Neutral		•		16
Saddle		•		19
Saddle		•		79#
Saddle	•			49

#Notch back or 60-40 seats

NINETY-EIGHT TRIM

COLOR	CLOTH	VINYL	LEATHER	CODE
Black		•		10
Black	•			40
Black	•			60#
Black	•			80#
Green	•			42
Green	•			62#
Green	•			82#
Blue	•			43
Blue	•			63#
Blue	•			83#
Chamois	•			44
Chamois	•			64#
Oxblood	•			45
Oxblood	•			85#
Neutral		•		16
Neutral		•		76#
Neutral	•			86#
White		•		17
Saddle		•		19

#Notch back or 60-40 seats

TORONADO TRIM

COLOR	CLOTH	VINYL	LEATHER	CODE
Black		•		10
Black	•			40
Black	•			60#
Green	•			42
Blue	•			43
Chamois	•			44
Oxblood	•			45
Neutral		•		16
Neutral	•			86#
Neutral	•			66#
White		•		17
Saddle		•		19

#Notch back or 60-40 seats

THE PAINT CODE furnishes the key to the paint colors used on the car. Two, two-digit codes indicate the bottom and top body colors respectively. NOTE: vinyl roof codes appear as a second set of digits.

COLOR	CODE
Cameo White	11
Ebony Black	19
Wedgewood Blue	24
Zodiac Blue	26
Eclipse Blue	29
Emerald Green	42
Crystal Green	44
Moss Gold	46
Brewster Green	48
Omega Yellow	51
Chamois Gold	56
Mayan Gold	60
Silver Taupe	64
Tanbark	66
Chestnut	68
Cranberry Red	74
Omega Red	75
Honey Beige	81
Omega Orange	97

VINYL ROOF COLORS

Color	Code
White	AA
Black	BB
Blue	DD
Green	GG
Maroon	HH
Black	BB
Brown	RR
Beige	TT

ENGINE NUMBER

An Oldsmobile engine is stamped with two different identification codes. One is the engine production code which identifies the engine and its approximate production date. The other code is the engine serial number — it matches the VIN (vehicle identification number).

OLDSMOBILE ENGINES

ENGINE CODE	NO. CYL.	CID	HORSE-POWER	COMP. RATIO	CARB	TRANS
CCC,CCD	6	250	100	8.2:1	1 BC	SMT
CCA,CCB	6	250	100	8.2:1	1 BC	Auto
QN,QO,QP	8	350	160	8.5:1	2 BC	Auto
QQ,QS,QT	8	350	160	8.5:1	2 BC	Auto
QA,QB,QJ	8	350	180	8.5:1	4 BC	Auto
QK,QU,QV	8	350	180	8.5:1	4 BC	Auto
QC,QD	8	350	180	8.5:1	4 BC	Std
QE,QL	8	350	180	8.5:1	4 BC	Std
UA,UB,US	8	455	225	8.5:1	4 BC	Auto
UT,UU,UV	8	455	225	8.5:1	4 BC	Auto
UD	8	455	225	8.5:1	4 BC	Std
	8	455	250	8.5:1	4 BC	
	8	455	270	8.5:1	4 BC	4-spd Man

1974 OLDSMOBILE CUTLASS

1974 OLDSMOBILE CUTLASS SUPREME CRUISER

1974 OLDSMOBILE DELTA 88

1974 OLDSMOBILE DELTA 88

1974 OLDSMOBILE TORONADO

1974 OLDSMOBILE TORONADO

1974 OLDSMOBILE 98

1974 OLDSMOBILE OMEGA

VEHICLE IDENTIFICATION NUMBER

```
 •   OLDSMOBILE
     3G37M4R100001      •
```

Located on the top of the dash on the driver's side and visible through the windshield from outside the car.

FIRST DIGIT: Identifies GM Division (3 is Oldsmobile)

SECOND DIGIT: Identifies the series

SERIES	CODE
Omega	B
Cutlass	F
Cutlass	G
Cutlass Station Wagon	H
Cutlass Supreme	J
Vista Cruiser	J
Delta 88	L
Delta 88 Royale	N
Custom Cruiser	Q
Custom Cruiser	R
Ninety-Eight	T
Ninety-Eight Luxury	V
Ninety-Eight Regency	X
Toronado Custom	Y
Toronado Brougham	Z
Special Sill Cowl Chassis	W
Toronado CKD Chassis	U

THIRD AND FOURTH DIGITS: Identify the body style

BODY STYLE	CODE
2-Door Omega Hatchback Coupe	17
2-Door Omega Pillar Coupe	27
4-Door Cutlass Pillar Sedan	29
4-door SW, 2-Seat	35
Hardtop Coupe	37
Delta 88 Hardtop Sedan	39
4-Door SW, 3-Seat	45
Hardtop Coupe (Opera Roof)	47
Toronado CKD Chassis	51
Delta 88/Toronado Hardtop Coupe	57
Special Sill Cowl Chassis	60
Convertible	67
4-Door Pillar Sedan	69

FIFTH DIGIT: Identifies the engine

ENGINE	CODE
V6-250 1 BC	D
V8-350 4 BC	K
V8-350 4 BC (Dual Ex.)	M
V8-455 4 BC	W
V8-455 4 BC	T
V8-455 4 BC (Dual Ex.)	U
V8-455 4 BC	V

SIXTH DIGIT: Identifies the year 1974

SEVENTH DIGIT: Identifies the assembly plant

ASSEMBLY PLANT	CODE
Linden, NJ	E
Doraville, GA	D
Framingham, MA	G
Van Nuys, CA	L
Lansing, MI	M
Arlington, TX	R
Willow Run, MI	W
Fairfax, KS	X

LAST SIX DIGITS: Represent the basic production numbers

BODY NUMBER PLATE

The body number plate is located on the firewall, just below the rear edge of the hood. This plate identifies the model year, car division, series, body style, body assembly plant, body numbers, trim combination, paint code and build date code.

```
            BODY BY FISHER
   ST 74   3CV37  LAN 123456 BDY
   TR 10                 19 19 PNT
   000

 •                                    •

   GENERAL MOTORS CORPORATION CERTIFIES
      TO THE DEALER THAT THIS VEHICLE
   CONFORMS TO ALL U.S., FEDERAL MOTOR
          VEHICLE SAFETY STANDARDS
    APPLICABLE AT TIME OF MANUFACTURE.
```

Example:

74	Model Year (1974)
3	Car Division (Oldsmobile)
CV	Series (Ninety-Eight Luxury)
37	Style (2-Door Hardtop)
LAN	Body Assembly Plant (Lansing, MI)
123456	Production Sequence
10	Black Vinyl Trim
19	Ebony Black Lower Body Color
19	Ebony Black Upper Body Color
000	Time Built Date

CUTLASS	CODE
2-Door	AF37
4-Door	AG29

*442 option available
*GMO option available

CUTLASS S	CODE
2-Door	AG37

*Hurst/Olds option available
*W-30 option available

CUTLASS SUPREME CRUISER	CODE
4-Door SW, 2-Seat	AH35
4-Door SW, 3-Seat	AH45

VISTA CRUISER	CODE
4-Door SW, 2-Seat	AJ35
4-Door SW, 3-Seat	AJ45

CUTLASS SUPREME	CODE
4-Door	AJ29
2-Door	AJ57

*Salon option available

DELTA 88	CODE
4-Door Hardtop	BL39
2-Door Hardtop	BL57
4-Door Sedan	BL69

DELTA 88 ROYALE	CODE
4-Door Hardtop	BN39
2-Door Hardtop	BN57
Convertible	BN67
4-Door Sedan	BN69

CUSTOM CRUISER

	CODE
4-Door SW, 2-Seat	BQ35
4-Door SW, 3-Seat	BQ45

CUSTOM CRUISER

	CODE
2-Seat	BR35
3-Seat	BR45

NINETY-EIGHT

	CODE
2-Door Hardtop	CT37
4-Door Hardtop	CT39

NINETY-EIGHT LUXURY

	CODE
2-Door Hardtop	CV37
4-Door Hardtop	CV39

NINETY-EIGHT REGENCY

	CODE
2-Door Hardtop	CX37
4-Door Hardtop	CX39

*Elegance option available

TORONADO CUSTOM

	CODE
Custom	EY47
Brougham	EZ47

OMEGA

	CODE
Hatchback	XB17
Coupe	XB27
Sedan	XB69

THE TRIM CODE furnishes the key to the interior color and material scheme.

OMEGA TRIM

COLOR	CLOTH	VINYL	LEATHER	CODE
Black		•		30*
Black	•			40
Green		•		12
Wdgwd. Blue		•		13
White		•		17
Saddle		•		19
Saddle		•		39*

*Bucket seats

CUTLASS TRIM

COLOR	CLOTH	VINYL	LEATHER	CODE
Black		•		10
Black		•		30*
Green		•		12
Wdgwd. Blue	•			43
Red		•		15
Red		•		35*
Beige		•		16
White		•		17
White		•		37*
Saddle		•		39*
Saddle	•			49

*Bucket seats

CUTLASS SUPREME PILLAR SEDAN TRIM

COLOR	CLOTH	VINYL	LEATHER	CODE
Black		•		10
Black		•		50*
Black		•		70#
Green	•			42
Green	•			22*
Green	•			62#
Wdgwd. Blue	•			43
Wdgwd. Blue	•			23*
Wdgwd. Blue	•			63#
Red	•			25*
Beige		•		16
Beige		•		76#
Saddle		•		59*
Saddle	•			49
Saddle	•			29*
Saddle	•			69#

*Bucket seats
#Notch back or 60-40 seats

CUTLASS SUPREME VISTA CRUISER TRIM

COLOR	CLOTH	VINYL	LEATHER	CODE
Green	•			12
Wdgwd. Blue	•			13
Red	•			15
Beige	•			16
Beige	•			76#
Saddle	•			19
Saddle	•			79#

#Notch back or 60-40 seats

CUTLASS SUPREME HARDTOP COUPE TRIM

COLOR	CLOTH	VINYL	LEATHER	CODE
Black		•		10
Black		•		30*
Black		•		70#
Black		•		50*
Green	•			42
Green	•			62#
Green	•			22*
Wdgwd. Blue	•			43
Wdgwd. Blue	•			63#
Wdgwd. Blue	•			23*
Red		•		15
Red		•		35*
Red	•			25*
Beige		•		16
Beige		•		76#
White		•		17
White		•		37*
White		•		77#
Saddle		•		39*
Saddle	•			49
Saddle		•		59*
Saddle	•			69#
Saddle	•			29*

*Bucket seats
#Notch back or 60-40 seats

DELTA 88 TRIM

COLOR	CLOTH	VINYL	LEATHER	CODE
Black		•		10
Green	•			42
Mid. Blue	•			43
White		•		17
Saddle		•		19
Saddle	•			49

DELTA ROYALE HT COUPE/SEDAN TRIM

COLOR	CLOTH	VINYL	LEATHER	CODE
Black	•			40
Black	•			60#
Green	•			42
Green	•			62#
Mid. Blue	•			43
Mid. Blue	•			63#
Red	•			45
Red	•			65#
White		•		17
White		•		77#
Saddle		•		19
Saddle		•		79#
Saddle	•			49
Saddle	•			69#

#Notch back or 60-40 seats

DELTA ROYALE CONVERTIBLE TRIM

COLOR	CLOTH	VINYL	LEATHER	CODE
Black		•		10
White		•		17

CUSTOM CRUISER TRIM

COLOR	CLOTH	VINYL	LEATHER	CODE
Green		•		12
Mid. Blue		•		13
Red		•		15
Beige		•		16
Beige		•		76#
Saddle		•		19
Saddle		•		79#
Saddle	•			49

#Notch back or 60-40 seats

NINETY-EIGHT TRIM

COLOR	CLOTH	VINYL	LEATHER	CODE
Black		•		10
Black	•			40
Black	•			60#
Black	•			80#
Green	•			42
Green	•			62#
Green	•			82#
Mid. Blue	•			43
Mid. Blue	•			63#
Mid. Blue	•			83#
Red	•			45
Red	•			65#
Red	•			85#
Beige		•		16
Beige		•		76#
White		•		17
Saddle	•			49
Saddle	•			69#
Saddle	•			89#

#Notch back or 60-40 seats

TORONADO TRIM

COLOR	CLOTH	VINYL	LEATHER	CODE
Black	•			40
Black	•			60#
Green	•			42
Green	•			62#
Mid. Blue	•			43
Mid. Blue	•			63#
Red	•			45
Red	•			65#
White		•		17
White		•		77#
Saddle		•		19
Saddle	•			69#

#Notch back or 60-40 seats

THE PAINT CODE furnishes the key to the paint colors used on the car. Two, two-digit codes indicate the bottom and top body colors respectively. NOTE: vinyl roof codes appear as a second set of digits.

COLOR	CODE
Cameo White	11
Ebony Black	19
Wedgewood Blue	24
Zodiac Blue	26
Eclipse Blue	29
Reef Turquoise	36
Omega Lime	40
Sage Green	44
Cypress Green	46
Balsam Green	49
Colonial Cream	50
Omega Maize	51
Omega Gold	53
Colonial Gold	55
Citation Bronze	59
Silver Taupe	64
Cinnamon	66
Clove Brown	69
Cranberry	74
Omega Red	75

VINYL ROOF COLORS

White	AA
Black	BB
Blue	DD
Cream	EE
Green	GG
Cranberry	HH
Saddle	RR

ENGINE NUMBER

An Oldsmobile engine is stamped with two different identification codes. One is the engine production code which identifies the engine and its approximate production date. The other code is the engine serial number — it matches the VIN (vehicle identification number).

OLDSMOBILE ENGINES

ENGINE CODE	NO. CYL.	CID	HORSE-POWER	COMP. RATIO	CARB	TRANS
CCC,CCD	6	250	100	8.5:1	1 BC	Auto
CCA,CCB	6	250	100	8.5:1	1 BC	Std.
QB,QC,QL	8	350	180	8.5:1	4 BC	Auto
QO,QU,QW	8	350	180	8.5:1	4 BC	Auto
TB,TC	8	350	180	8.5:1	4 BC	Auto
TL,TO	8	350	180	8.5:1	4 BC	Auto
	8	350	200	8.5:1	4 BC	
VA,VB,VC	8	455	210	8.5:1	4 BC	Auto
VD,VL,VO	8	455	210	8.5:1	4 BC	Auto
VP,UA,UB	8	455	210	8.5:1	4 BC	Auto
UC,UD,UL	8	455	210	8.5:1	4 BC	Auto
UN,UP,UR	8	455	210	8.5:1	4 BC	Auto
UO,UV,UX	8	455	210	8.5:1	4 BC	Auto
	8	455	230	8.5:1	4 BC	
	8	455	275	8.5:1	4 BC	

1975 OLDSMOBILE OMEGA

1975 OLDSMOBILE CUTLASS

1975 OLDSMOBILE STARFIRE

1975 OLDSMOBILE CUSTOM CRUISER

1975 OLDSMOBILE TORONADO

1975 OLDSMOBILE DELTA 88 ROYALE

1975 OLDSMOBILE VISTA CRUISER

1975 OLDSMOBILE 98 REGENCY

VEHICLE IDENTIFICATION NUMBER

OLDSMOBILE
3G37M5M10001

Located on the top of the dash on the driver's side and visible through the windshield from outside the car.

FIRST DIGIT: Identifies GM Division (3 is Oldsmobile)

SECOND DIGIT: Identifies the series

SERIES	CODE
Starfire	D
Omega	B
Omega Salon	C
Cutlass	F
Cutlass S	G
Cutlass Supreme Cruiser	H
Cutlass Supreme	J
Vista Cruiser	K
Cutlass Salon	K
Delta 88	L
Delta 88 Royale	N
Custom Cruiser	Q
Custom Cruiser	R
Toronado CKD	U
Ninety-Eight Luxury	V
Driveaway Chassis	W
Ninety-Eight Regency	X
Toronado Custom	Y
Toronado Brougham	Z

THIRD AND FOURTH DIGITS: Identify the body style

BODY STYLE	CODE
2-Door Sport Coupe	07
2-Door Hatchback	17
2-Door Coupe	27
Colonnade Sedan	29
4-Door SW, 2-Seat Vista Cruiser	35
Colonnade Hardtop Coupe	37
4-Door Hardtop	39
4-Door SW, 3-Seat	45
Driveaway Chassis	51
2-Door Hardtop Coupe	57
Toronado CKD	60
2-Door Convertible	67
4-Door Town Sedan	69

FIFTH DIGIT: Identifies the engine

ENGINE	CODE
V6-231 1 BC	C
L6-250 1 BC	D
V8-260 2 BC	F
V8-350 2 BC	H
V8-350 2 BC	J
V8-350 4 BC	K
V8-350 4 BC (Dual Ex.)	M
V8-400 2 BC	R
V8-400 4 BC	S
V8-455 4 BC	T
V8-455 4 BC	W

SIXTH DIGIT: Identifies the year 1975

SEVENTH DIGIT: Identifies the assembly plant

ASSEMBLY PLANT	CODE
Doraville, GA	D
Linden, NJ	E
Kansas City, MO	K
Van Nuys, CA	L
Lansing, MI	M
Arlington, TX	R
Willow Run, MI	W
Fairfax, KS	X
St. Therese, CAN	2

LAST SIX DIGITS: Represent the basic production numbers

BODY NUMBER PLATE

The body number plate is located on the firewall, just below the rear edge of the hood. This plate identifies the model year, car division, series, body style, body assembly plant, body numbers, trim combination, paint code and build date code.

```
              BODY BY FISHER
  ST 75   3CV37  LAN 123456 BDY
  TR 40                  19 19 PNT
  000

  GENERAL MOTORS CORPORATION CERTIFIES
  TO THE DEALER THAT THIS VEHICLE
  CONFORMS TO ALL U.S., FEDERAL MOTOR
       VEHICLE SAFETY STANDARDS
  APPLICABLE AT TIME OF MANUFACTURE.
```

Example:

75	Model Year (1975)
3	Car Division (Oldsmobile)
CV	Series (Ninety-Eight Luxury)
37	Style (2-Door Hardtop)
LAN	Body Assembly Plant (Lansing, MI)
123456	Production Sequence
40	Black Cloth Trim
19	Ebony Black Lower Body Color
19	Ebony Black Upper Body Color
000	Time Built Date

CUTLASS	CODE
2-Door	AF37
4-Door	AG29
S 2-Door	AG37

*442 Option available

CUTLASS SUPREME CRUISER	CODE
4-Door SW, 2-Seat	AH35
4-Door SW, 3-Seat	AH45
2-Door	AK29
4-Door	AJ29

*Hurst/Olds option available

VISTA CRUISER	CODE
4-Door SW, 2-Seat	AJ35
4-Door SW, 3-Seat	AJ45

CUTLASS SALON

	CODE
2-Door	AJ57
4-Door	AK57

DELTA 88

	CODE
4-Door Hardtop	BL39
2-Door Hardtop	BL57
4-Door Sedan	BL69

DELTA 88 ROYALE

	CODE
4-Door Hardtop	BN39
2-Door Hardtop	BN57
Convertible	BN67
4-Door Sedan	BN69

CUSTOM CRUISER

	CODE
4-Door SW, 2-Seat	BQ35
4-Door SW, 3-Seat	BQ45
4-Door SW, 2-Seat	BR35
4-Door SW, 3-Seat	BR45

NINETY-EIGHT LUXURY

	CODE
2-Door Hardtop	CV37
4-Door Hardtop	CV39

NINETY-EIGHT REGENCY

	CODE
2-Door Hardtop	CX37
4-Door Hardtop	CX39

TORONADO CUSTOM

	CODE
Custom	EY57
Brougham	EZ47
Brougham	EZ57

STARFIRE

	CODE
Hatchback	HD07

OMEGA

	CODE
Hatchback	XB17
Coupe	XB69
Salon Hatchback	XC17
Salon Coupe	XC27
Salon Sedan	XC69

*Salon option available

THE TRIM CODE furnishes the key to the interior color and material scheme.

STARFIRE TRIM

COLOR	CLOTH	VINYL	LEATHER	CODE
Black		•		30*
Black			•	L0*
Dk. Blue		•		33*
Dk. Blue	•			03*
Dk. Oxblood	•			05*
Sandstone			•	L5*
White		•		37*
Dk. Saddle		•		39*
Dk. Saddle			•	L9*

*Bucket seats

OMEGA TRIM

COLOR	CLOTH	VINYL	LEATHER	CODE
Black		•		50*
Black	•			40
Dk. Blue	•			43
Dk. Blue	•			23*
Dk. Oxblood		•		15
Dk. Oxblood	•			25*

COLOR	CLOTH	VINYL	LEATHER	CODE
White		•		17
White		•		37*
White		•		57*
Dk. Saddle		•		19
Dk. Saddle	•			29*
Dk. Saddle		•		39*

*Bucket seats

CUTLASS TRIM

COLOR	CLOTH	VINYL	LEATHER	CODE
Black		•		10
Black		•		30*
Black	•			40
Med. Green	•			42
Dk. Blue		•		13
Dk. Oxblood		•		15
Dk. Oxblood	•			45
White		•		17
White		•		37*
Dk. Saddle		•		19
Dk. Saddle	•			49
Dk. Saddle	•			09*

*Bucket seats

CUTLASS COUPE/SEDAN TRIM

COLOR	CLOTH	VINYL	LEATHER	CODE
Black		•		10
Black		•		70#
Black		•		30*
Black		•		50*
Med. Green		•		12
Med. Green		•		72#
Med. Green	•			22*
Dk. Blue	•			43
Dk. Blue	•			63#
Dk. Blue	•			23*
Dk. Oxblood	•			45
Dk. Oxblood	•			65#
Dk. Oxblood		•		35*
Dk. Oxblood	•			25*
White		•		17
White		•		37*
White		•		57*
White		•		77#
Dk. Saddle		•		19
Dk. Saddle		•		39*
Dk. Saddle		•		59*
Dk. Saddle	•			49
Dk. Saddle	•			69#
Dk. Saddle	•			29*

*Bucket seats
#Notch back or 60-40 seats

CUTLASS SUPREME CRUISER TRIM

COLOR	CLOTH	VINYL	LEATHER	CODE
Med. Green		•		12
Med. Green		•		72#
Dk. Blue		•		13
Dk. Blue		•		73#
Dk. Oxblood		•		15
Dk. Oxblood		•		75#
Dk. Saddle		•		19
Dk. Saddle		•		79#

#Notch back or 60-40 seats

DELTA 88 TRIM

COLOR	CLOTH	VINYL	LEATHER	CODE
Black		•		10
Med. Green	•			42
Dk. Blue		•		43
Dk. Oxblood		•		15
Sandstone		•		16
White		•		17
Dk. Saddle		•		19
Dk. Saddle	•			49

DELTA ROYALE COUPE/SEDAN TRIM

COLOR	CLOTH	VINYL	LEATHER	CODE
Black	•			40
Black	•			60#
Med. Green	•			42
Med. Green	•			62#
Dk. Blue	•			43
Dk. Blue	•			63#
Dk. Oxblood	•			45
Dk. Oxblood	•			65#
Sandstone		•		16
Sandstone		•		76#
White		•		17
White		•		77#
Dk. Saddle		•		19
Dk. Saddle		•		79#
Dk. Saddle	•			49
Dk. Saddle	•			69#

#Notch back or 60-40 seats

DELTA ROYALE CONVERTIBLE TRIM

COLOR	CLOTH	VINYL	LEATHER	CODE
Dk. Oxblood		•		15
Dk. Oxblood		•		75#
White		•		17
White		•		77#

#Notch back or 60-40 seats

CUSTOM CRUISER TRIM

COLOR	CLOTH	VINYL	LEATHER	CODE
Med. Green		•		12
Med. Green		•		72#
Dk. Blue		•		13
Dk. Blue		•		73#
Dk. Oxblood		•		15
Dk. Oxblood		•		75#
Sandstone		•		16
Sandstone		•		76#
Dk. Saddle		•		19
Dk. Saddle		•		79#

#Notch back or 60-40 seats

NINETY-EIGHT TRIM

COLOR	CLOTH	VINYL	LEATHER	CODE
Black	•			40
Black	•			60#
Black	•			80#
Silver**	•			81#
Med. Green	•			42
Med. Green	•			62#
Med. Green	•			82#
Dk. Blue	•			43
Dk. Blue	•			63#
Dk. Blue	•			83#
Dk. Oxblood	•			45
Dk. Oxblood	•			65#
Dk. Oxblood	•			85#
White		•		17
White		•		77#
White		•		97#
Dk. Saddle	•			49
Dk. Saddle	•			69#
Dk. Saddle	•			89#

#Notch back or 60-40 seats
**Regency only

TORONADO TRIM

COLOR	CLOTH	VINYL	LEATHER	CODE
Black	•			40
Black	•			60#
Silver		•		71#
Med. Green	•			42
Med. Green	•			62#
Dk. Blue	•			43
Dk. Blue	•			63#
Dk. Oxblood	•			45
Dk. Oxblood	•			65#
White		•		17
White		•		77#
Dk. Saddle		•		19
Dk. Saddle		•		69#

#Notch-Back or 60-40 Seats

THE PAINT CODE furnishes the key to the paint colors used on the car. Two, two-digit codes indicate the bottom and top body colors respectively. NOTE: vinyl roof codes appear as a second set of digits.

COLOR	CODE
Cameo White	11
Inca Silver	13
Dove Gray	15
Shadow Gray	16
Ebony Black	19
Glacier Blue	21
Horizon Blue	24
Spectra Blue	26
Midnight Blue	29
Sage Green	44
Forest Green	49
Colonial Cream	50
Sebring Yellow	51
Sandstone	55
Bronze	58
Sable Brown	59
Canyon Copper	63
Persimmon	64
Crimson Red	72
Cranberry	74
Rallye Red	75
Burgundy	79
Sunfire Orange	80

VINYL ROOF COLORS

White	AA
Black	BB
Cordovan	CC
Blue	DD
Green	GG
Cranberry	HH
Red	RR
Sandstone	SS

CONVERTIBLE TOP COLORS

White	AA
Black	BB

ENGINE NUMBER

An Oldsmobile engine is stamped with two different identification codes. One is the engine production code which identifies the engine and its approximate production date. The other code is the engine serial number — it matches the VIN (vehicle identification number).

OLDSMOBILE ENGINES

ENGINE CODE	NO. CYL.	CID	HORSE-POWER	COMP. RATIO	CARB	TRANS
CJU	6	250	105	8.2:1	1 BC	Std.
CJT, CJL	6	250	105	8.2:1	1 BC	Auto
FP	6	231	110	8.0:1	2 BC	Std.
FR,FS	6	231	110	8.0:1	2 BC	Auto
QA,QK,QD	8	260	110	8.5:1	2 BC	Std.
QB,QC,QK	8	260	110	8.5:1	2 BC	
QN,TA,TK	8	260	110	8.5:1	2 BC	Std.
TD,TN	8	260	110	8.5:1	2 BC	Std.
QE,QP,QJ	8	260	110	8.5:1	2 BC	Auto
QJ,QQ,TE	8	260	110	8.5:1	2 BC	Auto
TP,TJ,TQ	8	260	110	8.5:1	2 BC	Auto
RW,QL,RX	8	350	165	8.0:1	4 BC	
Q2,Q3,Q4	8	350	165	8.0:1	4 BC	
Q5,QL	8	350	165	8.0:1	4 BC	
PA,PB	8	350	165	8.0:1	4 BC	
QO,QX,RN	8	350	165	8.0:1	4 BC	Auto
TL,RO,TO	8	350	165	8.0:1	4 BC	Auto
TX	8	350	165	8.0:1	4 BC	Auto
RS,RT	8	350	145	8.1:1	2 BC	
	8	350	170	8.5:1	4 BC	
YH,YJ	8	400	170	8.0:1	2 BC	
	8	400	175	8.5:1	4 BC	
YM,YT	8	400	190	7.6:1	4 BC	Auto
UB,UE,UP	8	455	190	8.5:1	4 BC	Auto
UC,UD,UP	8	455	190	8.5:1	4 BC	Auto
VB,VE,VP	8	455	190	8.5:1	4 BC	Auto
VC,VD,VP	8	455	190	8.5:1	4 BC	Auto
	8	455	215	8.5:1	4 BC	

1976 OLDSMOBILE CUTLASS S

1976 OLDSMOBILE OMEGA

1976 OLDSMOBILE CUTLASS STATION WAGON

1976 OLDSMOBILE STARFIRE

1976 OLDSMOBILE DELTA 88

1976 OLDSMOBILE TORONADO

1976 OLDSMOBILE 98

1976 OLDSMOBILE CUTLASS

VEHICLE IDENTIFICATION NUMBER

OLDSMOBILE
3G37T6R103133

Located on the top of the dash on the driver's side and visible through the windshield from outside the car.

FIRST DIGIT: Identifies GM Division (3 is Oldsmobile)

SECOND DIGIT: Identifies the series

SERIES	CODE
Starfire SX	D
Starfire	T
Omega	B
Omega Brougham	E
Omega F-85	S
Cutlass S	G
Cutlass Supreme	H
Cutlass Supreme	J
Cutlass Salon	K
Cutlass Supreme Brougham	M
Delta 88	L
Delta 88 Royale	N
Custom Cruiser	Q
Custom Cruiser	R
Ninety-Eight Luxury	V
Ninety-Eight Regency	X
Toronado Custom	Y
Toronado Brougham	Z
Special Sill Cowl	W
Toronado CKD	U

THIRD AND FOURTH DIGITS: Identify the body style

BODY STYLE	CODE
Sport Coupe	07
Hatchback Coupe	17
Coupe	27
Sedan	29
Station Wagon	35
Hardtop Coupe	37
Hardtop Sedan	39
Station Wagon 3-Seat	45
Hardtop Coupe	57
Sedan	69
Toronado CKD	51

FIFTH DIGIT: Identifies the engine

ENGINE	CODE
V4-140 1 BC	B
V6-231 1 BC	C
V6-250 1 BC	D
V8-260 2 BC	F
V8-350 2 BC	H
V8-350 4 BC	J
V8-350 4 BC	R
V8-455 4 BC	S
V8-455 4 BC	T

SIXTH DIGIT: Identifies the year 1976

SEVENTH DIGIT: Identifies the assembly plant

ASSEMBLY PLANT	CODE
South Gate, CA	C
Doraville, GA	D
Linden, NJ	E
Van Nuys, CA	L
Lansing, MI	M
Arlington, TX	R
Willow Run, MI	W
Fairfax, KS	X
St. Therese, Que., CAN	2

LAST SIX DIGITS: Represent the basic production numbers

BODY NUMBER PLATE

The body number plate is located on the firewall, just below the rear edge of the hood. This plate identifies the model year, car division, series, body style, body assembly plant, body numbers, trim combination, paint code and build date code.

```
           BODY BY FISHER
ST 76   3CV37  LAN 123456 BDY
TR 40                   19 19 PNT
000  A51

GENERAL MOTORS CORPORATION CERTIFIES
TO THE DEALER THAT THIS VEHICLE
CONFORMS TO ALL U.S., FEDERAL MOTOR
VEHICLE SAFETY STANDARDS
APPLICABLE AT TIME OF MANUFACTURE.
```

Example:

76	Model Year (1976)
3	Car Division (Oldsmobile)
CV	Series (Ninety-Eight Luxury)
37	Style (2-Door Hardtop)
LAN	Body Assembly Plant (Lansing, MI)
123456	Production Sequence
40	Black Cloth Trim
19	Ebony Black Lower Body Color
19	Ebony Black Upper Body Color
000	Time Built Date
A51	Modular Seat Code

CUTLASS	CODE
4-Door	AG29
S 2-Door	AG37
*442 option available	

CUTLASS SUPREME	CODE
Station Wagon	AH35
4-Door	AJ29
Vista Cruiser	AJ35
2-Door	AJ57
Brougham 2-Door	AM57

CUTLASS SALON	CODE
4-Door	AK29
2-Door	AK57

DELTA 88

	CODE
4-Door Hardtop	BL39
2-Door Hardtop	BL57
4-Door Town Sedan	BL69

DELTA 88 ROYALE

	CODE
4-Door Hardtop	BN39
2-Door Hardtop	BN57
4-Door Town Sedan	BN69

*Crown Landau option available

CUSTOM CRUISER

	CODE
4-Door SW, 2-Seat	BQ35
4-Door SW, 3-Seat	BQ45
4-Door SW, 2-Seat	BR35
4-Door SW, 3-Seat	BR45

NINETY-EIGHT LUXURY

	CODE
2-Door	CV37
4-Door	CV39

NINETY-EIGHT REGENCY

	CODE
2-Door	CX37
4-Door	CX39

TORONADO

	CODE
Custom	EY57
Brougham	EZ57

STARFIRE

	CODE
Sport Coupe SX	HD07
Sport Coupe	HT07

*GT option available

OMEGA

	CODE
Hatchback	XB17
2-Door Coupe	XB27
4-Door Sedan	XB69
Brougham Hatchback	XE17
2-Door Brougham Coupe	XE27
4-Door Brougham Sedan	XE69
F85 2-Door Coupe	XS27

*SX option available

THE TRIM CODE furnishes the key to the interior color and material scheme.

STARFIRE TRIM

COLOR	CLOTH	VINYL	LEATHER	CODE
Blue	•			03*
Blue		•		30*
Red	•			04*
Red		•		34*
Black		•		30*
White		•		37*
Buckskin		•		38*

*Bucket seats

OMEGA TRIM

COLOR	CLOTH	VINYL	LEATHER	CODE
Mahogany		•		15
Mahogany	•			45
Mahogany	•			05*
White		•		17
White		•		37*
White		•		17
Buckskin		•		18
Buckskin		•		38*
Black	•			40
Blue	•			43
Blue	•			03*

*Bucket seats

CUTLASS S TRIM

COLOR	CLOTH	VINYL	LEATHER	CODE
Black		•		10
Black	•			40
Black		•		30*
Mahogany		•		15
Mahogany	•			45
Mahogany		•		35*
White		•		17
White		•		37*
Blue	•			43
Buckskin	•			48
Buckskin		•		18
Buckskin	•			08*

*Bucket seats

CUTLASS SUPREME/BROUGHAM TRIM

COLOR	CLOTH	VINYL	LEATHER	CODE
Black		•		10#
Black		•		70#
Black		•		30*
Black	•			60#
White		•		17#
White		•		77#
White		•		37*
Buckskin		•		18#
Buckskin	•			68#
Buckskin		•		38*
Blue	•			43#
Blue	•			63#
Mahogany	•			45#
Mahogany	•			65#
Mahogany	•			05*
Buckskin	•			48#
Buckskin		•		78#
Buckskin		•		38*
Buckskin	•			68#

*Bucket seats
#Notch back or 60-40 seats

CUTLASS SALON TRIM

COLOR	CLOTH	VINYL	LEATHER	CODE
Blue	•			23*
Mahogany	•			25*
Buckskin	•			28*
Buckskin		•		58*
Black		•		50*
White		•		57*

*Bucket seats

CRUISER/VISTA CRUISER TRIM

COLOR	CLOTH	VINYL	LEATHER	CODE
Blue		•		13#
Blue		•		73#
Mahogany		•		15#
Mahogany		•		75#
Buckskin		•		17#
Buckskin		•		78#

#Notch back or 60-40 seats

DELTA 88 TRIM

COLOR	CLOTH	VINYL	LEATHER	CODE
Mahogany		•		15
White		•		17
Buckskin		•		18
Buckskin	•			48
Black	•			40
Blue	•			43

DELTA 88 ROYALE TRIM

COLOR	CLOTH	VINYL	LEATHER	CODE
Black	•			40
Black	•			40#
Black	•			60#
Blue	•			43
Blue	•			43#
Blue	•			63#
Mahogany	•			45
Mahogany	•			45#
Mahogany	•			65#
Buckskin		•		18#
Buckskin	•			48
Buckskin	•			48#
Buckskin	•			68#
Buckskin		•		78#
White		•		17#
White		•		77#

#Notch back or 60-40 seats

CUSTOM CRUISER TRIM

COLOR	CLOTH	VINYL	LEATHER	CODE
Blue		•		13
Blue		•		73#
Mahogany		•		15
Mahogany		•		75#
Buckskin		•		18
Buckskin		•		78#

#Notch back or 60-40 seats

NINETY-EIGHT TRIM

COLOR	CLOTH	VINYL	LEATHER	CODE
White		•		17/17#
White		•		77#
Black	•			40/40#
Black	•			60#
Black	•			80#
Black			•	L0#
Blue	•			43/43#
Blue	•			63#
Blue	•			83#
Mahogany	•			45/45#
Mahogany	•			65#
Mahogany	•			85#
Buckskin	•			48/48#
Buckskin	•			68#
Buckskin	•			88#

#Notch back or 60-40 seats

TORONADO TRIM

COLOR	CLOTH	VINYL	LEATHER	CODE
White		•		17#
White	•			77#
Black	•			40#
Black	•			60#
Buckskin		•		18#
Buckskin	•			68#
Blue	•			43#
Blue	•			63#
Mahogany	•			45#
Mahogany	•			65#

#Notch back or 60-40 seats

THE PAINT CODE furnishes the key to the paint colors used on the car. Two, two-digit codes indicate the bottom and top body colors respectively. NOTE: vinyl roof codes appear as a second set of digits.

COLOR	CODE
White	11
Silver	13
Medium Gray	16
Ebony Black	19
Light Blue	28
Dark Blue	35
Red	36
Mahogany	37
Lime	40
Forest Green	49
Cream	50
Bright Yellow	51
Buckskin	65
Saddle	67
Crimson Red	72
Red Orange	78

VINYL ROOF COLORS

COLOR	CODE
White	AA
Black	BB
Dk. Blue Metallic	DD
Red Metallic	FF
Buckskin	KK
Mahogany Metallic	MM
Silver Metallic	TT

ENGINE NUMBER

An Oldsmobile engine is stamped with two different identification codes. One is the engine production code which identifies the engine and its approximate production date. The other code is the engine serial number — it matches the VIN (vehicle identification number).

OLDSMOBILE ENGINES

ENGINE CODE	NO. CYL.	CID	HORSE-POWER	COMP. RATIO	CARB	TRANS
BS,BK	4	140	80	8.0:1	2 BC	Std.
BT,BL	4	140	80	8.0:1	2 BC	Auto
CAY,CBL	4	140	87	8.0:1	2 BC	
FH,FO	6	231	110	8.0:1	2 BC	Std.
FI,FJ	6	231	110	8.0:1	2 BC	Auto
CCD,CCJ	6	250	105	8.5:1	1 BC	Std.
CCF,CCH	6	250	105	8.5:1	1 BC	Auto
CCC	6	250	105	8.5:1	1 BC	Auto
QA,QK,QD	8	260	110	8.0:1	2 BC	Std.
QN,TA,TD	8	260	110	8.0:1	2 BC	Std.
TK,TN	8	260	110	8.0:1	2 BC	Std.
QB,QP,Q7	8	260	110	8.0:1	2 BC	Auto
Q8,QC,QT	8	260	110	8.0:1	2 BC	Auto
TE,TP,T2	8	260	110	8.0:1	2 BC	Auto
T3,T4,T5	8	260	110	8.0:1	2 BC	Auto
T7,T8	8	260	110	8.0:1	2 BC	Auto
TJ,TT	8	260	110	8.0:1	2 BC	Auto
PA,PB	8	350	140	8.0:1	2 BC	Auto
PE,Q2,Q4	8	350	155	8.0:1	4 BC	Auto
Q6,PF,Q3	8	350	155	8.0:1	4 BC	Auto
Q5,PM,TL	8	350	155	8.0:1	4 BC	Auto
TY,PN,TO	8	350	155	8.0:1	4 BC	Auto
TW,TX,TG	8	350	155	8.0:1	4 BC	Auto
	8	350	170	8.5:1	4 BC	
UB,UE,U5	8	455	190	8.5:1	4 BC	Auto
U6,U7,U8	8	455	190	8.5:1	4 BC	Auto
UC,UD,U3	8	455	190	8.5:1	4 BC	Auto
U4,VB,VE	8	455	190	8.5:1	4 BC	Auto
V5,VD	8	455	190	8.5:1	4 BC	Auto
V3,V4	8	455	190	8.5:1	4 BC	Auto
	8	455	215	8.5:1	4 BC	

1977 OLDSMOBILE CUTLASS S

1977 OLDSMOBILE CUTLASS

1977 OLDSMOBILE CUSTOM
CRUISER STATION WAGON

1977 OLDSMOBILE OMEGA

1977 OLDSMOBILE DELTA 88

1977 OLDSMOBILE STARFIRE

1977 OLDSMOBILE 98

1977 OLDSMOBILE TORONADO

VEHICLE IDENTIFICATION NUMBER

OLDSMOBILE 3G37R7M103133

Located on the top of the dash on the driver's side and visible through the windshield from outside the car.

FIRST DIGIT: Identifies GM Division (3 is Oldsmobile)

SECOND DIGIT: Identifies the series

SERIES	CODE
Omega	B
Starfire SX	E
Omega Brougham	E
Cutlass S	G
Cutlass Supreme	H
Cutlass Supreme	J
Cutlass Salon	K
Delta 88	L
Cutlass Supreme Brougham	M
Delta 88 Royale	N
Custom Cruiser	Q
Omega F85	S
Starfire	T
Ninety-Eight Luxury	V
Ninety-Eight Regency	X
Toronado XSR	W
Toronado Brougham	Z

THIRD AND FOURTH DIGITS: Identify the body style

BODY STYLE	CODE
Sport Coupe	07
2-Door Hatchback	17
2-Door Coupe	27
Cruiser 2-Seat	35
Hardtop Coupe	37
CKD Chassis	51
2-Door Hardtop Coupe	57
Sedan	69

FIFTH DIGIT: Identifies the engine

ENGINE	CODE
4-140 2 BC	B
6-231 1 BC	C
8-260 2 BC	F
V8-305 2 BC	U
V8-350 2 BC	
V8-350 4 BC	L
V8-350 4 BC	R
V8-403 4 BC	K

SIXTH DIGIT: Identifies the year 1977

SEVENTH DIGIT: Identifies the assembly plant

ASSEMBLY PLANT	CODE
South Gate, CA	C
Doraville, GA	D
Linden, NJ	E
Framingham, MA	G
Van Nuys, CA	L
Lansing, MI	M
Arlington, TX	R
Willow Run, MI	W
Fairfax, KS	X
St. Therese, Que., CAN	2

BODY NUMBER PLATE

The body number plate is located on the firewall, just below the rear edge of the hood. This plate identifies the model year, car division, series, body style, body assembly plant, body numbers, trim combination, paint code and build date code.

```
        BODY BY FISHER
ST 77  3CV37  LAN 123456 BDY
TR 19C                11 11 PNT
000
```

GENERAL MOTORS CORPORATION CERTIFIES TO THE DEALER THAT THIS VEHICLE CONFORMS TO ALL U.S., FEDERAL MOTOR VEHICLE SAFETY STANDARDS APPLICABLE AT TIME OF MANUFACTURE.

Example:

77	Model Year (1977)
3	Car Division (Oldsmobile)
CV	Series (Ninety-Eight Luxury)
37	Style (2-Door)
LAN	Body Assembly Plant (Lansing, MI)
123456	Production Sequence
19C	Black Cloth & Vinyl Trim
11	White Lower Body Color
11	White Upper Body Color
000	Time Built Date

CUTLASS	CODE
4-Door	AG29
S 2-Door	AG37
*442 option available	

CUTLASS SUPREME	CODE
4-Door	AJ29
Vista Cruiser	AH35
2-Door	AJ57
Salon 2-Door	AK57
Brougham 4-Door	AM29
Brougham 2-Door	AM57

DELTA 88	CODE
2-Door Hardtop	BL37
4-Door Town Sedan	BL69

DELTA 88 ROYALE	CODE
2-Door Hardtop	BN37
4-Door Town Sedan	BN69

CRUISER	CODE
Custom	BQ35

NINETY-EIGHT LUXURY	CODE
2-Door	CV37
4-Door	CV69

NINETY-EIGHT REGENCY	CODE
2-Door	CX37
4-Door	CX69

TORONADO	CODE
XS or XSR	EW57
Brougham	EZ57

STARFIRE				CODE
Sport Coupe XS				HD07
Sport Coupe				HT07

*GT option available

OMEGA				CODE
Hatchback				XB17
2-Door Coupe				XB27
4-Door Sedan				XB69

*SX option available

OMEGA BROUGHAM				CODE
Hatchback				XE17
2-Door Coupe				XE27
4-Door Sedan				XE69
F85 2-Door Coupe				XS27

THE TRIM CODE furnishes the key to the interior color and material scheme.

CUTLASS TRIM

COLOR	CLOTH	VINYL	LEATHER	CODE
White		•		11N
Black	•	•		19C
Blue	•	•		24C
Buckskin				64N
Firethorn	•	•		71C

CUTLASS S TRIM

COLOR	CLOTH	VINYL	LEATHER	CODE
White		•		11V*
Black	•	•		19D
Black	•	•		19D*
Blue	•	•		24D
Buckskin		•		64V/64V*
Firethorn		•		71V/71V*

*Bucket seats

CUTLASS SUPREME 4-DOOR TRIM

COLOR	CLOTH	VINYL	LEATHER	CODE
Black		•		19W#
Blue	•	•		24E#
Buckskin	•	•		64E#
Buckskin		•		64W#
Firethorn	•	•		71E#

#Notch back or 60-40 seats

CUTLASS SUPREME 2-DOOR TRIM

COLOR	CLOTH	VINYL	LEATHER	CODE
White		•		11W*#
White		•		11Y*
Black		•		19W*#
Black		•		19Y*
Blue	•	•		24E#24G*
Green		•		44W#
Buckskin	•	•		64E#/64G*
Buckskin		•		64W*
Buckskin		•		64Y*
Firethorn	•	•		71E#*
Firethorn	•	•		71G*

*Bucket seats
#Notch back or 60-40 seats

CUTLASS SUPREME VISTA CRUISER TRIM

COLOR	CLOTH	VINYL	LEATHER	CODE
Blue		•		24W#
Buckskin		•		64W#
Firethorn		•		71W#

#Notch back or 60-40 seats

CUTLASS BROUGHAM TRIM

COLOR	CLOTH	VINYL	LEATHER	CODE
Black	•	•		19H#
Blue	•	•		24H#
Green	•	•		44H#
Buckskin	•	•		64H#
Firethorn	•	•		71H#

#Notch back or 60-40 seats

DELTA 88 TRIM

COLOR	CLOTH	VINYL	LEATHER	CODE
White		•		11R
Black	•	•		19B
Blue	•	•		24B
Buckskin	•	•		64B
Firethorn	•	•		71B

DELTA 88 ROYALE TRIM

COLOR	CLOTH	VINYL	LEATHER	CODE
White		•		11N#
Black	•	•		19C#
Blue	•	•		24C#
Green	•	•		44C#
Buckskin	•	•		64C#
Buckskin		•		64N#
Firethorn	•	•		71C#

#Notch back or 60-40 seats

CUSTOM CRUISER TRIM

COLOR	CLOTH	VINYL	LEATHER	CODE
Blue		•		24V/24V#
Buckskin	•	•		64D/64D#
Buckskin		•		64V/64V#
Firethorn		•		71V/71V#

#Notch back or 60-40 seats

NINETY-EIGHT LUXURY TRIM

COLOR	CLOTH	VINYL	LEATHER	CODE
White		•		11R/11R#
Black	•	•		19B/19B#
Blue	•	•		24B/24B#
Buckskin	•	•		64B/64B#
Firethorn	•	•		71B/71B#

#Notch back or 60-40 seats

NINETY-EIGHT LUXURY REGENCY TRIM

COLOR	CLOTH	VINYL	LEATHER	CODE
White		•		11N#
Black	•	•		19C#
Blue	•	•		24C#
Green	•	•		44C#
Buckskin	•	•		64C#
Buckskin			•	642#
Firethorn	•	•		71C#

#Notch back or 60-40 seats

TORONADO TRIM

COLOR	CLOTH	VINYL	LEATHER	CODE
White		•		11N#
Black	•	•		19C#
Blue	•	•		24C#
Buckskin	•	•		64C#
Firethorn	•	•		71C#

#Notch back or 60-40 seats

STARFIRE TRIM

COLOR	CLOTH	VINYL	LEATHER	CODE
White		•		11N*
Black				19V*/19N*
Blue	•	•		24B*
Blue		•		02N*
Buckskin		•		64V*/64N*
Buckskin		•		64N*
Buckskin		•		61N*
Firethorn		•		71V*/07N*
Firethorn	•			71B*
Mandarin		•		08N*
Dk. Aqua		•		03N*

*Bucket seats

OMEGA 2-DOOR COUPE TRIM

COLOR	CLOTH	VINYL	LEATHER	CODE
White		•		11R*#
Black	•	•		19E/19B
Blue	•	•		24B
Buckskin		•		64W/64R*
Firethorn		•		71R

*Bucket seats
#Notch back or 60-40 seats

OMEGA 4-DOOR/HATCHBACK TRIM

COLOR	CLOTH	VINYL	LEATHER	CODE
White		•		11R/11R*
Black	•	•		19B
Blue	•	•		24B
Buckskin		•		64R/64R*
Firethorn		•		71R

*Bucket seats

OMEGA BROUGHAM TRIM

COLOR	CLOTH	VINYL	LEATHER	CODE
White		•		11V/11V*
Blue	•	•		24D/24D*
Buckskin		•		64V/64V*
Firethorn	•	•		71D/71D*

*Bucket seats

THE PAINT CODE furnishes the key to the paint colors used on the car. Two, two-digit codes indicate the bottom and top body colors respectively. NOTE: vinyl roof codes appear as a second set of digits.

COLOR	CODE
White	11
Silver	13
Medium Gray	16
Black	19
Light Blue	22
Dark Blue	29
Firethorn Red	36
Dark Aqua	38
Medium Green	44
Dark Green	48
Yellow	50
Bright Yellow	51
Light Buckskin	61
Buckskin	63
Brown	69
Red	72
Bright Red	75
Mandarin Orange	78
Medium Blue	85

VINYL ROOF COLORS

COLOR	CODE
White	11T
Silver	13T
Black	19T
Light Blue	22T
Firethorn	36T
Medium Green	44T
Light Buckskin	61T

ENGINE NUMBER

An Oldsmobile engine is stamped with two different identification codes. One is the engine production code which identifies the engine and its approximate production date. The other code is the engine serial number — it matches the VIN (vehicle identification number).

OLDSMOBILE ENGINES

ENGINE CODE	NO. CYL.	CID	HORSE-POWER	COMP. RATIO	CARB	TRANS
CAY,CBS	4	140	84	8.0:1	2 BC	Std.
CAZ,CBK	4	140	84	8.0:1	2 BC	Std.
CBT,CBL	4	140	84	8.0:1	2 BC	Auto
SG,SU,SR	6	231	105	8.0:1	2 BC	Std.
SI,SK,SL	6	231	105	8.0:1	2 BC	Auto
SM,SN,SY	6	231	105	8.0:1	2 BC	Auto
SA,SB,SD	6	231	105	8.0:1	2 BC	
SE,SF,SQ	6	231	105	8.0:1	2 BC	
SW,FH,FO	6	231	105	8.0:1	2 BC	
FI,FJ	6	231	105	8.0:1	2 BC	
QS,QT	8	260	110	8.0:1	2 BC	Std.
QC,QD,QE	8	260	110	8.0:1	2 BC	Auto
QJ,QU,QV	8	260	110	8.0:1	2 BC	Auto
CPA,CRS	8	305	145	8.5:1	2 BC	Std.
CPY,CPX	8	305	145	8.5:1	2 BC	Auto
CRT,CRL	8	305	145	8.5:1	2 BC	
CRM	8	305	145	8.5:1	2 BC	
CHY,CVB	8	350	140	8.5:1	2 BC	
CKM,CLY	8	350	140	8.5:1	2 BC	
QK,QL,QN	8	350	170	8.0:1	4 BC	Auto
QO,QP,QQ	8	350	170	8.0:1	4 BC	Auto
CKR,TK	8	350	170	8.0:1	4 BC	Auto
TC,TB	8	350	170	8.0:1	4 BC	
TL,TN,TO	8	350	170	8.0:1	4 BC	Auto
TP,TQ,TV	8	350	170	8.0:1	4 BC	Auto
TX,TY,TU	8	350	170	8.0:1	4 BC	Auto
Q2,Q3,Q6	8	350	170	8.0:1	4 BC	Auto
Q7,Q8,Q9	8	350	170	8.0:1	4 BC	Auto
UA,UB,UC	8	403	185	8.0:1	4 BC	Auto
UD,UE	8	403	185	8.0:1	4 BC	Auto
VA,VB,VE	8	403	185	8.0:1	4 BC	Auto
VJ,VK,VL	8	403	185	8.0:1	4 BC	Auto
U2,U3,U6	8	403	185	8.0:1	4 BC	
	8	403	200	8.0:1	4 BC	

1978 OLDSMOBILE CUTLASS

1978 OLDSMOBILE DELTA 88

1978 OLDSMOBILE CUTLASS BROUGHAM

1978 OLDSMOBILE OMEGA

1978 OLDSMOBILE CUTLASS WAGON

1978 OLDSMOBILE 98 REGENCY

1978 OLDSMOBILE CUSTOM CRUISER WAGON

1978 OLDSMOBILE STARFIRE

VEHICLE IDENTIFICATION NUMBER

OLDSMOBILE 3V37K8M100001

Located on the top of the dash on the driver's side and visible through the windshield from outside the car.

FIRST DIGIT: Identifies GM Division (3 is Oldsmobile)

SECOND DIGIT: Identifies the series

SERIES	CODE
Omega	B
Starfire SX	D
Omega Brougham	E
Cutlass Salon	G
Cutlass Cruiser	H
Cutlass Salon Brougham	J
Cutlass Calais	K
Delta 88	L
Cutlass Supreme Brougham	M
Delta 88 Royale	N
Custom Cruiser	Q
Cutlass Supreme	R
Starfire	T
Ninety-Eight Luxury	V
Ninety-Eight Regency	X
Toronado Brougham	Z

THIRD AND FOURTH DIGITS: Identify the body style

BODY STYLE	CODE
Sport Coupe	07
Sedan	09
Hatchback Coupe	17
Coupe	27
2-Seat Vista Cruiser	35
Hardtop Coupe	37
Hardtop Coupe Brougham	57
4-Door Sedan	69

FIFTH DIGIT: Identifies the engine

ENGINE	CODE
V4-151 2 BC	V
V4-151 2 BC	1
V6-231 1 BC	A
V8-260 2 BC	F
V8-305 2 BC	U
V8-305 4 BC	H
V8-350 4 BC	L
V8-350 4 BC	R
V8-403 4 BC	K
V8 Diesel	N

SIXTH DIGIT: Identifies the year 1978

SEVENTH DIGIT: Identifies the assembly plant

ASSEMBLY PLANT	CODE
South Gate, CA	C
Doraville, GA	D
Linden, NJ	E
Framingham, MA	G
Lansing, MI	M
Arlington, TX	R
Lordstown, OH	U
Willow Run, MI	W
Fairfax, KS	X
St. Therese, Que., CAN	2

LAST SIX DIGITS: Represent the basic production numbers

BODY NUMBER PLATE

The body number plate is located on the firewall, just below the rear edge of the hood. This plate identifies the model year, car division, series, body style, body assembly plant, body numbers, trim combination, paint code and build date code.

```
          BODY BY FISHER
ST 78   3CV37   LAN 123456 BDY
TR 19B                  11 11 PNT
000  A51
```

GENERAL MOTORS CORPORATION CERTIFIES TO THE DEALER THAT THIS VEHICLE CONFORMS TO ALL U.S., FEDERAL MOTOR VEHICLE SAFETY STANDARDS APPLICABLE AT TIME OF MANUFACTURE.

Example:

78	Model Year (1978)
3	Car Division (Oldsmobile)
CV	Series (Ninety-Eight Luxury)
37	Style (2-Door)
LAN	Body Assembly Plant (Lansing, MI)
123456	Production Sequence
19B	Black Cloth & Vinyl Trim
11	White Lower Body Color
11	White Upper Body Color
000	Time Built Date
A51	Modular Seat Code

CUTLASS	CODE
4-Door Sedan	AG09
2-Door Coupe	AG87
Vista Cruiser Wagon	AH35

CUTLASS SALON BROUGHAM	CODE
4-Door	AJ09
2-Door	AJ87
Calais 2-Door	AK47

*442 option available

CUTLASS SUPREME	CODE
Brougham 2-Door	AM47
2-Door	AR47

DELTA 88	CODE
2-Door	BL37
4-Door	BL69

DELTA 88 ROYALE	CODE
2-Door	BN37
4-Door	BN69
Custom Cruiser Wagon	BO35

NINETY-EIGHT LUXURY	CODE
2-Door	CV37
4-Door	CV69

NINETY-EIGHT REGENCY	CODE
2-Door	CX37
4-Door	CX69

TORONADO

	CODE
XSR	EW57
Brougham	EZ57

STARFIRE

	CODE
SX 2-Door	HD07
2-Door	HT07

*GT option available
*Firenza option available

OMEGA

	CODE
2-Door Hatchback	XB17
2-Door Coupe	XB27
4-Door Sedan	XB69

OMEGA DELUXE

	CODE
2-Door Coupe	XE27
4-Door Sedan	XE69

*LS option available
*SX option available

THE TRIM CODE furnishes the key to the interior color and material scheme.

CUTLASS SALON TRIM

COLOR	CLOTH	VINYL	LEATHER	CODE
White		•		11N/11N*
Black		•		19N/19N*
Lt. Blue	•	•		24C
Dk. Camel Tan		•		62N/62N*
Dk. Carmine	•	•		74C/74C*

*Bucket seats

CUTLASS SALON BROUGHAM TRIM

COLOR	CLOTH	VINYL	LEATHER	CODE
White		•		11V#/11V*
Black		•		19V#/19V*
Lt. Blue	•	•		24D#
Dk. Sage Green		•		44V#
Camel Tan	•	•		62D#
Dk. Cml. Tan		•		62V#/62V*
Dk. Carmine	•	•		74D#/74D*

*Bucket seats
#Notch back or 60-40 seats

CUTLASS SUPREME TRIM

COLOR	CLOTH	VINYL	LEATHER	CODE
White		•		11V#/11V*
White		•		11W*
Black		•		19V#/19V*
Black		•		19W*
Black	•	•		19G#
Lt. Blue	•	•		24D#/24G*
Sage Grn.	•	•		44G*
Camel Tan	•	•		62D#/62G#
Dk. Cml. Tan		•		62V#/62V*
Dk. Cml. Tan		•		62W*
Dk. Carmine	•	•		74D#/74D*
Dk. Carmine		•		62G#

*Bucket seats
#Notch back or 60-40 seats

CUTLASS VISTA CRUISER WAGON TRIM

COLOR	CLOTH	VINYL	LEATHER	CODE
White		•		11V#/11V*
Lt. Blue		•		24V#
Dk. Camel Tan		•		62V#/62V*
Dk. Carmine		•		74V#

*Bucket seats
#Notch back or 60-40 seats

DELTA 88 TRIM

COLOR	CLOTH	VINYL	LEATHER	CODE
White		•		11R/11R*
Lt. Blue	•			24B/24B*
Camel Tan	•			62B/62B*
Dk. Cml. Tan		•		62R/62R*
Dk. Carmine		•		74R/74R*

*Bucket seats

DELTA 88 ROYALE TRIM

COLOR	CLOTH	VINYL	LEATHER	CODE
White		•		11N#
Black	•			19C#
Black			•	192*
Lt. Blue	•			24C#
Sage Grn.	•			44C#
Camel Tan	•			62C#
Dk. Cml. Tan		•		62N#
Dk. Cml. Tan			•	622#
Dk. Carmine	•	•		74C#

*Bucket seats
#Notch back or 60-40 seats

DELTA 88 CUSTOM CRUISER WAGON TRIM

COLOR	CLOTH	VINYL	LEATHER	CODE
White		•		11V/11V#
Lt. Blue		•		24V/24V#
Camel Tan	•	•		62D/62D#
Dk. Cml. Tan		•		62V/62V#
Dk. Carmine		•		74V/74V#

#Notch back or 60-40 seats

NINETY-EIGHT LUXURY TRIM

COLOR	CLOTH	VINYL	LEATHER	CODE
White		•		11R/11R#
Black	•			19B/19B#
Lt. Blue	•			24B/24B#
Lt. Blue		•		24R/24R#
Camel Tan	•	•		62B/62B#
Dk. Cml. Tan	•			62R/62R#
Dk. Carmine	•		•	74B/74B#

#Notch back or 60-40 seats

NINETY-EIGHT REGENCY TRIM

COLOR	CLOTH	VINYL	LEATHER	CODE
White		•		11N#/11R#
Black	•			19C#
Black			•	192#
Lt. Blue	•	•		24C#
Sage Grn.	•	•		44C#
Camel Tan	•	•		62C#
Dk. Cml Tan			•	622#/623#
Dk. Carmine	•			74C#

#Notch back or 60-40 seats

TORONADO TRIM

COLOR	CLOTH	VINYL	LEATHER	CODE
White		•		11N#
Black	•	•		19C#
Black			•	192#
Lt. Blue	•	•		24C#
Camel Tan	•	•		62C#
Dk. Cml. Tan			•	622#
Dk. Carmine	•	•		74C#
Dk. Carmine			•	742#

#Notch back or 60-40 seats

STARFIRE TRIM

COLOR	CLOTH	VINYL	LEATHER	CODE
White		•		11N*
Black		•		19N*
Dk. Cml. Tan		•		62N*

*Bucket seats

OMEGA TRIM

COLOR	CLOTH	VINYL	LEATHER	CODE
White		•		11R/11R*
Black	•	•		19D/19D*
Lt. Blue	•	•		24D/24D*
Camel Tan	•	•		62D/62D*
Dk. Cml. Tan		•		62R/62R*
Dk. Carmine	•	•		74D/74D*
Dk. Carmine		•		74R/74R*

*Bucket seats

THE PAINT CODE furnishes the key to the paint colors used on the car. Two, two-digit codes indicate the bottom and top body colors respectively. NOTE: vinyl roof codes appear as a second set of digits.

COLOR	CODE
White	11
Silver Poly	15
Gray Poly	16
Black	19
Pastel Blue	21
Light Blue Poly	22
Bright Blue Poly	24
Dark Blue Poly	29
Light Green Poly	44
Medium Green Poly	45
Dark Green Poly	48
Bright Yellow	51
Medium Gold Poly	56
Light Camel Beige	61
Medium Camel Poly	63
Russet Poly	67
Dark Camel Poly	69
Bright Red	75
Carmine Red Poly	77
Dark Carmine Poly	79
Med. Blue Irid	85

VINYL ROOF COLORS

COLOR	CODE
White	AA
Black	BB
Light Camel Beige	CC
Light Blue Metallic	DD
Light Green Metallic	GG
Dark Carmine Red Metallic	MM
Silver Metallic	TT

ENGINE NUMBERS

An Oldsmobile engine is stamped with two different identification codes. One is the engine production code which identifies the engine and its approximate production date. The other code is the engine serial number — it matches the VIN (vehicle identification number).

OLDSMOBILE ENGINES

ENGINE CODE	NO. CYL.	CID	HORSE-POWER	COMP. RATIO	CARB	TRANS
XL,XN	4	151	85	8.3:1	2 BC	Auto
ZK,ZJ	4	151	85	8.3:1	2 BC	Auto
WB,ZA,ZB	4	151	85	8.3:1	2 BC	
WD,WH	4	151	85	8.3:1	2 BC	Man.
EA,EB,EM	6	231	105	8.0:1	2 BC	Std.
EC,EK,EL	6	231	105	8.0:1	2 BC	Auto
EE,OH,OK	6	231	105	8.0:1	2 BC	Auto
EG	6	231	105	8.0:1	2 BC	Auto
OA,OD,OF	6	231	105	8.0:1	2 BC	Man
ED,OB,OE	6	231	105	8.0:1	2 BC	Auto
OC,ZJ	6	231	105	8.0:1	2 BC	Auto
OH,ZK	6	231	105	8.0:1	2 BC	
QD,QE	8	260	110	7.5:1	2 BC	Std.
QJ,QL,QK	8	260	110	7.5:1	2 BC	Auto
QN,QT,QU	8	260	110	7.5:1	2 BC	Auto
TK,TJ	8	260	110	7.5:1	2 BC	Auto
CTA	8	305	145	8.5:1	2 BC	Man
CTB,CTF	8	305	145	8.5:1	2 BC	Auto
CTD	8	305	145	8.5:1	2 BC	Auto
CTH,CRW	8	305	145	8.5:1	2 BC	Std.
CPF,CTJ	8	305	145	8.5:1	2 BC	Auto
CRY,CRZ	8	305	145	8.5:1	2 BC	Auto
CPZ	8	305	145	8.5:1	2 BC	Auto
TO,TP,TQ	8	350	160	8.5:1	4 BC	Auto
TS,CHJ	8	350	160	8.5:1	4 BC	Auto
Q2,Q3,QO	8	350	160	8.5:1	4 BC	Auto
CHL,CMC	8	350	160	8.5:1	4 BC	Auto
QP,QQ,QS	8	350	160	8.5:1	4 BC	Auto
MA,MB	8	350	160	8.5:1	4 BC	Auto
QB,QC	8	350	120	22.5:1	Diesel	Auto
VA,VB,VC	8	403	185	8.0:1	4 BC	Auto
U2,U3,U4	8	403	185	8.0:1	4 BC	Auto
UA,UB,UC	8	403	185	8.0:1	4 BC	Auto
UD,UE	8	403	185	8.0:1	4 BC	Auto
	8	403	190	8.0:1	4 BC	

1979 OLDSMOBILE DELTA 88

1979 OLDSMOBILE TORONADO

1979 OLDSMOBILE OMEGA

1979 OLDSMOBILE CUTLASS

1979 OLDSMOBILE 98 REGENCY

1979 OLDSMOBILE CUTLASS SALON

1979 OLDSMOBILE STARFIRE

1979 OLDSMOBILE CUTLASS WAGON

VEHICLE IDENTIFICATION NUMBER

OLDSMOBILE
3J87R9M103133

Located on the top of the dash on the driver's side and visible through the windshield from outside the car.

FIRST DIGIT: Identifies GM Division (3 is Oldsmobile)

SECOND DIGIT: Identifies the series

SERIES	CODE
Omega	B
Starfire SX	D
Omega Brougham	E
Cutlass Salon or Cruiser	G
Cutlass Cruiser Brougham	H
Cutlass Salon Brougham	J
Cutlass Calais	K
Delta 88	L
Cutlass Supreme Brougham	M
Delta 88 Royale	N
Custom Cruiser	Q
Cutlass Supreme	R
Starfire	T
Ninety-Eight Luxury	V
Ninety-Eight Regency	X
Toronado Brougham	Z

THIRD AND FOURTH DIGITS: Identify the body style

BODY STYLE	CODE
Starfire 2-Door	07
4-Door Sedan	09
2-Door Hatchback	17
2-Door Coupe	27
4-Door Station Wagon	35
Hardtop Coupe	37
2-Door Coupe Cutlass	47
2-Door Coupe Toronado	57
4-Door Sedan	69
2-Door Coupe	87

FIFTH DIGIT: Identifies the engine

ENGINE	CODE
V4-151	1
V6-231	2
V4-151	9
V6-231	A
V8-260	F
V8-305	G
V8-305 4 BC	H
V8-403	K
V8-350 4 BC	L
V8-350 Diesel	N
V8-260 Diesel	P
V8-350 4 BC	R
V4-151	V
V8-301	Y

SIXTH DIGIT: Identifies the year 1979

SEVENTH DIGIT: Identifies the assembly plant

ASSEMBLY PLANT	CODE
Doraville, GA	D
Linden, NJ	E
Framingham, MA	G
Lansing, MI	M
Arlington, TX	R
Willow Run, MI	W
Fairfax, KS	X
St. Therese, Que., CAN	2
Lordstown, OH	7

LAST SIX DIGITS: Represent the basic production numbers

BODY NUMBER PLATE

The body number plate is located on the firewall, just below the rear edge of the hood. This plate identifies the model year, car division, series, body style, body assembly plant, body numbers, trim combination, paint code and build date code.

```
         BODY BY FISHER
ST 79   3CV37  LAN 123456 BDY
TR 74B       15L 16T  19A L PNT
000  A51
```

GENERAL MOTORS CORPORATION CERTIFIES TO THE DEALER THAT THIS VEHICLE CONFORMS TO ALL U.S., FEDERAL MOTOR VEHICLE SAFETY STANDARDS APPLICABLE AT TIME OF MANUFACTURE.

Example:

79	Model Year (1979)
3	Car Division (Oldsmobile)
CV	Series (Ninety-Eight Luxury)
37	Style (2-Door)
LAN	Body Assembly Plant (Lansing, MI)
123456	Production Sequence
74B	Carmine Cloth & Vinyl Trim
15L	Silver Lower Body Color
16T	Gray Upper Body Color
19A	Black Accent Color
L	Paint Type
000	Time Built Date
A51	Modular Seat Code

CUTLASS SALON	CODE
4-Door Sedan	AG09
Vista Cruiser Wagon	AG35
2-Door Coupe	AG87
Brougham Cruiser Wagon	AH35
Brougham 4-Door	AJ09
Brougham 2-Door	AJ87

*442 Option available

CUTLASS CALAIS	CODE
2-Door	AK47

*Hurst/Olds option available

CUTLASS SUPREME

	CODE
Brougham 2-Door	AM47
2-Door	AR47

DELTA 88

	CODE
2-Door	BL37
4-Door	BL69

DELTA 88 ROYALE

	CODE
2-Door	BN37
4-Door	BN69
Custom Cruiser Wagon	BQ35

NINETY-EIGHT LUXURY

	CODE
2-Door	CV37
4-Door	CV69

NINETY-EIGHT REGENCY

	CODE
2-Door	CX37
4-Door	CX69

TORONADO

	CODE
Brougham	CZ57

STARFIRE

	CODE
SX 2-Door	HD07
2-Door	HT07

*GT option available
*Firenza option available

OMEGA

	CODE
2-Door Hatchback	XB17
2-Door Coupe	XB27
4-Door Sedan	XB69
Deluxe 2-Door Coupe	XE27
Deluxe 4-Door Sedan	XE69

*SX option available
*LS option available

THE TRIM CODE furnishes the key to the interior color and material scheme.

CUTLASS SALON TRIM

COLOR	CLOTH	VINYL	LEATHER	CODE
Oyster		•		12N/12N*
Black		•		19N/19N*
Lt. Blue	•	•		24C
Camel Tan		•		62N/62N*
Carmine	•	•		74C/74C*

*Bucket seats

CUTLASS VISTA CRUISER WAGON TRIM

COLOR	CLOTH	VINYL	LEATHER	CODE
Blue		•		24V#
W. Green		•		44V#*
Cml. Tan		•		62N
Cml. Tan		•		62V#*
Cml. Tan	•	•		62H#*/62D#*
Carmine	•	•		74D#*

*Bucket seats
#Notch back or 60-40 seats

CUTLASS SALON BROUGHAM TRIM

COLOR	CLOTH	VINYL	LEATHER	CODE
Oyster		•		12V#*
Black		•		19V#*
Blue	•	•		24D#*
W. Green		•		44V#*
Cml. Tan	•	•		62H#
Cml. Tan	•	•		62D#*
Cml. Tan		•		62V#*
Carmine	•	•		74D#*

*Bucket seats
#Notch back or 60-40 seats

CUTLASS SUPREME TRIM

COLOR	CLOTH	VINYL	LEATHER	CODE
Oyster		•		12V#*/12W*
Black		•		19V#*/19W*
Black	•	•		19B#*/19G#
Blue	•	•		24D*/24E*
Blue	•	•		24B#*/24G#
W. Green	•			44G#
W. Green		•		44V#*
Cml. Tan	•	•		62D#*/62E*
Cml. Tan		•		62V#*/62W*
Cml. Tan	•	•		62G#/62J#
Cml. Tan			•	622#
Carmine	•	•		74D#*/74E*
Carmine	•	•		74B#*/74G#*
Carmine			•	742#

*Bucket seats
#Notch back or 60-40 seats

DELTA 88 TRIM

COLOR	CLOTH	VINYL	LEATHER	CODE
Oyster		•		12R/12R*
Blue	•	•		24B/24B*
Cml. Tan	•	•		62B/62B*
Cml. Tan		•		62R/62R*
Carmine		•		74R/74R*

*Bucket seats

DELTA 88 ROYALE TRIM

COLOR	CLOTH	VINYL	LEATHER	CODE
Black	•	•		19C#
Blue	•	•		24C#/24E#
W. Green	•	•		44C#/44E#
Cml. Tan	•	•		62C#/62E#
Cml. Tan			•	622#
Carmine	•	•		74C#/74E#

#Notch back or 60-40 seats

DELTA 88 CUSTOM CRUISER WAGON TRIM

COLOR	CLOTH	VINYL	LEATHER	CODE
Blue		•		24V/24V#
W. Green		•		44V/44V#
Cml. Tan	•	•		62D/62D#
Cml. Tan		•		62V/62V#
Carmine		•		74V/74V#

#Notch back or 60-40 seats

NINETY-EIGHT LUXURY TRIM

COLOR	CLOTH	VINYL	LEATHER	CODE
Blue	•			24B/24B#
Blue		•		24R/24R#
W. Green	•			44B/44B#
Cml. Tan	•			62B/62B#
Cml. Tan		•		62R/62R#
Carmine	•			74B/74B#

#Notch back or 60-40 seats

NINETY-EIGHT REGENCY TRIM

COLOR	CLOTH	VINYL	LEATHER	CODE
Black	•	•		19C#
Black			•	192#
Blue	•	•		24C#
W. Green	•	•		44C#
Cml. Tan	•	•		62C#
Cml. Tan			•	622#
Carmine	•	•		74C#
Carmine			•	742#

#Notch back or 60-40 seats

TORONADO BROUGHAM TRIM

COLOR	CLOTH	VINYL	LEATHER	CODE
Black	•	•		19B#
Black			•	192#
Blue	•	•		24B#
W. Green	•	•		44B#
Cml. Tan	•	•		62B#
Cml. Tan			•	622#
Carmine	•	•		74B#
Carmine			•	742#

#Notch back or 60-40 seats

STARFIRE TRIM

COLOR	CLOTH	VINYL	LEATHER	CODE
Oyster		•		12N*
Black		•		19N*
Blue	•	•		24B*
Cml. Tan		•		62N*
Carmine	•	•		74B*

*Bucket seats

OMEGA TRIM

COLOR	CLOTH	VINYL	LEATHER	CODE
Black	•	•		19B
Blue	•	•		24B
Cml. Tan		•		62R/62R*
Carmine		•		74R
White		•		11R/11R*

*Bucket seats

OMEGA DELUXE TRIM

COLOR	CLOTH	VINYL	LEATHER	CODE
Black	•	•		19D/19D*
Blue	•	•		24D/24D*
Cml. Tan	•	•		62D/62D*
Carmine	•	•		74D/74D*

*Bucket seats

THE PAINT CODE furnishes the key to the paint colors used on the car. Two, two-digit codes indicate the bottom and top body colors respectively. NOTE: vinyl roof codes appear as a second set of digits.

COLOR	CODE
White	11
Silver Irid	15
Gray Irid	16
Pastel Blue	21
Light Blue Irid	22
Bright Blue Irid	24
Dark Blue Irid	29
Caramel Firemist	33
Pastel Green	40
Medium Green Irid	44
Bright Yellow	51
Light Yellow	54
Medium Beige	61
Camel Irid	63
Dark Brown Irid	69
Red	75
Carmine Irid	77
Dark Carmine Irid	79
Medium Blue Irid	85
Charcoal Firemist	98
Saffron Firemist	99
Black	19
Gold Poly	55

VINYL ROOF COLORS

White	A
Black	B
Medium Beige	C
Light Blue Metallic	D
Pastel Green	G
Dark Carmine Metallic	M
Silver Metallic	T

ENGINE NUMBER

An Oldsmobile engine is stamped with two different identification codes. One is the engine production code which identifies the engine and its approximate production date. The other code is the engine serial number — it matches the VIN (vehicle identification number).

OLDSMOBILE ENGINES

ENGINE CODE	NO. CYL.	CID	HORSE-POWER	COMP. RATIO	CARB	TRANS
XJ,XK	4	151	90	8.3:1	2 BC	Auto
ZP,ZR	4	151	90	8.3:1	2 BC	Auto
WJ,WM	4	151	90	8.3:1	2 BC	Man
AF,AH	4	151	90	8.3:1	2 BC	Man
NB,NM	6	231	115	8.0:1	2 BC	Auto
NH,NE	6	231	115	8.0:1	2 BC	Auto
NA,NC	6	231	115	8.0:1	2 BC	Man
RG,RW,RY	6	231	115	8.0:1	2 BC	Auto
RJ,NJ,NK	6	231	115	8.0:1	2 BC	Auto
NL,RB	6	231	115	8.0:1	2 BC	Auto
RC,RX	6	231	115	8.0:1	2 BC	Auto
NG,RA	6	231	115	8.0:1	2 BC	Std
VC,U5	8	260	105	7.5:1	2 BC	Auto
UE,UJ,UK	8	260	105	7.5:1	2 BC	Auto
UL,UN,UO	8	260	105	7.5:1	2 BC	Auto
UP,UQ	8	260	105	7.5:1	2 BC	Auto
UC,UD	8	260	105	7.5:1	2 BC	Std
UW,UX	8	260	105	7.5:1	2 BC	Std
XP,XR	8	301	135	8.2:1	2 BC	Auto
DTL,DND	8	305	130	8.5:1	2 BC	Auto
DTK	8	305	130	8.5:1	2 BC	Man
DNX,DNY	8	305	130	8.5:1	2 BC	Auto
DTA,DNJ	8	305	130	8.5:1	2 BC	Auto
DNT,DNW	8	305	130	8.5:1	2 BC	Auto
DTX	8	305	130	8.5:1	2 BC	Auto
DNS,DTM	8	305	130	8.5:1	2 BC	Std
VA,VK	8	350	160	8.5:1	4 BC	Auto
DRJ,DRX	8	350	160	8.5:1	4 BC	Auto
U2,U9	8	350	160	8.5:1	4 BC	Auto
DRY,SA	8	350	160	8.5:1	4 BC	Auto
SB,UA,US	8	350	160	8.5:1	4 BC	Auto
UT,UU,UV	8	350	160	8.5:1	4 BC	Auto
U3,V4,V6	8	350	125	22.5:1	Diesel	
UB,VN,VO	8	350	125	22.5:1	Diesel	
VP,VQ	8	350	125	22.5:1	Diesel	
TB,Q3,QB	8	403	175	7.8:1	4 BC	Auto

1970 PONTIAC JUDGE

1970 PONTIAC LEMANS

1970 PONTIAC GRAND PRIX

1970 PONTIAC GTO

1970 PONTIAC FIREBIRD

1970 PONTIAC FIREBIRD

1970 PONTIAC BONNEVILLE

1970 PONTIAC CATALINA

VEHICLE IDENTIFICATION NUMBER

┌─────────────────────────────┐
│ ●   **PONTIAC**   ● │
│   **233270P300039**   │
└─────────────────────────────┘

Located on the top of the dash on the driver's side and visible through the windshield from outside the car.

FIRST DIGIT: Identifies GM Division (2 is Pontiac)

SECOND AND THIRD DIGITS: Identifies the series

SERIES	CODE
Firebird	23
Firebird Esprit	24
Firebird Formula 400	26
Firebird Trans Am	28
Tempest or T-37	33
LeMans	35
LeMans Sport	37
Tempest GTO	42
Catalina	52
Executive	56
Bonneville	62
Grand Prix	76

FOURTH AND FIFTH DIGITS: Identify the body style

BODY STYLE	CODE
2-Door Coupe	27
4-Door SW, 2-Seat	35
4-Door SW, 2-Seat Sport	36
2-Door Hardtop	37
4-Door Hardtop	39
4-Door SW, 3-Seat	46
2-Door Hardtop (Grand Prix)	57
2-Door Convertible	67
4-Door Sedan	69
2-Door Hardtop	87

SIXTH DIGIT: Identifies the year 1970

SEVENTH DIGIT: Identifies the assembly plant

ASSEMBLY PLANT	CODE
Atlanta, GA	A
Baltimore, MD	B
South Gate, CA	C
Linden, NJ	E
Framingham, MA	G
Van Nuys, CA	L
Norwood, OH	N
Pontiac, MI	P
Arlington, TX	R
Kansas City, KS	X
Fremont, CA	Z
Oshawa, Ont., CAN	1
St. Therese, Que., CAN	2

LAST SIX DIGITS: Represent the basic production numbers

BODY NUMBER PLATE

The body number plate is located on the firewall, just below the rear edge of the hood. This plate identifies the model year, car division, series, body style, body assembly plant, body numbers, trim combination, paint code and build date code.

┌───┐
│   **BODY BY FISHER**   │
│ ST 70   23327   LIN 123456 BDY   │
│ TR 231   10 10 PNT   │
│ 000   │
│ ●   ● │
│ GENERAL MOTORS CORPORATION CERTI-   │
│ FIES TO THE DEALER THAT THIS VEHICLE   │
│ CONFORMS TO ALL U.S., FEDERAL MOTOR   │
│   VEHICLE SAFETY STANDARDS   │
│ APPLICABLE AT TIME OF MANUFACTURE.   │
└───┘

Example:

70	Model Year (1970)
2	Car Division (Pontiac)
33	Series (Tempest)
27	Style (2-Door Coupe)
LIN	Body Assembly Plant (Linden, NJ)
123456	Production Sequence
231	Blue Cloth Trim
10	Polar White Lower Body Color
10	Polar White Upper Body Color
000	Time Built Date

FIREBIRD	CODE
2-Door Hardtop	2387
2-Door Hardtop Esprit	2487
2-Door Hardtop Formula 400	2687
2-Door Hardtop Trans Am	2887

TEMPEST	CODE
2-Door Coupe	3327
2-Door Hardtop T-37	3337
4-Door Sedan	3369

*GT option available

LEMANS	CODE
2-Door Coupe	3527
4-Door SW, 2-Seat	3535
2-Door Hardtop	3537
4-Door Hardtop	3539
4-Door Sedan	3569

LEMANS SPORT	CODE
2-Door Coupe	3727
2-Door Hardtop	3737
4-Door Hardtop	3739
2-Door Convertible	3767
4-Door SW, 2-Seat	3736

GTO	CODE
2-Door Hardtop	4237
2-Door Convertible	4267

*Judge option available

CATALINA

	CODE
4-Door SW, 2-Seat	5236
2-Door Hardtop	5237
4-Door Hardtop	5239
4-Door SW, 3-Seat	5246
2-Door Convertible	5267
4-Door Sedan	5269

EXECUTIVE

	CODE
4-Door SW, 2-Seat	5636
2-Door Hardtop	5637
4-Door Hardtop	5639
4-Door SW, 3-Seat	5646
4-Door Sedan	5669

*Turnpike Cruise option available

BONNEVILLE

	CODE
2-Door Hardtop	6237
4-Door Hardtop	6239
4-Door SW, 3-Seat	6246
2-Door Convertible	6267
4-Door Sedan	6269

*Safari Wagon option available
*Brougham option available

GRAND PRIX

	CODE
2-Door Hardtop	7657

*SJ option available

THE TRIM CODE furnishes the key to the interior color and material scheme.

GRAND PRIX HARDTOP COUPE TRIM

COLOR	CLOTH	VINYL	LEATHER	CODE
Blue	•			270*
Blue		•		280*
Gold	•			272*
Gold	•			292#
Green	•			276*
Green		•		286*
Black	•			278*
Black		•		288*
Black	•			259#
Black		•		299#
Black			•	298*
Brown		•		283*
Saddle		•		285*
Saddle			•	295*
Sandlewood		•		287*
Sandlewood		•		297#

*Bucket seats
#Notch back or 60-40 seats

BONNEVILLE STATION WAGON TRIM

COLOR	CLOTH	VINYL	LEATHER	CODE
Brown				573
Saddle				575
Green	•			576
Black				578

BONNEVILLE CONVERTIBLE TRIM

COLOR	CLOTH	VINYL	LEATHER	CODE
Brown				563#
Saddle				565
Green				566#
Sandalwood				567#
Black				568#

#Notch back or 60-40 seats

BONNEVILLE HARDTOP COUPE TRIM

COLOR	CLOTH	VINYL	LEATHER	CODE
Blue				560#
Gold	•			582#
Gold	•			512#
Gold				562#
Brown				563#
Green	•			586#
Green	•			516#
Green				567#
Sandlewood				567#
Black	•			588#
Black	•			518#
Black				568#

#Notch back or 60-40 seats

BONNEVILLE 4-DOOR HARDTOP TRIM

COLOR	CLOTH	VINYL	LEATHER	CODE
Blue	•			590
Blue				560
Blue	•			522
Gold	•			592
Gold	•			222#
Gold				562
Gold	•			526
Brown				563
Green	•			596
Green	•			226#
Green				566
Green	•			528
Sandlewood				567
Black	•			598
Black	•			229#
Black				568
Black		•		528

BONNEVILLE 4-DOOR SEDAN TRIM

COLOR	CLOTH	VINYL	LEATHER	CODE
Gold				572
Gold	•			522
Green	•			526
Black				578

EXECUTIVE 4-DR HT/COUPE & 4-DR SEDAN TRIM

COLOR	CLOTH	VINYL	LEATHER	CODE
Blue				550
Blue	•			540#
Gold	•			542
Saddle				555
Green				556
Green	•			546
Sandalwood				557*
Black				558
Black	•			548**

*Available 4-Dr. Hardtop and coupe only
**Available 4-Dr. Hardtop only
#Available in 4-Dr. Sedan only

CATALINA 4-DR HT/COUPE & 4-DR SEDAN TRIM

COLOR	CLOTH	VINYL	LEATHER	CODE
Blue				550
Blue				540#
Blue		•		501
Blue				531#
Blue				501
Gold				532#
Gold				542
Gold		•		502
Saddle				555
Green				556
Green				535#
Green				546
Green				506
Green		•		557*
Sandalwood				558
Black				538#
Black				548*
Black		•		508

*Available 4-Dr. hardtop/coupe only
#Available 4-Dr. sedan

CATALINA 2-SEAT/3-SEAT SW TRIM

COLOR	CLOTH	VINYL	LEATHER	CODE
Blue				531
Brown				553
Saddle				555
Saddle				535
Green				556
Green				536
Black				538

CATALINA 2-DR HT/4-DR HT TRIM

COLOR	CLOTH	VINYL	LEATHER	CODE
Blue				531
Gold				532
Brown				533
Green				536
Sandalwood				537
Black				538

CATALINA CONVERTIBLE TRIM

COLOR	CLOTH	VINYL	LEATHER	CODE
Saddle				535
Green				536
Sandalwood				537
Black				538

GTO HT COUPE/CONVERTIBLE TRIM

COLOR	CLOTH	VINYL	LEATHER	CODE
Blue		•		250*
Brown		•		253*
Brown		•		253**
Red		•		254*
Saddle		•		255*
Green		•		256*
Sandalwood		•		267*
Sandalwood		•		257*
Black		•		268*
Black		•		258*

*Bucket seats
**Available in Hardtop coupe only

LEMANS SPORT HT COUPE/CONVERTIBLE TRIM

COLOR	CLOTH	VINYL	LEATHER	CODE
Blue		•		250*
Brown		•		253#*
Red		•		254*
Saddle		•		255*
Green		•		256*
Sandalwood		•		257*
Black		•		258*

*Bucket seats
#Not available on convertible

LEMANS SPORT 4-DOOR HARDTOP TRIM

COLOR	CLOTH	VINYL	LEATHER	CODE
Blue		•		260#
Gold		•		262#
Green		•		266#
Black		•		268#

#Notch back or 60-40 seats

LEMANS SPORT HARDTOP COUPE/CONVERTIBLE TRIM

COLOR	CLOTH	VINYL	LEATHER	CODE
Sandalwood		•		267#
Black		•		268#

#Notch back or 60-40 seats

LEMANS SPORT SAFARI TRIM

COLOR	CLOTH	VINYL	LEATHER	CODE
Blue				241
Saddle				245
Green				246
Black				248

LEMANS COUPE/HT COUPE/SW TRIM

COLOR	CLOTH	VINYL	LEATHER	CODE
Blue				241
Saddle				245
Green				246
Sandalwood				247*
Black				248

*Available in coupe only

LEMANS 4-DR SEDAN/4-DR HARDTOP TRIM

COLOR	CLOTH	VINYL	LEATHER	CODE
Med. Blue				241
Med. Gold				242
Dk. Green				246
Black				248

LEMANS SPORT 2-DR COUPE TRIM

COLOR	CLOTH	VINYL	LEATHER	CODE
Gold		•		252*
Green		•		256*
Black		•		258*

*Bucket seats

TEMPEST COUPE/4-DOOR SEDAN TRIM

COLOR	CLOTH	VINYL	LEATHER	CODE
Blue	•			231
Blue				231
Gold				232
Gold	•			232*
Green				236
Green	•			236*
Black				249*

*Morrokide

THE PAINT CODE furnishes the key to the paint colors used on the car. Two, two-digit codes indicate the bottom and top body colors respectively. NOTE: vinyl roof codes appear as a second set of digits.

COLOR	CODE
Polar White	10
Palladium Silver	14
Starlight Black	19
Bermuda Blue	25
Lucerne Blue	26
Atoll Blue	28
Mint Turquoise	34
Keylime Green	43
Palisade Green	45
Verdoro Green	47
Pepper Green	48
Sierra Yellow	50
Coronado Gold	53

COLOR	CODE
Baja Gold	55
Granada Gold	58
Palomino Copper	63
Castillian Bronze	67
Cardinal Red	75
Burgundy	78

VINYL TOP COLORS

	CODE
White	1
Black	2
Sandalwood	5
Dark Gold	7
Dark Green	9

CONVERTIBLE TOP COLORS

	CODE
White	1
Black	2
Sandalwood	5
Dark Gold	7

ENGINE NUMBER

Two identification numbers are used on all Pontiac engines. One identifies the engine code letters and production number. The second is an engine vehicle identification number which identifies proper engine-chassis combinations. A Pontiac 6 engine is identified by a letter code stamped on the distributor mounting pad, at the right side of the block. A Pontiac V8 letter code is stamped below the engine production number on the front of the block, just below the right-hand cylinder head.

PONTIAC ENGINES

ENGINE CODE	NO. CYL.	CID	HORSE-POWER	COMP. RATIO	CARB	TRANS
CG,RF	6	250	155	8.5:1	1 BC	
ZB	6	250	155	8.5:1	1 BC	3-Spd
ZG	6	250	155	8.5:1	1 BC	Auto
WU	8	350	255	8.8:1	2 BC	3-Spd/4-Spd
YU	8	350	255	8.8:1	2 BC	Auto
W7	8	350	255	8.8:1	2 BC	Manual
X7	8	350	255	8.8:1	2 BC	Auto
XX,YB	8	400	265	8.8:1	2 BC	Auto
WE	8	400	290	10.0:1	2 BC	3-Spd
YD	8	400	290	10.0:1	2 BC	Auto
WT*	8	400	330	10.25:1	4 BC	3-Spd
YS,XV,XZ	8	400	330	10.25:1	4 BC	Auto
WS*	8	400	345	10.5:1	4 BC	3-Spd
YZ*	8	400	345	10.5:1	4 BC	Auto
WT#,WX	8	400	350	10.0:1	4 BC	3-Spd
YS,XH	8	400	350	10.0:1	4 BC	Auto
WS#	8	400	366	10.5:1	4 BC	3-Spd
YZ#	8	400	366	10.5:1	4 BC	Auto
WW,WH	8	400	370	10.5:1	4 BC	3-Spd
XP,XN	8	400	370	10.5:1	4 BC	Auto
YH	8	455	360	10.0:1	4 BC	Auto
WA,WG	8	455	370	10.25:1	4 BC	3-Spd
YC,YA,XF	8	455	370	10.25:1	4-BC	Auto

*Firebird
#Tempest & GTO

1971 PONTIAC FIREBIRD TRANS AM

1971 PONTIAC GT 37

1971 PONTIAC JUDGE

1971 PONTIAC GRAND VILLE

1971 PONTIAC LEMANS SPORT

1971 PONTIAC GRAND PRIX

1971 PONTIAC BONNEVILLE

1971 PONTIAC SAFARI

VEHICLE IDENTIFICATION NUMBER

PONTIAC
268491P300039

Located on the top of the dash on the driver's side and visible through the windshield from outside the car.

FIRST DIGIT: Identifies GM Division (2 is Pontiac)

SECOND AND THIRD DIGITS: Identify the series

SERIES	CODE
Ventura II	13
Firebird	23
Firebird Esprit	24
Firebird Formula 400	26
Firebird Trans Am	28
T-37	33
LeMans	35
LeMans Sport	37
Tempest GTO	42
Catalina	52
Catalina Brougham	58
Bonneville	62
Grand Ville	68
Grand Prix	76

FOURTH AND FIFTH DIGITS: Identify the body style

BODY STYLE	CODE
2-Door Coupe	27
4-Door SW, 2-Seat (Catalina)	35
4-Door SW, 2-Seat (LeMans)	36
2-Door Hardtop	37
4-Door Hardtop	39
4-Door SW, 3-Seat	45
4-Door SW, 3-Seat (LeMans)	46
2-Door Hardtop (Grand Ville)	47
4-Door Hardtop (Grand Ville)	49
2-Door Hardtop (Grand Prix, Bonneville, Catalina)	57
2-Door Convertible	67
4-Door Sedan	69
2-Door Hardtop (Firebird)	87

SIXTH DIGIT: Identifies the year 1971

SEVENTH DIGIT: Identifies the assembly plant

ASSEMBLY PLANT	CODE
Atlanta, GA	A
Baltimore, MD	B
Southgate, CA	C
Doraville, GA	D
Linden, NJ	E
Van Nuys, CA	L
Norwood, OH	N
Pontiac, MI	P
Arlington, TX	R
Kansas City, KS	X
Fremont, CA	Z
Oshawa, Ont., CAN	1
St. Therese, Que., CAN	2

LAST SIX DIGITS: Represent the basic reproduction numbers

BODY NUMBER PLATE

The body number plate is located on the firewall, just below the rear edge of the hood. This plate identifies the model year, car division, series, body style, body assembly plant, body numbers, trim combination, paint code and build date code.

BODY BY FISHER
ST 71   23527   LIN 123456 BDY
TR 249   19 19 PNT
000

GENERAL MOTORS CORPORATION CERTIFIES TO THE DEALER THAT THIS VEHICLE CONFORMS TO ALL U.S., FEDERAL MOTOR VEHICLE SAFETY STANDARDS APPLICABLE AT TIME OF MANUFACTURE.

Example:

71	Model Year (1971)
2	Car Division (Pontiac)
35	Series (LeMans)
27	Style (2-Door Coupe)
LIN	Body Assembly Plant (Linden, NJ)
123456	Production Sequence
249	Black Cloth & Vinyl Trim
19	Starlight Black Lower Body Color
19	Starlight Black Upper Body Color
000	Time Built Date

VENTURA II	CODE
Coupe	1327
4-Door Sedan	1369

*Sprint option available

FIREBIRD	CODE
2-Door Hardtop	2387
Esprit	2487
Formula	2687
Trans Am	2887

*Formula 350 option available
*Formula 400 option available
*Formula 455 option available

T-37	CODE
2-Door Coupe	3327
2-Door Hardtop	3337
4-Door Sedan	3369

*GT option available

LEMANS	MODEL CODE
2-Door Coupe	3527
4-Door SW, 2-Seat	3536
2-Door Hardtop	3537
4-Door Hardtop	3539
4-Door SW, 3-Seat	3546
4-Door Sedan	3569

LEMANS SPORT	CODE
2-Door Hardtop	3537
4-Door Hardtop	3739
Convertible	3767

GTO — **CODE**
2-Door Hardtop 4237
Convertible 4267
*Judge option available

CATALINA — **CODE**
4-Door SW, 2-Seat 5235
4-Door Hardtop 5239
4-Door SW, 3-Seat 5245
2-Door Hardtop 5257
Convertible 5267
4-Door Sedan 5269

CATALINA BROUGHAM — **CODE**
4-Door Hardtop 5839
2-Door Hardtop 5857
4-Door Sedan 5869

BONNEVILLE — **CODE**
4-Door SW, 2-Seat 6235
4-Door Hardtop 6239
4-Door SW, 3-Seat 6245
2-Door Hardtop 6257
4-Door Sedan 6269

GRAND VILLE — **CODE**
2-Door Hardtop 6847
4-Door Hardtop 6849
2-Door Convertible 6867
*Custom option available

GRAND PRIX — **CODE**
2-Door Hardtop 7657
*SJ option available
*Hurst option available

THE TRIM CODE furnishes the key to the interior color and material scheme.

VENTURA II 2-DR COUPE/4-DR SEDAN TRIM

COLOR	CLOTH	VINYL	LEATHER	CODE
Dk. Blue	•	•		795
Dk. Blue		•		782
Sandalwood	•	•		796
Sandalwood		•		783
Dk. Jade	•	•		797
Dk. Jade		•		784
Black		•		793
Black		•		754*
Dk. Saddle		•		794
Dk. Saddle		•		767*

*Bucket seats

GRAND PRIX HT COUPE TRIM

COLOR	CLOTH	VINYL	LEATHER	CODE
Dk. Jade	•	•		285*
Sandalwood	•	•		287*
Sandalwood	•	•		270#
Black	•	•		289*
Black		•		270#
Dk. Blue		•		291*
Ivory		•		292*
Dk. Saddle		•		293*
Dk. Sienna		•		294*
Dk. Jade		•		296*
Sandalwood		•		297*
Sandalwood		•		/278#
Black		•		299*

*Bucket seats
#Notch back or 60-40 seats

GRAND VILLE HT COUPE TRIM

COLOR	CLOTH	VINYL	LEATHER	CODE
Dk. Jade	•	•		545#

Sandalwood	•		•	568#
Black	•		•	549#
Black	•		•	560#

#Notch back or 60-40 seats

GRAND VILLE HT COUPE/CONVERTIBLE TRIM

COLOR	CLOTH	VINYL	LEATHER	CODE
Dk. Blue		•		551#+
Ivory		•		552#
Dk. Saddle		•		553#
Dk. Jade		•		556#+
Sandalwood		•		557#+
Black		•		559#

#Notch back or 60-40 seats
+Not available on convertible

GRAND VILLE 4-DR HT TRIM

COLOR	CLOTH	VINYL	LEATHER	CODE
Dk. Blue	•	•		561
Dk. Blue		•		571
Ivory		•		572
Dk. Saddle		•		573
Dk. Jade	•	•		565
Dk. Jade	•	•		585
Dk. Jade	•	•		595#
Dk. Jade		•		576
Sandalwood	•	•		567
Sandalwood	•	•		587
Sandalwood	•	•		597#
Sandalwood		•		577
Black	•	•		569
Black	•	•		580
Black		•		579
Black	•	•		599#

#Notch back or 60-40 seats

BONNEVILLE 4-DR HT/COUPE/SEDAN TRIM

COLOR	CLOTH	VINYL	LEATHER	CODE
Dk. Blue	•	•		521+
Dk. Jade	•	•		525
Sandalwood	•	•		527
Ivory		•		532\
Dk. Saddle		•		533\
Dk. Sienna		•		534\
Dk. Jade		•		536
Sandalwood		•		537
Black	•	•		529**
Black		•		539

+Not available on hardtop coupe
**Not available on HT coupe and 4-dr. sedan
\Not available on 4-dr. hardtop

GRAND SAFARI SW TRIM

COLOR	CLOTH	VINYL	LEATHER	CODE
Dk. Blue		•		511
Dk. Blue		•		541+
Dk. Saddle		•		513
Dk. Sienna		•		544+
Dk. Jade		•		516
Dk. Jade		•		546+
Sandalwood		•		517
Sandalwood		•		548+
Black		•		519

+Expanded Morrokide

**CATALINA BROUGHAM 4-DR/HT COUPE/
4-DR SEDAN TRIM**

COLOR	CLOTH	VINYL	LEATHER	CODE
Dk. Blue	•	•		521*
Ivory		•		532#
Dk. Saddle		•		533#
Dk. Sienna		•		534#
Dk. Jade	•	•		525

COLOR	CLOTH	VINYL	LEATHER	CODE
Dk. Jade		•		536
Sandalwood	•	•		527
Sandalwood		•		537
Black	•	•		529+
Black		•		539

*Not available on hardtop coupe
#Not available on 4-dr. sedan
+Not available on HT coupe/4-dr. sedan

CATALINA 4-DR HT/HT COUPE/4-DR SEDAN TRIM

COLOR	CLOTH	VINYL	LEATHER	CODE
Dk. Blue	•	•		501
Dk. Blue		•		511
Ivory		•		512#
Dk. Jade	•	•		505
Dk. Jade		•		516
Dk. Saddle		•		513
Dk. Sienna		•		514+
Sandalwood	•	•		507
Sandalwood		•		517
Black		•		509
Black		•		519

#Not available on 4-door sedan
+Not available on HP coupe

CATALINA CONVERTIBLE TRIM

COLOR	CLOTH	VINYL	LEATHER	CODE
Ivory		•		512
Dk. Sienna		•		514
Black		•		519

LEMANS SPORT HT COUPE/4-DR HT TRIM

COLOR	CLOTH	VINYL	LEATHER	CODE
Dk. Jade		•		276+
Sandalwood		•		277
Black		•		279

+Not available on hardtop coupe

LEMANS SPORT HT COUPE/CONVERTIBLE TRIM

COLOR	CLOTH	VINYL	LEATHER	CODE
Dk. Blue		•		261*
Ivory		•		262*
Dk. Saddle		•		263*#
Dk. Sienna		•		264*
Dk. Jade		•		266*#
Sandalwood		•		267*#
Black		•		269*

*Bucket seats
#Not available on convertible

LEMANS COUPE/HT COUPE/4-DR HT/ 4-DR SEDAN TRIM

COLOR	CLOTH	VINYL	LEATHER	CODE
Dk. Blue	•	•		241*
Dk. Jade	•	•		245#
Sandalwood	•	•		247##
Black	•	•		249+

*Available on 4-dr. sedan only
#Available on 4-dr HT/4-dr. sedan only
##Available on coupe/HT coupe only
+Not available on coupe

LEMANS COUPE/4-DR HT/4-DR SEDAN/2-SEAT SW/ 3-SEAT SW TRIM

COLOR	CLOTH	VINYL	LEATHER	CODE
Dk. Blue		•		251*
Dk. Saddle		•		253#
Dk. Jade		•		256
Sandalwood		•		257
Black		•		259**

*Available on 4-dr sedan only
#Available on SW only
**Available on coupe only

LEMANS HARDTOP COUPE TRIM

COLOR	CLOTH	VINYL	LEATHER	CODE
Dk. Blue		•		251
Ivory		•		252
Dk. Saddle		•		253
Dk. Jade		•		256
Sandalwood		•		257
Black		•		259

GTO HARDTOP COUPE/CONVERTIBLE TRIM

COLOR	CLOTH	VINYL	LEATHER	CODE
Dk. Blue		•		261*
Ivory		•		262*
Dk. Saddle		•		263*+
Dk. Sienna		•		264*
Dk. Jade		•		266*+
Sandalwood		•		277#
Sandalwood		•		267*+
Black		•		279#
Black		•		269*

*Bucket seats
#Notch back or 60-40 seats
+Not available on convertible

T-37 COUPE/HT COUPE/4-DR SEDAN TRIM

COLOR	CLOTH	VINYL	LEATHER	CODE
Black	•	•		239
Black	•	•		230*
Ivory		•		232+
Dk. Blue	•	•		231
Dk. Jade	•			236
Dk. Jade		•		236
Sandalwood	•			237#
Sandalwood		•		238
Sandalwood		•		237#

*Not available on 4-dr. sedan
#Available on 4-dr. sedan only
+Available on HT coupe only

FIREBIRD HT COUPE/FORMULA HT COUPE/ TRANS AM HT COUPE TRIM

COLOR	CLOTH	VINYL	LEATHER	CODE
Dk. Blue		•		201*
Dk. Saddle		•		203*
Dk. Jade		•		206*
Sandalwood		•		207*
Black		•		209*

*Bucket seats

ESPRIT HT COUPE/FORMULA HT COUPE/ TRANS AM HT COUPE TRIM

COLOR	CLOTH	VINYL	LEATHER	CODE
Dk. Blue		•		211*
Ivory		•		212*
Dk. Saddle		•		213*
Dk. Sienna		•		214*
Dk. Jade		•		216*
Sandalwood		•		217*
Black		•		219*

*Bucket seats

ESPRIT HT COUPE/FORMULA HT COUPE/ TRANS AM HT COUPE TRIM

COLOR	CLOTH	VINYL	LEATHER	CODE
Sandalwood	•			227*
Sandalwood		•		227*
Black	•	•		229*

*Bucket seats

THE PAINT CODE furnishes the key to the paint colors used on the car. Two, two-digit codes indicate the bottom and top body colors respectively. NOTE: vinyl roof codes appear as a second set of digits.

COLOR	CODE
Cameo White	11
Nordic Silver	13
Bluestone Gray	16
Starlight Black	19
Adriatic Blue	24
Lucerne Blue	26
Regency Blue	29
Aquarius Green	39
Limekist Green	42
Tropical Lime	43
Laurentian Green	49
Quezal Gold	53
Baja Gold	55
Aztec Gold	59
Sandalwood	61
Canyon Copper	62
Bronzini Gold	66
Castillian Bronze	67
Cardinal Red	75
Rosewood	78

CONVERTIBLE TOP COLORS

White	1
Black	2
Sandalwood	5
Dark Green	9

VINYL TOP COLORS

White	1
Black	2
Sandalwood	5
Dark Brown	7
Dark Green	9

ENGINE NUMBERS

Two identification numbers are used on all Pontiac engines. One identifies the engine code letters and production number. The second is an engine vehicle identification number which identifies proper engine-chassis combinations. A Pontiac 6 engine is identified by a letter code stamped on the distributor mounting pad, at the right side of the block. A Pontiac V8 letter code is stamped below the engine production number on the front of the block, just below the right-hand cylinder head.

PONTIAC ENGINES

ENGINE CODE	NO. CYL.	CID	HORSE-POWER	COMP. RATIO	CARB	TRANS
ZB,CAA	6	250	145	8.5:1	1 BC	3-Spd
ZG,CAB	6	250	145	8.5:1	1 BC	Auto
CCA	8	307	200	8.5:1	2 BC	3-Spd
CCC	8	307	200	8.5:1	2 BC	Auto
WR,WU	8	350	250	8.0:1	2 BC	3-Spd
YU,XR	8	350	250	8.0:1	2 BC	Auto
WN,WP	8	350	250	8.0:1	2 BC	
YN,YP	8	350	250	8.0:1	2 BC	
WS,WX	8	400	265	8.2:1	2 BC	3-Spd
XX,YX	8	400	265	8.2:1	2 BC	Auto
WT,WK	8	400	300	8.2:1	4 BC	3-Spd
YS	8	400	300	8.2:1	4 BC	Auto
WG	8	455	280	8.2:1	2 BC	3-Spd
YG	8	455	280	8.2:1	2 BC	Auto
WJ	8	455	325	8.2:1	4 BC	3-Spd
YC	8	455	325	8.2:1	4 BC	Auto
WL,WC	8	455	335	8.4:1	4 BC	3-Spd
YE,YA	8	455	335	8.4:1	4 BC	Auto

1972 PONTIAC CATALINA

1972 PONTIAC FIREBIRD FORMULA

1972 PONTIAC GRAND PRIX

1972 PONTIAC GRAND VILLE

1972 PONTIAC LUXURY LE MANS

1972 PONTIAC VENTURA II SPRINT

VEHICLE IDENTIFICATION NUMBER

PONTIAC
2P49W2P100001

Located on the top of the dash on the driver's side and visible through the windshield from outside the car.

FIRST DIGIT: Identifies GM Division (2 is Pontiac)

SECOND DIGIT: Identifies the series

SERIES	CODE
LeMans	D
LeMans Luxury	G
Grand Prix	K
Catalina	L
Catalina Brougham	M
Bonneville	N
Grand Ville	P
Firebird	S
Firebird Esprit	T
Firebird Formula	U
Firebird Trans Am	V
Ventura II	Y

THIRD AND FOURTH DIGITS: Identify the body style

BODY STYLE	CODE
2-Door Sedan	27
4-Door SW, 2-Seat (Catalina)	35
4-Door SW, 2-Seat (LeMans)	36
2-Door Hardtop	37
4-Door Sport Sedan	39
SWB Cowl	40
4-Door SW, 3-Seat	45
4-Door SW, 3-Seat (LeMans)	46
Sport Coupe (Grand Ville)	47
4-Door Sport Sedan	49
Sport Coupe (Catalina/Bonne)	57
Convertible	67
4-Door Sedan	69
Hardtop Coupe (Firebird)	87
LWB Cowl	90

FIFTH DIGIT: Identifies the engine

ENGINE	CODE
V6-250 1V	D
V8-307 2V	F
V8-350 2V, SE	M
V8-350 2V DE	N
V8-400 2V DE	P
V8-400 2V SE	R
V8-400 4V SE	S
V8-400 4V DE	T
V8-455 2V DE	U
V8-455 2V SE	V
V8-455 4V SE	W
V8-455 4V Perf	X
V8-455 4V DE	Y

SIXTH DIGIT: Identifies the year 1972

SEVENTH DIGIT: Identifies the assembly plant

ASSEMBLY PLANT	CODE
Atlanta, GA	A
South Gate, CA	C
Doraville, GA	D
Framingham, MA	G
Van Nuys, CA	L
Norwood, OH	N
Pontiac, MI	P
Willow Run, MI	W
Kansas City, KS	X
Fremont, CA	Z
St. Therese, Que., CAN	2

LAST SIX DIGITS: Represent the basic production numbers

BODY NUMBER PLATE

The body number plate is located on the firewall, just below the rear edge of the hood. This plate identifies the model year, car division, series, body style, body assembly plant, body numbers, trim combination, paint code and build date code.

BODY BY FISHER
ST 72   22387   NOR 123456 BDY
TR 161   19 19 PNT
000 A51

GENERAL MOTORS CORPORATION CERTIFIES TO THE DEALER THAT THIS VEHICLE CONFORMS TO ALL U.S., FEDERAL MOTOR VEHICLE SAFETY STANDARDS APPLICABLE AT TIME OF MANUFACTURE.

Example:

72	Model Year (1972)
2	Car Division (Pontiac)
23	Series (Firebird)
87	Style (Espirit 2-Door Hardtop)
NOR	Body Assembly Plant (Norwood, OH)
123456	Production Sequence
161	Black Vinyl Trim
19	Starlight Black Lower Body Color
19	Starlight Black Upper Body Color
000	Time Built Date
A51	Modular Seat Code

VENTURA II	CODE
Coupe	1327
4-Door Sedan	1369

*SD option available
*Sprint option available

FIREBIRD	CODE
2-Door Hardtop	2387
Esprit	2487
Formula	2687
Trans Am	2887

LEMANS	CODE
2-Door Coupe	3527
4-Door SW, 2-Seat	3536
2-Door Hardtop	3537
4-Door Sedan	3569
4-Door SW, 3-Seat	3546

*GTO option available
*Sport option available
*GT option available

LEMANS SPORT — CODE
Convertible 3867

LEMANS LUXURY — CODE
2-Door Hardtop 4437
4-Door Hardtop 4439

CATALINA — CODE
4-Door SW, 2-Seat 5235
4-Door Hardtop 5239
4-Door SW, 3-Seat 5245
2-Door Hardtop 5257
Convertible 5267
4-Door Sedan 5269

CATALINA BROUGHAM — CODE
4-Door Hardtop 5839
2-Door Hardtop 5857
4-Door Sedan 5869

BONNEVILLE — CODE
4-Door SW, 2-Seat 5235
4-Door Hardtop 6239
4-Door SW, 3-Seat 6245
2-Door Hardtop 6257
4-Door Sedan 6269

GRAND VILLE — CODE
2-Door Hardtop 6847
4-Door Hardtop 6849
Convertible 6867

GRAND PRIX — CODE
2-Door Hardtop 7657
*SJ option available

THE TRIM CODE furnishes the key to the interior color and material scheme.

GRAND VILLE HT COUPE TRIM
COLOR	CLOTH	VINYL	LEATHER	CODE
Keswick pattern cloth and Morrokide				
Pewter	•	•		805#
Dk. Blue	•	•		815#
Dk. Green	•	•		845#
Lt. Beige	•	•		855#
Black	•	•		865#

#Notch back or 60-40 seats

GRAND VILLE 4-DR HT TRIM
COLOR	CLOTH	VINYL	LEATHER	CODE
Keswick pattern cloth and Morrokide				
Pewter	•	•		802
Pewter	•	•		806#
Dk. Blue	•	•		812
Dk. Green	•	•		842
Dk. Green	•	•		846#
Lt. Beige	•	•		852
Lt. Beige	•	•		856#
Black	•	•		862
Black	•	•		866#

#Notch back or 60-40 seats

GRAND VILLE HT COUPE TRIM
COLOR	CLOTH	VINYL	LEATHER	CODE
Pampa pattern cloth and Morrokide				
Pewter	•	•		605#
Dk. Blue	•	•		615#
Dk. Blue	•	•		715#+
Dk. Green	•	•		645#
Dk. Saddle		•		735#+
Lt. Beige	•	•		655#
Lt. Beige	•	•		755#+
Black	•	•		665#

#Notch back or 60-40 seats
+Elk and Madrid Morrokide

GRAND VILLE 4-DR HT TRIM
COLOR	CLOTH	VINYL	LEATHER	CODE
Pampa pattern cloth and Morrokide				
Pewter	•	•		602
Dk. Blue	•	•		612
Dk. Blue	•	•		712+
Dk. Green	•	•		642
Dk. Green	•	•		742+
Lt. Beige	•	•		652
Lt. Beige	•	•		752+
Black	•	•		662
Black	•	•		762+

+Elk and Madrid Morrokide

GRAND VILLE CONVERTIBLE TRIM
COLOR	CLOTH	VINYL	LEATHER	CODE
Elk Morrokide				
Dk. Saddle		•		735#
Dk. Green		•		745#
Lt. Beige		•		755#

#Notch back or 60-40 seats

GRAND PRIX HT COUPE TRIM
COLOR	CLOTH	VINYL	LEATHER	CODE
Potomac pattern cloth and Morrokide				
Pewter	•	•		801*
Pewter	•	•		901*+
Pewter	•	•		805#
Dk. Green	•	•		841*
Dk. Green	•	•		941*+
Lt. Beige	•	•		851*
Lt. Beige	•	•		855#
Lt. Beige	•	•		955#+
Ivory		•		921*+
Dk. Saddle		•		931*+
Black	•	•		861*
Black	•	•		961*+
Black		•		965#+

*Bucket seats
#Notch back or 60-40 seats
+Perforated Roulet Morrokide

GRAND SAFARI 2-SEAT SW/3-SEAT SW TRIM
COLOR	CLOTH	VINYL	LEATHER	CODE
All Morrokide				
Dk. Blue		•		212/512
Dk. Saddle		•		232/532
Dk. Green		•		242/542
Lt. Beige		•		252/552

CATALINA BROUGHAM HT COUPE/4-DR HT/ 4-DR SEDAN TRIM
COLOR	CLOTH	VINYL	LEATHER	CODE
Pacarro pattern, prima bolster cloths and Morrokide				
Dk. Blue	•	•		312
Dk. Green	•	•		342
Lt. Beige	•	•		352
Black	•	•		362

CATALINA BROUGHAM HT COUPE TRIM

COLOR	CLOTH	VINYL	LEATHER	CODE
All Morrokide				
Ivory		•		422
Ivory		•		422*
Dk. Blue		•		412*
Dk. Saddle		•		432
Dk. Green		•		442
Dk. Green		•		442*
Dk. Green		•		442**
Lt. Beige		•		452**
Black		•		462*

*4-Dr hardtop
**4-Dr sedan

CATALINA 4-DR HT/4-DR SEDAN TRIM

COLOR	CLOTH	VINYL	LEATHER	CODE
All Morrokide				
Dk. Blue		•		212
Dk. Saddle		•		232
Dk. Green		•		242
Lt. Beige		•		252
Black		•		262*

*4-Dr. hardtop only

CATALINA HT COUPE/4-DR HT/4-DR SEDAN TRIM

COLOR	CLOTH	VINYL	LEATHER	CODE
Paxton pattern cloth and Morrokide				
Dk. Blue	•	•		112
Dk. Blue	•	•		212*
Dk. Green	•	•		142
Dk. Green	•	•		242*
Ivory		•		222*
Lt. Beige	•	•		152
Black	•	•		162
Black	•	•		262*
Dk. Saddle		•		232*

*All Morrokide, hardtop coupe only

CATALINA CONVERTIBLE TRIM

COLOR	CLOTH	VINYL	LEATHER	CODE
Grained Morrokide				
Ivory		•		222
Dk. Saddle		•		232
Black		•		262

BONNEVILLE HT COUPE/4-DR HT/4-DR SEDAN TRIM

COLOR	CLOTH	VINYL	LEATHER	CODE
Pacarro pattern, prima bolster cloths and Morrokide				
Dk. Blue	•	•		312
Dk. Green	•	•		342
Lt. Beige	•	•		353
Black	•	•		362

BONNEVILLE HTP COUPE TRIM

COLOR	CLOTH	VINYL	LEATHER	CODE
All Morrokide				
Ivory		•		422
Ivory		•		422*
Dk. Saddle		•		432
Dk. Green		•		442
Dk. Green		•		442*
Dk. Green		•		442**
Lt. Beige		•		452**
Black		•		462
Black		•		462*
Dk. Blue		•		412*

*4-Dr hardtop
**4-Dr sedan

LEMANS LUXURY HT COUPE/4-DR HT TRIM

COLOR	CLOTH	VINYL	LEATHER	CODE
Potomac pattern cloth				
Pewter	•	•		605#
Pewter	•	•		705#
Ivory		•		725#
Dk. Blue	•	•		615#
Dk. Saddle		•		735#
Dk. Green	•	•		645#
Dk. Green		•		745#
Lt. Beige	•	•		655#
Black	•	•		665#
Black	•	•		765#

700 numbers are Elk Morrokide
#Notch back or 60-40 seats

LUXURY LEMANS HT COUPE TRIM

COLOR	CLOTH	VINYL	LEATHER	CODE
Elk Morrokide				
Pewter		•		701*
Ivory		•		721*
Dk. Saddle		•		731*
Dk. Green		•		741*
Black		•		761*

*Bucket seats

LEMANS SPORT CONVERTIBLE TRIM

COLOR	CLOTH	VINYL	LEATHER	CODE
All Morrokide				
Pewter		•		701*
Ivory		•		721*
Dk. Saddle		•		731*
Dk. Green		•		741*
Black		•		761*

*Bucket seats

LEMANS COUPE/HT COUPE/4-DR SEDAN TRIM

COLOR	CLOTH	VINYL	LEATHER	CODE
All Morrokide				
Ivory		•		522
Dk. Saddle		•		532
Dk. Green		•		542
Black		•		562

LEMANS SW 2-SEAT/3-SEAT TRIM

COLOR	CLOTH	VINYL	LEATHER	CODE
All Morrokide				
Dk. Blue		•		012
Dk. Saddle		•		032
Dk. Green		•		042
Black		•		062

LEMANS 2-DR COUPE/HT COUPE/4-DR SEDAN TRIM

COLOR	CLOTH	VINYL	LEATHER	CODE
Piccard pattern cloth				
Dk. Blue	•	•		412
Dk. Green	•	•		442
Dk. Green	•	•		741*
Lt. Beige	•	•		452
Pewter		•		701*
Ivory		•		721*
Dk. Saddle		•		731*
Black		•		761*

*Bucket seats
700 Numbers All Morrokide, HT coupe only

FIREBIRD HT COUPE/FORMULA HT COUPE/ TRANS AM HT COUPE TRIM

COLOR	CLOTH	VINYL	LEATHER	CODE
All Morrokide				
Ivory		•		121*
Dk. Saddle		•		131*
Dk. Green		•		141*
Black		•		161*

*Bucket seats

ESPRIT HT COUPE/FORMULA HT COUPE/ TRANS AM TRIM

HT coupe standard interior, all others roulet Morrokide

COLOR	CLOTH	VINYL	LEATHER	CODE
Dk. Blue		•		211*
Ivory		•		221*
Dk. Saddle		•		231*
Dk. Green		•		241*
Lt. Beige		•		251*
Lt. Beige		•		351*
Black		•		261*
Black		•		361*

*Bucket seats

300 Numbers Potomac cloth and Morrokide

VENTURA II 2-DR COUPE/4-DR SEDAN TRIM

Royal pattern cloth and Morrokide

COLOR	CLOTH	VINYL	LEATHER	CODE
Black	•	•		502
Black	•	•		512+
Black		•		531*++
Black		•		532++
Dk. Blue	•	•		562
Dk. Green		•		602+
Lt. Beige		•		632+
Lt. Beige		•		642++
Med. Tan		•		661*++

*Bucket seats
+All Morrokide (Pinta Grained)
++All Morrokide (Grained Vinyl)

THE PAINT CODE furnishes the key to the paint colors used on the car. Two, two-digit codes indicate the bottom and top body colors respectively. NOTE: vinyl roof codes appear as a second set of digits.

COLOR	CODE
Cameo White	11
Revere Silver	14
Antique Pewter	18
Starlight Black	19
Adriatic Blue	24
Lucerne Blue	26
Cumberland Blue	28
Julep Green	36
Springfield Green	43
Wilderness Green	48
Brittany Beige	50
Quezal Gold	53
Arizona Gold	54
Shadow Gold	55
Monarch Gold	56
Brasila Gold	57
Spice Beige	62
Anaconda Gold	63
Sundance Orange	65
Cinnamon Bronze	69
Cardinal Red	75

ENGINE NUMBER

Two identification numbers are used on all Pontiac engines. One identifies the engine code letters and production number. The second is an engine vehicle identification number which identifies proper engine-chassis combinations. A Pontiac 6 engine is identified by a letter code stamped on the distributor mounting pad, at the right side of the block. A Pontiac V8 letter code is stamped below the engine production number on front of the block, just below the right-hand cylinder head.

PONTIAC ENGINES

ENGINE CODE	NO. CYL.	CID	HORSE-POWER	COMP. RATIO	CARB	TRANS
W6,CBG	6	250	110	8.5:1	1 BC	3-Spd
Y6,CBJ	6	250	110	8.5:1	1 BC	Auto
CBA,CBC*	6	250	110	8.5:1	1 BC	
CKG,CAY CKH,CAZ	8	307	130	8.5:1	2 BC	3-Spd
CTK,CMA	8	307	130	8.5:1	2 BC	Auto
WR	8	350	160	8.2:1	2 BC	4-Spd
YU,YV,YR	8	350	160	8.2:1	2 BC	Auto
YX,ZX	8	400	180	8.2:1	2 BC	Auto
WS	8	400	200	8.2:1	4 BC	3-Spd
WK	8	400	200	8.2:1	4 BC	4-Spd
YS,ZS	8	400	200	8.2:1	4 BC	Auto
	8	400	250	8.2:1	4 BC	
YH,ZH	8	455	190	8.2:1	2 BC	Auto
YC,YA	8	455	220	8.2:1	4 BC	Auto
WD,WM	8	455	300	8.4:1	4 BC	4-Spd
YB,YE	8	455	300	8.4:1	4 BC	Auto
	8	455	210	8.2:1	2 BC	
	8	455	240	8.2:1	4 BC	
	8	455	200	8.2:1	4 BC	

*Available in California only

1973 PONTIAC GRAND AM

1973 PONTIAC GRAND PRIX

1973 PONTIAC FIREBIRD

1973 PONTIAC GRAND VILLE

1973 PONTIAC CATALINA

1973 PONTIAC LEMANS

1973 PONTIAC CATALINA

1973 PONTIAC VENTURA

VEHICLE IDENTIFICATION NUMBER

PONTIAC
2K57T3P113856

Located on the top of the dash on the driver's side and visible through the windshield from outside the car.

FIRST DIGIT: Identifies GM Division (2 is Pontiac)

SECOND DIGIT: Identifies the series

SERIES	CODE
LeMans	D
LeMans Sport	F
LeMans Luxury	G
Grand Am	H
Grand Prix	K
Catalina	L
Bonneville	N
Grand Ville	P
Firebird	S
Firebird Esprit	T
Firebird Formula	U
Firebird Trans Am	V
Ventura	Y
Ventura Custom	Z

THIRD AND FOURTH DIGITS: Identify the body style

BODY STYLE	CODE
2-Door Hatchback Sedan	17
2-Door Sedan	27
4-Door Sedan	29
4-Door SW, 2-Seat	35
Sport Coupe	37
4-Door Sport Sedan	39
SWB Cowl	40
4-Door SW, 3-Seat	45
Sport Coupe	47
4-Door Sport Sedan	49
Sport Coupe	57
4-Door Sedan	69
Hardtop Coupe (Firebird)	87
LWB Cowl	90

FIFTH DIGIT: Identifies the engine

ENGINE	CODE
V6-250 1V	D
V8-307 2V (In Canada only)	F
V8-350 2V SE	M
V8-350 2V DE	N
V8-400 4V DE	P
V8-400 2V SE	R
V8-400 4V SE	S
V8-400 2V DE	T
V8-455 4V SE	W
V8-455 4V Perf SD	X
V8-455 4V DE	Y

SIXTH DIGIT: Identifies the year 1973

SEVENTH DIGIT: Identifies the assembly plant

ASSEMBLY PLANT	CODE
Atlanta, GA	A
South Gate, CA	C
Doraville, GA	D
Framingham, MA	G
Van Nuys, CA	L
Norwood, OH	N
Pontiac, MI	P
Kansas City, KS	X
Fremont, CA	Z

LAST SIX DIGITS: Represent the basic production numbers

BODY NUMBER PLATE

The body number plate is located on the firewall, just below the rear edge of the hood. This plate identifies the model year, car division, series, body style, body assembly plant, body numbers, trim combination, paint code and build date code.

BODY BY FISHER
ST 73   2BN39   PON 345687 BDY
TR 546   11 11 PNT
000 A51

GENERAL MOTORS CORPORATION CERTIFIES TO THE DEALER THAT THIS VEHICLE CONFORMS TO ALL U.S., FEDERAL MOTOR VEHICLE SAFETY STANDARDS APPLICABLE AT TIME OF MANUFACTURE.

Example:

73	Model Year (1973)
2	Car Division (Pontiac)
BN	Series (Bonneville)
39	Style (2-Door Hardtop)
PON	Body Assembly Plant (Pontiac, MI)
345687	Production Sequence
546	Black Cloth & Leather Trim
11	Cameo White Lower Body Color
11	Cameo White Upper Body Color
000	Time Built Date
A51	Modular Seat Code

LEMANS	CODE
4-Door	AD29
4-Door SW, 2-Seat	AD35
2-Door	AD37
4-Door SW, 3-Seat	AD45
*GT option available	

LEMANS SPORT	CODE
2-Door	AF37
*GTO option available	

LUXURY LEMANS	CODE
4-Door	AG29
2-Door	AG37
4-Door SW, 3-Seat	AG45

GRAND AM	CODE
4-Door	AH29
2-Door	AH37

CATALINA — CODE
4-Door SW, 2-Seat ... BL35
4-Door Hardtop ... BL39
4-Door SW, 3-Seat ... BL45
2-Door Hardtop ... BL57
4-Door Sedan ... BL69

BONNEVILLE — CODE
4-Door Hardtop ... BN39
2-Door Hardtop ... BN57
4-Door Sedan ... BN69
*RTS option available

GRAND VILLE — CODE
4-Door SW, 2-Seat ... BP35
4-Door SW, 3-Seat ... BP45
2-Door Hardtop ... BP47
4-Door Hardtop ... BP49
Convertible ... BP67

FIREBIRD — CODE
2-Door Hardtop ... FS87
Esprit ... FT87
Formula ... FU87
Trans Am ... FV87

GRAND PRIX — CODE
2-Door ... GK57
*SJ option available

VENTURA — CODE
Hatchback Coupe ... XY17
2-Door Coupe ... XY27
4-Door Sedan ... XY69
*Sprint option available

VENTURA CUSTOM — CODE
Hatchback Coupe ... XZ17
2-Door Coupe ... XZ27
4-Door Sedan ... XZ69

THE TRIM CODE furnishes the key to the interior color and material scheme.

LEMANS 2-DR TRIM
COLOR	CLOTH	VINYL	LEATHER	CODE
Green	•	•		264
Beige	•	•		265
Blue		•		271
White		•		272
Saddle		•		273
Black		•		276

LEMANS 4-DR TRIM
COLOR	CLOTH	VINYL	LEATHER	CODE
Blue	•	•		261
Green	•	•		264
Green		•		274
Beige	•	•		265
Beige		•		275
Saddle		•		273

LEMANS SW, 2-SEAT/3-SEAT TRIM
COLOR	CLOTH	VINYL	LEATHER	CODE
Saddle		•		273
Green		•		274
Beige		•		275
Oxblood		•		277

LEMANS SPORT 2-DR TRIM
COLOR	CLOTH	VINYL	LEATHER	CODE
Blue		•		251
White		•		252
Saddle		•		253
Black		•		556
Oxblood		•		257
Chamois		•		258

LUXURY LEMANS 2-DR/4-DR TRIM
COLOR	CLOTH	VINYL	LEATHER	CODE
Blue	•	•		281
Green	•	•		284
Beige	•	•		285
Black	•	•		286
Black		•		296*
Oxblood	•	•		287*
Oxblood		•		297*
White		•		292
Saddle		•		293
Chamois		•		298*

*2-Door only

GRAND AM 2-DR/4-DR TRIM
COLOR	CLOTH	VINYL	LEATHER	CODE
Beige	•			505
Beige		•		515*
Oxblood	•			507
Oxblood		•		517
Saddle		•		513
Black		•		516

*2-Door only

CATALINA 2-DR HT/4-DR HT/4-DR SEDAN TRIM
COLOR	CLOTH	VINYL	LEATHER	CODE
Blue	•			521
Blue		•		531
White		•		532
Saddle		•		533
Green	•			524
Green		•		534
Beige	•			525
Beige		•		535
Black	•			526
Oxblood		•		537

CATALINA SW 2-SEAT/3-SEAT TRIM
COLOR	CLOTH	VINYL	LEATHER	CODE
Saddle		•		533
Green		•		534
Beige		•		535
Oxblood		•		537

BONNEVILLE 4-DR HT/2-DR HT/4-DR SEDAN TRIM
COLOR	CLOTH	VINYL	LEATHER	CODE
Blue	•	•		541
Green	•	•		544
Beige	•	•		545
Beige		•		555*
Black	•	•		546
White		•		552
Saddle		•		553
Oxblood		•		557

*4-Door sedan only

GRAND VILLE SW 2-SEAT/3-SEAT TRIM
COLOR	CLOTH	VINYL	LEATHER	CODE
Saddle		•		573
Green		•		574
Beige		•		575
Oxblood		•		577

GRAND VILLE 2-DR HT/4-DR HT (STD) TRIM

COLOR	CLOTH	VINYL	LEATHER	CODE
Beige	•	•		245
Black	•	•		506

GRAND VILLE 2-DR HT/4-DR HT (CUST) TRIM

COLOR	CLOTH	VINYL	LEATHER	CODE
Blue	•	•		561
Green	•	•		564
Beige	•	•		565
Beige		•		575
Black	•	•		566
Oxblood	•	•		567
Oxblood		•		577
Saddle		•		573

GRAND VILLE CONVERTIBLE TRIM

COLOR	CLOTH	VINYL	LEATHER	CODE
White		•		572
Saddle		•		573
Oxblood		•		577

GRAND PRIX 2-DR TRIM

COLOR	CLOTH	VINYL	LEATHER	CODE
Beige	•	•		585
Beige		•		595
Black	•	•		586
Black		•		596
Oxblood		•		587
Oxblood		•		597
Blue		•		591

FIREBIRD (STANDARD) TRIM

COLOR	CLOTH	VINYL	LEATHER	CODE
White		•		232
Saddle		•		233
Black		•		236

FIREBIRD (CUSTOM) TRIM

COLOR	CLOTH	VINYL	LEATHER	CODE
Beige	•	•		255
White		•		242
Saddle		•		243
Black		•		246
Oxblood		•		247

VENTURA (STANDARD) TRIM

COLOR	CLOTH	VINYL	LEATHER	CODE
Beige		•		205
Beige		•		225*
Black		•		206
Black		•		256*

*4-Door sedan only

VENTURA (CUSTOM) TRIM

COLOR	CLOTH	VINYL	LEATHER	CODE
Black	•	•		226
Black	•	•		266*
Black		•		216
Blue		•		211
Blue		•		221*
Beige		•		215
Beige		•		235*

*4-Door sedan only

THE PAINT CODE furnishes the key to the paint colors used on the car. Two, two-digit codes indicate the bottom and top body colors respectively. NOTE: vinyl roof codes appear as a second set of digits.

COLOR	CODE
Cameo White	11
Starlight Black	19
Porcelain Blue	24
Regatta Blue	26
Admiralty Blue	29
Verdant Green	42
Slate Green	44
Golden Olive	46
Brewster Green	48
Sunlight Yellow	51
Desert Sand	56
Valencia Gold	60
Ascot Silver	64
Burnished Umber	66
Burma Brown	68
Florentine Red	74
Buccaneer Red	75
Mesa Tan	81
Navajo Orange	97

ENGINE NUMBER

Two identification numbers are used on all Pontiac engines. One identifies the engine code letters and production number. The second is an engine vehicle identification number which identifies proper engine-chassis combinations. A Pontiac 6 engine is identified by a letter code stamped on the distributor mounting pad, at the right side of the block. A Pontiac V8 letter code is stamped below the engine production number on the front of the block, just below the right-hand cylinder head.

PONTIAC ENGINES

ENGINE CODE	NO. CYL.	CID	HORSE-POWER	COMP. RATIO	CARB	TRANS
CCC,CCD	6	250	100	8.2:1	1 BC	3-Spd
CCA,CCB	6	250	100	8.2:1	1 BC	Auto
CDR, CDS	6	250	100	8.2:1	1 BC	
CAW	6	250	100	8.2:1	1 BC	
XR,XV	8	350	150	7.6:1	2 BC	3-Spd
Y2,YR,Y7	8	350	150	7.6:1	2 BC	Auto
YV,ZR,ZV	8	350	150	7.6:1	2 BC	Auto
YL,XC	8	350	150	7.6:1	2 BC	Auto
WV	8	350	175	7.6:1	2 BC	
ZB,ZD	8	350			2 BC	3-Spd
WD,XC,X2	8	350			2 BC	Auto
WF,WA,XF	8	350			2 BC	Auto
WC,WL,WN	8	350			2 BC	Auto
YW	8	350			2 BC	Auto
YP,Y4,YX	8	400	170	8.0:1	2 BC	Auto
Y1,ZX,ZK	8	400	170	8.0:1	2 BC	Auto
YZ	8	400	170	8.0:1	2 BC	Auto
	8	400	185	8.0:1	2 BC	
	8	400	200	8.0:1	4 BC	
WK,WS,WP	8	400	230	8.0:1	4 BC	3-Spd
YS,Y3,YN	8	400	230	8.0:1	4 BC	Auto
ZX,YY,ZN	8	400	230	8.0:1	4 BC	Auto
YT	8	400	230	8.0:1	4 BC	Auto
X4,X1,X3	8	400			2 BC	Auto
XH,W5	8	400			2 BC	Auto
Y6,YF,YG	8	400			4 BC	3-Spd
XN,XX,X5	8	400			4 BC	Auto
XZ,XK	8	400			4 BC	Auto
	8	455	215	8.0:1	4 BC	
WW,WT	8	455	250	8.0:1	4 BC	3-Spd
YC,YA,ZC	8	455	250	8.0:1	4 BC	Auto
ZA,YK,YD	8	455	250	8.0:1	4 BC	Auto
ZZ,ZE	8	455			4 BC	3-Spd
XE,XA,XJ	8	455			4 BC	Auto
XL,XO,XT	8	455			4 BC	Auto
X7,XY,XM	8	455			4 BC	Auto
ZJ	8	455SD	310	8.4:1	4 BC	3-Spd
XD	8	455SD	310	8.4:1	4 BC	Auto
W8	8	455SD	310	8.4:1	4 BC	3-Spd
Y8	8	455SD	310	8.4:1	4 BC	Auto

1974 PONTIAC VENTURA

1974 PONTIAC GRAND PRIX

1974 PONTIAC GRAND VILLE

1974 PONTIAC LEMANS

1974 PONTIAC FIREBIRD TRANS AM

1974 PONTIAC GTO

1974 PONTIAC CATALINA

1974 PONTIAC GRAND AM

VEHICLE IDENTIFICATION NUMBER

PONTIAC
2P49W4P325678

Located on the top of the dash on the driver's side and visible through the windshield from outside the car.

FIRST DIGIT: Identifies GM Division (2 is Pontiac)

SECOND DIGIT: Identifies the series

SERIES	CODE
LeMans	D
LeMans Sport Coupe	F
Luxury LeMans	G
Grand Am	H
Grand Prix	K
Catalina	L
Bonneville	N
Grand Ville	P
Firebird	S
Firebird Esprit	T
Firebird Formula	U
Firebird Trans Am	V
Ventura	Y
Ventura Custom	Z

THIRD AND FOURTH DIGITS: Identify the body style

BODY STYLE	CODE
2-Door Hatchback Sedan	17
2-Door Sedan (Ventura)	27
4-Door Sedan (LeMans)	29
4-Door SW, 2-Seat	35
2-Door Sedan (LeMans)	37
4-Door Sport Sedan	39
4-Door SW, 3-Seat	45
Sport Coupe	47
4-Door Sport Sedan	49
2-Door Sport Coupe	57
Convertible	67
4-Door Sedan	69
Hardtop Coupe (Firebird)	87

FIFTH DIGIT: Identify the engine

ENGINE	CODE
V6-250 1V	D
V8-350 4V SE	J
V8-350 4V DE	K
V8-350 2V SE	M
V8-350 2V DE	N
V8-400 2V DE	P
V8-400 2V SE	R
V8-400 4V SE	S
V8-400 4V DE	T
V8-455 4V SE	W
V8-455 SD	X
V8-455 4V DE	Y

SIXTH DIGIT: Identifies the year 1974

SEVENTH DIGIT: Identifies the assembly plant

ASSEMBLY PLANT	CODE
Atlanta, GA	A
South Gate, CA	C
Doraville, GA	D
Framingham, MA	G
Van Nuys, CA	L
Norwood, OH	N
Pontiac, MI	P
Willow Run, MI	W
Kansas City, KS	X
Fremont, CA	Z
Oshawa, Ont., CAN	1

LAST SIX DIGITS: Represent the basic production numbers

BODY NUMBER PLATE

The body number plate is located on the firewall, just below the rear edge of the hood. This plate identifies the model year, car division, series, body style, body assembly plant, body numbers, trim combination, paint code and build date code.

BODY BY FISHER
ST 74   2FS87   NOR 345687 BDY
TR 590   19 19 PNT
000 A51

GENERAL MOTORS CORPORATION CERTIFIES TO THE DEALER THAT THIS VEHICLE CONFORMS TO ALL U.S., FEDERAL MOTOR VEHICLE SAFETY STANDARDS APPLICABLE AT TIME OF MANUFACTURE.

Example:

74	Model Year (1974)
2	Car Division (Pontiac)
FS	Series (Firebird)
87	Style (2-Door Hardtop)
NOR	Body Assembly Plant (Norwood, OH)
345687	Production Sequence
590	Red Vinyl Trim
19	Starlight Black Lower Body Color
19	Starlight Black Upper Body Color
000	Time Built Date
A51	Modular Seat Code

LEMANS	CODE
4-Door	AD29
4-Door SW, 2-Seat	AD35
2-Door	AD37
4-Door SW, 3-Seat	AD45

LEMANS SPORT	CODE
2-Door	AF37

*GT option available

LUXURY LEMANS	CODE
4-Door	AG29
4-Door SW, 2-Seat	AG35
2-Door	AG37
4-Door SW, 3-Seat	AG45

GRAND AM	CODE
4-Door	AH29
2-Door	AH37

CATALINA

	CODE
4-Door SW, 2-Seat	BL35
4-Door Hardtop	BL39
4-Door SW, 3-Seat	BL45
2-Door Hardtop	BL57
4-Door Sedan	BL69

BONNEVILLE

	CODE
4-Door Hardtop	BN39
2-Door Hardtop	BN57
4-Door Sedan	BN69

GRAND VILLE

	CODE
4-Door SW, 2-Seat	BP35
4-Door SW, 3-Seat	BP45
2-Door Hardtop	BP47
4-Door Hardtop	BP49
Convertible	BP67

FIREBIRD

	CODE
2-Door Coupe	FS87
Esprit	FT87
Formula	FU87
Trans Am	FV87

GRAND PRIX

	CODE
2-Door	GK57

*SJ option available

VENTURA

	CODE
Hatchback Coupe	XY17
2-Door Coupe	XY27
4-Door Sedan	XY69

*GTO option available
*Sprint option available

VENTURA CUSTOM

	CODE
Hatchback Coupe	XZ17
2-Door Coupe	XZ27
4-Door Sedan	XZ69

THE TRIM CODE furnishes the key to the interior color and material scheme.

LEMANS 4-DR TRIM

COLOR	CLOTH	VINYL	LEATHER	CODE
Green	•	•		204s
Green	•	•		239c
Green		•		214s
Green		•		266c
Beige	•	•		295s
Beige	•	•		243c
Beige		•		268c
Oxblood	•	•		589c
Oxblood		•		217s
Oxblood		•		588c
Blue	•	•		201s
Blue	•	•		238c
Blue		•		211s
Blue		•		247c
Saddle		•		213s
Saddle	•			259c

s Standard
c Custom

LEMANS STATION WAGON 2-SEAT/3-SEAT TRIM

COLOR	CLOTH	VINYL	LEATHER	CODE
Blue		•		211
Saddle		•		213
Green		•		214
Oxblood		•		217

LEMANS 2-DR TRIM

COLOR	CLOTH	VINYL	LEATHER	CODE
Blue		•		211
Blue	•			201
White		•		212
Saddle		•		213
Green	•			204
Green		•		214
Beige	•			205
Black		•		216
Oxblood		•		217

LEMANS SPORT 2-DR TRIM

COLOR	CLOTH	VINYL	LEATHER	CODE
Blue		•		231
White		•		232
Saddle		•		233
Green		•		234
Black		•		236
Oxblood		•		220
Beige		•		235

LUXURY LEMANS 2-DR/4-DR TRIM

COLOR	CLOTH	VINYL	LEATHER	CODE
Green	•	•		244
Green		•		254
Beige	•	•		245
Beige		•		255+
Oxblood	•	•		271
Oxblood		•		276+
Blue	•	•		241
Blue		•		251
White		•		252
Saddle		•		253
Black		•		256+

+2-Door only

LUXURY LEMANS SW 2-SEAT/3-SEAT TRIM

COLOR	CLOTH	VINYL	LEATHER	CODE
Blue		•		280
Saddle		•		290
Green		•		508
Oxblood		•		217

GRAND AM 2-DR/4-DR TRIM

COLOR	CLOTH	VINYL	LEATHER	CODE
Saddle	•			263
Saddle		•		273
Green	•			264
Green		•		274
Beige	•			265
Beige		•		275
Oxblood	•			267
Oxblood		•		277
White		•		551

CATALINA SW 2-SEAT/3-SEAT TRIM

COLOR	CLOTH	VINYL	LEATHER	CODE
Blue		•		511
Saddle		•		513
Green		•		514
Oxblood		•		517

CATALINA 4-DR HT/2-DR HT/4-DR SEDAN TRIM

COLOR	CLOTH	VINYL	LEATHER	CODE
Green	•			504
Green		•		514
Beige	•			505
Beige		•		515
Black	•			506
Blue	•			501
Blue		•		511
White		•		512+
Saddle		•		513

+2-Door and 4-Door Hardtop only

BONNEVILLE HDTP/SEDAN TRIM

COLOR	CLOTH	VINYL	LEATHER	CODE
Green	•			524
Green		•		534+
Beige	•			525
Beige		•		535
Black	•			526
Blue	•			521
White		•		532+
Saddle		•		533

+Not available on 4-Door sedan

GRAND VILLE SW 2-SEAT/3-SEAT TRIM

COLOR	CLOTH	VINYL	LEATHER	CODE
Saddle	•			543
Saddle		•		553
Blue		•		577
Green		•		554
Oxblood		•		557

GRAND VILLE 2-DR/4-DR TRIM

COLOR	CLOTH	VINYL	LEATHER	CODE
Green	•			544
Green		•		554
Beige	•			545
Beige		•		555
Oxblood	•			547
Oxblood		•		557
Black	•			546
Blue	•			541
Taupe	•			548
Saddle		•		553

GRAND VILLE CONVERTIBLE TRIM

COLOR	CLOTH	VINYL	LEATHER	CODE
White		•		578
Saddle		•		553
Green		•		554
Oxblood		•		557
Beige		•		555

FIREBIRD TRIM

COLOR	CLOTH	VINYL	LEATHER	CODE
Saddle	•			583c
Saddle		•		593c
Saddle		•		573s
Black	•			586c
Black		•		576s
Black		•		596c
White		•		572s
White		•		592c
Green		•		594c
Red		•		590c

s Standard
c Custom

GRAND PRIX TRIM

COLOR	CLOTH	VINYL	LEATHER	CODE
Saddle	•			283
Saddle		•		293
Green	•			284
Green		•		294
Oxblood	•			287
Oxblood		•		297
Black	•			286
Black		•		296
Blue		•		291
White		•		292
Beige		•		295

VENTURA HATCHBACK/2-DR COUPE TRIM

COLOR	CLOTH	VINYL	LEATHER	CODE
Black	•			502+
Black	•			523++
Black		•		552+
Saddle		•		503
Green		•		574

+Black/White/Red plaid
++Black/White/Green plaid

VENTURA 4-DR SEDAN TRIM

COLOR	CLOTH	VINYL	LEATHER	CODE
Black	•			516+
Black		•		536+

+Black/White/Red plaid

VENTURA CUSTOM HATCHBACK/2-DR COUPE TRIM

COLOR	CLOTH	VINYL	LEATHER	CODE
Green	•			564
Green		•		584
Black	•			522
Saddle		•		563
White		•		542
Red		•		550

VENTURA CUSTOM 4-DR SEDAN TRIM

COLOR	CLOTH	VINYL	LEATHER	CODE
Black	•			556
Black		•		566

THE PAINT CODE furnishes the key to the paint colors used on the car. Two, two-digit codes indicate the bottom and top body colors respectively. NOTE: vinyl roof codes appear as a second set of digits.

COLOR	CODE
Cameo White	11
Starlight Black	19
Porcelain Blue	24
Regatta Blue	26
Admiralty Blue	29
Gulfmist Aqua	36
Fernmist Green	40
Lakemist Green	44
Limefire Green	46
Pinemist Green	49
Carmel Beige	50
Sunstorm Yellow	51
Denver Gold	53
Colonial Gold	55
Crestwood Brown	59
Ascot Silver	64
Fire Coral Bronze	66
Shadowmist Brown	69
Honduras Maroon	74
Buccaneer Red	75

ENGINE NUMBER

Two identification numbers are used on all Pontiac engines. One identifies the engine code letters and production number. The second is an engine vehicle identification number which identifies proper engine-chassis combinations. A Pontiac 6 engine is identified by a letter code stamped on the distributor mounting pad, at the right side of the block. A Pontiac V8 letter code is stamped below the engine production number on front of the block, just below the right-hand cylinder head.

PONTIAC ENGINES

ENGINE CODE	NO. CYL.	CID	HORSE-POWER	COMP. RATIO	CARB	TRANS
CCR	6	250	100	8.2:1	1 BC	3-Spd
CCX,CCW	6	250	100	8.2:1	1 BC	3-Spd
*	6	250	110	8.5:1	1 BC	3-Spd/Auto
*	8	350	150	8.0:1	2 BC	Auto
WA,WB	8	350	155	7.6:1	2 BC	3 Spd
YA,YB,YC	8	350	155	7.6:1	2 BC	Auto
AA,ZA,ZB	8	350	155	7.6:1	2 BC	Auto
*	8	350	170	7.6:1	4 BC	Auto
	8	350	170	7.6:1	2 BC	
WN,WP	8	350	170	7.6:1	4 BC	3-Spd
YN,YP	8	350	170	7.6:1	4 BC	Auto
YS,ZP	8	350	170	7.6:1	4 BC	Auto
	8	350	200	7.6:1	4 BC	
*	8	400	170	8.0:1	2 BC	Auto
YH,YJ,AH	8	400	175	8.0:1	2 BC	Auto
Zh,ZJ	8	400	175	8.0:1	2 BC	Auto
	8	400	190	8.0:1	2 BC	
*	8	400	200	8.0:1	4 BC	Auto
WT	8	400	200	8.0:1	4 BC	3-Spd
YT,AT	8	400	200	8.0:1	4 BC	Auto
ZT,YZ	8	400	200	8.0:1	4 BC	Auto
	8	400	225	8.0:1	4 BC	
*	8	455	215	8.0:1	4 BC	Auto
YY,YU,YX	8	455	215	8.0:1	4 BC	Auto
AU,ZU,ZX	8	455	215	8.0:1	4 BC	Auto
YW,ZW,YR	8	455	215	8.0:1	4 BC	Auto
	8	455	250	8.0:1	4 BC	
W8	8	455SD	290	8.4:1	4 BC	3-Spd
Y8	8	455SD	290	8.4:1	4 BC	Auto
*	8	455SD	310	8.4:1	4 BC	4-Spd/Auto

*California only

1975 PONTIAC FIREBIRD

1975 PONTIAC GRANDVILLE

1975 PONTIAC GRAND AM

1975 PONTIAC GRAND SAFARI STATION WAGON

1975 PONTIAC GRAND PRIX

1975 PONTIAC LEMANS

1975 PONTIAC ASTRE STATION WAGON

1975 PONTIAC VENTURA SPRINT

1975 PONTIAC BONNEVILLE

1975 PONTIAC CATALINA

VEHICLE IDENTIFICATION NUMBER

PONTIAC
2P49W5P324567

Located on the top of the dash on the driver's side and visible through the windshield from outside the car.

FIRST DIGIT: Identifies GM Division (2 is Pontiac)

SECOND DIGIT: Identifies the series

SERIES	CODE
Ventura S.J.	B
LeMans	D
LeMans Sport	F
Grand LeMans	G
Grand Am	H
Grand Prix	K
Catalina	L
Bonneville/Grand Safari	P
Grand Ville Brougham	R
Firebird	S
Firebird Esprit	T
Firebird Formula	U
Astre	V
Firebird Trans Am	W
Astre S.J.	X
Ventura	Y
Ventura Custom	Z

THIRD AND FOURTH DIGITS: Identify the body style

BODY STYLE	CODE
Notchback 2-Door Coupe	11
2-Door SW, 2-Seat	15
2-Door Hatchback Sedan	17
2-Door Sedan	27
4-Door Sedan (LeMans)	29
Grand Safari SW 2 Seat	35
2-Door Sedan (LeMans)	37
4-Door SW, 3-Seat	45
Sport Coupe	47
4-Door Sport Sedan	49
2-Door Sport Coupe	57
4-Door Sedan	69
2-Door Hatchback Coupe	77
Hardtop Coupe (Firebird)	87

FIFTH DIGIT: Identifies the engine

ENGINE	CODE
4-V 140 1 BC	A
4-V 140 2 BC	B
6-V 250	D
V-8-350 4 BC	E
V-8 260	F
V-8 350 2 BC	H
V-8 350 4 BC	J
V-8 350 2 BC	M
V-8 400 2 BC	R
V-8 400 4 BC	S
V-8 455	W

SIXTH DIGIT: Identifies the year 1975

SEVENTH DIGIT: Identifies the assembly plant

ASSEMBLY PLANT	CODE
Atlanta, GA	A
South Gate, CA	C
Framingham, MA	G
Van Nuys, CA	L
Norwood, OH	N
Pontiac, MI	P
Tarrytown, NY	T
Lordstown, OH	U
Willow Run, MI	W
Kansas City, KS	X
Oshawa, Ont., CAN	1

LAST SIX DIGITS: Represent the basic production numbers

BODY NUMBER PLATE

The body number plate is located on the firewall, just below the rear edge of the hood. This plate identifies the model year, car division, series, body style, body assembly plant, body numbers, trim combination, paint code and build date code.

```
              BODY BY FISHER
ST 75   2FS87   NOR 345677 BDY
TR 26WC                24 24 PNT
000 A51


GENERAL MOTORS CORPORATION CERTI-
FIES TO THE DEALER THAT THIS VEHICLE
CONFORMS TO ALL U.S., FEDERAL MOTOR
     VEHICLE SAFETY STANDARDS
APPLICABLE AT TIME OF MANUFACTURE.
```

Example:

75	Model Year (1975)
2	Car Division (Pontiac)
FS	Series (Firebird)
87	Style (2-Door Hardtop)
NOR	Body Assembly Plant (Norwood, OH)
345677	Production Sequence
26WC	Blue Vinyl Trim
24	Artic Blue Lower Body Color
24	Artic Blue Upper Body Color
000	Time Built Date
A51	Modular Seat Code

LEMANS	CODE
4-Door Sedan	AD29
SW, 2-Seat	AD35
2-Door	AD37
SW, 3-Seat	AD45

LEMANS SPORT	CODE
2-Door	AF37

*GT option available

GRAND LEMANS	CODE
4-Door	AG29
SW, 2-Seat	AG35
2-Door	AG37
SW, 3-Seat	AG45

GRAND AM	CODE
4-Door	AH29
2-Door	AH37

CATALINA	CODE
SW, 2-Seat	BL35
SW, 3-Seat	BL45
2-Door Hardtop	BL57
4-Door Sedan	BL69

BONNEVILLE	CODE
SW, 2-Seat	BP35
SW, 3-Seat	BP45
2-Door Hardtop	BP47
4-Door Hardtop	BP49

GRAND VILLE	CODE
2-Door Hardtop	BR47
4-Door Hardtop	BR49
Convertible	BR67

FIREBIRD	CODE
2-Door Coupe	FS87
Esprit	FT87
Formula	FU87
Trans Am	FW87

GRAND PRIX	CODE
2-Door	GK57
*LJ option available	
*SJ option available	

ASTRE	CODE
Station Wagon	HX15
Hatchback	HV77
Coupe	HV11
*Custom option available	
*GT option available	
*S option available	

ASTRE SJ	CODE
Station Wagon	HX15
Hatchback	HX77

VENTURA SJ	CODE
Hatchback Coupe	XB17
2-Door Coupe	XB27
4-Door Sedan	XB69

VENTURA	CODE
Hatchback Coupe	XY17
2-Door Coupe	XY27
4-Door Sedan	XY69
*Sprint option available	
*S option available	

VENTURA CUSTOM	CODE
Hatchback Coupe	XZ17
2-Door Coupe	XZ27
4-Door Sedan	XZ69

THE TRIM CODE furnishes the key to the interior color and material scheme.

LEMANS 4-DOOR SEDAN TRIM

COLOR	CLOTH	VINYL	LEATHER	CODE
Blue	•	•		26Cs
Blue	•	•		26Mc
Blue		•		26Vs
Blue		•		26Jc
Green		•		44Vs
Green		•		44Jc
Saddle	•	•		63Cs
Saddle	•	•		63Mc
Saddle		•		63Vs
Saddle		•		63Jc
Oxblood	•	•		73Mc
Oxblood		•		73Vs
Oxblood		•		73Jc
White		•		11Vs
White		•		11Jc

s Standard
c Custom

LEMANS STATION WAGON 2-SEAT TRIM

COLOR	CLOTH	VINYL	LEATHER	CODE
Blue		•		26Vs
Blue		•		26Yc
Green		•		44Vs
Green		•		44Yc
Saddle		•		63Vs
Saddle		•		63Yc
Oxblood		•		73Vs
Oxblood		•		73Yc
White		•		11Vs
White		•		11Yc

s Standard
c Custom

LEMANS 2-DOOR TRIM

COLOR	CLOTH	VINYL	LEATHER	CODE
Black	•	•		19C
Black		•		19V
Blue	•	•		26C
Blue		•		26V
Saddle	•	•		63C
Saddle		•		63V
Green		•		44V
Oxblood		•		73V
White		•		11V

LEMANS SW, 3-SEAT TRIM

COLOR	CLOTH	VINYL	LEATHER	CODE
Blue		•		26V
Green		•		44V
Saddle		•		63V
Oxblood		•		73V
White		•		11V

LEMANS SPORT 2-DOOR TRIM

COLOR	CLOTH	VINYL	LEATHER	CODE
Black		•		19W
Blue		•		26W
Green		•		44W
Saddle		•		63W
Oxblood		•		73W
White		•		11W

GRAND LEMANS 2-DR/4-DR TRIM

COLOR	CLOTH	VINYL	LEATHER	CODE
Blue	•	•		26E
Blue		•		26Y
Black		•		19Y
Green		•		44Y
Saddle	•	•		63E
Saddle		•		63Y
Oxblood	•	•		73E
Oxblood		•		73Y
White		•		11Y
Black		•		19Y+

+ 2-Door only

GRAND LEMANS SW 2-SEAT/3-SEAT TRIM

COLOR	CLOTH	VINYL	LEATHER	CODE
Blue		•		26Y
Green		•		44Y
Saddle		•		63Y
Oxblood		•		73Y
White		•		11Y

GRAND AM 2-DOOR/4-DOOR TRIM

COLOR	CLOTH	VINYL	LEATHER	CODE
Black	•			19G
Black		•		19Z+
Blue	•			26G
Blue		•		26Z
Green	•			44G
Green		•		44Z
Saddle	•			63G
Saddle		•		63Z
Oxblood	•			73G
Oxblood		•		73Z
White		•		11Z

+ 2-Door only

CATALINA SW 2-SEAT/3-SEAT TRIM

COLOR	CLOTH	VINYL	LEATHER	CODE
Blue		•		26V
Green		•		44V
Saddle		•		63V
Oxblood		•		73V

CATALINA 2-DOOR HT/4-DOOR SEDAN TRIM

COLOR	CLOTH	VINYL	LEATHER	CODE
Black	•	•		19Cs
Black	•	•		19Dc
Blue	•	•		26Cs
Blue	•	•		26Dc
Blue		•		26Vs
Blue		•		26Wc++
Green	•	•		44Cs
Green	•	•		44Dc
Green		•		44Vs
Green		•		44Wc+
Saddle	•	•		63Cs+
Saddle		•		63Vs
Saddle		•		63Wc
Oxblood	•	•		73Dc++
Oxblood		•		73Vs
Oxblood		•		73Wc+
White		•		11V+
White		•		11W+

+ 2-Door hardtop only
++4-Door sedan only

BONNEVILLE SW 2-SEAT/3-SEAT TRIM

COLOR	CLOTH	VINYL	LEATHER	CODE
Saddle	•	•		63G
Saddle		•		63Z
Blue		•		26Z
Green		•		44Z
Oxblood		•		73Z

BONNEVILLE 2-DOOR/4-DOOR HT TRIM

COLOR	CLOTH	VINYL	LEATHER	CODE
Black	•	•		19E
Blue	•	•		26E
Blue		•		26H+
Green	•	•		44E
Green		•		44H+
Saddle		•		63H
Oxblood	•	•		73E
Oxblood		•		73H++
White		•		11H++

+ 4-Door hardtop only
++ 2-Door hardtop Only

GRAND VILLE 2-DOOR/4-DOOR TRIM

COLOR	CLOTH	VINYL	LEATHER	CODE
Black	•	•		19B
Black		•		19Y+
Blue	•	•		26B
Saddle	•	•		63B
Saddle		•		63Y+
Oxblood	•	•		73B

+ Available on convertible also

FIREBIRD TRIM

COLOR	CLOTH	VINYL	LEATHER	CODE
Black		•		19Vs
Black		•		19Wc
Blue		•		26Wc
Saddle		•		63Vs
Saddle		•		63Wc
Oxblood		•		73Wc
White		•		11Vs
White		•		11Wc

s Standard
c Custom

GRAND PRIX TRIM

COLOR	CLOTH	VINYL	LEATHER	CODE
Black	•			19Bs
Black	•			19Nc
Black		•		19Hs
Green	•			44Bs
Green		•		44Hs
Saddle	•			63Bs
Saddle		•		63Hs
Oxblood	•			73Bs
Oxblood	•			73Nc
Oxblood		•		73Hs
Blue		•		26Hs
White		•		11Hs

s Standard
c Custom

ASTRE SW/HATCHBACK TRIM

COLOR	CLOTH	VINYL	LEATHER	CODE
Black	•	•		19E
Black		•		19Y
Saddle	•	•		63E
Saddle		•		63Y
Oxblood	•	•		73E
Oxblood		•		73Y
Sandstone		•		55Y
White		•		HY

ASTRE SJ SW/HATCHBACK TRIM

COLOR	CLOTH	VINYL	LEATHER	CODE
Black	•			19G
Blue	•			26G
Oxblood	•			63G

VENTURA SJ HATCHBACK/2-DOOR/4-DOOR TRIM

COLOR	CLOTH	VINYL	LEATHER	CODE
Black		•		19E
Saddle		•		63Z
Oxblood		•		73Z
White		•		11Z

VENTURA HATCHBACK/2-DOOR/4-DOOR TRIM

COLOR	CLOTH	VINYL	LEATHER	CODE
Black	•	•		19Cs
Black	•	•		19Dc
Black		•		19Wc
Sandstone	•	•		55Cs
Sandstone	•	•		55Dc
Blue		•		19Wc+
Saddle		•		63Wc
Saddle		•		63Vs++
Oxblood		•		73Wc+
White		•		11Vs+
White		•		11Wc

c Custom
s Standard
+ Not available on 4-Door sedan
++ Available on 4-Door sedan only

THE PAINT CODE furnishes the key to the paint colors used on the car. Two, two-digit codes indicate the bottom and top body colors respectively. NOTE: vinyl roof codes appear as a second set of digits.

COLOR	CODE
Cameo White	11
Sterling Silver	13
Graystone	15
Starlight Black	19
Arctic Blue	24
Bimini Blue	26
Stellar Blue	29
Gray	31
Burgundy	39
Lakemist Green	44
Augusta Green	45
Alpine Green	49
Carmel Beige	50
Sunstorm Yellow	51
Sandstone	55
Ginger Brown	58
Oxford Brown	59
Copper Mist	63
Persimmon	64
Fire Coral Bronze	66
Roman Red	72
Honduras Maroon	74
Buccaneer Red	75
Tampico Orange	80

VINYL ROOF COLORS

White	1
Black	2
Sandstone	3
Cordovan	4*
Green	5
Burgundy	6
Blue	7
Red	8*
Silver	9

* Not available on Catalina, Bonneville, Grand Ville Brougham and Grand Prix 2-Door Hardtop Coupes

CONVERTIBLE TOP COLORS

White	1
Black	2

ENGINE NUMBER

Two identification numbers are used on all Pontiac engines. One identifies the engine code letters and production number. The second is an engine vehicle identification number which identifies proper engine-chassis combinations. A Pontiac 6 engine is identified by a letter code stamped on the distributor mounting pad, at the right side of the block. A Pontiac V8 letter code is stamped below the engine production number on the front of the block, just below the right-hand cylinder head.

PONTIAC ENGINES

ENGINE CODE	NO. CYL.	CID	HORSE-POWER	COMP. RATIO	CARB	TRANS
BB	4	140	78	8.0:1	1 BC	3-Spd
BC	4	140	78	8.0:1	1 BC	Auto
AM,AS	4	140	87	8.0:1	2 BC	3-Spd
AR,AT	4	140	87	8.0:1	2 BC	Auto
CAM,CAW	4	140	87	8.0:1	2 BC	3-Spd
CBB,CBD	4	140	87	8.0:1	2 BC	3-Spd
CAR,CAU	4	140	87	8.0:1	2 BC	Auto
CBC,CBF	4	140	87	8.0:1	2 BC	Auto
CAS*	4	140	80	8.0:1	2 BC	3-Spd
CAT*	4	140	80	8.0:1	2 BC	Auto
JU	6	250	105	8.2:1	1 BC	3-Spd
JT,JL*	6	250	105	8.2:1	1 BC	Auto
QA,QD	8	260	110	8.5:1	2 BC	3-Spd
QE,QJ	8	260	110	8.5:1	2 BC	Auto
TE*,TJ*	8	260	110	8.5:1	2 BC	Auto
RI,RS	8	350	145	8.1:1	2 BC	Auto
RW,RX	8	350	165	8.0:1	4 BC	Auto
YA,YB	8	350	155	8.0:1	2 BC	Auto
WN	8	350	175	8.0:1	4 BC	Auto
YN	8	350	175	8.0:1	4 BC	3-Spd
ZP*	8	350	175	8.0:1	4 BC	Auto
RN*,RO*	8	350	175	8.1:1	4 BC	Auto
YH*	8	400	170	7.6:1	2 BC	Auto
YT,YM,YS	8	400	185	7.6:1	4 BC	Auto
WT	8	400	185	7.6:1	4 BC	3-Spd
ZT*	8	400	185	7.6:1	4 BC	Auto
YW,YU	8	455	200	7.6:1	4 BC	Auto
ZU*,ZW*	8	455	200	7.6:1	4 BC	Auto
WX	8	455	200	7.6:1	4 BC	

*California

1976 PONTIAC ASTRE

1976 PONTIAC GRAND LeMANS

1976 PONTIAC BONNEVILLE

1976 PONTIAC CATALINA

1976 PONTIAC FIREBIRD

1976 PONTIAC LEMANS

1976 PONTIAC SUNBIRD

1976 PONTIAC GRAND PRIX

1976 PONTIAC VENTURA

1976 PONTIAC ASTRE STATION WAGON

VEHICLE IDENTIFICATION NUMBER

PONTIAC
2P49W6P324568

Located on the top of the dash on the driver's side and visible through the windshield from outside the car.

FIRST DIGIT: Identifies GM Division (2 is Pontiac)

SECOND DIGIT: Identifies the series

SERIES	CODE
Astre	C
LeMans	D
LeMans Sport	F
Grand LeMans	G
Grand Prix	J
Grand Prix SJ	K
Catalina	L
Sunbird	M
Bonneville/Grand Safari	P
Bonneville Brougham	R
Firebird	S
Firebird Esprit	T
Firebird Formula	U
Firebird Trans Am	W
Ventura	Y
Ventura SJ	Z

THIRD AND FOURTH DIGITS: Identify the body style

BODY STYLE	CODE
2-Door Notchback Coupe	11
2-Door SW 2-Seat	15
2-Door Hatchback Sedan	17
2-Door Sedan (Ventura)	27
2-Dr. Notchback Coupe (Sunbird)	27
4-Door Sedan (LeMans)	29
SW, 2-Seat	35
2-Door Sedan (LeMans)	37
2-Door Sport Coupe	47
4-Door Sport Sedan	49
2-Door Sport Coupe	57
4-Door Sedan	69
2-Door Hatchback Coupe	77
Hardtop Coupe (Firebird)	87

FIFTH DIGIT: Identifies the engine

ENGINE	CODE
4V-140 1 BC	A
4V-140 2 BC	B
V6-231	C
L6-250	D
V8-350 4 BC	E
V8-260 2 BC	F
V8-350 2 BC	H
V8-350 4 BC	J
V8-350 2 BC	M
V8-400 2 BC	R
V8-400 4 BC	S
V8-455	W

SIXTH DIGIT: Identifies the year 1976

SEVENTH DIGIT: Identifies the assembly plant

ASSEMBLY PLANT	CODE
Atlanta, GA	A
South Gate, CA	C
Framingham, MA	G
Van Nuys, CA	L
Norwood, OH	N
Pontiac, MI	P
Tarrytown, NY	T
Lordstown, OH	U
Willow Run, MI	W
Kansas City, KS	X
St. Therese, Que., CAN	2

LAST SIX DIGITS: Represent the basic production numbers

BODY NUMBER PLATE

The body number plate is located on the firewall, just below the rear edge of the hood. This plate identifies the model year, car division, series, body style, body assembly plant, body numbers, trim combination, paint code and build date code.

BODY BY FISHER
ST 76 2FS87 N   345677 BDY
TR 19M   19 19 PNT
000 A51

GENERAL MOTORS CORPORATION CERTIFIES TO THE DEALER THAT THIS VEHICLE CONFORMS TO ALL U.S., FEDERAL MOTOR VEHICLE SAFETY STANDARDS APPLICABLE AT TIME OF MANUFACTURE.

Example:

76	Model Year (1976)
2	Car Division (Pontiac)
FS	Series (Firebird)
87	Style (2-Door Hardtop)
N	Body Assembly Plant (Norwood, OH)
345677	Production Sequence
19M	BLack Cloth Trim
19	Starlight Black Lower Body Color
19	Starlight Black Upper Body Color
000	Time Built Date
A51	Modular Seat Code

LEMANS	CODE
4-Door Hardtop	AD29
Station Wagon	AD35
2-Door Hardtop	AD37

LEMANS SPORT	CODE
Coupe	AF37

GRAND LEMANS	CODE
4-Door	AG29
SW, 2-Seat	AG35
2-Door	AG37

CATALINA	CODE
SW, 2-Seat	BL35
2-Door	BL57
4-Door Sedan	BL69

BONNEVILLE	CODE
SW, 3-Seat	BP35
2-Door Hardtop	BP47
4-Door Hardtop	BP49

BONNEVILLE BROUGHAM	CODE
2-Door	BR47
4-Door	BR49

FIREBIRD	CODE
2-Door Coupe	FS87
Esprit	FT87
Formula	FU87
Trans Am	FW87

*Trans Am Limited Edition option available

GRAND PRIX	CODE
2-Door Hardtop	GJ57
SJ 2-Door Hardtop	GK57

*Golden Anniversary option available
*SJ option available
*LJ option available

ASTRE	CODE
Notchback	HC11
Station Wagon	HC15
Hatchback	HC77

*GT option available

SUNBIRD	CODE
2-Door Notchback Coupe	HM27

*Formula option available

VENTURA	CODE
Hatchback Coupe	XY17
2-Door Coupe	XY27
4-Door Sedan	XY69

VENTURA SJ	CODE
Hatchback Coupe	XZ17
2-Door Coupe	XZ27
4-Door Sedan	XZ69

THE TRIM CODE furnishes the key to the interior color and material scheme.

LEMANS TRIM

COLOR	CLOTH	VINYL	LEATHER	CODE
White	•			11M/11V
White				11W/11Y
Black		•		19B/19C
Black				19D/19E
Black	•			91M/91N
Black	•			91V
Black				19V/91W
Black				19Y
Black				91Y
Blue		•		26B/26C
Blue		•		26D
Blue	•			26M/92M
Blue				26N
Blue				92N/26V
Blue				92V
Blue				26W/92W
Blue				26Y

		COLOR	CODE
		Blue	92Y
•		Buckskin	64M/64N
•		Buckskin	64V
		Buckskin	64W/64Y
	•	Buckskin	64E/64J
	•	Buckskin	643
•		Firethorn	71M/97M
•		Firethorn	71N
		Firethorn	97N/71V
		Firethorn	97V
		Firethorn	71W/97W
		Firethorn	71Y
		Firethorn	97Y/
	•	Firethorn	71C/71D
	•	Firethorn	71E
•		Mahogany	98Y
	•	Mahogany	74J/743

CATALINA TRIM

COLOR	CLOTH	VINYL	LEATHER	CODE
White	•			11M/110
White	•			11V
Black			•	19B/19D
Black			•	19E
Black				19G
Black	•			19M
Blue			•	26B/26D
Blue			•	26E
Blue				26G
Blue	•			26M/92M
Blue	•			260
Blue				920/26V
Blue				92V
Blue				92W
Buckskin			•	64B/64D
Buckskin			•	64E
Buckskin				64G
Buckskin	•			64M/640
Buckskin	•			64V
Buckskin				64W
Mahogany			•	74B/74D
Mahogany			•	74E
Mahogany				74G
Mahogany	•			74M/98M
Mahogany	•			740
Mahogany				980/74V
Mahogany				98V
Mahogany				98W/74W

BONNEVILLE TRIM

COLOR	CLOTH	VINYL	LEATHER	CODE
White	•			11M/110
White	•			11V
Black			•	19B/19D
Black			•	19E
Black				19G
Black	•			19M
Blue			•	26B/26D
Blue			•	26E
Blue				26G
Blue	•			26M/92M
Blue	•			260
Blue				920/26V
Blue				92V
Blue				92W
Buckskin			•	64B/64D
Buckskin				64E
Buckskin				64G
Buckskin	•			64M/640
Buckskin	•			64V
Buckskin				64W
Mahogany			•	74B/74D

Mahogany				74E
Mahogany				74G
Mahogany	•			74M/98M
Mahogany	•			740
Mahogany				980/74V
Mahogany				98V
Mahogany				98W/74W

FIREBIRD TRIM

COLOR	CLOTH	VINYL	LEATHER	CODE
White	•			11M/11N
Black	•			19M/91M
Black	•			19N
Black				91N
Blue	•			26N/92N
Buckskin	•			64M/64N
Firethorn	•			71N/97N

VENTURA TRIM

COLOR	CLOTH	VINYL	LEATHER	CODE
White	•			11M/11V
White				11N/11W
Black		•		19B/19E
Black		•		19C
Black				19D
Blue	•			26M/92M
Blue	•			92V
Blue			•	26B
Buckskin	•			64M/64V
Buckskin	•			64N
Buckskin				64W
Firethorn	•			97M/71V
Firethorn	•			97V
Firethorn				71N/71W
Firethorn				97W
Firethorn			•	71D

GRAND PRIX TRIM

COLOR	CLOTH	VINYL	LEATHER	CODE
White	•			110/11Z
Black			•	198/19G
Black			•	19H
Black	•			91Z/19Z
Blue	•			260/92Z
Blue	•			26Z
Blue			•	268
Buckskin	•			640/64Z
Buckskin			•	64G/64H
Buckskin			•	642
Firethorn	•			710/71Z
Firethorn	•			91Z
Firethorn			•	718/71G
Mahogany			•	74H/742

ASTRE TRIM

COLOR	CLOTH	VINYL	LEATHER	CODE
White	•			11V/11Z
Black			•	19B/19E
Black			•	19G
Black	•			19V/91V
Black	•			19W
Black				19Z/91Z
Black			•	19M
Blue	•			26V/O2V
Blue	•			92V
Blue				26Z/O2Z
Blue				92Z
Lime	•			O3Z
Buckskin		•		64M
Buckskin	•			64V/64W
Buckskin				64Z
Firethorn			•	71B/71E
Firethorn			•	71G
Firethorn		•		71M
Firethorn	•			71V/O7V
Firethorn	•			97V
Firethorn				71Z/O7Z
Firethorn				97Z

THE PAINT CODE furnishes the key to the paint colors used on the car. Two, two-digit codes indicate the bottom and top body colors respectively. NOTE: vinyl roof codes appear as a second set of digits.

COLOR	CODE
Cameo White	11
Sterling Silver	13
Medium Gray	16
Starlight Black	19
Athena Blue	28
Polaris Blue	35
Firethorn Red	36
Cordovan Maroon	37
Metalime Green	40
Alpine Green	49
Bavarian Cream	50
Goldenrod Yellow	51
Anniversary Gold	55
Cream Gold	57
Buckskin Tan	65
Durango Bronze	67
Roman Red	72
Carousel Red	78

ENGINE NUMBER

Two identification numbers are used on all Pontiac engines. One identifies the engine code letters and production number. The second is an engine vehicle identification number which identifies proper engine-chassis combinations. A Pontiac 6 engine is identified by a letter code stamped on the distributor mounting pad, at the right side of the block. A Pontiac V8 letter code is stamped below the engine production number on front of the block, just below the right-hand cylinder head.

PONTIAC ENGINES

ENGINE CODE	NO. CYL.	CID	HORSE-POWER	COMP. RATIO	CARB	TRANS
CBH	4	140	70	8.0:1	1 BC	3-Spd
CBJ	4	140	70	8.0:1	1 BC	Auto
CBS,CBK*	4	140	80	8.0:1	2 BC	3-Spd
CBT,CBL*	4	140	80	8.0:1	2 BC	Auto
	4	140	87	8.0:1	2 BC	
CBW,CBX	4	140		8.0:1		3-Spd
CBU,CCM	4	140		8.0:1		Auto
CBZ,CAY	4	140		8.0:1		3-Spd
CBY*,CAZ*	4	140		8.0:1		3-Spd
FI,FK	6	231	110	8.0:1	2 BC	Auto
FJ*	6	231	110	8.0:1	2 BC	Auto
FH,FM	6	231	110	8.0:1	2 BC	3-Spd
FO*	6	231	110	8.0:1	2 BC	3-Spd
CD,CJ	6	250	105	8.2:1	1 BC	3-Spd
CL*	6	250	105	8.2:1	1 BC	3-Spd
CF,CH	6	250	105	8.2:1	1 BC	Auto
CC*	6	250	105	8.2:1	1 BC	Auto
QA,QD	8	260	110	7.5:1	2 BC	3-Spd
TA*,TD*	8	260	110	7.5:1	2 BC	3-Spd
TE*,TJ*	8	260	110	7.5:1	2 BC	3-Spd
QB,QC	8	260	110	7.5:1	2 BC	Auto
Q7,Q8*	8	260	110	7.5:1	2 BC	Auto
T2*,T3*	8	260	110	7.5:1	2 BC	Auto
T7*,T8*	8	260	110	7.5:1	2 BC	Auto
QK,QN	8	260	110	7.5:1	2 BC	3-Spd
TK*,TP*	8	260	110	7.5:1	2 BC	3-Spd
TP*,TT*	8	260	110	7.5:1	2 BC	3-Spd
QP,QT	8	260	110	7.5:1	2 BC	Auto
T4*,T5*	8	260	110	7.5:1	2 BC	Auto
YA,YK,YP	8	350	160	7.6:1	2 BC	Auto
YL,YB,YR	8	350	160	7.6:1	2 BC	Auto
ZW,ZH,XH	8	350	160	7.6:1	2 BC	Auto
XN	8	350	160	7.6:1	2 BC	Auto
PA,PB,PO	8	350#	140	8.0:1	2 BC	Auto
XD,XR,XU	8	350	165	7.6:1	4 BC	Auto
XW,XX	8	350	165	7.6:1	4 BC	Auto
ZX*,ZC*	8	350	165	7.6:1	4 BC	Auto
PE,PF,PP	8	350#	155	8.0:1	4 BC	Auto
XB,XD,XM	8	350	165	7.6:1	4 BC	Auto
PM*,PN*	8	350#	155	8.0:1	4 BC	Auto
YC,YJ,XZ	8	400	170	7.6:1	2 BC	Auto
Y6,Y7,X9	8	400	185	7.6:1	4 BC	Auto
YT,YY,XS	8	400	185	7.6:1	4 BC	Auto
Y9,YS,YZ	8	400	185	7.6:1	4 BC	Auto
ZL,ZJ,XA	8	400	185	7.6:1	4 BC	
XC,XJ,Z8	8	400	185	7.6:1	4 BC	
WU,X4,X6	8	400	185	7.6:1	4 BC	3-Spd
X7	8	400	185	7.6:1	4 BC	
ZA*,ZK*	8	400	185	7.6:1	4 BC	Auto
Y8,Y3	8	455	200	7.6:1	4 BC	Auto
Y3,Y4	8	455	200	7.6:1	4 BC	Auto
Z6*,Z3*	8	455	200	7.6:1	4 BC	Auto
Z4*	8	455	200	7.6:1	4 BC	Auto

\# Ventura only
* California

1977 PONTIAC LEMANS

1977 PONTIAC ASTRE

1977 PONTIAC GRAND LEMANS

1977 PONTIAC BONNEVILLE

1977 PONTIAC SUNBIRD

1977 PONTIAC VENTURA

1977 PONTIAC FIREBIRD

1977 PONTIAC CATALINA

1977 PONTIAC GRAND PRIX

1977 PONTIAC GRAND SAFARI STATION WAGON

VEHICLE IDENTIFICATION NUMBER

PONTIAC 2J57R7P300039

Located on the top of the dash on the driver's side and visible through the windshield from outside the car.

FIRST DIGIT: Identifies GM Division (2 is Pontiac)

SECOND DIGIT: Identifies the series

SERIES	CODE
Astre	C
LeMans, LeMans Safari	D
LeMans Sport	F
Grand LeMans	G
Grand Prix SJ	H
Grand Prix	J
Grand Prix LJ	K
Catalina or Safari	L
Sunbird	M
Bonneville or Grand Safari	N
Bonneville Brougham	Q
Firebird	S
Firebird Esprit	T
Firebrid Formula	U
Firebird Trans Am	W
Phoenix	X
Ventura	Y
Ventura SJ	Z

THIRD AND FOURTH DIGITS: Identify the body style

BODY STYLE	CODE
2-Door Hatchback Coupe	07
2-Door Notchback Coupe	11
2-Door SW, 2-Seat	15
2-Door Hatchback Sedan	17
2-Door Notchback Coupe	27
4-Door Sedan (LeMans)	29
SW, 2-Seat (Safari)	35
2-Door Sport Coupe	37
2-Door Coupe (Grand Prix)	57
4-Door Sedan	69
Hardtop Coupe (Firebird)	87

FIFTH DIGIT: Identifies the engine

ENGINE	CODE
V4-140	B
V6-231	C
V8-403	K
V8-350	L
V8-350	P
V8-350	R
V8-305	U
V4-151	V
V8-301	Y
V8-400	Z

SIXTH DIGIT: Identifies the year 1977

SEVENTH DIGIT: Identifies the assembly plant

ASSEMBLY PLANT	CODE
Atlanta, GA	A
Southgate, CA	C
Framingham, MA	G
Leeds, MO	K
Van Nuys, CA	L

ASSEMBLY PLANT	CODE
Norwood, OH	N
Pontiac, MI	P
Tarrytown, NY	T
Lordstown, OH	U
Willow Run, MI	W
Kansas City, KS	X
Oshawa, CAN	1
St. Therese, Que., CAN	2

LAST SIX DIGITS: Represent the basic production numbers

BODY NUMBER PLATE

The body number plate is located on the firewall, just below the rear edge of the hood. This plate identifies the model year, car division, series, body style, body assembly plant, body numbers, trim combination, paint code and build date code.

BODY BY FISHER

ST 77 2FS87 N   345677 BDY
TR 19B   19 19 PNT
000 A51

GENERAL MOTORS CORPORATION CERTI- FIES TO THE DEALER THAT THIS VEHICLE CONFORMS TO ALL U.S., FEDERAL MOTOR VEHICLE SAFETY STANDARDS APPLICABLE AT TIME OF MANUFACTURE.

Example:

77	Model Year (1977)
2	Car Division (Pontiac)
FS	Series (Firebird)
87	Style (2-Door Hardtop)
N	Body Assembly Plant (Norwood, OH)
345677	Production Sequence
19B	BLack Cloth & Vinyl Trim
19	Starlight Black Lower Body Color
19	Starlight Black Upper Body Color
000	Time Built Date
A51	Modular Seat Code

LEMANS	CODE
4-Door Hardtop	AD29
Station Wagon	AD35
2-Door Hardtop	AD37

LEMANS SPORT	CODE
Coupe	AF37

*GT option available
*Can AM option available

GRAND LEMANS	CODE
4-Door Hardtop	AG29
Station Wagon	AG35
2-Door Hardtop	AG37

GRAND PRIX SJ	CODE
2-Door Hardtop Coupe	GH57
Grand Prix	GJ57
Grand Prix LJ	GK57

CATALINA

	CODE
Station Wagon	BL35
2-Door Hardtop	BL37
4-Door Sedan	BL69

BONNEVILLE

	CODE
Station Wagon	BN35
2-Door Hardtop	BN37
4-Door Sedan	BN69

BONNEVILLE BROUGHAM

	CODE
2-Door Hardtop	BQ37
4-Door Hardtop	BQ69

FIREBIRD

	CODE
Std. 2-Door Hardtop Coupe	FS87
Esprit	FT87
Formula	FU87
Trans Am	FW87

*Trans Am Special Edition option available

ASTRE

	CODE
Notchback Coupe	HC11
Station Wagon	HC15
Hatchback Coupe	HC77

*Formula option available

SUNBIRD

	CODE
Hatchback Coupe	HM07
Notchback Coupe	HM27

*Formula option available

VENTURA

	CODE
2-Door Hatchback Coupe	XY17
2-Door Coupe	XY27
4-Door Sedan	XY69

VENTURA SJ

	CODE
2-Door Hatchback Coupe	XZ17
2-Door Coupe	XZ27
4-Door Sedan	XZ69

PHOENIX

	CODE
2-Door	XZ27
4-Door	XZ69

THE TRIM CODE furnishes the key to the interior color and material scheme.

LEMANS 4-DOOR HT TRIM

COLOR	CLOTH	VINYL	LEATHER	CODE
Black	•	•		19B/197
Black	•			19C#
Black		•		19R*
Black		•		19N#
Blue	•	•		24B/247
Blue	•			24C#
Blue		•		24R*
Blue		•		24N#
Buckskin		•		64R/64R*
Buckskin		•		64N#
Buckskin	•	•		64C#
Firethorn		•		71R/71R*
Firethorn		•		71N#
Firethorn	•	•		71C#

*Bucket seats
#Notch back or 60-40 seats

LEMANS STATION WAGON TRIM

COLOR	CLOTH	VINYL	LEATHER	CODE
Blue		•		24R/24Y
Blue		•		24N#
Blue		•		24W*#
Buckskin		•		64R/64Y
Buckskin		•		64N#
Buckskin		•		64W*#
Firethorn		•		71R/71Y
Firethorn		•		71N#
Firethorn		•		71W*#

*Bucket seats
#Notch back or 60-40 seats

LEMANS 2-DOOR HT TRIM

COLOR	CLOTH	VINYL	LEATHER	CODE
White		•		11R*/11R
White		•		11N#
Black	•	•		19B/197
Black	•			19C#
Black		•		19R/19R*
Black		•		19N#
Blue	•	•		24B/247
Blue		•		24C#
Blue		•		92R/92R*
Blue		•		24N#
Blue		•		92N#
Buckskin		•		64R*/64R
Buckskin	•	•		64C#
Buckskin		•		64N#
Firethorn		•		71R*/71R
Firethorn		•		97R/97R*
Firethorn	•	•		71C#
Firethorn		•		71N#

*Bucket seats
#Notch back or 60-40 seats

GRAND LEMANS TRIM

COLOR	CLOTH	VINYL	LEATHER	CODE
White+		•		11W*#
Black	•	•		19D#
Black	•	•		19J*#
Black		•		19W*#
Blue	•	•		24D#
Blue		•		35J*#
Blue		•		24W*#
Blue		•		92W*#
Buckskin	•	•		64D#
Buckskin	•	•		64J*#
Buckskin		•		64W*#
Firethorn	•	•		71D#
Firethorn	•	•		71J*#
Firethorn		•		71W*#
Firethorn		•		97W*#

*Bucket seats
#Notch back or 60-40 seats
+ 2-Door hardtop only

CATALINA TRIM

COLOR	CLOTH	VINYL	LEATHER	CODE
White+		•		11R
Black	•	•		19B
Blue	•	•		24B
Blue		•		24R/92R
Blue		•		24Z/24Z#
Buckskin		•		64B/64D
Buckskin		•		64R/64Z
BUckskin		•		64Z#
Firethorn	•	•		71B
Firethorn		•		71R/97R
Firethorn		•		71Z/71Z#

#Notch back or 60-40 seats   + 2-Door hardtop only

BONNEVILLE STATION WAGON TRIM

COLOR	CLOTH	VINYL	LEATHER	CODE
Blue		•		24V/24V#
Sage Green		•		44V/44V#
Buckskin	•	•		64E/64E#
Buckskin		•		64V/64V#
Firethorn		•		71V/71V#

#Notch back or 60-40 seats

BONNEVILLE 2-DOOR/4-DOOR TRIM

COLOR	CLOTH	VINYL	LEATHER	CODE
White		•		11V#
White		•		11W#
Black	•	•		19E/19E#
Black	•	•		19G#
Blue	•	•		24E/24E#
Blue	•	•		24G#
Blue		•		24V/24V#
Blue		•		92V/92V#
Sage Green	•	•		44G#
Sage Green		•		44V/44V#
Sage Green		•		94V/94V#
Buckskin	•	•		64E/64E#
Buckskin	•	•		64G#
Buckskin	•	•		64H#
Buckskin		•		64V/64V#
Buckskin		•		64W#
Firethorn	•	•		71E/71E#
Firethorn	•	•		71G#
Firethorn		•		71V/71V#
Firethorn		•		97V/97V#

#Notch back or 60-40 seats

FIREBIRD TRIM

COLOR	CLOTH	VINYL	LEATHER	CODE
White		•		11R*
White		•		11N*
Black		•		19R*
Black		•		19N*
Black	•	•		19B*
Blue	•	•		24B*
Blue		•		24N*
Blue		•		92N*
Buckskin		•		64N*
Buckskin		•		64R*
Firethorn	•	•		71B*
Firethorn		•		71R*
Firethorn		•		71N*
Firethorn		•		97R*
Firethorn		•		97N*

*Bucket seats

GRAND PRIX TRIM

COLOR	CLOTH	VINYL	LEATHER	CODE
White		•		11V*#
White		•		11Z*
Black	•	•		19E*#
Black	•	•		19G*
Black	•	•		19H*#
Black			•	192*
Black		•		19V*#
Black		•		19Z*
Blue	•	•		24E*#
Blue	•	•		24G*
Blue	•	•		24H*#
Blue		•		24V*#

COLOR	CLOTH	VINYL	LEATHER	CODE
Blue		•		24Z*
Blue		•		92Z*#
Sage Green		•		44V*#
Sage Green		•		94V*#
Buckskin	•	•		64E*#
Buckskin	•	•		64G*
Buckskin	•	•		64H*#
Buckskin		•		64V*#
Buckskin		•		64Z*
Firethorn	•	•		71E*#
Firethorn	•	•		71G*#
Firethorn	•	•		71H*#
Firethorn		•		71V*#
Firethorn		•		97V*#
Firethorn		•		71Z*#
Firethorn		•		97Z*#

*Bucket seats
#Notch back or 60-40 seats

ASTRE TRIM

COLOR	CLOTH	VINYL	LEATHER	CODE
White		•		11W*
White		•		11V*
Black		•		19R*
Black		•		19W*
Black	•	•		19C*
Black	•	•		19D*
Buckskin		•		64R*
Buckskin		•		64W*
Buckskin		•		06W*
Buckskin		•		64V*
Buckskin		•		06V*
Firethorn	•	•		71D*
Firethorn	•	•		71C*
Firethorn		•		71W*
Firethorn		•		07W*
Firethorn		•		97W*
Firethorn		•		07W*
Firethorn		•		97V*
Firethorn		•		07V*
Aqua		•		03W*
Aqua		•		03V*

*Bucket seats

SUNBIRD TRIM

COLOR	CLOTH	VINYL	LEATHER	CODE
White		•		11N*
White		•		11Z*
Black	•	•		19H*
Black	•	•		19G*
Black		•		19N*
Buckskin		•		64N*
Buckskin		•		06N*
Buckskin		•		64Z*
Buckskin		•		06Z*
Firethorn	•	•		71H*
Firethorn	•	•		71G*
Firethorn		•		71N*
Firethorn		•		97N*
Firethorn		•		07N*
Firethorn		•		07Z*
Firethorn			•	972*
Aqua		•		03N*
Aqua		•		03Z*

*Bucket seats

VENTURA TRIM

COLOR	CLOTH	VINYL	LEATHER	CODE
White		•		11R/11R*
White		•		11N/11N#
Black	•	•		19E/19B
Black	•	•		19C#
Black		•		19R/19R*
Blue	•	•		24E/24B
Blue	•	•		24C#
Blue		•		24R/24R*
Blue		•		92R/94R*
Buckskin		•		64R/64R*
Buckskin		•		64N/64N*
Firethorn	•	•		71C/71C#
Firethorn		•		71R/71R*
Firethorn		•		71N/71N#

*Bucket seats
#Notch back or 60-40 seats

VENTURA SJ TRIM

COLOR	CLOTH	VINYL	LEATHER	CODE
White		•		11V
White		•		11V*#
Black	•	•		19D
Black	•	•		19D*#
Blue	•	•		24D
Blue	•	•		24D*#
Blue		•		92V
Blue		•		92V*#
Buckskin		•		64V
Buckskin		•		64V*#
Firethorn	•	•		71D
Firethorn	•	•		71D*#
Firethorn		•		71V
Firethorn		•		71V*#
Firethorn		•		97V
Firethorn		•		97V*#

*Bucket seats
#Notch back or 60-40 seats

THE PAINT CODE furnishes the key to the paint colors used on the car. Two, two-digit codes indicate the bottom and top body colors respectively. NOTE: vinyl roof codes appear as a second set of digits.

COLOR	CODE
Cameo White	11
Sterling Silver	13
Gray	15
Starlight Black	19
Lombard Blue	21
Glacier Blue	22
Nautilus Blue	29
Royal Lime	32
Firethorn Red	36
Cordovan Maroon	37
Aquamarine	38
Bahia Green	44
Berkshire Green	48
Cream Gold	50
Goldenrod Yellow	51
Mojave Tan	61
Buckskin	63
Fiesta Orange	64
Brentwood Brown	69
Roman Red	72
Buccaneer Red	75
Mandarin Orange	78

VINYL ROOF COLORS

	CODE
White	11T
Silver	13T
Black	19T
Light Blue	22T
Firethorn	36T
Medium Green	44T
Light Buckskin	61T

ENGINE NUMBER

Two identification numbers are used on all Pontiac engines. One identifies the engine code letters and production number. The second is an engine vehicle identification number which identifies proper engine-chassis combinations. A Pontiac 6 engine is identified by a letter code stamped on the distributor mounting pad, at the right side of the block. A Pontiac V8 letter code is stamped below the engine production number on front of the block, just below the right-hand cylinder head.

ENGINE CODE	NO. CYL.	CID	HORSE-POWER	COMP. RATIO	CARB	TRANS
CBS,CBZ	4	140	84	8.0:1	2 BC	3-Spd
CAY,CAK	4	140	84	8.0:1	2 BC	3-Spd
CBT,CBU	4	140	84	8.0:1	2 BC	Auto
CBK*,CBY*	4	140	79	8.0:1	2 BC	3-Spd
CAZ*,CBW	4	140	79	8.0:1	2 BC	5-Spd
CBL*,CBX	4	140	79	8.0:1	2 BC	Auto
CAA,CAC	4	140		8.0:1	2 BC	3-Spd
CAB	4	140		8.0:1	2 BC	Auto
WC#,WD#	4	151	87	8.3:1	2 BC	3-Spd
YL#,YM#	4	151	87	8.3:1	2 BC	Auto
WF,WH,ZF	4	151	87	8.3:1	2 BC	3-Spd
YR,YS,ZD	4	151	87	8.3:1	2 BC	Auto
ZJ#*,ZH#*	4	151	88	8.3:1	2 BC	Auto
ZP*,ZN*	4	151	88	8.3:1	2 BC	Auto
SA,SG	6	231	105	8.0:1	2 BC	3-Spd
SD,SI,SJ	6	231	105	8.0:1	2 BC	Auto
SB*,SU*	6	231	110	8.0:1	2 BC	3-Spd
SY*,SK*	6	231	110	8.0:1	2 BC	Auto
SL*	6	231	110	8.0:1	2 BC	Auto
SM,SN,SX	6	231	105	8.0:1	2 BC	Auto
ST,SO,SB	6	231	105	8.0:1	2 BC	
YW,YX	8	301	135	8.2:1	2 BC	Auto
YH,YK	8	301	135	8.2:1	2 BC	Auto
WB,HK	8	301	135	8.2:1	2 BC	3-Spd
CPY,CPR	8	305	145	8.5:1	2 BC	Auto
CPA	8	305	145	8.5:1	2 BC	
CEB*,CED*	8	305	145	8.5:1	2 BC	Auto
YA,YB	8	350	170	8.5:1	4 BC	Auto
XB,XC,Y9	8	350	170	8.5:1	4 BC	Auto
QP,QQ	8	350	170	8.5:1	4 BC	Auto
TN,TO,TK	8	350*	170	8.5:1	4 BC	Auto
TL,TS,TT	8	350*	170	8.5:1	4 BC	Auto
TX,TY	8	350*	170	8.5:1	4 BC	Auto
YG,YC,YD	8	350	170	8.5:1	4 BC	
CKR	8	350*	170	8.5:1	4 BC	Auto
CKM	8	350	170	8.5:1	4 BC	Auto
Q2,Q3,Q6	8	350	170	8.5:1	4 BC	Auto
Q7,Q8,Q9	8	350	170	8.5:1	4 BC	Auto
Q4,Q5	8	350	170	8.5:1	4 BC	Auto
WA	8	400	200	8.0:1	4 BC	3-Spd
XA,Y6	8	400	200	8.0:1	4 BC	Auto
XH,XJ,XD	8	400	180	7.6:1	4 BC	Auto
XF,YU,Y4	8	400	180	7.6:1	4 BC	Auto
Y7,XK	8	400	180	7.6:1	4 BC	Auto
UA,UB	8	403	185	8.0:1	4 BC	Auto
VA,VB	8	403*	185	8.0:1	4 BC	Auto
VJ,VK	8	403*	185	8.0:1	4 BC	Auto
U2,U3	8	403	185	8.0:1	4 BC	Auto

#Astre
*California

1978 PONTIAC GRAND AM

1978 PONTIAC LEMANS WAGON

1978 PONTIAC PHOENIX

1978 PONTIAC GRAND PRIX

1978 PONTIAC GRAND SAFARI WAGON

1978 PONTIAC SUNBIRD

1978 PONTIAC LEMANS

1978 PONTIAC BONNEVILLE

1978 PONTIAC FIREBIRD

1978 PONTIAC CATALINA

VEHICLE IDENTIFICATION NUMBER

PONTIAC 2U87L8L325678

Located on the top of the dash on the driver's side and visible through the windshield from outside the car.

FIRST DIGIT: Identifies GM Division (2 is Pontiac)

SECOND DIGIT: Identifies the series

SERIES	CODE
LeMans	D
Sunbird	E
Grand LeMans	F
Grand Am	G
Grand Prix SJ	H
Grand Prix	J
Grand Prix LJ	K
Catalina	L
Sunbird Sport	M
Bonneville/Grand Safari	N
Bonneville Brougham	Q
Firebird	S
Firebird Esprit	T
Firebird Formula	U
Firebird Trans Am	W
Phoenix	Y
Phoenix LJ	Z

THIRD AND FOURTH DIGITS: Identify the body style

BODY STYLE	CODE
2-Door Hatchback Coupe	07
2-Door Sport Safari SW	15
2-Door Hatchback	17
4-Door Notchback Sedan	19
2-Door Notchback Sedan	27
4-Door Grand Safari SW	35
2-Door Notchback Sport Coupe	37
4-Door Notchback Pillar Sedan	69
2-Door Hardtop Coupe (Firebird)	87

FIFTH DIGIT: Identifies the engine

ENGINE	CODE
4V-151	1
V6-231	A
V8-305	H
V8-403	K
V8-350	L
V8-350	R
V8-305	U
V4-151	V
V8-301	W
V8-350	X
V8-301	Y
V8-400	Z

SIXTH DIGIT: Identifies the year 1978

SEVENTH DIGIT: Identifies the assembly plant

ASSEMBLY PLANT	CODE
Atlanta, GA (Lakewood)	A
Baltimore, MD	B
South Gate, CA	C
Doraville, GA	D
Linden, NJ	E
Framingham, MA	G
Janesville, WI	J
Leeds, MO	K
Van Nuys, CA	L
Lansing, MI	M
Norwood, OH	N
Pontiac, MI	P
Detroit, MI	Q
Arlington, TX	R
St. Louis, MO	S
Tarrytown, NY	T
Lordstown, OH	U
Willow Run, MI	W
Fairfax, KS	X
Wilmington, DE	Y
Fremont, CA	Z
Oshawa, Ont., CAN	1
St. Therese, Que., CAN	2

LAST SIX DIGITS: Represent the basic production numbers

BODY NUMBER PLATE

The body number plate is located on the firewall, just below the rear edge of the hood. This plate identifies the model year, car division, series, body style, body assembly plant, body numbers, trim combination, paint code and build date code.

BODY BY FISHER
ST 78   2FS87 N   345677 BDY
TR 19B   19 19 PNT
000 A51

GENERAL MOTORS CORPORATION CERTIFIES TO THE DEALER THAT THIS VEHICLE CONFORMS TO ALL U.S., FEDERAL MOTOR VEHICLE SAFETY STANDARDS APPLICABLE AT TIME OF MANUFACTURE.

Example:

78	Model Year (1978)
2	Car Division (Pontiac)
FS	Series (Firebird)
87	Style (2-Door Hardtop)
N	Body Assembly Plant (Norwood, OH)
345677	Production Sequence
19B	BLack Cloth & Vinyl Trim
19	Starlight Black Lower Body Color
19	Starlight Black Upper Body Color
000	Time Built Date
A51	Modular Seat Code

LEMANS	CODE
4-Door Sedan	AD19
2-Door Coupe	AD27
Safari Station Wagon	AD35

GRAND LEMANS	CODE
4-Door Sedan	AF19
2-Door Coupe	AF27
Safari Station Wagon	AF35

GRAND AM

	CODE
4-Door Sedan	AG19
2-Door Coupe	AG27

CATALINA

	CODE
Safari Station Wagon	BL35
2-Door Coupe	BL37
4-Door Sedan	BL69

BONNEVILLE

	CODE
Safari Station Wagon	BN35
2-Door Coupe	BN37
4-Door Sedan	BN69

BONNEVILLE BROUGHAM

	CODE
2-Door Coupe	BQ37
4-Door Sedan	BQ69

FIREBIRD

	CODE
2-Door Coupe	FS87
Esprit	FT87
Formula	FU87
Trans Am	FW87

*Special Edition option available
*Skybird option available
*Red Bird option available

GRAND PRIX

	CODE
2-Door	GJ37
SJ 2-Door	GH37
LJ 2-Door	GK37

SUNBIRD

	CODE
2-Door Notchback	HE27
Sport 2-Door Hatchback	HM07
Safari Station Wagon	HM15
Sport 2-Door Notchback	HM27

*Formula option available

PHOENIX

	CODE
2-Door Hatchback	XY17
2-Door Coupe	XY27
4-Door Sedan	XY69
LJ 2-Door Coupe	XZ27
LJ 4-Door Sedan	XZ69

THE TRIM CODE furnishes the key to the interior color and material scheme.

LEMANS 2-DOOR/4-DOOR TRIM

COLOR	CLOTH	VINYL	LEATHER	CODE
White		•		11R
Black	•	•		19B
Black			•	245
Lt. Blue	•	•		24B
Lt. Blue		•		24R
Lt. Blue			•	625
Camel Tan	•	•		62B
Camel Tan		•		62R
Carmine		•		74R

LEMANS STATION WAGON TRIM

COLOR	CLOTH	VINYL	LEATHER	CODE
Lt. Blue		•		24R
Lt. Blue		•		24N*#
Sage Green		•		44N*#
Camel Tan	•	•		62C*#
Camel Tan		•		62R*#
Camel Tan		•		62N*#
Carmine		•		74R*#
Carmine		•		74N*#

*Bucket seats
#Notch back or 60-40 seats

GRAND AM 2-DOOR/4-DOOR TRIM

COLOR	CLOTH	VINYL	LEATHER	CODE
White		•		11N*#
Black	•	•		19C*#
Black		•		19N*#
Lt. Blue	•	•		24C*#
Lt. Blue		•		24N*#
Sage Green		•		44N*#
Camel Tan		•		62N*#
Camel Tan	•	•		62C*#
Carmine	•	•		74C*#
Carmine		•		74N*#

*Bucket seats
#Notch back or 60-40 seats

GRAND LEMANS 2-DOOR/4-DOOR TRIM

COLOR	CLOTH	VINYL	LEATHER	CODE
White		•		11N*#
Black		•		19N*#
Black	•	•		19G*#
Lt. Blue	•	•		24G*#
Lt. Blue		•		24N*#
Sage Green	•	•		44G*#
Sage Green		•		44N*#
Camel Tan	•	•		62G*#
Camel Tan		•		62N*#
Carmine	•	•		74G*#
Carmine		•		74N*#

*Bucket seats
#Notch back or 60-40 seats

GRAND LEMANS STATION WAGON TRIM

COLOR	CLOTH	VINYL	LEATHER	CODE
Camel Tan	•	•		62C*#
Lt. Blue		•		24Y
Lt. Blue		•		24N*#
Sage Green		•		44N*#
Camel Tan		•		62Y
Camel Tan		•		62N*#
Carmine		•		74Y
Carmine		•		74N*#

*Bucket seats
#Notch back or 60-40 seats

CATALINA 2-DOOR/4-DOOR TRIM

COLOR	CLOTH	VINYL	LEATHER	CODE
Black	•	•		19B
Black			•	246/242
Black		•		19R/19R*
Lt. Blue	•	•		24B
Lt. Blue		•		24R/24R*
Lt. Blue			•	626/622
Sage Green			•	746/742
Camel Tan	•	•		62B
Camel Tan		•		62R/62R*
Carmine	•	•		74B
Carmine		•		74R/74R*

*Bucket seats

CATALINA SAFARI WAGON TRIM

COLOR	CLOTH	VINYL	LEATHER	CODE
Black			•	242
Lt. Blue		•		24R/24R*
Lt. Blue		•		24V#
Lt. Blue			•	622
Sage Green			•	742
Sage Green		•		44V#
Camel Tan		•		62R/62R*
Camel Tan		•		62V#
Camel Tan	•	•		62H#
Camel Tan	•	•		62E#
Carmine		•		74R/74R*
Carmine		•		74V#

*Bucket seats
#Notch back or 60-40 seats

BONNEVILLE 2-DOOR/4-DOOR TRIM

COLOR	CLOTH	VINYL	LEATHER	CODE
White		•		11V#
Black	•	•		19E#
Black	•	•		19G#
Lt. Blue	•	•		24E#
Lt. Blue	•	•		24G#
Lt. Blue		•		24V#
Sage Green	•	•		44E#
Sage Green	•	•		44G#
Sage Green		•		44V#
Camel Tan	•	•		62E#
Camel Tan	•	•		62G#
Camel Tan	•	•		62H#
Camel Tan		•		62V#
Carmine	•	•		74E#
Carmine	•	•		74G#
Carmine	•	•		74H#
Carmine		•		74V#

#Notch back or 60-40 seats

BONNEVILLE SAFARI WAGON TRIM

COLOR	CLOTH	VINYL	LEATHER	CODE
Lt. Blue		•		24N/24V#
Sage Green		•		44V#
Camel Tan	•	•		62E#
Camel Tan	•	•		62H#
Camel Tan		•		62N
Camel Tan		•		62V#
Carmine		•		74N
Carmine		•		74V#

#Notch back or 60-40 seats

FIREBIRD TRIM

COLOR	CLOTH	VINYL	LEATHER	CODE
White		•		11R*
White		•		11N*
Black	•	•		19B*
Black		•		19R*
Balck		•		19N*
Lt. Blue	•	•		24B*
Lt. Blue		•		24N*
Camel Tan	•	•		62B*
Camel Tan		•		62R*
Camel Tan		•		62N*
Carmine		•		74B*
Carmine		•		74R*
Carmine		•		74N*

*Bucket seats

GRAND PRIX TRIM

COLOR	CLOTH	VINYL	LEATHER	CODE
White		•		11V*#
White		•		11W*
Black	•	•		19D*#
Black	•	•		19E*#
Black		•		19V*#
Black		•		19W*
Black			•	193*
Black			•	194*
Lt. Blue	•	•		24D*#
Lt. Blue	•	•		24E*#
Lt. Blue		•		24V*#
Lt. Blue		•		24W*
Lt. Blue			•	244*
Sage Green	•	•		44E*#
Sage Green		•		44V*#
Camel Tan	•	•		62D*#
Camel Tan	•	•		62E*#
Camel Tan		•		62V*#
Camel Tan		•		62W*
Camel Tan			•	623*
Camel Tan			•	624*
Carmine	•	•		74D*#
Carmine	•	•		74E*#
Carmine		•		74V*#
Carmine		•		74W*
Carmine			•	743*
Carmine			•	744*

*Bucket seats
#Notch back or 60-40 seats

SUNBIRD TRIM

COLOR	CLOTH	VINYL	LEATHER	CODE
White		•		11N*
White		•		11Z*
Black		•		19W*
Black		•		19N*
Black		•		19R*
Lt. Blue	•	•		24G*
Camel Tan	•	•		62G*
Camel Tan		•		62W*
Camel Tan		•		62N*
Camel Tan		•		62Z*
Camel Tan		•		62R*
Carmine	•	•		74G*
Carmine		•		74N*
Carmine		•		74Z*
Carmine		•		74R*

*Bucket seats

PHOENIX TRIM

COLOR	CLOTH	VINYL	LEATHER	CODE
White		•		11R*
White		•		11N#
Black		•		19R*
Black		•		19N#
Black	•	•		19C#
Lt. Blue	•	•		24B
Lt. Blue	•	•		24C#
Lt. Blue		•		24R*
Lt. Blue		•		24N#
Camel Tan	•	•		62B
Camel Tan	•	•		62C#
Camel Tan		•		62R*
Camel Tan		•		62N#
Carmine	•	•		74C#
Carmine		•		74R*
Carmine		•		74N#

*Bucket seats
#Notch back or 60-40 seats

PHOENIX LJ/SJ TRIM

COLOR	CLOTH	VINYL	LEATHER	CODE
White		•		11V*#
Black	•	•		19D*#
Black		•		19V*#
Lt. Blue	•	•		24D*#
Lt. Blue		•		24V*#
Camel Tan	•	•		62D*#
Camel Tan		•		62V*#
Carmine	•	•		74D*#
Carmine		•		74V*#

*Bucket seats

#Notch back or 60-40 seats

THE PAINT CODE furnishes the key to the paint colors used on the car. Two, two-digit codes indicate the bottom and top body colors respectively. NOTE: vinyl roof codes appear as a second set of digits.

COLOR	CODE
Cameo White	11
Platinum Poly	15
Gray Poly	16
Starlight Black	19
Dresden Blue	21
Glacier Blue Poly	22
Martinique Blue Poly	24

	CODE
Nautilus Blue Poly	29
Lombard Blue	30
Seafoam Green Poly	44
Mayfair Green Poly	45
Berkshire Green Poly	48
Gold	50
Sundance Yellow	51
Gold	55
Burnished Gold Poly	56
Blue	58
Desert Sand	61
Laredo Brown Poly	63
Ember Mist Poly	67
Chesterfield Brown Poly	69
Roman Red	72
Mayan Red	75
Carmine Poly	77
Claret Poly	79
Med. Blue Irid	85

VINYL ROOF COLORS

	CODE
White	11T
Platinum Poly	15T
Black	19T
Lt. Blue Poly	22T
Med. Green Poly	44T
Camel Tan	61T
Dk. Carmine Poly	79T

ENGINE NUMBER

Two identification numbers are used on all Pontiac engines. One identifies the engine code letters and production number. The second is an engine vehicle identification number which identifies proper engine-chassis combinations. A Pontiac 6 engine is identified by a letter code stamped on the distributor mounting pad, at the right side of the block. A Pontiac V8 letter code is stamped below the engine production number on front of the block, just below the right-hand cylinder head.

PONTIAC ENGINES

ENGINE CODE	NO. CYL.	CID	HORSE-POWER	COMP. RATIO	CARB	TRANS
WB,WD,WH	4	151	85	8.0:1	2 BC	3-Spd
XL,XN	4	151	85	8.0:1	2 BC	Auto
ZJ*,ZK*	4	151	85	8.0:1	2 BC	Auto
YB,YC	4	151	85	8.0:1	2 BC	Auto
ZA*,ZB*	4	151	85	8.0:1	2 BC	Auto
EI,EJ,EC	6	231	105	8.0:1	2 BC	Auto
OR,OB,OH	6	231	105	8.0:1	2 BC	Auto
EA,OA	6	231	105	8.0:1	2 BC	3-Spd
OD*	6	231	105	8.0:1	2 BC	3-Spd
OF	6	231	105	8.0:1	2 BC	3-Spd
OC	6	231	105	8.0:1	2 BC	Auto
EK*,EL*	6	231	105	8.0:1	2 BC	Auto
EE*,OE*	6	231	105	8.0:1	2 BC	Auto
OK*	6	231	105	8.0:1	2 BC	Auto
XA,XC,YL	8	301	140	8.2:1	2 BC	Auto
YM,XD,XP	8	301	140	8.2:1	2 BC	Auto
YP,YN	8	301	140	8.2:1	2 BC	Auto
XF,XH	8	301	150	8.2:1	4 BC	Auto
XU,XW	8	301	150	8.2:1	4 BC	Auto
CRU,CSC	8	305	135	8.4:1	2 BC	Auto
CSD,CTM	8	305	135	8.4:1	2 BC	Auto
CTW,DAF	8	305	135	8.4:1	2 BC	Auto
CTH,CTA	8	305	135	8.4:1	2 BC	3-Spd
CEM,CRX	8	305	135	8.4:1	2 BC	Auto
CTU,CTR	8	305	135	8.4:1	2 BC	Auto
CTX,CTB	8	305	135	8.4:1	2 BC	Auto
CRY,CTS	8	305*	135	8.4:1	2 BC	Auto
CTY,CRZ	8	305*	135	8.4:1	2 BC	Auto
CTY,CRZ	8	305*	135	8.4:1	2 BC	Auto
CTK,CTT	8	305*	135	8.4:1	2 BC	Auto
CTZ,CTF	8	305*	135	8.4:1	2 BC	Auto
CPH,CPZ	8	305*	135	8.4:1	2 BC	Auto
CTU,CTD	8	305*	135	8.4:1	2 BC	Auto
CPF	8	305	145	8.4:1	4 BC	Auto
	8	350	155	8.0:1	4 BC	
CHJ	8	350*	160	8.2:1	4 BC	Auto
CMC,CHL	8	350	160	8.2:1	4 BC	Auto
MA,MB	8	350	170	8.5:1	4 BC	Auto
TO,TP	8	350	170	7.9:1	4 BC	Auto
TQ,TS	8	350	170	7.9:1	4 BC	Auto
QS,Q3	8	350	170	7.9:1	4 BC	Auto
CHR	8	350	160	8.2:1	4 BC	3-Spd
XJ,XK,YK	8	400	180	7.7:1	4 BC	Auto
YH,YS,YT	8	400	180	7.7:1	4 BC	Auto
X9,YU,YR	8	400	180	7.7:1	4 BC	Auto
YW	8	400	180	7.7:1	4 BC	Auto
WC	8	400	220	8.1:1	4 BC	3-Spd
X7	8	400	220	8.1:1	4 BC	Auto
YA,YU	8	400	180	8.1:1	4 BC	Auto
XJ,XK,YK	8	400	180	8.1:1	4 BC	Auto
YH,Y,X9	8	400	180	8.1:1	4 BC	Auto
YJ	8	400	180	8.1:1	4 BC	Auto
VA,VB	8	403*	185	7.9:1	4 BC	Auto
VD,VE	8	403*	185	7.9:1	4 BC	Auto
U2,U3	8	403	185	7.9:1	4 BC	Auto
U5,U6	8	403	185	7.9:1	4 BC	Auto

*California

1979 PONTIAC PHOENIX

1979 PONTIAC GRAND AM

1979 PONTIAC SUNBIRD

1979 PONTIAC GRAND PRIX

1979 PONTIAC SUNBIRD HATCHBACK

1979 PONTIAC LEMANS

1979 PONTIAC SUNBIRD WAGON

1979 PONTIAC LEMANS WAGON

1979 PONTIAC BONNEVILLE

1979 PONTIAC FIREBIRD

VEHICLE IDENTIFICATION NUMBER

PONTIAC 2J37R9N300039

Located on the top of the dash on the driver's side and visible through the windshield from outside the car.

FIRST DIGIT: Identifies the GM Division (2 is Pontiac)

SECOND DIGIT: Identifies the series

SERIES	CODE
LeMans	D
Sunbird	E
Grand LeMans	F
Grand Am	G
Grand Prix SJ	H
Grand Prix	J
Grand Prix LJ	K
Catalina	L
Sunbird Sport	M
Bonneville/Grand Safari	N
Bonneville Brougham	Q
Firebird	S
Firebird Esprit	T
Firebird Formula	U
Firebird Trans Am	W
Phoenix	Y
Phoenix LJ	Z

THIRD AND FOURTH DIGITS: Identify the body style

BODY STYLE	CODE
2-Door Hatchback	07
2-Door Station Wagon	15
2-Door Hatchback	17
4-Door Notchback Sedan	19
2-Door Notchback Coupe	27
4-Door Station Wagon	35
2-Door Notchback Hardtop Coupe	37
4-Door Notchback Pillar	69
2-Door Plain Back Hardtop Coupe	87

FIFTH DIGIT: Identifies the engine

ENGINE	CODE
V4-151	1
V6-231	2
V4-151	9
V6-231	A
V8-305	G
V8-305	H
V8-403	K
V8-350	L
V8-350	R
V4-151	V
V8-301	W
V8-350	X
V8-301	Y
V8-400	Z

SIXTH DIGIT: Identifies the year 1979

SEVENTH DIGIT: Identifies the assembly plant

ASSEMBLY PLANT	CODE
Lakewood, GA	A
Baltimore, MD	B
South Gate, CA	C
Doraville, GA	D
Linden, NJ	E
Framingham, MA	G
Janesville, WI	J
Leeds, MO	K
Van Nuys, CA	L
Lansing, MI	M
Norwood, OH	N
Pontiac, MI	P
Detroit, MI	Q
Arlington, TX	R
St. Louis, MO	S
Tarrytown, NY	T
Lordstown, OH	U
Willow Run, MI	W
Fairfax, KS	X
Wilmington, DE	Y
Fremont, CA	Z
Oshawa, Ont., CAN	1
St. Therese, Que., CAN	2

LAST SIX DIGITS: Represent the basic production numbers

BODY NUMBER PLATE

The body number plate is located on the firewall, just below the rear edge of the hood. This plate identifies the model year, car division, series, body style, body assembly plant, body numbers, trim combination, paint code and build date code.

```
        BODY BY FISHER
ST 79  2FS87  N      345677 BDY
TR 19R                 15 15 PNT
000 A51
```

GENERAL MOTORS CORPORATION CERTIFIES TO THE DEALER THAT THIS VEHICLE CONFORMS TO ALL U.S., FEDERAL MOTOR VEHICLE SAFETY STANDARDS APPLICABLE AT TIME OF MANUFACTURE.

Example:

79	Model Year (1979)
2	Car Division (Pontiac)
FS	Series (Firebird)
87	Style (2-Door Hardtop)
N	Body Assembly Plant (Norwood, OH)
345677	Production Sequence
19R	BLack Vinyl Trim
15	Silver Lower Body Color
15	Silver Upper Body Color
000	Time Built Date
A51	Modular Seat Code

LEMANS	CODE
4-Door Sedan	AD19
2-Door Coupe	AD27
Safari Station Wagon	AD35

GRAND LEMANS	CODE
4-Door Sedan	AF19
2-Door Coupe	AF27
Safari Station Wagon	AF35

GRAND AM

	CODE
4-Door Sedan	AG19
2-Door Coupe	AG27

CATALINA

	CODE
Safari Station Wagon	BL35
4-Door Sedan	BL69

BONNEVILLE

	CODE
Safari Station Wagon	BN35
2-Door Coupe	BN37
4-Door Sedan	BN69

BONNEVILLE BROUGHAM

	CODE
2-Door Coupe	BQ37
4-Door Sedan	BQ69

FIREBIRD

	CODE
2-Door Coupe	FS87
Esprit	FT87
Formula	FU87
Trans Am	FW87

*10th Anniversary Edition option available
*Special Edition option available
*Red Bird option available

GRAND PRIX

	CODE
2-Door SJ	GH37
2-Door	GJ37
2-Door LJ	GK37

SUNBIRD

	CODE
2-Door Notchback	K#27
2-Door Hatchback	HM07
Sport Safari SW	HM15
Sport 2-Door Notchback	HM27

*Formula option available

PHOENIX

	CODE
2-Door Hatchback	XY17
2-Door Notchback	XY27
4-Door Sedan	XY69

PHOENIX LJ

	CODE
2-Door Coupe	XZ27
4-Door Sedan	XZ69

THE TRIM CODE furnishes the key to the interior color and material scheme.

LEMANS 2-DOOR/4-DOOR TRIM

COLOR	CLOTH	VINYL	LEATHER	CODE
Lt. Blue	•	•		24B
Lt. Blue		•		24R
Camel Tan	•	•		62B
Camel Tan		•		62R
Carmine	•	•		74B
Carmine		•		74R

LEMANS SAFARI WAGON TRIM

COLOR	CLOTH	VINYL	LEATHER	CODE
Lt. Blue		•		24R
Lt. Blue		•		24N*#
Camel Tan	•	•		62C*#
Camel Tan		•		62R
Camel Tan		•		62N*#
Carmine		•		74R
Carmine		•		74N*#
Will. Grn.	•	•		44C*#

GRAND LEMANS 2-DOOR/4-DOOR TRIM

COLOR	CLOTH	VINYL	LEATHER	CODE
Oyster		•		12N*#
Black	•	•		19G*#
Black		•		19N*#
Lt. Blue	•	•		24G*#
Lt. Blue	•	•		24C*#
Lt. Blue		•		24N*#
Camel Tan	•	•		62G*#
Camel Tan	•	•		62C*#
Camel Tan		•		62N*#
Carmine	•	•		74G*#
Carmine	•	•		74C*#
Carmine		•		74N*#
Will. Grn.	•	•		44G*#
Will. Grn.	•	•		44C*#
Will. Grn.		•		44N*#

*Bucket seats
#Notch back or 60-40 seats

GRAND AM 2-DOOR/4-DOOR TRIM

COLOR	CLOTH	VINYL	LEATHER	CODE
Black	•	•		19G*#
Lt. Blue	•	•		24G*#
Camel Tan	•	•		62G*#
Carmine	•	•		74G*#
Will. Grn.	•	•		44G*#

*Bucket seats
#Notch back or 60-40 seats

GRAND PRIX TRIM

COLOR	CLOTH	VINYL	LEATHER	CODE
Oyster		•		12V*#
Oyster		•		12W*
Black	•			19E*#
Black		•		19V*#
Black		•		19W*
Black			•	193*
Lt. Blue	•	•		24D*#
Lt. Blue	•	•		24E*#
Lt. Blue		•		24V*#
Lt. Blue		•		24W*
Camel Tan	•	•		62D*#
Camel Tan	•	•		62E*#
Camel Tan		•		62V*#
Camel Tan		•		62W*
Camel Tan			•	743*
Will. Grn.	•	•		44D*#
Will. Grn.	•	•		44E*#

*Bucket seats
#Notch back or 60-40 seats

CATALINA TRIM

COLOR	CLOTH	VINYL	LEATHER	CODE
Oyster		•		12R
Lt. Blue	•	•		24B
Lt. Blue		•		24R
Camel Tan	•	•		62B/62E#
Camel Tan		•		62R
Carmine	•	•		74B
Carmine		•		74R
Will. Grn.	•	•		44B
Will. Grn.		•		44R

#Notch back or 60-40 seats

BONNEVILLE TRIM

COLOR	CLOTH	VINYL	LEATHER	CODE
Oyster		•		12V#
Black	•			19E#
Black	•	•		19G#
Black	•	•		18H#
Lt. Blue	•	•		24E*#

COLOR	CLOTH	VINYL	LEATHER	CODE
Lt. Blue	•	•		24G#
Lt. Blue	•	•		24D#
Lt. Blue		•		24N/24V#
Camel Tan	•	•		62E*#
Camel Tan	•	•		62G#
Camel Tan	•			62D#
Camel Tan	•	•		62N/62V#
Carmine	•	•		74E*#
Carmine	•	•		74G#
Carmine	•			74D#
Carmine		•		74N/74V#
Will. Grn.	•	•		44E#
Will. Grn.	•	•		44G#
Will. Grn.	•	•		44D#
Will. Grn.		•		44V#

FIREBIRD TRIM

COLOR	CLOTH	VINYL	LEATHER	CODE
Oyster		•		12R*
Oyster		•		12N*
Black		•		19R*
Black		•		19N*
Black	•	•		19B*
Lt. Blue	•	•		24B*
Lt. Blue		•		24N*
Camel Tan	•	•		62B*
Camel Tan		•		62R*
Camel Tan		•		62N*
Carmine	•	•		74B*
Carmine		•		74R*
Carmine		•		74N*
Silver			•	152*

*Bucket seats

SUNBIRD TRIM

COLOR	CLOTH	VINYL	LEATHER	CODE
Oyster		•		12N*
Oyster		•		12Z*
Black		•		19W*
Black		•		19N*
Lt. Blue		•		24R*
Lt. Blue		•		24N*
Lt. Blue	•	•		24G*
Camel Tan	•	•		62G*
Camel Tan		•		62R*
Camel Tan		•		62W*
Camel Tan		•		62N*
Camel Tan		•		62Z*
Carmine	•	•		74G*
Carmine		•		74R*
Carmine		•		74W*
Carmine		•		74N*

*Bucket seats

PHOENIX TRIM

COLOR	CLOTH	VINYL	LEATHER	CODE
Black		•		19R
Black	•	•		19C*#
Lt. Blue	•	•		24B
Lt. Blue	•	•		24C*#
Lt. Blue		•		24R
Lt. Blue		•		24N*#
Camel Tan	•			62B
Camel Tan	•	•		62C*#
Camel Tan		•		62R
Camel Tan		•		62N*#
Carmine	•	•		74C*#
Carmine		•		74R
Carmine		•		74N*#
White		•		11R
White		•		11N*#

*Bucket seats   #Notch back or 60-40 seats

PHOENIX LJ TRIM

COLOR	CLOTH	VINYL	LEATHER	CODE
Black	•	•		19D*#
Lt. Blue	•	•		24D*#
Lt. Blue		•		24V*#
Camel Tan	•	•		62D*#
Camel Tan		•		62V*#
Carmine	•	•		74D*#
Carmine		•		74V*#
White		•		11V*#

*Bucket seats
#Notch back or 60-40 seats

THE PAINT CODE furnishes the key to the paint colors used on the car. Two, two-digit codes indicate the bottom and top body colors respectively. NOTE: vinyl roof codes appear as a second set of digits.

COLOR	CODE
White	11
Silver Irid	15
Gray Irid	16*
Pastel Blue	21
Lt. Blue Irid	22
Bright Blue Irid	24
Dk. Blue Irid	29
Pastel Green	40
Med. Green Irid	44
Gold Irid	50#
Bright Yellow	51
Lt. Yellow	54
Med. Beige	61
Camel Irid	63
Dk. Brown Irid	69
Red	75
Carmine Irid	77
Dk. Carmine Irid	79
Red	80#
Med. Blue Irid	85*
Black (No Chip)	19
Gold Metallic	56

*Two-Tone Only
#Special Order Color

VINYL ROOF COLORS

	CODE
White	11T
Silver Poly	15T
Black	19T
Lt. Blue Poly	22T
Pastel Green	40T
Med. Beige	61T
Dk. Carmine Poly	79T

ENGINE NUMBER

Two identification numbers are used on all Pontiac engines. One identifies the engine code letters and production number. The second is an engine vehicle identification number which identifies proper engine-chassis combinations. A Pontiac 6 engine is identified by a letter code stamped on the distributor mounting pad, at the right side of the block. A Pontiac V8 letter code is stamped below the engine production number on front of the block, just below the right-hand cylinder head.

PONTIAC ENGINES

ENGINE CODE	NO. CYL.	CID	HORSE-POWER	COMP. RATIO	CARB	TRANS
WM,WJ	4	151	90	8.2:1	2 BC	3-Spd
XJ,XK	4	151	90	8.2:1	2 BC	Auto
WB,WD,WR	4	151	90	8.2:1	2 BC	
XL,YB	4	151	90	8.2:1	2 BC	
XN,YC	4	151	90	8.2:1	2 BC	
AF,AH	4	151*	85	8.3:1	2 BC	3-Spd
AC,AD	4	151	85	8.3:1	2 BC	
ZJ,ZK	4	151	85	8.3:1	2 BC	
ZP,ZR	4	151*		8.2:1	2 BC	Auto
AB,ZA,ZB	4	151		8.2:1	2 BC	
RA,NG,NA	6	231	115	8.0:1	2 BC	3-Spd
RB,RX,RC	6	231	115	8.0:1	2 BC	Auto
NB,NJ,NL	6	231	115	8.0:1	2 BC	Auto
NK,NM	6	231	115	8.0:1	2 BC	Auto
NC	6	231*	115	8.0:1	2 BC	3-Spd
RY,RG	6	231*	115	8.0:1	2 BC	Auto
RW,NH	6	231*	115	8.0:1	2 BC	Auto
NE	6	231	115	8.0:1	2 BC	Auto
	6	231	155	8.0:1	4 BC	
PX7,PXF	8	301	135	8.2:1	2 BC	Auto
PX9,PXH	8	301	135	8.2:1	2 BC	Auto
PXP,PXR	8	301	135	8.2:1	2 BC	Auto
PWB,PWA	8	301	150	8.1:1	4 BC	3-Spd
PXL,PXS	8	301	150	8.1:1	4 BC	Auto
PXN,PXT	8	301	150	8.1:1	4 BC	Auto
PXU,PX4	8	301	150	8.1:1	4 BC	Auto
PX6,PXW	8	301	150	8.1:1	4 BC	Auto
DTK,DTM	8	305	130	8.5:1	2 BC	3-Spd
DTL,DNJ	8	305	130	8.5:1	2 BC	Auto
DND,DNK	8	305	130	8.5:1	2 BC	Auto
DND	8	305*	130	8.5:1	2 BC	Auto
DNX,DNY	8	305*	160	8.5:1	4 BC	Auto
DTA	8	305*	160	8.5:1	4 BC	Auto
DRJ	8	350*	170	8.5:1	4 BC	Auto
DRY,DNX	8	350	170	8.5:1	4 BC	Auto
DRX,DRF	8	350	170	8.5:1	4 BC	
DRK,DRZ	8	350	170	8.5:1	4 BC	
SA,SB	8	350			4 BC	Auto
U9,VK	8	350			4 BC	Auto
PWH	8	400	220	8.1:1	4 BC	3-Spd
QE,QJ,QL	8	403	175	8.5:1	4 BC	Auto
TB,TD,TE	8	403*	175	8.5:1	4 BC	Auto
Q3,QK,Q6	8	403	175	8.5:1	4 BC	

*California

1970 FORD FALCON FUTURA

1970 FORD CUSTOM 500

1970 FORD MUSTANG

1970 FORD FAIRLANE 500

1970 FORD MAVERICK

1970 FORD MUSTANG MACH 1

1970 FORD XL

1970 FORD LTD

1970 FORD TORINO

1970 FORD THUNDERBIRD

VEHICLE IDENTIFICATION NUMBER

| • | FORD
F 0E51M123456 F | • |

Located on the top of the dash on the driver's side and visible through the windshield from outside the car.

FIRST DIGIT: Identifies the year 0 = 1970

SECOND DIGIT: Identifies the assembly plant

ASSEMBLY PLANT	CODE
Atlanta, GA	A
Oakville, Ont., CAN	B
Dallas, TX	D
Mahwah, NJ	E
Dearborn, MI	F
Chicago, IL	G
Lorain, OH	H
Los Angeles, CA	J
Kansas City, KS	K
Michigan Truck	L
Norfolk, VA	N
Twin Cities, MN	P
San Jose, CA	R
Allen Park (Pilot Plant)	S
Metuchen, NJ	T
Louisville, KY	U
Wayne, MI	W
St. Thomas, Ont., CAN	X
Wixom, MI	Y

THIRD AND FOURTH DIGITS: Identify the body serial code

THUNDERBIRD	CODE
2-Dr. Hardtop**	83
2-Dr. Hardtop*	83
2-Dr. Landau***	84
2-Dr. Landau*	84
4-Dr. Landau**	87
4-Dr. Landau*	87

* Bench seat
** Split bench
*** Bucket seats

FALCON	CODE
2-Dr. Sedan*	10
4-Dr. Sedan*	11
2-Dr. Sedan Futura*	20
4-Dr. Sedan Futura*	21
4-Dr. Standard Station Wagon*	12
4-Dr. Futura Station Wagon*	23
4-Dr. Station Wagon	

* Bench seat

MAVERICK	CODE
2-Dr. Sedan Standard	91

MUSTANG	CODE
2-Dr. Hardtop Standard***	01
2-Dr. Fastback Standard***	02
Convertible Standard***	03
2-Dr. Hardtop "Grande"***	04
2-Dr. Fastback "Mach I"***	05

*** Bucket seats

FORD	CODE
4-Dr. Sedan Custom*	51
4-Dr. Sedan Custom 500*	53
4-Dr. Sedan Galaxie 500*	54
2-Dr. Hardtop Fastback Galaxie 500*	55
2-Dr. Hardtop Formal Galaxie 500*	58
4-Dr. Hardtop Galaxie 500*	56
2-Dr. Hardtop Fastback Ford XL*/***	60
Convertible Ford XL*/***	61
4-Dr. Sedan Ford LTD & Brougham*/**	64
2-Dr. Hardtop Formal Ford LTD & Brougham*/**	62
4-Dr. Hardtop Ford LTD & Brougham*/**	66
6-Pass. Ranchwagon Station Wagon*	70
6-Pass. Custom 500 Ranchwagon Station Wagon*	71
Custom 500 Ranchwagon-Dual Face Rear Station Wagon*	72
6-Pass. Country Sedan Station Wagon*	73
Country Sedan-Dual Face Rear Station Wagon*	74
6-Pass. Country Squire Station Wagon*	75
Country Squire-Dual Face Rear Station Wagon*	76

* Bench seat
** Split bench
*** Bucket seats

FAIRLANE	CODE
4-Dr. Sedan Fairlane 500*	28
2-Dr. Hardtop Fairlane 500*	29
2-Dr. Hardtop Torino*	30
4-Dr. Sedan Torino*	31
4-Dr. Hardtop Torino*	32
2-Dr. Hardtop Formal Torino Brougham*	33
4-Dr. Hardtop Torino Brougham*	36
2-Dr. Hardtop Fastback Torino GT*	35
Convertible Torino GT*	37
2-Dr. Hardtop Fastback Cobra*	38
Fairlane 500 Station Wagon 4-Dr.*	41
Torino Station Wagon 4-Dr.*	42
Torino Squire (Brougham) Station Wagon 4-Dr.*	43

* Bench seat
*** Bucket seats

FIFTH DIGIT: Identifies the engine code

ENGINE	CODE
V8-460	A
6-240 (Police)	B
V8-429	C
V8-302 (Police/Taxi)	D
6-240 (Taxi)	E
V8-302	F
V8-302	G
V8-351	H
V8-429	J
V8-429	K
6-250	L
V8-351	M
V8-429	N
V8-428 (Police)	P
V8-429 370 HP	Q
V8-428	R
V8-390	S
6-200	T
6-170	U
6-240	V
V8-390	X
V8-390	Y
V8-429	Z
6-200 (Low Comp-Export)	2
6-250 (Low Comp)	3
6-240 (Low Comp)	5
V8-302 (Low Comp)	6

LAST SIX DIGITS: Represent the basic production numbers

EXAMPLE:

0	E	51	M	123456
Model Year	Asm Plant	Body Serial Code	Engine	Production Sequence Number

VEHICLE CERTIFICATION LABEL

THE VEHICLE CERTIFICATION LABEL is attached to the rear face of the driver's door. The upper half of the label contains the name of the manufacturer, the month and year of manufacture and the certification statement. The V.C. label also contains the Vehicle Identification Number. The remaining information on the V.C. label consists of pertinent vehicle identification codes: ie. body, color, trim, axle, transmission and the domestic special order (DSO) codes.

```
MANUFACTURED BY
FORD MOTOR COMPANY

7/70 THIS VEHICLE CONFORMS TO ALL
APPLICABLE FEDERAL MOTOR VEHICLE
SAFETY STANDARDS IN EFFECT ON
DATE OF MANUFACTURE SHOWN ABOVE

0E51N123456          54E      M
NB        4          W        33

NOT FOR TITLE OR REGISTRATION
MADE IN U.S.A.
```

EXAMPLE:
0E51M123456 .... Vehicle Identification Number (VIN)
54E ....Body Type Code (4-Dr. Sedan Custom)
M ....Color Code (White)
NB ....Trim Code (Blue Vinyl)
4 ....Rear Axle Code (2.80:1)
W ....Transmission Code (C4 Automatic)
33 ....District Special Equipment Code (Detroit)

THE BODY CODE is two numerals and a letter identifying the body style.

THUNDERBIRD   CODE
2-Dr. Hardtop*** 65A
2-Dr. Hardtop* 65C
2-Dr. Landau*** 65B
2-Dr. Landau* 65D
4-Dr. Landau** 57B
4-Dr. Landau* 57C
* Bench seat
** Split bench
*** Bucket seats

FALCON   CODE
2-Dr. Sedan Standard* 62A
4-Dr. Sedan Standard* 54A
2-Dr. Sedan Futura* 62B
4-Dr. Sedan Futura* 54B
4-Dr. Standard Station Wagon* 71A
4-Dr. Futura Station Wagon* 71B
4-Dr. Station Wagon 71D
* Bench seat

MAVERICK   CODE
2-Dr. Sedan Standard 62A

MUSTANG   CODE
2-Dr. Hardtop Standard*** 65A
2-Dr. Fastback Standard*** 63A
Convertible Standard*** 76A
2-Dr. Hardtop "Grande"*** 65E
2-Dr. Fastback "Mach I"*** 63C
*** Bucket seats
*Boss 302 option available
*Boss 429 option available
*Twister option available

FORD   CODE
4-Dr. Sedan Custom* 54E
4-Dr. Sedan Custom 500* 54B
2-Dr. Hardtop Fastback Galaxie 500* 63B
2-Dr. Hardtop Formal Galaxie 500* 65C
4-Dr. Hardtop Galaxie 500* 57B
2-Dr. Hardtop Fastback Ford XL*/*** 63C
Convertible Ford XL*/*** 76B
4-Dr. Sedan Ford LTD & Brougham*/** 54C
2-Dr. Hardtop Formal Ford LTD & Brougham*/** 65A
4-Dr. Hardtop Ford LTD & Brougham*/** 57F
6-Pass. Ranchwagon Station Wagon* 71D
6-Pass. Custom 500 Ranchwagon Station Wagon* 71H
Custom 500 Ranchwagon-Dual Face Rear Station Wagon* 71J
6-Pass. Country Sedan* 71B
Country Sedan-Dual Face Rear Station Wagon* 71C
6-Pass. Country Squire Station Wagon* 71E
Country Squire-Dual Face Rear Station Wagon* 71A
* Bench seat
** Split bench
*** Bucket seats

FAIRLANE   CODE
4-Dr. Sedan Fairlane 500* 54B
2-Dr. Hardtop Fairlane 500* 65B
2-Dr. Hardtop Torino*/*** 65C
4-Dr. Sedan Torino* 54C
4-Dr. Hardtop Torino* 57C
2-Dr. Hardtop-Formal Torino Brougham* 65E
4-Dr. Hardtop Torino Brougham* 57E
2-Dr. Hardtop-Fastback Torino GT*/*** 63F
Convertible Torino GT*/*** 76F
2-Dr. Hardtop-Fastback Cobra*/*** 63H
Fairlane 500 4-Dr. Station Wagon* 71B
Torino 4-Dr. Station Wagon* 71C
Torino Squire (Brougham) 4-Dr. Station Wagon* 71E
* Bench seat
*** Split bench
Torino Twister option available

THE COLOR CODE is a number or letter (or both) indicating the exterior paint color.

COLOR   CODE
Black ...... A
Dk. Maroon ...... B
Dk. Ivy Green Metallic C
Brt. Yellow, Competition Yellow ...... D
Lt. Blue ...... E
Dk. Aqua Met. (Brt.), Dk. Aqua Met. ...... F
Med. Avacado Met., Med. Lime Met. ...... G
Lt. Green ...... H
Dk. Orchid Met. I
Brt. Blue Met. (Astra), Deep Blue Met. ...... J

COLOR	CODE
Yellow Met., Brt. Gold Met., Deep Gold Met.	K
Lt. Gray Met.	L
White	M
Platinum, Pastel Blue	N
Burnt Orange Met.	O
Med. Ivy Green Met.	P
Med. Blue Met.	Q
Dk. Brown Met.	R
Nugget Gold Met., Med. Gold Met.	S
Red	T
Med. Aqua Met.	U
Yellow	W
Dk. Blue	X
Chestnut Met., Chestnut Bronze Met., Med. Bronze Met.	Y
Dk. Slate Gray Met., Dk. Gray Met.	Z
Calypso Coral, Vermilion, Competition Orange	1
Lt. Ivy Yellow	2
Ginger Met., Med. Brown Met.	5
Med. Brt. Blue Met., Bright Blue Met., Hulla Blue/Maver.	6
Med. Peppermint Met.	7
Lt. Gold	8
Yellow/Pastel Yellow	9

GLAMOUR PAINTS - OPTIONAL

COLOR	CODE
Ivy Bronze Met., Green Fire, Green Stardust	19
Olive Bronze Met., Olive Fire, Olive Stardust	09
Fall Bronze Met., Bronze Fire, Bronze Stardust	89
Med. Red Met., Burgundy Fire, Red Stardust	59

THE TRIM CODE consists of a two-letter or a number-letter combination designating the interior trim.

CUSTOM AND RANCH WAGON*	CODE
Black	NA
Blue	NB
Nugget	NY

* Vinyl bench

CUSTOM 500*	CODE
Black	3A
Blue	3B
Ivy	3G
Nugget Gold	3Y

* CLoth & vinyl bench

CUSTOM 500 RANCH WAGONS*	CODE
Black	7A
Blue	7B
Ginger	7F
Ivy	7G

* Vinyl bench

GALAXIE 500, LTD, AND XL	CODE
Black (1)	5A/6A
Black (2)	6A
Blue (1)	5B/6B
Blue (2)	6B
Ivy (1)	5G/6G
Ivy (2)	6G
Aqua (1)	5K
Nugget (1)	5Y/6Y
Nugget (2)	6Y
Red (1), (2)	6D
Ginger (1), (2)	6F/6G
White (1), (2)	6W

(1) Cloth & Vinyl bench
(2) Vinyl bench

GALAXIE 500, LTD AND XL*#	CODE
Black	JA
White	JW

\# Not available on convertibles
* Comfortweave vinyl bench
Reclining bench available on all 2-Dr. models

GALAXIE 500 AND FORD XL*#	CODE
Black	8A
Blue	8B
Red	8D
Ginger	8F
Ivy (1)	8G
White	8W

* Comfortweave vinyl bucket
\# Two-Door models and convertible only
1 - Not available on convertible

GALAXIE 500 COUNTRY SEDAN*	CODE
Black	WA
Nugget	WY

* Comfortweave vinyl bench

GALAXIE 500 LUXURY COUNTRY SEDAN*	CODE
Black	KA/HA
Nugget	KY/HY

* Comfortweave vinyl bench

GALAXIE 500 COUNTRY SEDAN*	CODE
Black	MA/SA
Red	MD/SD

* Plaid cloth & vinyl bench

FORD LTD*	CODE
Black	DA
Blue	DB
Red	DD
Ivy	DG
Aqua	DK
Nugget	DY

* Luxury cloth & vinyl bench

LTD BROUGHAM*	CODE
Black*	9A/YA
Black	EA
Blue	9B
Red	9D
Ivy	9G/YG
Ivy Gold	EG
Aqua	9K
Nugget	9Y/YY
Nugget Gold	EY

* Cloth & vinyl bench

LTD COUNTRY SQUIRE	CODE
Black (1)	FA/KA
Black (1)	HA
Black (2)	RA/TA
Blue (1)	FB
Red (1)	FD
Red (2)	RD/TD
Ginger (1)	FF
Ivy (1)	FG
Nugget (1)	KY
Nugget (1)	HY

1 - Vinyl bench
2 - Plaid cloth and vinyl bench

FAIRLANE 500 SEDAN AND HARDTOP*	CODE
Black	3A
Blue	3B
Nugget	3Y

* Cloth & vinyl bench

FAIRLANE 500 4-DOOR STATION WAGON*	CODE
Black	5A
Blue	5B
Ginger	5F

*All vinyl bench

COBRA SPORTSROOF	CODE
Black (1)	3A
Black (2)	RA
Black (4)	CA
Blue (1)	3B
Blue (2)	RB
Blue (4)	CB
Nugget (1)	3Y
Red (2)	RD
Red (3)	PD
Red (4)	CD
Ginger (2)	RF
Ginger (3)	PF
Ginger (4)	CF

1 - Cloth and vinyl bench
2 - All vinyl bench
3 - Blazer stripe bench
4 - Comfortweave vinyl bucket seat

TORINO GT SPORTSROOF AND CONVERTIBLE	CODE
Black (1)	6A
Black (2)	WA
Black (3)	YA
Blue (1)	6B
Blue (3)	YB
Red (1)	6D
Red (3)	YD
Red (4)*	ED
Ivy (1)*	6G
Ginger (1)	6F
Ginger (3)*	YF
Ginger (4)*	EF
Ivy (3)*	YG
White (1)*	6W
White (2)	WW
White (3)	YW

* Sportsroof only
1 - All vinyl bench
2 - Comfortweave vinyl bench
3 - Comfortweave vinyl bucket
4 - Blazer stripe bench

TORINO SEDAN AND HARDTOPS	CODE
Black (1)	7A
Black (2)	JA
Black (3)	KA
Blue (1)	7B
Blue (2)	JB
Red (2)	JD
Ginger (2)	JF
Ivy (1)	7G
Ivy (2)	JG
White (2)	JW
White (3)	KW
Nugget (1)	7Y
Nugget (2)	JY
Nugget (3)	KY

1 - Cloth & vinyl bench
2 - All vinyl bench
3 - Comfortweave vinyl bench

TORINO 2-DOOR FORMAL HARDTOP	CODE
Black (1)	8A
Blue (1)	8B
Red (1)	8D
Red (2)	DD
Ginger (1)	8F
Ginger (2)	DF
Ivy (1)	8G
White (1)	8W

1 - Comfortweave vinyl bucket
2 - Blazer stripe bench

TORINO STATION WAGON	CODE
Black (1)	GA
Black (2)	VA
Black (3)	BA
Blue (1)	GB
Red (1)	GD
Red (3)	BD
Ginger (1)	GF
Ginger (2)	VF

1 - All vinyl bench
2 - Comfortweave vinyl bench
3 - Plaid cloth & vinyl bench

TORINO BROUGHAM HARDTOPS*	CODE
Black	HA
Blue	HB
Red	HD
Ivy	HG
Nugget	HY

* Cloth & vinyl bench

TORINO BROUGHAM STATION WAGON	CODE
Black (1)	9A
Black (2)	NA
Black (3)	AA
Blue (1)	9B
Red (1)	9D
Red (3)	AD
Ginger (1)	9F
Ginger (2)	NF
Ivy (1)	9G

1 - All vinyl bench
2 - Comfortweave vinyl bench
3 - Plaid cloth & vinyl bench

FALCON SEDAN AND COUPES*	CODE
Black	1A
Blue	1B
Nugget Gold	1Y

* All vinyl, except station wagons

FALCON STATION WAGON AND SEDANS*	CODE
Black	2A
Blue	2B
Nugget Gold	2Y
Med. Ginger	2F

* All vinyl

FUTURA SEDANS AND COUPES*	CODE
Black	3A
Blue	3B
Nugget Gold	3Y

* Cloth and vinyl

FUTURA SEDANS/COUPES/STATION WAGONS*	CODE
Black	4A
Blue	4B
Red	4D
Nugget Gold	4Y

* All vinyl

MAVERICK TRIM SCHEME*

	CODE
Black Standard Cloth & Vinyl	2A
Black Optional All Vinyl	1A
Blue Standard Cloth & Vinyl	2B
Red Standard Cloth & Vinyl	2D
Red Optional All Vinyl	1D
Red Optional Blazer Stripe	FD
Nugget Optional All Vinyl	1Y
Nugget Optional Blazer Stripe	FY

MUSTANG HARDTOP/SPORTSROOF/CONVERTIBLE*

	CODE
Black	BA
Blue	BB
Vermillion	BE
Ginger	BF
Ivy	BG
White	BW

* All vinyl

MUSTANG CONVERTIBLE

	CODE
Black (1)	EA
Blue (1)	EB
Ivy (1)	EG
Vermillion (2)	CE
Ginger (2)	CF

1 - Comfortweave vinyl
2 - Blazer stripe cloth & vinyl

MUSTANG HARDTOP AND SPORTSROOF

	CODE
Black (1)	TA
Blue (1)	TB
Ivy (1)	TG
White (1)	TW
Vermillion (2)	UE
Ginger (2)	UF

1 - Comfortweave vinyl
2 - Blazer stripe cloth & vinyl

MUSTANG GRANDE HARDTOP*

	CODE
Black	AA
Blue	AB
Vermillion	AE
Ginger	AF
Ivy	AG

*Houndstooth cloth & vinyl

MUSTANG MACH I SPORTSROOF*

	CODE
Black	3A
Blue	3B
Ivy	3G
White	3W
Vermillion	3E
Ginger	3F

*Comfortweave vinyl

THUNDERBIRD HARDTOP AND LANDAU

	CODE
Black (1)	4A
Black (2)	2A
Black (3)	8A
Black (4)	3A
Black (5)	1A
Blue (1)	4B
Blue (2)	2B
Blue (4)	3B
Blue (5)	1B
Ivy (1)	4G
Ivy (2)	2G
Ivy (5)	1G
Ivy Gold (4)	3G
White (1)	4W
White (2)	2W

THUNDERBIRD HARDTOP AND LANDAU

	CODE
Red (3)	8D
Red (4)	3D
Red (5)	1D
Ginger (3)	8F
Ginger (4)	3F
Ginger (5)	1F
Nugget Gold (4)	3Y

1 - All vinyl bench
2 - Vinyl bucket seat
3 - Brougham leather bucket seat
4 - Brougham cloth & vinyl bench
5 - Brougham cloth & vinyl bucket seat

THUNDERBIRD 4-DOOR LANDAU

	CODE
Black (1)	5A
Black (2)	6A
Blue (1)	5B
Red (1)	5D
Red (2)	6D
Ivy (1)	5G
Nugget (1)	5Y
Tobacco (1)	5Z
Tobacco (2)	6Z

1 - Brougham cloth & vinyl split bench
2 - Brougham leather split bench

THE AXLE CODE is a number or letter indicating the rear axle ratio and standard or locking type axles.

CONVENTIONAL	LOCKING	RATIO
0		2.50:1
2	K	2.75:1
3		2.79:1
4	M	2.80:1
5		2.83:1
6	O	3.00:1
7		3.10:1
8		3.20:1
9	R	3.25:1
A	S	3.50:1
B		3.07:1
C		3.08:1
F	X	2.33:1
	V	3.91:1
	W	4.30:1

THE TRANSMISSION CODE is a number or letter indicating the type of transmission; numerals for manual and letters for automatic or semi-automatic.

TYPE	CODE
3-Speed Manual	1
4-Speed Manual wide ratio	5
4-Speed Manual close ratio	6
Semi-Automatic Stick Shift	V
Automatic (C4)	W
Automatic (C6)	U
Automatic (FMX)	X
Automatic (C6 Special)	Z

THE DSO CODE, consisting of two numbers, designates the district in which the car was ordered and may appear in conjunction with a Domestic Special Order or Foreign Special Order number when applicable. Ford of Canada DSO codes consist of a letter and a number except for export codes, which are designated by two numbers.

FORD DISTRICT	CODE
Boston	11
New York	13
Newark	15
Philadelphia	16
Washington	17
Atlanta	21
Charlotte	22
Jacksonville	24
Richmond	25
Louisville	28
Cleveland	32
Detroit	33
Indianapolis	34
Lansing	35
Buffalo	37
Pittsburgh	38
Chicago	41
Fargo	42
Milwaukee	43
Twin Cities	44
Indianapolis	46
Cincinnati	47
Denver	51
Des Moines	52
Kansas City	53
Omaha	54
St. Louis	55
Davenport	56
Dallas	61
Houston	62
Memphis	63
New Orleans	64
Oklahoma City	65
Los Angeles	71
San Jose	72
Salt Lake City	73
Seattle	74
Phoenix	75
Government	83
Home Office Reserve	84
American Red Cross	85
Transportation Services	89
Export	90-99

FORD OF CANADA DISTRICT	CODE
Central	B1
Eastern	B2
Atlantic	B3
Export	I1-I7
Midwestern	B4
Western	B6
Pacific	B7

ENGINE IDENTIFICATION

ENGINE TAG
Since 1964, Ford engines can be identified by a tag attached to the engine. The tag contains the year and cubic inch displacement.

CASTING NUMBERS
While helpful in identifying Ford engine components, casting numbers are not conclusive in pin-pointing the exact year of manufacture. A better method is to search for the original host vehicle's VIN (Vehicle Identification Number) stamped on the driver's side at the rear of the engine block below the cylinder head.

ENGINE TAG EXAMPLE
240   70
0-A   123A

DECODED EXAMPLE
240   CID
70   Model Year (1970)
0   Production Year (1970)
A   Production Month (January)
123A   Engine Code Number

FULL SIZE MODEL ENGINES

CID	NO. CYL.	HORSE-POWER	COMP. RATIO	CARB
240	6	150	9.2	1 BC
302	8	210	9.5	2 BC
351	8	250	9.5	2 BC
390	8	270	9.5	2 BC
429	8	320	10.5	2 BC
429	8	360	11.0	4 BC

COMPACT & INTERMEDIATE MODEL ENGINES

CID	NO. CYL.	HORSE-POWER	COMP. RATIO	CARB
170	6	105	9.1	1 BC
200	6	120	8.8	1 BC
250	6	155	9.1	1 BC
302	8	210	9.5	2 BC
302 "Boss"	8	300	10.5	4 BC
351	8	250	9.5	2 BC
351	8	300	11.0	4 BC
428 "CJ"	8	335	10.6	4 BC
428	8	335	10.6	4 BC
429	8	360	11.0	4 BC
429 "CJ"	8	370	11.5	4 BC
429 "Boss"	8	375	10.5	4 BC

1971 FORD MAVERICK

1971 FORD PINTO

1971 FORD MUSTANG

1971 FORD TORINO GT

1971 FORD LTD

1971 FORD THUNDERBIRD

VEHICLE IDENTIFICATION NUMBER

FORD
F 1E51M123456 F

Located on the top of the dash on the driver's side and visible through the windshield from outside the car.

FIRST DIGIT: Identifies the year 1 = 1971

SECOND DIGIT: Identifies the assembly plant

ASSEMBLY PLANT	CODE
Atlanta, GA	A
Oakville, Ont., CAN	B
Dallas, TX	D
Mahwah, NJ	E
Dearborn, MI	F
Chicago, IL	G
Lorain, OH	H
Los Angeles, CA	J
Kansas City, KS	K
Norfolk, VA	N
Twin Cities, MN	P
San Jose, CA	R
Allen Park, NJ	S
Metuchen, NJ	T
Louisville, KY	U
Wayne, MI	W
St. Thomas, Ont., CAN	X
Wixom, MI	Y
St. Louis, MO	Z

THIRD AND FOURTH DIGITS: Identify the body serial code

TORINO	CODE
4-Dr. Sedan	27
2-Dr. Hardtop	25
2-Dr. HT-Sportsroof Torino 500	34
2-Dr. HT Torino 500	30
4-Dr. Sedan Torino 500	31
4-Dr. Hardtop	32
2-Dr. HT-Formal Torino Brougham	33
4-Dr. HT Torino Brougham	36
2-Dr. HT-Sportsroof Torino GT	35
Convertible Torino GT	37
2-Dr. HT-Sportsroof Cobra	38
Torino SW 4-Dr.	40
Torino 500 SW 4-Dr.	42
Torino Squire (Brougham) SW 4-Dr.	43

FORD	CODE
4-Dr. Sedan Custom	51
4-Dr. Sedan Custom 500	53
4-Dr. Sedan Galaxie 500	54
2-Dr. Hardtop Galaxie 500	58
4-Dr. Hardtop Galaxie 500	56
Convertible LTD	61
4-Dr. Hardtop LTD	64
2-Dr. Hardtop LTD	62
4-Dr. HT Sedan LTD	63
4-Dr. HT Sedan LTD Brougham	66
4-Dr. HT LTD Brougham	67
2-Dr. HT LTD Brougham	68
4-Dr. SW Custom Ranch	70
4-Dr. SW Custom 500 Ranch	72
4-Dr. SW Country Sedan	74
4-Dr. SW Country Squire	76

MAVERICK	CODE
2-Dr. Sedan Standard	91
4-Dr. Sedan Standard	92
2-Dr. Sport Sedan Standard	93

PINTO	CODE
2-Dr. Sedan	10
3-Dr. Runabout	11

MUSTANG	CODE
2-Dr. Hardtop Standard	01
2-Dr. Sportsroof Standard	02
Convertible Standard	03
2-Dr. Hardtop Grande	04
2-Dr. Sportsroof Mach I	05

THUNDERBIRD	CODE
2-Dr. Hardtop	83
2-Dr. Landau	84
4-Dr. Landau	87

FIFTH DIGIT: Identifies the engine code

ENGINE	CODE
6-240 (Police)	B
V8-429	C
V8-302 HO	D
6-240	E
V8-302	F
V8-302	G
V8-351	H
V8-429	J
V8-429	K
6-250	L
V8-351	M
V8-429	N
V8-429	P
V8-351	Q
V8-351 Boss	R
V8-400	S
6-200	T
6-170	U
6-240	V
4-98	W
4-122	X
V8-390	Y
6-200	2
6-250	3
6-240	5
V8-302	6

LAST SIX DIGITS: Identifies the basic production numbers

EXAMPLE:

1	E	51	M	123456
Model Year	Asm Plant	Body Serial Code	Engine	Production Sequence Number

VEHICLE CERTIFICATION LABEL

THE VEHICLE CERTIFICATION LABEL is attached to the rear face of the driver's door. The upper half of the label contains the name of the manufacturer, the month and year of manufacture and the certification statement. The V.C. label also contains the Vehicle Identification Number. The remaining information on the V.C. Label consists of pertinent vehicle identification codes: ie. body, color, trim, axle, transmission and the domestic special order (DSO) codes.

MANUFACTURED BY
FORD MOTOR COMPANY

7/71 THIS VEHICLE CONFORMS TO ALL APPLICABLE FEDERAL MOTOR VEHICLE SAFETY STANDARDS IN EFFECT ON DATE OF MANUFACTURE SHOWN ABOVE

● 1E51M123456   54B   M ●

BB   4   W   33

NOT FOR TITLE OR REGISTRATION
MADE IN U.S.A.

EXAMPLE:

1E51M123456	Vehicle Identification Number (VIN)
54B	Body Type Code(Custom 4-Dr. Sedan)
M	Color Code (White)
BB	Trim Code (Blue Cloth & Vinyl)
4	Rear Axle Code (2.80:1)
W	Transmission Code (C4 Automatic)
33	District Special Equipment Code (Detroit)

THE BODY CODE is two numerals and a letter identifying the body style.

TORINO	CODE
4-Dr. Sedan Torino	54A
2-Dr. Hardtop Torino	65A
2-Dr. HT Sportsroof Torino 500	63C
2-Dr. HT Torino 500	65C
4-Dr. Sedan Torino 500	54C
4-Dr. Hardtop Torino 500	57C
2-Dr. HT Formal Torino Brougham	65E
4-Dr. HT Torino Brougham	57E
2-Dr. HT Sportsroof Torino GT	63F
Convertible Torino GT	76F
2-Dr. HT Sportsroof Cobra	63H
Torino SW 4-Dr.	71D
Torino 500 SW 4-Dr.	71C
Torino Squire (Brougham) SW 4-Dr.	71E

FORD	CODE
4-Dr. Sedan Custom	54B
4-Dr. Sedan Custom 500	54D
4-Dr. Sedan Galaxie 500	54F
2-Dr. HT Galaxie 500	65F
4-Dr. HT Galaxie 500	57F
Convertible LTD	76H
4-Dr. HT LTD	65H
4-Dr. HT Sedan LTD	53H
4-Dr. HT Sedan LTD Brougham	53K
4-Dr. HT LTD Brougham	57K
2-Dr. HT LTD Brougham	65K
4-Dr. SW Custom Ranch	71B
4-Dr. SW Custom 500 Ranch	71D
4-Dr. SW Country Sedan	71F
4-Dr. SW Country Squire	71H

MAVERICK	CODE
2-Dr. Sedan Standard	62A
4-Dr. Sedan Standard	54A
2-Dr. Sport Sedan Grabber	62D

PINTO	CODE
2-Dr. Sedan	62B
3-Dr. Runabout	64B
*Rallye option available	

MUSTANG	CODE
2-Dr. HT Standard	65D
2-Dr. Sportsroof Standard	63D
Convertible Standard	76D
2-Dr. HT Grande	65F
2-Dr. Sportsroof Mach I	63R

THUNDERBIRD	CODE
2-Dr. Hardtop	65A
2-Dr. Hardtop	65C
2-Dr. Landau	65B
2-Dr. Landau	65D
4-Dr. Landau	57B
4-Dr. Landau	57C

THE COLOR CODE is a number or letter (or both) indicating the exterior paint color.

COLOR	CODE
Black	A
White	M
Calypso Coral	1
Red	T
Bright Red	3
Maroon Met.	B
Lt. Gray Met.	L
Dk. Slate Gray Met.	K
Platinum	N
Med. Blue Met.	Q
Dk. Blue Met.	X
Bright Blue Met.	6
Grabber Blue	J
Bright Astra Blue Met.	Y
Med. Bright Aqua Met.	F
Lt. Green	H
Med. Green Met.	P
Dk. Green Met.	C
Grabber Green Met.	Z
Dk. Vintage Green	G
Bright Lime Green	I
Lt. Gold	8
Med. Gray Gold Met.	S
Yellow	W
Bright Yellow	D
Lt. Goldenrod Yellow	O
Med. Goldenrod Yellow	E
Grabber Orange	U
Med. Tan	2
Lt. Pewter Met.	V
Dk. Brown Met.	R
Med. Ginger Met.	5

GLAMOUR PAINTS - OPTIONAL

COLOR	CODE
Med. Ivy Bronze Met.	49
Med. Ginger Bronze Met.	79
Med. Ivy Bronze Met.	E9
Med. Ginger Bronze Met.	39
Med. Blue Met.	D9
Med. Red Met.	C9

THE TRIM CODE consists of a two-letter or a number-letter combination designating the interior trim.

CUSTOM AND RANCH WAGON*	CODE
Black	NA
Medium Blue	NB
Medium Green (1)	NR
Light Gray Gold (2)	NY

* All vinyl bench
1 - Ranch Wagon only
2 - Custom only

CUSTOM 500*	CODE
Black	3A
Medium Blue	3B
Medium Green	3R
Light Gray Gold	3Y

* Cloth & vinyl bench

CUSTOM 500 RANCH WAGONS*	CODE
Black	7A
Medium Blue	7B
Medium Ginger	7F
Medium Green	7R

* All vinyl bench

GALAXIE 500	CODE
Black (1)	5A
Black (2)	WA
Black (3)	8A
Medium Blue (1)	5B
Medium Blue (2)	WD
Dark Red (2)	WD
Dark Red (3)	8D
Medium Ginger (1)	5F
Medium Ginger (2)	WF
Medium Green (1)	5R
Medium Green (2)	WR
Light Gray Gold (1)	5Y
Light Gray Gold (2)	WY
White (2)	WW
White (3)	8W

1 - Cloth & vinyl bench
2 - Vinyl bench
3 - Vinyl bucket

GALAXIE 500 COUNTRY SEDAN	CODE
Black (1)	WA
Black (2)	RA
Medium Blue (1)	WB
Dark Red (1)	WD
Dark Red (2)	RD
Medium Ginger (1)	WF
Medium Green (1)	WR

1 - All vinyl bench
2 - Plaid cloth & vinyl bench

LTD	CODE
Black (1)	FA
Black (2)	GA
Black (3)	DA
Medium Blue (1)	FB
Medium Blue (3)	DB
Dark Red (1)	FD
Dark Red (2)	GD
Dark Red (3)	DD
Medium Ginger (1)	FF
Medium Ginger (3)	DF
Medium Green (1)	FR
Medium Green (3)	DR
White (1)	FW
White (2)	GW
Light Gray Gold (1)	FY
Light Gray Gold (3)	DY

1 - Vinyl bench
2 - Vinyl bucket
3 - Cloth & vinyl bench

LTD BROUGHAM	CODE
Black (1)	EA
Black (2)	9A
Black (3)	ZA
Medium Blue (1)	EB
Medium Blue (2)	9B
Medium Blue (3)	ZB
Dark Red (1)	ED
Dark Red (2)	9D
Dark Red (3)	ZD
Medium Ginger (2)	9F
Medium Ginger (3)	ZF
Medium Green (1)	ER
Medium Green (2)	9R
Medium Green (3)	ZR
Light Gray Gold (1)	EY
Light Gray Gold (2)	9Y
Light Gray Gold (3)	ZY

1 - Cloth & vinyl hi-back split bench
2 - Cloth & vinyl bench
3 - Cloth & vinyl hi-back bench

LTD COUNTRY SQUIRE	CODE
Black (1)	BA
Black (2)	FA
Black (3)	VA
Medium Blue (2)	FB
Dark Red (2)	FD
Dark Red (3)	VD
Medium Ginger (1)	BF
Medium Ginger (2)	FF
Medium Green (1)	BR
Medium Green (2)	FR

1 - Squire Luxury vinyl bench
2 - All vinyl bench
3 - Plaid cloth & vinyl bench

TORINO AND TORINO STATION WAGON*	CODE
Black	2A
Medium Blue	2B
Light Gray Gold	2Y

* All vinyl bench

TORINO 500	CODE
Black (1)	7A
Black (2)	8A
Black (3)	KA/JA
Medium Blue (1)	7B
Medium Blue (2)	8B
Medium Blue (3)	JB
Medium Vermillion (2)	8E
Medium Vermillion (3)	JE
Medium Ginger (2)	8F
Medium Ginger (3)	JF
Medium Green (1)	7R
Medium Green (2)	8R
Medium Green (3)	JR
Light Gray Gold (1)	7Y
Light Gray Gold (3)	KY/JY
White (2)	8W
White (3)	KW/JW

1 - Cloth & vinyl bench
2 - Vinyl bucket
3 - Vinyl bench

TORINO 500	CODE
Black (1)	JA
Black (2)	VA
Black (3)	BA
Medium Blue (1)	JB
Medium Vermillion (1)	JE
Medium Vermillion (3)	BE
Medium Ginger (1)	JF
Medium Green (1)	JR
White (1)	JW
Light Gray Gold (1)	JY

1 - Vinyl bench
2 - Knitted vinyl bench
3 - Plaid cloth & vinyl bench

TORINO BROUGHAM*	CODE
Black	HA
Medium Blue	HB
Medium Green	HR
Light Gray Gold	HY

* Cloth & vinyl bench

TORINO GT	CODE
Black (1)	6A
Black (2)	WA
Black (3)	YA
Medium Blue (1)	6B
Medium Blue (3)	YB
Medium Vermillion (1)	6E
Medium Vermillion (3)	YE
Medium Ginger (1)	6F
Medium Ginger (3)	YF
Medium Green (1)	6R
Medium Green (3)	YR
White (1)	6W
White (2)	WW
White (3)	YW

1 - Vinyl bench
2 - Knitted vinyl bench
3 - Knitted vinyl bucket

TORINO SQUIRE STATION WAGON	CODE
Black (1)	9A
Black (2)	AA
Black (3)	NA
Medium Blue (1)	9B
Medium Vermillion (1)	9E
Medium Vermillion (2)	AE
Medium Ginger (1)	9F
Medium Green (1)	9R

1 - Vinyl bench
2 - Cloth & vinyl bench
3 - Knitted vinyl bench

COBRA	CODE
Black (1)	CA
Black (2)	RA
Medium Blue (1)	CB
Medium Blue (2)	RB
Medium Vermillion (1)	CE
Medium Vermillion (2)	RE
Medium Ginger (1)	CF
Medium Ginger (2)	RF

1 - Knitted vinyl bucket
2 - Vinyl bench

MUSTANG HT/SPORTSROOF/BOSS 351/ MACH I/CONVERTIBLE*	CODE
Black	1A
Medium Blue	2B
Vermillion	1E
Medium Ginger (1)	1F
Medium Green	1R
White	1W

* All vinyl
1 - N.A. on convertible

MUSTANG HARDTOP AND SPORTSROOF*	CODE
Black	3A
White	3W

* Knitted vinyl
Optional Decor Group - N.A. on Mach I or Grande

MUSTANG HT, SPORTSROOF & BOSS 351*	CODE
Vermillion	2E
Medium Ginger	2F
Medium Blue	2B
Medium Green	2R

* Cloth & vinyl
Optional Decor Group

MACH I SPORTS INTERIOR*	CODE
Black	5A
White	5W
Vermillion	5E
Medium Blue	5B
Medium Green	5R
Medium Ginger	5F

* Knitted vinyl (optional)

CONVERTIBLE*	CODE
Black	CA
White	CW
Vermillion	CE
Medium Blue	CB
Medium Green	CR
Medium Ginger	CF

* Knitted vinyl
Optional Decor Group

GRANDE HARDTOP* CODE
Black 4A
Medium Blue 4B
Vermillion 4E
Medium Ginger 4F
Medium Green 4R
* Cloth & vinyl

MAVERICK STANDARD 2 AND 4-DOOR SEDANS* CODE
Black 2A
Medium Blue 2B
Gray Gold 2Y
* Std. cloth & vinyl bench

MAVERICK STANDARD SEDANS AND GRABBER CODE
Black (1) 1A
Black (2) 3A
Black (3) 5A
Black (5) 8A
Medium Blue (2) 3B
Medium Blue (3) 5B
Medium Blue (5) 8B
Vermillion (2) 3E
Vermillion (3) 5E
Vermillion (4) 9E
Vermillion (5) 8E
Gray Gold (1) 1Y
Gray Gold (2) 3Y
Gray Gold (3) 5Y
Gray Gold (4) 9Y
Gray Gold (5) 8Y
1 - Vinyl bench
2 - Deluxe cloth & vinyl bench
3 - Deluxe woven vinyl bench
4 - Cloth & vinyl bucket
5 - Deluxe woven vinyl bucket

SEDAN CODE
Black (1) 1A
Black (2) 2A
Black (3) 3A
Medium Blue (1) (2) 2B
Medium Blue (3) 3B
Medium Ginger (2) 2F
Medium Ginger (3) 3F
Medium Green (1) 1R
Medium Green (2) 2R
Medium Green (3) 3R
1 - Vinyl bucket
2 - Cloth & vinyl bucket
3 - Knitted vinyl bucket

THUNDERBIRD HARDTOP AND LANDAU CODE
Black (1) 4A
Black (2) 2A
Black (3) 8A
Black (4) ....CA
Black (5) ....AA
Black (6) ....FA
Black (7) ....EA
Dark Red (3) 8D
Dark Red (4) ....CD
Dark Red (5) ....AD
Dark Red (6) ....FD
Dark Red (7) ....ED
Medium Ginger (3) 8F
Medium Ginger (4) ....CF
Medium Ginger (5) ....AF
Dark Blue (1) 4B
Dark Blue (2) 2B
Dark Blue (4) ....CB
Dark Blue (5) ....AB

THUNDERBIRD HARDTOP AND LANDAU CODE
Dark Blue (7) ....EB
Dark Green (1) 4R
Dark Green (2) 2R
Dark Green (4) ....CR
Dark Green (5) ....AR
Dark Green (7) ....ER
White (1) 4W
Light Gray Gold (4) ....CY
Light Gray Gold (7) ....EY
Dark Tobacco (6) ....FZ
Dark Tobacco (7) ....EZ
1 - Vinyl bench
2 - Vinyl high-back bucket
3 - Brougham leather & vinyl high back bucket
4 - Brougham cloth & vinyl bench
5 - Brougham cloth & vinyl high back bucket
6 - Brougham leather & vinyl split bench
7 - Brougham cloth & vinyl split bench

THE AXLE CODE is a number or letter indicating the rear axle ratio and standard or locking type axles.

CONVENTIONAL	LOCKING	RATIO
0		2.50:1
2	K	2.75:1
3		2.79:1
4	M	2.80:1
5		2.83:1
6	O	3.00:1
9	R	3.25:1
A	S	3.50:1
B		3.07:1
	V	3.91:1
	W	4.30:1
	X	2.33:1
	Y	4.11:1

THE TRANSMISSION CODE is a number or letter indicating the type of transmission; numerals for manual and letters for automatic or semi-automatic.

TYPE	CODE
3-Speed Manual	1
4-Speed Manual wide ratio	5
4-Speed Manual close ratio	6
Automatic (C4)	W
Automatic (C6)	U
Semi-Automatic	V
Automatic (FMX)	X
Automatic (C6 Special)	Z

THE DSO CODE, consisting of two numbers, designates the district in which the car was ordered and may appear in conjunction with a Domestic Special Order or Foreign Special Order number when applicable. Ford of Canada DSO codes consist of a letter and a number except for export codes, which are designated by two numbers.

FORD DISTRICT	CODE
Boston	11
New York	13
Newark	15
Philadelphia	16
Washington	17
Atlanta	21
Charlotte	22
Jacksonville	24
Richmond	25
Louisville	28
Cleveland	32
Detroit	33
Lansing	35
Buffalo	37
Pittsburgh	38
Chicago	41
Fargo	42
Milwaukee	43
Twin Cities	44
Indianapolis	46
Cincinnati	47
Denver	51
Des Moines	52

FORD DISTRICT	CODE
Kansas City	53
Omaha	54
St. Louis	55
Davenport	56
Dallas	61
Houston	62
Memphis	63
New Orleans	64
Oklahoma City	65
Los Angeles	71
San Jose	72
Salt Lake City	73
Seattle	74
Phoenix	75
Government	83
Home Office Reserve	84
American Red Cross	85
Body Company	87
Transportation Services	89
Export	90-99

FORD OF CANADA DISTRICT	CODE
Central	B1
Eastern	B2
Atlantic	B3
Midwestern	B4
Western	B6
Pacific	B7
Export	12

ENGINE IDENTIFICATION

ENGINE TAG
Since 1964, Ford engines can be identified by a tag attached to the engine. The tag contains the year and cubic inch displacement.

CASTING NUMBERS
While helpful in identifying Ford engine components, casting numbers are not conclusive in pin-pointing the exact year of manufacture. A better method is to search for the original host vehicle's VIN (Vehicle Identification Number) stamped on the driver's side at the rear of the engine block below the cylinder head.

ENGINE TAG EXAMPLE
240　　　71
1-A　　 23A

DECODED EXAMPLE
240	CID
71	Model Year (1971)
1	Production Year
A	Production Month (January)
123A	Engine Code Number

FORD ENGINES
CID	NO. CYL.	HORSE-POWER	COMP. RATIO	CARB.
240	6	140	8.9:1	1 BC
302	8	210	9.0:1	2 BC
351	8	240	9.0:1	2 BC
390	8	255	8.6:1	2 BC
400	8	260	9.0:1	2 BC
429	8	320	10.5:1	2 BC
429	8	360	10.5:1	4 BC

TORINO ENGINES
CID	NO. CYL.	HORSE-POWER	COMP. RATIO	CARB.
250	6	145	9.0:1	1 BC
302	8	210	9.0:1	2 BC
351	8	240	9.0:1	2 BC
351	8	285	10.7:1	4 BC
429*	8	370	11.3:1	4 BC
429*	8	370	11.3:1	4 BC

* "CJ"

PINTO ENGINES
CID	NO. CYL.	HORSE-POWER	COMP. RATIO	CARB.
98	4	75	8.4:1	1 BC
122	4	100	9.0:1	2 BC

MAVERICK ENGINES
CID	NO. CYL.	HORSE-POWER	COMP. RATIO	CARB.
170	6	100	8.7:1	1 BC
200	6	115	8.7:1	1 BC
250	6	145	9.0:1	1 BC
302	8	210	9.0:1	2 BC

MUSTANG ENGINES
CID	NO. CYL.	HORSE-POWER	COMP. RATIO	CARB.
250	6	145	9.0:1	1 BC
302***	8	210	9.0:1	2 BC
351	8	240	9.0:1	2 BC
351	8	330	11.7:1	4 BC
351**	8	285	10.7:1	4 BC
429*	8	370	11.3:1	4 BC
429*	8	370	11.3:1	4 BC
429	8	375	11.5:1	4 BC

* "CJ"
** Available with Boss 351 only
*** Standard on Mach 1

THUNDERBIRD ENGINES
CID	NO. CYL.	HORSE-POWER	COMP. RATIO	CARB.
429	8	360	10.5:1	4 BC

1972 FORD PINTO

1972 FORD GRAN TORINO

1972 FORD THUNDERBIRD

1972 FORD MAVERICK GRABBER

1972 FORD LTD

1972 FORD MUSTANG

1972 FORD GALAXIE

1972 FORD LTD COUNTRY SQUIRE

VEHICLE IDENTIFICATION NUMBER

```
FORD
2E51H123456
```

Located on the top of the dash on the driver's side and visible through the windshield from outside the car.

FIRST DIGIT: Identifies the year 2 = 1972

SECOND DIGIT: Identifies the assembly plant

ASSEMBLY PLANT	CODE
Atlanta, GA	A
Oakville, Ont., CAN	B
Mahwah, NJ	E
Dearborn, MI	F
Chicago, IL	G
Lorain, OH	H
Los Angeles, CA	J
Kansas City, KS	K
Norfolk, VA	N
Twin Cities, MN	P
San Jose, CA	R
Allen Park (Pilot Plant)	S
Metuchen, NJ	T
Louisville, KY	U
Wayne, MI	W
St. Thomas, Ont., CAN	X
Wixom, MI	Y
St. Louis, MO	Z

THIRD AND FOURTH DIGITS: Identify the body serial code

TORINO	CODE
4-Dr. Sedan Hardtop	27
2-Dr. Hardtop	25
2-Dr. Hardtop Gran Torino	30
4-Dr. Sedan HT Gran Torino	31
2-Dr. Fastback Gran Torino Sport	35
2-Dr. HT Gran Torino Sport	38
Torino SW 4-Dr.	40
Gran, Torino SW 4-Dr.	42
Torino Squire SW 4-Dr.	43

FORD	CODE
4-Dr. Sedan Custom	51
4-Dr. Sedan Custom 500	53
4-Dr. Sedan Galaxie 500	54
4-Dr. HT Galaxie 500	56
2-Dr. HT Galaxie 500	58
Convertible LTD	61
2-Dr. HT LTD	62
4-Dr. Sedan HT LTD	63
4-Dr. Hardtop LTD	64
4-Dr. Sedan HT LTD Brougham	66
4-Dr. HT LTD Brougham	67
2-Dr. HT LTD Brougham	68
4-Dr. SW Custom Ranch	70
4-Dr. SW Custom 500 Ranch	72
4-Dr. SW Country Sedan	74
4-Dr. SW Country Squire	76

MAVERICK	CODE
2-Dr. Sedan Standard	91
4-Dr. Sedan Standard	92
2-Dr. Sport Sedan Standard	93

MUSTANG	CODE
2-Dr. Hardtop Standard	01
2-Dr. Sportsroof Standard	02
Convertible Standard	03
2-Dr. Hardtop Grande	04
2-Dr. Sportsroof Mach 1	05

PINTO	CODE
2-Dr. Sedan Runabout	10
3-Dr. Runabout	11
2-Dr. SW Runabout	12

THUNDERBIRD	CODE
2-Dr. Hardtop	87

FIFTH DIGIT: Identifies the engine code

ENGINE	CODE
6-170	U
6-200	T
6-200*	2
6-250	L
6-250*	3
6-240	V
6-240 (Taxi)	E
V8-302	F
V8-302*	6
V8-302 (Taxi & Police)	D
V8-351	H
V8-351	Q
V8-351	R
V8-400	S
V8-429	N
V8-429 (Police)	P
V8-460	A
4-98	W
4-122	X
6-240 (Police)	B

LAST SIX DIGITS: Identifies the basic production numbers

EXAMPLE:

2	E	51	H	123456
Model Year	Asm Plant	Body Serial Code	Engine	Production Sequence Number

VEHICLE CERTIFICATION LABEL

THE VEHICLE CERTIFICATION LABEL is attached to the rear face of the driver's door. The upper half of the label contains the name of the manufacturer, the month and year of manufacture and the certification statement. The V.C. label also contains the Vehicle Identification Number. The remaining information on the V.C. label consists of pertinent vehicle identification codes: ie. body, color, trim, axle, transmission and the Domestic Special Order (DSO) codes.

```
MANUFACTURED BY
FORD MOTOR COMPANY

7/72 THIS VEHICLE CONFORMS TO ALL
APPLICABLE FEDERAL MOTOR VEHICLE
SAFETY STANDARDS IN EFFECT ON
DATE OF MANUFACTURE SHOWN ABOVE

2E51H123456        54B    1C
AA          U        W    48

NOT FOR TITLE OR REGISTRATION
MADE IN U.S.A.
```

EXAMPLE
2E51H123456 .... Vehicle Identification Number (VIN)
54B .... Body Type Code (Custom 4-Dr. Sedan)
1C .... Color Code (Black)
AA .... Trim Code (Black Vinyl)
4 .... Rear Axle Code (2.80:1)
U .... Transmission Code (C6 Automatic)
48 .... District Special Equipment Code (Detroit)

THE BODY CODE is two numerals and a letter identifying the body style.

TORINO	CODE
4-Dr. Sedan HT Torino	53B
2-Dr. HT Torino	65B
2-Dr. HT Gran Torino	65D
4-Dr. Sedan HT Gran Torino	53D
2-Dr. Fastback Gran Torino Sport	63R
2-Dr. HT Gran Torino Sport	65R
Torino SW 4-Dr.	71B
Gran Torino SW 4-Dr.	71D
Torino Squire SW 4-Dr.	71K

*Rallye option available

FORD	CODE
4-Dr. Sedan Custom	54B
4-Dr. Sedan Custom 500	54D
4-Dr. Sedan Galaxie 500	54F
4-Dr. HT Galaxie 500	57F
2-Dr. HT Galaxie 500	65F
Convertible LTD	76H
2-Dr. HT LTD	65H
4-Dr. Sedan HT LTD	53H
4-Dr. HT LTD	57H
4-Dr. Sedan HT LTD Brougham	53K
4-Dr. HT LTD Brougham	57K
2-Dr. HT LTD Brougham	65K
4-Dr. SW Custom Ranch	71B
4-Dr. SW Custom 500 Ranch	71D
4-Dr. SW Country Sedan	71F
4-Dr. SW Country Squire	71H

MAVERICK	CODE
2-Dr. Sedan Standard	62A
4-Dr. Sedan Standard	54A
2-Dr. Sport Sedan Grabber	62D

MUSTANG	CODE
2-Dr. HT Standard	65D
2-Dr. Sportsroof Standard	63D
Convertible Standard	76D
2-Dr. HT Grande	65F
2-Dr. Sportsroof Mach I	63R

*Spring option available

PINTO	CODE
2-Dr. Sedan Runabout	62B
3-Dr. Runabout	64B
2-Dr. SW Runabout	73B

*Squire Wagon option available

THUNDERBIRD	CODE
2-Dr. Hardtop	65K

THE COLOR CODE is a number and letter indicating the exterior paint color.

COLOR	CODE
Light Gray Metallic	1A
Black	1C
Silver Metallic	1D
Calypso Blue	2A
Bright Red	2B
Red	2E
Medium Red Metallic	2G
Maroon	2J
Light Blue	3B
Medium Blue Metallic	3C
Medium Blue Metallic	3D
Grabber Blue	3F
Dark Blue Metallic	3H
Bright Blue Metallic	3J
Pastel Lime	4A
Bright Green Gold Metallic	4B
Ivy Bronze Metallic	4C
Medium Ivy Bronze Metallic	4D
Bright Lime	4E
Medium Lime Metallic	4F
Medium Ivy Bronze Metallic	4G
Medium Green Metallic	4P
Dark Green Metallic	Q
Light Pewter Metallic	5A
Ginger Bronze Metallic	5C
Ginger Bronze Metallic	5D
Dark Brown Metallic	5F
Light Copper Metallic	5G
Ginger Metallic	5H
Medium Ginger Bronze Metallic	5J
Tan	5L
Light Goldenrod	6B
Medium Goldenrod	6C
Yellow	6D
Medium Bright Yellow	6E
Bright Yellow Gold Metallic	6F
Light Copper Metallic	6G
Gray Gold Metallic	6J
White	9A

THE TRIM CODE consists of a two-letter or a letter-number combination designating the interior trim.

THUNDERBIRD	CODE
Black (1)	HA
Black (2)	KA
Black (3)	GA
Dark Blue (1)	HB
Dark Blue (2)	KB
Dark Blue (3)	GB
Dark Red (1)	HD
Dark Red (2)	KD
Dark Red (3)	GD
Ginger (2)	KF
Ginger (3)	GF
Dark Green (1)	HR
Dark Green (2)	KR
Dark Green (3)	GR
Tobacco (1)	HZ
Tobacco (2)	KZ
White/Black (2)	KW
White/Blue (2)	KL
White/Green (2)	K5
White/Tobacco (2)	K9

1 - Cloth & vinyl split-bench
2 - Leather & vinyl split-bench
3 - Cloth & vinyl hi-back bucket

PINTO SEDAN AND RUNABOUT ALL VINYL BUCKET-STANDARD	CODE
Black (1)	AA
Black (2)	BA
Black (3)	CA
Medium Blue (1)	AB
Medium Blue (2)	BB
Medium Blue (3)	CB
Medium Ginger (1)	AF
Medium Ginger (2)	BF
Medium Ginger (3)	CR
Medium Green (1)	AR
Medium Green (2)	BR
Medium Beige (1)	AT
Medium Beige (2)	BT
Medium Beige (3)	CT
White/Black (1)	AW
White/Black (2)	BW
White/Black (3)	CW
White/Blue (1)	AL
White/Blue (2)	BL
White/Blue (3)	CL
White/Ginger (1)	AS
White/Ginger (2)	BS
White/Ginger (3)	CS
White/Green (1)	A5
White/Green (2)	B5
White/Green (3)	C5

1 - Vinyl bucket
2 - Cloth & vinyl bucket
3 - Knitted vinyl bucket

MAVERICK STANDARD 2 AND 4-DOOR SEDANS STANDARD CLOTH & VINYL BENCH	CODE
Black (1)	BA
Black (2)	AA
Black (3)*	CA
Black (4)	EA
Black (6)	FA
Medium Blue (1)	BB
Medium Blue (3)*	CB
Medium Blue (4)	EB
Medium Blue (6)	FB
Vermillion (3)**	CE

MAVERICK STANDARD 2 AND 4-DOOR SEDANS STANDARD CLOTH & VINYL BENCH	CODE
Vermillion (4)	EE
Vermillion (5)	GE
Vermillion (6)	FE
Light Gray Gold (1)	BY
Light Gray Gold (2)	AY
Light Gray Gold (3)	CY
Light Gray Gold (4)	EY
Light Gray Gold (5)	GY
Light Gray Gold (6)	FY

1 - Cloth & vinyl bench
2 - Vinyl bench
3 - Deluxe cloth & vinyl bench
4 - Deluxe woven vinyl bench
5 - cloth & vinyl bucket
6 - Deluxe woven vinyl bucket
* N/A on 2-Door and Grabber
** N/A on 4-Door

MUSTANG HARDTOP, SPORTSROOF AND MACH I	CODE
Black (1)	AA/GA
Black*	CA
Black**	FA
Medium Blue (1)	AB/GB
Medium Blue*	CB
Medium Blue**	FB
Vermillion (1)	AE/GE
Vermillion*	CE
Vermillion**	FE
Medium Ginger (1)	AF/GF
Medium Ginger*	CF
Medium Ginger**	FF
Medium Green (1)	AR/GR
Medium Green*	CR
Medium Green**	FR
White (1)	AW/GW
White*	CW

1 - Vinyl
2 - Knitted vinyl
* Convertible - Knitted vinyl
** Grande HT - Lambeth cloth & vinyl

GRAN TORINO SPORT*	CODE
Black	MA
Medium Blue	MB
Ginger	MF
Medium Green	MR
White w/Black	MW
White w/Blue	ML
White w/Tobacco	M9
White w/Green	M5

* Knitted vinyl bucket

TORINO BROUGHAM AND SPORT*	CODE
Black	NA/EA
Medium Blue	NB
Medium Green	NR
Light Gray Gold	NY
Tobacco	NZ
Ginger	EF

* Cloth & vinyl bench

GRAN TORINO STATION WAGON*	CODE
Black	CA/GA
Black	JA/HA
Medium Blue	CB/GB
Ginger	CF/GF
Ginger	JF/HF
Medium Green	CR/GR

* Vinyl bench

TORINO (LOW SERIES)*/**	CODE
Black	AA
Medium Blue	AB
Medium Green	AR

* Includes Torino Station Wagon
** Vinyl bench

GRAN TORINO*	CODE
Black (1)	BA/CA
Black (1)	KA
Medium Blue (1)	BB/CB
Medium Blue (1)	KB
Medium Green (1)	BR/CR
Medium Green (1)	KR
Light Gray Gold (1)	BY
Tobacco (1)	BZ
Ginger (1)	CF/KF
White w/Black	CW/KW
White w/Blue	CL/KL
White w/Tobacco	C9/K9
White w/Green	C5/K5

1 - Cloth & vinyl bench
2 - Vinyl bench

GRAN TORINO SPORT	CODE
Black (1)	DA
Black (2)	FA
Medium Blue (2)	FB
Ginger (1)	DF
Ginger (2)	FF
Medium Green (2)	FR
White w/Black (2)	FW
White w/Blue (2)	FW
White w/Tobacco (2)	F9
White w/Green (2)	F5

1 - Sport cloth bench
2 - Vinyl bench

FORD LTD BROUGHAM*	CODE
Black	ZA/EA
Medium Blue	ZB/EB
Dark Red	ZD/ED
Medium Green	ZR/ER
Gray Gold	ZY/EY
Dark Tobacco	ZZ/EZ

* Cloth & vinyl hi-back bench

COUNTRY SQUIRE*	CODE
Black	BA
Medium Blue	BB
Ginger	BF
Medium Green	BR

* Knitted vinyl

LTD CONVERTIBLE & COUNTRY SQUIRE*	CODE
Black	FA
Medium Blue	FB
Dark Red	FD
Ginger	FF
Medium Green	FR
White (w/Black)**	FW**

* Vinyl bench
** White trim w/black components

CUSTOM AND CUSTOM RANCH WAGON*	CODE
Black	NA
Medium Blue	NB
Medium Green**	NR
Gray Gold***	NY

* Vinyl bench
** Ranch Wagon only
*** Custom only

CUSTOM 500 AND CUSTOM 500 RANCH WAGONS*	CODE
Black	HA/JA**
Medium Blue	HB/JB**
Medium Green	HR/JF**
Gray Gold	HY/JR**

* Cloth & vinyl bench
** Ranch Wagons - Vinyl

GALAXIE 500 AND COUNTRY SEDAN	CODE
Black (1)	KA
Black (2)	WA
Medium Blue (1)	KB
Medium Blue (2)	WB
Dark Red (2)	WD
Medium Ginger (1)	KF
Medium Ginger (2)	WF
Medium Green (1)	KR
Medium Green (2)	WR
Gray Gold (1)	KY
Gray Gold (2)	WY

1 - Cloth & vinyl bench
2 - Vinyl bench

COUNTRY SEDAN & COUNTRY SQUIRE*	CODE
Black (Country Sedan)	RA
Black (Country Squire)	VA

* Plaid cloth & vinyl bench

LTD	CODE
Black	FA*/DA**
Medium Blue	FB*/DB**
Dark Red	FD*/DD**
Ginger	FF*/DF**
Medium Green	FR*/DR**
Gray Gold	FY*/DY**
White (w/Black)***	FW

* Vinyl bench
** Cloth & vinyl bench
*** White trim w/black components

THE AXLE CODE is a number or letter indicating the rear axle ratio and standard or locking type axles.

CONVENTIONAL	LOCKING	RATIO
2	K	2.75:1
3		2.79:1
4	M	2.80:1
6	O	3.00:1
7		3.18:1
9	R	3.25:1
A	S	3.50:1
B		3.07:1
G		3.55:1
H		3.78:1
	V	3.91:1

THE TRANSMISSION CODE is a number or letter indicating the type of transmission.

TYPE	CODE
3-Speed Manual	1
4-Speed Manual	5
4-Speed Manual	E
Automatic (C4)	W
Automatic (C6)	U
Automatic (FMX)	X
Automatic (C6 Special)	Z

9 - 20

THE DSO CODE, consisting of two numbers, designates the district in which the car was ordered and may appear in conjunction with a Domestic Special Order or Foreign Special Order number when applicable. Ford of Canada DSO codes consist of a letter and a number.

FORD DISTRICT	CODE
Boston	11
Buffalo	12
New York	13
Pittsburgh	14
Newark	15
Philadelphia	16
Washington	27
Atlanta	21
Charlotte	22
Memphis	23
Jacksonville	24
Richmond	25
New Orleans	26
Louisville	28
Pittsburgh	38
Chicago	41
Cleveland	42
Milwaukee	43
Lansing	45
Indianapolis	46
Cincinnati	47
Detroit	48
Dallas	52
Kansas City	53
Omaha	54
St. Louis	55
Davenport	56
Houston	57
Twin City	58
Oklahoma City	65
Los Angeles	71
San Jose	72
Salt Lake City	73
Seattle	74
Phoenix	75
Denver	76
Government	83
Home Office Reserve	84
American Red Cross	85
Body Company	87
Transportation Services	89
Export	90-99

FORD OF CANADA DISTRICT	CODE
Central	B1
Eastern	B2
Atlantic	B3
Midwestern	B4
Western	B6
Pacific	B7
Export	12

ENGINE IDENTIFICATION

ENGINE TAG
Since 1964, Ford engines can be identified by a tag attached to the engine. The tag contains the year and cubic inch displacement.

CASTING NUMBERS
While helpful in identifying Ford engine components, casting numbers are not conclusive in pin-pointing the exact year of manufacture. A better method is to search for the original host vehicle's VIN (Vehicle Identification Number) stamped on the driver's side at the rear of the engine block below the cylinder head.

ENGINE TAG EXAMPLE
240	72
2-A	123A

DECODED EXAMPLE
240	CID
72	Model Year (1972)
2	Production Year
A	Production Month (January)
123A	Engine Code Number

FORD ENGINES
CID	NO. CYL.	HORSE-POWER	COMP. RATIO	CARB.
240	6	103	8.5:1	1 BC
302	8	140	8.5:1	2 BC
351	8	153	8.3:1	2 BC
351	8	163	8.4:1	2 BC
400	8	172	8.4:1	2 BC
429	8	208	8.5:1	4 BC

TORINO ENGINES
CID	NO. CYL.	HORSE-POWER	COMP. RATIO	CARB.
250	6	95	8.0:1	1 BC
302	8	140	8.5:1	2 BC
351	8	161	8.6:1	2 BC
351 "CJ"	8	248	8.6:1	4 BC
400	8	168	8.4:1	2 BC
429	8	205	8.5:1	4 BC

PINTO ENGINES
CID	NO. CYL.	HORSE-POWER	COMP. RATIO	CARB.
98	4	54	8.0:1	1 BC
122	4	86	8.2:1	2 BC

MAVERICK ENGINES
CID	NO. CYL.	HORSE-POWER	COMP. RATIO	CARB.
170	6	82	8.3:1	1 BC
200	6	91	8.3:1	1 BC
250	6	98	8.0:1	1 BC
302	8	143	8.5:1	2 BC

MUSTANG ENGINES
CID	NO. CYL.	HORSE-POWER	COMP. RATIO	CARB.
250	6	99	8.0:1	1 BC
302*	8	141	8.5:1	2 BC
351	8	177	8.6:1	2 BC
351	8	266	8.6:1	4 BC

* Standard on Mach 1

THUNDERBIRD ENGINES
CID	NO. CYL.	HORSE-POWER	COMP. RATIO	CARB.
429	8	212	8.5:1	4 BC
460	8	224	8.5:1	4 BC

1973 FORD LTD COUNTRY SQUIRE

1973 FORD LTD BROUGHAM

1973 FORD GALAXIE 500

1973 FORD PINTO

1973 FORD GRAN TORINO SQUIRE

1973 FORD THUNDERBIRD

1973 FORD MAVERICK

1973 FORD GRAN TORINO

1973 FORD MUSTANG MACH I

VEHICLE IDENTIFICATION NUMBER

• FORD F 3S56H123456 F •

Located on the top of the dash on the driver's side and visible through the windshield from outside the car.

FIRST DIGIT: Identifies the year 3 = 1973

SECOND DIGIT: Identifies the assembly plant

ASSEMBLY PLANT	CODE
Atlanta, GA	A
Oakville, Ont., CAN	B
Mahwah, NJ	E
Dearborn, MI	F
Chicago, IL	G
Lorain, OH	H
Los Angeles, CA	J
Kansas City, KS	K
Norfolk, VA	N
Twin Cities, MN	P
San Jose, CA	R
Allen Park (Pilot Plant)	S
Metuchen, NJ	T
Louisville, KY	U
Wayne, MI	W
St. Thomas, Ont., CAN	X
Wixom, MI	Y
St. Louis, MO	Z

THIRD AND FOURTH DIGITS: Identify the body serial code

TORINO	CODE
4-Dr. Sedan HT Torino	27
2-Dr. Hardtop Torino	25
2-Dr. Hardtop Gran Torino	30
4-Dr. Sedan HT Gran Torino	31
2-Dr. Fastback Gran Torino Sport	35
2-Dr. HT Gran Torino Sport	38
Torino SW 4-Dr.	40
Gran Torino SW 4-Dr.	42
Torino Squire SW 4-Dr.	43

FORD	CODE
4-Dr. Sedan Custom 500	53
4-Dr. Sedan Galaxie 500	54
4-Dr. HT Galaxie 500	56
2-Dr. HT Galaxie 500	58
2-Dr. HT LTD	62
4-Dr. Pillar HT LTD	63
4-Dr. HT LTD	64
4-Dr. Pillar HT LTD Brougham	66
4-Dr. HT LTD Brougham	67
2-Dr. HT LTD Brougham	68
4-Dr. SW Custom 500 Ranch	72
4-Dr. SW Country Sedan	74
4-Dr. SW Country Squire	76

MAVERICK	CODE
2-Dr. Sedan	91
4-Dr. Sedan	92
2-Dr. Sport Sedan Grabber	93

MUSTANG	CODE
2-Dr. Hardtop	01
2-Dr. Sportsroof	02
Convertible	03
2-Dr. HT Grande	04
2-Dr. Sportsroof Mach I	05

PINTO	CODE
2-Dr. Sedan	10
3-Dr. Runabout	11
2-Dr. Station Wagon	12

THUNDERBIRD	CODE
2-Dr. Hardtop	87

FIFTH DIGIT: Identifies the engine code

ENGINE	CODE
V-8 460-4V	A
V-8 460-4V Police	C
V-8 302-2V	F
V-8 351-2V	H
6 250-1V	L
V-8 429-4V	N
V-8 351-4V (CJ)	Q
V-8 400-2V	S
6 200-1V	T
4 91-1V (1600 cc)	W
4 122-2V (2000 cc)	X
6 250-1V*	3
V-8 351 (H.O.)	R

* Low compression export

LAST SIX DIGITS: Represents the basic production numbers

EXAMPLE:

3	S	56	H	123456
Model Year	Asm Plant	Body Serial Code	Engine	Production Sequence Number

VEHICLE CERTIFICATION LABEL

THE VEHICLE CERTIFICATION LABEL is attached to the rear face of the driver's door. The upper half of the label contains the name of the manufacturer, the month and year of manufacture and the certification statement. The V.C. label also contains the Vehicle Identification Number. The remaining information on the V.C. label consists of pertinent vehicle identification codes: ie. body, color, trim, axle, transmission and the domestic special order (DSO) codes.

```
MANUFACTURED BY
FORD MOTOR COMPANY

7/73 THIS VEHICLE CONFORMS TO ALL
APPLICABLE FEDERAL MOTOR VEHICLE
SAFETY STANDARDS IN EFFECT ON
DATE OF MANUFACTURE SHOWN ABOVE

3S56H123456        57F    DA
DA         W        6      48

NOT FOR TITLE OR REGISTRATION
MADE IN U.S.A.
```

EXAMPLE:
3S56H123456	Vehicle Identification Number (VIN)
57F	Body Type Code (Galaxie 500 4-Dr. Hardtop)
DA	Color Code (Black)
DA	Trim Code (Black Cloth & Vinyl)
W	Transmission Code (C4 Automatic)
6	Rear Axle Code (3.00:1)
48	District Special Equipment Code (Detroit)

THE BODY CODE is two numerals and a letter identifying the body style.

TORINO — CODE
4-Dr. Sedan HT Torino	53B
2-Dr. HT Torino	65B
2-Dr. HT Gran Torino	65D
4-Dr. Sedan HT Gran Torino	53D
2-Dr. Fastback Gran Torino Sport	63R
2-Dr. HT Gran Torino Sport	65R
Torino Station Wagon 4-Dr.	71B
Gran Torino Station Wagon 4-Dr.	71D
Torino Squire Station Wagon 4-Dr.	71K

*Rallye option available

FORD — CODE
4-Dr. Sedan Custom 500	53D
4-Dr. Sedan Galaxie 500	53F
4-Dr. Hardtop Galaxie 500	57F
2-Dr. Hardtop Galaxie 500	65F
2-Dr. Hardtop LTD	65H
4-Dr. Pillar HT LTD	53H
4-Dr. Hardtop LTD	57H
4-Dr. Pillar HT LTD Brougham	53K
4-Dr. Hardtop LTD Brougham	57K
2-Dr. Hardtop LTD Brougham	65K
4-Dr. Wagon Custom 500 Ranch	71D
4-Dr. Wagon Country Sedan	71F
4-Dr. Wagon Country Squire	71H

MAVERICK — CODE
2-Dr. Sedan	62A
4-Dr. Sedan	54A
2-Dr. Sport Sedan Grabber 62D	

MUSTANG — CODE
2-Dr. Hardtop	65D
2-Dr. Sportsroof	63D
Convertible	76D
2-Dr. HT Grande	65F
2-Dr. Sportsroof Mach I	63R

PINTO — CODE
2-Dr. Sedan	62B
3-Dr. Runabout	64B
2-Dr. Station Wagon	73B

*Squire Wagon option available

THUNDERBIRD — CODE
2-Dr. Hardtop	65K

THE COLOR CODE is a number and letter indicating the exterior paint color.

COLOR — CODE
Lt. Gray Met.	1A
Black	1C
Silver Met.	1D
Brt. Red	2B
Red Met.	2C
Med. Red Met.	2G
Maroon	2J
Fuschia	2K
Platinum	3A
Lt. Blue	3B
Med. Blue Met.	3D
Brt. Dk. Blue Met.	3G
Brt. Blue Met.	3K
Silver Blue Met.	3L
Brt. Green Gold Met.	4B
Ivy Bronze Met.	4C
Dk. Ivy Bronze Met.	4D
Med. Aqua	4N
Med. Green Met.	4P
Dk. Green Met.	4Q
Lt. Green	4S
Brt. Lime Gold Met.	4U
Pewter Met.	5A
Ginger Bronze Met.	5D
Dk. Brown Met.	5F
Ginger Met.	5H
Med. Ginger Met.	5J
Dk. Gold Met.	5K
Tan	5L
Med. Chestnut Met.	5M
Med. Orange Met.	5N
Copper Met.	5P
Lt. Goldenrod	6B
Med. Goldenrod	6C
Yellow	6D
Med. Brt. Yellow	6E
Brt. Yellow Gold Met.	6F
Brt. Yellow Gold Met.	6G
Med. Gold Met.	6L
White	9A
White	9C

THE TRIM CODE consists of a two-letter or a letter-number combination designating the interior trim.

THUNDERBIRD

	CODE
Black (1)	HA/GA*
Black (2)	JA/KA**
Dark Blue (1)	HB/GB*
Dark Blue (2)	JB/KB**
Ginger (1)	HF/GF*
Ginger (2)	JF/KF**
Dark Green (1)	HR/GR*
Dark Green (2)	JR/KR**
Light Gold (1)	HY
Light Gold (2)	JY/KY**
Tobacco (1)	HZ
Tobacco (2)	JZ/KZ**
White w/Black (2)	JW/KW**
White w/Green (2)	J5/K5**
White w/Tobacco (2)	J9/K9**
White w/Blue (2)	JL/KL**

1 - Cloth & vinyl split bench
2 - Vinyl
* Cloth & vinyl high-back bucket
** Leather & vinyl

PINTO

	CODE
Black (1)	AA/CA
Black (2)	BA
Lt. Med. Blue (1)	AB/CB
Med. Blue (2)	BB
Med. Ginger (1)	AF/CF
Med. Ginger (2)	BF
Orange (3)	BC
Med. Lt. Avocado (1)	AG/CG
Lt. Avocado (2)	BG
Avocado (3)	BG
Lt. Beige (1)	AT/CT
Lt. Beige (2)	BT
Yellow (3)	BY
Tan (3)	BU
White/Black (1)	AW/CW
White/Blue (1)	AQ/CQ
White/Ginger (1)	A3/C3
White/Avocado (1)	A6/C6

1 - Vinyl
2 - Cloth & vinyl luxury
3 - Cloth & vinyl sports accent

MAVERICK SEDANS AND GRABBER

	CODE
Black (1)	BA
Black (2)	HA/KA/LA
Med. Blue (1)	BB
Med. Blue (2)	HB/KB/LB
Med. Orange (N/A Sedans) (2)	HC/KC/LC
Med. Ginger (1)	BF
Med. Ginger (2)	HF/KF/LF
Med. Lt. Avocado (1)	BT
Avocado (2)	HG/KG/LG
Light Beige (1)	BG
Light Beige (2)	HT/KT/LT
Light Tan (2)	PU

1 - Cloth & vinyl bench
2 - Vinyl bench

MUSTANG

	CODE
Black (1)	AA
Black (2)	CA/GA
Black (3)	FA
Med. Blue (1)	AB
Med. Blue (2)	CB/GB
Med. Blue (3)	FB

MUSTANG

	CODE
Med. Ginger (1)	AF
Med. Ginger (2)	CF/GF
Med. Ginger (3)	FF
Avocado (1)	AG
Avocado (3)	CG/GG
Avocado (3)	FG
White (1)	AW
White (2)	GW

1 - Vinyl
2 - Knitted vinyl
3 - Cloth & vinyl

TORINO

	CODE
Black (1)	BA/DA*
Black (1)	EA/NA
Black (2)	AA/CA/FA
Black (2)	MA/GA
Med. Blue (1)	BB/NB
Med. Blue (2)	AB/CB/FB
Med. Blue (2)	KB/MB/GB
Med. Green (1)	BR/NR
Med. Green (2)	AR/CR/FR
Med. Green (2)	KR/MR/GR
Beige (1)	BT/NT
Beige (2)	AT/CT/FT
Beige (2)	KT/MT
Tobacco (1)	BZ/NZ
Ginger (1)	EF/DF*
Ginger (2)	CF/FF/KF
Ginger (2)	MF/GF

1 - Cloth & vinyl
2 - Vinyl
* Sport cloth

FORD CUSTOM 500

	CODE
Black (1)	AA
Black (2)	BA
Med. Blue (1)	AB
Med. Blue (2)	BB
Med. Green (1)	AR
Med. Green (2)	BR
Lt. Beige (1)	AT
Lt. Beige (2)	BT

1 - Cloth & vinyl
2 - Vinyl

GALAXIE 500/LTD/COUNTRY SQUIRE*

	CODE
Black	DA/GA
Black	HA/JA
Med. Blue	DB/GB
Med. Blue	HB/JB
Med. Green	DR/GR
Med. Green	HR/JR
Med. Ginger	DF/GF
Lt. Beige	DT/GT
Lt. Beige	HT/JT
Tobacco	HZ/JZ

* Cloth & vinyl

COUNTRY SEDAN*

	CODE
Black	EA/FA
Black	CA/KA
Med. Blue	EB/FB
Med. Blue	CB/KB
Med. Ginger	EF/FF
Med. Ginger	KF
Med. Green	ER/FR
Med. Green	CR/KR
Lt. Beige	ET/FT/CT

* Vinyl

THE AXLE CODE is a number or letter indicating the rear axle ratio and standard or locking type axles.

CONVENTIONAL	LOCKING	RATIO
2	K	2.75:1
3	L	2.79:1
5	E	3.07:1
6	O	3.00:1
7	P	3.40:1
9	R	3.25:1
A	S	3.50:1
G	X	3.55:1
	V	3.91:1

THE TRANSMISSION CODE is a number or letter indicating the type of transmission.

TYPE	CODE
3-Speed Manual	1
4-Speed Manual	5
4-Speed Borg Warner	6
4-Speed Manual	E
Automatic (C4)	W
Automatic (C6)	U
Automatic (C3)	V
Automatic (FMX)	X
Automatic Borg Warner	Y
Automatic (C6 Special)	Z

THE DSO CODE, consisting of two numbers, designates the district in which the car was ordered and may appear in conjuction with a Domestic Special Order or Foreign Special Order number when applicable. Ford of Canada DSO codes consist of a letter and a number

FORD DISTRICT	CODE
Boston	11
Buffalo	12
New York	13
Pittsburgh	14
Newark	15
Philadelphia	16
Washington	27
Atlanta	21
Charlotte	22
Memphis	23

FORD DISTRICT	CODE
Jacksonville	24
Richmond	25
New Orleans	26
Louisville	28
Chicago	41
Cleveland	42
Milwaukee	43
Lansing	45
Indianapolis	46
Cincinnati	47
Detroit	48
Dallas	52
Kansas City	53
Omaha	54
St. Louis	55
Davenport	56
Houston	57
Twin City	58
Los Angeles	71
San Jose	72
Salt Lake City	73
Seattle	74
Phoenix	75
Denver	76
Government	83
Home Office Reserve	84
American Red Cross	85
Body Company	87
Transportation Services	89
Export	90-99

FORD OF CANADA DISTRICT	CODE
Central	B1
Eastern	B2
Atlantic	B3
Midwestern	B4
Western	B6
Pacific	B7
Export	12

ENGINE IDENTIFICATION

ENGINE TAG
Since 1964, Ford engines can be identified by a tag attached to the engine. The tag contains the year and cubic inch displacement.

CASTING NUMBERS
While helpful in identifying Ford engine components, casting numbers are not conclusive in pin-pointing the exact year of manufacture. A better method is to search for the original host vehicle's VIN (Vehicle Identification Number) stamped on the driver's side at the rear of the engine block below the cylinder head.

ENGINE TAG EXAMPLE
351   73
3-A   123A

DECODED EXAMPLE
351	CID
73	Model Year (1973)
3	Production Year
A	Production Month (January)
123A	Engine Code Number

FORD ENGINES

CID	NO. CYL.	HORSE-POWER	COMP. RATIO	CARB.
351	8	158	8.0:1	2 BC
351	8	161	8.0:1	2 BC
400	8	171	8.0:1	2 BC
429	8	202	8.0:1	4 BC
460*	8	267	8.6:1	4 BC

* Police interceptor

TORINO ENGINES

CID	NO. CYL.	HORSE-POWER	COMP. RATIO	CARB.
250	6	92	8.0:1	1 BC
302	8	137	8.0:1	2 BC
351	8	156	8.0:1	2 BC
351	8	159	8.0:1	2 BC
351	8	246	8.0:1	4 BC
400	8	168	8.0:1	2 BC
429	8	197	8.0:1	4 BC
429	8	201	8.0:1	4 BC
460*	8	274	8.8:1	4 BC

* Police interceptor

PINTO ENGINES

CID	NO. CYL.	HORSE-POWER	COMP. RATIO	CARB.
98	4	54	8.1:1	1 BC
122	4	85	8.2:1	2 BC

MAVERICK ENGINES

CID	NO. CYL.	HORSE-POWER	COMP. RATIO	CARB.
200	6	84	8.3:1	1 BC
250	6	88	8.0:1	1 BC
302	8	138	8.0:1	2 BC

MUSTANG ENGINES

CID	NO. CYL.	HORSE-POWER	COMP. RATIO	CARB.
250	6	99	8.0:1	1 BC
302	8	141	8.0:1	2 BC
351	8	177	8.0:1	2 BC
351	8	266	7.9:1	4 BC

THUNDERBIRD ENGINES

CID	NO. CYL.	HORSE-POWER	COMP. RATIO	CARB.
429	8	208	8.0:1	4 BC
460	8	208	8.0:1	4 BC

1974 FORD MAVERICK

1974 FORD MUSTANG II

1974 FORD LTD COUNTRY SQUIRE

1974 FORD PINTO

1974 FORD GRAN TORINO

1974 FORD THUNDERBIRD

1974 FORD GRAN TORINO SQUIRE

1974 FORD LTD BROUGHAM

VEHICLE IDENTIFICATION NUMBER

```
FORD
F 4S56H123456 F
```

Located on the top of the dash on the driver's side and visible through the windshield from outside the car.

FIRST DIGIT: Identifies the year (4 = 1974)

SECOND DIGIT: Identifies the assembly plant

ASSEMBLY PLANT	CODE
Atlanta, GA	A
Oakville, Ont., CAN	B
Mahwah, NJ	E
Dearborn, MI	F
Chicago, IL	G
Lorain, OH	H
Los Angeles, CA	J
Kansas City, KS	K
Norfolk, VA	N
Twin Cities, MN	P
San Jose, CA	R
Allen Park (Pilot Plant)	S
Metuchen, NJ	T
Louisville, KY	U
Wayne, MI	W
St. Thomas, Ont., CAN	X
Wixom, MI	Y
St. Louis, MO	Z

THIRD AND FOURTH DIGITS: Identify the body serial code

TORINO	CODE
2-Dr. HT Grand Torino Elite	21
4-Dr. Sedan HT Torino	27
2-Dr. HT Torino	25
4-Dr. Sedan HT Gran Torino	31
2-Dr. HT Gran Torino	30
4-Dr. Sedan HT Gran Torino Brougham	33
2-Dr. HT Gran Torino Brougham	32
2-Dr. HT Gran Torino Sport	38
Torino Station Wagon	40
Gran Torino 3 SW	42
Gran Torino Squire 3 SW	43

FORD CODE	
4-Dr. Sedan Custom 500	53
4-Dr. Sedan Galaxie 500	54
4-Dr. Hardtop Galaxie 500	56
2-Dr. Hardtop Galaxie 500	58
2-Dr. Hardtop LTD	62
4-Dr. Pillar HT LTD	63
4-Dr. Hardtop LTD	64
4-Dr. Pillar HT LTD Brougham	66
4-Dr. HT LTD Brougham	67
2-Dr. HT LTD Brougham	68
4-Dr. SW Custom 500 Ranch	72
4-Dr. SW Country Sedan	74
4-Dr. SW Country Squire	76

MAVERICK	CODE
2-Dr. Sedan	91
4-Dr. Sedan	92
2-Dr. Sport Sedan Grabber	93

MUSTANG	CODE
2-Dr. 4-Pass. Notchback	02
3-Dr. 4-Pass. Hatchback	03
2-Dr. 4-Pass. Notchback GHIA	04
3-Dr. 4-Pass. Hatchback Mach I	05

PINTO	CODE
2-Dr. Sedan	10
3-Dr. Runabout	11
2-Dr. Station Wagon	12

THUNDERBIRD	CODE
2-Dr. Hardtop	87

FIFTH DIGIT: Identifies the engine code

ENGINE	CODE
V-8 460-4V	A
V-8 460-4V (Police)	C
V-8 302-2V	F
V-8 351-2V	H
6 250-1V	L
V-8 351-4V (CJ)	Q
V-8 400-2V	S
6 200-1V	T
4 122-2V (2000 cc)	X
4 139-2V (2300 cc)	Y
6 169-2V (2800 cc)	Z
6 250 (Export)	3

LAST SIX DIGITS: Identifies the basic production numbers

EXAMPLE:

4	S	56	H	123456
Model Year	Asm Plant	Body Serial Code	Engine	Production Sequence Number

VEHICLE CERTIFICATION LABEL

THE VEHICLE CERTIFICATION LABEL is attached to the rear face of the driver's door. The upper half of the label contains the name of the manufacturer, the month and year of manufacture and the certification statement. The V.C. label also contains the Vehicle Identification Number. The remaining information on the V.C. label consists of pertinent vehicle identification codes: ie. body, color, trim, axle, transmission and the domestic special order (DSO) codes.

```
MANUFACTURED BY
FORD MOTOR COMPANY

7/74 THIS VEHICLE CONFORMS TO ALL
APPLICABLE FEDERAL MOTOR VEHICLE
SAFETY STANDARDS IN EFFECT ON
DATE OF MANUFACTURE SHOWN ABOVE

4S56H123456        57F    1C
DA        X        2      48

NOT FOR TITLE OR REGISTRATION
MADE IN U.S.A.
```

EXAMPLE:

4S56H123456	Vehicle Identification Number (VIN)
57F	Body Type Code (Galaxie 500 4-Dr. Hardtop)
1C	Color Code (Black)
DA	Trim Code (Black Cloth & Vinyl)
X	Transmission Code (FMX Automatic)
2	Rear Axle Code (2.75:1)
48	District Special Equipment Code (Detroit)

THE BODY CODE is two numerals and a letter identifying the body style.

TORINO	CODE
2-Dr. HT Grand Torino Elite	65M
4-Dr. Sedan HT Torino	53B
2-Dr. HT Torino	65B
4-Dr. Sedan HT Gran Torino	53D
2-Dr. HT Gran Torino	65D
4-Dr. Sedan HT Gran Torino Brougham	53K
2-Dr. HT Gran Torino Brougham	65K
2-Dr. HT Gran Torino Sport	65R
Torino Station Wagon	71B
Gran Torino 3 SW	71D
Gran Torino Squire 3 SW	71K

FORD	CODE
4-Dr. Sedan Custom 500	53D
4-Dr. Sedan Galaxie 500	53F
4-Dr. HT Galaxie 500	57F
2-Dr. HT Galaxie 500	65F
2-Dr. HT LTD	65H
4-Dr. Pillar HT LTD	53H
4-Dr. HT LTD	57H
4-Dr. Pillar HT LTD Brougham	53K
4-Dr. HT LTD Brougham	57K
2-Dr. HT LTD Brougham	65K
4-Dr. SW Custom 500 Ranch	71D
4-Dr. SW Country Sedan	71F
4-Dr. SW Country Squire	71H

MAVERICK	CODE
2-Dr. Sedan	62A
4-Dr. Sedan	54A
2-Dr. Sport Sedan Grabber	62D

MUSTANG	CODE
2-Dr. 4-Pass. Notchback	60F
3-Dr. 4-Pass. Hatchback	69F
2-Dr. 4-Pass. Notchback GHIA	60H
3-Dr. 4-Pass. Hatchback Mach I	69R

PINTO	CODE
2-Dr. Sedan	62B
3-Dr. Runabout	64B
2-Dr. Station Wagon	73B

*Squire Wagon option available

THUNDERBIRD	CODE
2-Dr. Hardtop	65K

THE COLOR CODE is a number and letter indicating the exterior paint color.

COLOR	CODE
Black	1C
Silver Met.	1D
Lt. Silver Cloud Met.	1E
Silver Met.	1G
Med. Slate Blue Met.	1H
Bright Red	2B
Red	2E
Med. Red Met.	2G
Med. Red	2M
Platinum	3A
Light Blue	3B
Med. Blue Met.	3D
Bright Blue Met.	3E
Bright Dark Blue Met.	3G
Silver Blue Met.	3L

COLOR	CODE
Silver Blue Met.	3M
Light Grabber Blue	3N
Med. Blue Met.	3P
Pastel Blue	3Q
Pastel Lime	4A
Bright Green Gold Met.	4B
Dark Green Met.	4Q
Med. Ivy Bronze Met.	4T
Dark Yellow Green Met.	4V
Med. Lime Yellow	4W
Dk. Ivy Bronze Met.	4Y
Ginger Met.	5H
Dk. Ginger Met.	5J
Med. Chestnut Met.	5M
Dk. Brown Met.	5Q
Brt. Gold Bronze Met.	5R
Med. Beige	5S
Saddle Bronze Met.	5T
Buff	5V
Orange	5W
Dk. Copper Met.	5Y
Unique Gold Met.	5Z
Med. Goldenrod	6C
Brt. Yellow Gold Met.	5G
Brt. Yellow Gold Met.	5F
Med. Gold Met.	6L
Med. Dk. Gold Met.	6M
Maize Yellow	6N
White Decor	9C
Ginger Bronze Met.	51
Copper Met.	52

THE TRIM CODE consists of a two-letter or a letter-number combination designating the interior trim.

THUNDERBIRD	CODE
Black (1)	HA
Black (2)	JA
Black (3)	KA
Med. Blue (1)	HB
Med. Blue (2)	JB
Med. Blue (3)	KB
Dk. Red (1)	HD
Dk. Red (2)	JD
Dk. Red (3)	KD
Med. Green (1)	HR
Med. Green (2)	JR
Med. Green (3)	KR
Lt. Tan (1)	HU
Lt. Tan (2)	JU
Lt. Tan (3)	KU
Med. Saddle (1)	HZ
Med. Saddle (2)	JZ
Med. Saddle (3)	KZ
White w/Black (2)	JW
White w/Black (3)	KW
White w/Blue (2)	JQ
White w/Blue (3)	KQ
White w/Green (2)	J5
White w/Green (3)	K5
White w/Saddle (2)	J9
White w/Saddle (3)	K9
White w/Red (2)	JN
White w/Red (3)	KN
White w/Gold (2)	J8
White w/Gold (3)	K8

1 - Cloth & vinyl
2 - Vinyl
3 - Leather & vinyl

PINTO*	**CODE**
Black (1)	AA/CA
Black (2)	BA
Med. Blue (1)	AB/CB
Med. Blue (2)	BB
Orange (2)	BC
Lt. Avocado (1)	AG/CG
Lt. Avocado (2)	BG
Lt. Tan (1)	AU/CU
Lt. Tan (2)	BU
Saddle (1)	CZ
Saddle (2)	BZ
Yellow (2)	BY

1 - Vinyl
2 - Cloth & vinyl

MAVERICK SEDANS AND GRABBER	**CODE**
Black (1)	BA/JA
Black (2)	HA/KA/LA
Med. Blue (1)	BB/JB
Med. Blue (2)	HB/KB
Med. Orange (Grabber only) (2)	HC/KC/LC
Med. Lt. Avocado (1)	BG/JG
Med. Lt. Avocado (2)	HG/KG/LG
Lt. Tan (1)	BU/JU
Lt. Tan (2)	HU/KU/LU
Silver Blue (3)	PE
Tan (3)	PU

1 - Cloth & vinyl
2 - Vinyl
3 - Luxury decor option

MUSTANG II*	**CODE**
Black	AA
Med. Blue	AB
Lt. Avocado	AG
Lt. Tan	AU
White w/Black	AW
White w/Blue	AQ
White w/Tan	AM
White w/Avocado	A6
White w/Red	AN

* All vinyl

GHIA	**CODE**
Black (1)	BA
Black (2)	DA
Med. Blue (1)	BB
Med. Blue (2)	DB/CB
Dk. Red (1)	BD
Dk. Red (2)	DD/CD
Lt. Avocado (1)	BG
Lt. Avocado (2)	DG/CG
Lt. Silver (1)	BP
Lt. Tan (1)	BU
Lt. Tan (2)	DU/CU
White w/Black (1)	BW
White w/Blue (1)	BQ
White w/Tan (1)	BM
White w/Red (1)	BN
White w/Avocado (1)	B6
Black w/Vermillion Strap (1)	EA

1 - All vinyl
2 - Cloth & vinyl

TORINO	**CODE**
Black (1)	JA/BA
Black (2)	CA/AA
Black (2)	GA/KA
Med. Blue (1)	JB/BB/LB
Med. Blue (2)	CB/AB
Med. Blue (2)	BG/KB
Dk. Red (2)	GD
Med. Green (1)	JR/BR/LR
Med. Green (2)	CR/AR
Med. Green (2)	GR/KR
Lt. Tan (1)	JU/BU/LU
Lt. Tan (2)	CU/AU
Lt. Tan (2)	GU/KU
Red (1)	LD
Saddle (1)	BZ
Med. Saddle (2)	CZ
White w/Blue (2)	GQ/CQ
White w/Black (2)	GW/CW
White w/Green (2)	G5/C5
White w/Tan (2)	GM
White w/Red (2)	GN
White w/Gold (2)	G8/C8
White w/Saddle (2)	C9

1 - Cloth & vinyl
2 - Vinyl

TORINO SPORT	**CODE**
Black/Vermillion (1)	DA/EA
Black (1)	GA/HA
Med. Blue/Lt. Blue (1)	DB/EB
Med. Blue (1)	GB/HB
Med. Blue (2)	FB
Med. Green (1)	GR/HR
Lt. Tan/Orange (1)	DU/EU
Lt. Tan (1)	GU
Lt. Tan (2)	FU
Lt. Gold (1)	GY
Lt. Gold (2)	FY
Med. Saddle (1)	GZ/HZ
White w/Black (1)	EW
White w/Blue (1)	EQ
White w/Saddle (1)	E9

1 - Vinyl
2 - Cloth & vinyl

FORD CUSTOM 500 AND GALAXIE	**CODE**
Black (1)	DA
Black (2)	EA
Med. Blue (1)	AB/DB
Med. Blue (2)	BB/EB
Med. Green (1)	AR/DR
Med. Green (2)	BR/ER
Lt. Beige (1)	AT/DT
Lt. Beige (Pass.) (2)	BT/ET
Med. Saddle (1)	DZ
Med. Saddle (2)	EZ
Tan (Ranch Wagon) (2)	BU

1 - Cloth & vinyl
2 - Vinyl

LTD AND COUNTRY SQUIRE CODE

Black (1)	GA/HA/JA
Black (2)	FA
Med. Blue (1)	GB/HB
Med. Blue (1)	JB/QB
Med. Blue (2)	FB/LB
Med. Blue (2)	KB/NB
Med. Green (1)	GR/HR/JR
Med. Green (2)	FR/LR
Med. Green (2)	KR/NR
Lt. Beige (1)	GT/HT/JT
Lt. Beige (2)	FT
Lt. Tan (2)	MU/KU
Med. Beige (1)	QT
Lt. Gold (1)	HY/JY
Med. Saddle (1)	GZ/HZ
Med. Saddle (1)	JZ/QZ
Med. Saddle (2)	FZ/LZ
Med. Saddle (2)	KZ/NZ
White w/Black (2)	FW/KW
White w/Blue (2)	FQ/KQ
White w/Green (2)	F5/K5
White w/Saddle (2)	F8/K8
White w/Gold (2)	F9/K9

1 Cloth & vinyl
2 Vinyl

THE TRANSMISSION CODE is a number or letter indicating the type of transmission.

TYPE	CODE
3-Speed Manual	1
4-Speed Manual	5
4-Speed Manual	6
4-Speed English	E
Automatic (C3)	V
Automatic (C4)	W
Automatic (FMX)	X
Automatic (FMX)	Y
Automatic (C6)	U
Automatic (C6 Special)	Z

THE AXLE CODE is a number or letter indicating the rear axle ratio and standard or locking type axles.

CONVENTIONAL	LOCKING	RATIO
2	K	2.75:1
3	L	2.79:1
5	E	3.07:1
6	O	3.00:1
7	P	3.40:1
9	R	3.25:1
A	S	3.50:1
G	X	3.55:1

THE DSO CODE, consisting of two numbers, designates the district in which the car was ordered and may appear in conjunction with a Domestic Special Order or Foreign Special Order number when applicable. Ford of Canada DSO codes consist of a letter and a number.

FORD DISTRICT	CODE
Boston	11
Buffalo	12
New York	13
Pittsburgh	14
Newark	15
Philadelphia	16
Washington	17
Atlanta	21
Charlotte	22
Memphis	23
Jacksonville	24
Richmond	25
New Orleans	26
Louisville	28
Chicago	41
Cleveland	42
Milwaukee	43
Lansing	45
Indianapolis	46
Cincinnati	47
Detroit	48
Dallas	52
Kansas City	53
Omaha	54
St. Louis	55
Davenport	56
Houston	57
Twin City	58
Los Angeles	71
San Jose	72
Salt Lake City	73
Seattle	74
Phoenix	75
Denver	76
Government	83
Home Office Reservw	84
American Red Cross	85
Body Company	87
Transportation Services	89
Export	90-99

FORD OF CANADA DISTRICT	CODE
Central	B1
Eastern	B2
Atlantic	B3
Midwestern	B4
Western	B6
Pacific	B7
Export	12

9 - 32

ENGINE IDENTIFICATION

ENGINE TAG
Since 1964, Ford engines can be identified by a tag attached to the engine. The tag contains the year and cubic inch displacement.

CASTING NUMBERS
While helpful in identifying Ford engine components, casting numbers are not conclusive in pin-pointing the exact year of manufacture. A better method is to search for the original host vehicle's VIN (Vehicle Identification Number) stamped on the driver's side at the rear of the engine block below the cylinder head.

ENGINE TAG EXAMPLE
400	74
4-A	123A

DECODED EXAMPLE
400	CID
74	Model Year (1974)
4	Production Year (1974)
A	Production Month (January)
123A	Engine Code Number

FORD ENGINES
CID	NO. CYL.	HORSE-POWER	COMP. RATIO	CARB.
351	8	162	8.0:1	2 BC
351	8	163	8.0:1	2 BC
400	8	170	8.0:1	2 BC
460	8	195	8.0:1	4 BC
460	8	275	8.8:1	4 BC

TORINO ENGINES
CID	NO. CYL.	HORSE-POWER	COMP. RATIO	CARB.
302	8	140	8.0:1	2 BC
351	8	162	8.0:1	2 BC
351	8	163	8.0:1	2 BC
351	8	255	8.0:1	4 BC
400	8	170	8.0:1	2 BC
460	8	220	8.0:1	4 BC
460	8	195	8.0:1	4 BC

PINTO ENGINES
CID	NO. CYL.	HORSE-POWER	COMP. RATIO	CARB.
122	4	80	8.2:1	2 BC
140	4	82	8.4:1	2 BC

MAVERICK ENGINES
CID	NO. CYL.	HORSE-POWER	COMP. RATIO	CARB.
200	6	84	8.0:1	1 BC
250	6	91	8.0:1	1 BC
302	8	140	8.0:1	2 BC

MUSTANG ENGINES
CID	NO. CYL.	HORSE-POWER	COMP. RATIO	CARB.
140	4	88	8.4:1	2 BC
171	6	105	8.2:1	2 BC

THUNDERBIRD ENGINES
CID	NO. CYL.	HORSE-POWER	COMP. RATIO	CARB.
460	8	220	8.0:1	4 BC

1975 FORD GRANADA

1975 FORD MUSTANG II

1975 FORD PINTO STATION WAGON

1975 FORD ELITE

1975 FORD THUNDERBIRD

1975 FORD LTD STATION WAGON

1975 FORD TORINO

1975 FORD MAVERICK

1975 FORD GRAN TORINO STATION WAGON

1975 FORD MUSTANG II

VEHICLE IDENTIFICATION NUMBER

FORD
F 5S63H123456 F

Located on the top of the dash on the driver's side and visible through the windshield from outside the car.

FIRST DIGIT: Identifies the year (5 = 1975)

SECOND DIGIT: Identifies the assembly plant

ASSEMBLY PLANT	CODE
Atlanta, GA	A
Oakville, Ont., CAN	B
Mahwah, NJ	E
Dearborn, MI	F
Chicago, IL	G
Lorain, OH	H
Los Angeles, CA	J
Kansas City, KS	K
Twin Cities, MN	P
San Jose, CA	R
Allen Park (Pilot Plant)	S
Metuchen, NJ	T
Louisville, KY	U
Wayne, MI	W
St. Thomas, Ont., CAN	X
Wixom, MI	Y
St. Louis, MO	Z

THIRD AND FOURTH DIGITS: Identify the body serial code

TORINO	CODE
2-Dr. Hardtop Elite	21
2-Dr. Hardtop Torino	25
4-Dr. Sedan Hardtop Torino	27
2-Dr. Hardtop Gran Torino	30
4-Dr. Sedan Hardtop Gran Torino	31
2-Dr. HT Gran Torino Brougham	32
4-Dr. Sedan HT Gran Torino Brougham	33
2-Dr. HT Gran Torino Sport	38
Torino Station Wagon	40
Gran Torino Station Wagon	42
Gran Torino Squire SW	43

FORD	CODE
2-Dr. Pillar HT LTD	62
4-Dr. Pillar HT LTD	63
4-Dr. Pillar HT LTD Landau	64
2-Dr. Pillar HT LTD Landau	65
4-Dr. Pillar HT LTD Brougham	66
2-Dr. Pillar HT LTD Brougham	68
4-Dr. SW LTD	74
4-Dr. SW Country Squire	76

GRANADA	CODE
4-Dr. Sedan	81
2-Dr. Sedan	82
4-Dr. Sedan Ghia	83
2-Dr. Sedan Ghia	84

MAVERICK	CODE
2-Dr. Sedan	91
4-Dr. Sedan	92
2-Dr. Sport Sedan Grabber	93

MUSTANG II	CODE
2-Dr. Sedan	02
3-Dr. Model	03
2-Dr. Sedan Ghia	04
3-Dr. Model Mach I	05

PINTO CODE	
2-Dr. Sedan	10
3-Dr. Runabout	11
2-Dr. Wagon	12

THUNDERBIRD CODE	
2-Dr. Hardtop	87

FIFTH DIGIT: Identifies the engine code

ENGINE	CODE
V-8 460-4V	A
V-8 460-4V (Police)	C
V-8 302-2V	F
V-8 351-2V	H
6 250-1V	L
V-8 400-2V	S
6 200-1V	T
4 139-2V (2.3L)	Y
6 169-2V (2.8L)	Z

LAST SIX DIGITS: Represents the basic production numbers

EXAMPLE:

5	S	63	H	123456
Model Year	Asm Plant	Body Serial Code	Engine	Production Sequence Number

VEHICLE CERTIFICATION LABEL

THE VEHICLE CERTIFICATION LABEL is attached to the rear face of the driver's door. The upper half of the label contains the name of the manufacturer, the month and year of manufacture and the certification statement. The V.C. label also contains the Vehicle Identification Number. The remaining information on the V.C. label consists of pertinent vehicle identification codes: ie. body, color, trim, axle, transmission and the domestic special order (DSO) codes.

MANUFACTURED BY FORD MOTOR COMPANY

7/75 THIS VEHICLE CONFORMS TO ALL APPLICABLE FEDERAL MOTOR VEHICLE SAFETY STANDARDS IN EFFECT ON DATE OF MANUFACTURE SHOWN ABOVE

5S56H123456   PASSENGER
53H 1C-DA DA X   2   48

NOT FOR TITLE OR REGISTRATION
MADE IN U.S.A.

EXAMPLE:

5S63H123456	Vehicle Identification Number (VIN)
53H	Body Type Code (LTD 4-Dr. Pillar Hardtop)
1C-DA	Body Color Code and Vinyl Roof Type/Color (Black & Black Levant Full Vinyl Top
DA	Trim Code (Black Cloth & Vinyl)
X	Transmission Code (FMX Automatic)
2	Rear Axle Code (2.75:1)
48	District Special Equipment Code (Detroit)

THE BODY CODE is two numerals and a letter identifying the body style.

TORINO	CODE
2-Dr. Hardtop Elite	65M
2-Dr. Hardtop Torino	65B
4-Dr. Sedan HT Torino	53B
2-Dr. HT Gran Torino	65D
4-Dr. Sedan HT Gran Torino	53D
2-Dr. HT Gran Torino Brougham	65K
4-Dr. Sedan HT Gran Torino Brougham	53K
2-Dr. HT Gran Torino Sport	65R
Torino Station Wagon	71B
Gran Torino Station Wagon	71D
Gran Torino Squire SW	71K

FORD	CODE
2-Dr. Pillar HT LTD	60H
4-Dr. Pillar HT LTD	53H
4-Dr. Pillar HT LTD Landau	53L
2-Dr. Pillar HT LTD Landau	60L
4-Dr. Pillar HT LTD Brougham	53K
2-Dr. Pillar HT LTD Brougham	60K
4-Dr. Wagon LTD	71H
4-Dr. Wagon Country Squire	71K

GRANADA	CODE
4-Dr. Sedan	54H
2-Dr. Sedan	66H
4-Dr. Sedan Ghia	54K
2-Dr. Sedan Ghia	66K

MAVERICK	CODE
2-Dr. Sedan	62A
4-Dr. Sedan	54A
2-Dr. Sport Sedan Grabber	62D

MUSTANG II	CODE
2-Dr. Sedan	60F
3-Dr. Model	69F
2-Dr. Sedan Ghia	60H
3-Dr. Model Mach I	69R

PINTO	CODE
2-Dr. Sedan	62B
3-Dr. Runabout	64B
2-Dr. Station Wagon	73B

THUNDERBIRD	CODE
2-Dr. Hardtop	65K

THE COLOR CODE is a number and letter indicating the exterior paint color code and vinyl roof type and color (if equipped).

EXTERIOR PAINT COLOR	CODE
Black	1C
Silver Met.	1G
Med. Slate Blue Met.	1H
Brt. Red	2B
Red	2E
Dk. Red	2M
Maroon Met.	2Q
Brt. Blue Met.	3E
Brt. Dk. Blue Met.	3G
Pastel Blue	3Q
Dk. Yellow Green Met.	4V
Lt. Green Gold Met.	4Z
Dk. Jade Met.	46
Lt. Green	47

EXTERIOR PAINT COLOR	CODE
Med. Chestnut Met.	5M
Dk. Brown Met.	5Q
Saddle Bronze Met.	5T
Dk. Copper Met.	5Y
Orange	5W
Yellow	6D
Brt. Yellow	6E
Maize Yellow	6N
Dk. Gold Met.	6Z
White	9D
Brt. Blue Met. (1)	3K
Silver Blue Met. (1)	3M
Med. Ivy Bronze Met. (1)	4T
Dk. Ginger Met. (1)	5J
Tan Met. (1)	5U
Med. Red Met. (2)	2G
Brt. Gold Yellow Met. (2)	6G
Silver Met. (3)	1J
Med. Taupe Met. (3)	2P
Med. Blue Met. (3)	3P
Silver Blue Met. (3)	3R
Brt. Lime Gold Met. (3)	41
Aqua Blue Met. (3)	45
Ginger Bronze Met. (3)	51
Copper Met. (3)	52
Unique Gold Met. (3)	54

1 - (RPO) Unique Colors (Non Polish)
2 - (RPO) Unique Colors (Polish)
3 - (RPO) Diamond Flare (Polish)

VINYL ROOF TYPE/COLOR CODES

VINYL TYPE (First Letter)	CODE
Cross Hatch Full 2-Door	B
Cross Hatch Halo Style 4-Dr.	C
Levant Full	D
Levant Half (1/2)	E
Normandie	F
Odense Full	G
Odense Three-Quarter (3/4)	H
Odense Embassy (Basket Handle)	J
Normandie Three-Quarter (3/4)	K
Normandie Half (1/2)	L
Odense Half (1/2)	N

VINYL COLOR (Second Letter)	CODE
Aqua	L
Black	A
Blue	B
Brown	T
Copper	K
Gold	Y
Gold Flare	M
Green (Light)	G
Jade	R
Red	D
Saddle	Z
Silver	P
Silver Blue	S
Tan	U
Taupe	J
White	W

THE **TRIM CODE** consists of a two-letter or a letter-number combination designating the interior trim.

THUNDERBIRD

	CODE
Black (1)	HA
Black (2)	JA
Black (3)	KA
Blue (1)	HB/FB
Blue (2)	JB
Blue (3)	KB
Dark Red (1)	FD
Dark Red (2)	JD
Dark Red (3)	KD
Green (1)	HG/FG
Green (2)	JG
Green (3)	KG
Saddle (1)	HZ/FZ
Saddle/Tan (2)	JU
Saddle/Tan (3)	KU
Saddle (2)	JZ
Saddle (3)	KZ
White/Red (2)	JN
White/Red (3)	KN
White/Blue (2)	JQ
White/Blue (3)	KQ
White/Black (2)	JW
White/Black (3)	KW
White/Green (2)	J5
White/Green (3)	K5
White/Copper (2)	J6
White/Copper (3)	K6
White/Saddle (2)	J9
White/Saddle (3)	K9
Silver Leather (4)	KP
Red Leather (4)	KC
Red Picton (4)	FD
Copper Leather (4)	KC
Copper Media (4)	MC

1 - Cloth & vinyl
2 - Vinyl
3 - Leather & vinyl
4 - Leather & velour

PINTO SEDANS/RUNABOUT/STATION WAGONS

	CODE
Black (1)	AA/CA
Black (2)	BA
Blue (1)	AB/CB
Blue (1)	EB/FB
Blue (2)	BB
Green (1)	AG/CG
Green (1)	EG/FG
Green (2)	BG
Tan (1)	AU/CU
Tan (1)	EU/FU
Tan (2)	BU
Orange (2)	BC

1 - Vinyl
2 - Cloth & vinyl

MAVERICK

	CODE
Black (1)	BA/JA
Black (2)	HA/KA/LA
Blue (1)	BB/JB
Blue (2)	HB/KB
Blue (2)	PB/LB
Green (1)	BG/JG
Green (2)	HG/KG
Tan (1)	BU/JU
Tan (2)	HU/KU
Tan (2)	PU/LU

1 - Cloth & vinyl
2 - Vinyl

MUSTANG II*

	CODE
Black	AA/BA
Blue	AB/BB
Red	BD
Green	AG/BG
Tan	AU/BU
White/Red	AN/BN
White/Blue	AQ/BQ
White/Black	AW/BW
White/Tan	A4/B4
White/Green	A5/B5
Black/Red	EA

* Vinyl

GHIA

	CODE
Black (1)	DA
Black (2)	BA/CA
Black/Red (2)	EA
Blue (1)	DB/CB
Blue (2)	BB
Red (1)	DD/CD
Red (2)	BD/CD
Red (3)	DD
Red (4)	FD
Silver/Blue (2)	CE
Silver/Blue (3)	DE
Silver/Blue (4)	FE
Green (1)	DG/CG
Green (2)	BG/CG
Green (3)	DG
Tan (1)	DU/CU
Tan (2)	BU/CU
Tan (3)	DU
Tan (4)	FU
White/Red (2)	BN
White/Blue (2)	BQ
White/Black (2)	BW
White/Tan (2)	BR
White/Green (2)	B5

1 - Cloth & vinyl
2 - Vinyl
3 - Cloth
4 - Leather

GRANADA*

	CODE
Black	AA
Red	AD
Silver/Blue	AE
Green	AG
Tan	AU

* Vinyl

GRAN TORINO

	CODE
Black (1)	BA
Black (2)	AA/CA
Black (2)	EA/DA
Blue (1)	BB
Blue (2)	AB/CB
Blue (2)	EB/DB
Green (1)	BG
Green (2)	AG/CG
Tan (1)	BU
Tan (2)	AU/CU
Tan (2)	EU/DU
Saddle (2)	CZ
White/Blue (2)	CQ/EQ/DQ
White/Black (2)	CW/EW/DW
White/Green (2)	C5/E5/D5
White/Saddle (2)	C9/E9/D9

1 - Cloth & vinyl
2 - Vinyl

GRAN TORINO BROUGHAM/SQUIRE WAGON

	CODE
Black (1)	FA
Black (2)	GA
Blue (1)	FB
Blue (2)	GB
Green (1)	FG
Green (2)	GG
Tan (1)	FU
Tan (2)	GU
Saddle (1)	FZ
Saddle (2)	GZ
White/Blue (2)	GQ
White/Black (2)	GW
White/Green (2)	G5
White/Saddle (2)	G9

1 - Cloth & vinyl
2 - Vinyl

GRAN TORINO SQUIRE STATION WAGONS*

	CODE
Blue	AB/CB
Blue	RB/GB
Green	AG/CG
Green	RG/GG
Tan	AU/CU
Tan	RU/GU
Saddle	CZ/GZ

* Vinyl

ELITE HARDTOPS

	CODE
Black (1)	JA
Black (2)	KA/GA
Blue (1)	JB
Blue (2)	KB/GB
Blue (3)	LB
Red (2)	GD
Red (3)	LD
Green (1)	JG
Green (2)	KG/GG
Green (3)	LG
Tan (1)	JU
Tan (2)	KU/GU
Tan (3)	LU
Saddle (1)	JZ
Saddle (2)	KZ/GZ
Saddle (3)	LZ
White/Red (2)	GN
White/Blue (2)	GQ
White/Black (2)	GW
White/Green (2)	G5
White/Saddle (2)	G9

1 - Cloth & vinyl
2 - Vinyl
3 - Cloth

FORD LTD AND CUSTOM 500*

	CODE
Black (1)	DA
Blue (1)	DB
Blue (2)	EB
Green (1)	DG
Green (2)	EG
Tan (1)	DU
Tan (2)	EU

* Custom 500 (Fleet only)
1 - Cloth & vinyl
2 - Vinyl

LTD BROUGHAM

	CODE
Black (1)	GA/RA
Blue (1)	GB/RB
Blue (2)	FB/NB/TB
Dark Red (1)	RD
Dark Red (2)	FD/ND
Green (1)	GG/RG
Green (2)	FG/NG/TG
Tan (1)	GU/RU
Tan (2)	FU/NU/TU
White/Red (2)	FN
White/Blue (2)	FQ
White/Black (2)	FW
White/Green (2)	F5
White/Saddle (2)	F9

1 - Cloth & vinyl
2 - Vinyl

LTD LANDAU

	CODE
Black (1)	HA
Blue (1)	HB/KB
Blue (2)	JB
Dark Red (1)	HD/KD
Dark Red (2)	JD
Green (1)	HG/KG
Green (2)	JG
Tan (1)	HU/KU
Tan (2)	JU
Saddle (1)	HZ/KZ
Saddle (2)	JZ
White/Red (2)	JN
White/Blue (2)	JQ
White/Black (2)	JW
White/Green (2)	J5
White/Saddle (2)	J9

1 - Cloth & vinyl
2 - Vinyl

FORD STATION WAGONS (FLEET ONLY)*

	CODE
Blue	EB/UB
Blue	NB/SB/MB
Dark Red	ND/SD/MD
Green	EG/UG
Green	NG/SG/MG
Tan	EU/UU
Tan	NU/SU/MU
Saddle	EZ/SZ/MZ

* Vinyl only

THE TRANSMISSION CODE is a number or letter indicating the type of transmission.

TYPE	CODE
3-Speed Manual	1
4-Speed Manual	5
4-Speed Manual	6
4-Speed (English)	E
XP Automatic (C-3)	V
XP Automatic (C-4)	W
FMX Automatic	X
FMX Automatic	Y
XPL Automatic (C-6)	U
XPL Automatic (Special)	Z

THE AXLE CODE is a number or letter indicating the rear axle ratio and standard or locking type axles.

CONVENTIONAL	LOCKING	RATIO
2	K	2.75
7	P	3.40
6	O	3.00
9	R	3.25
G	X	3.55
5		3.07
3		2.79
E		3.07
A	S	3.50
	V	3.91

THE DSO CODE, consisting of two numbers, designates the district in which the car was ordered and may appear in conjunction with a Domestic Special Order or Foreign Special Order number when applicable. Ford of Canada DSO codes consist of a letter and number.

FORD DISTRICT	CODE
Special	00
Boston	11
Buffalo	12
New York	13
Pittsburgh	14
Newark	15
Philadelphia	16
Washington	17
Atlanta	21
Charlotte	22
Memphis	23
Jacksonville	24
Richmond	25
New Orleans	26
Louisville	28
Chicago	41
Cleveland	42
Milwaukee	43
Lansing	45
Indianapolis	46
Cincinnati	47
Detroit	48
Dallas	52
Kansas City	53
Omaha	54
St. Louis	55
Davenport	56
Houston	57
Twin Cities	58
Los Angeles	71
San Jose	72
Salt Lake City	73
Seattle	74
Phoenix	75
Denver	76
Government	83
Home Office Reserve	84
American Red Cross	85
Recreational Vehicle Pool	86
Body Company	87
Transportation Services	89
Export	90's

FORD OF CANADA DISTRICT	CODE
Central	B1
Eastern	B2
Atlantic	B3
Midwestern	B4
Western	B6
Pacific	B7
Export	12

ENGINE IDENTIFICATION

ENGINE TAG
Since 1964, Ford engines can be identified by a tag attached to the engine. The tag contains the year and cubic inch displacement.

CASTING NUMBERS
While helpful in identifying Ford engine components, casting numbers are not conclusive in pin-pointing the exact year of manufacture. A better method is to search for the original host vehicle's VIN (Vehicle Identification Number) stamped on the driver's side at the rear of the engine block below the cylinder head.

FORD ENGINES

CID	NO. CYL.	HORSE-POWER	COMP. RATIO	CARB.
351	8	148	8.0:1	2 BC
400	8	158	8.0:1	2 BC
460	8	218	8.0:1	4 bc

ELITE ENGINES

CID	NO. CYL.	HORSE-POWER	COMP. RATIO	CARB.
351	8	148	8.0:1	2 BC
351	8	150	8.2:1	2 BC
400	8	158	8.0:1	2 BC
460	8	216	8.0:1	4 BC

TORINO ENGINES

CID	NO. CYL.	HORSE-POWER	COMP. RATIO	CARB.
351	8	148	8.0:1	2 BC
351	8	154	8.2:1	2 BC
400	8	158	8.0:1	2 BC
460	8	216	8.0:1	4 BC
460*	8	226	8.0:1	4 BC

* Police Interceptor

GRANADA ENGINES

CID	NO. CYL.	HORSE-POWER	COMP. RATIO	CARB.
200	6	75	8.3:1	1 BC
250	6	85	8.0:1	1 BC
302	8	129	8.0;1	2 BC
351	8	143	8.2:1	2 BC

PINTO ENGINES

CID	NO. CYL.	HORSE-POWER	COMP. RATIO	CARB.
140	4	87	8.4:1	2 BC
171	6	97	8.2:1	2 BC

MAVERICK ENGINES

CID	NO. CYL.	HORSE-POWER	COMP. RATIO	CARB.
200	6	75	8.3:1	1 BC
250	6	85	8.0:1	1 BC
302	8	122	8.0:1	2 bc

MUSTANG II/MACH I ENGINES

CID	NO. CYL.	HORSE-POWER	COMP. RATIO	CARB.
140	4	87	8.4:1	2 BC
171	6	97	8.2:1	2 BC
171	6	110	8.2:1	2 BC
302	8	140	8.0:1	2 BC

THUNDERBIRD ENGINES

CID	NO. CYL.	HORSE-POWER	COMP. RATIO	CARB.
460	8	216	8.0:1	4 BC

1976 FORD MAVERICK

1976 FORD ELITE

1976 FORD MUSTANG II

1976 FORD GRANADA

1976 FORD PINTO

1976 FORD LTD

1976 FORD PINTO STATION WAGON

1976 FORD TORINO

1976 FORD LTD STATION WAGON

1976 FORD THUNDERBIRD

VEHICLE IDENTIFICATION NUMBER

```
FORD
F 6S63H123456 F
```

Located on the top of the dash on the driver's side and visible through the windshield from outside the car.

FIRST DIGIT: Identifies the year (6 = 1976)

SECOND DIGIT: Identifies the assembly plant

ASSEMBLY PLANT	CODE
Atlanta, GA	A
Oakville, Ont., CAN	B
Mahwah, NJ	E
Dearborn, MI	F
Chicago, IL	G
Lorain, OH	H
Los Angeles, CA	J
Kansas City, KS	K
Twin Cities, MN	P
San Jose, CA	R
Allen Park (Pilot Plant)	S
Metuchen, NJ	T
Louisville, KY	U
Wayne, MI	W
St. Thomas, Ont., CAN	X
Wixom, MI	Y
St. Louis, MO	Z

THIRD AND FOURTH DIGITS: Identify the body serial code

TORINO	CODE
2-Dr. HT Gran Torino (XL) Elite	21
2-Dr. HT Torino	25
4-Dr. Sedan HT Torino	27
2-Dr. HT Gran Torino	30
4-Dr. Sedan HT Gran Torino	31
2-Dr. HT Gran Torino Brougham	32
4-Dr. Sedan HT Torino Brougham	33
Torino Station Wagon	40
Gran Torino SW	42
Gran Torino Squire SW	43

FORD	CODE
4-Dr. Pillar HT Custom 500	53
2-Dr. Pillar HT LTD	62
4-Dr. Pillar HT LTD	63
4-Dr. Pillar HT LTD Landau	64
2-Dr. Pillar HT LTD Landau	65
4-Dr. Pillar HT LTD Brougham	66
2-Dr. Pillar HT LTD Brougham	68
4-Dr. SW LTD	74
4-Dr. SW Country Squire	76

GRANADA	CODE
4-Dr. Sedan	81
2-Dr. Sedan	82
4-Dr. Sedan Ghia	83
2-Dr. Sedan Ghia	84

MAVERICK	CODE
2-Dr. Sedan Fastback	91
4-Dr. Sedan	92

MUSTANG	CODE
2-Dr. 4-Pass. Base	02
3-Dr. 4-Pass. Base	03
2-Dr. 4-Pass. Ghia	04
3-Dr. 4-Pass. Mach I	05

PINTO	CODE
2-Dr. Sedan	10
3-Dr. Sedan	11
2-Dr. Wagon	12

THUNDERBIRD	CODE
2-Dr. Hardtop	87

FIFTH DIGIT: Identifies the engine code

ENGINE	CODE
V-8 460-4V	A
V-8 460-4V (Police)	C
V-8 302-2V	F
V-8 351-2V	H
6 250-1V	L
V-8 400-2V	S
6 200-1V	T
4 139-2V (2.3L)	Y
6-169-2V (2.8L)	Z

LAST SIX DIGITS: Represent the basic production numbers

EXAMPLE:

6	S	63	H	123456
Model Year	Asm Plant	Body Serial Code	Engine	Production Sequence Number

VEHICLE CERTIFICATION LABEL

THE VEHICLE CERTIFICATION LABEL (V.C. Label) is affixed on the left front door lock face panel or door pillar. The upper half of the label contains the name of manufacturer, month and year of manufacture, Gross Vehicle Weight Rating (GVWR), Gross Axle Weight Rating (GAWR), and the certification statement. The V.C. label also contains the Vehicle Identification Number. The remaining information on the V.C. label consists of pertinent vehicle identification codes: ie. body, color, trim, axle, transmission and the domestic special order (DSO) codes.

```
MANUFACTURED BY
FORD MOTOR COMPANY

7/76 THIS VEHICLE CONFORMS TO ALL
APPLICABLE FEDERAL MOTOR VEHICLE
SAFETY STANDARDS IN EFFECT ON
DATE OF MANUFACTURE SHOWN ABOVE

6S63H123456        PASSENGER
53H  1C-DA  DA   X    2    48

NOT FOR TITLE OR REGISTRATION
MADE IN U.S.A.
```

EXAMPLE:

6S63H123456	Vehicle Identification Number (VIN)
53H	Body Type Code (LTD 4-Dr. Pillar Hardtop)
1CDA	Body Color Code and Vinyl Roof Type/Color (Black & Black Levant Full Vinyl Roof)
DA	Trim Code (Black Cloth & Leather)
X	Transmission Code (FMX Automatic)
2	Rear Axle Code (2.75:1)
48	District Special Equipment Code (Detroit)

THE BODY CODE is two numerals and a letter identifying the body style.

TORINO	CODE
2-Dr. HT Gran Torino (XL) Elite	65H
2-Dr. HT Torino	65B
4-Dr. Sedan HT Torino	53B
2-Dr. HT Gran Torino	65D
4-Dr. Sedan HT Gran Torino	53D
2-Dr. HT Gran Torino Brougham	65K
4-Dr. Sedan HT Torino Brougham	53K
Torino Station Wagon	71B
Gran Torino SW	71D
Gran Torino Squire SW	71K

FORD	CODE
4-Dr. Pillar HT Custom 500	53D
2-Dr. Pillar HT LTD	60H
4-Dr. Pillar HT LTD	53H
4-Dr. Pillar HT LTD Landau	53L
2-Dr. Pillar HT LTD Landau	60L
4-Dr. Pillar HT LTD Brougham	53K
2-Dr. Pillar HT LTD Brougham	60K
4-Dr. SW LTD	71H
4-Dr. SW Country Squire	71K

GRANADA	CODE
4-Dr. Sedan	54H
2-Dr. Sedan	66H
4-Dr. Sedan Ghia	54K
2-Dr. Sedan Ghia	66K

* Sports sedan option available

MAVERICK	CODE
2-Dr. Sedan Fastback	62A
4-Dr. Sedan	54A

* Stallion option available

MUSTANG	CODE
2-Dr. 4-Pass. Base	60F
3-Dr. 4-Pass. Base	69F
2-Dr. 4-Pass. Ghia	60H
3-Dr. 4-Pass. Mach I	69R

* Cobra II option available
* Stallion option available
* MPG option available

PINTO	CODE
2-Dr. Sedan	62B
3-Dr. Runabout	64B
2-Dr. Wagon	73B

* Pony option available
* Stallion option available
* Squire Wagon option available
* MPG option available

THUNDERBIRD	CODE
2-Dr. Hardtop	65K

THE COLOR CODE is a number and letter indicating the exterior paint color code and vinyl roof type and color (if equipped).

EXTERIOR PAINT COLOR	CODE
Black	1C
Silver Met.	1G
Med. Slate Blue Met.	1H
Brt. Red	2B
Candyapple Red	2E
Dk. Red	2M
Brt. Red	2R
Brt. Red	2U
Med. Blue Met.	3D
Brt. Blue Met.	3E

EXTERIOR PAINT COLOR	CODE
Brt. Dk. Blue Met.	3G
Lt. Blue	3S
Brt. Med. Blue	3T
Dk. Yellow Green Met.	4Y
Dk. Jade Met.	46
Lt. Green	47
Dk. Green	49
Copper Met.	5B
Med. Chestnut Met.	5M
Dk. Brown Met.	5Q
Saddle Bronze Met.	5T
Tan	5V
Yellow Orange	56
Brt. Yellow	6E
Cream	6P
Dk. Yellow	6R
Chrome Yellow	6S
Tan	6U
Lt. Gold	6W
Lt. Jade	7A
Med. Green Gold	7E
Med. Ginger Met.	8B
Dk. Brown	8D
Med. Orange Met.	8E
Tangerine	8F
White	9A
White	9D
Silver Blue Met. (1)	3M
Med. Ivy Bronze Met. (1)	4T
Med. Ivy Bronze Met. (1)	48
Tan Met. (1)	5U
Dk. Ginger Met. (1)	57
Ginger Bronze Met. (1)	58
Med. Dk. Gold Met. (1)	6T
Med. Gold Met. (1)	6V
Dk. Red Met. (2)	2S
Silver Met. (3)	1J
Med. Taupe Met. (3)	2P
Brt. Blue Met. (3)	3P
Silver Blue Met. (3)	3R
Brt. Yellow Gold Met. (3)	6Y
Aqua Blue Met. (3)	45
Ginger Bronze Met. (3)	51
Gold Bronze Met. (3)	54
Med. Chestnut Met. (3)	59
Med. Jade Met. (3)	7F
Rose Met. (4)	2T
Lt. Jade Met. (4)	7B
Lt. Apricot Met. (4)	8A

1 - (RPO) Unique Colors (Non Polish)
2 - (RPO) Diamond Brt. (Polish)
3 - (RPO) Diamond Flare (Polish)
4 - Crystals

VINYL ROOF TYPE/COLOR CODES

VINYL TYPE (First Letter)	CODE
Cross Hatch Full 2-Door	B
Cross Hatch Halo Style 4-Door	C
Levant Full	D
Levant (1/2)	E
Normandie Full	F
Odense Full	G
Odense (3/4)	H
Odense Embassy (Basket Handle)	J
Normandie (3/4)	K
Normandie (1/2)	L
Odense (1/2)	N
Cross-Hatch (3/4)	P
Cross-Hatch (1/2)	R
Levant (3/4)	S

VINYL COLOR (Second Letter)

Color	CODE
Black	A
Blue	B
Apricot	C
Red	D
Green	G
Rose	H
Taupe	J
Copper	K
Aqua	L
Gold Flare	M
Red Lipstick	N
Silver	P
Jade	R
Silver Blue	S
Brown	T
Tan	U
Cream	V
White	W
Gold	Y
Saddle	Z

THE TRIM CODE consists of a two-letter or a letter-number combination designating the interior trim.

FORD COLOR

Color	CODE
Black (1)	AA/DA
Black (1)	GA/HA/RA
Blue (1)	AB/DB
Blue (1)	GB/HB
Blue (1)	KB/RB
Blue (2)	BB/EB/FB
Blue (2)	JB/MB/SB
Blue (3)	NB/UB
Blue (4)	YB
Red (4)	YD
Dark Red (1)	HD/KD/RD
Dark Red (2)	FD/JD
Dark Red (2)	SD/MD
Dark Red (3)	ND/UD
Green (1)	DG/GG/HG
Green (1)	KG/RG
Green (2)	BG/EG/FG
Green (2)	JG/MG/SG
Green (3)	NG/UG
Green (4)	YG
Gold (1)	DY/HY
Gold (1)	KY/RY
Gold (2)	EY/FY/SY
Saddle (1)	AZ/DZ/HZ
Saddle (1)	GZ/KZ/RZ
Saddle (2)	BZ/EZ/FZ
Saddle (2)	MZ/SZ
Saddle/Tan (2)	JU
Saddle/Tan (3)	NU/YU
Saddle/Tan (4)	YU
Gold/Cream (2)	JV
White/Red (2)	EN/FN/JN
White/Blue (2)	EQ/FQ/JQ
White/Black (2)	EW/FW/JW
White/Green (2)	E5/F5/J5
White/Gold (2)	E8/F8/J8
White/Saddle (2)	E9/F9/J9

1 - Cloth & vinyl
2 - Vinyl
3 - Polyknit & vinyl
4 - Leather

PINTO

Color	CODE
Black (1)	GA
Black (2)	AA/HA
Blue (1)	DB/GD
Blue (2)	AB/HB
Green (1)	DG/GG
Green (2)	AG/HG
Tan (1)	DU/GU
Tan (2)	AU/HU

1 - Cloth & vinyl
2 - Vinyl

MAVERICK

Color	CODE
Black (1)	BA/JA
Black (2)	HA/KA/LA
Blue (1)	BB/JB
Blue (1)	QB/RB
Blue (2)	HB/KB
Blue (2)	LB/PB
Green (1)	BG/JG
Green (2)	HG/KG
Tan (1)	BU/JU
Tan (1)	QU/RU
Tan (2)	HU/KU
Tan (2)	LU/PU

1 - Cloth & vinyl
2 - Vinyl

MUSTANG

Color	CODE
Black (2)	AA/BA/DA
Blue (1)	CB
Blue (2)	AB/BB
Blue (2)	DB/EB
Cranberry (1)	CH
Red (2)	AD/BD
Red (2)	DD/ED
Tan (1)	CU
Tan (2)	AU/BU
Tan (2)	DU/EU
Cream (2)	BV
Gold/Cream (1)	CV
Gold/Cream (2)	DV/EV
White/Red (2)	BN
White/Blue (2)	BQ
White/Black (2)	BW
White/Tan (2)	B4

1 - Cloth & vinyl
2 - Vinyl

GRANADA

Color	CODE
Black (2)	AA/CA
Black (2)	EA/GA/JA
Red (1)	BD/DD
Red (1)	HD/ND
Red (2)	AD/CD
Red (2)	ED/GD/JD
Red (3)	FD/LD/MD
Silver Blue (1)	BE/DE/HE
Silver Blue (2)	AE/CE
Silver Blue (2)	EE/GE/JE
Silver Blue (3)	FE/LE
White/Red (2)	AN/CN
White/Red (2)	EN/GN/JN
White/Red (3)	FN/LN
Tan (1)	BU/DU
Tan (1)	HU/NU
Tan (2)	AU/CU
Tan (2)	EU/GU/JU
Tan (2)	FU/LU/MU
White/Black (2)	AW/CW
White/Black (2)	EW/GW/JW
White/Black (3)	FU/LW

GRANADA

	CODE
White/Tan (2)	A4/C4
White/Tan (2)	E4/G4/J4
White/Tan (3)	F4/L4
White/Silver Blue (2)	A7/C7
White/Silver Blue (2)	E7/G7/J7
White/Silver Blue (3)	F7/L7

1 - Cloth & vinyl
2 - Vinyl
3 - Leather

TORINO

	CODE
Black (1)	BA/FA/PA
Black (2)	AA/CA
Black (2)	GA/SA
Blue (1)	BB/FB/PB
Blue (2)	AB/CB
Blue (2)	GB/SB
Blue (3)	RB
Green (1)	BG/FG
Green (2)	AG/CG
Green (2)	GG/SG
Green (3)	RB
Tan (2)	AU/CU/GU
Tan (3)	RU
Saddle (1)	BZ/FZ/PZ
Saddle (2)	AZ/CZ
Saddle (2)	GZ/SZ
White/Blue (2)	CQ/GQ/SQ
White/Black (2)	CW/GW/SW
White/Green (2)	C5/G5/S5
White/Saddle (2)	C9/G9/S9

1 - Cloth & vinyl
2 - Vinyl
3 - Polyknit & vinyl

ELITE

	CODE
Black (1)	AA
Black (2)	BA/DA
Black (2)	EA/FA
Blue (1)	AB/CB
Blue (2)	BB/DB
Blue (2)	EB/FB
Red (1)	AD/CD
Red (2)	BD/DD
Red (2)	ED/FD
Green (1)	AG/CG
Green (2)	BG/DG
Green (2)	EG/FG
Gold (1)	AY/CY
Gold (2)	GY/DY/FY
Saddle (1)	AZ/CZ
Saddle (2)	BZ/DZ
Saddle (2)	EZ/FZ
White/Red (2)	DN/FN
White/Blue (2)	DQ/FQ
White/Black (2)	DW/FW
White/Green (2)	D5/F5
White/Gold (2)	D8/F8
White/Saddle (2)	D9/F9

1 - Cloth & vinyl
2 - Vinyl

THUNDERBIRD

	CODE
Black (1)	HA
Black (2)	JA
Black (4)	KA
Blue (1)	FB/HB
Blue (2)	JB
Blue (4)	KB
Red (1)	FD

THUNDERBIRD

	CODE
Red (3)	QD
Red (4)	KD
Red (5)	RD
Jade (1)	FR/HR
Jade (2)	JR
Jade (4)	KR
Saddle (1)	HZ
Saddle (2)	JZ
Saddle/Tan (1)	FU
Saddle/Tan (4)	KU
Gold (1)	FY
Gold (3)	QY
Gold (4)	KY
Gold/Cream (5)	RY
White/Red (2)	JN
White/Red (4)	KN
White/Blue (2)	JQ
White/Blue (4)	KQ
White/Black (2)	JW
White/Black (4)	KW
White/Jade (2)	J5
White/Jade (4)	K5
White/Gold (2)	J8
White/Gold (4)	K8
White/Saddle (2)	J9
White/Saddle (4)	K9

1 - Cloth & vinyl
2 - Vinyl
3 - Cloth
4 - Leather
5 - Leather & vinyl

THE TRANSMISSION CODE is a number or letter indicating the type of transmission.

TRANSMISSION	CODE
3-Speed Manual	1
4-Speed Manual	5
4-Speed Manual	6
4-Speed Manual	7
XP Automatic (C-3)	V
XP Automatic (C-4)	W
FMX Automatic	X
XPL Automatic (C-6)	U
XPL Automatic (Special)	Z

THE AXLE CODE is a number or letter indicating the rear axle ratio and standard or locking type axles.

CONVENTIONAL	LOCKING	RATIO
2	K	2.75
7	P	3.40
6	O	3.00
9	R	3.25
7G	X	3.55
5E	N	3.07
3	L	2.79
4	M	3.18

THE DSO CODE, consisting of two numbers, designates the district in which the car was ordered and may appear in conjunction with a Domestic Special Order or Foreign Special Order number when applicable. Ford of Canada DSO codes consist of a letter and number.

FORD DISTRICT CODE

Special	00
Boston	11
Buffalo	12
New York	13
Pittsburgh	14
Newark	15
Philadelphia	16
Washington	17
Atlanta	21
Charlotte	22
Memphis	23
Jacksonville	24
Richmond	25
New Orleans	26
Louisville	28
Chicago	41
Cleveland	42
Milwaukee	43
Lansing	45
Indianapolis	46
Cincinnati	47
Detroit	48
Dallas	52
Kansas City	53
Omaha	54
St. Louis	55
Davenport	56
Houston	57
Twin Cities	58
Los Angeles	71
San Jose	72
Salt Lake City	73
Seattle	74
Phoenix	75
Denver	76
Government	83
Home Office Reserve	84
American Red Cross	85
Recreational Vehicle Pool	86
Body Company	87
Transportation Services	89
Export	90's

FORD OF CANADA DISTRICT

DISTRICT	CODE
Central	B1
Eastern	B2
Atlantic	B3
Midwestern	B4
Western	B6
Pacific	B7
Export	12

ENGINE IDENTIFICATION

ENGINE TAG
Since 1964, Ford engines can be identified by a tag attached to the engine. The tag contains the year and cubic inch displacement.

CASTING NUMBERS
While helpful in identifying Ford engine components, casting numbers are not conclusive in pin-pointing the exact year of manufacture. A better method is to search for the original host vehicle's VIN (Vehicle Identification Number) stamped on the driver's side at the rear of the engine block below the cylinder head.

PINTO ENGINES

CID	NO. CYL.	HORSE-POWER	COMP. RATIO	CARB.
140	4	92	9.0:1	2 BC
170	6	103	8.7:1	2 BC

MUSTANG II ENGINES

CID	NO. CYL.	HORSE-POWER	COMP. RATIO	CARB.
140	4	92	9.0:1	2 BC
170	6	103	8.7:1	2 BC
302	8	134	8.0:1	2 BC

MAVERICK ENGINES

CID	NO. CYL.	HORSE-POWER	COMP. RATIO	CARB.
200	6	81	8.3:1	1 BC
250	6	90	8.0:1	1 BC
302	8	138	8.0:1	2 BC

GRANADA ENGINES

CID	NO. CYL.	HORSE-POWER	COMP. RATIO	CARB.
200	6	81	8.3:1	1 BC
250	6	87	8.0:1	1 BC
302	8	134	8.0:1	2 BC
351	8	143	8.0:1	2 BC

ELITE ENGINES

CID	NO. CYL.	HORSE-POWER	COMP. RATIO	CARB.
351	8	152	8.0:1	2 BC
351	8	154	8.0:1	2 BC
400	8	180	8.0:1	2 BC
460	8	202	8.0:1	4 BC

LTD ENGINES

CID	NO. CYL.	HORSE-POWER	COMP. RATIO	CARB.
351	8	152	8.0:1	2 BC
400	8	180	8.0:1	2 BC
460	8	202	8.0:1	4 BC

TORINO ENGINES

CID	NO. CYL.	HORSE-POWER	COMP. RATIO	CARB.
351	8	152	8.0:1	2 BC
351	8	154	8.1:1	2 BC
400	8	180	8.0:1	2 BC
460	8	202	8.0:1	4 BC

THUNDERBIRD ENGINES

CID	NO. CYL.	HORSE-POWER	COMP. RATIO	CARB.
460	8	202	8.0:1	4 BC

1977 FORD MAVERICK

1977 FORD GRANADA

1977 FORD MUSTANG II

1977 FORD LTD

1977 FORD PINTO

1977 FORD LTD II

1977 FORD THUNDERBIRD

1977 FORD LTD STATION WAGON

1977 FORD LTD II STATION WAGON

VEHICLE IDENTIFICATION NUMBER

```
•  FORD
   F 7S63H123456  •
```

Located on the top of the dash on the driver's side and visible through the windshield from outside the car.

FIRST DIGIT: Identifies the year (7 = 1977)

SECOND DIGIT: Identifies the assembly plant

ASSEMBLY PLANT	CODE
Atlanta, GA	A
Oakville, Ont., CAN	B
Mahwah, NJ	E
Dearborn, MI	F
Chicago, IL	G
Lorain, OH	H
Los Angeles, CA	J
Kansas City, KS	K
Twin Cities, MN	P
San Jose, CA	R
Allen Park (Pilot Plant)	S
Metuchen, NJ	T
Louisville, KY	U
Wayne, MI	W
St. Thomas, Ont., CAN	X
Wixom, MI	Y
St. Louis, MO	Z

THIRD AND FOURTH DIGITS: Identify the body serial code

PINTO	CODE
2-Dr. Sedan	10
3-Dr. Sedan	11
Station Wagon	12

MUSTANG II	CODE
2-Dr. Notchback	02
3-Dr. Hatchback	03
2-Dr. Notchback Ghia	04
3-Dr. Hatchback Mach I	05

MAVERICK	CODE
2-Dr. Sedan	91
4-Dr. Sedan	92

GRANADA	CODE
4-Dr. Sedan	81
2-Dr. Sedan	82
4-Dr. Sedan	83
2-Dr. Sedan	84

LTD II	CODE
2-Dr. HT LTD II S	25
4-Dr. Pillar HT LTD II S	27
2-Dr. HT LTD II	30
4-Dr. Pillar HT LTD II	31
2-Dr. HT Brougham	32
4-Dr. Pillar HT Brougham	33
LTD II S Station Wagon	40
LTD II SW	42
LTD II Squire Wagon	43

THUNDERBIRD	CODE
2-Dr. Pillar Hardtop	87

FORD	CODE
2-Dr. Pillar HT Custom 500 Fleet	52
4-Dr. Pillar HT Custom 500 Fleet	53
2-Dr. Pillar HT LTD	62
4-Dr. Pillar HT LTD	63
4-Dr. Pillar HT LTD Landau	64
2-Dr. Pillar HT LTD Landau	65
Custom 500 Ranch Wagon	72
LTD Wagon	74

FIFTH DIGIT: Identifies the engine code

ENGINE	CODE
V-8 460-4V	A
V-8 460-4V (Police)	C
V-8 302-2V	F
V-8 352-2V	H
6 250-1V	L
V-8 351-2V Modified	Q
V-8 400-2V	S
6 200-1V	T
4 139-2V (2.3L)	Y
6 169-2V (2.8L)	Y

LAST SIX DIGITS: Represent the basic production number

EXAMPLE:

7	S	63	H	123456
Model Year	Asm Plant	Body Serial Code	Engine	Production Sequence Number

VEHICLE CERTIFICATION LABEL

THE VEHICLE CERTIFICATION LABEL (V.C. Label) is affixed on the left front door lock face panel or door pillar. The upper half of the label contains the name of manufacturer, month and year of manufacture, Gross Vehicle Weight Rating (GVWR), Gross Axle Weight Rating (GAWR), and the certification statement. The V.C. label also contains the Vehicle Identification Number. The remaining information on the V.C. label consists of pertinent vehicle identification codes: ie. body, color, trim, axle, transmission and the domestic special order (DSO) codes.

```
     MANUFACTURED BY
    FORD MOTOR COMPANY

 7/77 THIS VEHICLE CONFORMS TO ALL
 APPLICABLE FEDERAL MOTOR VEHICLE
      SAFETY STANDARDS IN EFFECT ON
•  DATE OF MANUFACTURE SHOWN ABOVE  •

 7S63H123456      PASSENGER
 53H    1C-CA    ED  X  6    48

 NOT FOR TITLE OR REGISTRATION
       MADE IN U.S.A.
```

EXAMPLE:

7S63H123456	Vehicle Identification Number (VIN)
53H	Body Type Code (LTD 4-Dr. Pillar Hardtop)
1C-CA	Body Color Code and Vinyl Roof Type/Color (Black & Black Cross Hatch Halo Style Vinyl Roof)
ED	Trim Code (Red Cloth & Vinyl)
X	Transmission Code (FMX Automatic)
6	Rear Axle Code (3.00:1)
48	District Special Equipment Code (Detroit)

1977 FORD

THE BODY CODE is two numerals and a letter identifying the body style.

PINTO	CODE
2-Dr. Sedan	62B
3-Dr. Sedan	64B
Station Wagon	73B

* Sports Rallye option available
* Pony option available
* Squire Wagon option available

MUSTANG II	CODE
2-Dr. Notchback	60F
3-Dr. Hatchback	69F
2-Dr. Notchback Ghia	60H
3-Dr. Hatchback Mach I	69R

* Rallye option available
* Limited option available
* Cobra option available

MAVERICK	CODE
2-Dr. Sedan	62A
4-Dr. Sedan	54A

* Limited option available

GRANADA	CODE
4-Dr. Sedan	54H
2-Dr. Sedan	66H
4-Dr. Sedan	54K
2-Dr. Sedan	66K

* Limited option available

LTD II	CODE
2-Dr. HT LTD II S	65B
4-Dr. Pillar HT LTD II S	53B
2-Dr. HT LTD II	65D
4-Dr. Pillar HT LTD II	53D
2-Dr. HT Brougham	65K
4-Dr. Pillar HT Brougham	53K
LTD II S Wagon	71B
LTD II Station Wagon	71D
LTD II Squire Wagon	71K

THUNDERBIRD	CODE
2-Dr. Pillar Hardtop	60H

*Town Landau option available

FORD	CODE
2-Dr. Pillar HT Custom 500 Fleet	60D
4-Dr. Pillar HT Custom 500 Fleet	53D
2-Dr. Pillar HT LTD	60H
4-Dr. Pillar HT LTD	53H
4-Dr. Pillar HT LTD Landau	53L
2-Dr. Pillar HT LTD Landau	60L
Custom 500 Ranch Wagon	71D
LTD Wagon	71H

THE COLOR CODE is a number and letter indicating the exterior paint color code and vinyl roof type and color (if equipped).

EXTERIOR PAINT COLOR	CODE
Black	1C
Silver Met.	1G
Dove Gray	2N
Med. Gray Met. (Tie Tone Only)	1P
Med. Silver Met.	1Q
Dark Red	2M
Brt. Red	2R
Lipstick Red	2U
Brt. Dk. Blue Met.	3G

EXTERIOR PAINT COLOR	CODE
Lt. Blue	3U
Midnight Blue	31
Med. Blue	34
Dk. Jade Met.	46
Lt. Green	47
Dk. Yellow Green Met.	4V
Dk. Brown Met.	5Q
Brt. Yellow	6E
Cream	6P
Lt. Tan	6U
Lt. Aqua Met.	7Q
Dk. Emerald Met.	7S
Vista Orange	8G
Tan	8H
Brt. Saddle Met.	8K
Dk. Cordovan Met.	8N
Lt. Cordovan	8P
Champagne Met.	8Y
Chamois	83
Dk. Cordovan	84
White	9D
Rose Met. (1)	2Y
Brt. Blue Met. (1)	3V
Tan Met. (1)	6V
Med. Gold Met. (1)	6V
Brt. Aqua Met. (1)	7H
Lt. Jade Met. (1)	7L
Med. Emerald Met. (1)	7T
Med. Tan Met. (1)	8J
Chamois Met. (1)	8W
Dk. Red Met. (2)	2S
Med. Red Met. (2)	2G
Med. Blue Met. (2)	32
Med. Ember Met. (2)	8V
Med. Nectarine Met. (2)	8Z
Lt. Silver Met. (2)	1R
Silver Met. (3)	1J
Black Met. (3)	1L
Rose Met. (3)	2T
Brt. Yellow Gold Met. (3)	6Y
Crystal Jade Met. (3)	7B

1 - (RPO) Unique Colors (Non Polish) "D"
2 - (RPO) Diamond Bright (Polish) "W"
3 - (RPO) Diamond Flare (Polish) "G"

VINYL ROOF TYPE/COLOR CODES

Vinyl Type (First Letter)	CODE
Cross Hatch Full 2-Door	B
Cross Hatch Halo Style 4-Door	C
Odense Full	G
Odense (3/4)	H
Cayman Coach	J
Odense (1/2)	N
Cross Hatch (3/4)	P
Cayman Full	Q
Cross Hatch (1/2)	R
Valino Coach	T
Cayman (1/2)	U
Calino Full	V
Lugano Full	W
Lugano (1/2)	X
Valino (1/2)	Y

VINYL COLOR (Second Letter)	CODE
Black	A
Blue	B
Ember	C
Red	D
Rose	H
Taupe	J
Aqua	L
Lt. Jade	M
Red Lipstick	N

VINYL COLOR (Second Letter)

	CODE
Silver	P
Emerald Dk.	Q
Jade Dk.	R
Med. Blue	S
Brown	T
Chamois	U
Cream	V
White	W
Gold	Y

THE TRIM CODE consists of a two letter or a letter-number combination designating the interior trim.

PINTO

	CODE
Black (1)	GA/LA
Black (2)	AA/HA
Blue (1)	DB/GB
Blue (1)	KB/LB
Blue (2)	AB/HB
Blue (2)	JB/MB
Red (1)	DD/GD
Red (1)	KD/LD
Red (2)	AD/HD
Red (2)	JD/MD
Green (1)	DG/GG
Green (1)	KG/LG
Green (2)	AG/HG
Green (2)	JG/MG
Chamois (1)	DT/GT
Chamois (1)	KT/LT
Chamois (2)	AT/HT
Chamois (2)	JT/MT/NT

1 - Cloth & vinyl
2 - Vinyl

MUSTANG

	CODE
Black (2)	AA/BA
Black (2)	GA/HA/WA
Black (2)	SA/TA/YA
Red (1)	KD/QD
Red (1)	RD/VD/ZD
Red (2)	AD/BD
Red (2)	GD/HD/WD
Red (2)	SD/TD/YD
Aqua (1)	BK/CK/EK
Aqua (1)	QK/RK/UK
Aqua (2)	AK/BK
Aqua (2)	SK/TK
White/Red (2)	AN/BN
White/Red (2)	GN/HN/WN
White/Red (2)	SN/TN/YN
Chamois (1)	CT/UT
Chamois (2)	AT/BT/ST
Chamois (2)	DT/LT/TT
Cream (2)	AV/BV
Gold/Cream (1)	EV/UV/VV
White/Black (2)	AW/BW
White/Black (2)	GW/HW/WW
White/Black (2)	SW/TW/YW
White/Chamois (2)	A2/B2
White/Chamois (2)	S2/T2
White/Emerald (1)	E5/K5/V5
White/Emerald (2)	A5/B5
White/Emerald (2)	G5/H5/W5
White/Emerald (2)	S5/T5/Y5
White/Aqua (1)	V7
White/Aqua (2)	A7/B7
White/Aqua (2)	S7/T7
White/Gold (2)	A8/B8
White/Gold (2)	S8/T8

1 - Cloth & vinyl
2 - Vinyl

MAVERICK

	CODE
Black (1)	BA/UA
Black (2)	SA/VA
Blue (1)	BB/QB
Blue (1)	TB/UB
Blue (2)	SB/VB
Red (1)	BD
Red (2)	SD/VD
Green (1)	BG/QG
Green (1)	TG/UG
Green (2)	VG
Tan (1)	BU/QU
Tan (1)	TU/UU/WU
Tan (2)	SU/VU

1 - Cloth & vinyl
2 - Vinyl

GRANADA

	CODE
Blue (1)	BB/HB
Blue (2)	AB/CB/EB
Blue (2)	GB/JB
Blue (3)	FB
Red (1)	BD/HD/QD
Red (2)	AD/CD/ED
Red (2)	GD/JD/PD
Red (3)	FD/MD/RD
Jade (1)	BR/HR/QR
Jade (2)	AR/CR/ER
Jade (2)	GR/JR
Jade (3)	FR
Lt./Dk. Jade (3)	MM/RM
Gray (1)	BS/QS
Gray (1)	AS/CS
Gray (2)	ES/GS
Gray (3)	FS/MS/RS
Tan (1)	BU/HU/QU
Tan (2)	AU/CU/EU
Tan (2)	GU/JU/PU
Tan (3)	FU/MU/RU
Cream (2)	AV/CV/DV
Cream (2)	EV/GV/JV
Cream (3)	FV

1 - Cloth & vinyl
2 - Vinyl
3 - Leather

THUNDERBIRD

	CODE
Blue (1)	AB/DB
Blue (1)	HB/JB
Blue (2)	BB/CB
Blue (2)	EB/GB
Blue (3)	FB
Blue (4)	RB
Blue (5)	SB
Red (1)	AD/DD
Red (1)	HD/JD
Red (2)	BD/CD
Red (2)	ED/GD
Red (3)	FD
Red (4)	RD
Red (5)	SD
Jade (1)	AR/DR
Jade (1)	HR/JR
Jade (2)	BR/CR
Jade (2)	ER/GR
Jade (3)	FR
Jade (4)	RR
Jade (5)	SR
Gray (1)	AS/DS
Gray (1)	HS/JS
Gray (2)	BS/CS
Gray (2)	ES/GS
Gray (3)	FS
Gray (4)	RS
Gray (5)	SS
Chamois (1)	AT/DT

THUNDERBIRD	CODE
Chamois (1)	HT/JT
Chamois (2)	BT/CT
Chamois (2)	ET/GT
Chamois (3)	FT
Chamois (4)	RT
Chamois (5)	ST
Saddle (1)	AZ/DZ
Saddle (1)	HZ/JZ
Saddle (2)	BZ/CZ
Saddle (2)	EZ/GZ
Saddle (3)	FZ
Saddle/White (2)	E3/G3
Saddle/White (3)	F3
White/Lip. Red (2)	CL/EL/GL
White/Lip. Red (3)	FL
White/Red (2)	CN/EN/GN
White/Red (3)	FN
White/Blue (2)	CQ/EQ/GQ
White/Blue (3)	FQ
White/Chamois (2)	C2/E2/G2
White/Chamois (3)	D2
White/Jade (2)	C5/E5/G5
White/Jade (3)	F5
White/Saddle (2)	C9/E9/G9
White/Saddle (3)	F9
Gray/Red (2)	PS/QS

1 - Cloth & vinyl
2 - Vinyl
3 - Leather & vinyl
4 - Cloth
5 - Leather

LTD	CODE
Blue (1)	AB/CB
Blue (1)	EB/JB/LB
Blue (2)	BB/DB
Blue (2)	FB/GB
Blue (2)	HB/KB/MB
Red (1)	AD/CD
Red (1)	ED/JD/LD
Red (2)	BD/DD
Red (2)	FD/GD
Red (2)	HD/KD/MD
Jade (1)	AR/CR
Jade (1)	ER/JR/LR
Jade (2)	BR/DR
Jade (2)	FR/GR
Jade (2)	HR/KR/MR
Gray (1)	CS/ES
Gray (1)	JS/LS
Gray (2)	DS/FS/GS
Gray (2)	HS/KS/MS
Chamois (1)	AT/CT
Chamois (1)	ET/JT/LT
Chamois (2)	BT/DT
Chamois (2)	FT/GT
Chamois (2)	HT/KT/MT
Saddle (1)	CZ/EZ
Saddle (1)	JZ/LZ
Saddle (2)	DZ/FZ/GZ
Saddle (2)	HZ/KZ/MZ
Saddle/White (2)	F3/G3/H3
Cream/Blue (2)	PV

1 - Cloth & vinyl
2 - Vinyl

FORD	CODE
Blue (1)	AB/CB
Blue (1)	DB/FB
Blue (1)	HB/KB/PB
Blue (2)	BB/EB/GB
Blue (2)	JB/QB/SB
Blue (3)	KB/UB
Blue (4)	YB
Red (1)	AD/CD

FORD	CODE
Red (1)	DD/FD
Red (1)	HD/KD/PD
Red (2)	BD/ED/BD
Red (2)	JD/QD/SD
Red (3)	ND/UD
Red (4)	YD
Jade (1)	CR/DR/FR
Jade (1)	HR/KR/PR
Jade (2)	BR/ER/GR
Jade (2)	JR/QR/SR
Jade (3)	NR/UR
Jade (4)	YR
Gray (1)	DS/FS
Gray (1)	HS/KS/PS
Gray (2)	ES/GS
Gray (2)	JS/QS
Gray (4)	YS
Gold (1)	CY/DY/FY
Gold (1)	HY/KY/PY
Gold (2)	EY/GY
Gold (2)	JY/SY
Gold/Cream (2)	QV
Gold/Cream (4)	YV
Saddle (1)	AZ/CZ
Saddle (1)	DZ/FZ
Saddle (1)	HZ/KZ/PZ
Saddle (2)	BZ/EZ/GZ
Saddle (2)	JZ/QZ/SZ
Saddle (4)	YZ
Saddle/White (2)	Q3
Saddle/White (4)	Y3
Saddle/Tan (3)	NU/UU
Cream/Blue (2)	RV

1 - Cloth & vinyl
2 - Vinyl
3 - Polyknit & vinyl
4 - Leather

THE TRANSMISSION CODE is a number or letter indicating the type of transmission.

TRANSMISSION	CODE
3-Speed Manual	1
4-Speed Manual	6
4-Speed Manual	7
Jatco Automatic	S
XP Automatic (C-3)	V
XP Automatic (C-4)	W
FMX Automatic	X
XPL Automatic (C-6)	U
XPL Automatic (Special)	Z

THE AXLE CODE is a number or letter indicating the rear axle ratio and standard or locking type axles.

CONVENTIONAL	LOCKING	RATIO
B		2.47
1	J	2.50
8		2.73
2		2.75
3		2.79
6	O	3.00
4		3.18
7		3.40

THE DSO CODE, consisting of two numbers, designates the district in which the car was ordered and may appear in conjunction with a Domestic Special Order or Foreign Special Order number when applicable. Ford of Canada DSO codes consist of a letter and number.

FORD DISTRICT	CODE
Special	00
Boston	11
Buffalo	12
New York	13
Pittsburgh	14
Newark	15
Philadelphia	16
Washington	17
Atlanta	21
Charlotte	22
Memphis	23
Jacksonville	24
Richmond	25
New Orleans	26
Louisville	28
Chicago	41
Cleveland	42
Milwaukee	43
Lansing	45
Indianapolis	46
Cincinnati	47
Detroit	48
Dallas	52
Kansas City	53
Omaha	54
St. Louis	55
Davenport	56
Houston	57
Twin Cities	58
Los Angeles	71
San Jose	72
Salt Lake City	73
Seattle	74
Phoenix	75
Denver	76
Government	83
Home Office Reserve	84
American Red Cross	85
Recreational Vehicle Pool	86
Body Company	87
Transporation Services	89
Export	90's

FORD OF CANADA DISTRICT	CODE
Central	B1
Eastern	B2
Atlantic	B3
Midwestern	B4
Western	B6
Pacific	B7
Export	12

ENGINE IDENTIFICATION

ENGINE TAG
Since 1964, Ford engines can be identified by a tag attached to the engine. The tag contains the year and cubic inch displacement.

CASTING NUMBERS
While helpful in identifying Ford engine components, casting numbers are not conclusive in pin-pointing the exact year of manufacture. A better method is to search for the original host vehicle's VIN (Vehicle Identification Number) stamped on the driver's side at the rear of the engine block below the cylinder head.

PINTO ENGINES

CID	NO. CYL.	HORSE-POWER	COMP. RATIO	CARB.
140	4	89	9.0:1	2 BC
171	6	93	8.7:1	2 BC

MUSTANG II ENGINES

CID	NO. CYL.	HORSE-POWER	COMP. RATIO	CARB.
140	4	89	9.0:1	2 BC
171	6	93	8.7:1	2 BC
302	8	129	8.4:1	2 BC
302	8	139	8.4:1	2 BC

GRANADA ENGINES

CID	NO. CYL.	HORSE-POWER	COMP. RATIO	CARB.
200	6	96	8.5:1	1 BC
250	6	98	8.1:1	1 BC
302	8	122	8.4:1	2 BC
302	8	134	8.4:1	2 BC
351	8	135	8.3:1	2 BC

MAVERICK ENGINES

CID	NO. CYL.	HORSE-POWER	COMP. RATIO	CARB.
200	6	96	8.5:1	1 BC
250	6	98	8.1:1	1 BC
302	8	137	8.4:1	2 BC

LTD ENGINES

CID	NO. CYL.	HORSE-POWER	COMP. RATIO	CARB.
302	8	130	8.4:1	2 BC
351	8	161	8.0:1	2 BC
351	8	149	8.3:1	2 BC
400	8	173	8.0:1	2 BC

THUNDERBIRD ENGINES

CID	NO. CYL.	HORSE-POWER	COMP. RATIO	CARB.
302	8	130	8.4:1	2 BC
351	8	149	8.3:1	2 BC
351	8	161	8.0:1	2 BC
400	8	168	8.0:1	2 BC
400	8	173	8.0:1	2 BC

FORD ENGINES

CID	NO. CYL.	HORSE-POWER	COMP. RATIO	CARB.
302	8	134	8.4:1	2 BC
351	8	149	8.3:1	2 BC
400	8	173	8.0:1	2 BC
460	8	197	8.0:1	4 BC

1978 FORD LTD II

1978 FORD THUNDERBIRD

1978 FORD LTD WAGON

1978 FORD FAIRMONT

1978 FORD MUSTANG II

1978 FORD FAIRMONT WAGON

1978 FORD PINTO

1978 FORD GRANADA

1978 FORD LTD II

1978 FORD LTD

VEHICLE IDENTIFICATION NUMBER

**FORD
F 8S63H123456**

Located on the top of the dash on the driver's side and visible through the windshield from outside the car.

FIRST DIGIT: Identifies the year (8 = 1978)

SECOND DIGIT: Identifies the assembly plant

ASSEMBLY PLANT	CODE
Atlanta, GA	A
Oakville, Ont., CAN	B
Mahwah, NJ	E
Dearborn, MI	F
Chicago, IL	G
Lorain, OH	H
Los Angeles, CA	J
Kansas City, KS	K
Twin Cities, MN	P
San Jose, CA	R
Allen Park (Pilot Plant)	S
Metuchen, NJ	T
Louisville, KY	U
Wayne, MI	W
St. Thomas, Ont., CAN	X
Wixom, MI	Y
St. Louis, Mo	Z

THIRD AND FOURTH DIGITS: Identify the body serial code

PINTO	CODE
2-Dr. Sedan	10
3-Dr. Sedan	11
Wagon	12

MUSTANG II	CODE
2-Dr. Base	02
3-Dr. Base	03
2-Dr. Ghia	04
3-Dr. Mach I	05

GRANADA	CODE
4-Dr. Sedan	82
2-Dr. Sedan	81
2-Dr. Ghia	84
4-Dr. Ghia	83

LTD II	CODE
2-Dr. Hardtop LTD II S	25
4-Dr. Pillar HT LTD II S	27
2-Dr. HT LTD II	30
4-Dr. Pillar HT LTD II	31

FAIRMONT	CODE
4-Dr. Sedan	92
2-Dr. Sedan	91
2-Dr. Sedan Sport Coupe Futura	93
Station Wagon	94

THUNDERBIRD	CODE
2-Dr. Pillar Hardtop	87

FORD	CODE
2-Dr. Pillar HT Custom 500 Fleet	52
4-Dr. Pillar HT Custom 500 Fleet	53
2-Dr. Pillar HT LTD	62
4-Dr. Pillar HT LTD	63
4-Dr. Pillar HT LTD Landau	64
2-Dr. Pillar HT LTD Landau	65
Custom 500/LTD Wagon Fleet	72
LTD Station Wagon	74
Country Squire SW	76

FIFTH DIGIT: Identifies the engine code

ENGINE	CODE
V-8 460-4V	A
V-8 460-4V (Police Interceptor)	C
V-8 302-2V	F
V-8 351-2V	H
6 250-1V	L
V-8 400-2V	S
6 200-1V	T
4 139-2V (2.3L)	Y
6 169-2V (2.8L)	Z
351 Modified	Q

LAST SIX DIGITS: Represents the basic production numbers

EXAMPLE:

8	S	63	H	123456
Model Year	Asm Plant	Body Serial Code	Engine	Production Sequence Number

VEHICLE CERTIFICATION LABEL

THE VEHICLE CERTIFICATION LABEL (V.C. Label) is affixed on the left front door lock face panel or door pillar. The upper half of the label contains the name of manufacturer, month and year of manufacture, Gross Vehicle Weight Rating (GVWR), Gross Axle Weight Rating (GAWR), and the certification statement. The V.C. label also contains the Vehicle Identification Number (VIN). The remaining information on the V.C. label consists of pertinent vehicle identification codes: ie. body, color, trim, axle, transmission and the domestic special order (DSO) codes.

MANUFACTURED BY FORD MOTOR COMPANY

7/78 THIS VEHICLE CONFORMS TO ALL APPLICABLE FEDERAL MOTOR VEHICLE SAFETY STANDARDS IN EFFECT ON DATE OF MANUFACTURE SHOWN ABOVE

8S63H123456   PASSENGER
53H   3E   DB X 6   48

NOT FOR TITLE OR REGISTRATION
MADE IN U.S.A.

EXAMPLE:
8S63H123456	Vehicle Identification Number (VIN)
53H	Body Type Code (LTD 4-Dr. Pillar Hardtop)
3E	Body Color Code (Diamond Blue Metallic)
DB	Trim Code (Blue Cloth & Vinyl)
X	Transmission Code (FMX Automatic)
6	Rear Axle Code (3.00:1)
48	District Special Equipment Code (Detroit)

THE BODY CODE is two numerals and a letter identifying the body style.

PINTO CODE	
2-Dr. Sedan	62B
3-Dr. Sedan	64B
Station Wagon	73B

* Runabout option available
* Pony option available
* Squire Wagon available

MUSTANG II	CODE
2-Dr. Base	60F
3-Dr. Base	69F
2-Dr. Ghia	60H
3-Dr. Mach I	69R
* King Cobra option available	
* Cobra option available	

GRANADA	CODE
4-Dr. Sedan	54H
2-Dr. Sedan	66H
2-Dr. Ghia	66K
4-Dr. Ghia	54K

LTD II	CODE
2-Dr. Hardtop LTD II S	65B
4-Dr. Pillar HT LTD II S	53B
2-Dr. Hardtop LTD II	65D
4-Dr. Pillar HT LTD II	53D
LTD II Squire Wagon	71K

FAIRMONT	CODE
4-Dr. Sedan	54B
2-Dr. Sedan	66B
2-Dr. Sedan Sport Coupe Futura	66R
Station Wagon	74B
* Squire Wagon option available	
* E.S. option available	

THUNDERBIRD	CODE
2-Dr. Pillar Hardtop	60H
* Diamond Jubilee Edition option available	
* Town Landau option available	

FORD	CODE
2-Dr. Pillar HT Custom 500 Fleet	60D
4-Dr. Pillar HT Custom 500 Fleet	53D
2-Dr. Pillar HT LTD	60H
4-Dr. Pillar HT LTD	53H
4-Dr. Pillar HT LTD Landau	53L
2-Dr. Pillar HT LTD Landau	60L
Custom 500/LTD Wagon Fleet	71D
LTD Station Wagon	71H
Country Squire SW	71H

THE COLOR CODE is a two-letter or a number-letter indicating the exterior paint color code and vinyl roof type and color (if equipped).

EXTERIOR PAINT COLOR	CODE
Black	1C
Silver Metallic	1G
Dove Grey	1N
Dark Red	2M
Bright Red	2R
Bright Russet Red	21
Dark Midnight Blue	3A
Diamond Blue Metallic	3E
Dark Blue Metallic	3G
Light Blue	3U
Medium Blue	34
Dark Jade Metallic	46
Medium Chestnut Metallic	5M
Dark Brown Metallic	5Q
Ember Metallic	5Y
Bright Yellow	6E
Creme	6P
Antique Cream	62
Light Aqua Metallic	7Q
Medium Jade	7W
Cordovan Metallic	8N
Champagne Metallic	8Y
Russet Metallic	81
Light Chamois	83
Tangerine	85

EXTERIOR PAINT COLOR	CODE
Pastel Beige	86
Polar White	9D
Bright Blue Glow*	3V
Bright Aqua Glow*	7H
Light Jade Glow*	7L
Camel Glow*	8J
Chamois Glow*	8W
*Metallic Glow Paints optional at extra cost	

VINYL ROOF TYPE/COLOR CODES

Vinyl Type (First Letter)	CODE
Lugano Full	W
Lugano Half	X
Lugano Front Half	K
Lugano Coach	M
Milano Full	D
Milano Half	E
Milano Halo	F
Cayman Full	Q
Cayman Half	U
Valino Full	V
Valino Half	Y
Valino Front Half	Z
Valino Coach	T
Crosshatch Full	B
Crosshatch Half	R
Levant Full	S
Levant Half Rear	E
Odense Full	G
Odense Half	N
Odense Front Half	A

VINYL COLOR (Second Letter)	CODE
Black	A
Medium Blue	B
Midnight Blue	S
Wedgewood Blue	5
Dark Brown	T
Light Camel	V
Medium Camel	Y
Chamois	U
Light Champagne	6
Midnight Champagne	J
Cordovan	F
Light Cordovan	K
Galveston Gold	E
Dove Gray	E
Dark Jade	R
Light Jade	M
Medium Jade	4
Wedgewood Jade	3
Red/Russet	D
Silver	P
White	W

THE TRIM CODE consists of a two-letter or a letter number combination designating the interior trim.

PINTO	CODE
Black (1)	GA
Black (2)	AA/HA
Blue (1)	GB/DB
Blue (2)	AB/HB
Red (1)	GD/DD
Red (2)	AD/HD
Tangerine (1)	DJ
Tangerine (2)	HJ
Jade (1)	DR/GR
Jade (2)	AR/HR
Chamois (1)	DT/GT
Chamois (2)	AT/HT
1 - Cloth & vinyl	
2 - Vinyl	

FAIRMONT — CODE

White/Black (2)	AW/BW
White/Black (2)	EW/GW/KW
White/Russet (2)	A7/B7
White/Russet (2)	E7/G7/K7
White/Chamois (2)	A2/B2
White/Chamois (2)	E2/G2/K2
White/Blue (2)	AQ/BQ
White/Blue (2)	EQ/GQ/KQ
Chamois (1)	CT/LT
Chamois (1)	FT/HT
Chamois (2)	AT/BT
Chamois (2)	ET/GT/KT
Chamois/Black (2)	AU/BU/GU
Russet (1)	CE/LE
Russet (1)	FE/HE
Russet (2)	AE/BE
Russet (2)	EE/GE/KE
Blue (1)	CB/LB
Blue (1)	FB/HB
Blue (2)	AB/BB
Blue (2)	EB/GB/KB
Black (1)	HA/LA/FA
Black (2)	AA/BA
Black (2)	EA/GA/KA

1 - Cloth & vinyl
2 - Vinyl

MUSTANG II — CODE

White/Aqua (2)	A7/M7/B7
White/Chamois (2)	A2/M2/B2
White/Black (2)	AW/MW
White/Black (2)	GW/BW
White/Red (2)	AN/MN
White/Red (2)	GN/BN
Chamois (1)	JT/NT
Chamois (1)	PT/CT/ET
Chamois (2)	AT/MT
Chamois (2)	FT/BT
Aqua (1)	JK/NK
Aqua (1)	PK/CK/EK
Aqua (2)	AK/MK/BK
Tangerine (1)	NJ/PJ/EJ
Red (1)	JD/ND/ED
Red (2)	AD/MD
Red (2)	GD/BD
Black (1)	JA
Black (2)	AA/MA
Black (2)	GA/BA
Black/Gold (1)	FA
White/Gold (1)	F8
Dove Gray/Red (1)	PD
Dove Gray/Black (1)	PA

1 - Cloth & vinyl
2 - Vinyl

GRANADA — CODE

Camel (1)	KY/HY
Camel (1)	BY/DY/QY
Camel (2)	LY/EY/AY
Camel (2)	GY/PY/CY
Camel (3)	FY/RY/MY
Dove Gray (1)	HS/BS
Dove Gray (1)	/DS/QS
Dove Gray (2)	ES/AS
Dove Gray (2)	GS/PS/CS
Dove Gray (3)	FS/RS/MS
Red (1)	KD/HD
Red (1)	BD/DD/QD

GRANADA — CODE

Red (2)	LD/ED/AD
Red (2)	GD/PD/CD
Red (3)	FD/RD/MD
Blue (1)	KB/HB
Blue (1)	BB/DB
Blue (2)	LB/EB/AB
Blue (2)	GB/PB/CB
Blue (3)	FB
Jade (1)	KR/HR
Jade (1)	BR/DR
Jade (2)	LR/ER/AR
Jade (2)	GR/PR/CR
Jade (3)	FR
Cordovan (1)	BF/DF
Cordovan (2)	EF/AF
Cordovan (2)	GF/PF/CF
Cordovan (3)	FF

1 - Cloth & vinyl
2 - Vinyl
3 - Leather & vinyl

LTD II — CODE

Saddle (1)	LZ/HZ
Saddle (1)	EZ/KZ
Saddle (2)	MZ/JZ
Saddle (2)	FZ/GZ
Chamois (1)	AT/LT
Chamois (1)	HT/ET/KT
Chamois (2)	BT/MT
Chamois (2)	JT/FT/GT
Dove Gray (1)	LS/HS
Dove Gray (1)	ES/KS
Dove Gray (2)	MS/JS
Dove Gray (2)	FS/GS
Jade (1)	AR/LR
Jade (1)	HR/ER/KR
Jade (2)	BR/MR
Jade (2)	JR/FR/GR
Russet (1)	AE/LE
Russet (1)	HE/EE/KE
Russet (2)	BE/ME
Russet (2)	JE/FE/GE
Blue (1)	AB/LB
Blue (1)	HB/EB/KB
Blue (2)	BB/MB
Blue (2)	JB/FB/GB

1 - Cloth & vinyl
2 - Vinyl

FORD LTD — CODE

Saddle (1)	DZ/FZ
Saddle (1)	HZ/KZ/PZ
Saddle (2)	EZ/GZ
Saddle (2)	JZ/QZ
Saddle (3)	YZ
Saddle/Tan (4)	UU
Camel (1)	DY/FY
Camel (1)	HY/KY/PY
Camel (2)	EY/GY
Camel (2)	JY/QY
Camel (3)	YY
Dove Gray (1)	DS/FS
Dove Gray (1)	HS/KS/PS
Dove Gray (2)	ES/GS
Dove Gray (2)	JS/QS
Dove Gray (3)	YS
Jade (1)	DR/FR

FORD LTD

FORD LTD	CODE
Jade (1)	HR/KR/PR
Jade (2)	ER/GR
Jade (2)	JR/QR
Jade (3)	YR
Jade (4)	UR
Red (1)	DD/FD
Red (1)	HD/KD/PD
Red (2)	ED/GD
Red (2)	JD/QD
Red (3)	YD
Red (4)	UD
Blue (1)	DB/FB
Blue (1)	HB/KB/PB
Blue (2)	EB/GB
Blue (2)	JB/QB
Blue (3)	YB
Blue (4)	UB

1 - Cloth & vinyl
2 - Vinyl
3 - Leather & vinyl
4 - Duraweave

LTD WAGON & COUNTRY SQUIRE

LTD WAGON & COUNTRY SQUIRE	CODE
Saddle/Tan (1)	UU/NU
Saddle (2)	EZ/SU/QU
Saddle (3)	YU
Camel (1)	UY/NY
Camel (2)	EY/SY/QY
Camel (3)	YY
Jade (1)	UR/NR
Jade (2)	ER/SR/QR
Jade (3)	YR
Red (1)	UD/ND
Red (2)	ED/SD/QD
Red (3)	YD
Blue (1)	UB/NB
Blue (2)	EB/SB/QB
Blue (3)	YB

1 - Duraweave
2 - Vinyl

THUNDERBIRD

THUNDERBIRD	CODE
Saddle (1)	AZ/HZ
Saddle (1)	DZ/JZ
Saddle (2)	BZ/CZ
Saddle (2)	EZ/GZ
Saddle (3)	FZ/SZ
Saddle (4)	RZ
Chamois (1)	AT/HT
Chamois (1)	DT/JT
Chamois (2)	BT/CT
Chamois (2)	ET/GT
Chamois (3)	FT/ST
Chamois (4)	RT
Chamois (5)	TT
Dove Gray (1)	AS/HS
Dove Gray (1)	DS/JS
Dove Gray (2)	BS/CS
Dove Gray (2)	ES/GS
Dove Gray (3)	FS/SS
Dove Gray (4)	RS
Jade (1)	AR/HR
Jade (1)	DR/JR
Jade (2)	BR/CR
Jade (2)	ER/GR
Jade (3)	FR/SR
Jade (4)	RR
Russet (1)	AE/HE
Russet (1)	DE/JE
Russet (2)	BE/CE
Russet (2)	EE/GE
Russet (3)	FE/SE
Russet (4)	RE
Blue (1)	AB/HB
Blue (1)	DB/JB

THUNDERBIRD

THUNDERBIRD	CODE
Blue (2)	BB/CB
Blue (2)	EB/GB
Blue (3)	FB/SB
Blue (4)	RB
Blue (5)	TB
White/Saddle (2)	C9/E9/G9
White/Saddle (3)	F9/S9
White/Russet (2)	C7/E7/G7
White/Russet (3)	F7/S7
White/Jade (2)	C5/E5/G5
White/Jade (3)	F5/S5
White/Chamois (2)	C2/E2/G2
White/Chamois (3)	F2/S2
White/Blue (2)	CQ/EQ/GQ
White/Blue (3)	FQ/SQ

1 - Cloth & vinyl
2 - Vinyl
3 - Leather & vinyl
4 - Velour
5 - Cloth

THE TRANSMISSION CODE is a number or letter indicating the type of transmission.

TRANSMISSION	CODE
3-Speed Manual	1
4-Speed Overdrive	5
4-Speed Manual	6
4-Spped Manual	7
XP Automatic (C-3)	V
XP Automatic (C-4)	W
FMX Automatic	X
XPL Automatic (C-6)	U
XPL Automatic (Special)	Z

THE AXLE CODE is a number or letter indicating the rear axle ratio and standard or locking type axles.

CONVENTIONAL	LOCKING	RATIO
Y		3.08
B		2.47
1	J	2.50
8		2.73
2		2.75
3		2.79
6	O	3.00
4		3.18
7		3.40

THE DSO CODE, consisting of two numbers, designates the district in which the car was ordered and may appear in conjunction with a Domestic Special Order or Foreign Special Order number when applicable. Ford of Canada DSO codes consist of a letter and number.

FORD DISTRICT	CODE
Special	00
Boston	11
Buffalo	12
New York	13
Pittsburgh	14
Newark	15
Philadelphia	16
Washington	17
Atlanta	21
Charlotte	22
Memphis	23
Jacksonville	24
Richmond	25
New Orleans	26
Louisville	28
Chicago	41
Cleveland	42
Milwaukee	43
Lansing	45
Indianapolis	46
Cincinnati	47
Detroit	48
Dallas	52
Kansas City	53
Omaha	54
St. Louis	55
Davenport	56
Houston	57
Twin Cities	58
Los Angeles	71
San Jose	72
Salt Lake City	73
Seattle	74
Phoenix	75
Denver	76
Government	83
Home Office Reserve	84
American Red Cross	85
Recreational Vehicle Pool	86
Body Company	87
Transportation Services	89
Export	90's

FORD OF CANADA DISTRICT	CODE
Central	B1
Eastern	B2
Atlantic	B3
Midwestern	B4
Western	B6
Pacific	B7
Export	12

ENGINE IDENTIFICATION

ENGINE TAG

Since 1964, Ford engines can be identified by a tag attached to the engine. The tag contains the year and cubic inch displacement.

CASTING NUMBERS

While helpful in identifying Ford engine components, casting numbers are not conclusive in pin-pointing the exact year of manufacture. A better method is to search for the original host vehicle's VIN (Vehicle Identification Number) stamped on the driver's side at the rear of the engine block below the cylinder head.

PINTO ENGINES

CID	NO. CYL.	HORSE-POWER	COMP. RATIO	CARB.
140	4	88	9.0:1	2 BC
171	6	90	8.7:1	2 BC

FAIRMONT ENGINES

CID	NO. CYL.	HORSE-POWER	COMP. RATIO	CARB.
140	4	88	9.0:1	2 BC
200	6	85	8.5:1	1 BC
302	8	139	8.4:1	2 BC

MUSTANG II ENGINES

CID	NO. CYL.	HORSE-POWER	COMP. RATIO	CARB.
140	4	88	9.0:1	2 BC
171	6	90	8.7:1	2 BC
302	8	139	8.4:1	2 BC

GRANADA ENGINES

CID	NO. CYL.	HORSE-POWER	COMP. RATIO	CARB.
250	6	97	8.5:1	1 BC
302	8	139	8.4:1	2 BC

FORD ENGINES

CID	NO. CYL.	HORSE-POWER	COMP. RATIO	CARB.
302	8	134	8.4:1	2 BC
351	8	145	8.0:1	2 BC
400	8	160	8.0:1	2 BC
460	8	202	8.0:1	4 BC

THUNDERBIRD ENGINES

CID	NO. CYL.	HORSE-POWER	COMP. RATIO	CARB.
302	8	134	8.4:1	2 BC
351	8	152	8.0:1	2 BC
351	8	144	8.3:1	2 BC
400	8	166	8.0:1	2 BC

LTD II ENGINES

CID	NO. CYL.	HORSE-POWER	COMP. RATIO	CARB.
351	8	152	8.0:1	2 BC
302	8	139	8.4:1	2 BC
302	8	134	8.4:1	2 BC
351	8	144	8.3:1	2 BC
400	8	166	8.0:1	2 BC

1979 FORD MUSTANG

1979 FORD GRANADA

1979 FORD PINTO

1979 FORD LTD

1979 FORD PINTO WAGON

1979 FORD LTD II

1979 FORD THUNDERBIRD

1979 FORD LTD WAGON

1979 FORD FAIRMONT

1979 FORD FAIRMONT WAGON

VEHICLE IDENTIFICATION NUMBER

```
┌─────────────────────────┐
│  •    FORD         •     │
│    F 9S63H123456         │
└─────────────────────────┘
```

Located on the top of the dash on the driver's side and visible through the windshield from outside the car.

FIRST DIGIT: Identifies the year (9 = 1979)

SECOND DIGIT: Identifies the assembly plant

ASSEMBLY PLANT	CODE
Atlanta, GA	A
Chicago, IL	G
Dearborn, MI	F
Kansas City, KS	K
Lorain, OH	H
Los Angeles, CA	J
Louisville, KY	U
Mahwah, NJ	E
Metuchen, NJ	T
Allen Park (Pilot Plant)	S
St. Louis, Mo	Z
San Jose, CA	R
Wayne, MI	W
Wixom, MI	Y
Oakville, Ont.,CAN	B
St. Thomas, Ont., CAN	X

THIRD AND FOURTH DIGITS: Identify the body serial code

PINTO	CODE
2-Dr. Sedan	10
3-Dr. Sedan	11
2-Dr. Wagon	12

MUSTANG	CODE
2-Dr. Notchback	02
3-Dr. Hatchback	03
3-Dr. Hatchback Ghia	05
2-Dr. Notchback Ghia	04

FAIRMONT	CODE
4-Dr. Sedan	92
2-Dr. Sedan	91
2-Dr. Sedan Sporty Coupe Futura	93
4-Dr. Wagon	94

GRANADA	CODE
4-Dr. Sedan	82
2-Dr. Sedan	81

LTD II	CODE
4-Dr. Pillar HT LTD II S	27
2-Dr. Hardtop LTD II S	25
4-Dr. Pillar HT LTD II	31
2-Dr. Hardtop LTD II	30

FORD	CODE
4-Dr. Sedan LTD	63
2-Dr. Sedan LTD	62
4-Dr. Sedan LTD Landau	65
2-Dr. Sedan LTD Landau	64
4-Dr. LTD Wagon	74
Country Squire	76

THUNDERBIRD	CODE
2-Dr. Pillar Hardtop	87

FIFTH DIGIT: Identifies the engine code

ENGINE	CODE
I4 139-2V	Y
I4 139-2V Turbo Charged	W
V6 169-2V	Z
I6 200/1V	T
I6 250-1V	L
V8 302-2V	F
V8 351-2V	H
V8 400-2V	S

LAST SIX DIGITS: Represent the basic production numbers

EXAMPLE:

9	S	63	H	123456
Model Year	Asm Plant	Body Serial Code	Engine	Production Sequence Number

VEHICLE CERTIFICATION LABEL

THE VEHICLE CERTIFICATION LABEL (V.C. Label) is affixed on the left front door lock face panel or door pillar. The upper half of the label contains the name of manufacturer, month and year of manufacture, Gross Vehicle Weight Rating (GVWR), Gross Axle Weight Rating (GAWR), and the certification statement. The V.C. label also contains the Vehicle Identification Number (VIN). The remaining information on the V.C. label consists of pertinent vehicle identification codes: ie. color, DSO code, body, trim, schedule date, axle, transmission and A.C. code (if applicable).

```
┌──────────────────────────────────────┐
│          MANUFACTURED BY               │
│        FORD MOTOR COMPANY              │
│                                        │
│    7/79 THIS VEHICLE CONFORMS TO ALL   │
│   APPLICABLE FEDERAL MOTOR VEHICLE     │
│        SAFETY STANDARDS IN EFFECT ON   │
│ • DATE OF MANUFACTURE SHOWN ABOVE •    │
│                                        │
│   9S63H123456      PASSENGER           │
│   1CYA 48 54H DD 08H 6 X A             │
│                                        │
│   NOT FOR TITLE OR REGISTRATION        │
│          MADE IN U.S.A.                │
└──────────────────────────────────────┘
```

EXAMPLE:

9S63H123456	Vehicle Identification Number (VIN)
1CYA	Body Color and Vinyl Roof Type/Color Codes (Black & Black Valino Half Vinyl Roof)
48	District Special Equipment Code (Detroit)
54H	Body Type Code (LTD 4-Dr. Sedan)
DD	Trim Code (Red Cloth & Vinyl)
08H	Scheduled Build Date
6	Rear Axle Code (3.00:1)
X	Transmission Code (FMX Automatic)
A	Air Conditioning

THE COLOR CODE consists of two or four digits. The first two digits represent the exterior body color. If the vehicle is equipped with a vinyl roof, the second two digits will indicate the style and color of the vinyl roof.

EXTERIOR PAINT COLOR

Color	CODE
Black	1C
Silver Metallic	1G
Dove Grey	1N
Med. Grey Metallic	1P
Maroon	2J
Bright Red	2P
Dark Red	2M
Light Medium Blue	3F
Bright Blue	3J
Dark Blue Metallic	3L
Wedgewood Blue	34
Dark Pine Metallic	4D
Dark Jade Metallic	46
Pastel Chamois	5P
Dark Brown Metallic	5Q
Light Champagne	52
Cream	6P
Light Gold	6W
Antique Gold	62
Bright Yellow	64
Light Medium Pine	76
Dk. Cordovan Metallic	8N
Light Chamois	83
Tangerine	85
White	9D
Medium Red Metallic (1)	2H
Lt. Wedgewood Blue Met. (1)	3H
Med. Dark Orange Met. (1)	5N
Med. Vaquero Met. (1)	5W
Med. Jade Metallic (1)	7L
Med. Pine Metallic (1)	75
Med. Tan Metallic (1)	8J
Chamois Metallic (1)	8W
Med. Gray Metallic (2)	1S
Silver Metallic (2)	1S
Light Red Metallic (2)	2W
Lt. Amethyst Metallic (2)	2D
Dk. Red Metallic (2)	23
Dk. Blue Metallic (2)	3Q
Diamond Blue Metallic (2)	38
Dark Beryl Metallic (2)	4B
Med. Beryl Metallic (2)	4B
Med. Beryl Metallic (2)	4C
Dk. Champagne Met. (2)	5A
Lt. Champagne Met. (2)	5C
Dk. Cordovan Met. (2)	5R
Jubilee Gold Met. (2)	66
Lt. Apricot Met. (2)	88

1 - Glamour Colors "D" Non Polish
2 - Clear Coat (Polish)

VINYL ROOF TYPE/COLOR CODES

Vinyl Type (First Letter)	CODE
Grande Full	H
Grande Half	P
Lugano Full	W
Lugano Half	X
Lugano Front Half	K
Valino Full	V
Valino Half	Y
Valino Front Half	Z
Valino Coach	T
Convertible Rood, Simulated, Diamond*	C
Cavalry Twill-Coach	J

*When a Vinyl Roof is installed, the type and color codes will be reflected after the two digit Exterior Paint Color Code.

VINYL COLOR (Second Letter)

Color	CODE
Amethyst	7
Medium Beryl	K
Black	A
Light Diamond/Blue	B
Midnight Blue	Q
Camel/Cream	V
Chamois	T
Dark Champagne	J
Light Champagne	U
Dark Cordovan	F
Light Cordovan	N
Jubilee Gold	Y
Dove Gray	S
Dark Midnight Jade	R
Pine	M
Red Dark (Versailles Only)/ Red Midnight	8
Red Dark (Others)/Red Bright/ Red Medium	D
Silver	P
Vaquero	Z
White	W

THE DSO CODE is two digits, designating the sales district where the vehicle was ordered.

FORD DISTRICT

District	CODE
Special	00
Boston	11
Buffalo	12
New York	13
Pittsburgh	14
Newark	15
Philadelphia	16
Washington	17
Atlanta	21
Charlotte	22
Memphis	23
Jacksonville	24
Richmond	25
New Orleans	26
Louisville	28
Chicago	41
Cleveland	42
Milwaukee	43
Lansing	45
Indianapolis	46
Cincinnati	47
Detroit	48
Dallas	52
Kansas City	53
Omaha	54
St. Louis	55
Davenport	56
Houston	57
Twin Cities	58
Los Angeles	71
San Jose	72
Salt Lake City	73
Seattle	74
Phoenix	75
Denver	76
Government	83
Home Office Reserve	84
American Red Cross	85
Recreational Vehicle Pool	86
Body Company	87
Transportaion Services	89
Export	90's

FORD OF CANADA DISTRICT	CODE
Central	B1
Eastern	B2
Atlantic	B3
Midwestern	B4
Western	B6
Pacific	B7
Great Lakes	B8
Export	12

THE BODY CODE consists of two numerals and one letter indicating the car line and body style.

PINTO	CODE
2-Dr. Sedan	62B
3-Dr. Sedan	64B
2-Dr. Wagon	73B

* Rallye option available
* Runabout option available
* Cruising Wagon option available
* Squire Wagon option available
* ESS option available

MUSTANG	CODE
2-Dr. Notchback	66B
3-Dr. Hatchback	61R
3-Dr. Hatchback Ghia	61H
2-Dr. Notchback Ghia	66H

* Cobra option available
* Indy Pace car option available

FAIRMONT	CODE
4-Dr. Sedan	54B
2-Dr. Sedan	66B
2-Dr. Sedan Sporty Coupe Futura	36R
4-Dr. Wagon	74B

* Squire Wagon option avaiable
* ESS option available

GRANADA	CODE
4-Dr. Sedan	54H
2-Dr. Sedan	66H

* Ghia option available

LTD II	CODE
4-Dr. Pillar HT LTD II S	53B
2-Dr. Hardtop LTD II S	65B
4-Dr. Pillar HT LTD II	53D
2-Dr. Hardtop LTD II	65D

FORD	CODE
4-Dr. Sedan LTD	54H
2-Dr. Sedan LTD	66H
4-Dr. Sedan LTD Landau	54K
2-Dr. Sedan LTD Landau	66K
4-Dr. LTD Wagon	74H
Country Squire	74K

THUNDERBIRD	CODE
2-Dr. Pillar Hardtop	60H

* Heritage option available
* Town Landau option available

THE TRIM CODE consists of two letters. The first letter indicates the type of trim and the second letter indicates the color of the trim.

FORD LTD	CODE
Blue (1)	AB/CB/DB
Blue (1)	GB/JB/MB
Blue (2)	BB/EB
Blue (2)	HB/KB/NB
Blue (3)	LB
Red (1)	AD/CD/DD

FORD LTD	CODE
Red (1)	GD/JD/MD
Red (2)	BD/ED
Red (2)	HD/KD/ND
Red (3)	LD
Cordovan (1)	AF/CF/DF
Cordovan (1)	GF/JF/MF
Cordovan (2)	BF/EF
Cordovan (2)	HF/KF/NF
Cordovan (3)	LF
Pine Green (1)	AR/CR/DR
Pine Green (1)	GR/JR/MR
Pine Green (2)	BR/ER
Pine Green (2)	HR/KR/NR
Pine Green (3)	LR
Dove Gray (1)	DS/GS
Dove Gray (1)	JS/MS
Dove Gray (2)	BS/ES
Dove Gray (2)	HS/KS/NS
Camel (1)	AY/CY/DY
Camel (1)	GY/JY/MY
Camel (2)	BY/EY
Camel (2)	HY/KY/NY
Camel (3)	LY

1 - Cloth & vinyl
2 - Vinyl
3 - Duraweave

LTD WAGON AND COUNTRY SQUIRE	CODE
Blue (1)	MB
Blue (2)	BB/EB/NB
Blue (3)	CB/FB
Red (1)	MD
Red (2)	BD/ED/ND
Red (3)	CD/FD
Cordovan (1)	MF
Cordovan (2)	BF/EF/NF
Cordovan (3)	CF/FF
Pine Green (1)	MR
Pine Green (2)	BR/ER/NR
Pine Green (3)	CR/FR
Camel (1)	MY
Camel (2)	BY/EY/NY
Camel (3)	CY/FY

1 - Cloth & vinyl
2 - Vinyl
3 - Duraweave

THUNDERBIRD	CODE
Blue (1)	KB/HB/DB
Blue (1)	JB/RB/TB
Blue (2)	LB/CB
Blue (2)	EB/GB
Blue (3)	SB
Red (1)	KD/HD/DD
Red (1)	JD/RD/TD
Red (2)	LD/CD
Red (2)	ED/GD
Red (3)	SD
Cordovan (1)	KF/HF
Cordovan (1)	DF/JF/RF
Cordovan (2)	LF/CF
Cordovan (2)	EF/GF
Cordovan (3)	SF
Jade (1)	KR/HR
Jade (1)	DR/JR/RR
Jade (2)	LR/CR
Jade (2)	ER/GR
Jade (3)	SR
Dove Gray (1)	KS/HS
Dove Gray (1)	DS/JS/RS
Dove Gray (2)	LS/CS
Dove Gray (2)	ES/GS
Dove Gray (3)	SS
Chamois (1)	KT/HT
Chamois (1)	DT/JT/RT

THUNDERBIRD	CODE
Chamois (2)	LT/CT
Chamois (2)	ET/GT
Chamois (3)	ST
White/Red (2)	CN/EN/GN
White/Red (3)	SN
White/Blue (2)	CQ/EQ/GQ
White/Blue (3)	SQ
White/Chamois (2)	C2/E2/G2
White/Chamois (3)	S2
White/Jade (2)	C5/E5/G5
White/Jade (3)	S5
White/Cordovan (2)	C6/E6/G6
White/Cordovan (3)	S6

1 - Cloth & vinyl
2 - Vinyl
3 - Leather & vinyl

LTD II	CODE
Blue (1)	AB/LB/JB
Blue (2)	BB/MB/HB
Red (1)	AD/LD/JD
Red (2)	BD/MD/HD
Jade (1)	JR
Jade (2)	MR/HR
Cordovan (1)	LF
Cordovan (2)	MF/HF
Dove Gray (1)	LS/JS
Dove Gray (2)	MS/HS
Chamois (1)	AT/LT/JT
Chamois (2)	BT/MT/HT

1 - Cloth & vinyl
2 - Vinyl

LTD II BROUGHAM	CODE
Blue (1)	EB/KB
Blue (2)	FB/GB
Red (1)	ED/KD
Red (2)	FD/GD
Cordovan (1)	EF
Cordovan (2)	FF/GF
Jade (1)	ER/KR
Jade (2)	FR/GR
Dove Gray (1)	ES/KS
Dove Gray (2)	FS/GS
Chamois (1)	ET/KT
Chamois (2)	FT/GT

1 - Cloth & vinyl
2 - Vinyl

GRANADA	CODE
Blue (1)	JB/BB/DB
Blue (2)	KB/GB/CB
Blue (3)	MB
Red (1)	JD/BD/DD
Red (2)	KD/GD/CD
Red (3)	MD
Cordovan (1)	BF/DF
Cordovan (2)	GF/CF
Cordovan (3)	MF
Jade (1)	JR/BR/DR
Jade (2)	KR/GR/CR
Jade (3)	MR
Dove Gray (1)	BS/DS
Dove Gray (2)	GS/CS
Dove Gray (3)	MS
Camel (1)	JY/BY/DY
Camel (2)	KY/GY/CY
Camel (3)	MY

1 - Cloth & vinyl
2 - Vinyl
3 - Leather & vinyl

GRANADA GHIA	CODE
Blue (1)	BB/DB
Blue (2)	GB/CB
Blue (3)	MB
Red (1)	BD/DD
Red (2)	GD/CD
Red (3)	MD
Cordovan (1)	BF/DF
Cordovan (2)	GF/CF
Cordovan (3)	MF
Jade (1)	BR/DR
Jade (2)	GR
Jade (3)	MR
Dove Gray (1)	BS/DS
Dove Gray (2)	GS/CS
Dove Gray (3)	MS
Camel (1)	BY/DY
Camel (2)	GY/CY
Camel (3)	MY

1 - Cloth & vinyl
2 - Vinyl

GRANADA ESS	CODE
Blue (1)	BB/DB
Blue (2)	GB/PB
Blue (3)	MB
Red (1)	BD/DD
Red (2)	GD/PD
Red (3)	MD
Cordovan (1)	BF/DF
Cordovan (2)	GF/PF
Cordovan (3)	MF
Jade (1)	BR/DR
Jade (2)	GR/PR
Jade (3)	MR
Dove Gray (1)	BS/DS
Dove Gray (2)	GS/PS
Dove Gray (3)	MS
Camel (1)	BY/DY
Camel (2)	GY/PY
Camel (3)	MY

1 - Cloth & vinyl
2 - Vinyl
3 - Leather & vinyl

FAIRMONT	CODE
Black (1)	FA/HA
Black (2)	AA/BA
Black (2)	EA/GA
Black (2)	KA/VA/WA
Blue (1)	CB/LB
Blue (1)	FB/HB
Blue (2)	AB/BB
Blue (2)	EB/GB/KB
Red (1)	CD/LD
Red (1)	FD/HD
Red (2)	AD/BD
Red (2)	ED/GD
Red (2)	VD/WD/KD
Chamois (1)	CT/LT
Chamois (1)	FT/HT/AU
Chamois (1)	BU/VU/WU
Chamois (2)	AT/BT
Chamois (2)	ET/GT
Chamois (2)	VT/WT/KT
White/Red (2)	EN/GN/KN
White/Blue (2)	EQ/GQ/KQ
White/Black (2)	EW/GW/KW
White/Chamois (2)	E2/G2/K2

1 - Cloth & vinyl
2 - Vinyl

FAIRMONT FUTURA

	CODE
Black (1)	SA/HA
Black (2)	RA/TA/KA
Blue (1)	SB/UB/HB
Blue (2)	RB/TB/KB
Red (1)	SD/UD/HD
Red (2)	RD/TD/KD
Chamois (1)	ST/UT/HT
Chamois (2)	RT/TT/KT
White/Red (2)	RN/TN/KN
White/Blue (2)	RQ/TQ/KQ
White/Black (2)	RW/TW/KW
White/Chamois (2)	RZ/TZ/KZ
Cream/Gold (1)	SV/HV
Cream/Gold (2)	RV/TV/KV

1 - Cloth & vinyl
2 - Vinyl

MUSTANG

	CODE
Black (1)	BA/DA
Black (2)	CA
Black (3)	FA
Blue (1)	BB/DB
Blue (2)	AB/CB
Blue (3)	FB
Red (1)	BD/DD
Red (2)	AD/CD
Red (3)	ED
Chamois (1)	BT/DT
Chamois (2)	AT/CT
Chamois (3)	ET
Vaquero (1)	BZ/DZ
Vaquero (2)	AZ/CZ
Vaquero (3)	EZ
White/Red (2)	AN/CH
White/Red (3)	EN
White/Blue (2)	AQ/CQ
White/Blue (3)	EQ
White/Black (2)	AW/CW
White/Black (3)	EW
White/Chamois (2)	A2/C2
White/Chamois (3)	E2
White/Vaquero (2)	A9/C9
White/Vaquero (3)	E9

1 - Cloth & vinyl
2 - Vinyl
3 - Velour & vinyl

PINTO

	CODE
Black (1)	GA
Black (2)	AA/HA
Black (3)	A
Black (4)	A
Blue (1)	GB/DB
Blue (2)	AB/HB
Blue (3)	B
Red (1)	GD/DD
Red (2)	AD/HD
Red (3)	D
Red (4)	D
Tangerine (1)	DJ/HJ
Tangerine (3)	T
Tangerine (4)	J
Chamois (1)	GT/DT
Chamois (2)	AT/HT
Chamois (3)	V

1 - Cloth & vinyl
2 - Vinyl
3 - ESS option
4 - Cruising Wagon

THE SCHEDULE DATE is a three-digit code designating the day and month the vehicle was scheduled to be built.

THE AXLE CODE consists of a single number. The number indicates the ratio and type of axle installed in the vehicle.

CONVENTIONAL	LOCKING	RATIO
G		2.26
B	C	2.47
1	J	2.50
8	H	2.73
2	K	2.75
3	L	2.79
6	O	3.00
Y		3.08
F	W	3.45

THE TRANSMISSION CODE is a single letter indicating the type and model of the transmission installed in the vehicle.

TYPE	CODE
4-Speed Overdrive Manual	5
4-Speed Manual	6
4-Speed Manual	7
XP Automatic (C-3)	V
XP Automatic (C-4)	W
FMX Automatic	X
XPL Automatic (C-6)	U
XPL Automatic (Special)	Z
Jatco Automatic	S
Borg Warner Automatic	Y

THE A.C. CODE is the letter "A". It will be shown on the label if the vehicle is air conditioned.

ENGINE IDENTIFICATION

ENGINE TAG
Since 1964, Ford engines can be identified by a tag attached to the engine. The tag contains the year and cubic inch displacement.

CASTING NUMBERS
While helpful in identifying Ford engine components, casting numbers are not conclusive in pin-pointing the exact year of manufacture. A better method is to search for the original host vehicle's VIN (Vehicle Identification Number) stamped on the driver's side at the rear of the engine block below the cylinder head.

PINTO ENGINES

CID	NO. CYL.	HORSE-POWER	COMP. RATIO	CARB.
140	4	88	9.0:1	2 BC
171	6	102	8.7:1	2 BC

FAIRMONT ENGINES

CID	NO. CYL.	HORSE-POWER	COMP. RATIO	CARB.
140	4	88	9.0:1	2 BC
200	6	85	8.5:1	1 BC
302	8	140	8.4:1	2 BC

MUSTANG ENGINES

CID	NO. CYL.	HORSE-POWER	COMP. RATIO	CARB.
140	4	88	9.0:1	2 BC
171	6	109	8.7:1	2 BC
302	8	140	8.4:1	2 BC

GRANADA ENGINES

CID	NO. CYL.	HORSE-POWER	COMP. RATIO	CARB.
250	6	97	8.6:1	1 BC
302	8	137	8.4:1	2 BC

FORD ENGINES

CID	NO. CYL.	HORSE-POWER	COMP. RATIO	CARB.
302	8	129	8.4:1	2 BC
351	8	142	8.3:1	2 BC

LTD II ENGINES

CID	NO. CYL.	HORSE-POWER	COMP. RATIO	CARB.
302	8	133	8.4:1	2 BC
351	8	151	8.0:1	2 BC

THUNDERBIRD ENGINES

CID	NO. CYL.	HORSE-POWER	COMP. RATIO	CARB.
302	8	133	8.4:1	2 BC
351	8	142	8.3:1	2 BC
351	8	151	8.0:1	2 BC

1970 MERCURY COUGAR

1970 MERCURY CYCLONE

1970 LINCOLN CONTINENTAL

1970 CONTINENTAL MARK III

1970 MERCURY MARQUIS

1970 MERCURY MONTEGO

1970 MERCURY MONTEREY

1970 MERCURY COUGAR

VEHICLE IDENTIFICATION NUMBER

· LINCOLN MERCURY ·
F 0F46N123456 F

Located on a metal tab that is riveted to the instrument panel close to the windshield on the driver's side of the car and is visible from outside.

FIRST DIGIT: Identifies the year (9 = 1970)

SECOND DIGIT: Identifies the assembly plant

ASSEMBLY PLANT	CODE
Oakville, Ont., CAN	B
Dearborn, MI	F
Lorain, OH	H
San Jose, CA	R
Allen Park (Pilot Plant)	S
Wixom, MI	Y
St. Louis, MO	Z

THIRD AND FOURTH DIGITS: Identify the body serial code

LINCOLN	CODE
4-Dr. Sedan	82
2-Dr. Hardtop	81
2-Dr. Hardtop (Mark III)	89

COUGAR	CODE
2-Dr. HT Standard	91
Convertible Standard	92
2-Dr. HT XR-7 Luxury	93
Convertible XR-7 Luxury	94

MERCURY	CODE
4-Dr. Sedan Monterey	44
2-Dr. HT Monterey	46
4-Dr. HT Monterey	48
Convertible Monterey	45
4-Dr. Sedan Monterey-Custom	54
2-Dr. HT Monterey-Custom	56
4-Dr. HT Monterey-Custom	58
4-Dr. HT Sedan Marquis	63
2-Dr. HT Marquis	66
4-Dr. HT Marquis	68
Convertible Marquis	65
4-Dr. HT Sedan Brougham	62
2-Dr. HT Brougham	64
4-Dr. HT Brougham	67
2-Dr. HT Marauder	60
2-Dr. HT Marauder X100	61
4-Dr. Monterey Wagon	72
4-Dr. Monterey Custom Wagon	74
4-Dr. Marquis Colony Park	76

MONTEGO	CODE
2-Dr. HT Montego	01
4-Dr. Sedan Montego	02
4-Dr. Sedan Montego MX	06
2-Dr. HT Montego MX	07
2-Dr. Sedan Montego MX Brougham	10
2-Dr. HT Montego MX Brougham	11
4-Dr. HT Montego MX Brougham	12
2-Dr. HT Cyclone	15
2-Dr. HT Cyclone Spoiler	17
2-Dr. HT Cyclone GT	16
4-Dr. Montego MX SW	08
4-Dr. Montego MX (Woodgrain Villager) SW	18

FIFTH DIGIT: Identifies the engine code

ENGINE	CODE
6-Cyl. 250 CID 1V	L
6-Cyl. 250 CID 1V	3
8-Cyl. 302 CID 2V	F
8-Cyl. 302 CID 2V	6
8-Cyl. 302 CID 2V Taxi	D
8-Cyl. 302 CID 4V HO	G
8-Cyl. 351 CID 2V	H
8-Cyl. 351 CID 4V	M
8-Cyl. 390 CID 2V Regular	Y
8-Cyl. 428 CID 4V CJ	Q
8-Cyl. 428 CID 4V CJ Ram Air	R
8-Cyl. 428 CID 4V Police	P
8-Cyl. 429 CID 2V	K
8-Cyl. 429 CID 4V	N
8-Cyl. 429 4V CJ	C
8-Cyl. 429 CID 4V HO	Z
8-Cyl. 429 CID 4V CJ	J
8-Cyl. 429 CID 4V CJ Ram Air	J
8-Cyl. 460 CID 4V	A

LAST SIX DIGITS: Represent the basic production numbers

EXAMPLE:

0	F	46	N	123456
Model Year	Assy. Plant	Body Serial Code	Engine	Production Sequence Number

VEHICLE CERTIFICATION LABEL

THE VEHICLE CERTIFICATION LABEL (V.C. Label) is attached to the rear face of the driver's door. The upper half of the label contains the name of the manufacturer, the month and year of manufacture and the certification statement. The V.C. label also contains the Vehicle Identification Number. The remaining information on the V.C. Label consists of pertinent vehicle identification codes: ie. body, color, trim, axle, transmission and DSO codes.

MANUFACTURED BY
FORD MOTOR COMPANY

09/70 THIS VEHICLE CONFORMS TO ALL APPLICABLE FEDERAL MOTOR VEHICLE SAFETY STANDARDS IN EFFECT ON DATE OF MANUFACTURE SHOWN ABOVE

0F46N123456	65A	M
1B	4	W	33

NOT FOR TITLE OR REGISTRATION
MADE IN U.S.A.

EXAMPLE:

0F46N123456	Vehicle Identification Number
65A	Body Type Code (Monterey 2-Dr. Hardtop)
M	Color Code (White)
1B	Trim Code (Medium Blue Cloth & Vinyl)
4	Rear Axle Code (2.80:1)
W	Transmission Code (C4 Automatic)
33	District Special Equipment Code (Cleveland)

THE BODY CODE is two numerals and a letter identifying the body style.

LINCOLN CONTINENTAL	CODE
4-Dr. Sedan	53A
2-Dr. Hardtop	65A
2-Dr. Hardtop (Mark III)	65A
* Town Car option available	

COUGAR	CODE
2-Dr. Hardtop Standard	65A
Convertible Standard	76A
2-Dr. Hardtop XR-7 Luxury	65B
Convertible XR-7 Luxury	76B
* Eliminator option available	

MERCURY	CODE
4-Dr. Sedan Monterey	54A
2-Dr. Hardtop Monterey	65A
4-Dr. Hardtop Monterey	57A
Convertible Monterey	76A
4-Dr. Sedan Monterey-Custom	54C
2-Dr. HT Monterey-Custom	65B
4-Dr. HT Monterey-Custom	57B
4-Dr. HT Sedan Marquis	53F
2-Dr. HT Marquis	65F
4-Dr. HT Marquis	57F
Convertible Marquis	76F
4-Dr. HT Sedan Brougham	53C
2-Dr. HT Brougham	65C
4-Dr. HT Brougham	57C
2-Dr. HT Marauder	63G
2-Dr. HT Marauder X100	63H
4-Dr. 2-Seat Monterey Wagon	71B
4-Dr. 3-Seat Monterey Wagon	71C
4-Dr. 2-Seat Monterey Custom Wagon	71F
4-Dr. 3-Seat Monterey Custom Wagon	71G
4-Dr. 2-Seat Marquis Colony Park	71E
4-Dr. 3-Seat Marquis Colony Park	71A

MONTEGO	CODE
2-Dr. HT Montego	65A
4-Dr. Sedan Montego	54A
4-Dr. Sedan Montego MX	54A
2-Dr. HT Montego MX	54B
4-Dr. Sedan Montego MX Brougham	54D
2-Dr. HT Montego MX Brougham	65D
4-Dr. HT Montego MX Brougham	57D
2-Dr. HT Montego MX	65E
4-Dr. HT Montego MX	57B
2-Dr. HT Cyclone	65F
2-Dr. HT Cyclone Spoiler	65G
2-Dr. HT Cyclone GT	65H
4-Dr. Montego MX SW	71C
4-Dr. Montego MX (Woodgrain Villager) SW	71A

THE COLOR CODE is a number or letter (or both) indicating the exterior paint color code.

COLOR	CODE
Black	A
Dk. Maroon	B
Dk. Ivy Green Met.	C
Brt. Yellow, Competition Yellow	D
Lt. Blue	E
Dk. Aqua Met. (Brt.) Dk. Aqua Met.	F
Med. Avocado Met., Med. Lime Met.	G
Lt. Green	H
Dk. Orchid Met.	I
Brt. Blue Met (Astra), Deep Blue Met.	J
Yellow Met., Brt. Gold Met., Deep Gold Met.	K
Lt. Gray Met.	L
White	M
Platinum, Pastel Blue	N

COLOR	CODE
Burnt Orange Met.	O
Med. Ivy Green Met.	P
Med. Blue Met.	Q
Dk. Brown Met.	R
Nugget Gold Met., Med. Gold Met.	S
Red	T
Med. Aqua Met.	U
Yellow	W
Dk. Blue	X
Chestnut Met., Chestnut Bronze Met., Med. Bronze Met.	Y
Dk. Slate Gray Met., Dk. Gray Met.	Z
Calypso Coral, Vermillion, Competition Orange	1
Lt. Ivy Yellow	2
Ginger Met., Med. Brown Met.	5
Med. Brt. Blue Met., Bright Blue Met.	6
Med. Peppermint Met.	7
Lt. Gold	8
Yellow/Pastel Yellow	9

GLAMOUR PAINT COLOR (OPTION)	CODE
Ivy Bronze Met., Green Fire, Green Stardust	19
Olive Bronze Met., Olive Fire, Olive Stardust	09
Fall Bronze Met., Bronze Fire, Bronze Stardust	89
Med. Red Met., Burgundy Fire, Red Stardust	59

THE TRIM CODE consists of a number-letter or a two-letter combination designating the interior trim.

LINCOLN CONTINENTAL	CODE
Black (1)	6A/1A
Black (2)	KA/3A
Black 92	7A/2A
Dark Blue (1)	1B
Dark Blue (2)	KB/3B
Dark Blue (2)	7B/2B
Dark Red (1)	1D
Dark Red (2)	KD/3D
Dark Red (2)	7D/2D
Medium Brown (2)	KF/3F/2F
Dark Green (1)	1G
Dark Green (2)	KG/3G
Dark Green (2)	7G/2G
Light Aqua (2)	KK/3K/2K
Medium Gray (1)	1P
Medium Gray (2)	KP/3P/2P
White (2)	KW/3W
White (2)	7W/2W
Light Gold (1)	1Y
Light Gold (2)	KY/3Y/2Y
Dark Brown (2)	KZ/3Z/2Z

1 - Cloth & vinyl
2 - Vinyl w/leather

MERCURY/MARAUDER/MARQUIS	CODE
Black (1)	TA/1A/KA
Black (1)	5A/ZA/3A
Black (2)	4A/VA/2A
Black (2)	8A/9A/6A
Med. Blue (1)	1B/KB
Med. Blue (1)	5B/3B
Med. Blue (2)	4B/VB
Med. Blue (2)	2B/8B/6B
Dk. Red (1)	TD/1D
Dk. Red (1)	KD/5D/3D
Dk. Red (2)	4D/VD
Dk. Red (2)	2D/8D/6D
Med. Brown (2)	4F/VF
Med. Brown (2)	2F/8F/6F
Med. Green (1)	1G/KG
Med. Green (1)	5G/ZG/3G
Med. Green (2)	4G/VG
Med. Green (2)	8G/2G
Med. Green (2)	9G/6G/MG

MERCURY/MARAUDER/MARQUIS

	CODE
Dk. Brown (1)	KZ/5Z/6Z
Lt. Gold (1)	1Y/KY
Lt. Gold (1)	5Y/3Y/6Y
Lt. Gold (2)	2Y/4Y
White (2)	8W/2W
White (2)	6W/VW/4W

1 - Cloth & vinyl
2 - Vinyl

MONTEGO

	CODE
Black (1)	6A/1A/5A
Black (1)	AA/BA/4A
Black (2)	6A/2A/UA
Black (2)	WA/GA/KA
Med. Blue (1)	5B/1B/4B
Med. Blue (1)	6B/2B
Med. Blue (2)	WB/GB
Dk. Red (1)	5D/TD
Dk. Red. (1)	AD/BD
Dk. Red (2)	6D/2D/GD
Med. Brown (1)	TF
Med. Brown (2)	6F/2F/GF
Med. Green (1)	5G/1G
Med. Green (2)	6G/2G
White (2)	2W/UW/6W
Lt. Gold (1)	5Y/1Y/4Y
Lt. Gold (2)	2Y/UY/KY

1 - Cloth & vinyl
2 - Vinyl

CYCLONE

	CODE
Black (1)	WA/KA
Black (1)	DA/RA
Black (2)	8A/MA
Med. Blue (1)	WB/DB/RB
Med. Blue (2)	8B/MB
Dk. Red (1)	WD/RD
Dk. Red (2)	8D
Med. Brown (1)	WF/RF
Med. Brown (2)	8F
Med. Green (1)	WG/RG
Med. Green (2)	8G
Lt. Gold (1)	KY
White (2)	8W/RW

1 - Cloth & vinyl
2 - Vinyl

COUGAR

	CODE
Black (1)	3A/7A
Black (2)	1A/5A
Black (2)	6A/2A
Black (3)	6A
Dk. Red (2)	5D/6D/1D
Dk. Red (3)	6D
Med. Brown (1)	7F
Med. Brown (2)	5F/3F/6F
Med. Brown (3)	6F
Med. Green (2)	5G/6G/1G
Med. Green (3)	6G
Med. Blue (2)	1B/5B/6B
Med. Blue (3)	6B
Dk. Brown (2)	6Z
Dk. Brown (3)	6Z
White/Black (2)	AA/EA/FA
White/Black (3)	FA

1 - Cloth & vinyl
2 - Vinyl

THE AXLE CODE is a number or letter indicating the rear axle ratio and standard or locking type axles.

CONVENTIONAL	LOCKING	RATIO
0		2.50:1
2	K	2.75:1
3		2.79:1
4	M	2.80:1
5		2.83:1
6	O	3.00:1
7		3.10:1
8		3.20:1
9	R	3.25:1
A	S	3.50:1
B		3.07:1
C		3.08:1
F	X	2.33:1
	V	3.91:1
	W	4.30:1
	Y	4.11:1

THE TRANSMISSION CODE is a number or letter indicating the type of transmission, numerals indicate manual and letters indicate automatic or semi-automatic.

TYPE	CODE
3-Speed Manual	1
4-Speed Manual wide ratio	5
4-Speed Manual close ratio	6
Semi-Automatic Stick Shift	V
Automatic (C4)	W
Automatic (C6)	U
Automatic (FMX)	X
Automatic (C6 Special)	Z

THE DSO CODE, consisting of two numbers, designates the district in which the car was ordered and may appear in conjunction with a Domestic Special Order or Foreign Special Order number when applicable. Ford of Canada DSO codes consist of a letter and a number, except for export codes which are designated by two numbers.

LINCOLN-MERCURY DISTRICT	CODE
Boston	11
New York	15
Philadelphia	16
Washington	17
Atlanta	21
Dallas	22
Jacksonville	23
Memphis	26
Buffalo	31
Cincinnati	32
Cleveland	33
Detroit	34
Chicago	41
St. Louis	42
Twin Cities	46
Denver	51
Los Angeles	52
Oakland	53
Seattle	54
Home Office Reserve	84
Export	90

ENGINE IDENTIFICATION

ENGINE TAG

Since 1964, Lincoln-Mercury engines can be identified by a tag attached to the engine. The tag contains the year and cubic inch displacement.

CASTING NUMBERS

While helpful in identifying Ford engine components, casting numbers are not conclusive in pin-pointing the exact year of manufacture. A better method is to search for the original host vehicle's VIN (Vehicle Identification Number) stamped on the driver's side at the rear of the engine block below the cylinder head.

COUGAR ENGINES

CID	NO. CYL.	HORSE-POWER	COMP. RATIO	CARB.
302	8	290	10.5:1	4 BC
351	8	250	9.5:1	2 BC
351	8	300	11.0:1	4 BC
428 CJ	8	335	10.6:1	4 BC
429	8	375	10.5:1	4 BC

CYCLONE ENGINES

CID	NO. CYL.	HORSE-POWER	COMP. RATIO	CARB.
351	8	250	9.5:1	2 BC
351	8	300	11.0:1	4 BC
429	8	360	10.5:1	4 BC
429	8	370	10.5:1	4 BC
429 (Boss)	8	375	10.5:1	4 BC

MERCURY ENGINES

CID	NO. CYL.	HORSE-POWER	COMP. RATIO	CARB.
250	6	155	9.0:1	1 BC
302	8	220	9.5:1	2 BC
351	8	300	11.0:1	4 BC
390	8	270	9.5:1	2 BC
429	8	320	10.5:1	2 BC
429	8	360	10.5:1	4 BC
429	8	375	10.5:1	4 BC

LINCOLN ENGINES

CID	NO. CYL.	HORSE-POWER	COMP. RATIO	CARB.
460	8	365	10.5:1	4 BC

1971 MERCURY COUGAR

1971 MERCURY CYCLONE GT

1971 MERCURY MONTEREY

1971 MERCURY MONTEGO

1971 LINCOLN CONTINENTAL MARK III

1971 LINCOLN CONTINENTAL MARK III

1971 MERCURY COMET

1971 LINCOLN CONTINENTAL

VEHICLE IDENTIFICATION NUMBER

• LINCOLN MERCURY •
F 1S93F123456 F

Located on a metal tab that is riveted to the instrument panel close to the windshield on the driver's side of the car and is visible from outside.

FIRST DIGIT: Identifies the year (1 = 1971)

SECOND DIGIT: Identifies the assembly plant

ASSEMBLY PLANT	CODE
Oakville, Ont., CAN	B
Dearborn, MI	F
Lorain, OH	H
Kansas City, KS	K
San Jose, CA	R
Allen Park (Pilot Plant)	S
Wixom, MI	Y
St. Louis, MO	Z

THIRD AND FOURTH DIGITS: Identify the body serial code

COMET	CODE
4-Dr. Sedan Standard	30
2-Dr. Sedan Standard	31

COUGAR	CODE
2-Dr. Hardtop Standard	91
Convertible Standard	92
2-Dr. HT XR-7 Luxury	93
Convertible XR-7 Luxury	94

LINCON	CODE
4-Dr. Sedan	82
2-Dr. Hardtop	81
2-Dr. Hardtop (Mark III)	89

MERCURY	CODE
4-Dr. Sedan Monterey	44
2-Dr. Hardtop Monterey	46
4-Dr. Hardtop Monterey	48
4-Dr. Sedan Monterey-Custom	54
2-Dr. HT Monterey-Custom	56
4-Dr. HT Monterey-Custom	58
4-Dr. HT Sedan Marquis	63
2-Dr. HT Marquis	66
4-Dr. HT Marquis	68
4-Dr. HT Sedan Brougham	62
2-Dr. HT Brougham	64
4-Dr. HT Brougham	67
4-Dr. 6-Pass. Monterey Wagon	72
4-Dr. 6-Pass. Marquis	74
4-Dr. 6-Pass. Marquis Colony Park	76

MONTEGO	CODE
2-Dr. Hardtop Montego	01
4-Dr. Sedan Montego	02
4-Dr. Sedan Montego MX	06
2-Dr. Hardtop Montego MX	07
4-Dr. Sedan Montego MX Brougham	10
2-Dr. Hardtop Montego MX Brougham	11
4-Dr. Hardtop Montego MX Brougham	12
2-Dr. Hardtop Cyclone	15
2-Dr. Hardtop Cyclone Spoiler	17
2-Dr. Hardtop Cyclone GT	16
4-Dr. Montego MX SW	08
4-Dr. Montego MX Villager SW	18

FIFTH DIGIT: Identifies the engine code

ENGINE	CODE
I6 170	U
I6 200-1V	T
I6 250-1V	L
I6 250-1V*	3
V-8 302-2V	F
V8 302-2V*	6
V8 3-2-2V Taxi	D
V8 351-2V	H
V8 351-4V	M
V8 351-4V GT	Q
V8 351 Boss	R
V8 400-2V	S
V8 429-2V	K
V8 429-4V	N
V8 429-4V CJ	C
V8 429-4V CJ Ram Air	J
V8 429-4V Police	P
V8 460-4V	A

*Low Compression Export

LAST SIX DIGITS: Represent the basic production numbers

EXAMPLE:

1	S	93	F	123456
Model Year	Assy. Plant	Body Serial Code	Engine Sequence	Production Number

VEHICLE CERTIFICATION LABEL

THE VEHICLE CERTIFICATION LABEL (V.C. Label) is attached to the rear face of the driver's door. The upper half of the label contains the name of the manufacturer, the month and year of manufacture and the certification statement. The V.C. label also contains the Vehicle Identification Number. The remaining information on the V.C. label consists of pertinent vehicle identification codes: ie. body, color, trim, axle, transmission and DSO codes.

MANUFACTURED BY FORD MOTOR COMPANY

09/71 THIS VEHICLE CONFORMS TO ALL APPLICABLE FEDERAL MOTOR VEHICLE SAFETY STANDARDS IN EFFECT ON DATE OF MANUFACTURE SHOWN ABOVE

1S93F123456	65F	J
3B	2	W	33

NOT FOR TITLE OR REGISTRATION
MADE IN U.S.A.

EXAMPLE:
1S93F123456 .... Vehicle Identification Number
65F .... Body Type Code (XR-7 Luxury 2-Dr. Hardtop)
J .... Color Code (Grabber Blue)
3B .... Trim Code (Medium Blue Cloth & Vinyl)
2 .... Rear Axle Code (2.75:1)
W .... Transmission Code (C4 Automatic)
33 .... District Special Equipment Code (Cleveland)

THE BODY CODE is two numerals and a letter identifying the body style.

COMET	CODE
4-Dr. Sedan Standard	54B
2-Dr. Sedan Standard	62B
*GT option available	

COUGAR	CODE
2-Dr. Hardtop Standard	65D
Convertible Standard	76D
2-Dr. Hardtop XR-7 Luxury	65F
Convertible XR-7 Luxury	76F
* GT option available	

LINCON	CODE
4-Dr. Sedan	53A
2-Dr. Hardtop	65A
2-Dr. Hardtop (Mark III)	65A
* Town Car option available	
* Golden Anniversary option available	

MERCURY	CODE
4-Dr. Sedan Monterey	53B
2-Dr. Hardtop Monterey	65B
4-Dr. Hardtop Monterey	57B
4-Dr. Sedan Monterey-Custom	53F
2-Dr. HT Monterey-Custom	65F
4-Dr. HT Monterey-Custom	57F
4-Dr. HT Sedan Marquis	53H
2-Dr. HT Marquis	65H
4-Dr. HT Marquis	57H
4-Dr. HT Sedan Brougham	53K
2-Dr. HT Brougham	65K
4-Dr. HT Brougham	57K
4-Dr. 6-Pass. Monterey Wagon	71B
4-Dr. 6-Pass. Marquis	71H
4-Dr. 6-Pass. Marquis Colony Park	71K

MONTEGO	CODE
2-Dr. HT Montego	65A
4-Dr. Sedan Montego	54A
4-Dr. Sedan Montego MX	54B
2-Dr. HT Montego MX	65B
4-Dr. Sedan Montego MX Brougham	54D
2-Dr. HT Montego MX Brougham	65D
4-Dr. HT Montego MX Brougham	57D
2-Dr. HT Cyclone	65F
2-Dr. HT Cyclone Spoiler	65G
2-Dr. HT Cyclone GT	65H
4-Dr. Montego MX SW	71C
4-Dr. Montego MX Villager SW	71A

THE COLOR CODE is a number or letter (or both) indicating the exterior paint color code.

COLOR	CODE
Black	A
White	M
Calypso Coral	1
Red	T
Bright Red	3
Maroon Met.	B
Lt. Gray Met.	L
Dk. Slat Gray Met.	K
Platinum	N
Med. Blue Met.	Q
Dk. Blue Met.	X
Bright Blue Met.	6
Grabber Blue	J
Bright Astra Blue Met.	Y
Med. Bright Aqua Met.	F
Lt. Green	H
Med. Green Met.	P

COLOR	CODE
Dk. Green Met.	C
Grabber Green Met.	Z
Dk. Vintage Green	G
Bright Lime Green	I
Lt. Gold	8
Med. Gray Gold Met.	S
Yellow	W
Bright Yellow	D
Lt. Goldenrod Yellow	O
Med. Goldenrod Yellow	E
Grabber Orange	U
Med. Tan	2
Lt. Pewter Met.	V
Dk. Brown Met.	R
Med. Ginger Met.	5
Med. Ivy Bronze Met.*	49
Med. Ginger Bronze Met.*	79
Med. Ivy Bronze Met.*	E9
Med. Ginger Bronze Met.*	39
Med. Blue Met.*	D9
Med. Red Met.*	C9

*Glamour paints

THE TRIM CODE consists of a number-letter or two-letter combination designating the interior trim.

LINCOLN	CODE
Black (1)	1A/AA
Black (1)	6A/3A
Black (2)	KA/7A/4A
Med. Ginger (1)	AF
Med. Ginger (2)	KF/4F
Lt. Aqua (1)	AK
Lt. Aqua (2)	KK/4K
Med. Gray (1)	AP/3P
Med. Gray (2)	KP/4P
Lt. Gray Gold (1)	AY/3Y
Lt. Gray Gold (2)	KY/4Y
Dk. Blue (1)	1B/3B
Dk. Blue (2)	KB/7B/4B
Dk. Red (1)	1D/3D
Dk. Red (2)	KD/7D/4D
Dk. Green (1)	1R/3R
Dk. Green (2)	KR/7R/4R
Dk. Tobacco (1)	1Z
Dk. Tobacco (2)	KZ/4Z
White (2)	KW/7W/4W

1 - Cloth & vinyl
2 - Leather & vinyl

MERCURY	CODE
Black (1)	1A/3A/5A
Black (1)	ZA/7A/KA
Black (2)	2A/4A
Black (2)	6A/VA/9A
Med. Blue (1)	1B/3B/5B
Med. Blue (1)	ZB/7B/KB
Med. Blue (2)	2B/4B
Med. Blue (2)	6B/VB/9B
Med. Ginger (1)	3F
Med. Ginger (2)	2F/4F
Med. Ginger (2)	6F/VF/9F
Dk. Red (1)	1D/3D/5D
Dk. Red (1)	ZD/7D/KD
Dk. Red (2)	2D/4D
Dk. Red (2)	6D/VD/9D
Med. Green (1)	1R/3R/5R
Med. Green (1)	ZR/7R/KR
Med. Green (2)	2R/4R
Med. Green (2)	6R/VR/9R
Lt. Gray Gold (1)	1Y/5Y
Lt. Gray Gold (1)	ZY/7Y/KY
Lt. Gray Gold (2)	2Y/4Y

MERCURY

	CODE
Lt. Gray Gold (2)	6Y/VY/9Y
White (2)	2W/4W
White (2)	6W/KZ
Dk. Tobacco (1)	5Z/ZZ/7Z
Dk. Tobacco (2)	VZ/9Z

1 - Cloth & vinyl
2 - Vinyl

MONTEGO

	CODE
Black (1)	4A/1A/5A
Black (2)	KA/2A/UA
Black (2)	RA/6A/GA
Med. Blue (1)	4B/1B/5B
Med. Blue (2)	2B/RB
Med. Blue (2)	6B/GB
Vermillion (2)	2E/RE
Vermillion (2)	GE/6E
Med. Ginger (2)	2F/RF
Med. Ginger (2)	GF/6F
Med. Green (1)	1R/5R
Med. Green (2)	2R/RR
Med. Green (2)	6R/GR
White (2)	2W/UW
White (2)	RW/6W
Lt. Gray Gold (1)	4Y/1Y/5Y
Lt. Gray Gold (2)	KY/2Y
Lt. Gray Gold (2)	UY/6Y

1 - Cloth & vinyl
2 - Vinyl

CYCLONE

	CODE
Black (1)	DA/WA
Black (2)	KA/MA/8A
Med. Blue (1)	DB/WB
Med. Blue (2)	MB/8B
Vermillion (1)	WE
Vermillion (2)	8E
Med. Ginger (1)	WF
Med. Ginger (2)	8F
Med. Green (1)	WR
Med. Green (2)	8R
Lt. Gray Gold (2)	KY
White (2)	8W

1 - Cloth & vinyl
2 - Vinyl

COUGAR

	CODE
Black (1)	3A/7A
Black (2)	1A/5A
Black (3)	6A
Med. Blue (1)	3B/7B
Med. Blue (2)	1B/5B
Med. Blue (3)	6B
Dk. Red (2)	1D/5D
Dk. Red (3)	6D
Med. Ginger (1)	3F/7F
Med. Ginger (2)	5F
Med. Ginger (3)	6F
Med. Green (1)	3R/7R
Med. Green (2)	1R/5R
Med. Green (3)	6R
White (2)	1W/5W
White (3)	6W

1 - Cloth & vinyl
2 - Vinyl
3 - Vinyl w/leather

COMET

	CODE
Black (1)	2A/3A
Black (2)	1A/5A/8A
Med. Blue (1)	2B/3B
Med. Blue (2)	5B/8B
Vermillion (1)	3E/9E
Vermillion (2)	5E/8E
Lt. Gray Gold (1)	2Y/3Y/9Y
Lt. Gray Gold (2)	1Y/5Y/8Y

1 - Cloth & vinyl
2 - Vinyl

THE AXLE CODE is a number or letter indicating the rear axle ratio and standard or locking type axles.

CONVENTIONAL	LOCKING	RATIO
2	K	2.75:1
3		2.79:1
4	M	2.80:1
5		2.83:1
6	O	3.00:1
7		3.10:1
8		3.20:1
9	R	3.25:1
A	S	3.50:1
B		3.07:1
C		3.08:1
F		2.33:1
G		3.55:1
O		2.50:1
	W	4.30:1
	X	2.33:1
	V	3.91:1
	Y	4.11:1

THE TRANSMISSION CODE is a number or letter indicating the type of transmission; numerals indicate manual and letters indicate automatic or semi-automatic.

TYPE	CODE
3-Speed Manual	1
4-Speed Manual wide ratio	5
4-Speed Manual close ratio	6
Automatic (C4)	W
Automatic (C6)	U
Automatic (FMX)	X
Automatic (C6 Special)	Z
Semi Automatic	V

THE DSO CODE, consisting of two numbers, designates the district in which the car was ordered and may appear in conjunction with a Domestic Special Order or Foreign Special Order number when applicable. Ford of Canada DSO codes consist of a letter and a number, except for export codes, which are designated by two numbers.

LINCOLN-MERCURY DISTRICT	CODE
Boston	11
New York	15
Philadelphia	16
Washington	17
Atlanta	21
Dallas	22
Jacksonville	23
Memphis	26
Buffalo	31
Cincinnati	32
Cleveland	33
Detroit	34
Chicago	41
St. Louis	42
Twin Cities	46
Denver	51
Los Angeles	52
Oakland	53
Seattle	54
Home Office Reserve	84
Export	90

ENGINE IDENTIFICATION

ENGINE TAG

Since 1964, Lincoln-Mercury engines can be identified by a tag attached to the engine. The tag contains the year and cubic inch displacement.

CASTING NUMBERS

While helpful in identifying Ford engine components, casting numbers are not conclusive in pin-pointing the exact year of manufacture. A better method is to search for the original host vehicle's VIN (Vehicle Identification Number) stamped on the driver's side at the rear of the engine block below the cylinder head.

COMET ENGINES

CID	NO. CYL.	HORSE-POWER	COMP. RATIO	CARB.
170	6	100	8.7:1	1 BC
200	6	115	8.7:1	1 BC
250	6	145	9.0:1	1 BC
302	8	210	9.0:1	2 BC

COUGAR ENGINES

CID	NO. CYL.	HORSE-POWER	COMP. RATIO	CARB.
351	8	240	9.0:1	2 BC
351	8	285	10.7:1	4 BC
429 CJ	8	370	11.3:1	4 BC

MERCURY ENGINES

CID	NO. CYL.	HORSE-POWER	COMP. RATIO	CARB.
351	8	240	9.0:1	2 BC
400	8	260	9.0:1	2 BC
429	8	320	10.5:1	2 BC
429	8	360	10.5:1	4 BC

MONTEGO/CYCLONE ENGINES

CID	NO. CYL.	HORSE-POWER	COMP. RATIO	CARB.
250	6	145	9.0:1	1 BC
302	8	210	9.0:1	2 BC
351	8	240	9.0:1	2 BC
351	8	285	10.7:1	4 BC
429 CJ	8	370	11.3:1	4 BC

LINCOLN ENGINES

CID	NO. CYL.	HORSE-POWER	COMP. RATIO	CARB.
460	8	365	10.2:1	4 BC

1972 MERCURY MONTEGO

1972 MERCURY MARQUIS

1972 MERCURY COMET

1972 MERCURY COUCAR

1972 LINCOLN CONTINENTAL MARK IV

1972 LINCOLN CONTINENTAL MARK IV

VEHICLE IDENTIFICATION NUMBER

LINCOLN MERCURY
F 2S54H123456 F

Located on a metal tab that is riveted to the instrument panel close to the windshield on the driver's side of the car and is visible from outside.

FIRST DIGIT: Identifies the year (2 = 1972)

SECOND DIGIT: Identifies the assembly plant

ASSEMBLY PLANT	CODE
Atlanta, GA	A
Oakville, Ont., CAN	B
Dearborn, MI	F
Lorain, OH	H
Kansas City, KS	K
San Jose, CA	R
Allen Park (Pilot Plant)	S
Wixom, MI	Y
St. Louis, MO	Z

THIRD AND FOURTH DIGITS: Identify the body serial code

COMET	CODE
4-Dr. Sedan	30
2-Dr. Sedan	31

COUGAR	CODE
2-Dr. Hardtop	91
Convertible	92
2-Dr. HT XR-7	93
Convertible XR-7	94

LINCOLN CONTINENTAL	CODE
2-Dr. Hardtop	81
4-Dr. Sedan HT	82
2-Dr. HT (Mark IV)	89

MERCURY	CODE
4-Dr. Sedan HT Monterey	44
2-Dr. HT Monterey	46
4-Dr. HT Monterey	48
4-Dr. Sedan HT Monterey Custom	54
2-Dr. HT Monterey Custom	56
4-Dr. HT Monterey Custom	58
4-Dr. Sedan HT Marquis	63
2-Dr. HT Marquis	66
4-Dr. HT Marquis	68
4-Dr. Sedan HT Brougham	62
2-Dr. HT Brougham	64
4-Dr. HT Brougham	67
4-Dr. 6-Pass. Monterey Wagon	72
4-Dr. 6-Pass. Marquis Wagon	74
4-Dr. 6-Pass. Marquis Colony Park Wagon	76

MONTEGO	CODE
4-Dr. Sedan HT Montego	02
2-Dr. HT Montego	03
4-Dr. Sedan HT Montego MX	04
2-Dr. HT Montego MX	07
4-Dr. Sedan HT Montego MX Brougham	10
2-Dr. HT Montego MX Brougham	11
2-Dr. Fastback Montego GT	16
4-Dr. Montego MX SW	08
4-Dr. Montego MX Villager SW	18

FIFTH DIGIT: Identifies the engine code

ENGINE	CODE
I6 170	U
I6 200-1V	T
I6 200-1V	2*
I6 250-1V	L
I6 250-1V	3*
V8 302-2V	F
V8 302-2V	6*
V8 302-2V Taxi	D
V8 351-2V	H
V8 351-4V	Q
V8 400-2V	S
V8 429-4V	N
V8 429-4V Police	P
V8 460-4V	A

*Low compression export

LAST SIX DIGITS: Represent the basic production numbers

EXAMPLE:

2	S	54	H	123456
Model Year	Assy. Plant	Body Serial Code	Engine	Production Sequence Number

VEHICLE CERTIFICATION LABEL

THE VEHICLE CERTIFICATION LABEL (V.C. Label) is attached to the rear face of the driver's door. The upper half of the label contains the name of the manufacturer, the month and year of manufacture and the certification statement. The V.C. label also contains the Vehicle Identification Number. The remaining information on the V.C. label consists of pertinent vehicle identification codes: ie. body, color, trim, axle, transmission and DSO codes.

MANUFACTURED BY
FORD MOTOR COMPANY

09/72 THIS VEHICLE CONFORMS TO ALL APPLICABLE FEDERAL MOTOR VEHICLE SAFETY STANDARDS IN EFFECT ON DATE OF MANUFACTURE SHOWN ABOVE

2S54H123456	53B	2B
AA	G	W	33

NOT FOR TITLE OR REGISTRATION
MADE IN U.S.A.

EXAMPLE:

2S54H123456	Vehicle Identification Number
53B	Body Type Code (Monterey 4-Dr. Sedan Hardtop)
2B	Color Code (Bright Red)
AA	Trim Code (Black Cloth & Vinyl)
G	Axle Code (3.78:1)
W	Transmission Code (C4 Automatic)
33	District Special Equipment Code (Cleveland)

THE BODY CODE is two numerals and a letter identifying the body style.

COMET	CODE
4-Dr. Sedan	54B
2-Dr. Sedan	2B

* Custom option available
* GT option available

COUGAR   **CODE**
- 2-Dr. Hardtop 65D
- Convertible 76D
- 2-Dr. HT XR-7 .... 65F
- Convertible XR-7 .... 76F

LINCOLN   **CODE**
- 2-Dr. Hardtop 65A
- 4-Dr. Sedan HT 53A
- 2-Dr. Hardtop (Mark IV) 65D

MERCURY   **CODE**
- 4-Dr. Sedan HT Monterey 53B
- 2-Dr. HT Monterey 65B
- 4-Dr. HT Monterey 57B
- 4-Dr. Sedan HT Monterey Custom 53F
- 2-Dr. HT Monterey Custom 65F
- 4-Dr. HT Monterey Custom 57F
- 4-Dr. Sedan HT Marquis 53H
- 2-Dr. HT Marquis 65H
- 4-Dr. HT Marquis 57H
- 4-Dr. Sedan HT Brougham 53K
- 2-Dr. HT Brougham 65K
- 4-Dr. HT Brougham 57K
- 4-Dr. 6-Pass. Monterey Wagon 71B
- 4-Dr. 6-Pass. Marquis Wagon 71H
- 4-Dr. 6-Pass. Marquis Colony Park Wagon ... 71K

MONTEGO   **CODE**
- 4-Dr. Sedan HT Montego 53B
- 2-Dr. HT Montego 65B
- 4-Dr. Sedan HT Montego MX 53D
- 2-Dr. HT Montego MX 65D
- 4-Dr. Sedan HT Montego MX Brougham 53K
- 2-Dr. HT Montego MX Brougham 65K
- 2-Dr. Fastback Montego GT 63R
- 4-Dr. Montego MX SW 71D
- 4-Dr. Montego MX Villager SW 71K

THE COLOR CODE is a number and letter indicating the exterior paint color.

COLOR   **CODE**
- Lt. Gray Met. 1A
- Black 1C
- Silver Met. 1D
- Calypso Blue 2A
- Bright Red 2B
- Red 2E
- Med. Red Met. 2G
- Maroon 2J
- Lt. Blue 3B
- Med. Blue Met. 3C
- Med. Blue Met. 3D
- Grabber Blue 3F
- Dk. Blue Met. 3H
- Bright Blue Met. 3J
- Pastel Lime 4A
- Bright Green Gold Met. 4B
- Ivy Bronze Met. 4C
- Med. Ivy Bronze Met. 4D
- Med. Lime Met. 4F
- Med. Ivy Bronze Met. 4G
- Med. Green Met. 4P
- Dk. Green Met. 4Q
- Lt. Pewter Met. 5A
- Ginger Bronze Met. 5C
- Ginger Bronze Met. 5D
- Dk. Brown Met. 5F
- Lt. Copper Met. 5G
- Ginger Met. 5H
- Med. Ginger Bronze Met. 5J
- Tan 5L
- Lt. Goldenrod 6B

COLOR   **CODE**
- Med. Goldenrod 6C
- Yellow 6D
- Med. Brt. Yellow 6E
- Brt. Yellow Gold Met. 6F
- Lt. Copper Met. 6G
- Gray Gold Met. 6J
- White 9A

THE TRIM CODE consists of a two-letter or a letter-number combination designating the interior trim.

LINCOLN   **CODE**
- Black (1) .... AA/BA/CA
- Black (2) .... DA/EA
- Black (2) .... FA/BA
- Dk. Blue (1) .... BB/AB
- Dk. Blue (2) .... DB/EB
- Dk. Blue (2) .... FB/BB
- Dk. Red (1) .... BD/AD
- Dk. Red (2) .... DD/ED
- Dk. Red (2) .... FD/BD
- Dk. Green (1) .... BR/AR/BR
- Dk. Green (2) .... DR/ER/FR
- Dk. Tobacco (1) .... BZ
- Dk. Tobacco (2) .... DZ/FZ/BZ
- Ginger w/Tobacco (1) .... AF/BF
- Ginger w/Tobacco (2) .... DF/FF
- White w/Black (2) .... DW/EW
- White w/Black (2) .... FW/BW
- White w/Blue (2) .... DL/EL
- White w/Blue (2) .... FL/BL
- White w/Green (2) D5/E5
- White w/Green (2) F5/B5
- White w/Tobacco (2) D9/E9
- White w/Tobacco (2) F9/B9
- Lt. Gray Gold (1) .... AY/CY
- Lt. Gray Gold (2) .... DY/FY/BY

1 - Cloth & vinyl
2 - Leather & vinyl

MERCURY/MONTEREY   **CODE**
- Black (1) .... AA/CA/EA
- Black (1) .... ZA/GA/KA
- Black (2) .... BA/DA
- Black (2) .... FA/VA/JA
- Med. Blue (1) .... AB/CB/EB
- Med. Blue (1) .... ZB/GB/KB
- Med. Blue (2) .... BB/DB
- Med. Blue (2) .... FB/VB/JB
- Dk. Red (1) .... ED/ZD
- Dk. Red (1) .... GD/KD
- Dk. Red (2) .... BD/DD
- Dk. Red (2) .... FD/VD/JD
- Med. Ginger (1) .... AF/CF
- Med. Ginger (2) .... BF/DF
- Med. Ginger (2) .... FF/VF/JF
- Med. Green (1) .... AR/CR
- Med. Green (1) .... ER/ZR/KR
- Med. Green (2) .... BR/DR/FR
- Med. Green (2) .... GR/VR/JR
- Lt. Gray Gold (1) .... AY/EY
- Lt. Gray Gold (1) .... ZY/GY/KY
- Lt. Gray Gold (2) .... BY/DY
- Lt. Gray Gold (2) .... FY/VY/JY
- Dk. Tobacco (1) .... EZ/ZZ
- Dk. Tobacco (1) .... GZ/KZ
- Dk. Tobacco (2) .... VZ/JZ
- White (2) .... BW/DW/FW

1 - Cloth & vinyl
2 - Vinyl

MONTEGO	CODE
Black (1)	AA/BA/CA/GA
Black (2)	JA/DA/KA
Black (2)	HA/EA/FA
Med. Blue (1)	AB/BB
Med. Blue (1)	CB/GB
Med. Blue (2)	JB/DB/KB
Med. Blue (2)	HB/EB/FB
Med. Ginger (2)	JF/DF/KF
Med. Ginger (2)	HF/EF/FF
Med. Green (1)	AR/BR
Med. Green (1)	CR/GR
Med. Green (2)	JR/DR/KR
Med. Green (2)	HR/ER/FR
Lt. Gray Gold (1)	CY/GY
Dk. Tobacco (1)	CZ/GZ
White w/Black (2)	DW/HW
White w/Black (2)	EW/FW
White w/Blue (2)	DL/HL
White w/Blue (2)	EL/FL
White w/Tobacco (2)	D9/H9
White w/Tobacco (2)	E9/F9
White w/Green (2)	D5/H5
White w/Green (2)	E5/F5

1 - Cloth & vinyl
2 - Vinyl

COUGAR	CODE
Black (1)	BA/EA
Black (2)	AA/CA
Black (3)	DA
Med. Blue (1)	BB/EB
Med. Blue (2)	AB/CB
Med. Blue (3)	DB
Dk. Red (2)	AD/CD
Dk. Red (3)	DD
Med. Ginger (1)	BF/EF
Med. Ginger (2)	CF
Med. Ginger (3)	DF
Med. Green (1)	BR/ER
Med. Green (2)	AR/CR
Med. Green (3)	DR
White w/Black (2)	AW/CW
White w/Black (3)	DW

1 - Cloth & vinyl
2 - Vinyl
3 - Leather & vinyl

COMET	CODE
Black (1)	JA
Black (2)	BA/HA
Black (2)	KA/NA/LA
Med. Blue (1)	JB
Med. Blue (2)	BB/HB/KB
Med. Ginger (1)	JF
Med. Ginger (2)	BF/HF
Med. Ginger (2)	KF/NF/LF
Lt. Beige (1)	JT
Lt. Beige (2)	BT/HT/KT
White w/Black (2)	KW/LW
White w/Blue (2)	KL/LL
White w/Ginger (2)	KS/LS
White w/Beige (2)	K6/L6

1 - Cloth & vinyl
2 - Vinyl

THE AXLE CODE is a number or letter indicating the rear axle ratio and standard or locking type axles.

CONVENTIONAL	LOCKING	RATIO
2	K	2.75:1
3		2.79:1
4	M	2.80:1
6	O	3.00:1
7		3.18:1
9	R	3.25:1
A	S	3.50:1
B		3.07:1
G		3.55:1
H		3.78:1
	V	3.91:1

THE TRANSMISSION CODE is a number or letter indicating the type of transmission.

TYPE	CODE
3-Speed Manual	1
4-Speed Manual	5
4-Speed Manual	E
Automatic (C4)	W
Automatic (C6)	U
Automatic (FMX)	X
Automatic (C6 Special)	Z

THE DSO CODE, consisting of two numbers, designates the district in which the car was ordered and may appear in conjunction with a Domestic Special Order or Foreign Special Order number when applicable.

LINCOLN-MERCURY

DISTRICT	CODE
Boston	11
New York	15
Philadelphia	16
Washington	17
Atlanta	21
Dallas	22
Jacksonville	23
Memphis	26
Buffalo	31
Cincinnati	32
Cleveland	33
Detroit	34
Chicago	41
St. Louis	42
Twin Cities	46
Denver	51
Los Angeles	52
Oakland	53
Seattle	54
Home Office Reserve	84
Export	90

ENGINE IDENTIFICATION

ENGINE TAG

Since 1964, Lincoln-Mercury engines can be identified by a tag attached to the engine. The tag contains the year and cubic inch displacement.

CASTING NUMBERS

While helpful in identifying Ford engine components, casting numbers are not conclusive in pin-pointing the exact year of manufacture. A better method is to search for the original host vehicle's VIN (Vehicle Identification Number) stamped on the driver's side at the rear of the engine block below the cylinder head.

MERCURY ENGINES

CID	NO. CYL.	HORSE-POWER	COMP. RATIO	CARB.
351	8	163	8.6:1	2 BC
400	8	172	8.4:1	2 BC
429	8	205	8.5:1	4 BC
429	8	208	8.5:1	4 BC
460	8	200	8.5:1	4 BC

MONTEGO ENGINES

CID	NO. CYL.	HORSE-POWER	COMP. RATIO	CARB.
250	6	97	8.0:1	1 BC
302	8	140	8.5:1	2 BC
351 CJ	8	248	8.5:1	2 BC
351	8	161	8.6:1	2 BC
400	8	168	8.4:1	2 BC
429	8	205	8.5:1	4 BC

COUGAR ENGINES

CID	NO. CYL.	HORSE-POWER	COMP. RATIO	CARB.
351	8	164	8.6:1	2 BC
351	8	262	8.6:1	4 BC
351 CJ	8	266	8.6:1	4 BC

COMET ENGINES

CID	NO. CYL.	HORSE-POWER	COMP. RATIO	CARB.
170	6	82	8.3:1	1 BC
200	6	91	8.3:1	1 BC
250	6	97	8.0:1	1 BC
302	8	143	8.5:1	2 BC

LINCOLN ENGINES

CID	NO. CYL.	HORSE-POWER	COMP. RATIO	CARB.
460	8	212	8.5:1	4 BC
460	8	224	8.5:1	4 BC

1973 MERCURY MARQUIS

1973 LINCOLN CONTINENTAL MARK IV

1973 LINCOLN CONTINENTAL

1973 MERCURY COUGAR

1973 MERCURY COMET

1973 MERCURY MONTEGO

1973 MERCURY MONTEREY

VEHICLE IDENTIFICATION NUMBER

• LINCOLN MERCURY •
F 3S56H123456 F

Located on a metal tab that is riveted to the instrument panel close to the windshield on the driver's side of the car and is visible from outside.

FIRST DIGIT: Identifies the year (3 = 1973)

SECOND DIGIT: Identifies the assembly plant

ASSEMBLY PLANT	CODE
Atlanta, GA	A
Oakville, Ont., CAN	B
Mahwah, NJ	E
Dearborn, MI	F
Lorain, OH	H
Kansas City, KS	K
San Jose, CA	R
Allen Park (Pilot)	S
Metuchen, NJ	T
Wixom, MI	Y
St. Louis, MO	Z

THIRD AND FOURTH DIGITS: Identify the body serial code

COMET	CODE
4-Dr. Sedan	30
2-Dr. Sedan	31

COUGAR	CODE
2-Dr. Hardtop	91
Convertible	92
2-Dr. HT XR-7	93
Convertible XR-7	94

LINCOLN	CODE
2-Dr. Hardtop	81
4-Dr. Sedan HT	82
2-Dr. Hardtop (Mark IV)	89

MERCURY	CODE
4-Dr. Pillar HT Monterey	44
2-Dr. HT Monterey	46
4-Dr. Pillar HT Monterey Custom	54
2-Dr. HT Monterey Custom	56
4-Dr. Pillar HT Marquis	63
2-Dr. HT Marquis	66
4-Dr. HT Marquis	68
4-Dr. Pillar HT Brougham	62
2-Dr. HT Brougham	64
4-Dr. HT Brougham	67
4-Dr. 6-Pass. Monterey Wagon	72
4-Dr. 6-Pass. Marquis Wagon	74
4-Dr. 6-Pass. Marquis Colony Park Wagon	76

MONTEGO	CODE
4-Dr. Sedan HT Montego	02
2-Dr. Hardtop Montego	03
4-Dr. Sedan HT Montego MX	04
2-Dr. HT Montego MX	07
4-Dr. Sedan HT Montego MX Brougham	10
2-Dr. HT Montego MX Brougham	11
2-Dr. Fastback Montego GT	16
4-Dr. Montego MX SW	08
4-Dr. Montego MX Villager SW	18

FIFTH DIGIT: Identifies the engine code

ENGINE	CODE
V8 460-4V	A
V8 460-4V Police	C
V8 302-2V	F
V8 351-2V	H
I6 250-1V	L
V8 429-4V	N
V8 351-4V CJ	Q
V8 400-2V	S
I6 200-1V	T
I6 251-1V Export	3
V8 351 H.O.	R

LAST SIX DIGITS: Represent the basic production numbers

EXAMPLE:

3	S	56	H	123456
Model Year	Assy. Plant	Body Serial Code	Engine	Production Sequence Number

VEHICLE CERTIFICATION LABEL

THE VEHICLE CERTIFICATION LABEL (V.C. Label) is attached to the rear face of the driver's door. The upper half of the label contains the name of the manufacturer, the month and year of manufacture, the Gross Vehicle Weight Rating (GVWR), the Gross Axle Weight Rating (GAWR), and the certification statement. The V.C. label also contains the Vehicle Identification Number. The remaining information on the V.C. label consists of pertinent vehicle identification codes: ie. body, color, trim, axle, transmission and DSO codes.

MANUFACTURED BY
FORD MOTOR COMPANY

09/73 THIS VEHICLE CONFORMS TO ALL APPLICABLE FEDERAL MOTOR VEHICLE SAFETY STANDARDS IN EFFECT ON DATE OF MANUFACTURE SHOWN ABOVE

3S56H123456　　　PASSENGER
65F　1C　　DA　　W　6　33

NOT FOR TITLE OR REGISTRATION
MADE IN U.S.A.

EXAMPLE:
3S56H123456 .... Vehicle Identification Number (VIN)
65F .... Body Type Code (Monterey Custom 2-Dr. Hardtop)
1C .... Color Code (Black)
DA .... Trim Code (Black Vinyl)
W .... Transmission Code (C4 Automatic)
6 .... Rear Axle Code (3.00:1)
33 .... District Special Equipment Code (Cleveland)

THE BODY CODE is two numerals and a letter identifying the body style.

COMET	CODE
4-Dr. Sedan	54B
2-Dr. Sedan	62B

* GT option available
* Custom available

COUGAR	CODE
2-Dr. Hardtop	65D
Convertible	76D
2-Dr. HT XR-7	65F
Convertible XR-7	76F

LINCOLN	CODE
2-Dr. Hardtop	65A
4-Dr. Sedan HT	53A
2-Dr. Hardtop (Mark IV)	65D
* Silver Luxury option available	
* Town Car option available	
* Town Coupe option available	
* Silver Mark option available	

MERCURY	CODE
4-Dr. Pillar HT Monterey	53B
2-Dr. HT Monterey	65B
4-Dr. Pillar HT Monterey Custom	53F
2-Dr. HT Monterey Custom	65F
4-Dr. Pillar HT Marquis	53H
2-Dr. HT Marquis	65H
4-Dr. HT Marquis	57H
4-Dr. Pillar HT Brougham	53K
2-Dr. HT Brougham	65K
4-Dr. HT Brougham	57K
4-Dr. 6-Pass. Monterey Wagon	71B
4-Dr. 6-Pass. Marquis Wagon	71H
4-Dr. 6-Pass. Marquis Colony Park Wagon	71K

MONTEGO	CODE
4-Dr. Sedan HT Montego	53B
2-Dr. HT Montego	65B
4-Dr. Sedan HT Montego MX	53D
2-Dr. HT Montego MX	65D
4-Dr. Sedan HT Montego MX Brougham	53K
2-Dr. HT Montego MX Brougham	65K
2-Dr. Fastback Montego GT	63R
4-Dr. Montego MX SW	71D
4-Dr. Montego MX Villager SW	71K

THE COLOR CODE is a number and letter indicating the exterior paint color.

COLOR	CODE
Lt. Gray Met.	1A
Black	1C
Silver Met.	1D
Brt. Red	2B
Red Met.	2C
Med. Red Met.	2G
Maroon	2J
Fuschia	2K
Platinum	3A
Lt. Blue	3B
Med. Blue Met.	3D
Brt. Dk. Blue Met.	3G
Brt. Blue Met.	3K
Silver Blue Met.	3L
Brt. Green Gold Met.	4B
Ivy Bronze Met.	4C
Dk. Ivy Bronze Met.	4D
Med. Aqua	4N
Med. Green Met.	4P
Dk. Green Met.	4Q
Lt. Green	4S
Brt. Lime Gold Met.	4U
Pewter Met.	5A
Ginger Bronze Met.	5D
Dk. Brown Met.	5F
Ginger Met.	5H
Med. Ginger Met.	5J
Dk. Gold Met.	5K
Tan	5L

COLOR	CODE
Med. Chestnut Met.	5M
Med. Orange Met.	5N
Copper Met.	5P
Lt. Goldenrod	6B
Med. Goldenrod	6C
Yellow	6D
Med. Brt. Yellow	6E
Brt. Yellow Gold Met.	6F
Brt. Yellow Gold Met.	6G
Med. Gold Met.	6L
White	9A
White	9C

THE TRIM CODE consists of a two-letter or a letter-number combination designating the interior trim.

LINCOLN	CODE
Black (1)	BA/CA/AA
Black (2)	GA
Black (3)	DA/EA/HA
Dk. Blue (1)	BB/CB/AB
Dk. Blue (3)	DB/EB/BD
Dk. Red (1)	AD
Dk. Red (3)	DD/ED/BD
Med. Ginger (1)	AF/FF
Med. Ginger (3)	DF/EF/BF
Cranberry (2)	AH
Lt. Silver Blue (1)	AP/BP
Lt. Silver Blue (1)	FP/CP
Lt. Silver Blue (2)	GP
Lt. Silver Blue (3)	DP/EP/HP
Dk. Green (1)	BR/CR
Dk. Green (1)	DR/BL
Dk. Green (3)	DR/ER
Lt. Beige (2)	GT
Lt. Beige (3)	DT/ET
Lt. Beige (3)	HT/BT
Lt. Gold (1)	AY/BY
Lt. Gold (1)	FY/CY
Lt. Gold (3)	DY/EY
Dk. Tobacco (1)	BZ/CZ/DZ
Dk. Tobacco (3)	DZ/EZ
White (3)	DQ/EQ/BQ
White (3)	DW/EW/BW
White (3)	D5/E5/B5
White (3)	D9/E9/B9
1 - Cloth & vinyl	
2 - Velour	
3 - Leather	

MERCURY/MONTEREY	CODE
Black (1)	CA/GA/KA
Black (1)	JA/NA/MA
Black (2)	DA/HA
Black (2)	LA/ZA/SA
Med. Blue (1)	CB/GB/KB
Med. Blue (1)	JB/NB/MB
Med. Blue (2)	DB/HB
Med. Blue (2)	LB/ZB/SB
Med. Green (1)	CR/GR/KR
Med. Green (1)	JR/NR/MR
Med. Green (2)	DR/HR
Med. Green (2)	LR/ZR/SR
Med. Ginger (2)	LF/SF/ZF
Lt. Beige (1)	CT/GT/KT
Lt. Beige (1)	JT/NT/MT
Lt. Beige (2)	DT/HT
Lt. Beige (2)	LT/ZT/ST

MERCURY/MONTEREY	CODE
Dk. Tobacco (1)	KZ/JZ
Dk. Tobacco (1)	NZ/MZ
Dk. Tobacco (2)	LZ/ZZ/SZ
White w/Blue (2)	ZQ/SQ
White w/Black (2)	ZW/SW
White w/Green (2)	Z5/S5
White w/Tobacco (2)	Z9/S9

1 - Cloth & vinyl
2 - Vinyl

MONTEGO	CODE
Black (1)	AA/CA/GA
Black (2)	BA/JA/DA
Black (2)	HA/EA/FA
Med. Blue (1)	AB/CB/GB
Med. Blue (2)	BB/JB/DB
Med. Blue (2)	HB/EB/FB
Med. Ginger (2)	DF/JF
Med. Ginger (2)	HF/EF/FF
Med. Green (1)	AR/CR/GR
Med. Green (2)	BR/JR/DR
Med. Green (2)	HR/ER/FR
Beige (1)	CT/GT/DT
Beige (2)	JT/HT
Beige (2)	ET/FT
Dk. Tobacco (1)	CZ/GZ
Maize Gold (1)	LY
White w/Blue (2)	DQ/HQ
White w/Black (2)	DW/HW
White w/Green (2)	D5/H5
White w/Tobacco (2)	D9/H9

1 - Cloth & vinyl
2 - Vinyl

COUGAR	CODE
Black (1)	BA/EA
Black (2)	AA/CA
Black (3)	DA
Med. Blue (1)	BB/EB
Med. Blue (2)	AB/CB
Med. Blue (3)	DB
Med. Ginger (1)	BF/EF
Med. Ginger (2)	AF/CF
Med. Ginger (3)	DF
Avocado (1)	BG/EG
Avocado (2)	AG/CG
Avocado (3)	DG
White w/Blue (2)	AQ/CQ
White w/Blue (3)	DQ
White w/Black (2)	AW/CW
White w/Black (3)	DW
White w/Ginger (2)	A3/C3
White w/Ginger (3)	D3
White w/Avocado (2)	A6/C6
White w/Avocado (3)	D6

1 - Cloth & vinyl
2 - Vinyl
3 - Leather

COMET	CODE
Black (1)	BA/JA
Black (2)	HA/KA/LA
Med. Blue (1)	BB/JB
Med. Blue (2)	HB/KB/LB
Orange (2)	HC/KC/LC
Med. Ginger (1)	BF/JF
Med. Ginger (2)	HF/KF/LF
Avocado (1)	BG/JG
Avocado (2)	HG/KG/LG

COMET	CODE
Tan (2)	PU
Beige w/Beige (1)	BT/JT
Beige w/Beige (2)	HT/KT/LT
Beige w/Ginger (1)	B3/J3
Beige w/Ginger (2)	H3/K3

1 - Cloth & vinyl
2 - Vinyl

THE AXLE CODE is a number or letter indicating the rear axle ratio and standard or locking type axles.

CONVENTIONAL	LOCKING	RATIO
2	K	2.75:1
3		2.79:1
6	O	3.00:1
9	R	3.25:1
A	S	3.50:1

THE TRANSMISSION CODE is a number or letter indicating the type of transmission.

TYPE	CODE
3-Speed Manual	1
4-Speed Manual	5
Automatic (C4)	W
Automatic (C6)	U
Automatic (FMX)	X
Automatic (C6 Special)	Z
Automatic (C3)	V

THE DSO CODE, consisting of two numbers, designates the district in which the car was ordered and may appear in conjunction with a Domestic Special Order or Foreign Special Order number when applicable.

LINCOLN-MERCURY DISTRICT	CODE
Boston	11
New York	15
Philadelphia	16
Washington	17
Atlanta	21
Dallas	22
Jacksonville	23
Memphis	26
Buffalo	31
Cincinnati	32
Cleveland	33
Detroit	34
Chicago	41
St. Louis	42
Twin Cities	46
Denver	51
Los Angeles	52
Oakland	53
Seattle	54
Home Office Reserve	84
Export	90

ENGINE IDENTIFICATION

ENGINE TAG
Since 1964, Lincoln-Mercury engines can be identified by a tag attached to the engine. The tag contains the year and cubic inch displacement.

CASTING NUMBERS
While helpful in identifying Ford engine components, casting numbers are not conclusive in pin-pointing the exact year of manufacture. A better method is to search for the original host vehicle's VIN (Vehicle Identification Number) stamped on the driver's side at the rear of the engine block below the cylinder head.

COMET ENGINES

CID	NO. CYL.	HORSE-POWER	COMP. RATIO	CARB.
200	6	84	8.3:1	1 BC
250	6	88	8.0:1	1 BC
302	8	138	8.0:1	2 BC

MONTEGO ENGINES

CID	NO. CYL.	HORSE-POWER	COMP. RATIO	CARB.
250	6	92	8.0:1	1 BC
302	8	137	8.0:1	2 BC
302	8	135	8.0:1	2 BC
351	8	159	8.0:1	2 BC
351	8	156	8.0:1	2 BC
351	8	246	8.0:1	4 BC
400	8	168	8.0:1	2 BC
429	8	201	8.0;1	4 BC
460	8	244	8.8:1	4 BC

MERCURY ENGINES

CID	NO. CYL.	HORSE-POWER	COMP. RATIO	CARB.
351	8	161	8.0:1	2 BC
400	8	171	8.0:1	2 BC
400	8	167	8.0:1	2 BC
429	8	201	8.0:1	4 BC
429	8	198	8.0:1	4 BC
460	8	202	8.0:1	4 BC
460	8	198	8.0:1	4 BC
460	8	267	8.8:1	4 BC

LINCOLN ENGINES

CID	NO. CYL.	HORSE-POWER	COMP. RATIO	CARB.
460	8	208	8.0:1	4 BC
460	8	219	8.0:1	4 BC

COUGAR ENGINES

CID	NO. CYL.	HORSE-POWER	COMP. RATIO	CARB.
351	8	168	8.0:1	2 BC
351	8	264	8.0:1	4 BC

1974 MERCURY COUGAR

1974 MERCURY COMET

1974 MERCURY MARQUIS

1974 MERCURY MONTEREY

1974 LINCOLN CONTINENTAL

1974 LINCOLN CONTINENTAL MARK IV

1974 MERCURY MONTEGO

VEHICLE IDENTIFICATION NUMBER

LINCOLN MERCURY
F 4S93H123456 F

Located on a metal tab that is riveted to the instrument panel close to the windshield on the driver's side of the car and is visible from outside.

FIRST DIGIT: Identifies the year (4 = 1974)

SECOND DIGIT: Identifies the assembly plant

ASSEMBLY PLANT	CODE
Atlanta, GA	A
Oakville, Ont., CAN	B
Mahwah, NJ	E
Lorain, OH	H
Kansas City, KS	K
San Jose, CA	R
Allen Park (Pilot)	S
Metuchen, NJ	T
Wayne, MI	W
Wixom, MI	Y
St. Louis, MO	Z

THIRD AND FOURTH DIGITS: Identify the body serial code

COMET	CODE
4-Dr. Sedan	30
2-Dr. Sedan	31

COUGAR	CODE
2-Dr. Hardtop XR-7	93

LINCOLN	CODE
2-Dr. Hardtop	81
4-Dr. Sedan HT	82
2-Dr. Hardtop (Mark IV)	89

MERCURY	CODE
4-Dr. Pillared HT Monterey	44
2-Dr. Hardtop	46
4-Dr. Pillared HT Monterey Custom	54
2-Dr. HT Monterey Custom	56
4-Dr. Pillared HT Marquis	63
2-Dr. HT Marquis	66
4-Dr. HT Marquis	68
4-Dr. Pillared HT Brougham	62
2-Dr. HT Brougham	64
4-Dr. HT Brougham	67
4-Dr. 6-Pass. Monterey Wagon	72
4-Dr. 6-Pass. Marquis Wagon	74
4-Dr. 6-Pass. Marquis Colony Park Wagon	76

MONTEGO	CODE
4-Dr. Sedan HT Montego	02
2-Dr. HT Montego	03
4-Dr. Sedan HT Montego MX	04
2-Dr. HT Montego MX	07
4-Dr. Sedan HT Montego Brougham	10
2-Dr. HT Montego Brougham	11
4-Dr. Montego MX SW	08
4-Dr. Montego MX Villager SW	18

FIFTH DIGIT: Identifies the engine code

ENGINE	CODE
V8 460-4V	A
V8 460-4V Police	C
V8 302-2V	F
V8 351-2V	H
I6 250-1V	L
V8 351-4V CJ	Q
V8 400-2V	S
I6 200-1V	T
I6 250 Export	3

LAST SIX DIGITS: Represent the basic production numbers

EXAMPLE:

4	S	56	H	123456
Model Year	Assy. Plant	Body Serial Code	Engine	Production Sequence Number

VEHICLE CERTIFICATION LABEL

THE VEHICLE CERTIFICATION LABEL (V.C. Label) is attached to the rear face of the driver's door. The upper half of the label contains the name of the manufacturer, the month and year of manufacture, the Gross Vehicle Weight Rating (GVWR), the Gross Axle Weight Rating (GAWR), and the certification statement. The V.C. label also contains the Vehicle Identification Number. The remaining information on the V.C. label consists of pertinent vehicle identification codes: ie. body, color, trim, axle, transmission and DSO codes.

MANUFACTURED BY
FORD MOTOR COMPANY

09/74 THIS VEHICLE CONFORMS TO ALL APPLICABLE FEDERAL MOTOR VEHICLE SAFETY STANDARDS IN EFFECT ON DATE OF MANUFACTURE SHOWN ABOVE

4S93H123456   PASSENGER
65F   3Q   AQ   X   2   34

NOT FOR TITLE OR REGISTRATION
MADE IN U.S.A.

EXAMPLE:

4S93H123456	Vehicle Identification Number
65F	Body Type Code (XR-7 2-Dr. Hardtop)
3Q	Color Code (Pastel Blue)
AQ	Trim Code (White w/Blue Vinyl)
X	Transmission Code (FMX Automatic)
2	Axle Code (2.75:1)
34	District Special Equipment Code (Detroit)

THE BODY CODE is two numerals and a letter identifying the body style.

COMET	CODE
4-Dr. Sedan	54B
2-Dr. Sedan	62B

* GT option available
* Custom option available

COUGAR	CODE
2-Dr. HT XR-7	65F

LINCOLN

	CODE
2-Dr. Hardtop	65A
4-Dr. Sedan HT	53A
2-Dr. Hardtop (Mark IV)	65D

* Town Car option available
* Town Coupe option available

MERCURY

	CODE
4-Dr. Pillared HT Monterey	53B
2-Dr. Hardtop Monterey	65B
4-Dr. Pillared HT Monterey Custom	53B
2-Dr. HT Monterey Custom	65F
4-Dr. Pillared HT Marquis	53H
2-Dr. Hardtop Marquis	65H
4-Dr. Hardtop Marquis	57H
4-Dr. Pillared HT Brougham	53K
2-Dr. HT Brougham	65K
4-Dr. HT Brougham	57K
4-Dr. 6-Pass. Monterey Wagon	71B
4-Dr. 6-Pass. Marquis Wagon	71H
4-Dr. 6-Pass. Marquis Colony Park Wagon	71K

MONTEGO

	CODE
4-Dr. Sedan HT Montego	53B
2-Dr. HT Montego	65B
4-Dr. Sedan HT Montego MX	53D
2-Dr. HT Montego MX	65D
4-Dr. Sedan HT Montego Brougham	53K
2-Dr. HT Montego Brougham	65K
4-Dr. Montego MX SW	71D
4-Dr. Montego MX Villager SW	71K

THE COLOR CODE is a number and letter indicating the exterior paint color.

COLOR	CODE
Black	1C
Silver Met.	1D
Light Silver Cloud Met.	1E
Silver Metallic	1G
Med. Slate Blue Met.	1H
Bright Red	2B
Red	2E
Med. Red Met.	2G
Medium Red	2M
Platinum	3A
Light Blue	3B
Medium Blue Met.	3D
Bright Blue Met.	3E
Bright Dark Blue Met.	3G
Silver Blue Met.	3L
Silver Blue Met.	3M
Light Grabber Blue	3N
Medium Blue Met.	3P
Pastel Blue	3Q
Pastel Lime	4A
Bright Green Gold Met.	4B
Dark Green Met.	4Q
Medium Ivy Bronze Met.	4T
Dark Yellow Green Met.	4V
Medium Lime Yellow	4W
Dark Ivy Bronze Met.	4Y
Ginger Metallic	5H
Dark Ginger Met.	5J
Medium Chestnut Met.	5M
Dark Brown Met.	5Q
Bright Gold Bronze Met.	5R
Medium Beige	5S
Saddle Bronze Met.	5T
Buff	5V
Orange	5W
Dark Copper Met.	5Y
Unique Gold Met.	5Z
Medium Goldenrod	6C

COLOR	CODE
Bright Yellow Gold Met.	6G
Bright Yellow Gold Met.	6F
Medium Gold Met.	6L
Medium Dark Gold Met.	6M
Maize Yellow	6N
White Decor	9C
Ginger Bronze Met.	51
Copper Met.	52

THE TRIM CODE consists of a two-letter or a letter-number combination designating the interior trim.

LINCOLN	CODE
Black (1)	BA/EA
Black (2)	JA
Black (3)	FA/HA
Black (3)	EA/KA/BA
Blue (1)	BB/EB
Blue (3)	FB/EB/BB
Silver Blue (1)	BE/EE
Silver Blue (2)	JE/AE
Silver Blue (3)	FE/HE
Silver Blue (3)	EE/KE/BE
Green (1)	BR/ER
Green (2)	AR/BR
Green (3)	FR/HR
Green (3)	ER/KR
Tan (1)	EU
Tan (3)	BU
Tan **	DU
Gold (1)	BY/EY
Gold (2)	JY/AY
Gold (3)	FY/HY
Gold (3)	EY/KY/BY
Lt. Beige (2)	JT
Lt. Beige (3)	HT/ET/KT
Red (1)	ED
Red (2)	JD/KD
Red (3)	ED
Red *	BD
Saddle (1)	BZ
Saddle (3)	FZ/EZ/BZ
Saddle **	DZ
Cranberry *	AH
White w/Black (3)	DW/BW
White w/Blue (3)	DQ/BQ
White w/Yellow (3)	DN/BN
White w/Green (3)	D5/B5
White w/Gold (3)	D8/B8
White w/Saddle (3)	D9/B9

1 - Cloth
2 - Velour
3 - Leather
* Silver Lux group
** Gold Lux group

MERCURY	CODE
Black (1)	CA/GA/KA
Black (1)	PA/RA/TA
Black (2)	DA/HA
Black (2)	LA/ZA/SA
Med. Blue (1)	CB/GB/KB
Med. Blue (1)	PB/RB/TB
Med. Blue (2)	DB/HB/LB
Med. Blue (2)	ZB/SB/QB
Med. Green (1)	CR/GR/KR
Med. Green (1)	PR/RR/TR
Med. Green (2)	DR/HR/LR
Med. Green (2)	ZR/SR/QR

MERCURY	CODE
Beige (1)	GT/KT
Beige (1)	PT/RT/TT
Beige (2)	HT/LT
Beige (2)	ZT/ST
Gold (1)	GY/KY
Gold (1)	PY/RY/TY
Gold (2)	HY/LY
Gold (2)	ZY/SY
Saddle (1)	CZ/GZ/KZ
Saddle (1)	PZ/RZ/TZ
Saddle (2)	DZ/HZ/LZ
Saddle (2)	ZZ/SZ/QZ
Tan (2)	DU/LU
Tan (2)	ZU/SU
Tan (3)	JU
Tan (4)	FU
White w/Black (2)	ZW/SW
White w/Blue (2)	ZQ/SQ
White w/Green (2)	Z5/S5
White w/Gold (2)	Z8
White w/Saddle (2)	Z9/S9

1 - Cloth
2 - Vinyl
3 - Cloth & Leather
4 - Leather

MONTEGO	CODE
Black (1)	CA/GA
Black (2)	AA/BA
Black (2)	DA/HA/EA
Med. Blue (1)	CB/GB
Med. Blue (2)	AB/BB
Med. Blue (2)	DB/HB/EB
Med. Blue (3)	KB
Med. Green (1)	CR/GR
Med. Green (2)	DR/HR/ER
Tan (1)	CU/GU
Tan (2)	AU/BU
Tan (2)	DU/HU
Gold (1)	CY/GY
Gold (2)	DY/HY
Gold (3)	KY
Saddle (1)	CZ/GZ
Saddle (2)	DZ/HZ/EZ
White w/Black (2)	DW/HW
Whie w/Blue (2)	DQ/HQ
White w/Green (2)	D5/H5
White w/Gold (2)	D8/H8
White w/Saddle (2)	D9/H9

1 - Cloth
2 - Vinyl
3 - Cloth & vinyl

COUGAR	CODE
Black (2)	AA/BA
Black (3)	FA/DA
Blue/Silver Blue (1)	EB
Blue/Silver Blue (2)	AB/HB
Blue/Silver Blue (3)	FB/DB
Dk. Red (1)	ED
Dk. Red (2)	AD/HD
Dk. Red (3)	FD/DD
Med. Green (1)	ER
Med. Green (2)	AR/HR
Med. Green (3)	DR
Tan (1)	EU
Tan (2)	AU/HU
Tan (3)	FU/DU
Saddle/Tan (1)	EZ
Saddle/Tan (2)	AZ/HZ
Saddle/Tan (3)	FZ/DZ
White w/Black (2)	AW/HW
White w/Black (3)	FW/DW
White w/Blue (2)	AQ
White w/Blue (3)	FQ

COUGAR	CODE
White w/Green (2)	A5
White w/Green (3)	F5
White w/Tan (2)	AM
White w/Tan (3)	FM
White w/Saddle (2)	A9
White w/Saddle (3)	F9

1 - Velour
2 - Vinyl
3 - Leather

COMET	CODE
Black (1)	BA
Black (2)	HA/KA/LA
Black (3)	JA
Med. Blue (1)	BB
Med. Blue (2)	HB/KB
Med. Blue (3)	JB
Silver Blue (2)	PE
Orange (2)	HC/KC/LC
Avocado (1)	BG
Avocado (2)	HG/KG/LG
Avocado (3)	JG
Tan (1)	BU
Tan (2)	HU/KU/LU/PU
Tan (3)	JU

1 - Cloth & vinyl
2 - Vinyl
3 - Cloth

THE TRANSMISSION CODE is a number or letter indicating the type of transmission.

TYPE	CODE
3-Speed Manual	1
Automatic (C-4)	W
Automatic (FMX)	X
Automatic (C-6)	U
Automatic (C-6 Special)	Z

THE AXLE CODE is a number or letter indicating the rear axle ratio and standard or locking type axles.

CONVENTIONAL	LOCKING	RATIO
2	K	2.75:1
3	L	2.79:1
5	E	3.07:1
6	O	3.00:1
7		3.40:1
9	R	3.25:1
A	S	3.50:1
G		3.55:1

THE DSO CODE, consisting of two numbers, designates the district in which the car was ordered and may appear in conjunction with a Domestic Special Order or Foreign Special Order number when applicable.

LINCOLN-MERCURY DISTRICT	CODE
Boston	11
New York	15
Philadelphia	16
Washington	17
Atlanta	21
Dallas	22
Jacksonville	23
Memphis	26
Buffalo	31
Cincinnati	32
Cleveland	33
Detroit	34
Chicago	41
St. Louis	42
Twin Cities	46
Denver	51
Los Angeles	52
Oakland	53
Seattle	54
Home Office Reserve	84
Export	90

ENGINE IDENTIFICATION

ENGINE TAG

Since 1964, Lincoln-Mercury engines can be identified by a tag attached to the engine. The tag contains the year and cubic inch displacement.

CASTING NUMBERS

While helpful in identifying Ford engine components, casting numbers are not conclusive in pin-pointing the exact year of manufacture. A better method is to search for the original host vehicle's VIN (Vehicle Identification Number) stamped on the driver's side at the rear of the engine block below the cylinder head.

COMET ENGINES

CID	NO. CYL.	HORSE-POWER	COMP. RATIO	CARB.
200	65	84	8.3:1	1 BC
250	6	91	8.0;1	1 BC
302	8	140	8.0:1	2 BC

MONTEGO ENGINES

CID	NO. CYL.	HORSE-POWER	COMP. RATIO	CARB.
302	8	140	8.0:1	2 BC
351	8	162	8.0:1	2 BC
351	8	163	8.0:1	2 BC
351	8	255	8.0:1	2 BC
400	8	170	8.0:1	2 BC
460	8	195	8.0:1	4 BC
460	8	220	8.0:1	4 BC

MERCURY ENGINES

CID	NO. CYL.	HORSE-POWER	COMP. RATIO	CARB.
351	8	162	8.0:1	2 BC
351	8	163	8.0:1	2 BC
351	8	255	8.0:1	4 BC
400	8	170	8.0:1	2 BC
460	8	195	8.0:1	4 BC

COUGAR ENGINES

CID	NO. CYL.	HORSE-POWER	COMP. RATIO	CARB.
351	8	162	8.0:1	2 BC
351	8	163	8.0:1	2 BC
351	8	255	8.0:1	4 BC
400	8	170	8.0:1	2 BC
460	8	220	8.0:1	4 BC

LINCOLN ENGINES

CID	NO. CYL.	HORSE-POWER	COMP. RATIO	CARB.
460	8	215	8.0:1	4 BC
460	8	220	8.0:1	4 BC

1975 LINCOLN CONTINENTAL TOWN CAR

1975 MERCURY COUGAR

1975 MERCURY COMET

1975 MERCURY MARQUIS STATION WAGON

1975 LINCOLN CONTINENTAL

1975 LINCOLN CONTINENTAL MARK IV

1975 MERCURY MONTEGO

1975 MERCURY MONARCH

1975 MERCURY MONTEGO STATION WAGON

VEHICLE IDENTIFICATION NUMBER

┌─────────────────────────┐
│ • LINCOLN MERCURY •   │
│   5S63H123456   │
└─────────────────────────┘

Located on a metal tab that is riveted to the instrument panel close to the windshield on the driver's side of the car and is visible from outside.

FIRST DIGIT: Identifies the year (5 = 1975)

SECOND DIGIT: Identifies the assembly plant

ASSEMBLY PLANT	CODE
Atlanta, GA	A
Oakville, Ont., CAN	B
Mahwah, NJ	E
Dearborn, MI	F
Lorain, OH	H
Kansas City, KS	K
San Jose, CA	R
Allen Park (Pilot)	S
Metuchen, NJ	T
Wayne, MI	W
Wixom, MI	Y
St. Louis, MO	Z

THIRD AND FOURTH DIGITS: Identify the body serial code

ELITE	CODE
2-Dr. Hardtop	21

COMET	CODE
4-Dr. Sedan	30
2-Dr. Sedan	31

COUGAR	CODE
2-Dr. Hardtop XR-7	93

LINCOLN	CODE
2-Dr. Hardtop	81
4-Dr. Sedan HT	82
2-Dr. Hardtop (Mark IV)	89

MERCURY	CODE
4-Dr. Pillared HT Grand Marquis	60
2-Dr. HT Grand Marquis	61
4-Dr. Pillared HT Marquis Brougham	62
2-Dr. HT Marquis Brougham	64
4-Dr. Pillared HT Marquis	63
2-Dr. HT Marquis	66
4-Dr. SW Marquis	74
4-Dr. SW Marquis Brougham Colony Park	76

MONARCH	CODE
4-Dr. Sedan	34
2-Dr. Sedan	35
4-Dr. Sedan Ghia	37
2-Dr. Sedan Ghia	38

MERCURY BOBCAT	CODE
3-Dr. Runabout	20
2-Dr. Villager	22

MONTEGO	CODE
4-Dr. Sedan/HT Montego	02
2-Dr. HT Montego	03
4-Dr. Sedan HT Montego MX	04
2-Dr. HT Montego MX	07
4-Dr. Sedan HT Montego Brougham	10
2-Dr. HT Montego Brougham	11
4-Dr. Montego MX SW	08
4-Dr. Villager (Woodgrain) SW	18

FIFTH DIGIT: Identifies the engine code

ENGINE	CODE
V8 460-4V	A
V8 460-4V Police	C
V8 302-2V	F
V8 351-2V	H
I6 250-1V	L
V8 351 Modified	Q
V8 400-2V	S
I6 200-1V	T
I4 139-2V (2.3L)	Y
I6 169-2V (2.8L)	Z

LAST SIX DIGITS: Represent the basic production numbers

EXAMPLE:

5	S	63	H	123456
Model Year	Assy. Plant	Body Serial Code	Engine	Production Sequence Number

VEHICLE IDENTIFICATION NUMBER

THE VEHICLE CERTIFICATION LABEL (V.C. Label) is affixed on the left front door lock face panel or door pillar. The upper half of the label contains the name of the manufacturer, month and year of manufacture, Gross Vehicle Weight Rating (GVWR), Gross Axle Weight Rating (GAWR), and the certification statement. The V.C. label also contains the Vehicle Identification Number (VIN). The remaining information on the V.C. Label consists of the following vehicle identification codes: body, color, trim, axle, transmission and DSO codes.

┌───────────────────────────────────┐
│ MANUFACTURED BY   │
│ FORD MOTOR COMPANY   │
│ 09/75 THIS VEHICLE CONFORMS TO ALL │
│ APPLICABLE FEDERAL MOTOR VEHICLE   │
│ SAFETY STANDARDS IN EFFECT ON   │
│ DATE OF MANUFACTURE SHOWN ABOVE   │
│ 5S63H123456   PASSENGER   │
│ 63H 1C GA X 2   34   │
│ NOT FOR TITLE OR REGISTRATION   │
│ MADE IN U.S.A.   │
└───────────────────────────────────┘

EXAMPLE:
5S63H123456 .... Vehicle Identification Number (VIN)
63H .... Body Type Code (Marquis 4-Dr. Pillared Hardtop)
1C .... Body Color Code and Vinyl Roof Type/Color (Black)
GA .... Trim Code (Black Cloth)
X .... Transmission Code (FMX Automatic)
2 .... Rear Axle Code (2.75:1)
34 .... District Special Equipment Code (Detroit)

THE BODY CODE is two numerals and a letter identifying the body style.

COMET	CODE
4-Dr. Sedan	54B
2-Dr. Sedan	62B

* GT option available
* Custom option available
* Limited option available

COUGAR	CODE
2-Dr. Hardtop XR-7	65F

LINCOLN	CODE
2-Dr. Hardtop	60B
4-Dr. Sedan Hardtop	53B
2-Dr. Hardtop (Mark IV)	65D

* Town Car option available
* Town Coupe option available
* Versailles option available

MERCURY	CODE
4-Dr. Pillared HT Grand Marquis	53L
2-Dr. HT Grand Marquis	65L
4-Dr. Pillared HT Marquis Brougham	53K
2-Dr. HT Marquis Brougham	65K
4-Dr. Pillared HT Marquis	53H
2-Dr. HT Marquis	65H
4-Dr. SW Marquis	71H
4-Dr. SW Marquis Brougham Colony Park	71K

MONARCH	CODE
4-Dr. Sedan	54H
2-Dr. Sedan	66H
4-Dr. Sedan Ghia	54K
2-Dr. Sedan Ghia	66K

MERCURY BOBCAT	CODE
3-Dr. Runabout	64H
2-Dr. Villager	73H

* MPG option available

MONTEGO	CODE
4-Dr. Sedan/HT Montego	53B
2-Dr. HT Montego	65B
4-Dr. Sedan HT Montego MX	53D
2-Dr. HT Montego MX	65D
4-Dr. Sedan HT Montego Brougham	53K
2-Dr. HT Montego Brougham	65K
4-Dr. Montego MX SW	71D
4-Dr. Villager (Woodgrain) SW	71K

THE COLOR CODE is a number and letter indicating the exterior paint color code and vinyl roof type and color (if equipped).

EXTERIOR COLOR	CODE
Black	1C
Silver Met.	1G
Med. Slate Blue Met.	1H
Brt. Red	2B
Red	2E
Dk. Red	2M
Maroon Met.	2Q
Brt. Blue Met.	3E
Brt. Dk. Blue Met.	3G
Pastel Blue	3Q
Dk. Yellow Green Met.	4V
Lt. Green Gold Met.	4Z
Dk. Jade Met.	46
Lt. Green	47
Med. Chestnut Met.	5M
Dk. Brown Met.	5Q
Saddle Bronze Met.	5T
Dk. Copper Met.	5Y
Orange	5W
Yellow	6D
Brt. Yellow	6E
Maize Yellow	6N
Dk. Gold Met.	6Q
White	9D
Brt. Blue Met.	3K
Silver Blue Met.	3M
Med. Ivy Bronze Met.	4T
Dk. Ginger Met.	5J

EXTERIOR COLOR	CODE
Tan Met.	5U
Med. Red Met.	2G
Brt. Gold Yellow Met.	6G
Silver Met.	1J
Med. Taupe Met.	2P
Med. Blue Met.	3P
Silver Blue Met.	3R
Brt. Lime Gold Met.	41
Aqua Blue Met.	45
Ginger Bronze Met.	51
Copper Met.	52
Unique Gold Met.	54

VINYL TYPE (First Letter)	CODE
Cross-Hatch Full 2-Dr.	B
Cross-Hatch Halo Style 4-Dr.	C
Levant Full	D
Levant Half	E
Normandie	F
Odense Full	G
Odense Three-Quarter	H
Odense Embassy (Basket Handle)	J
Normandie Three-Quarter	K
Normandie Half	L
Odense Half	N

VINYL COLOR (Second Letter)	CODE
Aqua	L
Black	A
Blue	B
Brown	T
Copper	K
Gold	Y
Gold Flare	M
Green (Light)	G
Jade	R
Red	D
Saddle	Z
Silver	P
Silver Blue	S
Tan	U
Taupe	J
White	W

THE TRIM CODE consists of a two-letter or a letter-number combination designating the interior trim.

LINCOLN	CODE
Black (1)	BA/FA/EA
Black (2)	DA/EA/BA
Blue (1)	BB/FB/EB
Blue (2)	DB/EB
Blue (2)	KB/HB/BB
Blue (3)	JB
Dk. Red (1)	BD/FD/ED
Dk. Red (2)	DD/ED
Dk. Red (2)	KD/HD/BD
Dk. Red (3)	JD/AD
Green (1)	BG/FG/EG
Green (2)	DG/EG
Green (2)	KG/HG/BG
Green (3)	JG
Taupe (1)	BJ/FJ
Taupe (2)	DJ/EJ
Taupe (2)	KJ/HJ
Taupe (3)	JJ
Aqua Blue (2)	BK
Aqua Blue (4)	FK
Silver (2)	BP
Tan (1)	BU/FU/EU
Tan (2)	DU/EU
Tan (2)	KU/HU/BU
Tan (3)	JU

LINCOLN

	CODE
Gold (1)	BY/FY
Gold (2)	DY/EY
Gold (2)	KY/HY
Gold (3)	JY
Saddle (2)	BZ
White w/Red (2)	DN/EN/BN
White w/Blue (2)	DQ/EQ/BQ
White w/Black (2)	DW/EW/BW
White w/Taupe (2)	D3/E3
White w/Tan (2)	D4/E4
White w/Green (2)	D5/E5/B5
White w/Gold (2)	D8/E8
White w/Saddle (2)	B9/DZ
Tan w/Saddle (2)	DU

1 - Cloth
2 - Leather
3 - Velour
4 - Velour & vinyl

MERCURY

	CODE
Black (1)	GA/TA
Black (2)	SA
Black (3)	JA
Black (4)	FA
Blue (1)	GB/RB/TB
Blue (2)	HB/SB
Blue (2)	EB/QB
Blue (3)	JB
Blue (4)	FB
Dk. Red (1)	RD/TD
Dk. Red (2)	SD/HD
Dk. Red (2)	ED/QD
Dk. Red (3)	JD
Dk. Red (4)	FD
Green (1)	GG/RG/TG
Green (2)	HG/SG
Green (2)	EG/QG
Green (3)	JG
Green (4)	FG
Tan (1)	GU/RU/TU
Tan (2)	HU/SU
Tan (2)	EU/QU
Tan (3)	JU
Tan (4)	FU
Saddle (1)	GZ/RZ/TZ
Saddle (2)	SZ/HZ/EZ
White w/Red (2)	SN
White w/Red (4)	FN
White w/Blue (2)	SQ
White w/Blue (4)	FQ
White w/Black (2)	SW
White w/Black (4)	FW
White w/Green (2)	S5
White w/Green (4)	F5
White w/Saddle (2)	S9
White w/Saddle (4)	F9

1 - Cloth
2 - Vinyl
3 - Cloth & vinyl
4 - Leather

MONTEGO

	CODE
Black (1)	AA/CA/GA
Black (2)	BA/DA/HA
Blue (1)	AB/CB/GB
Blue (2)	BB/DB
Blue (2)	HB/PB/EB
Blue (3)	KB
Green (1)	CG/GG
Green (2)	DG/HG
Green (2)	PG/EG
Green (3)	KG
Tan (1)	AU/CU/GU
Tan (2)	BU/DU
Tan (2)	HU/PU/EU

MONTEGO

	CODE
Tan (3)	KU
Saddle (1)	CZ/GZ
Saddle (2)	DZ/HZ/EZ
White w/Blue (2)	DQ/HQ
White w/Black (2)	DW
White w/Green (2)	D5/H5
White w/Saddle (2)	D9/H9

1 - Cloth
2 - Vinyl

COUGAR

	CODE
Black (2)	AA/HA
Black (3)	DA
Dk. Red (1)	ED
Dk. Red (2)	AD/HD
Dk. Red (3)	DD
Green (1)	EG
Green (2)	AG/HG
Green (3)	DG
Blue/Silver Blue(1)	ES
Blue/Silver Blue(2)	AS/HS
Blue/Silver Blue (3)	DS
Tan (1)	EU
Tan (2)	AU/HU
Tan (3)	DU
Saddle/Tan (1)	EZ
Saddle/Tan (2)	AZ/HZ
Saddle/Tan (3)	DZ
Blue (1)	EB
Blue (2)	HB
Blue (3)	DB
White w/Red (2)	AN/HN
White w/Red (3)	DN
White w/Blue (2)	AQ/HQ
White w/Blue (3)	DQ
White w/Black (2)	AW/HW
White w/Black (3)	DW
White w/Green (2)	A5/H5
White w/Green (3)	D5
White w/Saddle (2)	A9/H9
White w/Saddle (3)	D9

1 - Cloth
2 - Vinyl

MONARCH

	CODE
Black (2)	AA/CA
Dk. Red (1)	DD
Dk. Red (2)	AD/CD
Dk. Red (3)	FD
Silver Blue (1)	DE
Silver Blue (2)	AE/CD
Silver Blue (3)	FE
Green (1)	DG
Green (2)	AG/CG
Tan (1)	DU
Tan (2)	AU/CU
Tan (3)	FU

1 - Cloth
2 - Vinyl
3 - Leather

COMET

	CODE
Black (1)	MA
Black (2)	KA/PA
Blue (1)	MB
Blue (2)	KB/PB
Green (1)	MG
Green (2)	KG
Tan (1)	MU
Tan (2)	KU/PU

1 - Cloth
2 - Vinyl

THE AXLE CODE is a number or letter indicating the rear axle ratio and standard or locking type axles.

CONVENTIONAL	LOCKING	RATIO
2	K	2.75:1
7		3.40:1
6	O	3.00:1
9	R	3.25:1
G		3.55:1
5		3.07:1
3		2.79:1

THE TRANSMISSION CODE is a number or letter indicating the type of transmission.

TYPE	CODE
3-Speed Manual	1
4-Speed Manual	5
Automatic XP (C-3)	V
Automatic XP (C-4)	W
FMX Automatic	X
XPL Automatic (C-6)	U
XPL Automatic (Special)	Z

THE DSO CODE, consisting of two numbers, designates the district in which the car was ordered and may appear in conjunction with a Domestic Special Order or Foreign Special Order number when applicable.

LINCOLN-MERCURY DISTRICT	CODE
Special	00
Boston	11
New York	15
Philadelphia	16
Washington	17
Atlanta	21
Dallas	22
Jacksonville	23
Memphis	26
Buffalo	31
Cincinnati	32
Cleveland	33
Detroit	34
Chicago	41
St. Louis	42
Twin Cities	46
Denver	51
Los Angeles	52
Oakland	53
Seattle	54
Home Office Reserve	84
Export	90's

ENGINE IDENTIFICATION

ENGINE TAG

Since 1964, Lincoln-Mercury engines can be identified by a tag attached to the engine. The tag contains the year and cubic inch displacement.

CASTING NUMBERS

While helpful in identifying Ford engine components, casting numbers are not conclusive in pin-pointing the exact year of manufacture. A better method is to search for the original host vehicle's VIN (Vehicle Identification Number) stamped on the driver's side at the rear of the engine block below the cylinder head.

COMET ENGINES

CID	NO. CYL.	HORSE-POWER	COMP. RATIO	CARB.
200	6	75	8.3:1	1 BC
250	6	72	8.0:1	1 BC
302	8	122	8.0:1	2 BC

MONARCH ENGINES

CID	NO. CYL.	HORSE-POWER	COMP. RATIO	CARB.
200	6	75	8.3:1	1 BC
250	6	72	8.0:1	1 BC
302	8	129	8.0:1	2 BC
351	8	143	8.2:1	2 BC

COUGAR ENGINES

CID	NO. CYL.	HORSE-POWER	COMP. RATIO	CARB.
351	8	148	8.0:1	2 BC
351	8	154	8.2:1	2 BC
400	8	158	8.0:1	2 BC
460	8	216	8.0:1	4 BC

MONTEGO ENGINES

CID	NO. CYL.	HORSE-POWER	COMP. RATIO	CARB.
351	8	154	8.2:1	2 BC
351	8	148	8.0:1	2 BC
400	8	158	8.0:1	2 BC
460	8	216	8.0:1	4 BC
460 P.I.	8	226	8.0:1	4 BC

MERCURY ENGINES

CID	NO. CYL.	HORSE-POWER	COMP. RATIO	CARB.
400	8	158	8.0:1	2 BC
460	8	218	8.0:1	4 BC
460 P.I.	8	226	8.0:1	4 BC

LINCOLN

CID	NO. CYL.	HORSE-POWER	COMP. RATIO	CARB.
460	8	194	8.0:1	4 BC
460	8	206	8.0:1	4 BC

1976 LINCOLN CONTINENTAL TOWN CAR

1976 LINCOLN CONTINENTAL MARK IV

1976 MERCURY COUGAR

1976 MERCURY BOBCAT

1976 LINCOLN CONTINENTAL

1976 MERCURY COLONY PARK STATION WAGON

1976 MERCURY MONTEGO STATION WAGON

1976 MERCURY MONARCH

1976 MERCURY COMET

VEHICLE IDENTIFICATION NUMBER

```
┌─────────────────────────────┐
│ • LINCOLN MERCURY •          │
│     6S63H123456              │
└─────────────────────────────┘
```

Located on a metal tab that is riveted to the instrument panel close to the windshield on the driver's side of the car and is visible from outside.

FIRST DIGIT: Identifies the year (6 = 1976)

SECOND DIGIT: Identifies the assembly plant

ASSEMBLY PLANT	CODE
Atlanta, GA	A
Oakville, Ont., CAN	B
Mahwah, NJ	E
Dearborn, MI	F
Lorain, OH	H
Kansas City, KS	K
San Jose, CA	R
Allen Park (Pilot)	S
Metuchen, NJ	T
Wayne, MI	W
Wixom, MI	Y
St. Louis, MO	Z

THIRD AND FOURTH DIGITS: Identify the body serial code

COMET	CODE
4-Dr. Sedan	30
2-Dr. Sedan Fastback	31

COUGAR	CODE
2-Dr. Hardtop XR-7	93

LINCOLN	CODE
2-Dr. Hardtop	81
4-Dr. Sedan HT	82
2-Dr. Hardtop (Mark IV)	89

MERCURY	CODE
4-Dr. Pillared HT Grand Marquis	60
2-Dr. HT Grand Marquis	61
4-Dr. Pillared HT Marquis Brougham	62
2-Dr. HT Marquis Brougham	64
4-Dr. Pillared HT Marquis	63
2-Dr. HT Marquis	66
4-Dr. Wagon Marquis	74
4-Dr. Wagon Marquis Brougham	76

MONARCH	CODE
4-Dr. Sedan	34
2-Dr. Sedan	35
4-Dr. Sedan Ghia	37
2-Dr. Sedan Ghia	38

MERCURY BOBCAT	CODE
3-Dr. Runabout	20
2-Dr. Villager	22

MONTEGO	CODE
4-Dr. Sedan HT Montego	02
2-Dr. HT Montego	03
4-Dr. Sedan HT Montego MX	04
2-Dr. HT Montego MX	07
4-Dr. Sedan HT Montego Brougham	10
2-Dr. HT Montego Brougham	11
4-Dr. Montego MX SW	08
4-Dr. Villager (Woodgrain) SW	18

FIFTH DIGIT: Identifies the engine code

ENGINE	CODE
V8 460-4V	A
V8 460-4V Police	C
V8 302-2V	F
V8 351-2V	H
I6 250-1V	L
V8 351 Modified	Q
V8 400-2V	S
I6 200-1V	T
I4 139-2V (2.3L)	Y
I6 169-2V (2.8L)	Z

LAST SIX DIGITS: Represent the basic production numbers

EXAMPLE:

6	S	63	H	123456
Model Year	Assy. Plant	Body Serial Code	Engine	Production Sequence Number

VEHICLE CERTIFICATION LABEL

THE VEHICLE CERTIFICATION LABEL (V.C. Label) is affixed on the left front door lock face panel or door pillar. The upper half of the label contains the name of the manufacturer, month and year of manufacture, Gross Vehicle Weight Rating (GVWR), Gross Axle Weight (GAWR), and the certification rating statement. The V.C. label also contains the Vehicle Identification Number (VIN). The remaining information on the V.C. label consists of the following vehicle identification codes: body, color, trim, axle, transmission and DSO codes.

```
┌────────────────────────────────────────┐
│           MANUFACTURED BY               │
│          FORD MOTOR COMPANY             │
│                                         │
│   09/76 THIS VEHICLE CONFORMS TO ALL    │
│    APPLICABLE FEDERAL MOTOR VEHICLE     │
│      SAFETY STANDARDS IN EFFECT ON      │
│   DATE OF MANUFACTURE SHOWN ABOVE       │
│ •                                     • │
│   6S63H123456        PASSENGER          │
│   53H   1C   DA   X   2      34          │
│                                         │
│    NOT FOR TITLE OR REGISTRATION        │
│          MADE IN U.S.A.                  │
└────────────────────────────────────────┘
```

EXAMPLE:

6S63H123456	Vehicle Identification Number (VIN)
53H	Body Type Code (Marquis 4-Dr. Pillared Hardtop)
1C	Body Color Code and Vinyl Roof Type/Color (Black)
DA	Trim Code (Black Leather & Vinyl)
X	Transmission Code (FMX Automatic)
2	Rear Axle Code (2.75:1)
34	District Special Equipment Code (Detroit)

THE BODY CODE is two numerals and a letter identifying the body style.

COMET	CODE
4-Dr. Sedan	54B
2-Dr. Sedan Fastback	62B

* Custom option available
* GT option available

COUGAR	CODE
2-Dr. Hardtop XR-7	65F

LINCOLN

	CODE
2-Dr. Hardtop	60B
4-Dr. Sedan Hardtop	53B
2-Dr. Hardtop (Mark IV)	65D

* Designer Series option available
* Town Car option available
* Town Coupe option available

MERCURY

	CODE
4-Dr. Pillared HT Grand Marquis	53L
2-Dr. HT Grand Marquis	65L
4-Dr. Pillared HT Marquis Brougham	53K
2-Dr. HT Marquis Brougham	65K
4-Dr. Pillared HT Marquis	53H
2-Dr. HT Marquis	65H
4-Dr. SW Marquis	71H
4-Dr. SW Marquis Brougham	71K

MONARCH

	CODE
4-Dr. Sedan	54H
2-Dr. Sedan	66H
4-Dr. Sedan Ghia	54K
2-Dr. Sedan Ghia	66K

MERCURY BOBCAT

	CODE
3-Dr. Runabout	64H
2-Dr. Villager	73H

* MPG option available

MONTEGO

	CODE
4-Dr. Sedan HT Montego	53B
2-Dr. HT Montego	65B
4-Dr. Sedan HT Montego MX	53D
2-Dr. HT Montego MX	65D
4-Dr. Sedan HT Montego Brougham	53K
2-Dr. HT Montego Brougham	65K
4-Dr. Montego MX SW	71D
4-Dr. Villager (Woodgrain) SW	71K

THE COLOR CODE is a number and letter indicating the exterior paint color and vinyl roof type and color (if equipped).

EXTERIOR COLOR

	CODE
Black	1C
Silver Met.	1G
Med. Slate Blue Met.	1H
Brt. Red	2B
Candyapple Red	2E
Dk. Red	2M
Brt. Red	2R
Brt. Red	2U
Med. Blue Met.	3D
Brt. Blue Met.	3E
Brt. Dk. Blue Met.	3G
Lt. Blue	3S
Brt. Med. Blue	3T
Dk. Yellow Green Met.	4Y
Dk. Jade Met.	46
Lt. Green	47
Dk. Green	49
Copper Met.	4B
Med. Chestnut Met.	5M
Dk. Brown Met.	5Q
Saddle Bronze Met.	5T
Tan	5V
Yellow Orange	56
Brt. Yellow	6E
Cream	6P
Dk. Yellow	6R
Chrome Yellow	6S
Tan	6U
Lt. Gold	6W
Lt. Jade	7A

EXTERIOR COLOR

	CODE
Med. Green Gold	7E
Med. Ginger Met.	8B
Dk. Brown	8D
Med. Orange Met.	8E
Tangerine	8F
White	9A
White	9D
Silver Blue Met.	3M
Med. Ivy Bronze Met.	4T
Med. Ivy Bronze Met.	48
Tan Met.	5U
Dk. Ginger Met.	57
Ginger Bronze Met.	58
Med. Dk. Gold Met.	6T
Med. Gold Met.	6V
Dk. Red Met.	2S
Silver Met.	1J
Med. Taupe Met.	2P
Brt. Blue Met.	3P
Silver Blue Met.	3R
Brt. Yellow Gold Met.	6Y
Aqua Blue Met.	45
Ginger Bronze Met.	51
Gold Bronze Met.	54
Med. Chestnut Met.	59
Med. Jade Met.	7F
Rose Met.	2T
Lt. Jade Met.	7B
Lt. Apricot Met.	8A

VINYL ROOF TYPE (First Letter)

	CODE
Cross-Hatch Full 2-Door	B
Cross-Hatch Halo Style 4-Door	C
Levant Full	D
Levant Half	E
Normandie Full	F
Odense Full	G
Odense Three-Quarter	H
Odense Embassy (Basket Handle)	J
Normandie Three-Quarter	K
Normandie Half	L
Odense Half	N
Cross-Hatch Three-Quarter	P
Cross-Hatch Half	R
Levant Three-Quarter	S

VINYL ROOF COLOR (Second Letter)

	CODE
Black	A
Blue	B
Apricot	C
Red	D
Green	G
Rose	H
Taupe	J
Copper	K
Aqua	L
Gold Flare	M
Red Lipstick	N
Silver	P
Jade	R
Silver Blue	S
Brown	T
Tan	U
Cream	V
White	W
Gold	Y
Saddle	Z

THE TRIM CODE consists of a two-letter or a letter-number combination designating the interior trim.

LINCOLN	CODE
Black (2)	DA/EA
Black (2)	HA/KA/BA
Black (3)	JA/LA
Med. Blue (1)	BB/FB
Med. Blue (2)	DB/EB
Med. Blue (2)	HB/KB/BB
Med. Blue (3)	JB/LB/GB
Dk. Red (1)	BD/FD
Dk. Red (2)	DD/ED
Dk. Red (2)	HD/KD/BD
Dk. Red (3)	JD/LD/GD
Red Rose (2)	DH
Blue Diamond (2)	DK
Blue Diamond (4)	CK
Dove Gray (2)	KS
Dove Gray (3)	JS
Jade (1)	BR/FR
Jade (2)	DR/ER
Jade (2)	HR/KR
Jade (3)	JR/GR
Taupe (1)	BJ/FJ
Taupe (2)	DJ/EJ
Taupe (2)	HJ/KJ
Taupe (3)	JJ
Tan (1)	BU/FU
Tan (2)	DU/EU
Tan (2)	HU/KU/BU
Tan (3)	JU/LU/GU
Gold (1)	BY/FY
Gold (2)	DY/EY
Gold (2)	HY/KY/BY
Gold (3)	JY/LY
Gold/Cream (2)	DV
Saddle (2)	BZ
Saddle (3)	LZ
White w/Black (2)	DW/EW
White w/Black (2)	KW/BW
White w/Blue (2)	DQ/EQ
White w/Blue (2)	KQ/BQ
White w/Red (2)	DN/EN
White w/Red (2)	KN/BN/DN
White w/Jade (2)	D5/E5
White w/Jade (2)	K5/B5
White w/Taupe (2)	D3/E3/K3
White w/Tan (2)	D4/E4/K4
White w/Gold (2)	D8/K8/B8
White w/Saddle (2)	B9/D9

1 - Cloth & vinyl
2 - Leather & vinyl
3 - Velour
4 - Velour & vinyl

MONTEGO	CODE
Black (1)	AA/CA
Black (1)	GA/KA
Black (2)	BA/DA
Black (2)	HA/LA
Med. Blue (1)	AB/CB
Med. Blue (1)	GB/KB/PB
Med. Blue (2)	BB/DB
Med. Blue (2)	HB/LB/EB
Green (1)	CG/GG
Green (1)	KG/PG
Green (2)	DG/HG
Green (2)	LG/EG
Tan (1)	PU
Tan (2)	DU/HU/EU
Saddle (1)	AZ/CZ
Saddle (1)	GZ/KZ
Saddle (2)	BZ/DZ
Saddle (2)	HZ/LZ/EZ

MONTEGO	CODE
White w/Black (2)	DW/HW/LW
White w/Blue (2)	DQ/HQ/LQ
White w/Green (2)	D5/H5/L5
White w/Saddle (2)	D9/H9/L9

1 - Cloth & vinyl
2 - Vinyl

COUGAR	CODE
Black (2)	EA/AA/BA
Black (3)	DA
Med. Blue (1)	CB
Med. Blue (2)	EB/AB/BB
Med. Blue (3)	DB
Dk. Red (1)	CD
Dk. Red (2)	ED/AD/BD
Dk. Red (3)	DD
Green (1)	CG
Green (2)	EG/AG/BG
Green (3)	DG
Gold (1)	CY
Cream/Gold (2)	AV/BV
Cream/Gold (3)	DV
Saddle/Tan (1)	CU
Saddle/Tan (2)	AU/BU
Saddle/Tan (3)	DU
White w/Black (2)	AW/BW
White w/Black (3)	DW
White w/Blue (2)	AQ/BQ
White w/Blue (3)	DQ
White w/Red (2)	AN/BN
White w/Red (3)	DN
White w/Green (2)	A5/B5
White w/Green (3)	D5
White w/Gold (2)	A8/B8
White w/Gold (3)	D8
White w/Saddle (2)	A9/B9
White w/Saddle (3)	D9

1 - Velour & vinyl
2 - Vinyl
3 - Leather & vinyl

MONARCH	CODE
Black (2)	AA/EA
Black (2)	CA/GA
Dk. Red (1)	HD/DD
Dk. Red (1)	BD/ND
Dk. Red (2)	JD/AD
Dk. Red (2)	ED/CD/GD
Dk. Red (3)	FD/LD/MD
Silver Blue (1)	HE/DE/BE
Silver Blue (2)	JE/AE
Silver Blue (2)	EE/CE/GE
Silver Blue (3)	FE/LE
Tan (1)	HU/DU/BU
Tan (2)	JU/AU
Tan (2)	EU/CU/GU
Tan (3)	FU/LU
White w/Black (2)	AW/EW
White w/Black (2)	CW/GW
White w/Black (3)	FW/LW
White w/Dk. Red (2)	AN/EN
White w/Dk. Red (2)	CN/GN
White w/Dk. Red (3)	FN/LN
White w/Silver Blue (2)	A7/E7
White w/Silver Blue (2)	C7/G7
White w/Silver Blue (3)	F7/L7
White w/Tan (2)	A4/E4
White w/Tan (2)	C4/G4
White w/Tan (3)	F4/L4
White w/Tobacco (3)	M9

1 - Cloth & vinyl
2 - Vinyl
3 - Leather & vinyl

COMET

	CODE
Black (1)	JA
Black (2)	KA/LA
Med. Blue (1)	JB/RB/QB
Med. Blue (2)	KB/LB/PB
Lt. Green (1)	JG
Lt. Green (2)	KG
Tan (1)	JU/RU/QU
Tan (2)	KU/LU/PU

1 - Cloth & vinyl
2 - Vinyl

BOBCAT

	CODE
Black (1)	GA
Black (2)	AA/HA
Med. Blue (1)	GB/DB
Med. Blue (2)	AB/HB
Lt. Green (1)	GG/DG
Lt. Green (2)	AG/HG
Tan (1)	GU/DU
Tan (2)	AU/HU
Bright Red (1)	DD
Bright Red (2)	HD

1 - Cloth & vinyl
2 - Vinyl

THE AXLE CODE is a number or letter indicating the rear axle ratio and standard or locking type axles.

CONVENTIONAL	LOCKING	RATIO
2	K	2.75:1
4		3.40:1
6	O	3.00:1
9	R	3.25:1
5		3.07:1
3		2.79:1

THE TRANSMISSION CODE is a number or letter indicating the type of transmission.

TYPE	CODE
3-Speed Manual	1
4-Speed Manual	5
XP Automatic (C-3)	V
XP Automatic (C-4)	W
FMX Automatic	X
XPL Automatic (C-6)	U
XPL Automatic (Special)	Z

THE DSO CODE, consisting of two numbers, designates the district in which the car was ordered and may appear in conjunction with a Domestic Special Order or Foreign Special Order number when applicable.

LINCOLN-MERCURY DISTRICT	CODE
Special	00
Boston	11
New York	15
Philadelphia	16
Washington	17
Atlanta	21
Dallas	22
Jacksonville	23
Memphis	26
Buffalo	31
Cincinnati	32
Cleveland	33
Detroit	34
Chicago	41
St. Louis	42
Twin Cities	46
Denver	51

LINCOLN-MERCURY DISTRICT	CODE
Los Angeles	52
Oakland	53
Seattle	54
Home Office Reserve	84
Export	90's

ENGINE IDENTIFICATION

ENGINE TAG

Since 1964, Lincoln-Mercury engines can be identified by a tag attached to the engine. The tag contains the year and cubic inch displacement.

CASTING NUMBERS

While helpful in identifying Lincoln-Mercury engines components, casting numbers are not conclusive in pin-pointing the exact year of manufacture. A better method is to search for the original host vehicle's VIN (Vehicle Identification Number) stamped on the driver's side at the rear of the engine block below the cylinder head.

BOBCAT ENGINES

CID	NO. CYL.	HORSE-POWER	COMP. RATIO	CARB
140	4	92	9.0:1	2 BC
170	6	100	8.7:1	2 BC

COMET ENGINES

CID	NO. CYL.	HORSE-POWER	COMP. RATIO	CARB
200	6	81	8.3:1	1 BC
250	6	90	8.0:1	1 BC
302	8	138	8.0:1	2 BC

MONARCH ENGINES

CID	NO. CYL.	HORSE-POWER	COMP. RATIO	CARB
200	6	81	8.3:1	1 BC
250	6	90	8.0:1	1 BC
302	8	134	8.0:1	2 BC
351	8	152	8.0:1	2 BC

MONTEGO ENGINES

CID	NO. CYL.	HORSE-POWER	COMP. RATIO	CARB
351	8	154	8.1:1	2 BC
351	8	152	8.0:1	2 BC
400	8	180	8.0:1	2 BC
460	8	202	8.0:1	4 BC

COUGAR ENGINES

CID	NO. CYL.	HORSE-POWER	COMP. RATIO	CARB
351	8	152	8.0:1	2 BC
351	8	154	8.0:1	2 BC
400	8	180	8.0:1	2 BC
460	8	202	8.0:1	4 BC

MERCURY ENGINES

CID	NO. CYL.	HORSE-POWER	COMP. RATIO	CARB
400	8	180	8.0:1	2 BC
460	8	202	8.0:1	4 BC

LINCOLN ENGINES

CID	NO. CYL.	HORSE-POWER	COMP. RATIO	CARB
460	8	202	8.0:1	4 BC

1977 MERCURY MARQUIS

1977 MERCURY BOBCAT

1977 LINCOLN CONTINENTAL MARK V

1977 MERCURY COUGAR STATION WAGON

1977 MERCURY COMET

1977 LINCOLN CONTINENTAL

1977 MERCURY COUGAR XR-7

1977 MERCURY COUGAR

1977 MERCURY MONARCH

VEHICLE IDENTIFICATION NUMBER

```
• LINCOLN MERCURY •
    7S63H123456
```

Located on a metal tab that is riveted to the instrument panel close to the windshield on the driver's side of the car and is visible from outside.

FIRST DIGIT: Identifies the year (7 = 1977)

SECOND DIGIT: Identifies the assembly plant

ASSEMBLY PLANT	CODE
Atlanta, GA	A
Oakville, Ont., CAN	B
Mahwah, NJ	E
Lorain, OH	H
Kansas City, KS	K
San Jose, CA	R
Allen Park (Pilot)	S
Metuchen, NJ	T
Wayne, MI	W
Wixom, MI	Y
St. Louis, MO	Z

THIRD AND FOURTH DIGITS: Identify the body serial code

BOBCAT	CODE
3-Dr. Sedan	20
Wagon	22

COMET	CODE
4-Dr. Sedan	30
2-Dr. Sedan	31

MONARCH	CODE
4-Dr. Sedan	34
2-Dr. Sedan	35
4-Dr. Sedan Ghia	37
2-Dr. Sedan Ghia	38

COUGAR	CODE
4-Dr. Pillared HT Cougar	90
2-Dr. HT Cougar	91
Cougar Wagon	92
2-Dr. HT Cougar XR	93
4-Dr. Pillared HT Cougar Brougham	94
2-Dr. HT Cougar Brougham	95
Cougar Villager Wagon	96

MERCURY	CODE
4-Dr. Pillared HT Grand Marquis	60
2-Dr. HT Grand Marquis	61
4-Dr. Pillared HT Marquis Brougham	62
4-Dr. Pillared HT Marquis	63
2-Dr. HT Marquis Brougham	64
2-Dr. HT Marquis	66
Marquis Wagon*	76

*Also Colony Park and Decor Option

LINCOLN	CODE
2-Dr. Pillared Hardtop	81
4-Dr. Pillared Hardtop	82
4-Dr. Sedan (Versailles)	84
2-Dr. Hardtop (Mark V)	89

FIFTH DIGIT: Identifies the engine code

ENGINE	CODE
V8 460-4V	A
V8 460-4V Police	C
V8 302-2V	F
V8 351-2V	H
V6 250-1V	L
V8 400-2V	S
V6 200-1V	T
V4 139-2V (2.3L)	Y
V6 169-2V (2.8L)	Z
V8 351 Modified	Q

LAST SIX DIGITS: Represent the basic production numbers

EXAMPLE:

7	S	63	H	123456
Model Year	Assy. Plant	Body Serial Code	Engine	Production Sequence Number

VEHICLE CERTIFICATION LABEL

THE VEHICLE CERTIFICATION LABEL (V.C. Label) is affixed on the left front door lock face panel or door pillar. The upper half of the label contains the name of the manufacturer, month and year of manufacture, Gross Vehicle Weight Rating (GVWR), Gross Axle Weight (GAWR), and the certification rating statement. The V.C. label also contains the Vehicle Identification Number (VIN). The remaining information on the V.C. Label consists of the following vehicle identification codes: body, color, trim, transmission, axle and DSO codes.

```
MANUFACTURED BY
FORD MOTOR COMPANY

09/77 THIS VEHICLE CONFORMS TO ALL
APPLICABLE FEDERAL MOTOR VEHICLE
SAFETY STANDARDS IN EFFECT ON
DATE OF MANUFACTURE SHOWN ABOVE

7S63H123456       PASSENGER
53H    1C    MS    X    6    34

NOT FOR TITLE OR REGISTRATION
MADE IN U.S.A.
```

EXAMPLE:
7S63H123456	Vehicle Identification Number (VIN)
53H	Body Serial Code (Marquis 4-Dr. Pillared Hardtop)
1C	Body Color Code and Vinyl Roof Type/Color (Black)
MS	Trim Code (Dove Gray Cloth)
X	Transmission Code (FMX Automatic)
6	Rear Axle Code (3.00:1)
34	District Special Equipment Code (Detroit)

THE BODY CODE is two numerals and a letter identifying the body style.

BOBCAT	CODE
3-Dr. Sedan	64H
Wagon 73H	

* S option available
* Villager option available

COMET	CODE
4-Dr. Sedan	54B
2-Dr. Sedan	62B
* Custom option available	

MONARCH	CODE
4-Dr. Sedan	54H
2-Dr. Sedan	66H
4-Dr. Sedan Ghia	54K
2-Dr. Sedan Ghia	66K
* Grand Touring Sedan option available	
* S option available	

COUGAR	CODE
4-Dr. Pillared HT Cougar	53D
2-Dr. HT Cougar	65D
Cougar Wagon	71D
2-Dr. HT Cougar XR	65L
4-Dr. Pillared HT Cougar Brougham	53K
2-Dr. HT Cougar Brougham	65K
Cougar Villager Wagon	71K

MERCURY	CODE
4-Dr. Pillared HT Grand Marquis	53L
2-Dr. HT Grand Marquis	65L
4-Dr. Pillared HT Marquis Brougham	53K
4-Dr. Pillared HT Marquis	53H
2-Dr. HT Marquis Brougham	65K
2-Dr. HT Marquis	65H
Marquis Wagon	71K
* Colony Park option available	

LINCOLN	CODE
2-Dr. Pillared HT	60B
4-Dr. Pillared HT	53B
4-Dr. Sedan (Versailles)	54M
2-Dr. Hardtop (Mark V)	65D
* Town Coupe option available	
* Town Car option available	
* Designer Series option available	
* Williamsburg option available	

THE COLOR CODE is a number and letter indicating the exterior paint color and vinyl roof type and color (if equipped).

EXTERIOR COLOR	CODE
Black	1C
Silver Met.	1G
Dove Gray	1N
Med. Gray Met. (Tie Tone only)	1P
Med. Silver Met.	1Q
Dark Red	2M
Brt. Red	2R
Lipstick Red	2U
Brt. Dk. Blue Met.	3G
Lt. Blue	3U
Midnight Blue	31
Med. Blue	34
Dk. Jade Met.	46
Lt. Green	47
Dk. Yellow Green Met.	4V
Dk. Brown Met.	5Q
Brt. Yellow	6E
Cream	6P
Lt. Tan	6U
Lt. Aqua Met.	7Q
Dk. Emerald Met.	7S
Vista Orange	8G
Tan	8H
Brt. Saddle Met.	8K
Dk. Cordovan Met.	8N
Lt. Cordovan	8P
Champagne Met.	8Y
Chamois	83

EXTERIOR COLOR	CODE
Dk. Cordovan	84
White	9D
Rose Met.	2Y
Brt. Blue Met.	3V
Tan Met.	6V
Med. Gold Met.	6V
Brt. Aqua Met.	7H
Lt. Jade Met.	7L
Med. Emerald Met.	7T
Med. Tan Met.	8J
Chamois Met.	8W
Dk. Red Met.	2S
Med. Red Met.	2G
Med. Blue Met.	32
Med. Ember Met.	8V
Med. Nectarine Met.	8Z
Lt. Silver Met.	1R
Silver Met.	1J
Black Met.	1L
Rose Met.	2T
Brt. Yellow Gold Met.	6Y
Crystal Jade Met.	7B

VINYL TYPE (First Letter)	CODE
Cross-Hatch Full 2-Dr.	B
Cross-Hatch Halo Style 4-Dr.	C
Odense Full	G
Odense Three-Quarter	H
Cayman Coach	J
Odense Half	N
Cross Hatch Three-Quarter	P
Cayman Full	Q
Cross Hatch Half	R
Valino Coach	T
Cayman Half	U
Valino Full	V
Lugano Full	W
Lugano Half	X
Valino Half	Y

VINYL COLOR (Second Letter)	CODE
Black	A
Blue	B
Ember	C
Red	D
Rose	H
Taupe	J
Aqua	L
Lt. Jade	M
Lipstick Red	N
Silver	P
Dk. Emerald	Q
Dk. Jade	R
Med. Blue	S
Brown	T
Chamois	U
Cream	V
White	W
Gold	Y

THE TRIM CODE consists of a two-letter or a letter-number combination designating the interior trim.

LINCOLN	CODE
Black (1)	BA/FA
Black (2)	DA/EA
Black (2)	HA/KA/BA
Black (3)	JA/AA
Red (1)	BD/FD
Red (2)	DD/ED
Red (2)	HD/KD/BD
Red (3)	JD/AD/GD
Blue (1)	BB/FB
Blue (2)	DB/EB

LINCOLN

	CODE
Blue (2)	HB/KB/BB
Blue (3)	JB/AB/GB
Jade (1)	BR/FR
Jade (2)	DR/ER
Jade (2)	HR/KR/BR
Jade (3)	JR/AR/GR
Gold (1)	BY/FY
Gold (2)	DY/EY
Gold (2)	HY/KY/BY
Gold (3)	JY/AY
Cordovan (1)	BF/FF
Cordovan (2)	DF/EF
Cordovan (2)	HF/KF/BF
Cordovan (3)	JF/AF/CF
Chamois (1)	BT/FT
Chamois (2)	DT/ET
Chamois (2)	HT/KT/BT
Chamois (3)	JT/AT
Dove Gray (2)	KS
Dove Gray (2)	JS/FS
Red/Rose (2)	DH
Lt. Jade/Jade (2)	DR
Gold/Cream (2)	DV
Gold/Cream (3)	CY
Blue/Cream (2)	EB
White w/Black (2)	DW/EW
White w/Black (2)	KW/BW
White w/Red (2)	DN/EN
White w/Red (2)	KN/BN
White w/Blue (2)	DQ/EQ
White w/Blue (2)	KQ/BQ
White w/Jade (2)	D5/E5
White w/Jade (2)	K5/B5
White w/Gold (2)	D8/E8
White w/Gold (2)	K8/B8
White w/Cordovan (2)	D6/E6/LF
White w/Cordovan (2)	MF/K6/B6
White w/Chamois (2)	D2/E2
White w/Chamois (2)	K2/B2

1 - Cloth
2 - Leather & vinyl
3 - Velour

COMET

	CODE
Black (1)	BA/JA
Black (2)	HA/SA
Black 92)	KA/LA
Med. Blue (1)	BB/TB
Med. Blue (1)	JB/RB/QB
Med. Blue (2)	HB/SB
Med. Blue (2)	KB/LB/PB
Bright Red (1)	BD
Bright Red (2)	HD/SD
Bright Red (2)	KD/LD
Tan (1)	BU/TU
Tan (1)	JU/RU/QU
Tan (2)	HU/SU
Tan (2)	KU/LU/PU
Lt. Green (1)	BG/TG
Lt. Green (1)	JG/RG/QG
Lt. Green (2)	HG/KG

1 - Cloth
2 - Vinyl

COUGAR

	CODE
Dove Gray (1)	AS/CS
Dove Gray (1)	GS/TS/VS
Dove Gray (2)	BS/DS/FS
Dove Gray (2)	SS/HS/YS
Dove Gray (2)	US/WS/ZS
Dove Gray (3)	ES
Dk. Red (1)	AD/CD/GD
Dk. Red (1)	RD/TD/VD
Dk. Red (2)	BD/DD/FD
Dk. Red (3)	SD/HD/YD

COUGAR

	CODE
Dk. Red (3)	UD/WD/ZD
Dk. Red (3)	ED
Dk. Red (4)	LD
Med. Blue (1)	AB/CB/GB
Med. Blue (1)	TB/TB/VB
Med. Blue (2)	BB/DB/FB
Med. Blue (2)	SB/HB/YB
Med. Blue (2)	UB/WB/ZB
Med. Blue (3)	EB
Med. Blue (4)	LB
Jade (1)	AR/CR/GR
Jade (1)	RR/TR/VR
Jade (2)	BR/DR/FR
Jade (2)	SR/HR/YR
Jade (2)	UR/WR/ZR
Jade (3)	ER
Jade (4)	LR
Chamois (1)	AT/CT/GT
Chamois (1)	RT/TT/VT
Chamois (2)	BT/DT/FT
Chamois (2)	ST/HT/YT
Chamois (2)	UT/WT/ZT
Chamois (3)	ET
Saddle (1)	AZ/CZ/GZ
Saddle (1)	RZ/TZ/VZ
Saddle (2)	BZ/DZ/FZ
Saddle (2)	SZ/HZ/YZ
Saddle (2)	UZ/WZ/ZZ
Saddle (3)	EZ
Saddle (4)	LZ
Saddle/White (2)	D3/F3
Saddle/White (2)	Y3/W3/Z3
Saddle/White (3)	E3
White Chamois (1)	N2/P2
White Chamois (3)	E2
White Lipstick (2)	BL/DL/FL
White Lipstick (3)	EL
White/Red (2)	BN/DN/FN
White/Red (3)	EN
White/Blue (2)	BQ/DQ/FQ
White/Blue (3)	EQ
White/Jade (2)	B5/D5/F5
White/Jade (3)	E5
White/Chamois (2)	B2/D2/F2
White/Chamois (3)	E2
White/Saddle (2)	B9/D9/F9
White/Saddle (3)	E9

1 - Cloth & vinyl
2 - Vinyl
3 - Leather
4 - Cloth

MERCURY

	CODE
Dove Gray (1)	MS/NS
Dove Gray (2)	VS
Dove Gray (3)	JS
Dove Gray (4)	FS
Dk. Red (1)	LD/RD/MD
Dk. Red (2)	HD/VD
Dk. Red (2)	HD/SD/VD
Dk. Red (3)	JD
Dk. Red (4)	FD
Med. Blue (1)	LB/RB/MB
Med. Blue (2)	HB/VB
Med. Blue (2)	HB/SB/VB
Med. Blue (3)	JB
Med. Blue (4)	FB
Jade (1)	LR/RR/MR
Jade (2)	HR/VR
Jade (2)	HR/VR
Jade (3)	JR
Lt. Jade/Jade (2)	VR/SR
Lt. Jade/Jade (4)	FR
Gold (1)	RY/MY/HY
Gold (2)	HY

10 - 39

MERCURY

	CODE
Gold (3)	JY
Cream/Gold (2)	VV/SV/VV
Cream/Gold (4)	FV
Saddle (1)	LZ/RZ/MZ
Saddle (2)	HZ/SZ/VZ
Saddle (3)	JZ
Saddle (4)	FZ
Saddle/White (4)	F3

1 - Cloth
2 - Vinyl
3 - Velour & leather
4 - Leather

MONARCH

	CODE
Dove Gray (2)	ES/AS
Dove Gray (2)	GS/CS/BS
Dove Gray (3)	FS/TS/US
Dove Gray (4)	SS/VS
Cream (2)	JV/EV
Cream (2)	AV/KV/MV
Cream (2)	PV/GV/CV
Cream (3)	FV
Dk. Red (1)	WD/HD
Dk. Red (1)	LD/BD
Dk. Red (2)	JD/ED
Dk. Red (2)	AD/KD/MD
Dk. Red (2)	PD/GD/CD
Dk. Red (3)	FD
Med. Blue (1)	WB/HB
Med. Blue (1)	LB/BB
Med. Blue (2)	JB/EB
Med. Blue (2)	AB/KB
Med. Blue (2)	MB/GB/CB
Med. Blue (3)	FB/TB/UB
Blue (4)	SB/VB
Jade (1)	HR/BR
Jade (2)	ER/AR
Jade (2)	GR/CR
Jade (3)	FR
Tan (1)	WU/HU
Tan (1)	LU/BU
Tan (2)	JU/EU
Tan (2)	AU/KU/MU
Tan (2)	PU/GU/CU
Tan (3)	FU
Chamois (3)	UT/TT
Chamois (4)	ST/VT
Cordovan (3)	TF/UF
Cordovan (4)	SF/VF
White/Blue (3)	TQ/UQ
White/Chamois (3)	T2/U2
White/Cordovan (3)	T6

1 - Cloth
2 - Vinyl
3 - Leather
4 - Cloth & vinyl

BOBCAT

	CODE
Black (1)	GA
Black (2)	AA/HA
Bright Red (1)	GD
Bright Red (2)	AD/HD
Bright Red (3)	DD
Med. Blue (1)	GB
Med. Blue (2)	AB/HB
Med. Blue (3)	DB
Lt. Green (1)	GG
Lt. Green (2)	AG/HG
Lt. Green (3)	DG
Chamois (1)	GT
Chamois (2)	AT/HT
Chamois (3)	DT

1 - Cloth & vinyl
2 - Vinyl
3 - Cloth

COMET

	CODE
Black (1)	BA/JA
Black (2)	HA/KA
Black (2)	SA/LA
Blue (1)	BB/JB
Blue (1)	TB/RB/QB
Blue (2)	HB/KB
Blue (2)	SB/LB/PB
Brt. Red (1)	BD
Brt. Red (2)	HD/KD
Brt. Red (2)	SD/LD
Lt. Green (1)	BG/JG
Lt. Green (1)	TG/RG/QG
Lt. Green (2)	HG/KG
Tan (1)	BU/JU
Tan (1)	TU/RU/QU
Tan (2)	HU/KU
Tan (2)	SU/LU/PU

1 - Cloth
2 - Vinyl

THE TRANSMISSION CODE is a number or letter indicating the type of transmission.

TYPE	CODE
3-Speed Manual	1
4-Speed Manual	6
4-Speed Manaul	7
XP Automatic (C-3)	V
XP Automatic (C-4)	W
FMX Automatic	X
XPL Automatic (C-6)	U
XPL Automatic (Special)	Z
Jatco Automatic	S

THE AXLE CODE is a number or letter indicating the rear axle ratio and standard or locking type axles.

CONVENTIONAL	LOCKING	RATIO
B		2.47:1
1	J	2.50:1
8		2.73:1
2		2.75:1
3		2.79:1
6	O	3.00:1
4		3.18:1
7		3.40:1

THE DSO CODE, consisting of two numbers, designates the district in which the car was ordered and may appear in conjunction with a Domestic Special Order or Foreign Special Order number when applicable.

LINCOLN-MERCURY

DISTRICT	CODE
Special	00
Boston	11
New York	15
Philadelphia	16
Washington	17
Atlanta	21
Dallas	22
Jacksonville	23
Memphis	26
Buffalo	31
Cincinnati	32
Cleveland	33
Detroit	34
Chicago	41
St. Louis	42
Twin Cities	46
Denver	51
Los Angeles	52
Oakland	53
Seattle	54
Home Office Reserve	84
Export	90's

ENGINE IDENTIFICATION

ENGINE TAG
Since 1964, Lincoln-Mercury engines can be identified by a tag attached to the engine. The tag contains the year and cubic inch displacement.

CASTING NUMBERS
While helpful in identifying Lincoln-Mercury engine components, casting numbers are not conclusive in pin-pointing the exact year of manufacture. A better method is to search for the original host vehicle's VIN (Vehicle Identification Number) stamped on the driver's side at the rear of the engine block below the cylinder head.

BOBCAT ENGINES
CID	NO. CYL.	HORSE-POWER	COMP. RATIO	CARB.
140	4	89	9.0:1	2 BC
171	6	93	8.7:1	2 BC
171	6	90	8.7:1	2 BC

COMET ENGINES
CID	NO. CYL.	HORSE-POWER	COMP. RATIO	CARB.
200	6	96	8.5:1	1 BC
250	6	98	8.1:1	1 BC
302	8	137	8.4:1	2 BC

MONARCH ENGINES
CID	NO. CYL.	HORSE-POWER	COMP. RATIO	CARB.
200	6	96	8.5:1	1 BC
250	6	98	8.1:1	1 BC
302	8	122	8.4:1	2 BC
302	8	134	8.4:1	2 BC
351	8	135	8.3:'	2 BC

COUGAR ENGINES
CID	NO. CYL.	HORSE-POWER	COMP. RATIO	CARB.
302	8	130	8.4:1	2 BC
351	8	161	8.0:1	2 BC
351	8	149	8.3:1	2 BC
400	8	173	8.0:1	2 BC

MERCURY ENGINES
CID	NO. CYL.	HORSE-POWER	COMP. RATIO	CARB.
400	8	173	8.0:1	2 BC
460	8	197	8.0:1	4 BC
460 P.I.	8	226	—	4 BC

LINCOLN ENGINES
CID	NO. CYL.	HORSE-POWER	COMP. RATIO	CARB.
400	8	179	8.0:1	2 BC
460	8	208	8.0:1	4 BC

1978 LINCOLN CONTINENTAL

1978 MERCURY BOBCAT

1978 LINCOLN CONTINENTAL MARK V

1978 MERCURY BOBCAT WAGON

1978 LINCOLN VERSAILLES

1978 MERCURY COUGAR

1978 MERCURY ZEPHYR

1978 MERCURY MARQUIS

1978 MERCURY ZEPHYR WAGON

1978 MERCURY MONARCH

VEHICLE IDENTIFICATION NUMBER

• LINCOLN MERCURY •
8W93H123456

Located on a metal tab that is riveted to the instrument panel close to the windshield on the driver's side of the car and is visible from outside.

FIRST DIGIT: Identifies the year (8 = 1978)

SECOND DIGIT: Identifies the assembly plant

ASSEMBLY PLANT	CODE
Atlanta, GA	A
Lorain, OH	H
Kansas City, KS	K
San Jose, CA	R
Metuchen, NJ	T
Wayne, MI	W
St. Thomas, Ont., CAN	X
Wixom, MI	Y
St. Louis, MO	Z

THIRD AND FOURTH DIGITS: Identify the body serial code

BOBCAT	CODE
3-Dr. Sedan	20
Wagon	22

MONARCH	CODE
4-Dr. Sedan	34
2-Dr. Sedan	33

COUGAR	CODE
4-Dr. Pillared HT Cougar	92
2-Dr. HT Cougar	91
2-Dr. HT Cougar XR-7	93

MERCURY	CODE
4-Dr. Pillared HT Marquis	62
2-Dr. HT Marquis	61
4-Dr. Pillared HT Grand Marquis	66
2-Dr. HT Grand Marquis	65
4-Dr. Pillared HT Marquis Brougham	64
2-Dr. HT Marquis Brougham	63
Marquis Wagon	63

CONTINENTAL MARK V	CODE
2-Dr. Hardtop	89

LINCOLN	CODE
2-Dr. Pillared Hardtop	81
4-Dr. Pillared Hardtop	82
4-Dr. Sedan (Versailles)	84
2-Dr. Hardtop (Mark V)	89

ZEPHYR	CODE
4-Dr. Sedan	32
2-Dr. Sedan	31
2-Dr. Sedan Sport Coupe	35
Station Wagon	36

FIFTH DIGIT: Identifies the engine code

ENGINE	CODE
V8 460—4V (7.5L)	A
V8 460-4V Police Interceptor (7.5L)	C
V8 302-2V (5.0L)	F
V8 351-2V (5.8L)	H
V6 250-1V (4.1L)	L
V8 351 Modified	Q
V8 400-2V (6.6L)	S
V6 200-1V (3.3L)	T
V4 139-2V (2.3L)	Y
V6 169-2V (2.8L)	Z

LAST SIX DIGITS: Represent the basic production numbers

EXAMPLE:

8	W	93	H	123456
Model Year	Assy. Plant	Body Serial Code	Engine	Production Sequence Number

VEHICLE CERTIFICATION LABEL

THE VEHICLE CERTIFICATION LABEL (V.C. Label) is affixed on the left front door lock face panel or door pillar. The upper half of the label contains the name of the manufacturer, month and year of manufacture, Gross Vehicle Weight Rating (GVWR), Gross Axle Weight rating (GAWR), and the certification statement. The V.C. label also contains the Vehicle Identification Number (VIN). The remaining information on the V.C. Label consists of the following vehicle identification codes: body, color, trim, transmission, axle and DSO codes.

MANUFACTURED BY
FORD MOTOR COMPANY

09/78 THIS VEHICLE CONFORMS TO ALL APPLICABLE FEDERAL MOTOR VEHICLE SAFETY STANDARDS IN EFFECT ON DATE OF MANUFACTURE SHOWN ABOVE

8W93H123456　　　PASSENGER
65L　1C　RE　X　6　　34

NOT FOR TITLE OR REGISTRATION
MADE IN U.S.A.

EXAMPLE:

8W93H123456	Vehicle Identification Number (VIN)
65L	Body Serial Code (XR-7 2-Dr. Hardtop)
1C	Body Color Code and Vinyl Roof Type/Color (Black)
RE	Trim Code (Russet Cloth & Vinyl)
X	Transmission Code (FMX Automatic)
6	Rear Axle Code (3.00:1)
34	District Special Equipment Code (Detroit)

THE BODY CODE is two numerals and a letter identifying the body style.

BOBCAT	CODE
3-Dr. Sedan	64H
Station Wagon	73H

* Villager option available
* Sport option available

MONARCH	CODE
4-Dr. Sedan	54H
2-Dr. Sedan	66H

* ES option available
* ESS option available
* Anniversary Edition option available

COUGAR	CODE
4-Dr. Pillared HT Cougar	53D
2-Dr. Hardtop Cougar	65D
2-Dr. Hardtop Cougar XR-7	65L

* Brougham option available

MERCURY	CODE
4-Dr. Pillared HT Marquis	53H
2-Dr. Hardtop Marquis	65H
4-Dr. Pillared HT Grand Marquis	53L
2-Dr. HT Grand Marquis	65L
4-Dr. Pillared HT Marquis Brougham	53K
2-Dr. HT Marquis Brougham	65K
Marquis Wagon	71K

* Colony Park Wagon option available
* Anniversary Edition option available

LINCOLN	CODE
2-Dr. Pillared Hardtop	60B
4-Dr. Pillared Hardtop	53B
4-Dr. Sedan (Versailles)	54M
2-Dr. Hardtop (Mark V)	65D

* Diamond Jubilee option available
* Designer Series option available
* Town Car option available
* Town Coupe option available

ZEPHYR	CODE
4-Dr. Sedan	54D
2-Dr. Sedan	66D
2-Dr. Sedan Sport Coupe	36R
Station Wagon	74D

* Villager option available

THE COLOR CODE is a number and letter indicating the exterior paint color and vinyl roof type and color (if equipped).

EXTERIOR PAINT COLOR	CODE
Black	1C
Silver Met.	1G
Dove Gray	1N
Med. Gray Met. (Tie Tone only)	1P
Med. Silver Met.	1Q
Dark Red	2M
Brt. Red	2R
Lipstick Red	2U
Brt. Dk. Blue Met.	3G
Lt. Blue	3U
Midnight Blue	31
Med. Blue	34
Dk. Jade Met.	46
Lt. Green	47
Dk. Yellow Green Met.	4V
Dk. Brown Met.	4Q
Brt. Yellow	6E
Cream	6P
Lt. Tan	6U
Lt. Aqua Met.	7Q
Dk. Emerald Met.	7S
Vista Orange	8G
Tan	8H
Brt. Saddle Met.	8K
Dk. Cordovan Met.	8N
Lt. Cordovan	8P
Champagne Met.	8Y
Chamois	83

EXTERIOR PAINT COLOR	CODE
Dk. Cordovan	84
White	(D
Rose Met.	2Y
Brt. Blue Met.	3V
Tan Met.	6V
Med. Gold Met.	6V
Brt. Aqua Met.	7H
Lt. Jade Met.	7L
Med. Emerald Met.	7T
Med. Tan Met.	8J
Chamois Met.	8W
Dk. Red Met.	2S
Med. Red Met.	2G
Med. Blue Met.	32
Med. Ember Met.	8V
Med. Nectarine Met.	8Z
Lt. Silver Met.	1R
Dk. Red Met.	2S
Med. Red Met.	2G
Med. Blue Met.	32
Med. Ember Met.	8V
Med. Nectarine Met.	8Z
Lt. Silver Met.	1R
Silver Met.	1J
Black Met.	1L
Rose Met.	2T
Brt. Yellow Gold Met.	6Y
Crystal Jade Met.	7B

VINYL TYPE (First Letter)	CODE
Lugano Full	W
Lugano Half	X
Lugano Front Half	K
Lugano Coach	M
Milano Full	D
Milano Half	E
Milano Halo	F
Cayman Full	Q
Cayman Half	U
Valino Full	V
Valino Half	Y
Valino Front Half	Z
Valino Coach	T
Cross-Hatch Full	B
Cross-Hatch Half	R
Levant Full	S
Levant Half Rear	E
Odense Full	G
Odense Half	N
Odense Front Half	A

VINYL COLOR (Second Letter)	CODE
Black	A
Medium Blue	B
Midnight Blue	S
Wedgewood Blue	5
Dark Brown	T
Lt. Camel	V
Medium Camel	Y
Chamois	U
Light Champagne	6
Midnight Champagne	J
Cordovan	F
Light Cordovan	K
Galveston Gold	K
Dove Gray	E
Dark Jade	R
Light Jade	M
Medium Jade	4
Wedgewood Jade	3
Red/Russet	D
Silver	P
White	W

THE TRIM CODE consists of a two-letter or a letter-number combination designating the interior trim.

CONTINENTAL	CODE
Black (2)	BA/DA
Black (2)	EA/KA
Black (3)	AA/JA
Dk. Red (1)	SD
Dk. Red (2)	BD/BD
Dk. Red (2)	TD/ED/KD
Dk. Red (3)	AD/CD
Dk. Red (3)	JD/UD/DD
Wedgewood Blue (1)	KB/SB/BB
Wedgewood Blue (2)	BB/DB
Wedgewood Blue (2)	TB/UB
Wedgewood Blue (2)	DB/EB/KB
Wedgewood Blue (3)	AB/CB/JB
Red/Rose (2)	DH
Jade (1)	BR
Jade (1)	BR/DR
Jade (2)	ER/KR
Jade (3)	AR/CR/JR
Jade/Lt. Jade (2)	DM
Gold (1)	KY/BY
Gold (2)	BP/DY
Gold (2)	EY/KY
Gold (3)	AP/JY
Gold/Cream (2)	DP
Dove Gray (1)	SS
Dove Gray (2)	DS/TS
Dove Gray (2)	US/KS
Dove Gray (3)	CS/JS
Chamois (1)	ST/BT
Chamois (2)	BT/DT
Chamois (2)	TT/UT
Chamois (2)	DT/ET/KT
Chamois (3)	AT/JT
Champagne (1)	BV
Champagne (2)	BV/DV
Champagne (2)	EV/KV
Champagne (3)	AV/CV/JV
Cordovan (1)	SF/BF
Cordovan (2)	BF/TF/UF
Cordovan (2)	DF/EF/KF
Cordovan (3)	AF/CF/JF
Cordovan/White (2)	D3
White w/Blue (2)	BQ/TQ
White w/Blue (2)	UQ/KQ
White w/Black (2)	KW
White w/Jade (2)	B5/K5
White w/Gold (2)	B8/K8
White w/Chamois (2)	B2/T2
White w/Chamois (2)	U2/K2
White w/Champagne (2)	B4/K4
White w/Cordovan (2)	B6/T6
White w/Cordovan (2)	U6/K6
White w/Dk. Red (2)	BN/TN/UN

1 - Cloth
2 - Leather & vinyl
3 - Velour

MERCURY	CODE
Dove Gray (1)	LS/RS
Dove Gray (1)	MS/JS
Dove Gray (2)	HS/VS
Dove Gray (3)	FS
Dk. Red (1)	LD/RD
Dk. Red (1)	MD/JD
Dk. Red (2)	HD/VD/SD
Dk. Red (3)	FD
Med. Blue (1)	LB/RB
Med. Blue (1)	MB/JB
Med. Blue (2)	HB/VB/SB
Med. Blue (3)	FB
Dk. Jade (1)	LR/RR

MERCURY	CODE
Dk. Jade (1)	MR/JR
Dk. Jade (2)	HR/VR/SR
Dk. Jade (3)	FR
Camel (1)	LY/RY
Camel (1)	MY/JY
Camel (2)	HY/VY/SY
Camel (3)	FY
Saddle (1)	LZ/RZ
Saddle (1)	MZ/JZ
Saddle (2)	HZ/VZ/SZ
Saddle (3)	FZ

1 - Cloth
2 - Vinyl
3 - Leather

COUGAR	CODE
Dove Gray (1)	RS/TS/VS
Dove Gray (1)	AS/CS/GS
Dove Gray (2)	SS/HS/YS
Dove Gray (2)	US/WS/ZS
Dove Gray (2)	BS/DS/FS
Dove Gray (3)	ES
Russet (1)	RE/TE/VE
Russet (1)	AE/CE/GE
Russet (2)	SE/HE/YE
Russet (2)	UE/WE/ZE
Russet (2)	BE/DE/FE
Russet (3)	EE
Med. Blue (1)	RB/TB/VB
Med. Blue (1)	AB/CB/GB
Med. Blue (2)	SB/HB/YB
Med. Blue (2)	UB/WB/ZB
Med. Blue (2)	BB/DB/EB
Med. Blue (3)	EB
Dk. Jade (1)	RR/TR/VR
Dk. Jade (1)	AR/CR/GR
Dk. Jade (2)	SR/HR/YR
Dk. Jade (2)	UR/WR/ZR
Dk. Jade (2)	BR/DR/FR
Dk. Jade (3)	ER
Chamois (1)	RT/TT/VT
Chamois (1)	AT/CT/GT
Chamois (2)	ST/HT/YT
Chamois (2)	UT/WT/ZT
Chamois (2)	BT/DT/ET
Chamois (3)	ET
Saddle (1)	RZ/TZ/VZ
Saddle (1)	AZ/CZ/GZ
Saddle (2)	SZ/HZ/YZ
Saddle (2)	UZ/WZ/ZZ
Saddle (2)	BZ/DZ/EZ
Saddle (3)	EZ
Blue/Chamois (1)	QT
White/Russet (2)	B7/D7/F7
White/Russet (3)	E7
White/Blue (2)	BQ/BQ/FQ
White/Blue (3)	EQ
White/Jade (2)	B5/D5/F5
White/Jade (3)	E5
White/Chamois (2)	B2/D2/F2
White/Chamois (3)	E2
White/Saddle (2)	B9/D9/F9
White/Saddle (3)	E9

1 -Cloth & vinyl
2 - Vinyl
3 - Leather

MONARCH	CODE
Dove Gray (1)	HS/BS/DS
Dove Gray (2)	ES/AS
Dove Gray (2)	GS/CS/PS
Dove Gray (3)	FS
Dk. Red (1)	LD/HD
Dk. Red (1)	BD/DD
Dk. Red (2)	KD/ED/AD

MONARCH	CODE
Dk. Red (2)	GD/CD/PD
Dk. Red (3)	FD
Med. Blue (1)	LB/HB
Med. Blue (1)	BB/DB
Med. Blue (2)	KB/EB/AB
Med. Blue (2)	GB/CB/PB
Med. Blue (3)	FB
Jade (1)	LR/HR
Jade (1)	BR/DR
Jade (2)	KR/ER/AR
Jade (2)	GR/CR/PR
Jade (3)	FR
Camel (1)	LY/HY
Camel (1)	BY/DY
Camel (2)	KY/EY/AY
Camel (2)	GY/CY/PY
Camel (3)	FY
Cordovan (1)	BF/DF
Cordovan (2)	EF/AF
Cordovan (2)	GF/CF/PF
Cordovan (3)	FF

1 - Cloth
2 - Vinyl
3 - Leather

ZEPHYR	CODE
Russet (1)	CE/LE
Russet (1)	FE/HE
Russet (2)	AE/BE
Russet (2)	EE/GE/KE
Wedgewood Blue (1)	CB/LB
Wedgewood Blue (1)	FB/HB
Wedgewood Blue (2)	AB/BB
Wedgewood Blue (2)	EB/GB/KB
Black (2)	AA/BA
Black (2)	EA/GA
Black (2)	FA/HA/KA
Chamois (1)	CT/LT
Chamois (1)	FT/HT
Chamois (2)	AT/BT
Chamois (2)	ET/GT/KT
White w/Russet (2)	A7/B7
White w/Russet (2)	E7/G7/K7
White w/Wedgewood Blue (2)	AQ/BQ
White w/Wedgewood Blue (2)	EQ/GQ/KQ
White w/Black (2)	AW/BW
White w/Black (2)	EW/GW/KW
White w/Chamois (2)	A2/B2
White w/Chamois (2)	E2/G2/K2
Chamois/Black (2)	AU/BU
Chamois/Black (2)	EU/GU
Cream/Gold (1)	FV/HV
Cream/Gold (2)	EV/GV

1 - Cloth & vinyl
2 - Vinyl

BOBCAT	CODE
Black (1)	GA
Black (2)	AA/HA
Bright Red (1)	GD/DD
Bright Red (2)	AD/HD
Wedgewood Blue (1)	GB/DB
Wedgewood Blue (2)	AB/HB
Med. Jade (1)	GR/DR
Med. Jade (2)	AR/HR
Chamois (1)	GT/DT
Chamois (2)	AT/HT
Tangerine (1)	DJ
Tangerine (2)	HJ

1 - Cloth
2 - Vinyl

THE TRANSMISSION CODE is a number or letter indicating the type of transmission.

TYPE	CODE
3-Speed Manual	1
4-Speed Manual Overdrive	5
4-Speed Manual (Borg Warner)	6
4-Speed Manual (Hummer)	7
XP Automatic (C-3)	V
XP Automatic (C-4)	W
FMX Automatic	X
XPL Automatic (C-6)	U
XPL Automatic (Special)	Z

THE AXLE CODE is a number or letter indicating the rear axle ratio and standard or locking type axles.

CONVENTIONAL	LOCKING	RATIO
Y		3.08:1
B		2.47:1
1	J	2.50:1
8		2.73:1
2		2.75:1
3		2.79:1
6	O	3.00:1
4		3.18:1
7		3.40:1

THE DSO CODE, consisting of two numbers, designates the district in which the car was ordered and may appear in conjunction with a Domestic Special Order or Foreign Special Order number when applicable.

LINCOLN-MERCURY DISTRICT	CODE
Special	00
Boston	11
New York	15
Philadelphia	16
Washington	17
Atlanta	21
Dallas	22
Jacksonville	23
Memphis	26
Buffalo	31
Cincinnati	32
Cleveland	33
Detroit	34
Chicago	41
St. Louis	42
Twin Cities	46
Denver	51
Los Angeles	52
Oakland	53
Seattle	54
Home Office Reserve	84
Export	90's

ENGINE IDENTIFICATION

ENGINE TAG

Since 1964, Lincoln-Mercury engines can be identified by a tag attached to the engine. The tag contains the year and cubic inch displacement.

CASTING NUMBERS

While helpful in identifying Lincoln-Mercury engine components, casting numbers are not conclusive in pin-pointing the exact year of manufacture. A better method is to search for the original host vehicle's VIN (Vehicle Identification Number) stamped on the driver's side at the rear of the engine block below the cylinder head.

BOBCAT ENGINES

CID	NO. CYL.	HORSE-POWER	COMP. RATIO	CARB.
140	4	88	9.0:1	2 BC
171	6	90	8.7:1	2 BC

ZEPHYR ENGINES

CID	NO. CYL.	HORSE-POWER	COMP. RATIO	CARB.
140	4	88	9.0:1	2 BC
200	6	85	8.5:1	2 BC
302	8	139	8.4:1	2 BC

MONARCH ENGINES

CID	NO. CYL.	HORSE-POWER	COMP. RATIO	CARB.
250	6	97	8.5:1	1 BC
302	8	139	8.4:1	2 BC

COUGAR ENGINES

CID	NO. CYL.	HORSE-POWER	COMP. RATIO	CARB.
351	8	152	8.0:1	2 BC
302	8	134	8.4:1	2 BC
351	8	144	8.3:1	2 BC
400	8	166	8.0:1	2 BC

MERCURY ENGINES

CID	NO. CYL.	HORSE-POWER	COMP. RATIO	CARB.
351	8	145	8.0:1	2 BC
400	8	160	8.0:1	2 BC
460	8	202	8.0:1	4 BC

LINCOLN ENGINES

CID	NO. CYL.	HORSE-POWER	COMP. RATIO	CARB.
302	8	133	8.4:1	2 BC
400	8	166	8.0:1	2 BC
460	8	210	8.0:1	4 BC

1979 LINCOLN CONTINENTAL

1979 MERCURY BOBCAT

1979 LINCOLN CONTINENTAL MARK V

1979 MERCURY COUGAR

1979 LINCOLN VERSAILLES

1979 MERCURY MARQUIS

1979 MERCURY MONARCH

1979 MERCURY MARQUIS WAGON

1979 MERCURY ZEPHYR WAGON

1979 MERCURY ZEPHYR

VEHICLE IDENTIFICATION NUMBER

LINCOLN MERCURY
9S63H123456

Located on a metal tab that is riveted to the instrument panel close to the windshield on the driver's side of the car and is visible from outside.

FIRST DIGIT: Identifies the year (9 = 1979)

SECOND DIGIT: Identifies the assembly plant

ASSEMBLY PLANT	CODE
Dearborn, MI	F
Kansas City, KS	K
Lorain, OH	H
Mahwah, NJ	E
Metuchen, NJ	T
Allen Park (Pilot Plant)	S
St. Louis, MO	Z
San Jose, CA	R
Wayne, MI	W
Wixom, MI	Y
St. Thomas, Ont., CAN	X

THIRD AND FOURTH DIGITS: Identify the body serial code

BOBCAT	CODE
3-Door Sedan	20
2-Door Wagon	22

CAPRI	CODE
3-Door Fastback	14
3-Door Fastback Ghia	16

ZEPHYR	CODE
4-Door Sedan	32
2-Door Sedan	31
2-Door Sedan Sporty Coupe	35
4-Door Wagon	36

MONARCH	CODE
4-Door Sedan	34
2-Door Sedan	33

COUGAR	CODE
4-Dr. Pillared HT Cougar	92
2-Door HT Cougar	91
2-Door HT Cougar XR-7	93

MERCURY	CODE
4-Door Sedan Marquis	62
2-Door Sedan Marquis	61
4-Door Sedan Marquis Brougham	64
2-Door Sedan Marquis Brougham	63
4-Door Marquis Wagon	74

LINCOLN	CODE
4-Dr. Pillared HT	82
2-Dr. Pillared HT	81
4-Dr. Sedan (Versailles)	84
2-Dr. Hardtop (Mark V)	89

FIFTH DIGIT: Identifies the engine code

ENGINE	CODE
I4 2.3L 139/2V	Y
I4 2.3L 139/2V Turbo Charged	W
V6 2.8 169/2V	Z
I6 3.3L 200/1V	T
I6 4.1L 250/1V	L
V8 5.0L 302/2V	F
V8 5.8L 351/2V	H
V8 6.6L 400/2V	S

LAST SIX DIGITS: Represent the basic production numbers

EXAMPLE:

9	S	63	H	123456
Model Year	Assy. Plant	Body Serial Code	Engine	Production Sequence Number

VEHICLE CERTIFICATION LABEL

THE VEHICLE CERTIFICATION LABEL (V.C. Label) is affixed on the left front door lock face panel or door pillar. The upper half of the label contains the name of the manufacturer, month and year of manufacture, Gross Vehicle Weight Rating (GVWR), Gross Axle Weight Rating (GAWR), and the certification statement. The V.C. label also contains the Vehicle Identification Number (VIN). The remaining information on the V.C. Label consists of the following vehicle identification codes: ie. color, DSO code, body, trim schedule date, axle, transmission and A.C. codes.

MANUFACTURED BY FORD MOTOR COMPANY
09/79 THIS VEHICLE CONFORMS TO ALL APPLICABLE FEDERAL MOTOR VEHICLE SAFETY STANDARDS IN EFFECT ON DATE OF MANUFACTURE SHOWN ABOVE
9S63H123456   PASSENGER
1C 34 54K HF 08H 6 X   A
NOT FOR TITLE OR REGISTRATION MADE IN U.S.A.

EXAMPLE:

9S63H123456	Vehicle Identification Number (VIN)
1C	Body Color Code and Vinyl Roof Type/Color (Black)
34	District Special Equipment Code (Detroit)
54K	Body Serial Code (Marquis Brougham 4-Dr. Sedan)
HF	Trim Code (Cordovan Cloth & Vinyl)
08H	Schedule Build Date
X	Transmission Code (FMX Automatic)
6	Rear Axle Code (3.00:1)
A	Air Condition Code

THE COLOR CODE consists of two or four digits. The first two digits represent the exterior body color. If the vehicle is equipped with a vinyl roof, the second two digits will indicate the style and color of the vinyl roof.

EXTERIOR PAINT COLOR	CODE
Black	1C
Silver Met.	1G
Dove Gray	1N
Med. Gray Met.	1P
Maroon	2J
Bright Red	2P
Dark Red	2M
Light Medium Blue	3F
Bright Blue	3J
Dark Blue Met.	3L
Wedgewood Blue	34
Dark Pine Met.	4D
Dark Jade Met.	46
Pastel Chamois	5P
Dark Brown Met.	5Q
Light Champagne	52

EXTERIOR PAINT COLOR — **CODE**

Color	Code
Cream	5P
Light Gold	6W
Antique Gold	62
Bright Yellow	64
Light Medium Pine	76
Dk. Cordovan Met.	8N
Light Chamois	83
Tangerine	85
White	9D
Medium Red Met.	2H
Lt. Wedgewood Blue Met.	3H
Med. Dark Orange Met.	5N
Med. Vaquero Met.	5W
Med. Jade Met.	7L
Med. Pine Met.	75
Med. Tan Met.	8J
Chamois Met.	8W
Med. Gray Met.	1S
Silver Met.	1Y
Light Red Met.	2W
Lt. Amethyst Met.	2D
Dk. Red Met.	23
Dk. Blue Met.	3Q
Diamond Blue Met.	38
Dark Beryl Met.	4B
Med. Beryl Met.	4C
Dk. Champagne Met.	5A
Lt. Champagne Met.	5C
Dk. Cordovan Met.	5E
Jubilee Gold Met.	66
Lt. Apricot Met.	88

VINYL ROOF TYPE (First Letter) — **CODE**

Type	Code
Grande Full	H
Grande Half	P
Lugano Full	W
Lugano Half	X
Lugano Front Half	K
Valino Full	V
Valino Half	Y
Valino Front Half	Z
Valino Coach	T
Convertible Roof, Simulated, Diamond	C
Cavalry Twill Coach	J

VINYL ROOF COLOR (Second Letter) — **CODE**

Color	Code
Amethyst	7
Medium Beryl	K
Black	A
Diamond Blue/Lt. Blue	B
Midnight Blue	Q
Camel/Cream	V
Chamois	T
Dark Champagne	J
Light Champagne	U
Dark Cordovan	F
Light Cordovan	N
Jubilee Gold	Y
Dove Gray	S
Dk. Midnight Jade	R
Pine	M
Dk. Red/Midnight Red	8
Dark Red/Med. Red	D
Silver	P
Vaquero	Z
White	W

THE BODY CODE consists of two numerals and one letter, indicating the car line and body style.

BOBCAT — **CODE**

Model	Code
3-Door Sedan	64H
2-Door Wagon	73H

* Villager option available
* Sport option available

CAPRI — **CODE**

Model	Code
3-Door Fastback	61D
3-Door Fastback Ghia	61H

* R/S option available
* Turbo R/S option available

ZEPHYR — **CODE**

Model	Code
4-Door Sedan	54D
2-Door Sedan	66D
2-Door Sedan Sporty Coupe	36R
4-Door Wagon	74D

* Villager option available
* Ghia option available
* ESS option available

MONARCH — **CODE**

Model	Code
4-Door Sedan	54H
2-Door Sedan	66H

* Ghia option available
* ESS option available

COUGAR — **CODE**

Model	Code
4-Dr. Pillared HT Cougar	53D
2-Door HT Cougar	65D
2-Door HT Cougar XR-7	65L

MERCURY — **CODE**

Model	Code
4-Door Sedan Marquis	54H
2-Door Sedan Marquis	66H
4-Door Sedan Marquis Brougham	54K
2-Door Sedan Marquis Brougham	66K
4-Door Marquis Wagon	74H

* Grand Marquis option available
* Colony Park option available

LINCOLN — **CODE**

Model	Code
4-Dr. Pillared HT	53B
2-Dr. Pillared HT	60B
4-Dr. Sedan (Versailles)	54M
2-Dr. Hardtop (Mark V)	65D

* Designer Series option available
* Collector Edition option available
* Town Car option available
* Town Coupe option available

THE DISTRICT CODE (See 1978 Lincoln/Mercury for listing of District Codes)

THE TRIM CODE consists of two letters. The first letter indicates the type of trim and the second letter indicates the color of the trim.

MERCURY — **CODE**

Trim	Code
Dove Gray (1)	GS/JS
Dove Gray (2)	HS/KS/BS
Dove Gray (3)	NS
Dove Gray (4)	RS
Dk. Red (1)	AD/GD
Dk. Red (1)	JD/ND
Dk. Red (2)	HD/KD/BD
Dk. Red (3)	ND/CD
Dk. Red (3)	MD/JD
Dk. Red (4)	RD
Wedgewood Blue (1)	AB/GB
Wedgewood Blue (1)	JB/NB
Wedgewood Blue (2)	HB/KB/BB
Wedgewood Blue (3)	NB/CB
Wedgewood Blue (3)	MB/JB
Wedgewood Blue (4)	RB
Pine Green (1)	AR/GR
Pine Green (1)	JR/NR
Pine Green (2)	HR/KR/BR
Pine Green (3)	NR/CR
Pine Green (3)	MR/JR
Pine Green (4)	RR
Camel (1)	AY/GY
Camel (1)	JY/NY
Camel (2)	HY/KY/BY

MERCURY	CODE
Camel (3)	NY/MY/JY
Camel (4)	RY
Cordovan (1)	AF/GF
Cordovan (1)	JF/NF
Cordovan (2)	HF/KF/BF
Cordovan (3)	NF/CF
Cordovan (3)	MF/JF
Cordovan (4)	RF

1 - Cloth & vinyl
2 - Vinyl
3 - Cloth
4 - Leather & vinyl

CAPRI	CODE
Black (1)	BA/DA
Black (1)	FA/MA/PA
Black (2)	AA/CA
Black (2)	LA/NA
Black (3)	QA/EA/RA
Med. Red (1)	BD/DD
Med. Red (1)	FD/MD/PD
Med. Red (2)	AD/CD
Med. Red (2)	LD/ND
Med. Red (3)	QD/ED/RD
Wedgewood Blue (1)	BB/DB
Wedgewood Blue (1)	FB/MB/PB
Wedgewood Blue (2)	AB/CB
Wedgewood Blue (2)	LB/NB
Wedgewood Blue (3)	QB/EB/RB
Chamois (1)	BT/DT
Chamois (1)	FT/MT/PT
Chamois (2)	AT/CT
Chamois (2)	LT/NT
Chamois (3)	QT/ET/RT
Vaquero (1)	BZ/DZ
Vaquero (1)	FZ/MZ/PZ
Vaquero (2)	AZ/CZ
Vaquero (2)	LZ/NZ
Vaquero (2)	QZ/EZ/RZ
Black w/Black (2)	AW/CW
Black w/Black (2)	LW/NW
Black w/Black (3)	QW/EW/RW
Black w/Med. Red (2)	AN/CN
Black w/Med. Red (2)	LN/NN
Black w/Med. Red (3)	QN/EN/RN
Black w/Wedgewood Blue (2)	AQ/CQ
Black w/Wedgewood Blue (2)	LQ/NQ
Black w/Wedgewood Blue (3)	QQ/EQ/RQ
Black w/Chamois (2)	A2/C2
Black w/Chamois (2)	L2/N2
Black w/Chamois (3)	Q2/E2/R2
Black w/Vaquero (2)	A9/C9
Black w/Vaquero (2)	L9/N9
Black w/Vaquero (3)	Q9/E9/R9

1 - Cloth & vinyl
2 - Vinyl
3 - Leather & vinyl

BOBCAT	CODE
Black (1)	GA
Black (2)	AA/HA
Med. Red (1)	GD
Med. Red (2)	AD/HD
Med. Red (3)	DD
Wedgewood Blue (1)	GB
Wedgewood Blue (2)	AB/HB
Wedgewood Blue (3)	DB
Chamois (1)	GT
Chamois (2)	AT/HT
Chamois (3)	DT
Tangerine (2)	HJ
Tangerine (3)	DJ

1 - Cloth & vinyl
2 - Vinyl
3 - Cloth

ZEPHYR	CODE
Med. Red (1)	CD/FD
Med. Red (1)	LD/KD
Med. Red (1)	UD/SD/HD
Med. Red (2)	AD/BD/ED
Med. Red (2)	GD/VD/HD
Med. Red (2)	RD/TD/KD
Wedgewood Blue (1)	CB/FB
Wedgewood Blue (1)	LB/KB
Wedgewood Blue (1)	UB/SB/HB
Wedgewood Blue (2)	AB/BB
Wedgewood Blue (2)	EB/GB/HB
Wedgewood Blue (2)	RB/TB/KB
Black (1)	FA/LA
Black (1)	KA/SA/HA
Black (2)	AA/BA
Black (2)	EA/GA/HA
Black (2)	RA/TA/KA
Chamois (1)	CT/FT
Chamois (1)	LT/KT
Chamois (1)	UT/ST/HT
Chamois (2)	AT/BT
Chamois (2)	ET/GT/VT
Chamois (2)	HT/RT/KT
Cream/Gold (1)	SV/HV
Cream/Gold (2)	RV/TV/KV
Chamois w/Black (2)	AU/BU
Chamois w/Black (2)	VU/GU
White w/Med. Red (2)	EN/GN
White w/Med. Red (2)	RN/TN/KN
White w/Wedgewood Blue (2)	EQ/GQ
White w/Wedgewood Blue (2)	RQ/TQ/KQ
White w/Black (2)	EW/GW
White w/Black (2)	RW/TW/KW
White w/Chamois (2)	E2/G2
White w/Chamois (2)	R2/T2/K2

1 - Cloth & vinyl
2 - Vinyl

MONARCH	CODE
Dove Gray (1)	BS/DS
Dove Gray (2)	GS/CS/PS
Dove Gray (3)	MS
Dk. Red (1)	JD/BD/DD
Dk. Red (2)	KD/GD
Dk. Red (2)	CD/PD
Dk. Red (3)	MD
Med. Blue (1)	JB/BB/DB
Med. Blue (2)	KB/GB
Med. Blue (2)	CB/PB
Med. Blue (2)	MB
Dk. Jade (1)	JR/BR/DR
Dk. Jade (2)	KR/GR
Dk. Jade (2)	CR/PR
Dk. Jade (3)	MR
Camel (1)	JY/BY/DY
Camel (2)	KY/GY
Camel (2)	CY/PY
Camel (3)	MY
Cordovan (1)	BF/DF
Cordovan (2)	GF/CF/PF
Cordovan (3)	MF

1 - Cloth & vinyl
2 - Vinyl
3 - Leather & vinyl

COUGAR	CODE
Dove Gray (1)	RS/TS/VS
Dove Gray (1)	AS/CS/GS
Dove Gray (2)	SS/HS/YS
Dove Gray (2)	US/WS/ZS
Dove Gray (3)	BS/DS/FS
Dove Gray (3)	PS
Dove Gray (4)	ES
Dk. Red (1)	RD/TD/VD

COUGAR	CODE
Dk. Red (1)	AD/DD/GD
Dk. Red (2)	SD/HD/YD
Dk. Red (2)	UD/WD/ZD
Dk. Red (2)	BD/DD/FD
Dk. Red (3)	PD
Dk. Red (4)	ED
Med. Blue (1)	RB/TB/VB
Med. Blue (1)	AB/CB/GB
Med. Blue (2)	SB/HB/YB
Med. Blue (2)	UB/WB/ZB
Med. Blue (2)	BB/DB/FB
Med. Blue (3)	PB
Med. Blue (4)	EB
Dk. Jade (1)	RR/TR/VR
Dk. Jade (1)	AR/CR/GR
Dk. Jade (2)	SR/HR/YR
Dk. Jade (2)	UR/WR/ZR
Dk. Jade (2)	BR/DR/FR
Dk. Jade (3)	PR
Dk. Jade (4)	ER
Chamois (1)	RT/TT/VT
Chamois (1)	AT/CT/GT
Chamois (2)	ST/HT/YT
Chamois (2)	UT/WT/ZT
Chamois (2)	BT/DT/FT
Chamois (3)	PT
Chamois (4)	ET
Cordovan (1)	RF/TF/VF
Cordovan (1)	AF/CF/GF
Cordovan (2)	SF/HF/YF
Cordovan (2)	UF/WF/ZF
Cordovan (2)	BF/DF/FF
Cordovan (3)	PF
Cordovan (4)	EF
Chamois/Blue (1)	QT
Chamois/Saddle (1)	NT
White/Dk. Red (2)	BN/DN/FN
White/Dk. Red (4)	EN
White/Med. Blue (2)	BQ/DQ/FQ
White/Med. Blue (4)	EQ
White/Dk. Jade (2)	B5/D5/F5
White/Dk. Jade (4)	E5
White/Chamois (2)	B2/D2/F2
White/Chamois (4)	E2
White/Cordovan (2)	B6/D6/F6
White/Cordovan (4)	E6

1 - Cloth & vinyl
2 - Vinyl
3 - Velour
4 - Vinyl & leather

THE SCHEDULE DATE is a three digit code designating the day and month the vehicle was scheduled to be built.

THE AXLE CODE consists of a single number. The number indicates the ratio and type of axle installed in the vehicle.

CONVENTIONAL	LOCKING	RATIO
G		2.26:1
B	C	2.47:1
1	J	2.50:1
8	H	2.73:1
2	K	2.75:1
3	L	2.79:1
6	D	3.00:1
Y		3.08:1
F	W	3.45:1

THE TRANSMISSION CODE is a single letter indicating the type and model of transmission installed in the vehicle.

TYPE	CODE
4-Speed Overdrive Manual	5
4-Speed Manaul	6
4-Speed Manaul	7
XP Automatic (C-3)	V
XP Automatic (C-4)	W
FMX Automatic	X
XPL Automatic (C-6)	U
XPL Automatic (Special)	Z
Jatco	S
Borg Warner	Y

THE A.C. CODE is the letter "A". It will be shown on the label if the vehicle is air-conditioned.

ENGINE IDENTIFICATION

ENGINE TAG
Since 1964, Lincoln-Mercury engines can be identified by a tag attached to the engine. The tag contains the year and cubic inch displacement.

CASTING NUMBERS
While helpful in identifying Lincoln-Mercury engine components, casting numbers are not conclusive in pin-pointing the exact year of manufacture. A better method is to search for the original host vehicle's VIN (Vehicle Identification Number) stamped on the driver's side at the rear of the engine block below the cylinder head.

BOBCAT ENGINES

CID	NO. CYL.	HORSE-POWER	COMP. RATIO	CARB.
140	4	88	9.0:1	2 BC
171	6	102	8.7:1	2 BC

ZEPHYR ENGINES

CID	NO. CYL.	HORSE-POWER	COMP. RATIO	CARB.
140	4	88	8.0:1	2 BC
200	6	85	8.5:1	1 BC
302	8	140	8.4:1	2 BC

MONARCH ENGINES

CID	NO. CYL.	HORSE-POWER	COMP. RATIO	CARB.
250	6	97	8.6:1	1 BC
302	8	137	8.4:1	2 BC

COUGAR ENGINES

CID	NO. CYL.	HORSE-POWER	COMP. RATIO	CARB.
302	8	133	8.4:1	2 BC
351	8	135	8.3:1	2 BC
351	8	151	8.0:1	2 BC

MERCURY ENGINES

CID	NO. CYL.	HORSE-POWER	COMP. RATIO	CARB.
302	8	129	8.4:1	2 BC
351	8	138	8.3:1	2 BC

LINCOLN ENGINES

CID	NO. CYL.	HORSE-POWER	COMP. RATIO	CARB.
302	8	130	8.4:1	2 BC
400	8	159	8.0:1	2 BC

1970 IMPERIAL

1970 CHRYSLER 300

1970 CHRYSLER NEW YORKER

1970 CHRYSLER TOWN AND COUNTRY WAGON

1970 CHRYSLER NEWPORT

1970 IMPERIAL

VEHICLE IDENTIFICATION NUMBER

CHRYSLER
CH23T0C123456

Located on a plate attached to the left side of the instrument panel, visible through the windshield.

FIRST DIGIT: Identifies the car make

MAKE	CODE
Chrysler	C
Imperial	Y

SECOND DIGIT: Identifies the price class

CLASS	CODE
Economy	E
High	H
Low	L
Medium	M
Premium	P
Special	S

THIRD & FOURTH DIGITS: Identify the body type

TYPE	CODE
2-Dr. Sedan	21
2-Dr. Hardtop	23
Convertible Coupe	27
2-Dr. Sports Hardtop	29
4-Dr. Sedan	41
4-Dr. Hardtop	43
6-Pass. Wagon	45
9-Pass. Wagon	46

FIFTH DIGIT: Identifies the engine

CID	CODE
383 CID 2 BC 8-Cyl.	L
383 CID 4 BC Hi-Perf. 8-Cyl.	N
440 CID 4 BC 8-Cyl.	T
440 CID 4 BC Hi-Perf. 8-Cyl.	U
Special Order 8-Cyl.	Z

SIXTH DIGIT: Identifies the year
0 - 1970

SEVENTH DIGIT: Identifies the assembly plant

PLANT	CODE
Lynch Road, Detroit, MI	A
Hamtramck, MI	B
Jefferson Ave., Detroit, MI	C
Belvidere, IL	D
Los Angeles, CA	E
Newark, DE	F
St. Louis, MO	G
New Stanton, PA	H
Wyoming, MI	P
Windsor, Ontario, CAN	R

LAST SIX DIGITS: Identify the production sequence number

EXAMPLE

C	H	23	T	0	C	123456
Car Make	Price Class	Body Type	Engine	Model Year	Asm Plant	Production Sequence Number

BODY CODE PLATE

THE BODY CODE PLATE is located in the engine compartment on the left wheel housing, fender side shield or radiator yoke.

THE BODY CODE PLATE is read left to right, bottom to top. The information on the plate includes the car S.O. Number, and the trim and paint codes.

CHRYSLER MOTORS CORPORATION

				Line
XXX	XXX	XXX	XXX	6
XXX	XXX	XXX	XXX	5
XXX	XXX	XXX	XXX	4
XXX	XXX	XXX	XXX	3
XXX	XXX	XXX	XXX	2
XXX	XXX	XXX	XXX	1

LINE 1 - DIGITS 1, 2 & 3: Indicate engine codes

CID	CODE
383 2-BC	E61
383 4-BC	E63
440 4-BC	E85
440 4-BC Hi-Perf.	E86

LINE 1 - DIGITS 4, 5 & 6: Indicate transmission codes

TRANSMISSION		CODE
3-Spd. Manual Col. Shift	A903	D11
3-Spd. Manual Col. Shift	A230	D12
3-Spd. Manual Flr. Shift	A230	D13
3-Spd. Manual		D14
Auto. Trans.	A904	D31
Auto Trans.	A727	D32
Auto Trans.	A727	D34
H.D. Auto. Trans.	A727	D36

LINE 1 - DIGIT 7: Indicates car line

MAKE	CODE
Chrysler	C
Imperial	L

LINE 1 - DIGIT 8: Indicates price class

CLASS	CODE
Economy	E
High	H
Low	L
Medium	M
Premium	P
Special	S

LINE 1 - DIGITS 9 & 10: Indicate body type

TYPE	CODE
2-Dr. Sedan	21
4-Dr. Sedan	41
2-Dr. Hardtop	23
C.V. CP	27
2-Dr. Sports H/Top	29
6-Pass. Wagon	45
9-Pass. Wagon	46
4-Dr. Hardtop	43

LINE 1 - DIGIT 11: Indicates engine code

CID	CODE
383 CID 8-Cyl. 2 BC	L
383 CID 8-Cyl. Hi-Perf. 4 BC	N
440 CID 8-Cyl. 4 BC	T
440 CID 8-Cyl. Hi-Perf. 4 BC	U
Special Order 8-Cyl.	Z

LINE 1 - DIGIT 12: Indicates model year
0 - 1970

LINE 1 - DIGIT 13: Indicates the assembly plant

PLANT	CODE
Lynch Road, Detroit, MI	A
Hamtramck, MI	B
Jefferson Ave., Detroit, MI	C
Belvidere, IL	D
Los Angeles, CA	E
Newark, DE	F
St. Louis, MO	G
New Stanton, PA	H
Wyoming, MI	P
Windsor, Ontario, Canada	R

LINE 1 - LAST SIX DIGITS: Indicate production sequence number

LINE 2 - DIGITS 1, 2 & 3: Indicate lower body paint color

COLOR	CODE
Silver Metallic	EA4
Charcoal Metallic	EA9
Ice Blue Metallic	EB3
Blue Fire Metallic	EB5
Jamaica Blue Metallic	EB7
Violet Metallic	FC7
Rallye Red	FE5
Lime Green Metallic	FF4
Ivy Green Metallic	EF8
Dark Emerald Metallic	EF9
Limelight	FJ5
Sassy Grass Green	FJ6
Vitamin C	EK2
Burnt Orange Metallic	FK3
Deep Burnt Orange Metallic	FK5
Sand Pebble Beige	BL1
Moulon Rouge	FM3
Deep Plum	EM9
Frosted Teal Metallic	FP6
Scorch Red	ER6
Sahara Tan Metallic	FT3
Burnt Tan Metallic	FT6
Walnut Metallic	FT8
Tor-Red	EV2
Alpine White	EW1
Black Velvet	TX9
Lemon Twist	FY1
Sunfire Yellow	DY2
Yellow Gold	DY3
Citron Mist Metallic	FY4
Citron Gold Metallic	FY6
Petty Blue	C37D
Special Order	999

LINE 2 - DIGITS 4, 5, 6 & 7: Indicate trim code

LINE 2 - DIGIT 4: Indicates price class

PRICE CLASS	CODE
B-Class	B
Charger	C
Deluxe	D
Economy	E
Low	L
Medium	M
High	H
Premium	P
Sport	S
Police	K
Taxi	T

LINE 2 - DIGIT 5: Indicates seat and fabric type

SEAT	CODE
Cloth & Vinyl Bench	1
Vinyl Bench	2
Cloth & Vinyl Split Bench	3
Vinyl Split Bench	4
Cloth & Vinyl Bucket	5
Vinyl Bucket	6
Vinyl & Leather Bucket	R

LINE 2 - DIGITS 6 & 7: Indicate interior color

FABRIC COLOR	CODE
Gray	A5
Black Frost	A8
Dark Gray	A9
Light Blue	B3
Medium Blue	B5
Dark Blue	B7
White & Blue	BW
Red	E4
White & Red	EW
Light Green	F4
White & Green	FW
Green	F8
Burnt Orange	K4
White & Burnt Orange	KW
Beige	L2
Burgundy	M9
Teal	P6
Oxblood	R9
Light Tan	T3
Tan	T5
Tan & White	TW
Walnut & Beige	TT
Black	X9
Black & Charcoal	XA
Black & Peacock	XP
White & Black	XW
Black & Gold	XY
Gold & Black	YX
Gold	Y4

LINE 2 - DIGITS 8, 9 & 10: Indicate upper door frame color, not listed

LINE 2 - DIGIT 11: Indicates the month of manufacture

MONTH	CODE
January	1
February	2
March	3
April	4
May	5
June	6
July	7
August	8
September	9
October	A
November	B
December	C

LINE 2 - DIGITS 12 & 13: Indicate day of month

LINE 2 - LAST SIX DIGITS: Indicate production sequence number

LINE 3 - DIGITS 1, 2 & 3: Indicate upper body color or vinyl roof codes

COLOR	CODE
Paint-Mono Tone	V01
Paint-Two Tone	V02
Paint, Trim & Vinyl Roof Waiver	V08
Paint-Special Order	V09
Vinyl Roof	V10
Vinyl Roof Green	V1F
Vinyl Roof Gator Grain	V1G
Vinyl Roof Walnut Patterned	V1J
Vinyl Roof Champagne	V1L
Vinyl Roof White	V1W
Vinyl Roof Black	C1X
Vinyl Roof Turquoise Grain	V1Y
Vinyl Roof Special Order	V19
Paint-Hood Performance	V21
Delete Sport Hood Treatment	V22
Delete Lower Body Side Original Paint	V23
Paint-Hood Performance w/Eng Callout	V24
Convertible Top	V30
Convertible Top White	V3W
Convertible Top Black	V3X
Tape Stripe-Body Side White	V4W
Tape Stripe-Body Side Black	V4X
Mouldings-Protective Vinyl Body Side	V50
Mouldings-Protective Vinyl Body Side Bright Blue	V5B
Mouldings-Protective Vinyl Body Side Light Green	V5F
Mouldings-Protective Vinyl Body Side Burnt Orange	V5K
Mouldings-Protective Vinyl Body Side Red	V5R
Mouldings-Protective Vinyl Body Side Tan	V5T
Mouldings-Protective Vinyl Body Side White	V5W
Mouldings-Protective Vinyl Body Side Black	V5X
Mouldings-Protective Vinyl Body Side Citron Gold	V5Y
Sport Stripes Tape	V60
Sport Stripes Tape Blue	V6B
Sport Stripes Tape Green	V6F
Sport Stripes Tape Chartreuse	V6J
Sport Stripes Tape Burnt Orange	V6K
Sport Stripes Tape Magenta	V6M
Sport Stripes Red	V6R
Sport Stripes White	V6W
Sport Stripes Black	V6X
Sport Stripes Gold	V6Y
Sport Stripes Delete	V68
Accent Stripes Paint	V70
Accent Stripes Paint Blue	V7B
Accent Stripes Paint Green	V7F
Accent Stripes Paint Red	V7R
Accent Stripes Paint White	V7W
Accent Stripes Paint Black	V7X

COLOR	CODE
Accent Stripes Paint Delete	V78
Sport Stripes	V80
Sport Stripes Blue	V8B
Sport Stripes Green	V8F
Sport Stripes Red	V8R
Sport Stripes White	V8W
Sport Stripes Black	V8X
Sport Stripes Gold	V8Y
Sport Stripes Delete	V88

ENGINE NUMBER

THE ENGINE IDENTIFICATION NUMBER for V-8 engines are on the left side rear of block near oil pan flange on 383 and 440 blocks.

The following identification is included in the engine serial number:

THE FIRST TWO LETTERS designate the manufacturing plant

MANUFACTURING PLANT	CODE
Mound Road	PM
Trenton	PT
Marysville	NJ
Windsor	FW

The three numbers following the plant identification indicate the cubic inch displacement: ie. 383 - 440.

The four numbers following the model identification designate the build date. This is a date code for manufacturing purposes.

The four numbers following the build date are the engine sequence number.

EXAMPLE
PM44029251234

In the example above:

PM	Mound Road
440	Cubic Inch Displacement
2925	Build date code*
1234	Engine sequence number

*1970 build date codes run from 2895 thru 3259

NEWPORT ENGINES

CID	NO. CYL.	HORSE-POWER	COMP. RATIO	CARB.
383	8	290	8.7:1	2 BC
383	8	330	9.5:1	4 BC
440	8	375	9.7:1	4 BC

NEW YORKER ENGINES

CID	NO. CYL.	HORSE-POWER	COMP. RATIO	CARB.
440	8	350	9.7:1	4 BC
440	8	375	9.7:1	4 BC

TOWN & COUNTRY ENGINES

CID	NO. CYL.	HORSE-POWER	COMP. RATIO	CARB.
383	8	290	8.7:1	2 BC
383	8	330	9.5:1	4 BC
440	8	350	9.7:1	4 BC

IMPERIAL ENGINES

CID	NO. CYL.	HORSE-POWER	COMP. RATIO	CARB.
440	8	350	9.7:1	4 BC

1971 CHRYSLER THREE HUNDRED

1971 CHRYSLER TOWN & COUNTRY

1971 CHRYSLER NEWPORT ROYAL

1971 CHRYSLER NEWPORT ROYAL

1971 CHRYSLER IMPERIAL

1971 CHRYSLER IMPERIAL

VEHICLE IDENTIFICATION NUMBER

CHRYSLER
CH23T1C123456

Located on a plate attached to the left side of the instrument panel, visible through the windshield.

FIRST DIGIT: Identifies the car make

MAKE	CODE
Chrysler	C
Imperial	Y

SECOND DIGIT: Identifies the price class

CLASS	CODE
Economy	E
High	H
Low	L
Medium	M
Premium	P
Special	S

THIRD & FOURTH DIGITS: Identifies the body type

TYPE	CODE
2-Dr. Hardtop Coupe	23
4-Dr. Sedan	41
4-Dr. Hardtop Sedan	43
2-Seat Station Wagon	45
3-Seat Station Wagon	46

FIFTH DIGIT: Identifies the engine

CID	CODE
360 CID 2 BC 8-Cyl.	K
383 CID 2 BC 8-Cyl.	L
383 CID 4 BC 8-Cyl.	N
440 CID 4 BC 8-Cyl.	T
440 CID 4 BC Hi-Perf. 8-Cyl.	U
Special Order 8-Cyl.	Z

SIXTH DIGIT: Identifies the year
1 - 1971

SEVENTH DIGIT: Identifies the assembly plant

PLANT	CODE
Jefferson Ave., Detroit, MI	C
Newark, DE	F

REMAINING SIX DIGITS: Identify the production sequence number starting at each plant with 100001

EXAMPLE

C	H	23	T	1	C	123456
Car Make	Price Class	Body Type	Engine	Model Year	Asm Plant	Production Sequence Number

BODY CODE PLATE

THE BODY CODE PLATE is located in the engine compartment on the left wheel housing, fender side shield or radiator yoke.

THE BODY CODE PLATE is read left to right, bottom to top. The information on the plate includes the car S.O. Number and the trim and paint codes.

```
          CHRYSLER MOTORS
            CORPORATION

                                    Line
  XXX   XXX   XXX   XXX              6
  XXX   XXX   XXX   XXX              5
  XXX   XXX   XXX   XXX              4
  XXX   XXX   XXX   XXX              3
  XXX   XXX   XXX   XXX              2
  XXX   XXX   XXX   XXX              1
```

LINE 1 - DIGITS 1, 2 & 3: Indicate engine codes

CID	CODE
360	E57
383	E61
383	E63
440	E85
440	E86

LINE 1 - DIGITS 4, 5 & 6: Indicate transmission codes

TRANSMISSION		CODE
3-Spd. Manual Col. Shift	A903	D11
3-Spd. Manual Col. Shift	A230	D12
3-Spd. Manual Floor Shift	A230	D13
3-Spd. Manual		D14
4-Spd. Manual	A833	D21
Auto. Trans.	A904	D31
Auto. Trans.	A727	D32
Auto. Trans.		D34
H.D. Auto. Trans.	A727	D36
Special Order		D49

LINE 1 - DIGIT 7: Indicates car line

MAKE	CODE
Chrysler	C
Imperial	L

LINE 1 - DIGIT 8: Indicates price class

CLASS	CODE
Economy	E
High	H
Low	L
Medium	M
Premium	P
Special	S

LINE 1 - DIGITS 9 & 10: Indicate body type

TYPE	CODE
2-Dr. Hardtop Coupe	23
4-Dr. Sedan	41
4-Dr. Hardtop Sedan	43
2-Seat Station Wagon	45
3-Seat Station Wagon	46

LINE 1 - DIGIT 11: Indicates engine code

CID	CODE
360 CID 8-Cyl. 2 BC	K
383 CID 8-Cyl. 2 BC	L
383 CID 8-Cyl. Hi-Perf. 4 BC	N
440 CID 8-Cyl. 4 BC	T
440 CID 8-Cyl. Hi-Perf. 4 BC	U
Special Order 8-Cyl.	Z

LINE 1 - DIGIT 12: Indicates model year
1- 1971

LINE 1 - DIGIT 13: Indicates the assembly plant

PLANT	CODE
Jefferson Ave., Detroit, MI	C
Newark, DE	F

LINE 1 - LAST SIX DIGITS: Indicate production sequence number starting at each plant with 100001

LINE 2 - DIGITS 1, 2 & 3: Indicate lower body paint color

COLOR	CODE
Winchester Gray Metallic	GA4
Slate Gray Metallic	GA8
Glacial Blue Metallic	GB2
True Blue Metallic	GB5
Evening Blue Metallic	GB7
Violet Metallic	FC7
Mood Indigo Metallic	GC8
Rallye Red	FE5
Burnished Red Metallic	GE7
Amber Sherwood Metallic	GF3
Sherwood Green Metallic	GF7
April Green Metallic	GJ4
Sassy Grass Green	FJ6
Autumn Bronze Metallic	GK6
Sandalwood Beige	BL1
Bahama Yellow	EL5
Coral Turquoise Metallic	FQ5
Tunisian Tan Metallic	GT2
Tahitian Walnut Metallic	GT8
Tor-Red	EV2
Spinnaker White	EW1
Sno-White	GW3
Formal Black	TX9
Lemon Twist	FY1
Curious Yellow	GY3
Gold Leaf Metallic	GY8
Tawny Gold Metallic	GY9
Special Order	999

LINE 2 - DIGITS 4, 5 6 & 7: Indicate trim code

LINE 2 - DIGIT 4: Indicates price class

PRICE CLASS	CODE
Economy	E
High	H
Low	L
Medium	M
Premium	P
Special	S

LINE 2 - DIGIT 5: Indicates seat and fabric type

SEAT	CODE
Cloth & Vinyl Bench	1
Vinyl Bench	2
Cloth & Vinyl Split Bench	3
Vinyl Split Bench	4
Cloth & Vinyl Bucket	5
Vinyl Bucket	6
Vinyl & Leather Bucket	R

LINE 2 - DIGITS 6 & 7: Indicate interior color

FABRIC COLOR	CODE
Light Blue	B2
Medium Blue	B5
Dark Blue	B7
Russet	E8
Green	F7
Tan	T7
Light Gold	Y3
Medium Gold	Y5
Black	X9
Black & Orange	XV
Black & White	XX
Black & White	XW

LINE 2 - DIGITS 8, 9 & 10: Indicate upper door frame color, not listed

LINE 2 - DIGIT 11: Indicate month of manufacture

MONTH	CODE
January	1
February	2
March	3
April	4
May	5
June	6
July	7
August	8
September	9
October	A
November	B
December	C

LINE 2 - DIGITS 12 & 13: Indicate day of month of manufacture

LINE 2 - REMAINING SIX DIGITS: Indicate production sequence number starting at each plant with 100001

LINE 3 - DIGITS 1, 2 & 3: Indicate upper body color or vinyl roof codes

COLOR	CODE
Paint-Mono Tone	V01
Paint-Two Tone	V02
Paint, Trim & Vinyl Roof Waiver	V08
Paint-Special Order	V09
Full Vinyl Roof	V10
Full Vinyl Roof Gunmetal	V1A
Full Vinyl Roof Blue	V1B
Full Vinyl Roof Green	V1F
Full Vinyl Roof Paisley	V1J
Full Vinyl Roof Burgundy	V1M
Full Vinyl Roof Tan	V1T
Full Vinyl Roof White	V1W
Full Vinyl Roof Black	V1X
Full Vinyl Roof Gold	V1Y
Paint-Hood Performance	V21
Delete Sport Hood Treatment	V22
Paint-Hood Performance w/Eng. Callout	V24
Convertible Top	V30
Folding Sunroof	V30
Folding Sunroof White	V30
Folding Sunroof Black	V3X
Folding Sunroof Special Order	V39
Canopy Vinyl Roof	V40
Canopy Vinyl Roof Green	V4F
Canopy Vinyl Roof Parchment	V4L
Canopy Vinyl Roof White	V4W
Canopy Vinyl Roof Black	V4X
Canopy Vinyl Roof Gold	V4Y
Canopy Vinyl Roof Special Order	V49
Mouldings-Protective Vinyl Body Side	V50
Mouldings-Protective Vinyl Body Side Gunmetal	V5A
Mouldings-Protective Vinyl Body Side Blue	V5B
Mouldings-Protective Vinyl Body Side Green	V5F
Mouldings-Protective Vinyl Body Side Orange	V5K
Mouldings-Protective Vinyl Body Side Burgundy	V5M
Mouldings-Protective Vinyl Body Side Red	V5R
Mouldings-Protective Vinyl Body Side Tan	V5T
Mouldings-Protective Vinyl Body Side Black	V5X
Mouldings-Protective Vinyl Body Side Gold	V5Y
Sport Stripes	V60
Sport Stripes Blue	V6B
Sport Stripes Green	V6F
Sport Stripes Chartreuse	V6J
Sport Stripes Red	V6R
Sport Stripes Orange	V6V
Sport Stripes White	V6W
Sport Stripes Black	V6X
Sport Stripes Gold	V6Y
Sport Stripes Delete	V68
Accent Stripes	V70
Accent Stripes Blue	V7B
Accent Stripes Green	V7F
Accent Stripes Red	V7R
Accent Stripes White	V7W
Accent Stripes Black	V7X
Accent Stripes Gold	V7Y
Accent Stripes Delete	V78
Sport Stripes Tape	V80
Sport Stripes Red	V8R
Sport Stripes White	V8W
Sport Stripes Black	V8X
Sport Stripes Gold	V8Y
Sport Stripes Delete	V88
Tape Stripe	V90
Tape Stripe	V9W
Tape Stripe Black	V9X

ENGINE NUMBER

THE ENGINE IDENTIFICATION NUMBER for V-8 engines are on the left side rear of block near oil pan flange on 383 and 440 blocks.

The following identification is included in the engine serial number:

THE FIRST TWO LETTERS designate the manufacturing plant:

MANUFACTURING PLANT	CODE
Mound Road ....PM
Trenton ....PT
Marysville ....NJ
Windsor ....FW

THE THREE NUMBERS following the plant identification indicate the cubic inch displacement: ie. 383 - 440.

THE FOUR NUMBERS following the model identification designate the build date. This is a date code for manufacturing purposes.

THE FOUR NUMBERS following the build date are the engine sequence number.

EXAMPLE
PM44032611234

In the example above:

PM	Mound Road
440	Cubic Inch Displacement
3261	Build date code*
1234	Engine sequence number

*1971 build date codes run from 3260 thru 3624

NEWPORT ENGINES

CID	NO. CYL.	HORSE-POWER	COMP. RATIO	CARB.
383	8	275	8.5:1	2 BC
383	8	300	8.5:1	4 BC
440	8	370	9.5:1	4 BC

NEW YORKER ENGINES

CID	NO. CYL.	HORSE-POWER	COMP. RATIO	CARB.
440	8	335	8.5:1	4 BC
440	8	370	9.5:1	4 BC

TOWN & COUNTRY ENGINES

CID	NO. CYL.	HORSE-POWER	COMP. RATIO	CARB.
383	8	275	8.5:1	2 BC
383	8	300	8.5:1	4 BC
440	8	335	8.5:1	4 BC

IMPERIAL ENGINES

CID	NO. CYL.	HORSE-POWER	COMP. RATIO	CARB.
440	8	335	8.8:1	4 BC

1972 CHRYSLER NEWPORT

1972 CHRYSLER TOWN & COUNTRY

1972 CHRYSLER NEW YORKER

1972 CHRYSLER IMPERIAL

VEHICLE IDENTIFICATION NUMBER

CHRYSLER
CE41M2C123456

Located on a plate attached to the left side of the instrument panel, visible through the windshield.

FIRST DIGIT: Identifies the car make

MAKE	CODE
Chrysler	C
Imperial	Y

SECOND DIGIT: Identifies the price class

CLASS	CODE
Grand	G
High	H
Low	L
Medium	M
Premium	P
Special	S

THIRD & FOURTH DIGITS: Identify the body type

MAKE	CODE
2-Dr. Sedan	21
2-Dr. Hardtop	23
Convertible Coupe	27
2-Dr. Sports Hardtop	29
4-Dr. Sedan	41
4-Dr. Hardtop	43
2-Seat Wagon	45
3-Seat Wagon	46

FIFTH DIGIT: Identifies the engine

CID	CODE
360 2 BC 8-Cyl.	K
400 2 BC 8-Cyl.	M
400 4 BC Hi-Perf. 8-Cyl.	P
440 4 BC 8-Cyl.	T
440 4 BC Hi-Perf. 8-Cyl.	U
Special Order 8-Cyl.	Z

SIXTH DIGIT: Identifies the year
2 - 1972

SEVENTH DIGIT: Identifies the assembly plant

PLANT	CODE
Lynch Road, Detroit, MI	A
Hamtramck, Mi	B
Jefferson Ave., Detroit, MI	C
Belvidere, IL	D
Newark, DE	F
St. Louis, MO	G
Windsor, Ontario, CAN	R

LAST SIX DIGITS: Identify the production sequence number

EXAMPLE

C	E	41	M	2	C	123456
Car Make	Price Class	Body Type	Engine	Model Year	Asm Plant	Production Sequence Number

BODY CODE PLATE

THE BODY CODE PLATE is located in the engine compartment on the left wheel housing, fender side shield or radiator yoke.

THE BODY CODE PLATE is read left to right, bottom to top. The information on the plate includes the car S.O. Number and the trim and paint codes.

```
        CHRYSLER MOTORS
           CORPORATION

                              Line
   XXX   XXX   XXX   XXX        6
   XXX   XXX   XXX   XXX        5
   XXX   XXX   XXX   XXX        4
   XXX   XXX   XXX   XXX        3
   XXX   XXX   XXX   XXX        2
   XXX   XXX   XXX   XXX        1
```

LINE 1 - DIGITS 1, 2 & 3: Indicate engine codes

CID	CODE
360 CID 2 BC 8-Cyl.	E57
400 CID 2 BC 8-Cyl.	E63
400 CID 4 BC Hi-Perf. 8-Cyl.	E68
440 CID 4 BC 8-Cyl.	E85
440 CID 4 BC Hi-Perf. 8-Cyl.	E86

LINE 1 - DIGITS 4, 5 & 6: Indicate transmission codes

TRANSMISSION	CODE
3-Spd. Manual	D13
3-Spd. Manual	D14
3-Spd. Manual	D15
4-Spd. Manual	D21
3-Spd. Automatic	D34
3-Spd. Automatic	D35
H.D. Clutch 9 1/2"	D41
Special Order	D99

LINE 1 - DIGIT 7: Indicates car line

MAKE	CODE
Chrysler	C
Imperial	Y

LINE 1 - DIGIT 8: Indicates price class

CLASS	CODE
Grand	G
High	H
Low	L
Medium	M
Premium	P
Special	S

LINE 1 - DIGITS 9 & 10: Indicate body type

TYPE	CODE
2-Dr. Sedan	21
2-Dr. Hardtop	23
2-Dr. Sports Hardtop	29
4-Dr. Sedan	41
4-Dr. Hardtop	43
2-Seat Wagon	45
3-Seat Wagon	46

LINE 1 - DIGIT 11: Indicates engine code

CID	CODE
360 CID 2 BC 8-Cyl.	K
400 CID 2 BC 8-Cyl.	M
400 CID 4 BC Hi-Perf. 8-Cyl.	P
440 CID 4 BC 8-Cyl.	T
440 CID 4 BC Hi-Perf. 8-Cyl.	U
Special Order 8-Cyl.	Z

LINE 1 DIGIT 12: Indicates model year
2 - 1972

LINE 1 - DIGIT 13: Indicates the assembly plant

PLANT	CODE
Lynch Road, Detroit, MI	A
Hamtramck, MI	B
Jefferson Ave., Detroit, MI	C
Belvidere, IL	D
Newark, DE	F
St. Louis, MO	G
Windsor, Ontario, CAN	R

LINE 1 - LAST SIX DIGITS: Indicate production sequence number

LINE 2 - DIGITS 1, 2 & 3: Indicate lower body paint color

COLOR	CODE
Winchester Gray Metallic	GA4
Slate Gray Metallic	GA8
Charcoal Metallic	EA9
Blue Sky	HB1
Glacial Blue Metallic	GB2
Basin Street Blue	TB3
True Blue Metallic	GB5
Evening Blue Metallic	GB7
Midnight Blue Metallic	GB9
Midnight Blue Metallic	GB9
Rallye Red	FE5
Burnished Red Metallic	GE7
Amber Sherwood Metallic	GF3
Sherwood Green Metallic	GF7
Sahara Beige	HL4
Coral Turquoise Metallic	FQ5
Mojave Tan Metallic	HT6
Chestnut Metallic	HT8
Tor-Red	EV2
Spinnaker White	EW1
Formal Black	TX9
Lemon Twist	FY1
Sun Fire Yellow	DY2
Honeydew	GY4
Gold Leaf Metallic	GY8
Tawny Gold Metallic	GY9
Special Order	999

LINE 2 - DIGITS 4, 5, 6 & 7: Indicate trim code

LINE 2 - DIGIT 4: Indicates price class

CLASS	CODE
Grand	G
High	H
Police	K
Low	L
Medium	M
Premium	P
Special	S
Taxi	T
Fast Top	X

LINE 2 - DIGIT 5: Indicates seat and fabric type

SEAT	CODE
Cloth & Vinyl Bench	1
Vinyl Bench	2
Cloth & Leather Bench	A
Leather Bench	M
Cloth & Vinyl Bench Split Back	3
Vinyl Bench Split Back	4
Cloth & Leather Bench Split Back	B
Leather Bench Split Back	P
Cloth & Vinyl Bucket	5
Vinyl Bucket	6
Cloth & Leather Bucket	C
Leather Bucket	R
Cloth & Vinyl 50/50	7
Vinyl 50/50	8
Cloth & Leather 50/50	D
Leather 50/50	L
Cloth & Vinyl Special Design	9
Vinyl Special Design	H
Cloth & Leather Special Design	E
Leather Special Design	T

LINE 2 - DIGITS 6 & 7: Indicate interior color

COLOR	CODE
Gray	A9
Medium Blue	B5
Dark Blue	B8
Green	F6
Green & White	FW
White & Green	G6
Parchment	L3
Light Tan	T5
Black	X9
Black & White	XW
Light Gold	Y3
Gold	Y5

LINE 2 - DIGITS 8, 9 & 10: Indicate upper door frame color, not listed

LINE 2 - DIGIT 11: Indicates month of manufacture

MONTH	CODE
January	1
February	2
March	3
April	4
May	5
June	6
July	7
August	8
September	9
October	A
November	B
December	C

LINE 2 - DIGITS 12 & 13: Indicate the day of month of manufacture

LINE 2 - LAST SIX DIGITS: Indicate production sequence number

LINE 3 - DIGITS 1, 2 & 3: Indicate upper body color or vinyl roof codes

COLOR	CODE
Paint-Mono Tone	V01
Paint-Two Tone	V02
Paint, Trim & Vinyl Roof Waiver	V08
Paint-Special Order	V09
Full Vinyl Roof	V10
Full Vinyl Roof Gunmetal	V1A
Full Vinyl Roof Blue	V1B
Full Vinyl Roof Green	V1F
Full Vinyl Roof Mock Turtle	V1G
Full Vinyl Roof Burgundy	V1M
Full Vinyl Roof Walnut	V1T
Full Vinyl Roof White	V1W
Full Vinyl Roof Black	V1X
Full Vinyl Roof Gold	V1Y
Paint-Hood Performance	V21
Paint-Deck Performance	V25
Folding Sunroof	V30
Folding Sunroof White	V3W
Folding Sunroof Black	V3X
Canopy Vinyl Roof	V40
Canopy Vinyl Roof Green	V4F
Canopy Vinyl Roof Mock Turtle	V4G
Canopy Vinyl Roof White	V4W
Canopy Vinyl Roof Black	V4X
Canopy Vinyl Roof Gold	V4Y
Mouldings-Protective Vinyl Body Side	V50
Mouldings-Protective Vinyl Body Side Black	V5X
Sport Stripes	V60
Sport Stripes White	V6W
Sport Stripes Black	V6X
Sport Stripes Delete	V68
Accent Stripes Paint	V70
Accent Stripes White	V7W
Accent Stripes Black	V7X
Accent Stripes Delete	V78
Sport Stripes	V80
Sport Stripes White	V8W
Sport Stripes Black	V8X

ENGINE NUMBER

THE ENGINE IDENTIFICATION NUMBER for V-8 engines are on the left side rear of block near oil pan flange on 360, 400 and 440 blocks.

The following identification is included in the engine serial number:

THE FIRST TWO LETTERS designate the manufacturing plant.

PLANT	CODE
Mound Road	PM
Trenton	PT

THE THREE NUMBERS following the plant identification indicate the cubic inch displacement: ie. 360 - 400 - 440.

THE FOUR NUMBERS following the model identification designate the build date. This is a date code for manufacturing purposes.

THE FOUR NUMBERS following the build date are the engine sequence number.

EXAMPLE
PM31836301234

In the example above:

PM	Mound Road
318	Cubic Inch Displacement
3630	Build date code*
1234	Engine sequence number

*1972 build date codes run from 3625 thru 3990

NEWPORT ENGINES

CID	NO. CYL.	HORSE-POWER	COMP. RATIO	CARB
360	8	175	8.8:1	2 BC
400	8	190	8.2:1	2 BC
440	8	225	8.2:1	4 BC
440	8	245	8.2:1	4 BC

NEW YORKER ENGINES

CID	NO. CYL.	HORSE-POWER	COMP. RATIO	CARB
440	8	225	8.2:1	4 BC
440	8	245	8.2:1	4 BC

TOWN & COUNTRY ENGINES

CID	NO. CYL.	HORSE-POWER	COMP. RATIO	CARB
400	8	190	8.2:1	2 BC
440	8	225	8.2:1	4 BC

IMPERIAL ENGINES

CID	NO. CYL.	HORSE-POWER	COMP. RATIO	CARB
440	8	225	8.2:1	4 BC

1973 CHRYSLER NEW YORKER

1973 CHRYSLER NEW YORKER

1973 CHRYSLER IMPERIAL

1973 CHRYSLER IMPERIAL

1973 CHRYSLER NEWPORT

1973 CHRYSLER NEWPORT

VEHICLE IDENTIFICATION NUMBER

CHRYSLER
YH41M3R123456

Located on a plate attached to the left side of the instrument panel, visible through the windshield.

FIRST DIGIT: Identifies the car make

MAKE CODE

Chrysler	C
Chrysler Luxury	Y
Chrysler Specialty	S

SECOND DIGIT: Identifies the price class

CLASS	CODE
Low	L
Medium	M
High	H
Special	S
Premium	P

THIRD & FOURTH DIGITS: Identify the body type

TYPE	CODE
2-Dr. Hardtop Coupe	23
4-Dr. Sedan	41
4-Dr. Hardtop Sedan	43
2-Seat Wagon	45
3-Seat Wagon	46

FIFTH DIGIT: Identifies the engine

CID	CODE
400 CID 2 BC 8-Cyl.	M
440 CID 4 BC 8-Cyl.	T
440 4 BC Hi-Perf. 8-Cyl.	U

SIXTH DIGIT: Identifies the year
3 - 1973

SEVENTH DIGIT: Identifies the assembly plant

PLANT	CODE
Jefferson Ave., Detroit, MI	C
Belvidere, IL	D
Newark, DE	F
Windsor, Ontario, CAN	R

LAST SIX DIGITS: Identify the production sequence number starting at each plant with 100001.

EXAMPLE

Y	H	41	M	3	R	123456
Car Make	Price Class	Body Type	Engine	Model Year	Asm Plant	Production Sequence Number

BODY CODE PLATE

THE BODY CODE PLATE is located in the engine compartment on the left wheel housing, fender side shield or radiator yoke.

THE BODY CODE PLATE is read left to right, bottom to top. The information on the plate includes the car S.O. Number and the trim and paint codes.

```
        CHRYSLER MOTORS
          CORPORATION
                                Line
 •   XXX  XXX  XXX  XXX      6
     XXX  XXX  XXX  XXX      5
     XXX  XXX  XXX  XXX      4
     XXX  XXX  XXX  XXX      3
     XXX  XXX  XXX  XXX      2
     XXX  XXX  XXX  XXX      1
```

LINE 1 - DIGITS 1, 2 & 3: Indicate engine codes

CID	CODE
400 CID 2 BC 8-Cyl.	E63
440 CID 4 BC 8-Cyl.	E85
440 CID 4 BC Hi-Perf. 8-Cyl.	E86

LINE 1 - DIGITS 4, 5 & 6: Indicate transmission codes

TRANSMISSION CODE	
3-Spd. Manual Floor Shift	D13
3-Spd. Manual Clm. Shift	D14
3-Spd. Manual Clm. Shift	D15
4-Spd. Manual	D21
3-Spd. Automatic	D31
3-Spd. Automatic	D32
3-Spd. Automatic	D36

LINE 1 - DIGIT 7: Indicates car line

MAKE	CODE
Chrysler	C
Chrysler Luxury	Y
Chrysler Specialty	S

LINE 1 - DIGIT 8: Indicates price class

CLASS	CODE
Low	L
Medium	M
High	H
Special	S
Premium	P

LINE 1 - DIGITS 9 & 10: Indicate body type

TYPE	CODE
2-Dr. Hardtop	23
4-Dr. Sedan	41
4-Dr. Hardtop Sedan	43
2-Seat Wagon	45
3-Seat Wagon	46

LINE 1 - DIGIT 11: Indicates engine code

CID	CODE
400 CID 2 BC 8-Cyl.	M
440 CID 4 BC 8-Cyl.	T
440 4 BC Hi-Perf. 8-Cyl.	U

LINE 1 - DIGIT 12: Indicates model year
3 - 1973

LINE 1 - DIGIT 13: Indicates the assembly plant

PLANT	CODE
Jefferson Ave., Detroit, MI	C
Belvidere, IL	D
Newark, DE	F
Windsor, Ontario, CAN	R

LINE 1 - LAST SIX DIGITS: Indicate production sequence number

LINE 2 - DIGITS 1, 2 & 3: Indicate lower body paint color

COLOR	CODE
Silver Frost Metallic	JA5
Blue Sky	HB1
Basin Street Blue	TB3
True Blue Metallic	GB5
Regal Blue Metallic	JB9
Rallye Red	FE5
Burnished Red Metallic	GE7
Mist Green	JF1
Amber Sherwood Metallic	GF3
Forest Green Metallic	JF8
Autumn Bronze Metallic	GK6
Sahara Beige	HL4
Coral Turquoise Metallic	FQ5
Mojave Tan Metallic	HT6
Chestnut Metallic	HT8
Spinnaker White	EW1
Formal Black	TX9
Lemon Twist	FY1
Sunfire Yellow	DY2
Honey Gold	JY3
Golden Haze Metallic	JY6
Tahitian Gold Metallic	JY9
Special Order	999

LINE 2 - DIGITS 4, 5, 6 & 7: Indicate trim code

LINE 2 - DIGIT 4: Indicates price class

CLASS	CODE
Low	L
Medium	M
High	H
Special	S
Premium	P

LINE 2 - DIGIT 5: Indicates seat and fabric type

SEAT	CODE
Cloth & Vinyl Bench	1
Vinyl Bench	2
Cloth & Leather Bench	A
Leather Bench	M
Cloth & Vinyl Bench Split Back	3
Vinyl Bench Split Back	4
Cloth & Leather Bench Split Back	B
Leather Bench Split Back	P
Cloth & Vinyl Bucket	5
Vinyl Bucket	6
Cloth & Leather Bucket	C
Leather Bucket	R
Cloth & Vinyl 50/50	7
Vinyl 50/50	8
Cloth & Leather 50/50	D
Leather 50/50	L
Cloth & Vinyl Special Design	9
Vinyl Special Design	H
Cloth & Leather Special Design	E
Leather Special Design	T

LINE 2 - DIGITS 6 & 7: Indicate interior color

COLOR	CODE
Gray	A9
Medium Blue	B5
Dark Blue	B8
Red-Black-White	EW
Green	F6
Copper-Black-White	KW
Parchment	L3
Light Tan	T5
Black	X9
Black & White	XW
Gold	Y4
Gold-Black-White	YW

LINE 2 - DIGITS 8, 9 & 10: Indicate upper door frame color, not listed

LINE 2 - DIGIT 11: Indicates the month of manufacture

MONTH	CODE
January	1
February	2
March	3
April	4
May	5
June	6
July	7
August	8
September	9
October	A
November	B
December	C

LINE 2 - DIGITS 12 & 13: Indicate the day of month of manufacture

LINE 2 - LAST SIX DIGITS: Indicate production sequence number

LINE 3 - DIGITS 1, 2 & 3: Indicate upper body color or vinyl roof codes

COLOR	CODE
Paint-Mono Tone	V01
Paint-Two Tone	V02
Paint, Trim & Vinyl Roof Waiver	V08
Paint-Special Order	V09
Full Vinyl Roof	V10
Full Vinyl Roof Blue	V1B
Full Vinyl Roof Green	V1F
Full Vinyl Roof White	V1W
Full Vinyl Roof Black	V1X
Full Vinyl Roof Gold	V1Y
Paint-Hood Performance	V21
Halo Style Vinyl Roof	V40
Halo Style Vinyl Roof Blue	V4B
Halo Style Vinyl Roof Green	V4F
Halo Style Vinyl Roof White	V4W
Halo Style Vinyl Roof Black	V4X
Halo Style Vinyl Roof Gold	V4Y
Mouldings-Protective Vinyl Body Side	V50
Mouldings-Protective Vinyl Body Side Black	V5X
Sport Stripes	V60
Sport Stripes White	V6W
Sport Stripes Black	V6X
Accent Stripes	V70
Accent Stripes White	V7W
Accent Stripes Black	V7X
Sport Stripes	V80
Sport Stripes White	V8W
Sport Stripes Black	V8X
Hood Stripes	V90
Hood Stripes White	V9W
Hood Stripes Black	V9X

ENGINE NUMBER

THE ENGINE IDENTIFICATION NUMBER for 400 engines is found on the right side of the block adjacent to the distributor. The engine number for 440 engines is located on the left bank adjacent to the front tappet rail.

The following identification will be included in the engine serial number:

"A" ENGINE FAMILY

THE FIRST TWO LETTERS will designate the series and/or build plant.

THE THREE NUMBERS following the series and/or build plant are the cubic inch displacement: 400 - 440.

THE LETTER following the model identification is the engine type.

THE FOUR NUMBERS following the engine type are the build date code.

THE FOUR NUMBERS following the build date code are the daily production sequence number.

"B" AND "G" ENGINE FAMILY

THE FIRST LETTER will designate the series.

THE THREE NUMBERS AND LETTER following the series are the cubic inch displacement and type.

THE THREE NUMBERS following the model identification and type are the build date.

THE NUMBER following the build date is the shift built.

ENGINE SERIAL NUMBER CODES DEFINED:

High Performance	HP
Series (1973)	J
Low Compression	LC
Mound Road Plant	M
Premium Fuel Recommended	P
Regular Fuel may be used	R
Special Engine	S
Windsor Plant	W

EXAMPLE ("A" Engine Family)
JM400R39961234

J	Series (1973)
M	Mound Road Plant
400	Cubic Inch Displacement
R	Regular Fuel may be used
3996	Build date code*
1234	Engine sequence number

*1973 build date codes run from 3991 thru 4355

EXAMPLE ("B" AND "G" Engine Family)
J440R8-222

J	Series (1973)
440R	Cubic Inch Displacement and Type
8-22	Build date
2	Shift built

NEWPORT ENGINES

CID	NO. CYL.	HORSE-POWER	COMP. RATIO	CARB.
400	8	185	8.2:1	2 BC
440	8	215	8.2:1	4 BC

NEW YORKER ENGINES

CID	NO. CYL.	HORSE-POWER	COMP. RATIO	CARB.
440	8	215	8.2:1	4 BC

TOWN & COUNTRY ENGINES

CID	NO. CYL.	HORSE-POWER	COMP. RATIO	CARB.
440	8	215	8.2:1	4 BC

IMPERIAL LE BARON ENGINES

CID	NO. CYL.	HORSE-POWER	COMP. RATIO	CARB.
440	8	215	8.2:1	4 BC

1974 CHRYSLER IMPERIAL

1974 CHRYSLER NEWPORT

1974 CHRYSLER NEW YORKER

1974 CHRYSLER NEW YORKER

VEHICLE IDENTIFICATION NUMBER

• CHRYSLER
YH41N4R123456 •

Located on a plate attached to the left side of the instrument panel, visible through the windshield.

FIRST DIGIT: Identifies the car make

MAKE	CODE
Chrysler	C
Chrysler Luxury	Y
Chrysler Specialty	S

SECOND DIGIT: Identifies the price class

CLASS	CODE
Low	L
Medium	M
High	H
Special	S
Premium	P

THIRD & FOURTH DIGITS: Identify the body type

TYPE	CODE
2-Dr. Hardtop Coupe	23
4-Dr. Sedan	41
4-Dr. Hardtop Sedan	43
2-Seat Station Wagon	45
3-Seat Station Wagon	46

FIFTH DIGIT: Identifies the engine

CID	CODE
360 CID 4 BC 8-Cyl.	J
360 CID 2 BC 8-Cyl.	K
400 CID 2 BC 8-Cyl.	M
400 CID 4 BC 8-Cyl.	N
440 CID 4 BC 8-Cyl.	T
Special Order 8-Cyl.	Z

SIXTH DIGIT: Identifies the year
4 - 1974

SEVENTH DIGIT: Identifies the assembly plant

PLANT	CODE
Jefferson Ave., Detroit, MI	C
Belvidere, IL	D
Newark, DE	F
Windsor, Ontario, CAN	R

LAST SIX DIGITS: Identify the production sequence number starting at each plant with 100001

EXAMPLE						
Y	H	41	N	4	R	123456
Car Make	Price Class	Body Type	Engine	Model Year	Asm Plant	Production Sequence Number

BODY CODE PLATE

THE BODY CODE PLATE is located in the engine compartment on the left wheel housing, fender side shield or radiator yoke.

THE BODY CODE PLATE is read left to right, bottom to top. The information on the plate includes the S.O. Number and the trim and paint codes.

```
          CHRYSLER MOTORS
             CORPORATION
                                    Line
 •  XXX  XXX  XXX  XXX               6   •
    XXX  XXX  XXX  XXX               5
    XXX  XXX  XXX  XXX               4
    XXX  XXX  XXX  XXX               3
    XXX  XXX  XXX  XXX               2
    XXX  XXX  XXX  XXX               1
```

LINE 1 - DIGITS 1, 2 & 3: Indicate engine codes

CID	CODE
360 CID 4 BC 8-Cyl.	E56
360 CID 2 BC 8-Cyl.	E57
400 CID 2 BC 8-Cyl.	E63
400 CID 4 BC 8-Cyl.	E64
440 CID 8-Cyl.	E85

LINE 1 - DIGITS 4, 5 & 6: Indicate transmission codes

TRANSMISSION	CODES
3-Spd. Manual Floor Shift	D13
3-Spd. Std. Manual Clm. Shift	D14
H.D. 3-Spd. Manual Clm. Shift	D15
4-Spd. Manual	D21
Standard Automatic	D34
H.D. Automatic	D35

LINE 1 - DIGIT 7: Indicates car line

MAKE	CODE
Chrysler	C
Chrysler Luxury	Y
Chrysler Specialty	S

LINE 1 - DIGIT 8: Indicates price class

CLASS	CODE
Low	L
Medium	M
High	S
Special	S
Premium	P

LINE 1 - DIGITS 9 & 10: Indicate body type

TYPE	CODE
2-Dr. Hardtop Coupe	23
4-Dr. Sedan	41
4-Dr. Hardtop Sedan	43
2-Seat Station Wagon	45
3-Seat Station Wagon	46

LINE 1 - DIGIT 11: Indicates engine code

CID	CODE
360 CID 4 BC 8-Cyl.	J
360 CID 2 BC 8-Cyl.	K
400 CID 2 BC 8-Cyl.	M
400 CID 4 BC 8-Cyl.	N
440 CID 4 BC 8-Cyl.	T
Special Order 8-Cyl.	Z

LINE 1 - DIGIT 12: Indicates model year
4 - 1974

LINE 1 - DIGIT 13: Indicates the assembly plant

PLANT	CODE
Jefferson Ave., Detroit, MI	C
Belvidere, IL	D
Newark, DE	F
Windsor, Ontario, CAN	R

LINE 1 - LAST SIX DIGITS: Indicate production sequence number

LINE 2 - DIGITS 1, 2 & 3: Indicate lower body paint color

COLOR	CODE
Silver Frost Metallic	JA5
Powder Blue	KB1
Lucerne Blue Metallic	KB5
Starlight Blue Metallic	KB8
Rallye Red	FE5
Burnished Red Metallic	GE7
Frosty Green Metallic	KG2
Deep Sherwood Metallic	KG8
Avocado Gold Metallic	KJ6
Sahara Beige	HL4
Dark Moonstone Metallic	KL8
Sienna Metallic	KT5
Dark Chestnut Metallic	KT9
Spinnaker White	EW1
Formal Black	TX9
Sun Fire Yellow	DY2
Golden Fawn	KY4
Yellow Blaze	KY5
Golden Haze Metallic	JY6
Tahitian Godl Metallic	JY9
Special Order	999

LINE 2 - DIGITS 4, 5, 6 & 7: Indicate trim code

LINE 2 - DIGIT 4: Indicates price class

CLASS	CODE
Low	L
Medium	M
High	H
Special	S
Premium	P

LINE 2 - DIGIT 5: Indicates seat and fabric type

SEAT	CODE
Cloth & Vinyl Bench	1
Vinyl Bench	2
Cloth & Leather Bench	A
Leather Bench	M
Cloth & Vinyl Bench Split Back	3

SEAT

SEAT	CODE
Vinyl Bench Split Back	4
Cloth & Leather Bench Split Back	B
Leather Bench Split Back	P
Cloth & Vinyl Bucket	5
Vinyl Bucket	6
Cloth & Leather Bucket	C
Leather Bucket	R
Cloth & Vinyl 50/50	7
Vinyl 50/50	8
Cloth & Leather 50/50	D
Leather 50/50	L
Cloth & Vinyl Special Design	9
Vinyl Special Design	H
Cloth & Leather Special Design	E
Leather Special Design	T

LINE 2 - DIGITS 6 & 7: Indicate interior color

COLOR	CODE
Gray	A9
Blue	B6
Wimbleton	EW
Green	G6
Parchment	L3
Tangier	LL
Chestnut	T7
Orange, Black & White	VW
Black	X9
Black & White	XW
Gold	Y3
White & Gold	YW

LINE 2 - DIGITS 8, 9 & 10: Indicate upper door frame color, not listed

LINE 2 - DIGIT 11: Indicates the month of manufacture

MONTH	CODE
January	1
February	2
March	3
April	4
May	5
June	6
July	7
August	8
September	9
October	A
November	B
December	C

LINE 2 - DIGITS 12 & 13: Indicate the day of month of manufacture

LINE 2 - LAST SIX DIGITS: Indicate production sequence number

LINE 3 - DIGITS 1, 2 & 3: Indicate upper body color or vinyl roof codes

COLOR	CODE
Paint-Mono Tone	V01
Paint-Two Tone	V01
Paint, Trim & Vinyl Roof Waiver	V08
Paint-Special Order	V09
Full Vinyl Roof	V10
Full Vinyl Roof Blue	V1B
Full Vinyl Roof Green	V1G
Full Vinyl Roof Parchment	V1L
Full Vinyl Roof White	V1W
Full Vinyl Roof Black	V1X
Full Vinyl Roof Gold	V1Y
Paint-Hood Performance	V21
Decor Stripe Pkg. #2	V25
Halo Style Vinyl Roof	V40
Halo Style Vinyl Roof White	V4W
Halo Style Vinyl Roof Black	V4X
Halo Style Vinyl Roof Gold Reptile Grain	V4Y
Mouldings-Protective Vinyl Body Side	V50
Mouldings-Protective Vinyl Body Side Black	V5X
Sport Stripes	V60
Sport Stripes Red	V6R
Sport Stripes White	V6W
Sport Stripes Black	V6X
Sport Stripes Gold	V6Y
Sport Stripes Delete	V68
Accent Stripes	V70
Accent Stripes Blue Green	V7B
Accent Stripes Parchment	V7L
Accent Stripes Red	V7R
Accent Stripes White	V7W
Accent Stripes Black	V7X
Accent Stripes Gold	V7Y
Accent Stripes Delete	V78
Sport Stripes	V80
Sport Stripes Parchment	V8L
Sport Stripes Red	V8R
Sport Stripes White	V8W
Sport Stripes Black	V8X
Sport Stripes Delete	V88
Sport Stripes-Body Side & Roof	V90
Sport Stripes-Body Side & Roof Red	V9R
Sport Stripes-Body Side & Roof White	V9W
Sport Stripes-Body Side & Roof Black	V9X

ENGINE NUMBER

THE ENGINE IDENTIFICATION NUMBER for 360 CID V-8 engines is found at the left front of the block below the cylinder head. The engine number for 400 engines is found on the right side of the block adjacent to the distributor. The engine number for 440 engines is located on the left bank adjacent to the front tappet rail.

The following identification will be included in the engine serial number:

"A" ENGINE FAMILY

THE NUMBER AND LETTER designate the model year and/or build plant.

THE THREE NUMBERS following the model year and/or build plant are the cubic inch displacement.

THE LETTER following the model identification are the engine type.

THE FOUR NUMBERS following the engine type are the build date code.

THE FOUR NUMBERS following the build date code is the daily production sequence number.

"B" AND "G" ENGINE FAMILY

THE NUMBER AND LETTER will designate the model year and/or build plant.

THE THREE NUMBERS AND LETTLER following the model year and/or build plant are the cubic inch displacement and type.

THE THREE NUMBERS following the model identification and type are the build date.

THE NUMBER following the build date is the shift built.

ENGINE SERIAL NUMBER CODES DEFINED:

	CODE
High Performance	HP
Series (1974)	K
Low Compression	LC
Mound Road Plant	M
Premium Fuel Recommended	P
Regular Fuel may be used	R
Special Engine	S
Trenton Plant	T
Windsor Plant	W

NOTE: Series without "M" or "W" suffix indicates Trenton Engine Plant

EXAMPLE ("A" Engine Family)
4M400R44201234

4	Model year
M	Mound Road Plant
400	Cubic Inch Displacement
R	Regular Fuel may be used
4420	Build date code
1234	Engine sequence number

EXAMPLE ("B" And "G" Engine Family)
4T440R8-222

4	Model year
T	Build plant
440R	Cubic Inch Displacement and Type
8-22	Build date
2	Shift built

IMPERIAL ENGINES

CID	NO. CYL.	HORSE-POWER	COMP. RATIO	CARB.
440	8	230	8.2:1	4 BC

NEWPORT ENGINES

CID	NO. CYL.	HORSE-POWER	COMP. RATIO	CARB.
400	8	185	8.2:1	2 BC
360	8	200	8.4:1	4 BC
400	8	205	8.2:1	4 BC
440	8	230	8.2:1	4 BC

NEW YORKER ENGINES

CID	NO. CYL.	HORSE-POWER	COMP. RATIO	CARB.
440	8	230	8.2:1	4 BC

1975 CHRYSLER IMPERIAL LE BARON

1975 CHRYSLER CORDOBA

1975 CHRYSLER NEWPORT

1975 CHRYSLER IMPERIAL LE BARON

1975 CHRYSLER NEW YORKER

1975 CHRYSLER NEWPORT

1975 CHRYSLER TOWN AND COUNTRY STATION WAGON

1975 CHRYSLER NEW YORKER

VEHICLE IDENTIFICATION NUMBER

CHRYSLER SS22N5R123456

Located on a plate attached to the left side of the instrument panel, visible through the windshield.

FIRST DIGIT: Identifies the car make

MAKE	CODE
Chrysler	C
Chrysler Luxury	Y
Cordoba	S

SECOND DIGIT: Identifies the price class

CLASS	CODE
High	H
Low	L
Medium	M
Premium	P
Special	S

THIRD & FOURTH DIGITS: Identify the body type

TYPE	CODE
2-Dr. Specialty Hardtop	22
2-Dr. Hardtop Coupe	23
4-Dr. Sedan	41
4-Dr. Hardtop Sedan	43
2-Seat Station Wagon	45
3-Seat Station Wagon	46

FIFTH DIGIT: Identifies the engine

CID	CODE
318 CID 2 BC 8-Cyl.	G
360 CID 2 BC 8-Cyl.**	K
360 CID 4 BC 8-Cyl.*	J
400 CID 2 BC 8-Cyl.**	M
400 CID 4 BC 8-Cyl.	N
400 CID 4 BC Hi-Perf. 8-Cyl.	P
440 CID 4 BC 8-Cyl.	T
440 CID 4 BC Hi-Perf. 8-Cyl.	U

*With California emission package
**Not available with California emission package

SIXTH DIGIT: Identifies the year.
5 - 1975

SEVENTH DIGIT: Identifies the assembly plant

PLANT	CODE
Jefferson Ave., Detroit, MI	C
Belvidere, IL	D
Newark, DE	F
Windsor, Ontario, CAN	R

LAST SIX DIGITS: Identify the production sequence number starting at each plant with 100001

EXAMPLE

S	S	22	N	5	R	123456
Car Make	Price Class	Body Type	Engine	Model Year	Asm Plant	Production Sequence Number

BODY CODE PLATE

THE BODY CODE PLATE is located in the engine compartment on the left wheel housing, fender side shield or radiator yoke.

THE BODY CODE PLATE is read left to right, bottom to top. The information on the plate includes the S.O. Number and the trim and paint codes.

```
       CHRYSLER MOTORS
          CORPORATION
                              Line
   XXX  XXX  XXX  XXX          6
   XXX  XXX  XXX  XXX          5
   XXX  XXX  XXX  XXX          4
   XXX  XXX  XXX  XXX          3
   XXX  XXX  XXX  XXX          2
   XXX  XXX  XXX  XXX          1
```

LINE 1 - DIGITS 1, 2 & 3: Indicate engine codes

CID	CODE
318 CID 2 BC 8-Cyl.	E44
360 CID 2 BC 8-Cyl.**	E57
360 CID 4 BC 8-Cyl.*	E56
400 CID 2 BC 8-Cyl.**	E63
400 CID 4 BC 8-Cyl.	E64
400 CID 4 BC Hi-Perf. 8-Cyl.	E68
440 CID 4 BC 8-Cyl.	E85
440 CID 4 BC Hi-Perf. 8-Cyl.	E86

*With California emission package
**Not available with California emission package

LINE 1 - DIGITS 4, 5 & 6: Indicate transmission codes

TRANSMISSION	CODES
3-Spd. Manual Floor Shift	D13
3-Spd. Std. Manual Clm. Shift	D14
H.D. 3-Spd. Manual Clm. Shift	D15
4-Spd. Manual	D21
Standard Automatic	D34
H.D. Automatic	D35

LINE 1 - DIGIT 7: Indicates car line

MAKE	CODE
Chrysler	C
Chrysler Luxury	Y
Cordoba	S

LINE 1 - DIGIT 8: Indicates price class

CLASS	CODE
Dodge Taxi	G
High	H
Police	K
Low	L
Medium	M
Premium	P
Special	S
Taxi	T

LINE 1 - DIGITS 9 & 10: Indicate body type

TYPE	CODE
2-Dr. Specialty Hardtop	22
2-Dr. Hardtop Coupe	23
4-Dr. Sedan	41
4-Dr. Hardtop Sedan	43
2-Seat Station Wagon	45
3-Seat Station Wagon	46

LINE 1 - DIGIT 11: Indicates engine code

CID	CODE
318 CID 2 BC 8-Cyl.	G
360 CID 2 BC 8-Cyl.**	K
360 CID 4 BC 8-Cyl.*	J
400 CID 2 BC 8-Cyl.**	M
400 CID 4 BC 8-Cyl.	N
400 CID 4 BC Hi-Perf. 8-Cyl.	P
440 CID 4 BC 8-Cyl.	T
440 CID 4 BC Hi-Perf. 8-Cyl.	U

*With California emission package
**Not available with California emission package.

LINE 1 - DIGIT 12: Indicates model year
5 - 1975

LINE 1 - DIGIT 13: Indicates the assembly plant

PLANT	CODE
Jefferson Ave., Detroit, MI	C
Belvidere, IL	D
Newark, DE	F
Windsor, Ontario, CAN	R

LAST SIX DIGITS: Indicate production sequence number starting at each plant with 100001

LINE 2 - DIGITS 1, 2 & 3: Indicate lower body paint color

COLOR	CODE
Silver Cloud Metallic	LA2
Platinum Metallic	LJ2
Powder Blue	KB1
Lucerne Blue Metallic	KB5
Astral Blue Metallic	LB2
Starlight Blue Metallic	KB8
Rallye Red	FE5
Vintage Red Metallic	LE9
Bittersweet Metallic	LK3
Frosty Green Metallic	KG2
Deep Sherwood Metallic	KG8
Avocado Gold Metallic	KJ6
Sahara Beige	HL4
Moondust Metallic	LI5
Cinnamon Metallic	LT4
Sienna Metallic	KT5
Dark Chestnut Metallic	KT9
Spinnaker White	EW1
Formal Black	TX9
Yellow Blaze	KY5
Golden Fawn	KY4
Inca Gold Metallic	LY6
Spanish Gold Metallic	LY9

LINE 2 - DIGITS 4, 5, 6 & 7: Indicate trim code

LINE 2 - DIGIT 4: Indicates price class

CLASS	CODE
High	H
Low	L
Medium	M
Premium	P
Special	S

LINE 2 - DIGIT 5: Indicates seat and fabric type

SEAT	CODE
Cloth & Vinyl Bench	1
Vinyl Bench	2
Cloth & Leather Bench	A
Leather Bench	M
Cloth & Vinyl Bench Split Back	3
Vinyl Bench Split Back	4
Cloth & Leather Bench Split Back	B
Leather Bench Split Back	P
Cloth & Vinyl Bucket	5
Vinyl Bucket	6
Cloth & Leather Bucket	C
Leather Bucket	R
Cloth & Vinyl 50/50	7
Vinyl 50/50	8
Cloth & Leather 50/50	D
Leather 50/50	L
Cloth & Vinyl Special Design	9
Vinyl Special Design	H
Cloth & Leather Special Design	E
Leather Special Design	T

LINE 2 - DIGITS 6 & 7: Indicate interior color

COLOR	CODE
Medium Blue	B6
Blue & White	BW
Red	E7
Red	EE
Red, Black, White	EW
Green	G6
Green	GG
Green & White	GW
Copper, Black, White	KW
Parchment	L3
Parchment	LL
Chestnut	T7
Orange, Black, White	VW
Black	X9
Black & White	XW
Gold	Y3
Gold & White	YW

LINE 2 - DIGITS 8, 9 & 10: Indicate interior paint color, not listed

LINE 2 - DIGIT 11: Indicates the month of manufacture

MONTH	CODE
January	1
February	2
March	3
April	4
May	5
June	6
July	7
August	8
September	9
October	A
November	B
December	C

LINE 2 - DIGITS 12 & 13: Indicate the day of month of manufacture.

LINE 2 - LAST SIX DIGITS: Indicate production sequence number.

LINE 3 - DIGITS 1, 2 & 3: Indicate upper body color or vinyl roof codes.

COLOR	CODE
Halo Vinyl Roof White	V1W
Landau Vinyl Roof White	V3W
Halo Vinyl Roof Parchment	V1L
Landau Vinyl Roof Parchment	V3L
Halo Vinyl Roof Black	V1X
Landau Vinyl Roof Black	V3X
Halo Vinyl Roof Gold	V1Y
Landau Vinyl Roof Gold	V3Y
Halo Vinyl Roof Green	V1G
Landau Vinyl Roof Green	V3G
Halo Vinyl Roof Red	V1E
Landau Vinyl Roof Red	V3E
Landau Vinyl Roof Silver	V3A
Full Vinyl Roof Blue	V1B
Full Vinyl Roof Chestnut	V1T

ENGINE NUMBER

THE ENGINE IDENTIFICATION NUMBERS for 318 and 360 CID V-8 engines are found at the left front of the block below the cylinder head. The engine number for 400 engines is found on the right side of the block adjacent to the distributor. The engine number for 440 engines is located on the left bank adjacent to the front tappet rail.

The following identification will be included in the engine serial number:

"A" ENGINE FAMILY

THE NUMBER AND LETTER designate the model year and/or build plant.

THE THREE NUMBERS following the model year and/or build plant are the cubic inch displacement.

THE LETTER following the model identification is the engine type.

THE FOUR NUMBERS following the engine type are the build date code.

THE FOUR NUMBERS following the engine type is the daily production sequence number.

"B" AND "G" ENGINE FAMILY

THE NUMBER AND LETTER will designate the model year and/or build plant.

THE THREE NUMBERS AND LETTER following the model year and/or build plant are the cubic inch displacement and type.

THE THREE NUMBERS following the model identification and type are the build date.

THE NUMBER following the build date is the shift built.

ENGINE SERIAL NUMBER CODES DEFINED:

	CODE
High Performance	HP
Series (1975)	L
Low Compression	LC
Mound Road Plant	M
Premium Fuel Recommended	P
Regular Fuel may be used	R
Special Engine	S
Trenton Plant	T
Windsor Plant	W

NOTE: Series without "M" or "W" suffix indicates Trenton Engine Plant

EXAMPLE ("A" Engine Family)
5M318R09101234

5	Model year
M	Mound Road plant
318	Cubic Inch Displacement
R	Regular Fuel may be used
0910	Build date code
1234	Engine sequence number (optional usage)

EXAMPLE ("B" And "G" Engine Family)
5T440R8-222

5	Model year
T	Trenton plant
440R	Cubic Inch Displacement and Type
8-22	Build date code
2	Shift built

CORDOBA ENGINES

CID	NO. CYL.	HORSE-POWER	COMP. RATIO	CARB.
318	8	150	8.5:1	2 BC
360	8	180	8.4:1	2 BC
400	8	165	8.2:1	2 BC
400	8	190	8.2:1	4 BC
400	8	235	8.2:1	4 BC

NEWPORT ENGINES

CID	NO. CYL.	HORSE-POWER	COMP. RATIO	CARB.
360	8	180	8.4:1	2 BC
400	8	175	8.2:1	2 BC
360	8	190	8.4:1	4 BC
400	8	195	8.2:1	4 BC
440	8	215	8.2:1	4 BC

NEW YORKER ENGINES

CID	NO. CYL.	HORSE-POWER	COMP. RATIO	CARB.
400	8	175	8.2:1	2 BC
400	8	195	8.2:1	4 BC
440	8	215	8.2:1	4 BC

IMPERIAL ENGINES

CID	NO. CYL.	HORSE-POWER	COMP. RATIO	CARB.
440	8	215	8.2:1	4 BC

1976 CHRYSLER CORDOBA

1976 CHRYSLER CORDOBA

1976 CHRYSLER NEWPORT

1976 CHRYSLER NEWPORT

1976 CHRYSLER NEWPORT CUSTOM

1976 CHRYSLER TOWN & COUNTRY STATION WAGON

1976 CHRYSLER NEW YORKER

1976 CHRYSLER NEW YORKER

VEHICLE IDENTIFICATION NUMBER

```
CHRYSLER
SS22N6R123456
```

Located on a plate attached to the left side of the instrument panel, visible through the windshield.

EXAMPLE

S	S	22	N	6	R	123456
Car Make	Price Class	Body Type	Engine	Model Year	Asm Plant	Production Sequence Number

FIRST DIGIT: Identifies the car make

MAKE	CODE
Chrysler	S
Cordoba	S

SECOND DIGIT: Identifies the price class

CLASS	CODE
High	H
Police	K
Low	L
Medium	M
Premium	P
Special	S

THIRD & FOURTH DIGITS: Identify the body type

TYPE	CODE
2-Dr. Specialty Hardtop	22
2-Dr. Hardtop Coupe	23
4-Dr. Sedan	41
4-Dr. Hardtop Sedan	43
2-Seat Station Wagon	45
3-Seat Station Wagon	46

FIFTH DIGIT: Identifies the engine

CID	CODE
318 CID 2 BC 8-Cyl.	G
360 CID 4 BC 8-Cyl.*	J
360 CID 2 BC 8-Cyl.**	K
400 CID 2 BC 8-Cyl.**	M
400 CID 4 BC 8-Cyl.	N
400 CID 4 BC Hi-Perf. 8-Cyl.**	P
440 CID 4 BC 8-Cyl.	T
Special Order 8-Cyl.	Z

*With California emission package
**Not available with California emission package

SIXTH DIGIT: Identifies the year
6 - 1976

SEVENTH DIGIT: Identifies the assembly plant

PLANT	CODE
Jefferson Ave., Detroit, MI	C
Belvidere, IL	D
Newark, DE	F
Windsor, Ontario, CAN	R

LAST SIX DIGITS: Identify the production sequence number starting at each plant with 100001

BODY CODE PLATE

THE BODY CODE PLATE is located in the engine compartment on the left wheel housing, fender side shield or radiator yoke.

THE BODY CODE PLATE is read left to right, bottom to top. The information on the plate includes the S.O. Number and the trim and paint codes.

```
CHRYSLER MOTORS
CORPORATION
                          Line
XXX XXX XXX XXX            6
XXX XXX XXX XXX            5
XXX XXX XXX XXX            4
XXX XXX XXX XXX            3
XXX XXX XXX XXX            2
XXX XXX XXX XXX            1
```

LINE 1 - DIGITS 1, 2 & 3: Indicate engine codes

CID	CODE
318 CID 2 BC 8-Cyl.	E44
360 CID 4 BC 8-Cyl.*	E56
360 CID 2 BC 8-Cyl.**	E57
400 CID 2 BC 8-Cyl.**	E63
400 CID 4 BC 8-Cyl.	E64
400 CID 4 BC Hi-Perf. 8-Cyl.**	E68
440 CID 4 BC 8-Cyl.	E85

*With California emission package
**Not available with California emission package

LINE 1 - DIGITS 4, 5 & 6: Indicate transmission codes

TRANSMISSION	CODE
3-Spd. Manual Floor Shift	D13
3-Spd. Std. Manual Clm. Shift	D14
3-Spd. H.D. Manual Clm. Shift	D15
4-Spd. Standard	D21
4-Spd. O.D.	D24
Standard A904	D31
Standard A998	D32
Standard A999	D33
Standard Automatic	D34
H.D. A727	D35
Standard A727	D36
H.D. A904	D38

LINE 1 - DIGIT 7: Indicates car line

MAKE	CODE
Chrysler	S
Cordoba	S

LINE 1 - DIGIT 8: Indicates price class

CLASS	CODE
High	H
Police	K
Low	L
Medium	M
Premium	P
Special	S

LINE 1 - DIGITS 9 & 10: Indicate body type

TYPE	CODE
2-Dr. Specialty Hardtop	22
2-Dr. Hardtop Coupe	23
4-Dr. Sedan	41
4-Dr. Hardtop Sedan	43
2-Seat Station Wagon	45
3-Seat Station Wagon	46

LINE 1 - DIGIT 11: Indicates engine code

CID	CODE
318 CID 2 BC 8-Cyl.	G
360 CID 4 BC 8-Cyl.*	J
360 CID 2 BC 8-Cyl.**	K
400 CID 2 BC 8-Cyl.**	M
400 CID 4 BC 8-Cyl.	N
400 CID 4 BC Hi-Perf. 8-Cyl.**	P
440 CID 4 BC 8-Cyl.	T
Special Order 8-Cyl.	Z

*With California emission package
**Not available with California emission package

LINE 1 - DIGIT 12: Indicates model year
6 - 1976

LINE 1 - DIGIT 13: Indicates the assembly plant

PLANT	CODE
Jefferson Ave., Detroit, MI	C
Belvidere, IL	D
Newark, DE	F
Windsor, Ontario, CAN	R

LAST SIX DIGITS: Indicate production sequence number starting at each plant with 100001.

LINE 2 - DIGITS 1, 2 & 3: Indicate lower body paint color.

COLOR	CODE
Silver Cloud Metallic	LA2
Powder Blue	KB1
Astral Blue Metallic	LB2
Jamaican Blue Metallic	MB5
Starlight Blue Metallic	KB8
Rallye Red	FE5
Vintage Red Metallic	MF2
Jade Green Metallic	MF2
Deep Sherwood Metallic	KG8
Platinum Metallic	LJ2
Tropic Green Metallic	MJ5
Bittersweet Metallic	LK3
Sahara Beige	HL4
Moondust Metallic	LL5
Dark Chestnut Metallic	KT9
Saddle Tan	MU2
Caramel Tan Metallic	MU3
Light Chestnut Metallic	MU6
Spinnaker White	EW1
Formal Black	TX9
Golden Fawn	KY4
Yellow Blaze	KY5
Inca Gold Metallic	LY6
Spanish Gold Metallic	LY9
Vintage Red Sunfire Metallic	ME8
Deep Sherwood Sunfire Metallic	MG9

LINE 2 - DIGITS 4, 5, 6 & 7: Indicate trim code

LINE 2 - DIGIT 4: Indicates price class

CLASS	CODE
High	H
Police	K
Low	L
Medium	M
Premium	P
Special	S

LINE 2 - DIGIT 5: Indicates seat and fabric type

SEAT	CODE
Cloth & Vinyl Bench	1
Vinyl Bench	2
Cloth & Leather Bench	A
Leather Bench	M
Cloth & Vinyl Bench Split Back	3
Vinyl Bench Split Back	4
Cloth & Leather Bench Split Back	B
Leather Bench Split Back	P
Cloth & Vinyl Bucket	5
Vinyl Bucket	6
Cloth & Leather Bucket	C
Leather Bucket	R
Cloth & Vinyl 50/50	7
Vinyl 50/50	8
Cloth & Leather 50/50	D
Leather 50/50	L
Cloth & Vinyl Special Design	9
Vinyl Special Design	H
Cloth & Leather Special Design	E
Leather Special Design	T

LINE 2 - DIGITS 6 & 7: Indicate interior color

FABRIC COLOR	CODE
Medium Blue	B6
Blue & White	BW
Red	E7
Red	EE
Red & White	EW
Green	F6
Green	FF
Green & White	FW
Gold, Black, White	KW
Parchment	L3
Parchment	LL
Chestnut	T7
Tan	U5
Tan & White	UW
Black	X9
Black & White	XW
Gold	Y3
Gold & White	YW

LINE 2 - DIGITS 8, 9 & 10: Indicate interior paint color, not listed

LINE 2 - DIGIT 11: Indicates the month of manufacture

MONTH	CODE
January	1
February	2
March	3
April	4
May	5
June	6
July	7
August	8
September	9
October	A
November	B
December	C

LINE 2 - DIGITS 12 & 13: Indicate the day of month of manufacture

LINE 2 - LAST SIX DIGITS: Indicate production sequence number

LINE 3 - DIGITS 1, 2 & 3: Indicate upper body color or vinyl roof codes

COLOR	CODE
Halo Vinyl Roof Green	V1F
Full Vinyl Roof Green	V1F
Landau Vinyl Roof Green	V3F
Padded Canopy Vinyl Roof Green	V4F
Halo Vinyl Roof Gold	V1Y
Full Vinyl Roof Gold	V1Y
Landau Vinyl Roof Gold	V3Y
Padded Canopy Vinyl Roof Gold	V4Y
Halo Vinyl Roof Red	V1E
Full Vinyl Roof Red	V1E
Landau Vinyl Roof Red	V3E
Padded Canopy Vinyl Roof	V4E
Halo Vinyl Roof Black	V1X
Full Vinyl Roof Black	V1X
Landau Vinyl Roof Black	V3X
Padded Canopy Vinyl Roof Black	V4X
Halo Vinyl Roof White	V1W
Full Vinyl Roof White	V1W
Landau Vinyl Roof White	V3W
Padded Canopy Vinyl Roof White	V4W
Halo Vinyl Roof Tan	V1U
Landau Vinyl Roof Tan	V3U
Landau Vinyl Roof Silver	V3A
Padded Canopy Vinyl Roof Silver	V4A
Full Vinyl Roof Blue	V1B
Halo Vinyl Roof Blue	V1B
Padded Canopy Vinyl Roof Blue	V4B
Full Vinyl Roof Parchment	V1L
Halo Vinyl Roof Parchment	V1L
Padded Canopy Vinyl Roof Parchment	V4L
Full Vinyl Roof Chestnut	V1T
Halo Vinyl Roof Chestnut	V1T
Padded Canopy Vinyl Roof Chestnut	V4T

ENGINE NUMBER

THE ENGINE IDENTIFICATION NUMBERS for 318 and 360 CID V-8 engines are found at the left front of the block below the cylinder head. The engine number for 400 engines is found on the right side of the block adjacent to the distributor. The engine number for 440 engines is located on the left bank adjacent to the front tappet rail.

The following identification will be included in the engine serial number:

"A" ENGINE FAMILY

THE NUMBER AND LETTER designate the model year and/or build plant.

THE THREE NUMBERS following the model year and/or build plant are the cubic inch displacement.

THE LETTER following the engine type is the build date code.

THE FOUR NUMBERS following the engine type are the build date code.

THE FOUR NUMBERS following the engine type are the daily production sequence number.

"B" AND "G" ENGINE FAMILY

THE NUMBER AND LETTER will designate the model year and/or build plant.

THE THREE NUMBERS AND LETTER following the model year and/or build plant are the cubic inch displacement and type.

THE THREE NUMBERS following the model identification and type are the build date.

THE NUMBER following the build date is the shift built.

ENGINE SERIAL NUMBER CODES DEFINED:

	CODE
High Performance	HP
Series (1976)	
Low Compression	LC
Mound Road Plant	M
Premium Fuel recommended	P
Regular Fuel may be used	R
Special Engine	S
Trenton Plant	T
Windsor Plant	W

NOTE: Series without "M" or "W" suffix indicates Trenton Engine Plant

EXAMPLE ("A" Engine Family)
6M318R09101234

6	Model year
M	Mound Road plant
318	Cubic Inch Displacement
R	Regular Fuel may be used
0910	Build date code (0910 is September 10)
1234	Engine sequence number (optional usage)

EXAMPLE ("B" And "G" Engine Family)
6T440R8-222

6	Model year
T	Trenton plant
440R	Cubic Inch Displacement and Type
8-22	Build date code
2	Shift built

CORDOBA ENGINES

CID	NO. CYL.	HORSE-POWER	COMP. RATIO	CARB.
318	8	150	8.5:1	2 BC
360	8	170	8.4:1	2 BC
400	8	175	8.2:1	2 BC
360	8	175	8.4:1	4 BC
400	8	240	8.2:1	4 BC

NEWPORT ENGINES

CID	NO. CYL.	HORSE-POWER	COMP. RATIO	CARB.
360	8	170	8.4:1	2 BC
400	8	175	8.2:1	2 BC
360	8	175	8.4:1	4 BC
400	8	210	8.2:1	4 BC
440	8	205	8.0:1	4 BC

NEW YORKER ENGINES

CID	NO. CYL.	HORSE-POWER	COMP. RATIO	CARB.
400	8	175	8.2:1	2 BC
400	8	210	8.2:1	4 BC
440	8	205	8.0:1	4 BC

1977 CHRYSLER NEWPORT

1977 CHRYSLER NEWPORT

1977 CHRYSLER CORDOBA

1977 CHRYSLER CORDOBA

1977 CHRYSLER LE BARON

1977 CHRYSLER LE BARON

1977 CHRYSLER NEW YORKER

1977 CHRYSLER NEW YORKER

VEHICLE IDENTIFICATION NUMBER

CHRYSLER
SS22N7R123456

Located on a plate attached to the left side of the instrument panel, visible through the windshield.

FIRST DIGIT: Identifies the car make

MAKE	CODE
Chrysler	C
Chrysler Specialty & Cordoba	S

SECOND DIGIT: Identifies the price class

CLASS	CODE
High	H
Police	K
Low	L
Medium	M
Premium	P
Special	S

THIRD & FOURTH DIGITS: Identify the body type

TYPE	CODE
2-Dr. Specialty Hardtop	22
2-Dr. Hardtop Coupe	23
4-Dr. Sedan	41
4-Dr. Hardtop Sedan	43
2-Seat Station Wagon	45
3-Seat Station Wagon	46

FIFTH DIGIT: Identifies the engine

CID	CODE
318 CID 2 BC 8-Cyl.	G
360 CID 2 BC 8-Cyl.	K
400 CID 4 BC 8-Cyl.	N
440 CID 4 BC 8-Cyl.	T
Special Order 8-Cyl.	Z

SIXTH DIGIT: Identifies the year
7 - 1977

SEVENTH DIGIT: Identifies the assembly plant

PLANT	CODE
Jefferson Ave., Detroit, MI	C
Belvidere, IL	D
Newark, DE	F
Windsor, Ontario, CAN	R

LAST SIX DIGITS: Identify the production sequence number starting at each plant with 100001

EXAMPLE

S	S	22	N	7	R	123456
Car Make	Price Class	Body Type	Engine	Model Year	Asm Plant	Production Sequence Number

BODY CODE PLATE

THE BODY CODE PLATE is located in the engine compartment on the left wheel housing, fender side shield or radiator yoke.

THE BODY CODE PLATE is read left to right, bottom to top. The information on the plate includes the S.O. Number and the trim and paint codes.

CHRYSLER MOTORS CORPORATION

				Line
XXX	XXX	XXX	XXX	6
XXX	XXX	XXX	XXX	5
XXX	XXX	XXX	XXX	4
XXX	XXX	XXX	XXX	3
XXX	XXX	XXX	XXX	2
XXX	XXX	XXX	XXX	1

LINE 1 - DIGITS 1, 2 & 3: Indicate engine codes

CID	CODE
318 CID 2 BC 8-Cyl.	E44
360 CID 2 BC 8-Cyl.	E57
400 CID 4 BC 8-Cyl.	E64
440 CID 4 BC 8-Cyl.	E85
440 CID 4 BC Hi-Perf. 8-Cyl.	E86

LINE 1 - DIGITS 4, 5 & 6: Indicate transmission codes

TRANSMISSION	CODE
3-Spd. Manual Floor Shift	D13
3-Spd. Std. Manual Clm. Shift	D14
3-Spd. H.D. Manual Clm. Shift	D15
4-Spd. Standard	D21
4-Spd. O.D.	D24
Standard A904	D31
Standard A998	D32
Standard A999	D33
Standard Automatic	D34
H.D. A727	D35
Standard A727	D36
H.D. A904	D38

LINE 1 - DIGIT 7: Indicates car line

MAKE	CODE
Chrysler	C
Chrysler Specialty & Cordoba	S

LINE 1 - DIGIT 8: Indicates price class

CLASS	CODE
High	H
Police	K
Low	L
Medium	M
Premium	P
Special	S

LINE 1 - DIGITS 9 & 10: Indicate body type

TYPE	CODE
2-Dr. Specialty Hardtop	22
2-Dr. Hardtop Coupe	23
4-Dr. Sedan	41
4-Dr. Hardtop Sedan	43
2-Seat Station Wagon	45
3-Seat Station Wagon	46

LINE 1 - DIGIT 11: Indicates engine code

CID	CODE
318 CID 2 BC 8-Cyl.	G
360 CID 2 BC 8-Cyl.	K
400 CID 4 BC 8-Cyl.	N
440 CID 4 BC 8-Cyl.	T
Special Order 8-Cyl.	Z

LINE 1 - DIGIT 12: Indicates model year
7 - 1977

LINE 1 - DIGIT 13: Indicates the assembly plant

PLANT	CODE
Jefferson Ave., Detroit, Mi	C
Belvidere, IL	D
Newark, DE	F
Windsor, Ontario, CAN	R

LAST SIX DIGITS: Indicate production sequence number starting at each plant with 100001

LINE 2 - DIGITS 1, 2 & 3: Indicate lower body paint color

COLOR	CODE
Silver Cloud Metallic	LA2
Wedgewood Blue	PB2
Cadet Blue Metallic	PB3
French Racing Blue	PB5
Regatta Blue Metallic	PB6
Starlight Blue Sunfire Metallic	PB9
Rallye Red	FE5
Vintage Red Sunfire Metallic	ME8
Jade Green Metallic	MF2
Forest Green Sunfire Metallic	PF7
Burnished Copper Metallic	PK6
Mojave Beige	PL3
Moondust Metallic	LL5
Russet Sunfire Metallic	PR8
Coffee Sunfire Metallic	PT7
Lt. Mocha Tan	PT2
Caramel Tan Metallic	MU3
Spitfire Orange	MV1
Spinnaker White	EW1
Formal Black Sunfire Metallic	PX8
Jasmine Yellow	PY1
Golden Fawn	KY4
Yellow Blaze	KY5
Inca Gold Metallic	LY6
Spanish Gold Metallic	LY9
Harvest Gold	MY3

LINE 2 - DIGITS 4, 5, 6 & 7: Indicate trim code

LINE 2 - DIGIT 4: Indicates price class

CLASS	CODE
High	H
Police	K
Low	L
Medium	M
Premium	P
Special	S

LINE 2 - DIGIT 5: Indicates seat and fabric type

SEAT	CODE
Cloth & Vinyl Bench	1
Vinyl Bench	2
Cloth & Leather Bench	A
Leather Bench	M
Cloth & Vinyl Bench Split Back	3
Vinyl Bench Split Back	4
Cloth & Leather Bench Split Back	B
Leather Bench Split Back	P
Cloth & Vinyl Bucket	5
Vinyl Bucket	6
Cloth & Leather Bucket	C
Leather Bucket	R
Cloth & Vinyl 50/50	7
Vinyl 50/50	8
Cloth & Leather 50/50	D
Leather 50/50	L
Cloth & Vinyl Special Design	9
Vinyl Special Design	H
Cloth & Leather Special Design	E
Leather Special Design	T
Cloth 60/40	F
Cloth & Vinyl 60/40	W
Vinyl 60/40	X
Leather 60/40	Y

LINE 2 - DIGITS 6 & 7: Indicates interior color

FABRIC COLOR	CODE
Dove Silver	A3
Blue	B3
Medium Blue	B6
Blue & White	BW
Red	E7
Red & White	EW
Green	F6
Green	FF
Green & White	FW
Gold, Black, White	KW
Parchment	L3
Canyon Red	R4
Red & White	RW
Chestnut	T7
Tan	U5
Tan & White	UW
Black	X9
Black & White	XW
Gold	Y3
Gold & White	YW

LINE 2 - DIGITS 8, 9 & 10: Indicate interior paint color, not listed

LINE 2 - DIGIT 11: Indicates the month of manufacture

MONTH	CODE
January	1
February	2
March	3
April	4
May	5
June	6
July	7
August	8
September	9
October	A
November	B
December	C

LINE 2 - DIGITS 12 & 13: Indicate the day of month of manufacture

LINE 2 - LAST SIX DIGITS: Indicate production sequence number

LINE 3 - DIGITS 1, 2 & 3: Indicate upper body color or vinyl roof codes

TYPE	CODE
Full Roof Style	V1
Landau Roof Style	V3
Canopy Roof Style	V4
Halo Roof Style	V1
Canopy Roof Style w/Opera Window	V5

COLOR	CODE
Green	V1F, V4F, V3F, V5F
Parchment	V1L, V4L, V3L, V5L
Dark Red	V1E, V4E, V3E, V5E
Black	V1X, V4X, V3X, V5X
White	V1W, V4W, V3W, V5W
Blue	V1B, V4B, V3B, V5B
Tan	V1U, V3U
Silver	V1A, V3A, V5A
Gold	V1Y, V4Y, V5Y

ENGINE NUMBER

THE ENGINE IDENTIFICATION NUMBERS for 318 and 360 CID V-8 engines are found at the left front of the block below the cylinder head. The engine number for 400 engines is found on the right side of the block adjacent to the distributor. The engine number for 440 engines is located on the left bank adjacent to the front tappet rail.

The following identification will be included in the engine serial number:

318 & 360 ENGINES
7M31810242579

THE NUMBER AND LETTER designate the model year and/or plant.

THE THREE NUMBERS following the model year and/or plant are the cubic inch displacement.

THE FOUR NUMBERS following the model identification are the date code.

THE FOUR NUMBERS following the date code are the daily sequence number (optional usage).

400 & 440 ENGINES
7T400H10242A

THE NUMBER AND LETTER designate the model year and/or plant.

THE THREE NUMBERS following the model year and/or plant are the cubic inch displacement.

THE LETTER following the model identification is the engine type.

THE FOUR NUMBERS following the engine type are the date code.

THE NUMBER following the date code is the shift built.

THE LETTER following the shift built is a parts identification code. These codes are explained below.

ENGINE SERIAL NUMBER AND PARTS IDENTIFICATION CODES & SYMBOLS DEFINED:

	CODE
Oversize Cylinder Bore	A
Cast Crankshaft	E
Standard 4 BC	H
High Performance	HP
Toluca Engine Plant	K
Low Compressfion	LC
Mound Road Engine	M
Passenger Car Engine	R
Special Engine	S
Trenton Engine	T
Windsor Engine	W
O/S Valve Guide	X

LE BARON ENGINES

CID	NO. CYL.	HORSE-POWER	COMP. RATIO	CARB.
318	8	145	8.5:1	2 BC

CORDOBA ENGINES

CID	NO. CYL.	HORSE-POWER	COMP. RATIO	CARB.
318	8	145	8.5:1	2 BC
400	8	190	8.2:1	4 BC

NEWPORT ENGINES

CID	NO. CYL.	HORSE-POWER	COMP. RATIO	CARB.
360	8	155	8.4:1	2 BC
400	8	190	8.2:1	4 BC
440	8	195	8.2:1	4 BC

NEW YORKER ENGINES

CID	NO. CYL.	HORSE-POWER	COMP. RATIO	CARB.
400	8	190	8.2:1	4 BC
440	8	195	8.2:1	4 BC

1978 CHRYSLER LE BARON WAGON

1978 CHRYSLER LE BARON WAGON

1978 CHRYSLER NEW YORKER

1978 CHRYSLER NEW YORKER

1978 CHRYSLER NEWPORT

1978 CHRYSLER NEWPORT

1978 CHRYSLER CORDOBA

1978 CHRYSLER LE BARON

VEHICLE IDENTIFICATION NUMBER

```
  • CHRYSLER •
    FP41G8G123456
```

Located on a plate attached to the left side of the instrument panel, visible through the windsheild.

FIRST DIGIT: Identifies the car make

MAKE	CODE
Newport/New Yorker	C
Le Baron	F
Cordoba	S

SECOND DIGIT: Identifies the price class

CLASS	CODE
High	H
Police	K
Low	L
Medium	M
Premium	P
Special	S

THIRD & FOURTH DIGITS: Identify the body type

TYPE	CODE
2-Dr. Specialty Hardtop	22
2-Dr. Coupe Hardtop	23
4-Dr. Sedan	41
4-Dr. Sedan Hartop	43
2-Seat Station Wagon	45
3-Seat Station Wagon	46

FIFTH DIGIT: Identifies the engine

CID	CODE
3.7L 6-Cyl. 1 BC	C
3.7L 6-Cyl. 2 BC	D
5.2L V8 2 BC	G
5.2L V8 4 BC	H
360 CID 2 BC 8-Cyl.	K
360 CID 4 BC 8-Cyl.	J
360 CID 4 BC Hi-Perf. 8-Cyl.	L
440 CID 4 BC 8-Cyl.	T
440 CID 4 BC Hi-Perf. 8-Cyl.	U
400 CID 4 BC 8-Cyl.	N
400 CID Hi-Perf. 8-Cyl.	P

SIXTH DIGIT: Identifies the year
8 - 1978

SEVENTH DIGIT: Identifies the assembly plant

PLANT	CODE
Lynch Road, Detroit, MI	A
Hamtramck, MI	B
Jefferson Ave., Detroit, MI	C
Newark, DE	F
St. Louis, MO	G
Warren, OH	S
Windsor, Ontario, CAN	R

LAST SIX DIGITS: Identifies the production sequence number starting at each plant with 100001

EXAMPLE

F	P	41	G	8	G	123456
Car Make	Price Class	Body Type	Engine	Model Year	Asm Plant	Production Sequence Number

BODY CODE PLATE

THE BODY CODE PLATE is located in the engine compartment on the left wheel housing, fender side shield or radiator yoke.

THE BODY CODE PLATE is read left to right, bottom to top. The information on the plate includes the S.O. Number and the trim and paint codes.

```
           CHRYSLER MOTORS
             CORPORATION

                                      Line
  •  XXX  XXX  XXX  XXX                 6  •
     XXX  XXX  XXX  XXX                 5
     XXX  XXX  XXX  XXX                 4
     XXX  XXX  XXX  XXX                 3
     XXX  XXX  XXX  XXX                 2
     XXX  XXX  XXX  XXX                 1
```

LINE 1 - DIGIT 1, 2 & 3: Indicate engine codes

CID	CODE
225 1V	E24
225 1 BC	E25
225 2 BC	E26
318 2 BC	E44
318 2 BC	E45
318 4 BC	E46
360 2 BC	E55
360 4 BC	E56
360 2 BC	E57
360 4 BC Hi-Perf.	E58
400 4 BC	E64
400 4 BC Hi-Perf.	E68
440 4 BC	E85
440 4 BC Hi-Perf.	E86

LINE 1 - DIGITS 4, 5 & 6: Indicate transmission codes

TRANSMISSION	CODE
3-Spd. Manual Floor Shift	D13
3-Spd. Std. Manual Clm. Shift	D14
3-Spd. H.D. Manual Clm. Shift	D15
4-Spd. Standard	D21
4-Spd. Trans./Ax.	D22
4-Spd. O.D.	D24
Standard A904	D31
Standard A998	D32
Standard A999	D33
Standard Automatic	D34
H.D. A727	D35
Standard A727	D36
A404 Trans./Ax.	D37
H.D. A904	D38

LINE 1 - DIGIT 7: Indicates car line

MAKE	CODE
Newport/New Yorker	C
Le Baron	F
Cordoba	S

LINE 1 - DIGIT 8: Indicates price class

CLASS	CODE
High	H
Police	K
Low	L
Medium	M
Premium	P
Special	S

LINE 1 - DIGITS 9 & 10: Indicate body type

TYPE	CODE
2-Dr. Specialty Hardtop	22
2-Dr. Coupe Hardtop	23
4-Dr. Sedan	41
4-Dr. Sedan Hardtop	43
2-Seat Station Wagon	45
3-Seat Station Wagon	46

LINE 1 - DIGIT 11: Indicates engine code

CID	CODE
3.7L 6-Cyl. 1 BC	C
3.7L 6-Cyl. 2 BC	D
5.2L V8 2 BC	G
5.2L V8 4 BC	H
360 CID 2 BC 8-Cyl.	K
360 CID 4 BC 8-Cyl.	J
360 CID 4 BC Hi-Perf. 8-Cyl.	L
440 CID 4 BC 8-Cyl.	T
440 CID 4 BC Hi-Perf. 8-Cyl.	U
400 CID 4 BC 8-Cyl.	N
400 CID Hi-Perf. 8-Cyl.	P

LINE 1 - DIGIT 12: Indicates model year
8 - 1978

LINE 1 - DIGIT 13: Indicates the assembly plant

PLANT	CODE
Lynch Road, Detroit MI	A
Hamtramck, MI	B
Jefferson Ave., Detroit, MI	C
Newark, DE	F
St. Louis, MO	G
Warren, OH	S
Windsor, Ontario, CAN	R

LINE 1 - LAST SIX DIGITS: Indicate production sequence number starting at each plant with 100001

LINE 2 - DIGITS 1, 2 & 3: Indicate lower body paint color

COLOR	CODE
Charcoal Gray Sunfire Metallic	RA9
Pewter Gray Metallic	RA2
Dove Gray	RA1
Starlight Blue Sunfire Metallic	PB9
Cadet Blue Metallic	PB3
Mint Green Metallic	RF3
Augusta Green Sunfire Metallic	RF9
Jasmine Yellow	PY1
Classic Cream	RY3
Spanish Gold Metallic	LY9
Golden Fawn	KY4
Sable Tan Sunfire Metallic	RT9
Caramel Tan Metallic	MU3
Tapestry Red Sunfire Metallic	RR7
Spinnaker White	EW1
Formal Black	TX9

LINE 2 - DIGITS 4, 5, 6 & 7: Indicate trim code

LINE 2 - DIGIT 4: Indicates price class

CLASS	CODE
High	H
Police	K
Low	L
Medium	M
Premium	P
Special	S

LINE 2 - DIGIT 5: Indicates seat and fabric type

SEAT	CODE
Cloth & Vinyl Bench	1
Vinyl Bench	2
Cloth & Leather Bench	A
Leather & Vinyl Bench	M
Cloth Bench	N
Cloth & Vinyl Bench Split Back	3
Vinyl Bench Split Back	4
Cloth & Leather Bench Split Back	B
Leather & Vinyl Bench Split Back	P
Cloth Bench Split Back	G
Cloth & Vinyl Bucket	5
Vinyl Bucket	6
Cloth & Leather Bucket	C
Leather & Vinyl Bucket	R
Cloth Bucket	J
Cloth & Vinyl 50/50	7
Vinyl 50/50	8
Cloth & Leather 50/50	D
Leather & Vinyl 50/50	L
Cloth 50/50	Z
Cloth & Vinyl Recline 60/40	W
Vinyl Recline 60/40	X
Cloth & Leather Recline 60/40	K
Leather & Vinyl Recline 60/40	Y
Cloth Recline 60/40	F
Cloth & Vinyl Non-recline 60/40	9
Vinyl Non-recline 60/40	H
Cloth & Leather Non-recline 60/40	E
Leather & Vinyl Non-recline 60/40	T
Cloth Non-recline 60/40	V

LINE 2 - DIGITS 6 & 7: Indicates interior color

FABRIC COLOR	CODE
Dove Silver	A3
Blue	B3
Blue & White	BW
Green	F6
Green & White	FW
Canyon Red	R4
Red & White	RW
Tan	U5
Tan & White	UW
Black	X9
Black & White	XW
Gold	Y3
Gold & White	YW

LINE 2 - DIGITS 8, 9 & 10: Indicate interior paint color, not listed

LINE 2 - DIGIT 11: Indicates the month of manufacture

MONTH	CODE
January	1
February	2
March	3
April	4
May	5
June	6
July	7
August	8
September	9
October	A
November	B
December	C

LINE 2 - DIGITS 12 & 13: Indicate the day of month of manufacture

LINE 2 - LAST SIX DIGITS: Indicate production sequence number

LINE 3 - DIGITS 1, 2 & 3: Indicate upper body color or vinyl roof codes

COLOR	CODE
Halo Vinyl Roof Blue	V2B
Landau Vinyl Roof Blue	V3B
Full Vinyl Roof Blue	V1B
Padded Canopy Vinyl Roof Blue	V5B
Crown Landau Vinyl Roof Blue	V6B
Halo Vinyl Roof Green	V2F
Landau Vinyl Roof Green	V3F
Full Vinyl Roof Green	V1F
Padded Canopy Vinyl Roof Green	V5F
Crown Landau Vinyl Roof Green	V6F
Halo Vinyl Roof Red	V2R
Landau Vinyl Roof Red	V3R
Full Vinyl Roof Red	V1R
Padded Canopy Vinyl Roof Red	V5R
Crown Landau Vinyl Roof Red	V6R
Halo Vinyl Roof Black	V2X
Landau Vinyl Roof Black	V3X
Full Vinyl Roof Black	V1X
Padded Canopy Vinyl Roof Black	V5X
Crown Landau Vinyl Roof Black	V6X
Halo Vinyl Roof White	V2W
Landau Vinyl Roof White	V3W
Full Vinyl Roof White	V1W
Padded Canopy Vinyl Roof White	V5W
Crown Landau Vinyl Roof White	V6W
Halo Vinyl Roof Tan	V2U
Landau Vinyl Roof Tan	V3U
Full Vinyl Roof Tan	V1U
Crown Landau Vinyl Roof Tan	V6U
Halo Vinyl Roof Silver	V2A
Landau Vinyl Roof Silver	V3A
Full Vinyl Roof Silver	V1A
Padded Canopy Vinyl Roof Silver	V5A
Crown Landau Vinyl Roof Silver	V6A
Landau Vinyl Roof Cream	V3Y
Full Vinyl Roof Cream	V1Y
Halo Vinyl Roof Cream	V1Y
Crown Landau Vinyl Roof Cream	V6Y
Full Vinyl Roof Gold	V1Y
Padded Canopy Vinyl Roof Gold	V5Y

ENGINE NUMBER

THE ENGINE IDENTIFICATION NUMBER for 6-cylinder engines is located at the right side of the block below #6 spark plug.

ENGINE NUMBERS for 318 and 360 CID V-8 engines are found at the left front of the block below the cylinder head. The engine number for 400 engines is found on the right side of the block adjacent to the distributor. The engine number for 440 engines is located on the left bank pad adjacent to front tappet rail.

The following identification will be included in the engine serial number:

225 ENGINE
8225R21024A

THE FIRST DIGIT designates the model year and/or plant.

THE THREE NUMBERS following the model year and/or plant are the cubic inch displacement.

THE LETTER following the model identification is the engine usage code.

THE NUMBER following the engine usage is the shift built.

THE FOUR NUMBERS following the shift built are the date code.

THE LETTER following the date code is a parts identification code. These codes are explained below.

318 & 360 ENGINES
8M31810242579

THE NUMBER AND LETTER designate the model year and/or plant.

THE THREE NUMBERS following the model year and/or plant are the cubic inch displacement.

THE FOUR NUMBERS following the model identification are the date code.

THE FOUR NUMBERS following the date code are the daily sequence number (optional usage).

400 & 440 ENGINES
8T400H10242A

THE NUMBER AND LETTER designate the model year and/or plant.

THE THREE NUMBERS following the model year and/or plant are the cubic inch displacement.

THE LETTER following the model identification is the engine type.

THE FOUR NUMBERS following the engine type are the date code.

THE NUMBER following the date code is the shift built.

THE LETTER following the shift built is a parts identification code. These codes are explained below.

ENGINE SERIAL NUMBER AND PARTS IDENTIFICATION CODES
& SYMBOLS DEFINED:

	CODE
Oversize Cylinder Bore	A
Cast Crankshaft	E
Standard 4 BC	H
High Performance	HP
Toluca Engine Plant	K
Low Compression	LC
Mound Road Engine	M
Passenger Car Engine	R
Special Engine	S
Trenton Engine	T
Windsor Engine	W
O/S/ Valve Guide	X

LE BARON ENGINES

CID	NO. CYL.	HORSE-POWER	COMP. RATIO	CARB.
225	6	110	8.4:1	2 BC
318	8	140	8.5:1	2 BC
360	8	155	8.4:1	2 BC

CORDOBA ENGINES

CID	NO. CYL.	HORSE-POWER	COMP. RATIO	CARB.
318	8	140	8.5:1	2 BC
400	8	190	8.2:1	4 BC

NEWPORT ENGINES

CID	NO. CYL.	HORSE-POWER	COMP. RATIO	CARB.
360	8	155	8.4:1	2 BC
400	8	190	8.2:1	4 BC

NEW YORKER ENGINES

CID	NO. CYL.	HORSE-POWER	COMP. RATIO	CARB.
360	8	155	8.4:1	2 BC
400	8	190	8.2:1	4 BC
440	8	195	8.2:1	4 BC

1979 CHRYSLER CORDOBA

1979 CHRYSLER CORDOBA

1979 CHRYSLER LE BARON

1979 CHRYSLER LE BARON

1979 CHRYSLER LE BARON WAGON

1979 CHRYSLER LE BARON WAGON

1979 CHRYSLER NEW YORKER

1979 CHRYSLER NEW YORKER

1979 CHRYSLER NEWPORT

1979 CHRYSLER NEWPORT

VEHICLE IDENTIFICATION NUMBER

```
CHRYSLER
FP41G9G123456
```

Located on a plate attached to the left side of the instrument panel, visible through the windshield.

FIRST DIGIT: Identifies the car make

MAKE	CODE
LeBaron	F
Cordoba	S
Newport, New Yorker	T

SECOND DIGIT: Identifies the price class

CLASS	CODE
High	H
Police	K
Low	L
Medium	M
Premium	P
Special	S

THIRD & FOURTH DIGITS: Identify the body type

TYPE	CODE
2-Dr. Specialty Hardtop	22
4-Dr. Sedan	41
4-Dr. Sedan Hardtop	42
2-Seat Wagon	45

FIFTH DIGIT: Identifies the engine

CID	CODE
3.7L 1 BC 6-Cyl.	C
3.7L 1 BC 6-Cyl.	D
5.2L 2 BC 8-Cyl.	G
5.2L 4 BC 8-Cyl.	H
360 CID 2 BC 8-Cyl.	K
360 CID 4 BC 8-Cyl.	J
360 CID 4 BC Hi-Perf. 8-Cyl.	L

SIXTH DIGIT: Identifies the year
9 - 1979

SEVENTH DIGIT: Identifies the assembly plant

PLANT	CODE
Lynch Road, Detroit, MI	A
Hamtramck, MI	B
Jefferson Ave., Detroit, MI	C
Belvidere, IL	D
Newark, DE	F
St. Louis, MO	G
Windsor, Ontario, CAN	R

LAST SIX DIGITS: Identify the production sequence number starting at each plant with 100001

EXAMPLE

F	P	41	G	9	G	123456
Car Make	Price Class	Body Type	Engine	Model Year	Asm Plant	Production Sequence Number

BODY CODE PLATE

THE BODY CODE PLATE is located in the engine compartment on the left wheel housing, fender side shield or radiator yoke.

THE BODY CODE PLATE is read left to right, bottom to top. The information on the plate includes the S.O. Number and the trim and paint codes.

```
CHRYSLER MOTORS
CORPORATION
                                   Line
XXX  XXX  XXX  XXX                  6
XXX  XXX  XXX  XXX                  5
XXX  XXX  XXX  XXX                  4
XXX  XXX  XXX  XXX                  3
XXX  XXX  XXX  XXX                  2
XXX  XXX  XXX  XXX                  1
```

LINE 1 - DIGIT 1, 2 & 3: Indicate engine codes

CID	CODE
225 CID 1 BC	E24
225 CID 1 BC	E25
225 CID 2 BC	E26
225 CID 2 BC	E27
318 CID 2 BC	E44
318 CID 2 BC	E45
318 CID 4 BC	E46
318 CID 4 BC	E47
360 CID 4 BC	E56
360 CID 2 BC	E57
360 CID 4 BC	E58

LINE 1 - DIGITS 4, 5 & 6: Indicate transmission codes

TRANSMISSION	CODE
3-Spd. Manual Floor Shift	D13
3-Spd. Std. Manual Clm. Shift	D14
3-Spd. H.D. Manual Clm. Shift	D15
4-Spd. Standard	D21
4-Spd. Manaul Trans./Ax.	D22
4-Spd. O.D.	D24
Standard A904	D31
Standard A998	D32
Standard A999	D33
Standard Automatic	D34
H.D. A727	D35
Standard A727	D36
A404 Trans./Ax.	D37
H.D. A904	D38

LINE 1 - DIGIT 7: Indicates car line

MAKE	CODE
Newport, New Yorker	T
Cordoba	S
LeBaron	F

LINE 1 - DIGIT 8: Indicates price class

CLASS	CODE
High	H
Police	K
Low	L
Medium	M
Premium	P
Special	S

LINE 1 - DIGITS 9 & 10: Indicate body type

TYPE	CODE
2-Dr. Specialty Hardtop	22
4-Dr. Sedan	41
4-Dr. Sedan Hardtop	42
2-Seat Wagon	45

LINE 1 - DIGIT 11: Indicates engine code

CID	CODE
3.7L 1BC 6-Cyl.	C
3.7L 1BC 6-Cyl.	D
5.2L 2BC 8-Cyl.	G
5.2L 4BC 8-Cyl.	H
360 CID 2 BC 8-Cyl.	K
360 CID 4BC 8-Cyl.	J
360 CID 4BC Hi-Perf. 8-Cyl.	L

LINE 1 - DIGIT 12: Indicates model year
9 - 1979

LINE 1 - DIGIT 13: Indicates the assembly plant

PLANT	CODE
Lynch Road, Detroit, MI	A
Hamtramck, MI	B
Jefferson Ave., Detroit, MI	C
Belvidere, IL	D
Newark, DE	F
St. Louis, MO	G
Windsor, Ontario, CAN	R

LINE 1 - LAST SIX DIGITS: Indicate production sequence number starting at each plant with 100001

LINE 2 - DIGITS 1, 2 & 3: Indicate lower body paint color

COLOR	CODE
Dove Gray	RA1
Cadet Blue Metallic	PB3
Ensign Blue Metallic	SB7
Teal Frost Metallic	SG4
Chianti Red	SR5
Regent Red Sunfire Metallic	SR8
Teal Green Sunfire Metallic	SG8
Light Cashmere	ST1
Medium Cashmere Metallic	ST5
Sable Tan Sunfire Metallic	RT9
Formal Black	TX9
Frost Blue Metallic	SC2
Nightwatch Blue	SC9
Pearl Gray	SS1
Linen Cream	SY1
Designer's Cream	SL1
Designer's Beige	SL2
Oxford Gray	SA6
Garnet Red Sunfire Metallic	SR9

LINE 2 - DIGITS 4, 5, 6 & 7: Indicate trim code

LINE 2 - DIGIT 4: Indicates price class

CLASS	CODE
High	H
Police	K
Low	L
Medium	M
Premium	P
Special	S

LINE 2 - DIGIT 5: Indicates seat and fabric type

SEAT	CODE
Cloth & Vinyl Bench	1
Vinyl Bench	2
Cloth & Leather Bench	A
Leather & Vinyl Bench	M
Cloth Bench	N
Cloth & Vinyl Bench Split Back	3
Vinyl Bench Split Back	4
Cloth & Leather Bench Split Back	B
Leather & Vinyl Bench Split Back	P
Cloth Bench Split Back	G
Cloth & Vinyl Bucket	5
Vinyl Bucket	6
Cloth & Leather Bucket	C
Leather & Vinyl Bucket	R
Cloth Bucket	J
Cloth & Vinyl 50/50	7
Vinyl 50/50	8
Cloth & Leather 50/50	D
Leather & Vinyl 50/50	L
Cloth 50/50	Z
Cloth & Vinyl Recline 60/40	W
Vinyl Recline 60/40	X
Cloth & Leather Recline 60/40	K
Leather & Vinyl Recline 60/40	Y
Cloth Recline 60/40	F
Cloth & Vinyl Non-recline 60/40	9
Vinyl Non-recline 60/40	H
Cloth & Leather Non-recline 60/40	E
Leather & Vinyl Non-recline 60/40	T
Cloth Non-recline 60/40	V

LINE 2 - DIGITS 6 & 7: Indicates interior color

FABRIC COLOR	CODE
Blue	B3
Teal Green	G5
Gray	A3
Cashmere	T3
Red	R4
Midnight Blue	C8
White/Red	RW
White/Midnight Blue	CW
White/Teal Green	GW
White/Cashmere	TW
Champagne	L3

LINE 2 - DIGITS 8, 9 & 10: Indicate interior paint color, not listed

LINE 2 - DIGIT 11: Indicates the month of manufacture

MONTH	CODE
January	1
February	2
March	3
April	4
May	5
June	6
July	7
August	8
September	9
October	A
November	B
December	C

LINE 2 - DIGITS 12 & 13: Indicate the day of month of manufacture

LINE 2 - LAST SIX DIGITS: Indicate production sequence number

LINE 3 - DIGITS 1, 2 & 3: Indicate upper body color or vinyl roof codes.

COLOR	CODE
Landau Vinyl Roof Blue	V3B
Full Padded Vinyl Roof Blue	V1B
Landau Vinyl Roof Green	V3G
Full Padded Vinyl Roof Green	V1B
Landau Vinyl Roof Red	V3R
Full Padded Vinyl Roof Red	V1R
Landau Vinyl Roof Gray	V3S
Full Padded Vinyl Roof Gray	V1S
Landau Vinyl Roof Brown	V3T
Full Padded Vinyl Roof Brown	V1T
Landau Vinyl Roof White	V3W
Full Padded Vinyl Roof White	V1W
Landau Vinyl Roof Black	V3X
Full Padded Vinyl Roof Black	V1X
Landau Vinyl Roof Cream	V3Y
Full Padded Vinyl Roof Cream	V1Y
Full Vinyl Roof D. Blue	V1C
Landau Vinyl Roof Dk. Blue	V3C
Crown Landau Vinyl Roof Dk. Blue	V6C
Full Vinyl Roof Lt. Green	V1G
Landau Vinyl Roof Lt. Green	V3G
Crown Landau Vinyl Roof Lt. Green	V6G
Landau Vinyl Roof Red	V3R
Crown Landau Vinyl Roof Red	V6R
Landau Vinyl Roof Gray	V3S
Crown Landau Vinyl Roof Gray	V6S
Landau Vinyl Roof Brown	V3T
Crown Landau Vinyl Roof Brown	V6T
Full Vinyl Roof White	V1W
Landau Vinyl Roof White	V3W
Crown Landau Vinyl Roof White	V6W
Landau Vinyl Roof Black	V3X
Crown Landau Vinyl Roof Black	V6X
Landau Vinyl Roof Cream	V3Y
Crown Landau Vinyl Roof Cream	V6Y
Full Vinyl Roof Tan	V1U
Landau Vinyl Roof Tan	V3U
Landau Vinyl Roof Dk. Green	V3F

ENGINE NUMBER

THE ENGINE IDENTIFICATION NUMBER for 6-cylinder engines is located at the right side of the block below #6 spark plug.

ENGINE NUMBERS for 318 and 360 CID V-8 engines are found at the left front of the block below the cylinder head. The engine number for 400 engines is found on the right side of the block adjacent to the distributor. The engine number for 440 engines is located on the left bank pad adjacent to the front tappet rail.

The following identification will be included in the engine serial number:

225 ENGINE
9225R21024A

THE FIRST DIGIT designates the model year and/or plant.

THE THREE NUMBERS following the model identification are the cubic inch displacement.

THE LETTER following the model identification is the engine usage code.

THE NUMBER following the engine usage is the shift built.

THE FOUR NUMBERS following the shift built are the date code.

THE LETTER following the date code is a parts identification code. These codes are explained below.

318 & 360 ENGINES
9M31810242579

THE NUMBER AND LETTER designate the model year and/or plant.

THE THREE NUMBERS following the model year and/or plant are the cubic inch displacement.

THE FOUR NUMBERS following the model identification are the date code.

THE FOUR NUMBERS following the date code are the daily sequence number (optional usage).

400 & 440 ENGINES
9T400H10242A

THE NUMBER AND LETTER designate the model year and/or plant.

THE THREE NUMBERS following the model year and/or plant are the cubic inch displacement.

THE LETTER following the model identification is the engine type.

THE FOUR NUMBERS following the engine type are the date code.

THE NUMBER following the date code is the shift built.

THE LETTER following the shift built is a parts identification code. These codes are explained below.

ENGINE SERIAL NUMBER AND PARTS IDENTIFICATION CODES & SYMBOLS DEFINED:

	CODE
Oversize Cylinder Bore	A
Cast Crankshaft	E
Standard 4 BC	H
High Performance	HP
Toluca Engine Plant	K
Low Compression	LC
Mound Road Engine	M
Passenger Car Engine	R

LE BARON ENGINES

CID	NO. CYL.	HORSE-POWER	COMP. RATIO	CARB.
225	6	100	8.4:1	1 BC
225	6	110	8.4:1	2 BC
318	8	135	8.5:1	2 BC
360	8	150	8.4:1	2 BC
360	8	195	8.0;1	4 BC

CORDOBA ENGINES

CID	NO. CYL.	HORSE-POWER	COMP. RATIO	CARB.
318	8	135	8.5:1	2 BC
360	8	195	8.0;1	4 BC
360	8	195	8.0:1	4 BC

NEWPORT ENGINES

CID	NO. CYL.	HORSE-POWER	COMP. RATIO	CARB.
225	6	110	8.4:1	2 BC
318	8	135	8.5:1	2 BC

NEW YORKER ENGINES

CID	NO. CYL.	HORSE-POWER	COMP. RATIO	CARB.
318	8	135	8.5:1	2 BC
360	8	150	8.4:1	2 BC
360	8	195	8.0;1	4 BC

1970 DODGE MONACO

1970 DODGE POLARA

1970 DODGE CHALLENGER

1970 DODGE CHARGER

1970 DODGE CORONET

1970 DODGE DART

VEHICLE IDENTIFICATION NUMBER

```
• DODGE
  DL43G0F123456 •
```

Located on a plate attached to the left side of the instrument panel, visible through the windshield.

FIRST DIGIT: Identifies the car make

MAKE	CODE
Dodge	D
Challenger	J
Dart	L
Coronet	W
Charger	X

SECOND DIGIT: Identifies the price class

CLASS	CODE
High	H
Police	K
Low	L
Medium	M
Premium	P
Special	S
Taxi	T
New York Taxi	N
Superstock	O

THIRD & FOURTH DIGITS: Identify the body type

TYPE	CODE
2-Dr. Sedan	21
2-Dr. Hardtop	23
Convertible	27
2-Dr. Sports Hardtop	29
4-Dr. Sedan	41
4-Dr. Hardtop	43
2-Seat Wagon	45
3-Seat Wagon	46

FIFTH DIGIT: Identifies the engine

CID	CODE
198 CID 1 BC 6-Cyl.	B
225 CID 1 BC 6-Cyl.	C
Special Order 6-Cyl.	E
318 CID 2 BC 8-Cyl.	G
340 CID 4 BC 8-Cyl.	H
340 CID 3-2 BC 8-Cyl.	J
383 CID 2 BC 8-Cyl.	L
383 CID Hi-Perf. 4 BC 8-Cyl.	N
426 CID Hemi 2-4 BC 8-Cyl.	R
440 CID 4 BC 8-Cyl.	T
440 CID Hi-Perf. 4 BC 8-Cyl.	U
440 CID 3-2 BC 8-Cyl.	V
Special Order 8-Cyl.	Z

SIXTH DIGIT: Identifies the year
0 - 1970

SEVENTH DIGIT: Identifies the assembly plant

	CODE
Lynch Road, Detroit, MI	A
Hamtramck, MI	B
Jefferson Ave., Detroit, MI	C
Belvidere, IL	D
Los Angeles, CA	E
Newark, DE	F
St. Louis, MO	G
New Stanton, PA	H
Windsor, Ontario, CAN	R

LAST SIX DIGITS: Identify the production sequence number starting with 100001

EXAMPLE

D	L	43	G	0	F	123456
Car Make	Price Class	Body Type	Engine	Model Year	Asm Plant	Production Sequence Number

BODY CODE PLATE

THE BODY CODE PLATE is located on the left front fender side shield or wheel housing on all Challenger, Charger, Coronet and Dart models; and on the left side of upper radiator support on Monaco models.

THE BODY CODE PLATE is read left to right, bottom to top. The information on the plate includes the car S.O. Number and the trim and paint codes.

```
           CHRYSLER MOTORS
              CORPORATION
                                         Line
  •  XXX  XXX  XXX  XXX              •      6
     XXX  XXX  XXX  XXX                     5
     XXX  XXX  XXX  XXX                     4
     XXX  XXX  XXX  XXX                     3
     XXX  XXX  XXX  XXX                     2
     XXX  XXX  XXX  XXX                     1
```

LINE 1 - DIGITS 1, 2 & 3: Indicate engine codes

CID	CODE
Special Order 6-Cyl.	E06
Special Order 8-Cyl.	E08
198 1 BC 6-Cyl.	E22
225 1 BC 6-Cyl.	E24
225 1 BC 6-Cyl.	E25
318 2 BC 8-Cyl.	E44
340 4 BC 8-Cyl.	E55
383 2 BC 8-Cyl.	E61
383 4 BC Hi-Perf. 8-Cyl.	E63
426 2-4 BC Hi-Perf. 8-Cyl. Hemi	E74
440 4 BC 8-Cyl.	E85
440 4 BC Hi-Perf. 8-Cyl.	E86
440 3-2 BC Hi-Perf. 8-Cyl.	E87

LINE 1 - DIGITS 4, 5 & 6: Indicate transmission codes

TRANSMISSION	CODE
3-Spd. Manual	D11
3-Spd. Manual	D12
3-Spd. Manual	D13
4-Spd. Manual	D21
3-Spd. Automatic	D31
3-Spd. Automatic	D32
3-Spd. Automatic	D36
Special Order	D49

LINE 1 - DIGIT 7: Indicates car line

MAKE	CODE
Dart	L
Challenger	J
Coronet	W
Dodge	D
Charger	X

LINE 1 - DIGIT 8: Indicates price class

CLASS	CODE
High	H
Police	K
Low	L
Medium	M
Premium	P
Special	S
Taxi	T
New York Taxi	N
Superstock	O

LINE 1 - DIGITS 9 & 10: Indicate body type

TYPE	CODE
2-Dr. Sedan	21
2-Dr. Hardtop	23
Convertible	27
2-Dr. Sports Hardtop	29
4-Dr. Sedan	41
4-Dr. Hardtop	43
2-Seat Wagon	45
3-Seat Wagon	46

LINE 1 - DIGIT 11: Indicates engine code

CID	CODE
198 CID 1 BC 6-Cyl.	B
225 CID 1 BC 6-Cyl.	C
Special Order 6-Cyl.	E
318 CID 2 BC 8-Cyl.	G
340 CID 4 BC 8-Cyl.	H
340 CID 3-2 BC 8-Cyl.	J
383 CID 2 BC 8-Cyl.	L
383 CID Hi-Perf. 4 BC 8-Cyl.	N
426 CID Hemi 2-4 BC 8-Cyl.	R
440 CID 4 BC 8-Cyl.	T
440 CID Hi-Perf. 4 BC 8-Cyl.	U
440 CID 3-2 BC 8-Cyl.	V
Special Order 8-Cyl.	Z

LINE 1 - DIGIT 12: Indicates model year
0 - 1970

LINE 1 - DIGIT 13: Indicates the assembly plant

PLANT	CODE
Lynch Road, Detroit, MI	A
Hamtramck, MI	B
Jefferson Ave., Detroit, MI	C
Belvedere, IL	D
Los Angeles, CA	E
Newark, DE	F
St. Louis, MO	G
New Stanton, PA	H
Wyoming, MI	P
Windsor, Ontario, CAN	R

LINE 1 - DIGITS 14-19: Indicate production sequence number

LINE 2 - DIGITS 1, 2 & 3: Indicate body paint color, or fleet or special order paint code

COLOR	CODE
Silver Metallic	EA4
Dark Gray Metallic	EA9
Light Blue Metallic	EB3
Bright Blue Metallic	EB5
Medium Blue Metallic	EB7
Plum Crazy Metallic	FC7
Bright Red	FE5
Light Green Metallic	FF4
Dark Green Metallic	EF8
Sublime	FJ5
Green Go	FJ6
Go Mango	EK2
Dark Burnt Orange Metallic	FK5
Beige	BL1
Panther Pink	FM3
Light Turquoise Metallic	FQ3
Red	ER6
Burgundy Metallic	DR8
Tan Metallic	FT3
Dark Tan Metallic	FT6
Hemi Orange	EV2
Eggshell White	EW1
Black	TX9
Top Banana	FY1
Yellow	DY2
Cream	DY3
Light Gold Metallic	FY4
Gold Metallic	FY6
Corporate Blue	C37D
Special Order	999

LINE 2 - DIGITS 4, 5, 6 & 7: Indicate trim code

LINE 2 - DIGIT 4: Indicates price class

PRICE CLASS	CODE
High	H
Police	K
Low	L
Medium	M
Premium	P
Special	S
Taxi	T
New York Taxi	N
Superstock	O

LINE 2 - DIGIT 5: Indicates seat and fabric type

SEAT	CODE
Cloth & Vinyl Bench	1
Vinyl Bench	2
Cloth & Vinyl Split Bench	3
Vinyl Split Bench	4
Cloth & Vinyl Bucket	5
Vinyl Bucket	6
Vinyl & Leather Bucket	R

LINE 2 - DIGITS 6 & 7: Indicate interior color

FABRIC COLOR	CODE
Gray	A5
Black Frost	A8
Dark Gray	A9
Light Blue	B3
Medium Blue	B5
Dark Blue	B7
White & Blue	BW
Red	E4
White & Red	EW
Light Green	F4
White & Green	FW
Green	F8
Burnt Orange	K4
White & Burnt Orange	KW
Beige	L2
Burgundy	M9
Teal	P6
Oxblood	R9
Light Tan	T3
Tan	T5
Tan & White	TW
Walnut & Beige	TT
Black	X9
Black & Charcoal	XA
Black & Peacock	XP
White & Black	XW
Black & Gold	XY
Gold	Y4
Gold & Black	YX

NOTE: Vinyl & leather bucket seats:

CHARGER SE	CODE
Blue	CRB5
Green	CRF8
Tan	CRT5
Black & Charcoal	CRXA

CHALLENGER	CODE
Burnt Orange	HRK4
Tan	HRT5
Black	HRX9

LINE 2 - DIGITS 8, 9 & 10: Indicate upper door frame color, not listed

LINE 2 - DIGIT 11: Indicates the month of manufacture

MONTH	CODE
January	1
February	2
March	3
April	4
May	5
June	6
July	7
August	8
September	9
October	A
November	B
December	C

LINE 2 - DIGITS 12 & 13: Indicate the day of month of manufacture

LINE 2 - LAST SIX DIGITS: Indicate production sequence number

LINE 3 - DIGITS 1, 2 & 3: Indicate roof paint color, vinyl roof code or convertible top code

COLOR	CODE
Paint-Mono Tone	V01
Paint-Two Tone	V02
Paint, Trim & Vinyl Roof Waiver	V08
Paint-Special Order	V09
Vinyl Roof	V10
Vinyl Roof Green	V1F
Vinyl Roof Gator Grain (N/A Dart)	V1G
Vinyl Roof Walnut Patterned	V1J
Vinyl Roof Champagne	V1L
Vinyl Roof White	V1W
Vinyl Roof Black	V1X
Vinyl Roof Turquoise Grain	V1Y
Vinyl Roof Special Order	V19
Paint-Hood Performance	V21
Delete Sport Hood Treatment	V22
Delete Lower Body Side Org' Paint	V23
Paint-Hood Performance w/Eng. Callout	V24
Convertible Top	V30
Convertible Top White	V3W
Convertible Top Black	V3X
Mouldings-Protective Vinyl Body Side	V50
Mouldings-Protective Vinyl Body Side Bright Blue	V5B
Mouldings-Protective Vinyl Body Side Light Green	V5F
Mouldings-Protective Vinyl Body Side Burnt Orange	V5K
Mouldings-Protective Vinyl Body Side Red	V5R
Mouldings-Protective Vinyl Body Side Tan	V5T
Mouldings-Protective Vinyl Body Side White	V5W
Mouldings-Protective Vinyl Body Side Black	V5X
Mouldings-Protective Vinyl Body Side Citron Gold	V5Y
Sport Stripes-Longitudinal Tape	V60
Sport Stripes Tape Blue	V6B
Sport Stripes Tape Green	V6F
Sport Stripes Tape Trans Am Black	V6H
Sport Stripes Tape Chartreuse	V6J
Sport Stripes Tape Burnt Orange	V6K
Sport Stripes Tape Magenta	V6M
Sport Stripes Tape Red	V6R
Sport Stripes Tape White	V6W
Sport Stripes Tape Black	V6X
Sport Stripes Tape Gold	V6Y
Sport Stripes Tape Delete	V68
Accent Stripes Paint	V70
Accent Stripes Paint Blue	V7B
Accent Stripes Paint Green	V7F
Accent Stripes Paint Red	V7R
Accent Stripes Paint White	V7W
Accent Stripes Paint Black	V7X
Accent Stripes Paint Delete	V78
Sport Stripes Tape	V80
Sport Stripes Tape Blue	V8B
Sport Stripes Tape Green	V8F
Sport Stripes Tape Red	V8R
Sport Stripes Tape White	V8W
Sport Stripes Tape Black	V8X
Sport Stripes Tape Gold	V8Y
Sport Stripes Tape Delete	V88
Bumble Bee Paint Stripes	V90
Bumble Bee Paint Stripes Blue	V9B
Bumble Bee Paint Stripes Tan	V9T
Bumble Bee Paint Stripes White	V9W
Bumble Bee Paint Stripes Black	V9X
Bumble Bee Paint Stripes Gold	V9Y
Bumble Bee Paint Stripes Delete	V98

ENGINE NUMBER

THE ENGINE IDENTIFICATION NUMBER for 6-cylinder engines is located at the right front of the block below the cylinder head.

Engine numbers for 318 and 340 CID V-8 engines are found at the left front of the block below the cylinder head. Engine numbers for 383, 426 and 440 CID V-8 engines are found at the left rear of the block near the oil pan flange.

The following identification is included in the engine serial number:

THE FIRST TWO LETTERS designate the manufacturing plant

MANUFACTURING PLANT	CODE
Mound Road ....PM
Trenton ....PT
Marysville ....NM
Windsor ....FW

THE THREE NUMBERS following the plant identification indicate the cubic inch displacement: ie. 198 - 225 - 318 - 340 - 383 - 426 - 440.

THE FOUR NUMBERS following the model identification are the build date. This is a date code for manufacturing purposes.

THE FOUR NUMBERS following the build date are the engine production sequence number.

EXAMPLE
PM31831591234

In the example above:

PM	Mound Road
318	Cubic Inch Displacement
3159	Build date code*
1234	Engine sequence number

*1970 date codes run from 2895 to 3259

CHALLENGER ENGINES

CID	NO. CYL.	HORSE-POWER	COMP. RATIO	CARB.
225	6	145	8.4:1	1 BC
318	8	230	8.8:1	2 BC
340	8	275	8.8:1	4 BC
383	8	290	8.7:1	2 BC
383	8	330	9.5:1	4 BC
383	8	335	9.5:1	4 BC
440	8	375	9.7:1	4 BC
440	8	390	10.5:1	3-2 BC
426	8	425	10.25:1	2-4 BC

CHARGER ENGINES

CID	NO. CYL.	HORSE-POWER	COMP. RATIO	CARB.
225	6	145	8.4:1	1 BC
318	8	230	8.8:1	2 BC
383	8	290	8.7:1	2 BC
383	8	330	9.5:1	4 BC
383	8	335	9.5:1	4 BC
440	8	375	9.7:1	4 BC
440	8	390	10.5:1	3-2 BC
426	8	425	10.25:1	2-4 BC

CORONET ENGINES

CID	NO. CYL.	HORSE-POWER	COMP. RATIO	CARB.
225	6	145	8.4:1	1 BC
318	8	230	8.8:1	2 BC
383	8	290	8.7:1	2 BC
383	8	330	9.5:1	4 BC
383	8	335	9.5:1	4 BC
440	8	375	9.7:1	4 BC
440	8	390	10.5:1	3-2 BC
426	8	425	10.2:1	2-4 BC

DART ENGINES

CID	NO. CYL.	HORSE-POWER	COMP. RATIO	CARB.
198	6	125	8.4:1	1 BC
225	6	145	8.4:1	1 BC
318	8	230	8.8:1	2 BC
340	8	275	10.5:1	4 BC

DODGE ENGINES

CID	NO. CYL.	HORSE-POWER	COMP. RATIO	CARB.
318	8	230	8.8:1	2 BC
383	8	290	8.7:1	2 BC
440	8	350	9.7:1	4 BC

1971 DODGE CHALLENGER

1971 DODGE DEMON

1971 DODGE CHARGER 500

1971 DODGE DART SWINGER

1971 DODGE CORONET BROUGHAM

1971 DODGE POLARA BROUGHAM

VEHICLE IDENTIFICATION NUMBER

DODGE
DL43G1F123456

Located on a plate attached to the left side of the instrument panel, visible through the windshield.

FIRST DIGIT: Identifies the car make

MAKE	CODE
Dodge	D
Challenger	J
Dart	L
Coronet	W
Charger	X

SECOND DIGIT: Identifies the price class

CLASS	CODE
Economy	E
High	H
Police	K
Low	L
Medium	M
Premium	P
Taxi	T
Special	S

THIRD & FOURTH DIGITS: Identify the body type

TYPE	CODE
2-Dr. Sedan	21
2-Dr. Hardtop	23
Convertible Coupe	27
2-Dr. Sports Hardtop	29
4-Dr. Sedan	41
4-Dr. Hardtop	43
6-Pass. Wagon	45
9-Pass. Wagon	46

FIFTH DIGIT: Identifies the engine

CID	CODE
198 CID 1 BC 6-Cyl.	B
225 CID 1 BC 6-Cyl.	C
Special Order 6-Cyl.	E
318 CID 2 BC 8-Cyl.	G
340 CID Hi-Perf. 4 BC 8-Cyl.	H
340 CID Hi-Perf. 3-2 BC 8-Cyl.	J
360 CID 2 BC 8-Cyl.	K
383 CID 2 BC 8-Cyl.	L
383 CID Hi-Perf. 4 BC 8-Cyl.	N
426 CID Hemi 2-4 BC 8-Cyl.	R
440 CID 4 BC 8-Cyl.	T
440 CID Hi-Perf. 4 BC 8-Cyl.	U
440 CID 3-2 BC 8-Cyl.	V
Special Order 8-Cyl.	Z

SIXTH DIGIT: Identifies the year
1 - 1971

SEVENTH DIGIT: Identifies the assembly plant

PLANT	CODE
Lynch Road, Detroit, MI	A
Hamtramck, MI	B
Jefferson Ave., Detroit, MI	C
Belvidere, IL	D
Los Angeles, CA	E
Newark, DE	F
St. Louis, MO	G
Windsor, Ontario, CAN	R

REMAINING SIX DIGITS: Identify the production sequence number beginning with 100001

EXAMPLE

D	L	43	G	1	F	123456
Car Make	Price Class	Body Type	Engine	Model Year	Asm Plant	Production Sequence Number

BODY CODE PLATE

THE BODY CODE PLATE is located on the left front fender side shield or wheel housing on all Challenger, Charger, Coronet and Dart models; and on the left side of upper radiator support on Monaco models.

THE BODY CODE PLATE is read left to right, bottom to top. The information on the plate includes the car S.O. Number and the trim and paint codes.

```
        CHRYSLER MOTORS
          CORPORATION

                                    Line
    XXX   XXX   XXX   XXX            6
    XXX   XXX   XXX   XXX            5
    XXX   XXX   XXX   XXX            4
    XXX   XXX   XXX   XXX            3
    XXX   XXX   XXX   XXX            2
    XXX   XXX   XXX   XXX            1
```

LINE 1 - DIGITS 1, 2 & 3: Indicate engine codes

CID	CODE
Special Order 6-Cyl.	E06
Special Order 8-Cyl.	E08
198 1 BC 6-Cyl.	E22
225 1 BC 6-Cyl.	E24
225 1 BC 6-Cyl.	E25
318 2 BC 8-Cyl.	E44
340 4 BC 8-Cyl.	E55
360 CID 2 BC 8-Cyl.	E57
383 2 BC 8-Cyl.	E61
383 4 BC Hi-Perf. 8-Cyl.	E63
426 2-4 BC Hi-Perf. 8-Cyl. Hemi	E74
440 4 BC 8-Cyl.	E85
440 4 BC Hi-Perf. 8-Cyl.	E86
440 3-2 BC Hi-Perf. 8-Cyl.	E87

LINE 1 - DIGITS 4, 5 & 6: Indicate transmission code

TRANSMISSION	CODE
3-Spd. Manual	D13
3-Spd. Manual	D14
3-Spd. Manual	D15
4-Spd. Manual	D21
3-Spd. Automatic	D31
3-Spd. Automatic	D32
3-Spd. Automatic	D34
3-Spd. Automatic	D36
H.D. Clutch 9 1/2"	D41
Special Order	D49

LINE 1 - DIGIT 7: Indicates car line

MAKE	CODE
Dart	L
Challenger	J
Coronet	W
Dodge	D
Charger	X

LINE 1 - DIGIT 8: Indicates price class

CLASS	CODE
Economy	E
High	H
Police	K
Low	L
Medium	M
Premium	P
Taxi	T
Special	S

LINE 1 - DIGITS 9 & 10: Indicate body type

TYPE	CODE
2-Dr. Sedan	21
2-Dr. Hardtop	23
Convertible Coupe	27
2-Dr. Sports Hardtop	29
4-Dr. Sedan	41
4-Dr. Hardtop	43
6-Pass. Wgon	45
9-Pass. Wagon	46

LINE 1 - DIGIT 11: Indicates engine code

CID	CODE
198 CID 1 BC 6-Cyl.	B
225 CID 1 BC 6-Cyl.	C
Special Order 6-Cyl.	E
318 CID 2 BC 8-Cyl.	G
340 CID Hi-Perf. 4 BC 8-Cyl.	H
340 CID Hi-Perf. 3-2 BC 8-Cyl.	J
360 CID 2 BC 8-Cyl.	K
383 CID 2 BC 8-Cyl.	L
383 CID Hi-Perf. 4 BC 8-Cyl.	N
426 CID Hemi 2-4 BC 8-Cyl.	R
440 CID 4 BC8-Cyl.	T
440 CID Hi-Perf. 4 BC 8-Cyl.	U
440 CID 3-2 BC 8-Cyl.	V
Special Order 8-Cyl.	Z

LINE 1 - DIGIT 12: Indicates model year
1 - 1971

LINE 1 - DIGIT 13: Indicates the assembly plant

PLANT	CODE
Lynch Road, Detroit, MI	A
Hamtramck, MI	B
Jefferson Ave., Detroit, MI	C
Belvidere, IL	D
Los Angeles, CA	E
Newark, NJ	F
St. Louis, MO	G
Windsor, Ontario, CAN	R

LINE 1 - LAST SIX DIGITS: Indicate production sequence number

LINE 2 - DIGITS 1, 2 & 3: Indicate the body paint color, or fleet or special order paint code

COLOR	CODE
Light Gunmetal Metallic	GA4
Dark Gunmetal Metallic	GA8
Light Blue Metallic	GB2
Brite Blue Metallic	GB5
Dark Blue Metallic	GB7
Plum Crazy Metallic	FC7
Indigo Metallic	GC8
Bright Red	FE5
Burgundy Metallic	GE7
Medium Green Metallic	GF3
Dark Green Metallic	GF7
Moss Green Metallic	GJ4
Green Go	FJ6
Dark Bronze Metallic	GK6
Butterscotch	EL5
Turquoise Metallic	FQ5
Tan Metallic	GT2
Dark Tan Metallic	GT8
Hemi-Orange	EV2
White	EW1
Brite White	GW3
Black	TX9
Top Banana	FY1
Citron Yella	GY3
Gold	GY4
Gold Metallic	GY8
Dark Gold Metallic	GY9
Special Order	999
Special Order Panther Pink	148
Special Order Dk. Gunmetal Metallic	317

12 - 8

LINE 2 - DIGITS 4, 5, 6 & 7: Indicate trim code

LINE 2 - DIGIT 4: Indicates price class

CLASS	CODE
Deluxe	D
Economy	E
High	H
Police	K
Low	L
Medium	M
Premium	P
Taxi	T
Special	S

LINE 2 - DIGIT 5: Indicates seat and fabric type

SEAT	CODE
Cloth & Vinyl Bench	1
Vinyl Bench	2
Cloth & Vinyl Split Bench	3
Vinyl Split Bench	4
Cloth & Vinyl Bucket	5
Vinyl Bucket	6
	7
	8
Vinyl & Leather Bucket	R

LINE 2 - DIGITS 6 & 7: Indicate interior color

FABRIC COLOR	CODE
Light Blue	B2
Medium Blue	B5
Dark Blue	B7
Russet	E8
Green	F7
Tan	T7
Light Gold	Y3
Medium Gold	Y5
Black	X9
Black & Orange	XV
Black & White	XX
Black & White	XW

LINE 2 - DIGITS 8, 9 & 10: Indicate upper door frame color, not listed

LINE 2 - DIGIT 11: Indicates the month of manufacture

MONTH	CODE
January	1
February	2
March	3
April	4
May	5
June	6
July	7
August	8
September	9
October	A
November	B
December	C

LINE 2 - DIGITS 12 & 13: Indicate the day of month of manufacture

LINE 2 - LAST SIX DIGITS: Indicate production sequence number

LINE 3 - DIGITS 1, 2 & 3: Indicate roof paint color, vinyl roof code or convertible top code

COLOR	CODE
Paint-Mono Tone	V01
Paint-Two Tone	V02
Paint, Trim & Vinyl Roof Waiver	V08
Paint-Special order	V09
Full Vinyl Roof	V10
Full Vinyl Roof Gunmetal	V1A

COLOR	CODE
Full Vinyl Roof Blue	V1B
Full Vinyl Roof Green	V1F
Full Vinyl Roof Paisley	V1J
Full Vinyl Roof Burgundy	V1M
Full Vinyl Roof Tan	V1T
Full Vinyl Roof White	V1W
Full Vinyl Roof Black	V1X
Full Vinyl Roof Gold	V1Y
Paint-Hood Performance	V21
Delete Sport Hood Treatment	V22
Paint-Hood Performance w/Eng. Callout	V24
Convertible Top	V30
Folding Sunroof	V30
Folding Sunroof White	V3W
Folding Sunroof Black	V3X
Folding Sunroof Special Order	V39
Canopy Vinyl Roof	V40
Canopy Vinyl Roof Green	V4F
Canopy Vinyl Roof Parchment	V4L
Canopy Vinyl Roof White	V4W
Canopy Vinyl Roof Black	V4X
Canopy Vinyl Roof Gold	V4Y
Canopy Vinyl Roof Special Order	v49
Mouldings-Protective Vinyl Body Side	V50
Mouldings-Protective Vinyl Body Side Gunmetal	V5A
Mouldings-Protective Vinyl Body Side Blue	V5B
Mouldings-Protective Vinyl Body Side Green	V5F
Mouldings-Protective Vinyl Body Side Orange	V5K
Mouldings-Protective Vinyl Body Side Burgundy	V5M
Mouldings-Protective Vinyl Body Side Red	V5R
Mouldings-Protective Vinyl Body Side Tan	V5T
Mouldings-Protective Vinyl Body Side Black	V5X
Mouldings-Protective Vinyl Body Side Gold	V5Y
Sport Stripes Tape	V60
Sport Stripes Tape Blue	V6B
Sport Stripes Tape Green	V6F
Sport Stripes Tape Chartreuse	V6J
Sport Stripes Tape Red	V6R
Sport Stripes Tape Orange	V6V
Sport Stripes Tape White	V6V
Sport Stripes Tape White	V6W
Sport Stripes Tape Black	V6X
Sport Stripes Tape Gold	V6Y
Sport Stripes Tape Delete	V68
Accent Stripes Paint	V70
Accent Stripes Paint Blue	V7B
Accent Stripes Paint Green	V7F
Accent Stripes Paint Red	V7R
Accent Stripes Paint White	V7W
Accent Stripes Paint Black	V7X
Accent Stripes Paint Gold	V7Y
Accent Stripes Paint Delete	V78
Sport Stripes Tape	V80
Sport Stripes Tape Red	V8R
Sport Stripes Tape White	V8W
Sport Stripes Tape Black	V8X
Sport Stripes Tape Gold	V8Y
Sport Stripes Tape Delete	V88
Tape Stripe	V90
Tape Stripe White	V9W
Tape Stripe Black	V9X

ENGINE NUMBER

THE ENGINE IDENTIFICATION NUMBER for 6-cylinder engines is located at the right front of the block below the cylinder head.

Engine numbers for 318, 340 and 360 CID V-8 engines are found at the left front of the block below the cylinder head. Engine numbers for 383, 426 and 440 CID V-8 engines are found at the left rear of the block near the oil pan flange.

The following identification is included in the engine serial number:

THE FIRST TWO LETTERS designate the manufacturing plant

MANUFACTURING PLANT	CODE
Mound Road ....PM	
Trenton ....PT	

THE THREE NUMBERS following the plant identification indicate the cubic inch displacement: ie. 198 - 225 - 318 - 340 - 360 - 383 - 426 - 440.

THE FOUR NUMBERS following the model identification are the build date. This is a date code for manufacturing purposes.

THE FOUR NUMBERS following the build date are the engine production sequence number.

EXAMPLE
PM31832251234

In the example above:

PM	Mound Road
318	Cubic Inch Displacement
3225	Build date code*
1234	Engine sequence number

*1971 date codes run from 3260 to 3624

CHALLENGER ENGINES

CID	NO. CYL.	HORSE-POWER	COMP. RATIO	CARB.
198	6	125	8.4:1	2 BC
225	6	145	8.4:1	1 BC
318	8	230	8.6:1	2 BC
340	8	275	10.3:1	4 BC
383	8	275	8.5:1	2 BC
383	8	300	8.5:1	4 BC
426	8	425	10.2:1	2-4 BC
440	8	385	10.3:1	3-2 BC

CHARGER ENGINES

CID	NO. CYL.	HORSE-POWER	COMP. RATIO	CARB.
225	6	145	8.4:1	1 BC
318	8	230	8.6:1	2 BC
383	8	275	8.5:1	2 BC
383	8	300	8.5:1	4 BC
426	8	425	10.2:1	2-4 BC
440	8	370	9.5:1	4 BC
440	8	385	10.3:1	3-2 BC

DART ENGINES

CID	NO. CYL.	HORSE-POWER	COMP. RATIO	CARB.
198	6	125	8.4:1	1 BC
225	6	145	8.4:1	1 BC
318	8	230	8.6:1	2 BC
340	8	275	10.3:1	4 BC

DODGE ENGINES

CID	NO. CYL.	HORSE-POWER	COMP. RATIO	CARB.
225	6	145	8.4:1	1 BC
318	8	230	8.6:1	2 BC
360	8	255	8.7:1	2 BC
383	8	275	8.5:1	2 BC
383	8	300	8.5:1	4 BC
440	8	335	8.5:1	4 BC

1972 DODGE CHALLENGER

1972 DODGE COLT

1972 DODGE CHARGER

1972 DODGE CORONET CUSTOM

1972 DODGE DART SWINGER

1972 DODGE POLARA

1972 DODGE MONACO

VEHICLE IDENTIFICATION NUMBER

DODGE
• DL43G2F123456 •

Located on a plate attached to the left side of the instrument panel, visible through the windshield.

FIRST DIGIT: Identifies the car make

MAKE	CODE
Dodge	D
Challenger	J
Dart	L
Coronet, Charger	W

SECOND DIGIT: Identifies the price class

CLASS	CODE
Low	L
Medium	M
High	H
Premium	P
Special	S
Police	K
Taxi	T
Dodge Taxi	G

THIRD & FOURTH DIGITS: Identify the body type

TYPE	CODE
2-Dr. Sedan Coupe	21
2-Dr. Hardtop	23
2-Dr. Sports Hardtop	29
4-Dr. Sedan	41
4-Dr. Hardtop	43
6-Pass. Wagon	45
9-Pass. Wagon	46

FIFTH DIGIT: Indicates engine

CID	CODE
198 CID 1 BC 6-Cyl.	B
225 CID 1 BC 6-Cyl.	C
Special Order 6-Cyl.	E
318 CID 2 BC 8-Cyl.	G
340 CID 4 BC Hi-Perf. 8-Cyl.	H
360 CID 2 BC 8-Cyl.	K
400 CID 2 BC 8-Cyl.	M
400 CID 4 BC Hi-Perf. 8-Cyl.	P
440 CID 4 BC 8-Cyl.	T
440 CID 4 BC 8-Cyl.	U
440 CID 3-2 BC 8-Cyl.	V
Special Order 8-Cyl.	Z

SIXTH DIGIT: Identifies the year
2 - 1972

SEVENTH DIGIT: Identifies the assembly plant

PLANT	CODE
Lynch Road, Detroit, MI	A
Hamtramck, MI	B
Jefferson Ave., Detroit, MI	C
Belvidere, IL	D
Newark, DE	F
St. Louis, MO	G
Windsor, Ontario, CAN	R

REMAINING SIX DIGITS: Identify the production sequence number beginning with 100001

EXAMPLE						
D	L	43	G	2	F	123456
Car Make	Price Class	Body Type	Engine	Model Year	Asm Plant	Production Sequence Number

BODY CODE PLATE

THE BODY CODE PLATE is located on the left front fender side shield or wheel housing.

THE BODY CODE PLATE is read left to right, bottom to top. The information on the plate includes the car S.O. Number and the trim and paint codes.

CHRYSLER MOTORS CORPORATION

				Line
XXX	XXX	XXX	XXX	6
XXX	XXX	XXX	XXX	5
XXX	XXX	XXX	XXX	4
XXX	XXX	XXX	XXX	3
XXX	XXX	XXX	XXX	2
XXX	XXX	XXX	XXX	1

LINE 1 - DIGITS 1, 2 & 3: Indicate engine codes

CID	CODE
198 CID 1 BC 6-Cyl.	E22
225 CID 1 BC 6-Cyl.	E24
225 CID 1 BC 6-Cyl.	E25
318 CID 2 BC 8-Cyl.	E44
340 CID 4 BC 8-Cyl.	E55
360 CID 2 BC 8-Cyl.	E57
400 CID 2 BC 8-Cyl.	E63
400 CID 4 BC Hi-Perf. 8-Cyl.	E68
440 CID 4 BC 8-Cyl.	E85
440 CID 4 BC Hi-Perf. 8-Cyl.	E86
440 CID 3-2 BC 8-Cyl.	E87
Special Order	E99

LINE 1 - DIGITS 4, 5 & 6: Indicate transmission codes

TRANSMISSION	CODE
3-Spd. Manual	D13
3-Spd. Manual	D14
3-Spd. Manual	D15
4-Spd. Manual	D21
3-Spd. Automatic	D31
3-Spd. Automatic	D32
3-Spd. Automatic	D34
3-Spd. Automatic	D36
H.D. Clutch 9 1/2"	D41

LINE 1 - DIGIT 7: Indicates car line

MAKE	CODE
Dodge	D
Challenger	J
Dart	L
Coronet, Charger	W

LINE 1 - DIGIT 8: Indicates price class

CLASS	CODE
Low	L
Medium	M
High	H
Premium	P
Special	S
Police	K
Taxi	T
Dodge Taxi	T

LINE 1 - DIGITS 9 & 10: Indicate body type

TYPE	CODE
2-Dr. Sedan	21
2-Dr. Hardtop	23
2-Dr. Sports Hardtop	29
4-Dr. Sedan	41
4-Dr. Hardtop	43
2-Seat Wagon	45
3-Seat Wagon	46

LINE 1 - DIGIT 11: Indicates engine code

CID	CODE
198 CID 1 BC 6-Cyl.	B
225 CID 1 BC 6-Cyl.	C
Special Order 6-Cyl.	E
318 CID 2 BC 8-Cyl.	G
340 CID 4 BC Hi-Perf. 8=Cyl.	H
360 CID 2 BC 8-Cyl.	K
400 CID 2 BC 8-Cyl.	M
400 CID 4 BC Hi-Perf. 8-Cyl.	P
440 CID 4 BC 8-Cyl.	T
440 CID 4 BC 8-Cyl.	U
440 CID 3-2 BC 8-Cyl.	V
Special Order 8-Cyl.	Z

LINE 1 - DIGIT 12: Indicates model year
2 - 1972

LINE 1 - DIGIT 13: Indicates the assembly plant

PLANT	CODE
Lynch Road, Detroit, MI	A
Hamtramck, MI	B
Jefferson Ave., Detroit, MI	C
Belvidere, IL	D
Newark, NJ	F
St. Louis, MO	G
Windsor, Ontario, CAN	R

LINE 1 - LAST SIX DIGITS: Indicate production sequence number

LINE 2 - DIGITS 1, 2 & 3: Indicate the body paint color, or fleet or special order paint code

COLOR	CODE
Light Gunmetal Metallic	GA4
Dark Gunmetal Metallic	GA8
Dark Gray Metallic	EA9
Light Blue	HB1
Light Blue Metallic	GB2
Super Blue	TB3
Bright Blue Metallic	GB5
Dark Blue Metallic	GB7
Bright Red	FE5

COLOR	CODE
Light Green Metallic	GF3
Dark Green Metalic	GF7
Parchment	HL4
Turquoise Metallic	FQ5
Medium Tan Metallic	HT6
Dark Tan Metallic	HT8
Hemi-Orange	EV2
Eggshell White	EW1
Black	TX9
Top Banana	FY1
Yellow	DY2
Light Gold	GY4
Gold Metallic	GY8
Dark Gold Metallic	GY9
Special Order	999

LINE 2 - DIGITS 4, 5, 6 & 7: Indicate trim code

LINE 2 - DIGIT 4: Indicates price class

CLASS	CODE
A-Class	A
B-Class	B
Custom	C
Deluxe	D
Economy	E
F-Class	F
G-Class	G
High	H
Police	K
Low	L
Medium	M
Premium	P
Q-Class	Q
R-Class	R
Sport	S
Taxi	T
V-Class	V

LINE 2 - DIGIT 5: Indicates seat and fabric type

SEAT	CODE
Cloth & Vinyl Bench	1
Vinyl Bench	2
Cloth & Leather Bench	A
Leather Bench	M
Cloth & Vinyl Bench Split Back	3
Vinyl Bench Sp. Back	4
Cloth & Leather Bench Split Back	B
Leather Bench Split Back	P
Cloth & Vinyl Bucket	5
Vinyl Bucket	6
Cloth & Leather Bucket	C
Leather Bucket	R
Cloth & Vinyl 50/50	7
Vinyl 50/50	8
Cloth & Leather 50/50	D
Leather 50/50	L
Cloth & Vinyl Special Design	9
Vinyl Special Design	H
Cloth & Leather Special Design	E
Leather Special Design	T

LINE 2 - DIGITS 6 & 7: Indicate interior color

FABRIC COLOR	CODE
Gray	A9
Medium Blue	B5
Dark Blue	B8
Green	F6
Green & White	FW

FABRIC COLOR	CODE
White & Green	G6
Parchment	L3
Light Tan	T5
Black	X9
Black & White	XW
Light Gold	Y3
Gold	Y5

LINE 2 - DIGITS 8, 9 & 10: Indicate upper door frame color, not listed

LINE 2 - DIGIT 11: Indicates the month of manufacture

MONTH	CODE
January	1
February	2
March	3
April	4
May	5
June	6
July	7
August	8
September	9
October	A
November	B
December	C

LINE 2 - DIGITS 12 & 13: Indicate the day of month of manufacture

LINE 2 - LAST SIX DIGITS: Indicate production sequence number

LINE 3 - DIGITS 1, 2 & 3: Indicate roof paint color, vinyl roof code or convertible top code

COLOR	CODE
Paint-Mono Tone	V01
Paint-Two Tone	V02
Paint, Trim & Vinyl Roof Waiver	V08
Paint-Special Order	V09
Full Vinyl Roof	V10
Full Vinyl Roof Gunmetal	V1A
Full Vinyl Roof Blue (Cancelled)	V1B
Full Vinyl Roof Green	V1F
Full Vinyl Roof Mock Turtle	V1G
Full Vinyl Roof Burgundy	V1M
Full Vinyl Roof Walnut	V1T
Full Vinyl Roof White	V1X
Full Vinyl Roof Black	V1X
Full Vinyl Roof Gold	V1Y
Paint-Hood Performance	V21
Paint-Deck Performance	V25
Folding Sunroof	V30
Folding Sunroof White	V3W
Folding Sunroof Black	V3X
Canopy Vinyl Roof	V40
Canopy Vinyl Roof Green	V4F
Canopy Vinyl Roof Mock Turtle	V4G
Canopy Vinyl Roof White	V4W
Canopy Vinyl Roof Black	V4X
Canopy Vinyl Roof Gold	V4Y
Mouldings-Protective Vinyl Body Side	V50
Mouldings-Protective Vinyl Body Side Black	V5X
Sport Stripes	V60
Sport Stripes White	V6W
Sport Stripes Black	V6X
Sport Stripes Delete	V68
Accent Stripes Paint	V70
Accent Stripes Paint White	V7W
Accent Stripes Paint Black	V7X
Accent Stripes Paint Delete	V78
Sport Stripes Tape	V80
Sport Stripes Tape White	V8W
Sport Stripes Tape	V8X

ENGINE NUMBER

THE ENGINE IDENTIFICATION NUMBER for 6-cylinder engines is located at the right front of the block below the cylinder head.

ENGINE NUMBERS for 318, 340 and 360 CID V-8 engines are found at the left front of the block below the cylinder head. The engine number for 400 engines is located at the right side of the block adjacent to the distributor. The engine number for 440 CID V-8 engines is found at the left rear of the block near the oil pan flange.

The following identification is included in the engine serial number:

THE FIRST TWO LETTERS designate the manufacturing plant

MANUFACTURING PLANT	CODE
Mound Road	PM
Trenton	PT

THE THREE NUMBERS following the plant identification indicate the cubic inch displacement: ie. 198 - 225 - 318 - 340 - 360 - 400 - 440.

THE FOUR NUMBERS following the model identification are the build date. This is a date code for manufacturing purposes.

THE FOUR NUMBERS following the build date are the engine production sequence number.

EXAMPLE
PM31832401234

In the example above:
PM	Mound Road	
318	Cubic Inch Displacement	
3240	Build date code*	
1234	Engine sequence number	

*1972 date codes run from 3625 thru 3990

CHARGER ENGINES

CID	NO. CYL.	HORSE-POWER	COMP. RATIO	CARB.
225	6	110	8.4:1	1 BC
318	8	150	8.6:1	2 BC
340	8	240	8.5:1	4 BC
400	8	190	8.2:1	2 BC
400	8	255	8.2:1	4 BC
440	8	280	8.2:1	4 BC
440	8	330	10.3:1	6 BC

DART ENGINES

CID	NO. CYL.	HORSE-POWER	COMP. RATIO	CARB.
198	6	100	8.4:1	1 BC
225	6	110	8.4:1	1 BC
318	8	150	8.6:1	2 BC
340	8	240	8.5:1	4 BC

DODGE ENGINES

CID	NO. CYL.	HORSE-POWER	COMP. RATIO	CARB.
225	6	110	8.4:1	1 BC
318	8	150	8.6:1	2 BC
360	8	175	8.8:1	2 BC
400	8	190	8.2:1	2 BC
440	8	225	8.2:1	4 BC

1973 DODGE CHALLENGER

1973 DODGE DART

1973 DODGE CHARGER

1973 DODGE MONACO

1973 DODGE CORONET

1973 DODGE POLARA CUSTOM

VEHICLE IDENTIFICATION NUMBER

DODGE
WL41G3A123456

Located on a plate attached to the left side of the instrument panel, visible through the windshield.

FIRST DIGIT: Identifies the car make

MAKE	CODE
Dodge	D
Challenger	J
Dart	L
Coronet, Charger	W

SECOND DIGIT: Identifies the price class

CLASS	CODE
New York Taxi	G
High	H
Premium	P
Low	L
Medium	M
Special	S

THIRD & FOURTH DIGITS: Identify the body type

TYPE	CODE
2-Dr. Coupe	21
2-Dr. Hardtop	23
2-Dr. Sports Hardtop	29
4-Dr. Sedan	41
4-Dr. Hardtop Sedan	43
2-Seat Station Wagon	45
3-Seat Station Wagon	46

FIFTH DIGIT: Identifies the engine

CID	CODE
198 CID 1 BC 6-Cyl.	B
225 CID 1 BC 6-Cyl.	C
Special Order 6-Cyl.	E
318 CID 2 BC 8-Cyl.	G
340 CID Hi-Perf. 4 BC 8-Cyl.	H
360 CID 2 BC 8-Cyl.	K
400 CID 2 BC 8-Cyl.	M
400 CID 4 BC 8-Cyl.	P
440 CID 4 BC 8-Cyl.	T
440 CID Hi-Perf. 4 BC 8-Cyl.	U

SIXTH DIGIT: Identifies the year
3 - 1973

SEVENTH DIGIT: Identifies the assembly plant

PLANT	CODE
Lynch Road, Detroit, MI	A
Hamtramck, MI	B
Jefferson Ave., Detroit, MI	C
Belvidere, IL	D
Newark, DE	F
St. Louis, MO	G
New Stanton, RI	H
Windsor, Ontario, CAN	R

REMAINING SIX DIGITS: Identify the production sequence number starting at each plant with 100001

EXAMPLE						
W	L	41	G	3	A	123456
Car Make	Price Class	Body Type	Engine	Model Year	Asm Plant	Production Sequence Number

BODY CODE PLATE

THE BODY CODE PLATE is located on the left front fender side shield or wheel housing.

THE BODY CODE PLATE is read left to right, bottom to top. The information on the plate includes the car S.O. Number and the trim and paint codes.

CHRYSLER MOTORS CORPORATION

				Line
XXX	XXX	XXX	XXX	6
XXX	XXX	XXX	XXX	5
XXX	XXX	XXX	XXX	4
XXX	XXX	XXX	XXX	3
XXX	XXX	XXX	XXX	2
XXX	XXX	XXX	XXX	1

LINE 1 - DIGITS 1, 2 & 3: Indicate engine codes

CID	CODE
198 CID 1 BC 6-Cyl.	E22
225 CID 1 BC 6-Cyl.	E24
225 CID 1 BC 6-Cyl.	E25
318 CID 2 BC 8-Cyl.	E44
340 CID Hi-Perf. 4 BC 8-Cyl.	E55
360 CID 2 BC 8-Cyl.	E57
400 CID 2 BC 8-Cyl.	E63
400 CID 4 BC 8-Cyl.	E68
440 CID 4 BC 8-Cyl.	E85
440 CID Hi-Perf. 4 BC 8-Cyl.	E86
Special Order Engine	E99

LINE 1 - DIGITS 4, 5 & 6: Indicate transmission codes

TRANSMISSION	CODE
3-Spd. Manual Floor Shift	D13
3-Spd. Manual Clm. Shift	D14
3-Spd. Manual Clm. Shift	D15
4-Spd. Manual	D21
3-Spd. Automatic	D31
3-Spd. Automatic	D32
3-Spd. Automatic H.D.	D36

LINE 1 - DIGIT 7: Indicates car line

MAKE	CODE
Dodge	D
Challenger	J
Dart	L
Coronet, Charger	W

12 - 16

LINE 1 - DIGIT 8: Indicates price class

CLASS	CODE
New York Taxi	G
High	H
Premium	P
Low	L
Medium	M
Special	S

LINE 1 - DIGITS 9 & 10: Indicate body type

TYPE	CODE
2-Dr. Coupe	21
2-Dr. Hardtop	23
2-Dr. Sports Hardtop	29
4-Dr. Sedan	41
4-Dr. Hardtop Sedan	43
2-Seat Station Wagon	45
3-Seat Station Wagon	46

LINE 1 - DIGIT 11: Indicates engine code

CID	CODE
198 CID 1 BC 6-Cyl.	B
225 CID 1 BC 6-Cyl.	C
Special Order 6-Cyl.	E
318 CID 2 BC 8-Cyl.	G
340 CID Hi-Perf. 4 BC 8-Cyl.	H
360 CID 2 BC 8-Cyl.	K
400 CID 2 BC 8-Cyl.	M
400 CID 4 BC 8-Cyl.	P
440 CID 4 BC 8-Cyl.	T
440 CID Hi-Perf. 4 BC 8-Cyl.	U

LINE 1 - DIGIT 12: Indicates model year
3 - 1973

LINE 1 - DIGIT 13: Indicates the assembly plant

PLANT	CODE
Lynch Road, Detroit, MI	A
Hamtramck, MI	B
Jefferson Ave., Detroit, MI	C
Belvidere, IL	D
Newark, DE	F
St. Louis, MO	G
New Stanton, RI	H
Windsor, Ontario, CAN	R

LINE 1 - LAST SIX DIGITS: Indicate production sequence number

LINE 2 - DIGITS 1, 2 & 3: Indicate the body paint color, or fleet or special order paint code

COLOR	CODE
Dark Silver Metallic	JA5
Light Blue	HB1
Super Blue	TB3
Bright Blue Metallic	GB5
Dark Blue Metallic	JB9
Bright Red	FE5
Pale Green	JF1
Light Green Metallic	GF3
Dark Green Metallic	JF8
Bronze Metallic	GK6
Parchment	HL4
Turquoise Metallic	FQ5
Medium Tan Metallic	HT6
Dark Tan Metallic	HT8
Eggshell White	EW1
Black	TX9
Top Banana	FY1
Yellow	DY2
Light Gold	JY3
Gold Metallic	JY6
Dark Gold Metallic	JY9
Special Order	999

LINE 2 - DIGITS 4, 5, 6 & 7: Indicate trim code

LINE 2 - DIGIT 4: Indicates price class

CLASS	CODE
New York Taxi	G
High	H
Premium	P
Low	L
Medium	M
Special	S

LINE 2 - DIGIT 5: Indicates seat and fabric type

SEAT	CODE
Cloth & Vinyl Bench	1
Vinyl Bench	2
Cloth & Leather Bench	A
Leather Bench	M
Cloth & Vinyl Bench Split Back	3
Vinyl Bench Split Back	4
Cloth & Leather Split Back	B
Leather Split Back	P
Cloth & Vinyl Bucket	5
Vinyl Bucket	6
Cloth & Leather Bucket	C
Leather Bucket	R
Cloth & Vinyl 50/50	7
Vinyl 50/50	8
Cloth & Leather 50/50	D
Leather 50/50	L
Cloth & Vinyl Special Design	9
Vinyl Special Design	H
Cloth & Leather Special Design	E
Leather Special Design	T

LINE 2 - DIGITS 6 & 7: Indicate interior color

FABRIC COLOR	CODE
Gray	A9
Medium Blue	B5
Dark Blue	B8
Red-Black-White	EW
Green	F6
Copper-Black-White	KW
Parchment	L3
Light Tan	T5
Black	X9
Black & White	XW
Gold	Y4
Gold-Black-White	YW

LINE 2 - DIGITS 8, 9 & 10: Indicate upper door frame color, not listed

LINE 2 - DIGIT 11: Indicates the month of manufacture

MONTH	CODE
January	1
February	2
March	3
April	4
May	5
June	6
July	7
August	8
September	9
October	A
November	B
December	C

LINE 2 - DIGITS 12 & 13: Indicate the day of month of manufacture

LINE 2 - LAST SIX DIGITS: Indicate production sequence number

LINE 3 - DIGITS 1, 2 & 3: Indicate roof paint color, vinyl roof code or convertible top code

COLOR	CODE
Paint-Mono Tone	V01
Paint-Two Tone	V02
Paint, Trim & Vinyl Roof Waiver	V08
Paint-Special Order	V09
Full Vinyl Roof	V10
Full Vinyl Roof Blue	V1B
Full Vinyl Roof Green	V1F
Full Vinyl Roof White	V1W
Full Vinyl Roof Black	V1X
Full Vinyl Roof Gold	V1Y
Paint-Hood Performance	V21
Halo Style Vinyl Roof	V40
Halo Style Vinyl Roof Blue	V4B
Halo Style Vinyl Roof Green	V4F
Halo Style Vinyl Roof White	V4W
Halo Style Vinyl Roof Black	V4X
Halo Style Vinyl Roof Gold	V4Y
Mouldings-Protective Vinyl Body Side	V50
Mouldings-Protective Vinyl Body Side Black	V5X
Sport Stripes Tape	V60
Sport Stripes Tape White	V6W
Sport Stripes Tape Black	V6X
Accent Stripes Paint	V70
Accent Stripes Paint White	V70
Accent Stripes Paint Black	V7X
Sport Stripes Tape	V80
Sport Stripes Tape White	V8W
Sport Stripes Tape Black	V8X
Hood Stripes	V90
Hood Stripes White	V9W
Hood Stripes Black	V9X

ENGINE NUMBER

THE ENGINE IDENTIFICATION NUMBER for 6-cylinder engines is located at the right front of the block below #1 spark plug.

ENGINE NUMBERS for 318, 340 and 360 CID V-8 engines are found at the left front of the block below the cylinder head. The engine number for 400 engines is found on the right side of the block adjacent to the distributor. The engine number for 440 engines is located on the left bank adjacent to the front tappet rail.

The following identification will be included in the engine serial number:

"A" ENGINE FAMILY

THE FIRST TWO LETTERS will designate the series and/or build plant.

THE THREE NUMBERS following the series and/or build plant are the cubic inch displacement: ie 198 - 225 - 318 - 340 - 360 - 400 - 440.

THE LETTER following the model identification is the engine type.

THE FOUR LETTERS following the engine type are the build date code.

THE FOUR NUMBERS following the build date code are the daily production sequence number.

"B" AND "G" ENGINE FAMILY

THE FIRST LETTER will designate the series.

THE THREE NUMBERS AND LETTER following the series are the cubic inch displacement and type.

THE THREE NUMBERS following the model identification and type are the build date.

THE NUMBER following the build date is the shift built.

ENGINE SERIAL NUMBER CODES DEFINED:

	CODE
High Performance	HP
Series (1973)	J
Low Compression	LC
Mound Road Plant	M
Premium Fuel Recommended	P
Regular Fuel may be used	R
Special Engine	S
Windsor Plant	W

EXAMPLE ("A" Engine Family)
JM318R43511234

J	Series (1973)
M	Mound Road Plant
318	Cubic Inch Displacement
4351	Build date code*
1234	Daily engine sequence number

EXAMPLE ("B" and "G" Engine Family)
J440R8-222

J	Series (1973)
440R	Cubic Inch Displacement and Type
8-22	Build date code*
2	Shift built

*1973 date codes run from 3991 thru 4355.

CHARGER ENGINES

CID	NO. CYL.	HORSE-POWER	COMP. RATIO	CARB.
225	6	105	8.4:1	1 BC
318	8	150	8.6:1	2 BC
340	8	240	8.5:1	4 BC
400	8	175	8.2:1	2 BC
400	8	260	8.2:1	4 BC
440	8	280	8.2:1	4 BC

DART ENGINES

CID	NO. CYL.	HORSE-POWER	COMP. RATIO	CARB.
198	6	95	8.4:1	1 BC
225	6	105	8.4:1	1 BC
318	8	150	8.6:1	2 BC
340	8	240	8.5:1	4 BC

DODGE ENGINES

CID	NO. CYL.	HORSE-POWER	COMP. RATIO	CARB.
360	8	170	8.4:1	2 BC
400	8	185	8.2:1	2 BC
440	8	220	8.2:1	4 BC
318	8	150	8.6:1	2 BC

1974 DODGE CHALLENGER

1974 DODGE MONACO STATION WAGON

1974 DODGE CHARGER

1974 DODGE CORONET

1974 DODGE DART SWINGER

1974 DODGE DART CUSTOM

1974 DODGE MONACO

1974 DODGE CHALLENGER

VEHICLE IDENTIFICATION NUMBER

DODGE
WL41G4A123456

Located on a plate attached to the left side of the instrument panel, visible through the windshield.

FIRST DIGIT: Identifies the car make

MAKE	CODE
Monaco	D
Challenger	J
Dart	L
Coronet, Charger	W

SECOND DIGIT: Identifies the price class

CLASS	CODE
Low	L
Grand	G
High	H
Premium	P
Medium	M
Special	S

THIRD & FOURTH DIGITS: Identify the body type

TYPE	CODE
2-Dr. Hardtop Sedan Coupe	21
2-Dr. Hardtop	23
2-Dr. Spec. Hardtop	29
4-Dr. Sedan	41
4-Dr. Hardtop Sedan	43
2-Seat Station Wagon	45
3-Seat Station Wagon	46

FIFTH DIGIT: Identifies the engine

CID	CODE
198 CID 1 BC 6-Cyl.	B
225 CID 1 BC 6-Cyl.	C
Special Order 6-Cyl.	E
318 CID 2 BC 8-Cyl.	G
360 CID 4 BC 8-Cyl.	J
360 CID Hi-Perf. 4 BC 8-Cyl.	L
360 CID 2 BC 8-Cyl.	K
400 CID 2 BC 8-Cyl.	M
400 CID 4 BC 8-Cyl.	N
400 CID Hi-Perf. 4 BC 8-Cyl.	P
440 CID 4 BC 8-Cyl.	T
440 CID Hi-Perf. 4 BC 8-Cyl.	U

SIXTH DIGIT: Identifies the year
4 - 1974

SEVENTH DIGIT: Identifies the assembly plant

PLANT	CODE
Lynch Road, Detroit, MI	A
Hamtramck, MI	B
Jefferson Ave., Detroit, MI	C
Belvidere, IL	D
Newark, DE	F
St. Louis, MO	G
Japan	5
Japan	9

REMAINING SIX DIGITS: Identify the production sequence number beginning with 100001

EXAMPLE

W	L	41	G	4	A	123456
Car Make	Price Class	Body Type	Engine	Model Year	Asm Plant	Production Sequence Number

BODY CODE PLATE

THE BODY CODE PLATE is located on the left front fender side shield or wheel housing.

THE BODY CODE PLATE is read left to right, bottom to top. The information on the plate includes the car S.O. Number and the trim and paint codes.

CHRYSLER MOTORS CORPORATION

				Line
XXX	XXX	XXX	XXX	6
XXX	XXX	XXX	XXX	5
XXX	XXX	XXX	XXX	4
XXX	XXX	XXX	XXX	3
XXX	XXX	XXX	XXX	2
XXX	XXX	XXX	XXX	1

LINE 1 - DIGITS 1, 2 & 3: Indicate engine codes

CID	CODE
198 CID 1 BC 6-Cyl.	E22
225 CID 1 BC 6-Cyl.	E24
225 CID 1 BC 6-Cyl.	E25
318 CID 2 BC 8-Cyl.	E44
360 CID 4 BC 8-Cyl.	E56
360 CID Hi-Perf. 4 BC 8-Cyl.	E57
360 CID 2 BC 8-Cyl.	E58
400 CID 2 BC 8-Cyl.	E63
400 CID 4 BC 8-Cyl.	E64
400 CID 4 BC 8-Cyl.	E68
440 CID 4 BC 8-Cyl.	E85
440 CID Hi-Perf. 4 BC 8-Cyl.	E86
Special Order Engine	E99

LINE 1 - DIGITS 4, 5 & 6: Indicate transmission codes

TRANSMISSION	CODE
3-Spd. Manual Floor Shift	D13
3-Spd. Std. Man. Clm. Shift	D14
H.D. 3-Spd. Man. Clm. Shift	D15
4-Spd. Manual	D21
Standard Automatic	D34
H.D. Automatic	D35

LINE 1 - DIGIT 7: Indicates car line

MAKE	CODE
Monaco	D
Challenger	J
Dart	L
Coronet, Charger	W

LINE 1 - DIGIT 8: Indicates price class

CLASS	CODE
Low	L
Grand	G
High	H
Premium	P
Medium	M
Special	S

LINE 1 - DIGITS 9 & 10: Indicate body type

TYPE	CODE
2-Dr. Hardtop Sedan Coupe	21
2-Dr. Hardtop	23
2-Dr. Spec. Hardtop	29
4-Dr. Sedan	41
4-Dr. Hardtop Sedan	43
2-Seat Station Wagon	45
3-Seat Station Wagon	46

LINE 1 - DIGIT 11: Indicates engine code

CID	CODE
198 CID 1 BC 6-Cyl.	B
225 CID 1 BC 6-Cyl.	C
Special Order 6-Cyl.	E
318 CID 2 BC 8-Cyl.	G
360 CID 4 BC 8-Cyl.	J
360 CID Hi-Perf. 4 BC 8-Cyl.	L
360 CID 2 BC 8-Cyl.	K
400 CID 2 BC 8-Cyl.	M
400 CID 4 BC 8-Cyl.	N
400 CID Hi-Perf. 4 BC 8-Cyl.	P
440 CID 4 BC 8-Cyl.	T
440 CID Hi-Perf. 4 BC 8-Cyl.	U

LINE 1 - DIGIT 12: Indicates model year
4 - 1974

LINE 1 - DIGIT 13: Indicates the assembly plant

PLANT	CODE
Lynch Road, Detroit, MI	A
Hamtramck, MI	B
Jefferson Ave., Detroit, MI	C
Belvidere, IL	D
Newark, DE	F
St. Louis, MO	G
Japan	5
Japan	9

LINE 1 - LAST SIX DIGITS: Indicate production sequence number

LINE 2 - DIGITS 1, 2 & 3: Indicate the body paint color, or fleet or special order paint code

COLOR	CODE
Dark Silver Metallic	JA5
Powder Blue	KB1
Lucerne Blue Metallic	KB5
Starlight Blue Metallic	KB8
Bright Red	FE5
Burnished Red Metallic	GE7
Frosty Green Metallic	KG2
Deep Sherwood Metallic	KG8
Avocado Gold Metallic	KJ6
Parchment	HL4
Aztec Gold Metallic	JL6
Dark Moonstone Metallic	KL8
Sienna Metallic	KT5
Dark Chestnut Metallic	KT9
Eggshell White	EW1
Black	TX9
Yellow	DY2
Golden Fawn	KY4
Yellow Blaze	KY5
Gold Metallic	JY6
Dark Gold Metallic	JY9
Special Order	999

LINE 2 - DIGITS 4, 5, 6 & 7: Indicate trim code

LINE 2 - DIGIT 4: Indicates price class

CLASS	CODE
Low	L
Grand	G
High	H
Premium	P
Medium	M
Special	S

LINE 2 - DIGIT 5: Indicates seat and fabric type

SEAT	CODE
Cloth & Vinyl Bench	1
Vinyl Bench	2
Cloth & Leather Bench	A
Leather Bench	M
Cloth & Vinyl Bench Split Back	3
Vinyl Bench Split Back	4
Cloth & Leather Bench Split Back	B
Leather Bench Split Back	P
Cloth & Vinyl Bucket	5
Vinyl Bucket	6
Cloth & Leather Bucket	C
Leather Bucket	R
Cloth & Vinyl 50/50	7
Vinyl 50/50	8
Cloth & Leather 50/50	D
Leather 50/50	L
Cloth & Vinyl Special Design	9
Vinyl Special Design	H
Cloth & Leather Special Design	E
Leather Special Design	T

LINE 2 - DIGITS 6 & 7: Indicate interior color

FABRIC COLOR	CODE
Gray	A9
Blue	B6
Wimbleton	EW
Green	G6
Parchment	L3
Tangier	LL
Chestnut	T7
Orange, Black & White	VW
Black	X9
Black & White	XW
Gold	Y3
White & Gold	YW

LINE 2 - DIGITS 8, 9 & 10: Indicate upper door frame color, not listed

LINE 2 - DIGIT 11: Indicates the month of manufacture

MONTH	CODE
January	1
February	2
March	3
April	4
May	5
June	6
July	7
August	8
September	9
October	A
November	B
December	C

LINE 2 - DIGITS 12 & 13: Indicate the day of month of manufacture

LINE 2 - LAST SIX DIGITS: Indicate production sequence number

LINE 3 - DIGITS 1, 2 & 3: Indicate roof paint color, vinyl roof code or convertible top code

COLOR	CODE
Paint-Mono Tone	V01
Paint-Two Tone	V02
Paint, Trim & Vinyl Roof Waiver	V08
Paint-Special Order	V09
Full Vinyl Roof	V10
Full Vinyl Roof Blue	V1B
Full Vinyl Roof Green	V1G
Full Vinyl Roof Parchment	V1L
Full Vinyl Roof White	V1W
Full Vinyl Roof Black	V1X
Full Vinyl Roof Gold	V1Y
Paint-Hood Performance	V21
Decor Stripe Pkg. #2 (RH23)	V25
Delete "Dodge" Tape Block Letters	V38
Halo Style Vinyl Roof	V40
Halo Style Vinyl Roof White	V4W
Halo Style Vinyl Roof Black	V4X
Halo Style Vinyl Roof Gold Reptile Grain	V4Y
Mouldings-Protective Vinyl Body Side	V50
Mouldings-Protective Vinyl Body Side Black	V5X
Sport Stripes Tape	V60
Sport Stripes Tape Red	V6R
Sport Stripes Tape White	V6W
Sport Stripes Tape Black	V6X
Sport Stripes Tape Gold	V6Y
Sport Stripes Tape Delete	V68
Accent Stripes Paint	V70
Accent Stripes Paint Blue Green	V7B
Accent Stripes Paint Parchment	V7L
Accent Stripes Paint Red	V7R
Accent Stripes Paint White	V7W
Accent Stripes Paint Black	V7X
Accent Stripes Paint Gold	V7Y
Accent Stripes Paint Delete	V78
Sport Stripes Tape	V80
Sport Stripes Tape Parchment	V8L
Sport Stripes Tape Red	V8R
Sport Stripes Tape White	V8W
Sport Stripes Tape Black	V8X
Sport Stripes Tape Delete	V88
Sport Stripes-Body Side & Roof	V90
Sport Stripes-Body Side & Roof Red	V9R
Sport Stripes-Body Side & Roof White	V9W
Sport Stripes-Body Side & Roof Black	V9X

ENGINE NUMBER

THE ENGINE IDENTIFICATION NUMBER for 6-cylinder engines is located at the right side of the block below #1 spark plug.

ENGINE NUMBERS for 318 and 360 CID V-8 engines are found at the left front of the block below the cylinder head. The engine number for 400 CID V-8 engines is found on the right side of the block adjacent to the distributor. The engine number for 440 CID V-8 engines is found on the left bank adjacent to the front tappet rail.

The following identification is included in the engine serial number:

"A" ENGINE FAMILY

THE FIRST NUMBER AND LETTER will designate the model year and/or build plant.

THE THREE NUMBERS following the model year and/or build plant are the cubic inch displacement: ie. 198 - 225 - 318 - 360 - 400 - 440

THE LETTER following the model identification is the engine type.

THE FOUR NUMBERS following the engine type are the build date code.

THE FOUR NUMBERS following the build date code are the daily sequence number (optional usage).

"B" AND "G" ENGINE FAMILY

THE FIRST NUMBER AND LETTER will designate the model year and/or build plant.

THE THREE NUMBERS AND LETTER following the model year and/or build plant are the cubic inch displacement and type.

THE THREE NUMBERS following the model identification and type are the build date.

THE NUMBER following the build date is the shift built.

NOTE: Series without "M" or "W" suffix indicates Trenton Engine Plant.

ENGINE SERIAL NUMBER CODES DEFINED:

	CODE
High Performance	HP
Series (1974)	K
Low Compression	LC
Mound Road Plant	M
Premium Fuel Recommended	P
Regular Fuel may be used	R
Special Engine	S
Trenton Plant	T
Windsor Plant	W

EXAMPLE ("A" Engine Family)
4M318R043601234

4	Model year
M	Mound Road plant
318	Cubic Inch Displacement
R	Regular Fuel may be used
4360	Build date code
1234	Daily sequence number

EXAMPLE ("B" and "G" Engine Family)
4T440R8-222

4	Model year
T	Trenton engine plant
440R	Cubic Inch Displacement and type
8-22	Build date code
2	Shift built

CHARGER ENGINES

CID	NO. CYL.	HORSE-POWER	COMP. RATIO	CARB.
225	6	105	8.4:1	1 BC
318	8	150	8.6:1	2 BC
360	8	200	8.4:1	4 BC
360	8	245	8.4:1	4 BC
400	8	205	8.2:1	4 BC
400	8	250	8.2:1	4 BC
440	8	275	8.2:1	4 BC

DART ENGINES

CID	NO. CYL.	HORSE-POWER	COMP. RATIO	CARB.
198	6	95	8.4:1	1 BC
225	6	105	8.4:1	1 BC
318	8	150	8.6:1	2 BC
360	8	245	8.4:1	4 BC

DODGE ENGINES

CID	NO. CYL.	HORSE-POWER	COMP. RATIO	CARB.
360	8	180	8.4:1	2 BC
400	8	185	8.2:1	2 BC
400	8	205	8.2:1	4 BC
440	8	230	8.2:1	4 BC

1975 DODGE DART SPECIAL EDITION

1975 DODGE MONACO STATION WAGON

1975 DODGE DART SPORT

1975 DODGE COLT

1975 DODGE ROYAL MONACO

1975 DODGE CORONET

1975 DODGE COLT STATION WAGON

1975 DODGE CHARGER

VEHICLE IDENTIFICATION NUMBER

DODGE WL41G5A123456

Located on a plate attached to the left side of the instrument panel, visible through the windshield.

FIRST DIGIT: Identifies the car make

MAKE	CODE
Monaco	D
Dart	L
Coronet	W
Charger	X

SECOND DIGIT: Identifies the price class

CLASS	CODE
Dodge Taxi	D
High	H
Police	K
Low	L
Medium	M
Premium	P
Special	S
Taxi	T

THIRD & FOURTH DIGITS: Identify the body type

TYPE	CODE
2-Dr. Hardtop Coupe	21
2-Dr. Hardtop Coupe	22
2-Dr. Hardtop	23
2-Dr. Spec. Hardtop	29
4-Dr. Sedan	41
4-Dr. Hardtop Sedan	43
2-Seat Station Wagon	45
3-Seat Station Wagon	46

FIFTH DIGIT: Identifies the engine

CID	CODE
225 CID 1 BC 6-Cyl.	C
Special Order 6-Cyl.	E
318 CID 2 BC 8-Cyl.	G
360 CID 4 BC 8-Cyl.*	J
360 CID Hi-Perf. 4 BC 8-Cyl.*	L
360 CID 2 BC 8-Cyl.**	K
400 CID 2 BC 8-Cyl.**	M
400 CID 4 BC 8-Cyl.	N
400 CID 4 BC Hi-Perf. 8-Cyl.**	P
440 CID 4 BC 8-Cyl.	T
440 CID Hi-Perf. 4 BC 8-Cyl.	U
Special Order 8-Cyl.	Z

*With California emission package
**Not available with California emission package

SIXTH DIGIT: Identifies the year
5 - 1975

SEVENTH DIGIT: Identifies the assembly plant

PLANT	CODE
Lynch Road, Detroit, MI	A
Hamtramck, MI	B
Jefferson Ave., Detroit, MI	C
Belvidere, IL	D
Newark, DE	F
St. Louis, MO	G
Windsor, Ontario, CAN	R
Japan	5
Japan	9

REMAINING SIX DIGITS: Identify the production sequence number starting at each plant with 100001

EXAMPLE

W	L	41	G	5	A	123456
Car Make	Price Class	Body Type	Engine	Model Year	Asm Plant	Production Sequence Number

BODY CODE PLATE

THE BODY CODE PLATE is located on the left front fender side shield or wheel housing.

THE BODY CODE PLATE is read left to right, bottom to top. The information on the plate includes the car S.O. Number and the trim and paint codes.

CHRYSLER MOTORS CORPORATION

				Line
XXX	XXX	XXX	XXX	6
XXX	XXX	XXX	XXX	5
XXX	XXX	XXX	XXX	4
XXX	XXX	XXX	XXX	3
XXX	XXX	XXX	XXX	2
XXX	XXX	XXX	XXX	1

LINE 1 - DIGITS 1, 2 & 3: Indicate engine codes

CID	CODE
225 CID 1 BC 6-Cyl.	E24
225 CID 1 BC 6-Cyl.	E25
318 CID 2 BC 8-Cyl.	E44
360 CID 4 BC 8-Cyl.*	E56
360 CID Hi-Perf. 4 BC 8-Cyl.*	E58
360 CID 2 BC 8-Cyl.**	E57
400 CID 2 BC 8-Cyl.**	E63
400 CID 4 BC 8-Cyl.**	E64
400 CID 4 BC Hi-Perf. 8-Cyl.**	E68
440 CID 4 BC 8-Cyl.	E85
440 CID Hi-Perf. 4 BC 8-Cyl.	E86
Special Order Engine	E99

*With California emission package
**Not available with California emission package

LINE 1 - DIGITS 4, 5 & 6: Indicate transmission codes

TRANSMISSION	CODE
3-Spd. Manual Floor Shift	D13
3-Spd. Std. Manual Clm. Shift	D14
3-Spd. H.D. Manual Clm. Shift	D15
4-Spd. Manual	D21
Standard Automatic	D34
H.D. Automatic	D35

LINE 1 - DIGIT 7: Indicates car line

MAKE	CODE
Monaco	D
Dart	L
Coronet	W
Charger	X

LINE 1 - DIGIT 8: Indicates price class

CLASS	CODE
Dodge Taxi	D
High	H
Police	K
Low	L
Medium	M
Premium	P
Special	S
Taxi	T

LINE 1 - DIGITS 9 & 10: Indicate body type

TYPE	CODE
2-Dr. Hardtop Coupe	21
2-Dr. Hardtop Coupe	22
2-Dr. Hardtop	23
2-Dr. Spec. Hardtop	29
4-Dr. Sedan	41
4-Dr. Hardtop Sedan	43
2-Seat Station Wagon	45
3-Seat Station Wagon	46

LINE 1 - DIGIT 11: Indicates engine code

CID	CODE
225 CID 1 BC 6-Cyl.	C
Special Order 6-Cyl.	E
318 CID 2 BC 8-Cyl.	G
360 CID 4 BC 8-Cyl.*	J
360 CID Hi-Perf. 4 BC 8-Cyl.*	L
360 CID 2 BC 8-Cyl.**	K
400 CID 2 BC 8-Cyl.**	M
400 CID 4 BC 8-Cyl.	N
400 CID 4 BC Hi-Perf. 8-Cyl.**	P
440 CID 4 BC 8-Cyl.	T
440 CID Hi-Perf. 4 BC 8-Cyl.	U
Special Order 8-Cyl.	Z

*With California emission package
**Not available with California emission package

LINE 1 - DIGIT 12: Indicates model year
5 - 1975

LINE 1 - DIGIT 13: Indicates the assembly plant

PLANT	CODE
Lynch Road, Detroit, MI	A
Hamtramck, MI	B
Jefferson Ave., Detroit, MI	C
Belvidere, IL	D
Newark, DE	F
St. Louis, MO	G
Windsor, Ontario, CAN	R
Japan	5
Japan	9

LINE 1 - LAST SIX DIGITS: Indicate production sequence number

LINE 2 - DIGITS 1, 2 & 3: Indicate the body paint color, or fleet or special order paint code

COLOR	CODE
Silver Cloud Metallic	LA2
Platinum Metallic	LJ2
Powder Blue	KB1
Astral Blue Metallic	LB2
Lucerne Blue Metallic	KB5
Starlight Blue Metallic	KB8
Bright Red	FE5
Vintage Red Metallic	LE9
Bittersweet Metallic	LK3
Frosty Green Metallic	KG2
Deep Sherwood Metallic	KG8
Avocado Gold Metallic	KJ6
Moondust Metallic	LL5
Parchment	HL4
Cinnamon Metallic	LT4
Sienna Metallic	KT5
Dark Chestnut Metallic	KT9
Eggshell White	EW1
Black	TX9
Yellow Blaze	KY5
Golden Fawn	KY4
Inca Gold Metallic	LY6
Spanish Gold Metallic	LY9
Aztec Gold Metallic	JL6

LINE 2 - DIGITS 4, 5, 6 & 7: Indicate trim code

LINE 2 - DIGIT 4: Indicates price class

CLASS	CODE
Dodge Taxi	D
High	H
Police	K
Low	L
Medium	M
Premium	P
Special	S
Taxi	T

LINE 2 - DIGIT 5: Indicates seat and fabric type

SEAT	CODE
Cloth & Vinyl Bench	1
All Vinyl Bench	2
Cloth & Leather Bench	A
All Leather Bench	M
Cloth & Vinyl Bench Split Back	3
All Vinyl Bench Split Back	4
Cloth & Leather Bench Split Back	B
All Leather Bench Split Back	P
Cloth & Vinyl Bucket	5
All Vinyl Bucket	6
Cloth & Leather Bucket	C
All Leather Bucket	R
Cloth & Vinyl 50/50	7
All Vinyl 50/50	8
Cloth & Leather 50/50	L
All Leather 50/50	D
Cloth & Vinyl Special Design	9
All Vinyl Special Design	H
Cloth & Leather Special Design	E
All Leather Special Design	T

LINE 2 - DIGITS 6 & 7: Indicate interior color

FABRIC COLOR	CODE
Medium Blue	B6
Blue & White	BW
Red	E7
Red	EE
Red, Black, White	EW
Green	G6
Green	GG
Green & White	GW
Copper, Black, White	KW
Parchment	L3
Parchment	LL
Chestnut	T7
Orange, Black, White	VW
Black	X9
Black & White	XW
Gold	Y3
Gold & White	YW

LINE 2 - DIGITS 8, 9 & 10: Indicate upper door frame color, not listed

LINE 2 - DIGIT 11: Indicate the month of manufacture

MONTH	CODE
January	1
February	2
March	3
April	4
May	5
June	6
July	7
August	8
September	9
October	A
November	B
December	C

LINE 2 - DIGITS 12 & 13: Indicate the day of month of manufacture

LINE 2 - LAST SIX DIGITS: Indicate production sequence number

LINE 3 - DIGITS 1, 2 & 3: Indicate roof paint color, vinyl roof code or convertible top code

COLOR	CODE
Full Vinyl Roof White	V1W
Canopy Vinyl Roof White	V4W
Halo Vinyl Roof White	V3W
Landau Vinyl Roof White	V3W
Full Vinyl Roof Parchment	V1L
Canopy Vinyl Roof Parchment	V4L
Halo Vinyl Roof Parchment	V1L
Landau Vinyl Roof Parchment	V3L
Full Vinyl Roof Black	V1X
Canopy Vinyl Roof Black	V4X
Halo Vinyl Roof Black	V1X
Landau Vinyl Roof Black	V3X
Full Vinyl Roof Gold	V1Y
Canopy Vinyl Roof Gold	V4Y
Halo Vinyl Roof Gold	V1Y
Landau Vinyl Roof Gold	V3Y
Full Vinyl Roof Green	V1G
Canopy Vinyl Roof Green	V4G
Halo Vinyl Roof Green	V1G
Landau Vinyl Roof Green	V3G
Full Vinyl Roof Red	V1E
Canopy Vinyl Roof Red	V4E
Halo Vinyl Roof Red	V1E
Landau Vinyl Roof Red	V3E
Landau Vinyl Roof Silver	V3A
Full Vinyl Roof Blue	V1B

ENGINE NUMBER

THE ENGINE IDENTIFICATION NUMBER for 6-cylinder engines is located at the right side of the block below #1 spark plug.

ENGINE NUMBERS FOR 318 and 360 CID V-8 engines are found at the left front of the block below the cylinder head. The engine number for 400 CID V-8 engines is found on the right side of the block adjacent to the distributor. The engine number for 440 CID V-8 engines is found on the left bank adjacent to the front tappet rail.

The following identification is included in the engine serial number:

"A" ENGINE FAMILY

THE FIRST NUMBER AND LETTER will designate the model year and/or build plant.

THE THREE NUMBERS following the model year and/or build plant are the cubic inch displacement: ie. 225 - 318 - 360 - 400 - 440

THE LETTER following the model identification is the engine type.

THE FOUR NUMBERS following the engine type are the build date code.

THE FOUR NUMBERS following the build date code are the daily sequence number (optional usage).

"B" AND "G" ENGINE FAMILY

THE FIRST NUMBER AND LETTER will designate the model year and/or build plant.

THE THREE NUMBERS AND LETTER following the model year and/or build plant are the cubic inch displacement and type.

THE THREE NUMBERS following the model identification and type are the build date.

THE NUMBER following the build date is the shift built.

NOTE: Series without "M" or "W" suffix indicates Trenton Engine Plant.

ENGINE SERIAL NUMBER CODES DEFINED:

	CODE
High performance	HP
Series (1975)	L
Low Compression	LC
Mound Road Plant	M
Premium Fuel Recommended	P
Regular Fuel may be used	R
Special Engine	S
Trenton Plant	T
Windsor Plant	W

EXAMPLE ("A" Engine Family)
5M318R09101234

5	Model year
M	Mound Road plant
318	Cubic Inch Displacement
R	Regular Fuel may be used
0910	Build date code
1234	Daily sequence number

EXAMPLE ("B" and "G" Engine Family)
5T440R8-222

5	Model year
T	Trenton plant
440R	Cubic Inch Displacement and Type
8-22	Build date code
2	Shift built

CORONET ENGINES

CID	NO. CYL.	HORSE-POWER	COMP. RATIO	CARB.
225	6	95	8.4:1	1 BC
318	8	150	8.5:1	2 BC
360	8	180	8.4:1	2 BC
400	8	160	8.2:1	2 BC
400	8	190	8.2:1	4 BC
400	8	235	8.2:1	4 BC
318	8	135	8.5:1	2 BC
360	8	190	8.4:1	4 BC
400	8	165	8.2:1	2 BC
400	8	185	8.2:1	4 BC

DART ENGINES

CID	NO. CYL.	HORSE-POWER	COMP. RATIO	CARB.
225	6	95	8.4:1	1 BC
318	8	145	8.5:1	2 BC
360	8	230	8.4:1	4 BC

MONACO ENGINES

CID	NO. CYL.	HORSE-POWER	COMP. RATIO	CARB.
360	8	180	8.4:1	2 BC
318	8	150	8.5:1	2 BC
400	8	175	8.2:1	2 BC
440	8	215	8.2:1	4 BC

1976 DODGE CORONET

1976 DODGE CORONET STATION WAGON

1976 DODGE DART

1976 DODGE MONACO STATION WAGON

1976 DODGE MONACO

1976 DODGE MONACO

1976 DODGE ASPEN

1976 DODGE CHARGER

VEHICLE IDENTIFICATION NUMBER

DODGE
WL41G6A123456

Located on a plate attached to the left side of the instrument panel, visible through the windshield.

FIRST DIGIT: Identifies the car make

MAKE	CODE
Monaco	D
Dart	L
Aspen	N
Coronet/Charger	W
Charger S.E.	X

SECOND DIGIT: Identifies the price class

CLASS	CODE
High	H
Police	K
Low	L
Medium	M
Premium	P
Special	S

THIRD & FOURTH DIGITS: Identify the body type

TYPE	CODE
2-Dr. Coupe	22
2-Dr. Hardtop Coupe	23
2-Dr. Spec. Hardtop	29
4-Dr. Sedan	41
4-Dr. Hardtop	43
2-Seat Station Wagon	45
3-Seat Station Wagon	46

FIFTH DIGIT: Identifies the engine

CID	CODE
225 CID 1 BC 6-Cyl.	C
Special Order 6-Cyl.	E
318 CID 2 BC 8-Cyl.	G
360 CID 4 BC 8-Cyl.*	J
360 CID Hi-Perf. 4 BC 8-Cyl.	L
360 CID 2 BC 8-Cyl.**	K
400 CID 2 BC 8-Cyl.**	M
400 CID 4 BC 8-Cyl.	N
400 CID Hi-Perf. 4 BC 8-Cyl.**	P
440 CID 4 BC 8-Cyl.	T
440 CID Hi-Perf. 8-Cyl.	U
Special Order 8-Cyl.	Z

*With California emission package
**Not available with California emission package

SIXTH DIGIT: Identifies the year
6 - 1976

SEVENTH DIGIT: Identifies the assembly plant

PLANT	CODE
Lynch Road, Detroit, MI	A
Hamtramck, MI	B
Jefferson Ave., Detroit, MI	C
Belvidere, IL	D
Newark, DE	F
St. Louis, MO	G
Windsor, Ontario, CAN	R
Japan	5
Japan	7
Japan	8
Japan	9

REMAINING SIX DIGITS: Identify the production sequence number starting at each plant with 100001

EXAMPLE

W	L	41	G	6	A	123456
Car Make	Price Class	Body Type	Engine	Model Year	Asm Plant	Production Sequence Number

BODY CODE PLATE

THE BODY CODE PLATE is located on the left front fender side shield or wheel housing.

THE BODY CODE PLATE is read left to right, bottom to top. The information on the plate includes the car S.O. Number and the trim and paint codes.

CHRYSLER MOTORS CORPORATION

				Line
XXX	XXX	XXX	XXX	6
XXX	XXX	XXX	XXX	5
XXX	XXX	XXX	XXX	4
XXX	XXX	XXX	XXX	3
XXX	XXX	XXX	XXX	2
XXX	XXX	XXX	XXX	1

LINE 1 - DIGITS 1, 2 & 3: Indicate engine codes

CID	CODE
225 CID 1 BC 6-Cyl.	E24
225 CID 1 BC 6-Cyl.	E25
318 CID 2 BC 8-Cyl.	E44
360 CID 4 BC 8-Cyl.*	E56
360 CID Hi-Perf. 4 BC 8-Cyl.	E58
360 CID 2 BC 8-Cyl.**	E57
400 CID 2 BC 8-Cyl.**	E63
400 CID 4 BC 8-Cyl.**	E64
400 CID Hi-Perf. 4 BC 8-Cyl.**	E68
440 CID 4 BC 8-Cyl.	E85
440 CID Hi-Perf. 4 BC 8-Cyl.	E86
Special Order Engine	E99

*With California emission package
**Not available with California emission package

LINE 1 - DIGITS 4, 5 & 6: Indicate transmission codes

TRANSMISSION	CODE
3-Spd. Manual Floor Shift	D13
3-Spd. Std. Manual Clm. Shift	D14
3-Spd. H.D. Manual Clm. Shift	D15
4-Spd. Standard	D21
4-Spd. O.D.	D24
Standard A904	D31
Standard A998	D32
Standard A999	D33
Standard Automatic	D34
H.D. A727	D35
Standard A727	D36
H.D. A904	D38

LINE 1 - DIGIT 7: Indicates car line

MAKE	CODE
Monaco	D
Dart	L
Aspen	N
Coronet/Charger	W
Charger S.E.	X

LINE 1 - DIGIT 8: Indicates price class

CLASS	CODE
High	H
Police	K
Low	L
Medium	M
Premium	P
Special	S

LINE 1 - DIGITS 9 & 10: Indicate body type

TYPE	CODE
2-Dr. Coupe	22
2-Dr. Hardtop Coupe	23
2-Dr. Spec. Hardtop	29
4-Dr. Sedan	41
4-Dr. Hardtop	43
2-Seat Station Wagon	45
3-Seat Station Wagon	46

LINE 1 - DIGIT 11: Indicates engine code

CID	CODE
225 CID 1 BC 6-Cyl.	C
Special Order 6-Cyl.	E
318 CID 2 BC 8-Cyl.	G
360 CID 4 BC 8-Cyl.*	J
360 CID Hi-Perf. 4 BC 8-Cyl.	L
360 CID 2 BC 8-Cyl.**	K
400 CID 2 BC 8-Cyl.**	M
400 CID 4 BC 8-Cyl.	N
400 CID Hi-Perf. 4 BC 8-Cyl.**	P
440 CID 4 BC 8-Cyl.	T
440 CID Hi-Perf. 8-Cyl.	U
Special Order 8-Cyl.	Z

*With California emission package
**Not available with California emission package

LINE 1 - DIGIT 12: Indicates model year
6 - 1976

LINE 1 - DIGIT 13: Indicates the assembly plant

PLANT	CODE
Lynch Road, Detroit, MI	A
Hamtramck, MI	B
Jefferson Ave., Detroit, MI	C
Belvidere, IL	D
Newark, DE	F
St. Louis, MO	G
Windsor, Ontario, CAN	R
Japan	5
Japan	7
Japan	8
Japan	9

LINE 1 - LAST SIX DIGITS: Indicate production sequence number

LINE 2 - DIGITS 1, 2 & 3: Indicate the body paint color, or fleet or special order paint code

COLOR	CODE
Silver Cloud Metallic	LA2
Powder Blue	KB1
Astral Blue Metallic	LB2
Big Sky Blue	MB4
Jamaican Blue Metallic	MB5
Starlight Blue Metallic	KB8
Bright Red	FE5
Vintage Red Metallic	LE9
Jade Green Metallic	MF2
Deep Sherwood Metallic	KG8
Platinum Metallic	LJ2
Tropic Green Metallic	MJ5
Bittersweet Metallic	LK3
Parchment	HL4
Moondust Metallic	LL5
Claret Red	MR6
Cinnamon Metallic	LT4
Dark Chestnut Metallic	KT9
Saddle Tan	MU2
Carmel Tan Metallic	MU3
Light Chestnut Metallic	MU6
Spitfire Orange	MV1
Eggshell White	EW1
Black	TX9
Silver Cloud Metallic	9037

COLOR	CODE
Bright Blue Metallic	8717
Dark Green Metallic	7776
Bright Green Metallic	7807
Bright Tan Metallic	6486
White	1417
Light Gold	6442
White	1417
Yellow	2550
Light Green Metallic	7773
Sunstone	5207
Russet	3418
Golden Fawn	KY4
Yellow Blaze	KY5
Harvest Gold	MY3
Inca Gold Metallic	LY6
Spanish Gold Metallic	LY9
Deep Sherwood Sunfire Metallic	MG9
Vintage Red Sunfire Metallic	ME8
Bright Red	3116
Light Blue	8664
Chrome Yellow	2245

LINE 2 - DIGITS 4, 5, 6 & 7: Indicate trim code

LINE 2 - DIGIT 4: Indicates price class

CLASS	CODE
High	H
Police	K
Low	L
Medium	M
Premium	P
Special	S

LINE 2 - DIGIT 5: Indicates seat and fabric type

SEAT	CODE
Cloth & Vinyl Bench	1
All Vinyl Bench	2
Cloth & Leather Bench	A
All Leather Bench	M
Cloth & Vinyl Bench Split Back	3
All Vinyl Bench Split Back	4
Cloth & Leather Bench Split Back	B
All Leather Bench Split Back	P
Cloth & Vinyl Bucket	5
All Vinyl Bucket	6
Cloth & Leather Bucket	C
All Leather Bucket	R
Cloth & Vinyl 50/50	7
All Vinyl 50/50	8
Cloth & Leather 50/50	D
All Leather 50/50	L
Cloth & Vinyl Special Design	9
All Vinyl Special Design	H
Cloth & Leather Special Design	E
All Leather Special Design	T

LINE 2 - DIGITS 6 & 7: Indicate interior color

FABRIC COLOR	CODE
Medium Blue	B6
Blue & White	BW
Red	E7
Red	EE
Red & White	EW
Green	F6
Green	FF
Green & White	FW
Gold, Black, White	KW
Parchment	L3

FABRIC COLOR	CODE
Parchment	LL
Chestnut	T7
Tan	U5
Tan & White	UW
Black	X9
Black & White	XW
Gold	Y3
Gold & White	YW

LINE 2 - DIGITS 8, 9 & 10: Indicate upper door frame color, not listed

LINE 2 - DIGIT 11: Indicate the month of manufacture

MONTH	CODE
January	1
February	2
March	3
April	4
May	5
June	6
July	7
August	8
September	9
October	A
November	B
December	C

LINE 2 - DIGITS 12 & 13: Indicate the day of month of manufacture

LINE 2 - LAST SIX DIGITS: Indicate production sequence number

LINE 3 - DIGITS 1, 2 & 3: Indicate roof paint color, vinyl roof code or convertible top code

COLOR	CODE
Full Vinyl Roof Blue	V1B
Halo Vinyl Roof Blue	V1B
Landau Vinyl Roof Blue	V3B
Full Vinyl Roof Green	V1F
Halo Vinyl Roof Green	V1F
Canopy Vinyl Roof Green	V4F
Canopy Vinyl Roof Green	V5F
Full Vinyl Roof Parchment	V1L
Halo Vinyl Roof Parchment	V1L
Landau Vinyl Roof Parchment	V3L
Canopy Vinyl Roof Parchment	V4L
Canopy Vinyl Roof Parchment	V5L
Full Vinyl Roof Red	V1E
Halo Vinyl Roof Red	V1E
Landau Vinyl Roof Red	V3E
Canopy Vinyl Roof Red	V4E
Canopy Vinyl Roof Red	V5E
Full Vinyl Roof Black	V1X
Halo Vinyl Roof Black	V1X
Landau Vinyl Roof Black	V3X
Canopy Vinyl Roof Black	V4X
Canopy Vinyl Roof Black	V5X
Full Vinyl Roof White	V1W
Halo Vinyl Roof White	V1W
Landau Vinyl Roof White	V3W
Canopy Vinyl Roof White	V4W
Canopy Vinyl Roof White	V5W
Full Vinyl Roof Tan	V1U
Landau Vinyl Roof Tan	V3U
Full Vinyl Roof Silver	V1A
Landau Vinyl Roof Silver	V3A
Canopy Vinyl Roof Silver	V4A
Full Vinyl Roof Gold	V1Y
Canopy Vinyl Roof Gold	V4Y
Canopy Vinyl Roof Gold	V5Y

ENGINE NUMBER

THE ENGINE IDENTIFICATION NUMBER for 6-cylinder engines is located at the right side of the block below #1 spark plug.

ENGINE NUMBERS for 318 and 360 CID V-8 engines are found at the left front of the block below the cylinder head. The engine number for 400 CID V-8 engines is found on the right side of the block adjacent to the distributor. The engine number for 440 CID V-8 engines is found on the left bank adjacent to the front tappet rail.

The following identification is included in the engine serial number:

"A" ENGINE FAMILY

THE FIRST NUMBER AND LETTER will designate the model year and/or build plant.

THE THREE NUMBERS following the model year and/or build plant are the cubic inch displacement: ie. 225 - 318 - 360 - 400 - 440

THE LETTER following the model identification is the engine type.

THE FOUR NUMBERS following the engine type are the build date code.

THE FOUR NUMBERS following the build date code are the daily sequence number (optional usage).

"B" AND "G" ENGINE FAMILY

THE FIRST NUMBER AND LETTER will designate the model year and/or build plant.

THE THREE NUMBERS AND LETTER following the model year and/or build plant are the cubic inch displacement and type.

THE THREE NUMBERS following the model identification and type are the build date.

THE NUMBER following the build date is the shift built.

NOTE: Series without "M" or "W" suffix indicates Trenton Engine plant.

ENGINE SERIAL NUMBER CODES DEFINED:

	CODE
High Performance	HP
Series (1975)	L
Low Compression	LC
Mound Road Plant	M
Premium Fuel Recommended	P
Regular Fuel may be used	R
Special Engine	S
Trenton Plant	LT
Windsor Plant	W

EXAMPLE ("A" Engine Family)
6M318R09101234

6	Model year
M	Mound Road plant
318	Cubic Inch Displacement
R	Regular Fuel may be used
0910	Build date code (0910 is September 10)
1234	Daily sequence number

EXAMPLE ("B" and "G" Engine Family)
6T440R8-222

6	Model year
T	Trenton plant
440R	Cubic Inch Displacement and Type
8-22	Build date code
2	Shift built

ASPEN ENGINES

CID	NO. CYL.	HORSE-POWER	COMP. RATIO	CARB.
225	6	100	8.4:1	1 BC
318	8	150	8.5:1	2 BC
360	8	170	8.4:1	2 BC

CHARGER, CORONET ENGINES

CID	NO. CYL.	HORSE-POWER	COMP. RATIO	CARB.
225	6	100	8.4:1	1 BC
318	8	150	8.5:1	2 BC
360	8	170	8.4:1	2 BC
360	8	175	8.4:1	4 BC
400	8	175	8.2:1	2 BC
400	8	210	8.2:1	4 BC
400	8	240	8.2:1	4 BC

DART ENGINES

CID	NO. CYL.	HORSE-POWER	COMP. RATIO	CARB.
225	6	100	8.4:1	1 BC
318	8	150	8.5:1	2 BC
360	8	170	8.4:1	2 BC

MONACO ENGINES

CID	NO. CYL.	HORSE-POWER	COMP. RATIO	CARB.
318	8	150	8.5:1	2 BC
360	8	170	8.4:1	2 BC
360	8	175	8.2:1	4 BC
400	8	175	8.2:1	2 BC
400	8	210	8.2:1	4 BC
440	8	205	8.0:1	4 BC

1977 DODGE ASPEN

1977 DODGE COLT

1977 DODGE ASPEN STATION WAGON

1977 DODGE DIPLOMAT

1977 DODGE CHARGER

1977 DODGE MONACO

1977 DODGE ROYAL MONACO

1977 DODGE ROYAL MONACO STATION WAGON

VEHICLE IDENTIFICATION NUMBER

DODGE
WL41G7A123456

Located on a plate attached to the left side of the instrument panel, visible through the windshield.

FIRST DIGIT: Identifies the car make

MAKE	CODE
Royal Monaco	D
Diplomat	G
Aspen	N
Monaco	W
Charger S.E.	X

SECOND DIGIT: Identifies the price class

CLASS	CODE
High	H
Police	K
Low	L
Medium	M
Premium	P
Special	S

THIRD & FOURTH DIGITS: Identify the body type

TYPE	CODE
2-Dr. Coupe	22
2-Dr. Hardtop Coupe	23
2-Dr. Coupe	29
4-Dr. Sedan	41
4-Dr. Hardtop	43
2-Seat Station Wagon	45
3-Seat Station Wagon	46

FIFTH DIGIT: Identifies the engine

CID	CODE
225 CID 1 BC 6-Cyl.	C
225 CID 2 BC 6-Cyl.	D
318 CID 2 BC 8-Cyl.	G
360 CID 4 BC 8-Cyl.	J
360 CID Hi-Perf. 4 BC 8-Cyl.	L
360 CID 2 BC 8-Cyl.	K
400 CID 2 BC 8-Cyl.	N
400 CID 4 BC 8-Cyl.	P
440 CID 4 BC 8-Cyl.	T
440 CID Hi-Perf. 4 BC 8-Cyl.	U
Special Order 8-Cyl.	Z

SIXTH DIGIT: Identifies the year
7 - 1977

SEVENTH DIGIT: Identifies the assembly plant

PLANT	CODE
Lynch Road, Detroit, MI	A
Hamtramck, MI	B
Jefferson Ave., Detroit, MI	C
Belvidere, IL	D
Newark, DE	F
St. Louis, MO	G
Windsor, Ontario, CAN	R
Japan	5
Japan	7
Japan	8
Japan	9

REMAINING SIX DIGITS: Identify the production sequence number starting at each plant with 100001

EXAMPLE

W	L	41	G	7	A	123456
Car Make	Price Class	Body Type	Engine	Model Year	Asm Plant	Production Sequence Number

BODY CODE PLATE

THE BODY CODE PLATE is located on the left front fender side shield or wheel housing.

THE BODY CODE PLATE is read left to right, bottom to top. The information on the plate includes the car S.O. Number and the trim and paint codes.

CHRYSLER MOTORS CORPORATION

				Line
XXX	XXX	XXX	XXX	6
XXX	XXX	XXX	XXX	5
XXX	XXX	XXX	XXX	4
XXX	XXX	XXX	XXX	3
XXX	XXX	XXX	XXX	2
XXX	XXX	XXX	XXX	1

LINE 1 - DIGITS 1, 2 & 3: Indicate engine codes

CID	CODE
225 CID 1 BC 6-Cyl.	E24
225 CID 1 BC 6-Cyl.	E25
225 CID 2 BC 6-Cyl.	E26
318 CID 2 BC 8-Cyl.	E44
360 CID 4 BC 8-Cyl.	E56
360 CID Hi-Perf. 4 BC 8-Cyl.	E58
360 CID 2 BC 8-Cyl.	E57
400 CID 4 BC 8-Cyl.	E64
400 CID Hi-Perf. 4 BC 8-Cyl.	E68
440 CID 4 BC 8-Cyl.	E85
440 CID Hi-Perf. 4 BC 8-Cyl.	E86
Special Order Engine	E99

LINE 1 - DIGITS 4, 5 & 6: Indicate transmission codes

TRANSMISSION	CODE
3-Spd. Manual Floor Shift	D13
3-Spd. Std. Manual Clm. Shift	D14
3-Spd. H.D. Manual Clm. Shift	D15
4-Spd. Standard	D21
4-Spd. O.D.	D24
Standard A904	D31
Standard A998	D32
Standard A999	D33
Standard Automatic	D34
H.D. A727	D35
Standard A727	D36
H.D. A904	D38

LINE 1 - DIGIT 7: Indicates car line

MAKE	CODE
Royal Monaco	D
Diplomat	G
Aspen	N
Monaco	W
Charger S.E.	X

LINE 1 - DIGIT 8: Indicates price class

CLASS	CODE
High	H
Police	K
Low	L
Medium	M
Premium	P
Special	S

LINE 1 - DIGITS 9 & 10: Indicate body type

TYPE	CODE
2-Dr. Coupe	22
2-Dr. Hardtop Coupe	23
2-Dr. Coupe	29
4-Dr. Sedan	41
4-Dr. Hardtop	43
2-Seat Station Wagon	45
3-Seat Station Wagon	46

LINE 1 - DIGIT 11: Indicates engine code

CID	CODE
225 CID 1 BC 6-Cyl.	C
225 CID 2 BC 6-Cyl.	D
318 CID 2 BC 8-Cyl.	G
360 CID 4 BC 8-Cyl.	J
360 CID Hi-Perf. 4 BC 8-Cyl.	L
360 CID 2 BC 8-Cyl.	K
400 CID 2 BC 8-Cyl.	N
400 CID 4 BC 8-Cyl.	P
440 CID 4 BC 8-Cyl.	T
440 CID Hi-Perf. 4 BC 8-Cyl.	U
Special Order 8-Cyl.	Z

LINE 1 - 12: Indicates model year
7 - 1977

LINE 1 - DIGIT 13: Indicates the assembly plant

PLANT	CODE
Lynch Road, Detroit, MI	A
Hamtramck, MI	B
Jefferson Ave., Detroit, MI	C
Belvidere, IL	D
Newark, DE	F
St. Louis, MO	G
Windsor, Ontario, CAN	R
Japan	5
Japan	7
Japan	8
Japan	9

LINE 1 - LAST SIX DIGITS: Indicate production sequence number

LINE 2 - DIGITS 1, 2 & 3: Indicate the body paint color, or fleet or special order paint code.

COLOR	CODE
Silver Cloud Metallic	LA2
Wedgewood Blue	PB2
Cadet Blue Metallic	PB3
French Racing Blue	PB5
Regatta Blue Metallic	PB6
Starlight Blue Sunfire Metallic	PB9
Rallye Red	FE5
Vintage Red Sunfire Metallic	ME8
Jade Green Metallic	MF2
Forest Green Sunfire Metallic	PF7
Burnished Copper Metallic	PK6
Mojave Beige	PL3
Moondust Metallic	LL5
Russet Sunfire Metallic	PR8
Coffee Sunfire Metallic	PT7
Lt. Mocha Tan	PT2
Caramel Tan Metallic	MU3
Spitfire Orange	MV1
Spinnaker White	EW1
Formal Black Sunfire Metallic	PX8
Jasmine Yellow	PY1
Golden Fawn	KY4
Yellow Blaze	KY5
Inca Gold Metallic	LY6
Spanish Gold Metallic	LY9
Harvest Gold	MY3

LINE 2 - DIGITS 4, 5, 6 & 7: Indicate trim code

LINE 2 - DIGIT 4: Indicates price class

CLASS	CODE
High	H
Police	K
Low	L
Medium	M
Premium	P
Special	S

LINE 2 - DIGIT 5: Indicates seat and fabric type

SEAT	CODE
Cloth & Vinyl Bench	1
All Vinyl Bench	2
Cloth & Leather Bench	A
All Leather Bench	M
Cloth & Vinyl Bench Split Back	3
All Vinyl Bench Split Back	4
Cloth & Leather Bench Split Back	B
All Leather Bench Split Back	P
Cloth & Vinyl Bucket	5
All Vinyl Bucket	6
Cloth & Leather Bucket	C
All Leather Bucket	R
Cloth & Vinyl 50/50	7
All Vinyl 50/50	8
Cloth & Leather 50/50	D
All Leather 50/50	L
Cloth & Vinyl Special Design	9
All Vinyl Special Design	H
Cloth & Leather Special Design	E
All Leather Special Design	T
Cloth 60/40	F
Cloth & Vinyl 60/40	W
All Vinyl 60/40	X
All Leather 60/40	Y

LINE 2 - DIGITS 6 & 7: Indicate interior color

FABRIC COLOR	CODE
Dover Silver	A3
Blue	B3
Medium Blue	B6
Blue & White	BW
Red	E7
Red & White	EW
Green	F6
Green	FF
Green & White	FW
Gold, Black, White	KW
Parchment	L3
Canyon Red	R4
Red & White	RW
Chestnut	T7
Tan	U5
Tan & White	UW
Black	X9
Black & White	XW
Gold	Y3
Gold & White	YW

LINE 2 - DIGITS 8, 9 & 10: Indicate upper door frame color, not listed

LINE 2 - DIGIT 11: Indicate the month of manufacture

MONTH	CODE
January	1
February	2
March	3
April	4
May	5
June	6
July	7
August	8
September	9
October	A
November	B
December	C

LINE 2 - DIGIT 12 & 13: Indicate the day of month of manufacture

LINE 2 - LAST SIX DIGITS: Indicate production sequence number

LINE 3 - DIGITS 1, 2 & 3: Indicate roof paint color, vinyl roof code or convertible top code

COLOR	CODE
Full Vinyl Roof Blue	V1B
Halo Vinyl Roof Blue	V2B
Landau Vinyl Roof Blue	V3B
Canopy Vinyl Roof Blue	V4B
Canopy Vinyl Roof w/Opera Window Blue	V5B
Full Vinyl Roof Green	V1F
Halo Vinyl Roof Green	V2F
Landau Vinyl Roof Green	V3F
Canopy Vinyl Roof Green	V4F
Canopy Vinyl Roof w/Opera Window	V5F
Full Vinyl Roof Red	V1R
Halo Vinyl Roof Red	V2R
Landau Vinyl Roof Red	V3R
Canopy Vinyl Roof Red	V4R
Canopy Vinyl Roof w/Opera Window	V5R
Full Vinyl Roof Black	V1X
Halo Vinyl Roof Black	V2X
Landau Vinyl Roof Black	V3X
Canopy Vinyl Roof Black	V4X
Canopy Vinyl Roof w/Opera Window	V5X
Full Vinyl Roof White	V1W
Halo Vinyl Roof White	V2W
Landau Vinyl Roof White	V3W
Canopy Vinyl Roof White	V4W
Canopy Vinyl Roof w/Opera Window	V5W
Full Vinyl Roof Tan	V1U
Landau Vinyl Roof Tan	V3U
Full Vinyl Roof Silver	V1A
Halo Vinyl Roof Silver	V2A
Landau Vinyl Roof Silver	V3A
Canopy Vinyl Roof Silver	V4A
Canopy Vinyl Roof w/Opera Window Silver	V5A
Full Vinyl Roof Cream	V1Y
Landau Vinyl Roof Cream	V3Y
Full Vinyl Roof Gold	V1Y
Halo Vinyl Roof Gold	V2Y
Canopy Vinyl Roof Gold	V4Y
Canopy Vinyl Roof w/Opera Window Gold	V5Y

ENGINE NUMBER

THE ENGINE IDENTIFICATION NUMBER for 6-cylinder engines is located at the right side of the block below #1 spark plug.

ENGINE NUMBERS for 318 and 360 CID V-8 engines are found at the left front of the block below the cylinder head. The engine number for 400 CID V-8 engines is found on the right side of the block adjacent to the distributor. The engine number for 440 CID V-8 engines is found on the left bank adjacent to the front tappet rail.

The following identification is included in the engine serial number:

225 ENGINE
7225R21024A

THE FIRST DIGIT indicates the model year and/or plant.

THE THREE NUMBERS following the model year and/or plant are the cubic inch displacement.

THE LETTER following the model identification is the engine usage.

THE NUMBER following the engine usage is the shift built.

THE FOUR NUMBERS following the shift built are the date code.

THE LETTER following the date code is a parts identification code. These codes are explained below.

318 & 360 ENGINE
7M31810242579

THE NUMBER AND LETTER designate the model year and/or plant.

THE THREE NUMBERS following the model year and/or plant code are the cubic inch displacement.

THE FOUR NUMBERS following the model identification are the date code.

THE FOUR NUMBERS following the date code are the daily sequence number (optional).

400 & 440 ENGINE
7T400H10242A

THE NUMBER AND LETTER designate the model year and plant.

THE THREE NUMBERS following the model year and/or plant code are the cubic inch displacement.

THE LETTER following the model identification is the engine type.

THE FOUR NUMBERS following the engine type are the date code.

THE NUMBER following the date code is the shift built.

THE LETTER following the shift built code is a parts identification code. These codes are explained below.

ENGINE SERIAL NUMBER AND PARTS IDENTIFICATION CODES & SYMBOLS DEFINED:

	CODE
Oversize Cylinder Bore	A
Cast Crankshaft	E
Standard 4 BC	H
High Performance	HP
Toluca Engine Plant	K
Low Compression	LC
Mound Road Engine	M
Passenger Car Engine	R
Special Engine	S
Trenton Engine	T
Windsor Engine	W
O/S Valve Guide	X

EXAMPLE ("A" Engine Family)
7M318R09101234

In the example above:

7M	Model Year and/or Build Plant
318	Cubic Inch Displacement
R	Regular Fuel may be used
0910	Build date code (0910 is September 10)
1234	Daily sequence number (optional usage)

EXAMPLE ("B" and "G" Engine Family)
7T440R8-222

In the example above:

7T	Model Year and/or Build Plant
440R	CID and Type
8-22	Build date code
2	Shift built

ASPEN ENGINES

CID	NO. CYL.	HORSE-POWER	COMP. RATIO	CARB.
318	8	145	8.5:1	2 BC
225	6	100	8.4:1	1 BC
225	6	110	8.4:1	2 BC
360	8	155	8.4:1	2 BC
360	8	175	8.4:1	4 BC

DIPLOMAT ENGINE

CID	NO. CYL.	HORSE-POWER	COMP. RATIO	CARB.
318	8	145	8.5:1	2 BC

MONACO ENGINES

CID	NO. CYL.	HORSE-POWER	COMP. RATIO	CARB.
225	6	110	8.4:1	2 BC
318	8	145	8.5:1	2 BC
360	8	155	8.4:1	2 BC
400	8	190	8.2:1	4 BC

CHARGER ENGINES

CID	NO. CYL.	HORSE-POWER	COMP. RATIO	CARB.
318	8	145	8.5:1	2 BC
360	8	155	8.4:1	2 BC
400	8	190	8.2:1	4 BC

DODGE ENGINES

CID	NO. CYL.	HORSE-POWER	COMP. RATIO	CARB.
318	8	145	8.5:1	2 BC
360	8	155	8.4:1	2 BC
400	8	190	8.2:1	4 BC
440	8	195	8.2:1	4 BC

1978 DODGE COLT WAGON

1978 DODGE DIPLOMAT WAGON

1978 DODGE ASPEN WAGON

1978 DODGE ASPEN

1978 DODGE MONACO

1978 DODGE MAGNUM XE

1978 DODGE CHARGER

1978 DODGE DIPLOMAT

1978 DODGE CHALLENGER

1978 DODGE OMNI

VEHICLE IDENTIFICATION NUMBER

DODGE
GH45D8F123456

Located on a plate attached to the left side of the instrument panel, visible through the windshield.

FIRST DIGIT: Identifies the car make

MAKE	CODE
Aspen	N
Diplomat	G
Omni	Z
Monaco	W
Charger	X

SECOND DIGIT: Identifies the price class

CLASS	CODE
High	H
Police	K
Low	L
Medium	M
Premium	P
Special	S

THIRD & FOURTH DIGITS: Identify the body type

TYPE	CODE
2-Dr. Coupe	22
2-Dr. Coupe Hardtop	23
2-Dr. Hatchback	24
2-Dr. Coupe	29
4-Dr. Sedan	41
4-Dr. Hatchback	44
2-Seat Station Wagon	45
2-Seat Crestwood Station Wagon	46

FIFTH DIGIT: Identifies the engine

CID	CODE
104.7 CID (1.7L) 2 BC 4-Cyl.	A
225 CID 1 BC 6-Cyl.	C
225 CID 2 BC 6-Cyl. H.D.	D
Special Order 6-Cyl.	E
318 CID 2 BC 8-Cyl. S.D.	G
318 CID 4 BC 8-Cyl.	H
360 CID 4 BC 8-Cyl.	J
360 CID 2 BC 8-Cyl.	K
360 CID Hi-Perf. 4 BC 8-Cyl.	L
400 CID 4 BC 8-Cyl.	N
400 CID 4 BC 8-Cyl.	P
360 CID 4 BC 8-Cyl. H.D.	R
440 CID 4 BC 8-Cyl.	T
440 CID 8-Cyl. Hi-Perf.	U

NOTE:
S.D. - Standard Duty
H.D. - Heavy Duty

SIXTH DIGIT: Identifies the year
8 - 1978

SEVENTH DIGIT: Identifies the assembly plant

PLANT	CODE
Lynch Road, Detroit, MI	A
Belvidere, IL	D
Newark, NJ	F
St. Louis, Mo	G
Windsor, Ontario, CAN	R

REMAINING SIX DIGITS: Identify the production sequence number starting at each plant with 100001

EXAMPLE

G	H	45	D	8	F	123456
Car Make	Price Class	Body Type	Engine	Model Year	Asm Plant	Production Sequence Number

BODY CODE PLATE

THE BODY CODE PLATE is located on the left front fender side shield or wheel housing.

THE BODY CODE PLATE is read left to right, bottom to top. The information on the plate includes the car S.O. Number and the trim and paint codes.

CHRYSLER MOTORS CORPORATION

				Line
XXX	XXX	XXX	XXX	6
XXX	XXX	XXX	XXX	5
XXX	XXX	XXX	XXX	4
XXX	XXX	XXX	XXX	3
XXX	XXX	XXX	XXX	2
XXX	XXX	XXX	XXX	1

LINE 1 - DIGITS 1, 2 & 3: Indicate engine codes

CID	CODE
104.7 CID (1.7L) 2 BC 4-Cyl.	E12
225 CID 1 BC 6-Cyl.	E24
225 CID 1 BC 6-Cyl.	E25
225 CID 2 BC 6-Cyl. H.D.	E26
318 CID 2 BC 8-Cyl. S.D.	E44
318 CID 4 BC 8-Cyl.	E46
360 CID 4 BC 8-Cyl. H.D.	E53
360 CID 2 BC 8-Cyl.	E55
360 CID 4 BC 8-Cyl.	E56
360 CID Hi-Perf. 4 BC 8-Cyl.	E58
400 CID 4 BC 8-Cyl.	E64
400 CID 4 BC 8-Cyl.	E68
440 CID 4 BC 8-Cyl.	E85
440 CID 8-Cyl. Hi-Perf.	E86
Special Order 6-Cyl.	E99

LINE 1 - DIGITS 4, 5 & 6: Indicate transmission codes

TRANSMISSION	CODE
3-Spd. Manual Floor Shift	D13
3-Spd. Std. Manual Clm. Shift	D14
3-Spd. H.D. Manual Clm. Shift	D15
4-Spd. Standard	D21
4-Spd. Trans./Ax.	D22
4-Spd.O.D.	D24
Standard A904	D31
Standard A998	D32
Standard A999	D33
Standard Automatic	D34
H.D. A727	D35
Standard A727	D36
A404 Trans./Ax.	D37
H.D. A904	D38

LINE 1 - DIGIT 7: Indicates car line

MAKE	CODE
Aspen	N
Diplomat	G
Omni	Z
Monaco	W
Charger	X

LINE 1 - DIGIT 8: Indicates price class

CLASS	CODE
High	H
Police	K
Low	L
Medium	M
Premium	P
Special	S

LINE 1 - DIGITS 9 & 10: Indicate body type

TYPE	CODE
2-Dr. Coupe	22
2-Dr. Coupe Hardtop	23
2-Dr. Hatchback	24
2-Dr. Coupe	29
4-Dr. Sedan	41
4-Dr. Hatchback	44
2-Seat Station Wagon	45
2-Seat Crestwood Station Wagon	46

LINE 1 - DIGIT 11: Indicates engine code

CID	CODE
104.7 CID (1.7L) 2 BC 4-Cyl.	A
225 CID 1 BC 6-Cyl.	C
225 CID 2 BC 6-Cyl. H.D.	D
Special Order 6-Cyl.	E
318 CID 2 BC 8-Cyl. S.D.	G
318 CID 4 BC 8-Cyl.	H
360 CID 4 BC 8-Cyl.	J
360 CID 2 BC 8-Cyl.	K
360 CID Hi-Perf. 4 BC 8-Cyl.	L
400 CID 4 BC 8-Cyl.	N
400 CID 4 BC 8-Cyl.	P
360 CID 4 BC 8-Cyl. H.D.	R
440 CID 4 BC 8-Cyl.	T
440 CID 8-Cyl. Hi-Perf.	U

NOTE:
S.D. - Standard Duty
H.D. - Heavy Duty

LINE 1 - DIGIT 12: Indicates model year
8 - 1978

LINE 1 - DIGIT 13: Indicates the assembly plant

PLANT	CODE
Lynch Road, Detroit, MI	A
Belvidere, IL	D
Newark, NJ	F
St. Louis, Mo	G
Windsor, Ontario, CAN	R

LINE 1 - LAST SIX DIGITS: Indicate production sequence number

LINE 2 - DIGITS 1, 2 & 3: Indicate the body paint color, or fleet or special order paint code

COLOR	CODE
Charcoal Gray Sunfire Metallic	RA9
Pewter Gray Metallic	RA2
Dove Gray	RA1
Starlight Blue Sunfire Metallic	PB9
Cadet Blue Metallic	PB3
Wedgewood Blue	PB2
Mint Green Metallic	RF3
Augusta Green Sunfire Metallic	RF9
Citron Metallic	RJ3
Jasmine Yellow	PY1
Classic Cream	RY3
Spanish Gold Metallic	LY9
Golden Fawn	KY4
Sable Tan Sunfire Metallic	RT9
Caramel Tan Metallic	MU3
Light Mocha Tan	PT2
Spitfire Orange	MV1
Bright Canyon Red	RR4
Tapestry Red Sunfire Metallic	RR7
Black	TX9
Dark Silver Metallic	JA5
Crimson Red Sunfire Metallic	RR9

LINE 2 - DIGITS 4, 5, 6 & 7: Indicate trim code

LINE 2 - DIGIT 4: Indicates price class

CLASS	CODE
High	H
Police	K
Low	L
Medium	M
Premium	P
Special	S

LINE 2 - DIGIT 5: Indicates seat and fabric type

SEAT	CODE
Cloth & Vinyl Straight Bench	1
Vinyl Straight Bench	2
Cloth & Leather Straight Bench	A
Leather & Vinyl Straight Bench	M
Cloth Straight Bench	N
Cloth & Vinyl Bench Split Back w/Center Arm Rest	3
Vinyl Bench Split Back w/Center Arm Rest	4
Cloth & Leather Split Back w/Center Arm Rest	B
Leather & Vinyl Split Back w/Center Arm Rest	P
Cloth Split Back w/Center Arm Rest	G
Cloth & Vinyl Non-recline Bucket	5
Vinyl Non-recline Bucket	6
Cloth & Leather Non-recline Bucket	C
Leather & Vinyl Non-recline Bucket	R
Cloth Non-recline Bucket	J
Cloth & Vinyl 50/50 or Dual Recline Bucket	7
Vinyl 50/50 or Dual Recline Bucket	8
Cloth & Leather 50/50 or Dual Recline Bucket	D
Leather & Vinyl 50/50 or Dual Recline Bucket	L
Cloth 50/50 or Dual Recline Bucket	Z
Cloth & Vinyl Recline 60/40	W
Vinyl Recline 60/40	X
Cloth & Leather Recline 60/40	K
Leather & Vinyl Recline 60/40	Y
Cloth Recline 60/40	F
Cloth & Vinyl Non-recline 60/40	9
Vinyl Non-recline 60/40	H
Cloth & Leather Non-recline 60/40	E
Leather & Vinyl Non-recline 60/40	T
Cloth Non-recline 60/40	V

LINE 2 - DIGITS 6 & 7: Indicate interior color

FABRIC COLOR	CODE
Dove Silver	A3
Blue	B3
Blue & White	BW
Green	F6
Green & White	FW
Canyon Red	R4
Red & White	RW
Tan	U5
Tan & White	UW
Black	X9
Black & White	XW
Gold	Y3
Gold & White	YW

LINE 2 - DIGITS 8, 9 & 10: Indicate upper door frame color, not listed

LINE 2 - DIGIT 11: Indicate the month of manufacture

MONTH	CODE
January	1
February	2
March	3
April	4
May	5
June	6
July	7
August	8
September	9
October	A
November	B
December	C

LINE 2 - DIGIT 12 & 13: Indicate the day of month of manufacture

LINE 2 - LAST SIX DIGITS: Indicate production sequence number.

LINE 3 - DIGITS 1, 2 & 3: Indicate roof paint color, vinyl roof code or convertible top code

COLOR	CODE
Full Vinyl Roof Blue	V1B
Halo Vinyl Roof Blue	V2B
Landau Vinyl Roof Blue	V3B
Canopy Vinyl Roof Blue	V4B
Canopy Vinyl Roof w/Opera Window Blue	V5B
Full Vinyl Roof Green	V1F
Halo Vinyl Roof Green	V2F
Landau Vinyl Roof Green	V3F
Canopy Vinyl Roof Green	V4F
Canopy Vinyl Roof w/Opera Window	V5F
Full Vinyl Roof Red	V1R
Halo Vinyl Roof Red	V2R
Landau Vinyl Roof Red	V3R
Canopy Vinyl Roof Red	V4R
Canopy Vinyl Roof w/Opera Window	V5R
Full Vinyl Roof Black	V1X
Halo Vinyl Roof Black	V2X
Landau Vinyl Roof Black	V3X
Canopy Vinyl Roof Black	V4X
Canopy Vinyl Roof w/Opera Window	V5X
Full Vinyl Roof White	V1W
Halo Vinyl Roof White	V2W
Landau Vinyl Roof White	V3W
Canopy Vinyl Roof White	V4W
Canopy Vinyl Roof w/Opera Window	V5W
Full Vinyl Roof Tan	V1U
Landau Vinyl Roof Tan	V3U
Full Vinyl Roof Silver	V1A
Halo Vinyl Roof Silver	V2A
Landau Vinyl Roof Silver	V3A
Canopy Vinyl Roof Silver	V4A
Canopy Vinyl Roof w/Opera Window Silver	V5A
Full Vinyl Roof Cream	V1Y
Landau Vinyl Roof Cream	V3Y
Full Vinyl Roof Gold	V1Y
Halo Vinyl Roof Gold	V2Y
Canopy Vinyl Roof Gold	V4Y
Canopy Vinyl Roof w/Opera Window Gold	V5Y

SPECIAL NOTE: 1978 F-Body info

Super Coupe Package	(A67)
Street Kit Car Package	(A43)

ENGINE NUMBER

THE ENGINE IDENTIFICATION NUMBER for 6-cylinder engines is found at the right side of the block below #1 spark plug.

ENGINE NUMBERS for 318 and 360 CID V-8 engines are found at the left front of the block below the cylinder head. The engine number for 400 CID V-8 engines is found on the right side of the block adjacent to the distributor.

The following identification is included in the engine serial number:

225 ENGINE
8225R21024A

THE FIRST DIGIT designates the model year and/or plant.

THE THREE NUMBERS following the model year and/or plant are the cubic inch displacement.

THE LETTER following the model identification is the engine usage.

THE NUMBER following the engine usage is the shift built.

THE FOUR NUMBERS following the shift built are the date code.

THE LETTER following the date code is a parts identification code. These codes are explained below.

318 & 360 ENGINE
8M31810241234

THE NUMBER AND LETTER designate the model year and/or plant.

THE THREE NUMBERS following the model year and/or plant code are the cubic inch displacement.

THE FOUR NUMBERS following the model identification are the date code.

THE FOUR NUMBERS following the date code are the daily sequence number (optional usage).

400 ENGINE
8T400H10242A

THE NUMBER AND LETTER designate the model year and plant.

THE THREE NUMBERS following the model year and/or plant code are the cubic inch displacement.

THE LETTER following the model identification is the engine type.

THE FOUR NUMBERS following the engine type are the date code.

THE NUMBERS following the date code are the shift built.

THE LETTER following the shift built code is a parts identification code. These codes are explained below.

ENGINE SERIAL NUMBER AND PARTS IDENTIFICATION CODES & SYMBOLS DEFINED:

	CODE
Oversize Cylinder Bore	A
Cast Crankshaft	E
Standard 4 BC	H
High Performance	HP
Toluca Engine Plant	K
Low Compression	LC

	CODE
Mound Road Engine	M
Passenger Car Engine	R
Special Engine	S
Trenton Engine	T
Windsor Engine	W
O/S Valve Guide	X

EXAMPLE ("A" Engine Family)
8M318R09101234

In the example above:

8M	Model Year and/or Build Plant
318	Cubic Inch Displacement
R	Regular Fuel may be used
0910	Build date code (0910 is September 10)
1234	Daily sequence number (optional usage)

EXAMPLE ("B" and "G" Engine Family)
8T400R8-222

In the example above:

8T	Model Year and/or Build Plant
400R	CID and Type
8-22	Build date code
2	Shift built

OMNI ENGINE

CID	NO. CYL.	HORSE-POWER	COMP. RATIO	CARB.
104.7 (1.7L)	4	75	8.2:1	2 BC

ASPEN ENGINES

CID	NO. CYL.	HORSE-POWER	COMP. RATIO	CARB.
225	6	100	8.4:1	1 BC
225	6	110	8.5:1	2 BC
318	8	140	8.4:1	2 BC
360	8	155	8.4:1	2 BC
360	8	175	8.0:1	4 BC

DIPLOMAT ENGINES

CID	NO. CYL.	HORSE-POWER	COMP. RATIO	CARB.
225	6	110	8.4:1	2 BC
318	8	140	8.5:1	2 BC
360	8	155	8.4:1	2 BC

MONACO ENGINES

CID	NO. CYL.	HORSE-POWER	COMP. RATIO	CARB.
225	6	110	8.4:1	2 BC
318	8	140	8.5:1	2 BC
360	8	155	8.4:1	2 BC
400	8	190	8.2:1	4 BC

CHARGER S.E. ENGINES

CID	NO. CYL.	HORSE-POWER	COMP. RATIO	CARB.
318	8	140	8.5:1	2 BC
360	8	155	8.4:1	2 BC
400	8	190	8.2:1	4 BC

MAGNUM XE ENGINES

CID	NO. CYL.	HORSE-POWER	COMP. RATIO	CARB.
318	8	140	8.5:1	2 BC
360	8	155	8.4:1	2 BC
400	8	190	8.2:1	4 BC

1979 DODGE ST. REGIS

1979 DODGE DIPLOMAT

1979 DODGE ASPEN

1979 DODGE DIPLOMAT WAGON

1979 DODGE ASPEN WAGON

1979 DODGE MAGNUM XE

1979 DODGE CHALLENGER

1979 DODGE OMNI HATCHBACK

VEHICLE IDENTIFICATION NUMBER

DODGE
GH45D9F123456

Located on a plate attached to the left side of the instrument panel, visible through the windshield.

FIRST DIGIT: Identifies the car make

MAKE	CODE
Aspen	N
Omni	Z
Diplomat	G
St. Regis	E
Magnum	X
Challenger	2

SECOND DIGIT: Identifies the price class

CLASS	CODE
High	H
Police	K
Low	L
Medium	M
Premium	P
Special	S

THIRD & FOURTH DIGITS: Identify the body type

TYPE	CODE
2-Dr. Coupe	22
2-Dr. Hatchback	24
2-Dr. Coupe	29
4-Dr. Sedan	41
4-Dr. Pillared Hardtop	42
4-Dr. Hatchback	44
2-Seat Station Wagon	45

FIFTH DIGIT: Identifies the engine

CID	CODE
104.7 CID (1.7L) 2 BC 4-Cyl.	A
225 CID 1 BC 6-Cyl.	C
225 CID 2BC 6-Cyl. H.D.*	D
Special Order 6-Cyl.	E
318 CID 2 BC 8-Cyl. S.D.**	G
318 CID 4 BC 8-Cyl.	H
360 CID 4 BC 8-Cyl.	J
360 CID 2 BC 8-Cyl.	K
360 CID 4 BC 8-Cyl. Hi-Perf.	L
360 CID E.F.M.	R
Special Order 8-Cyl.	Z

*H.D. - Heavy Duty
**S.D. - Standard Duty

SIXTH DIGIT: Identifies the year
9 - 1979

SEVENTH DIGIT: Identifies the assembly plant

PLANT	CODE
Lynch Road, Detroit, MI	A
Jefferson Ave., Detroit, MI	C
Belvidere, IL	D
Newark, NJ	F
St. Louis, MO	G
Windsor, Ont.	R

REMAINING SIX DIGITS: Identify the production sequence number starting at each plant with 100001

EXAMPLE

G	H	45	D	9	F	123456
Car Make	Price Class	Body Type	Engine	Model Year	Asm Plant	Production Sequence Number

BODY CODE PLATE

THE BODY CODE PLATE is located on the left front fender side shield or wheel housing.

THE BODY CODE PLATE is read left to right, bottom to top. The information on the plate includes the car S.O. Number and the trim and paint codes.

CHRYSLER MOTORS CORPORATION

				Line
XXX	XXX	XXX	XXX	6
XXX	XXX	XXX	XXX	5
XXX	XXX	XXX	XXX	4
XXX	XXX	XXX	XXX	3
XXX	XXX	XXX	XXX	2
XXX	XXX	XXX	XXX	1

LINE 1 - DIGITS 1, 2 & 3: Indicate engine codes

CID	CODE
104.7 CID (1.7L) 2 BC 4-Cyl.	E12
225 CID 1 BC 6-Cyl.	E24
225 CID 1 BC 6-Cyl.	E25
225 CID 2 BC 6-Cyl. H.D.	E26
225 CID 2 BC 6-Cyl. H.D.	E27
318 CID 2 BC 8-Cyl. S.D.	E44
318 CID 2 BC 8-Cyl. S.D.	E45
318 CID 4 BC 8-Cyl.	E46
318 CID 4 BC 8-Cyl.	E47
360 CID E.F.M.	E53
360 CID 4 BC 8-Cyl.	E56
360 CID 2 BC 8-Cyl.	E57
360 CID 4 BC 8-Cyl. Hi-Perf.	E58
Special Order Engine	E99

LINE 1 - DIGITS 4, 5 & 6: Indicate transmission codes

TRANSMISSION	CODE
3-Spd. Manual Floor Shift	D13
3-Spd. Std. Manual Clm. Shift	D14
3-Spd. H.D. Manual Clm. Shift	D15
4-Spd. Standard	D21
4-Spd. Manual Trans./Ax.	D22
4-Spd. O.D.	D24
Standard A904	D31
Standard A999	D33
Standard Automatic	D34
H.D. A727	D35
Standard A727	D36
A404 Trans./Ax.	D37
H.D. A904	D38

LINE 1 - DIGIT 7: Indicates car line

MAKE	CODE
Aspen	N
Omni	Z
Diplomat	G
St. Regis	E
Magnum	X
Challenger	2

LINE 1 - DIGIT 8: Indicates price class

CLASS	CODE
High	H
Police	K
Low	L
Medium	M
Premium	P
Special	S

LINE 1 - DIGITS 9 & 10: Indicate body type

TYPE	CODE
2-Dr. Coupe	22
2-Dr. Hatchback	24
2-Dr. Coupe	29
4-Dr. Sedan	41
4-Dr. Pillared Hardtop	42
4-Dr. Hatchback	44
2-Seat Station Wagon	45

LINE 1- DIGIT 11: Indicates engine code

CID	CODE
104.7 CID (1.7L) 2 BC 4-Cyl.	A
225 CID 1 BC 6-Cyl.	C
225 CID 2BC 6-Cyl. H.D.*	D
Special Order 6-Cyl.	E
318 CID 2 BC 8-Cyl. S.D.**	G
318 CID 4 BC 8-Cyl.	H
360 CID 4 BC 8-Cyl.	J
360 CID 2 BC 8-Cyl.	K
360 CID 4 BC 8-Cyl. Hi-Perf.	L
360 CID E.F.M.	R
Special Order 8-Cyl.	Z

*H.D. - Heavy Duty
**S.D. - Standard Duty

LINE 1 - DIGIT 12: Indicates the model year
9 - 1979

LINE 1 - DIGIT 13: Indicates the assembly plant

PLANT	CODE
Lynch Road, Detroit, MI	A
Jefferson Ave., Detroit, MI	C
Belvidere, IL	D
Newark, NJ	F
St. Louis, MO	G
Windsor, Ontario, CAN	R

LINE 1 - LAST SIX DIGITS: Indicate production sequence number

LINE 2 - DIGITS 1, 2 & 3: Indicate the body paint color, or fleet or special order paint code

COLOR	CODE
Medium Cashmere Metallic	ST5
Cadet Blue Metallic	PB3
Ensign Blue Metallic	SB7
Nightwatch Blue	SC9
Sable Tan Sunfire Metallic	FT9
Teal Frost Metallic	SG4
Teal Green Sunfire Metallic	SG8
Flame Orange	SV3
Regent Red Sunfire Metallic	SR8
Light Cashmere	ST1
Dove Gray	RA1
Frost Blue Metallic	SC2
Oxford Gray	SA6
Black	TX9
Turquoise Metallic	SQ6
Smoked Gray Metallic	SA5
Garnet Red Sunfire Metallic	SR9
Flat Black	DX9
Chianti Red	SR5
Light Yellow	SY2
Pewter Gray Metallic	RA2
Bright Yellow	SY4
Eggshell White	EW1

LINE 2 - DIGITS 4, 5, 6 & 7: Indicate trim code

LINE 2 - DIGIT 4: Indicates price class

CLASS	CODE
High	H
Police	K
Low	L
Medium	M
Premium	P
Special	S

LINE 2 - DIGIT 5: Indicates seat and fabric type

SEAT	CODE
Cloth & Vinyl Straight Bench	1
Vinyl Straight Bench	2
Cloth & Leather Straight Bench	A
Leather & Vinyl Straight Bench	M
Cloth Straight Bench	N
Cloth & Vinyl Bench Split Back w/Center Arm Rest	3
Vinyl Bench Split Back w/Center Arm Rest	4
Cloth & Leather Split Back w/Center Arm Rest	B
Leather & Vinyl Split Back w/Center Arm Rest	P
Cloth Split Back w/Center Arm Rest	G
Cloth & Vinyl Non-recline Bucket	5
Vinyl Non-recline Bucket	6
Cloth & Leather Non-recline Bucket	C
Leather & Vinyl Non-recline Bucket	R
Cloth Non-recline Bucket	J
Cloth & Vinyl 50/50 or Dual Recline Bucket	7
Vinyl 50/50 or Dual Recline Bucket	8
Cloth & Leather 50/50 or Dual Recline Bucket	D
Leather & Vinyl 50/50 or Dual Recline Bucket	L
Cloth 50/50 or Dual Recline Bucket	Z
Cloth & Vinyl Recline 60/40	W
Vinyl Recline 60/40	X
Cloth & Leather Recline 60/40	K
Leather & Vinyl Recline 60/40	Y
Cloth Recline 60/40	F
Cloth & Vinyl Non-recline 60/40	9
Vinyl Non-recline 60/40	H
Cloth & Leather Non-recline 60/40	E
Leather & Vinyl Non-recline 60/40	T
Cloth Non-recline 60/40	V

LINE 2 - DIGITS 6 & 7: Indicate interior color

FABRIC COLOR	CODE
Blue	B3
Red	R4
Black	X9
Cashmere	T3
Teal Green	G5
Red/Black Plaid	VX
Yellow/Black Plaid	YX
Gray	A3
Midnight Blue	C8
White/Red	RW
White/Midnight Blue	CW
White/Teal Green	GW
White/Cashmere	TW

LINE 2 - DIGITS 8, 9 & 10: Indicate upper door frame color, not listed

LINE 2 - DIGIT 11: Indicate the month of manufacture

MONTH	CODE
January	1
February	2
March	3
April	4
May	5
June	6
July	7
August	8
September	9
October	A
November	B
December	C

LINE 2 - DIGIT 12 & 13: Indicate the day of month of manufacture

LINE 2 - LAST SIX DIGITS: Indicate production sequence number

LINE 3 - DIGITS 1, 2 & 3: Indicate roof paint color, vinyl roof code or convertible top code

COLOR	CODE
Full Vinyl Roof Silver	V1A
Halo Vinyl Roof Silver	V2A
Landau Vinyl Roof Silver	V3A
Full Vinyl Roof Blue	V1B
Halo Vinyl Roof Blue	V2B
Landau Vinyl Roof Blue	V3B
Full Vinyl Roof Green	V1G
Halo Vinyl Roof Green	V2G
Landau Vinyl Roof Green	V3G
Full Vinyl Roof Red	V1R
Halo Vinyl Roof Red	V2R
Landau Vinyl Roof Red	V3R
Full Vinyl Roof Tan	V1U
Halo Vinyl Roof Tan	V2U
Landau Vinyl Roof Tan	V3U
Full Vinyl Roof White	V1W
Halo Vinyl Roof White	V2W
Landau Vinyl Roof White	V3W
Full Vinyl Roof Cream	V1Y
Halo Vinyl Roof Cream	V2Y
Landau Vinyl Roof Cream	V3Y
Full Vinyl Roof Gray	V1S
Landau Vinyl Roof Gray	V3S
Full Vinyl Roof Brown	V1T
Landau Vinyl Roof Brown	V3T
Landau Vinyl Roof Dk. Blue	V3C
Landau Vinyl Roof Lt. Green	V3G
Vinyl Body-Side Lt. Blue	V1B
Vinyl Body-Side Dk. Blue	V1C
Vinyl Body-Side Lt. Green	V1G
Vinyl Body-Side Black	V1X

ENGINE NUMBER

THE ENGINE IDENTIFICATION NUMBER for 6-cylinder engines is found at the right side of the block below #1 spark plug.

ENGINE NUMBERS for 318 and 360 CID V-8 engines are found at the left front of the block below the cylinder head.

The following identification is included in the engine serial number:

225 ENGINE
9225R21024A

THE FIRST DIGIT designates the model year and/or plant.

THE THREE NUMBERS following the model year and/or plant are the cubic inch displacement.

THE LETTER following the model identification is the engine usage.

THE NUMBER following the engine usage is the shift built.

THE FOUR NUMBERS following the shift built are the date code.

THE LETTER following the date code is a parts identification code. These codes are explained below.

318 & 360 ENGINES
9M31810241234

THE NUMBER AND LETTER designate the model year and/or plant.

THE THREE NUMBERS following the model year and/or plant code are the cubic inch displacement.

THE FOUR NUMBERS following the model identification are the date code.

THE FOUR NUMBERS following the date code are the daily sequence number (optional usage).

ENGINE SERIAL NUMBER AND PARTS IDENTIFICATION CODES & SYMBOLS DEFINED:

	CODE
Oversize Cylinder Bore	A
Cast Crankshaft	E
Standard 4 BC	H
High Performance	HP
Toluca Engine Plant	K
Low Compression	LC
Mound Road Engine	M
Passenger Car Engine	R
Special Engine	S
Trenton Engine	T
Windsor Engine	W
O/S Valve Guide	X

EXAMPLE ("A" Engine Family)
9M318R09101234

In the example above:

9M	Model Year and/or Build Plant
318	Cubic Inch Displacement
R	Regular Fuel may be used
0910	Build date code (0910 is September 10)
1234	Daily sequence number (optional usage)

OMNI ENGINE

CID	NO. CYL.	HORSE-POWER	COMP. RATIO	CARB
104.7 (1.7L)	4	70	8.2:1	2 BC

ASPEN ENGINES

CID	NO. CYL.	HORSE-POWER	COMP. RATIO	CARB
225	6	100	8.4:1	1 BC
225	6	110	8.4:1	2 BC
318	8	135	8.5:1	2 BC
360	8	195	8.0:1	4 BC

DIPLOMAT ENGINES

CID	NO. CYL.	HORSE-POWER	COMP. RATIO	CARB
225	6	100	8.4:1	2 BC
225	6	110	8.4:1	2 BC
318	8	135	8.5:1	2 BC
360	8	150	8.4:1	2 BC
360	8	195	8.0:1	4 BC

MAGNUM XE ENGINES

CID	NO. CYL.	HORSE-POWER	COMP. RATIO	CARB
318	8	135	8.5:1	2 BC
360	8	150	8.4:1	2 BC
360	8	195	8.0:1	4 BC

ST. REGIS ENGINES

CID	NO. CYL.	HORSE-POWER	COMP. RATIO	CARB
225	6	110	8.4:1	2 BC
318	8	135	8.5:1	2 BC
360	8	150	8.4:1	2 BC

1970 PLYMOUTH BARRACUDA

1970 PLYMOUTH VALIANT

1970 PLYMOUTH DUSTER

1970 PLYMOUTH GTX

1970 PLYMOUTH SPORT SATELLITE

1970 PLYMOUTH ROAD RUNNER

1970 PLYMOUTH SPORT SATELLITE WAGON

1970 PLYMOUTH FURY III

VEHICLE IDENTIFICATION NUMBER

PLYMOUTH
VL29B0B123456

Located on a plate attached to the left side of the instrument panel, visible through the windshield.

FIRST DIGIT: Identifies the car make

MAKE	CODE
Barracuda	B
Valiant	V
Belvedere/Satellite	R
Fury	P

SECOND DIGIT: Identifies the price class

CLASS	CODE
Economy	E
Low	L
Medium	M
High	H
Premium	P
Special	S
Police	K
Taxi	T

THIRD & FOURTH DIGITS: Identify the body type

TYPE	CODE
2-Dr. Sedan Coupe	21
2-Dr. Hardtop Coupe	23
Convertible	27
2-Dr. Sports Hardtop	29
4-Dr Sedan	41
4-Dr. Hardtop	43
2-Seat Station Wagon	45
3-Seat Station Wagon	46

FIFTH DIGIT: Identifies the engine

CID	CODE
198 CID 6-Cyl.	B
225 CID 6-Cyl.	C
Special Order 6-Cyl.	E
318 CID 8-Cyl.	G
340 CID Hi-Perf. 8-Cyl.	H
340 CID 3-2 BC 8-Cyl.	J
383 CID 8-Cyl.	L
383 CID Hi-Perf. 8-Cyl.	N
426 CID Hemi 8-Cyl.	R
440 CID 8-Cyl.	T
440 CID Hi-Perf. 8-Cyl.	U
440 CID 3-2 BC 8-Cyl.	V
Special order 8-Cyl.	Z

SIXTH DIGIT: Identifies the year
0 - 1970

SEVENTH DIGIT: Identifies the assembly plant

PLANT	CODE
Lynch Road, Detroit, MI	A
Hamtramck, MI	B
Jefferson Ave., Detroit, MI	C
Belvidere, IL	D
Los Angeles, CA	E
Newark, DE	F
St. Louis, MO	G
New Stanton, PA	H
Wyoming (Detroit) Export	P
Windsor, Ontario, CAN	R

LAST SIX DIGITS: Identify the production sequence number starting with 100001 or 500005

EXAMPLE

V	L	29	B	0	B	123456
Car Make	Price Class	Body Type	Engine	Model Year	Asm Plant	Production Sequence Number

BODY CODE PLATE

THE BODY CODE PLATE is located in the engine compartment on the left wheel housing, fender side shield or radiator yoke.

THE BODY CODE PLATE is read left to right, bottom to top. The information on the plate includes the car S.O. Number and the trim and paint codes.

```
            CHRYSLER MOTORS
               CORPORATION

                                        Line
 •   XXX  XXX  XXX  XXX                   6    •
     XXX  XXX  XXX  XXX                   5
     XXX  XXX  XXX  XXX                   4
     XXX  XXX  XXX  XXX                   3
     XXX  XXX  XXX  XXX                   2
     XXX  XXX  XXX  XXX                   1
```

LINE 1 - DIGITS 1, 2 & 3: Indicate engine codes

CID	CODE
Special Order 6-Cyl.	E06
Special Order 8-Cyl.	E08
198 1 BC 6-Cyl.	E22
225 1 BC 6-Cyl.	E24
225 1 BC 6-Cyl.	E25
318 2 BC 8-Cyl.	E44
340 4 BC 8-Cyl.	E55
383 2 BC 8-Cyl.	E61
383 4 BC Hi-Perf. 8-Cyl.	E63
426 2-4 BC Hi-Perf. Hemi 8-Cyl.	E74
440 4 BC 8-Cyl.	E85
440 4 BC Hi-Perf. 8-Cyl.	E86
440 3-2 BC Hi-Perf. 8-Cyl.	E87

LINE 1 - DIGITS 4, 5 & 6: Indicate transmission codes

TRANSMISSION		CODE
3-Spd. Manual Col. Shift	A903	D11
3-Spd. Manual Col. Shift	A230	D12
3-Spd. Manual Fl. Shift	A230	D13
4-Spd. Manual	A833	D21
Automatic	A904	D31
Automatic	A727	D32
Automatic	A727	D34
H. D. Automatic	A727	D36

13 - 2

LINE 1 - DIGIT 7: Indicates car line

MAKE	CODE
Barracuda	B
Valiant	V
Belvedere/Satellite	R
Fury	P

LINE 1 - DIGIT 8: Indicates price class

CLASS	CODE
Economy	E
Low	L
Medium	M
High	H
Premium	P
Special	S
Police	K
Taxi	T

LINE 1 - DIGITS 9 & 10: Indicate body type

TYPE	CODE
2-Dr. Sedan Coupe	21
2-Dr. Hardtop Coupe	23
Convertible	27
2-Dr. Sports Hardtop	29
4-Dr. Sedan	41
4-Dr. Hardtop	43
2-Seat Station Wagon	45
3-Seat Station Wagon	46

LINE 1 - DIGIT 11: Indicates engine code

CID	CODE
198 CID 6-Cyl.	B
225 CID 6-Cyl.	C
Special Order 6-Cyl.	E
318 CID 8-Cyl.	G
340 CID Hi-Perf. 8-Cyl.	H
340 CID 3-2 BC 8-Cyl.	J
383 CID 8-Cyl.	L
383 CID Hi-Perf. 8-Cyl.	N
426 CID Hemi 8-Cyl.	R
440 CID 8-Cyl.	T
440 CID Hi-Perf. 8-Cyl.	U
440 CID 3-2 BC 8-Cyl.	V
Special Order 8-Cyl.	Z

LINE 1 - DIGIT 12: Indicates model year
0 - 1970

LINE 1 - DIGIT 13: Indicates the assembly plant

PLANT	CODE
Lynch Road, Detroit, MI	A
Hamtramck, MI	B
Jefferson Ave., Detroit, MI	C
Belvidere, IL	D
Los Angeles, CA	E
Newark, DE	F
St. Louis, MO	G
New Stanton, PA	H
Wyoming (Detroit) Export	P
Windsor, Ontario, CAN	R

LINE 1 - LAST SIX DIGITS: Indicate production sequence number

LINE 2 - DIGITS 1, 2 & 3: Indicate body paint color, or fleet or special order paint code

COLOR	CODE
Silver Metallic	EA4
Charcoal Metallic	EA9
Ice Blue Metallic	EB3
Blue Fire Metallic	EB5

COLOR	CODE
Jamaica Blue Metallic	EB7
Violet Metallic	FC7
Rallye Red	FE5
Lime Green Metallic	FF4
Ivy Green Metallic	EF8
Dark Emerald Metallic	EF9
Limelight	FJ5
Sassy Grass Green	FJ6
Vitamin C	EK2
Burnt Orange Metallic	FK3
Deep Burnt Orange Metallic	FK5
Sand Pebble Beige	BL1
Moulon Rouge	FM3
Deep Plum	EM9
Frosted Teal Metallic	FP6
Scorch Red	ER6
Sahara Tan Metallic	FT3
Burnt Tan Metallic	FT6
Walnut Metallic	FT8
Tor-Red	EV2
Alpine White	EW1
Black Velvet	TX9
Lemon Twist	FY1
Sunfire Yellow	DY2
Yellow Gold	DY3
Citron Mist Metallic	FY4
Citron Gold Metallic	FY6
Petty Blue	C37D
Special Order	999

*Extra cost/high impact paint

LINE 2 - DIGITS 4, 5, 6 & 7: Indicate trim code

LINE 2 - DIGIT 4: Indicates price class

PRICE CLASS	CODE
Economy	E
Low	L
Medium	M
High	H
Premium	P
Special	S
Police	K
Taxi	T

LINE 2 - DIGIT 5: Indicates seat and fabric type

SEAT	CODE
Cloth & Vinyl Bench	1
Vinyl Bench	2
Cloth & Vinyl Split Bench	3
Vinyl Split Bench	4
Cloth & Vinyl Bucket	5
Vinyl Bucket	6
	7
	8
Vinyl & Leather Bucket	R

LINE 2 - DIGITS 6 & 7: Indicate interior color

VINYL & FABRIC COLOR	CODE
Gray	A5
Black Frost	A8
Dark Gray	A9
Light Blue	B3
Medium Blue	B5
Dark Blue	B7
White & Blue	BW
Red	E4
White & Red	EW
Light Green	F4
White & Green	FW
Green	F8
Burnt Orange	K4

VINYL & FABRIC COLOR	CODE
White & Burnt Orange	KW
Beige	L2
Burgundy	M9
Teal	P6
Oxblood	R9
Light Tan	T3
Tan	T5
Tan & White	TW
Walnut & Beige	TT
Black	X9
Black & Charcoal	XA
Black & Peacock	XP
White & Black	XW
Black & Gold	XY
Gold	Y4
Gold & Black	YX

NOTE: Vinyl & leather buckets were available in Barracuda Grand Coupe and Cuda in the following trim codes only, all other N/A:

BARRACUDA	CODE
Tan	PRT5
Black	PRX9
White & Black	PRXW

LINE 2 - DIGITS 8, 9 & 10: Indicate upper door frame color, not listed

LINE 2 - DIGIT 11: Indicates the month of manufacture

MONTH	CODE
January	1
February	2
March	3
April	4
May	5
June	6
July	7
August	8
September	9
October	A
November	B
December	C

LINE 2 - DIGITS 12 & 13: Indicate the day of month of manufacture

LINE 2 - LAST SIX DIGITS: Indicate production sequence number

LINE 3 - DIGITS 1, 2 & 3: Indicate roof paint color, vinyl roof code or convertible top code

COLOR	CODE
Paint-Mono Tone	V01
Paint-Two Tone	V02
Paint, Trim & Vinyl Roof Waiver	V08
Paint-Special Order	V09
Vinyl Roof	V10
Vinyl Roof Green	V1F
Vinyl Roof Gator Grain	V1G
Vinyl Roof Walnut Patterned	V1J
Vinyl Roof Champagne	V1L
Vinyl Roof Mod Yellow (Barracuda Only)	V1P
Vinyl Roof Mod Blue (Barracuda Only)	V1Q

COLOR	CODE
Vinyl Roof White	V1W
Vinyl Roof Black	V1X
Vinyl Roof Torquoise Grain	V1Y
Vinyl Roof Special Order	V19
Paint-Hood Performance	V21
Delete Sport Hood Treatment	V22
Delete Lower Body Side Org. Paint	V23
Paint-Hood Performance w/Eng. Callout	V24
Convertible Top	V30
Convertible Top White	V3W
Convertible Top Black	V3X
Tape Stripe-Body Side (Barracuda Only)	V40
Lime Daylight Fluorescent ('Cuda Only)	V4J
Pink Daylight Fluorescent ('Cuda Only)	V4M
Tape Stripe-Body Side White	V4W
Tape Stripe-Body Side Black	V4X
Mouldings-Protective Vinyl Body Side	V50
Mouldings-Protective Vinyl Body Side Bright Blue	V5B
Mouldings-Protective Vinyl Body Side Light Green	V5F
Mouldings-Protective Vinyl Body Side Burnt Orange	V5K
Mouldings-Protective Vinyl Body Side Red	V5R
Mouldings-Protective Vinyl Body Side Tan	V5T
Mouldings-Protective Vinyl Body Side White	V5W
Mouldings-Protective Vinyl Body Side Black	V5X
Mouldings-Protective Vinyl Body Side Citron Gold	V5Y
Sport Stripes Tape	V60
Sport Stripes Tape Blue	V6B
Sport Stripes Tape Green	V6F
Sport Stripes Tape Trans Am Black	V6H
(T/A & AAR only)	
Sport Stripes Tape Chartreuse	V6J
Sport Stripes Tape Burnt Orange	V6K
Sport Stripes Tape Magenta	V6M
Sport Stripes Tape Red	V6R
Sport Stripes Tape White	V6W
Sport Stripes Tape Black	V6X
Sport Stripes Tape Gold	V6Y
(RM = Dust Trails)	
Sport Stripes Tape Delete	V68
Accent Stripes Paint	V70
Accent Stripes Paint Blue	V7B
Accent Stripes Paint Green	V7F
Accent Stripes Paint Red	V7R
Accent Stripes Paint White	V7W
Accent Stripes Paint Black	V7X
Accent Stripes Paint Delete	V78
Sport Stripes Tape	V80
Sport Stripes Tape Blue	V8B
Sport Stripes Tape Green	V8F
Sport Stripes Tape Red	V8R
Sport Stripes Tape White	V8W
Sport Stripes Tape Black	V8X
Sport Stripes Tape Gold	V8Y
Sport Stripes Tape Delete	V88

ENGINE NUMBER

THE ENGINE IDENTIFICATION NUMBER for 6-cylinder engines is located at the right front of the block below the cylinder head.

ENGINE NUMBERS for 318 and 340 CID V-8 engines are found at the left front of the block below the cylinder head. The engine number for 383 CID V-8 engines is located at the right side of the block adjacent to the distributor. The engine number for 440 engines is found on the left side of the block adjacent to the distributor. The engine number for 426 engines is located on the pan rail at the rear corner under the starter opening.

All high-performance engines will be painted orange.

The following identification will be included in the engine serial number:

THE FIRST TWO LETTERS will designate the manufacturing plant.

MANUFACTURING PLANT	CODE
Mound Road	PM
Trenton	PT
Marysville	NJ
Windsor	FW

THE THREE NUMBERS following the plant identification indicate the cubic inch displacement: ie. 198 -225 - 318 - 340 - 383 - 426 - 440.

THE FOUR NUMBERS following the model identification are the build date. This is a date code for manufacturing purposes.

THE FOUR NUMBERS following the build date are the engine production sequence number.

EXAMPLE
PT38331601234

In the example above:

PT	Trenton
383	Cubic Inch Displacement
3160	Build date code*
1234	Engine sequence number

*1970 date codes run from 2895 to 3259

BARRACUDA, BELVEDERE ENGINES

CID	NO. CYL.	HORSE-POWER	COMP. RATIO	CARB.
225	6	145	8.4:1	1 BC
318	8	230	8.8:1	2 BC
383	8	290	8.7:1	2 BC
383	8	330	9.5:1	4 BC

'CUDA ENGINES

CID	NO. CYL.	HORSE-POWER	COMP. RATIO	CARB.
383	8	335	9.5:1	4 BC
426	8	425	10.25:1	2-4 BC
440	8	275	10.5:1	4 BC
440	8	375	9.7:1	4 BC
440	8	390	10.5:1	3-2 BC

DUSTER ENGINES

CID	NO. CYL.	HORSE-POWER	COMP. RATIO	CARB.
198	6	125	8.4:1	1 BC
225	6	145	8.4:1	1 BC
318	8	230	8.8:1	2 BC
340	8	275	10.5:1	4 BC

FURY, SATELLITE ENGINES

CID	NO. CYL.	HORSE-POWER	COMP. RATIO	CARB.
225	6	145	8.4:1	1 BC
318	8	230	8.8:1	2 BC
383	8	290	8.7:1	2 BC
383	8	330	9.5:1	4 BC
440	8	350	9.7:1	4 BC
440	8	390	10.5:1	3-2 BC

GTX ENGINES

CID	NO. CYL.	HORSE-POWER	COMP. RATIO	CARB.
426	8	425	10.25:1	2-4 BC
440	8	375	9.7:1	4 BC
440	8	390	10.5:1	3-2 BC

ROAD RUNNER ENGINES

CID	NO. CYL.	HORSE-POWER	COMP. RATIO	CARB.
383	8	335	9.5:1	4 BC
426	8	425	10.25:1	2-4 BC
440	8	375	10.5:1	4 BC

VALIANT ENGINES

CID	NO. CYL.	HORSE-POWER	COMP. RATIO	CARB.
198	6	125	8.4:1	1 BC
225	6	145	8.4:1	1 BC
318	8	230	8.8:1	2 BC

1971 PLYMOUTH DUSTER

1971 PLYMOUTH BARRACUDA

1971 PLYMOUTH VALIANT

1971 PLYMOUTH SPORT FURY

1971 PLYMOUTH ROAD RUNNER

1971 PLYMOUTH BARRACUDA

1971 PLYMOUTH ROAD RUNNER

1971 PLYMOUTH SATELLITE

VEHICLE IDENTIFICATION NUMBER

PLYMOUTH
VL29B1B123456

Located on a plate attached to the left side of the instrument panel, visible through the windshield.

FIRST DIGIT: Identifies the car make

MAKE	CODE
Valiant	V
Barracuda	B
Belvedere/Satellite	R
Fury	P

SECOND DIGIT: Identifies the price class

CLASS	CODE
Economy	E
High	H
Police	K
Low	L
Medium	M
Premium	P
Special	S
Taxi	T
Fast Top	X

THIRD & FOURTH DIGITS: Identify the body type

TYPE	CODE
2-Dr. Sedan	21
2-Dr. Hardtop	23
Convertible Coupe	27
2-Dr. Sports Hardtop	29
4-Dr. Sedan	41
4-Dr. Hardtop	43
6-Pass. Wagon	45
9-Pass. Wagon	46

FIFTH DIGIT: Identifies the engine

CID	CODE
198 CID 6-Cyl.	B
225 CID 6-Cyl.	C
Special Order 6-Cyl.	E
318 CID 8-Cyl.	G
340 CID 8-Cyl.	H
340 CID 3-2 BC 8-Cyl.	J
360 CID 8-Cyl.	K
383 CID 8-Cyl.	L
383 CID Hi-Perf. 8-Cyl.	N
426 CID Hemi 8-Cyl.	R
440 CID 8-Cyl.	T
440 CID Hi-Perf. 8-Cyl.	U
440 CID 3-2 BC 8-Cyl.	V
Special Order 8-Cyl.	Z

SIXTH DIGIT: Identifies the year
1 - 1971

SEVENTH DIGIT: Identifies the assembly plant

PLANT	CODE
Lynch Road, Detroit, MI	A
Hamtramck, MI	B
Jefferson Ave., Detroit, MI	C
Belvidere, IL	D
Los Angeles, CA	E
Newark, DE	F
St. Louis, MO	G
Windsor, Ontario, CAN	R

LAST SIX DIGITS: Identify the production sequence number starting with 100001

EXAMPLE

V	L	29	B	1	B	123456
Car Make	Price Class	Body Type	Engine	Model Year	Asm Plant	Production Sequence Number

BODY CODE PLATE

THE BODY CODE PLATE is located in the engine compartment on the left wheel housing, fender side shield or radiator yoke.

THE BODY CODE PLATE is read left to right, bottom to top. The information on the plate includes the car S.O. Number and the trim and paint codes.

CHRYSLER MOTORS CORPORATION

				Line
XXX	XXX	XXX	XXX	6
XXX	XXX	XXX	XXX	5
XXX	XXX	XXX	XXX	4
XXX	XXX	XXX	XXX	3
XXX	XXX	XXX	XXX	2
XXX	XXX	XXX	XXX	1

LINE 1 - DIGITS 1, 2 & 3: Indicate engine codes

CID	CODE
Special Order 6-Cyl.	E06
Special Order 8-Cyl.	E08
198 CID 1 BC 6-Cyl.	E22
225 CID 1 BC 6-Cyl.	E24
225 CID 1 BC 6-Cyl.	E25
273 CID	E31
318 CID 2 BC 8-Cyl.	E44
340 CID 4 BC 8-Cyl.	E55
360 CID 2-BC 8-Cyl.	E57
383 CID 2 BC 8-Cyl.	E61
383 CID 4 BC Hi-Perf. 8-Cyl.	E63
383 CID 8-Cyl.	E65
426 2-4 BC Hi-Perf. Hemi 8-Cyl.	E74
440 4 BC 8-Cyl.	E85
440 4 BC Hi-Perf. 8-Cyl.	E86
440 3-2 BC Hi-Perf. 8-Cyl.	E87

LINE 1 - DIGITS 4, 5 & 6: Indicate transmission codes

TRANSMISSION		CODE
3-Spd. Manual Col. Shift	A903	D11
3-Spd. Manual Col. Shift	A230	D12
3-Spd. Manual Flr. Shift	A230	D13
4-Spd. Manual	A833	D21
Automatic	A904	D31
Automatic	A727	D32
Automatic	A727	D34
H.D. Automatic	A727	A36
Special Order		D49

LINE 1 - DIGIT 7: Indicates car line

MAKE	CODE
Barracuda	B
Valiant	V
Belvedere/Satellite	R
Fury	P

LINE 1 - DIGIT 8: Indicates price class

CLASS	CODE
Economy	E
High	H
Police	K
Low	L
Medium	M
Premium	P
Special	S
Taxi	T

LINE 1 - DIGITS 9 & 10: Indicate body type

TYPE	CODE
2-Dr.Sedan Coupe	21
2-Dr. Hardtop Coupe	23
Convertible Coupe	27
2-Dr. Sports Hardtop	29
4-Dr. Sedan	41
4-Dr. Hardtop	43
2-Seat Station Wagon	45
3-Seat Station Wagon	46

LINE 1 - DIGIT 11: Indicates engine code

CID	CODE
198 CID 6-Cyl.	B
225 CID 6-Cyl.	C
Special Order 6-Cyl.	E
318 CID 8-Cyl.	G
340 CID 8-Cyl.	H
340 CID 3-2 BC 8-Cyl.	J
360 CID 8-Cyl.	K
383 CID 8-Cyl.	L
383 CID Hi-Perf. 8-Cyl.	N
426 CID Hemi 8-Cyl.	R
440 CID 8-Cyl.	T
440 CID Hi-Perf. 8-Cyl.	U
440 CID 3-2 BC 8-Cyl.	V
Special Order 8-Cyl.	Z

LINE 1 - DIGIT 12: Indicates model year
1 - 1971

LINE 1 - DIGIT 13: Indicates the assembly plant

PLANT	CODE
Lynch Road, Detroit, MI	A
Hamtramck, MI	C
Jefferson Ave., Detroit, MI	D
Belvidere, IL	E
Los Angeles, CA	F
Newark, DE	F
St. Louis, MO	G
Windsor, Ontario, CAN	R

LINE 1 - LAST SIX DIGITS: Indicate production sequence number

LINE 2 - DIGITS 1, 2 & 3: Indicate body paint color, or fleet or special order paint code

COLOR	CODE
Winchester Gray Metallic	GA4
Slate Gray Metallic	GA8
Glacial Blue Metallic	GB2
True Blue Metallic	GB5
Evening Blue Metallic	GB7

COLOR	CODE
In-Violet Metallic	FC7
Mood Indigo Metallic	GC8
Rallye Red	FE5
Burnished Red Metallic	GE7
Amber Sherwood Metallic	GF3
Sherwood Green Metallic	GF7
April Green Metallic	GJ4
Sassy Grass Green	FJ6
Autumn Bronze Metallic	GK6
Sandalwood Beige	BL1
Bahama Yellow	EL5
Coral Turquoise Metallic	FQ5
Tunisian Tan Metallic	GT2
Tahitian Walnut Metallic	GT8
Tor-Red	EV2
Spinnaker White	EW1
Sno-White	GW3
Formal Black	TX9
Lemon Twist	FY1
Curious Yellow	GY3
Gold Leaf Metallic	GY8
Tawny Gold Metallic	GY9
Special Order	999

*Extra cost/high impact paint

LINE 2 - DIGITS 4, 5, 6 & 7: Indicate trim code

LINE 2 - DIGIT 4: Indicates price class

CLASS	CODE
Economy	E
High	H
Police	K
Low	L
Medium	M
Premium	P
Special	S
Taxi	T
Fast Top	X

LINE 2 - DIGIT 5: Indicates seat and fabric type

SEAT	CODE
Cloth & Vinyl Bench	1
Vinyl Bench	2
Cloth & Vinyl Split Bench	3
Vinyl Split Bench	4
Cloth & Vinyl Bucket	5
Vinyl Bucket	6
	7
	8
Vinyl & Leather Bucket	R

LINE 2 - DIGITS 6 & 7: Indicate interior color

FABRIC COLOR	CODE
Light Blue	B2
Medium Blue	B5
Dark Blue	B7
Russet	E8
Green	F7
Tan	T7
Light Gold	Y3
Medium Gold	Y5
Black	X9
Black & Orange	XV
Black & White	XX
Black & White	XW

LINE 2 - DIGITS 8, 9 & 10: Indicate upper door frame color, not listed

LINE 2 - DIGIT 11: Indicates the month of manufacture

MONTH	CODE
January	1
February	2
March	3
April	4
May	5
June	6
July	7
August	8
September	9
October	A
Novemmber	B
December	C

LINE 2 - DIGITS 12 & 13: Indicate the day of month of manufacture

LINE 2 - LAST SIX DIGITS: Indicate production sequence number

LINE 3 - DIGITS 1, 2 & 3: Indicate roof paint color, vinyl roof code or convertible top code

COLOR	CODE
Paint-Mono Tone	V01
Paint-Two Tone	V02
Paint, Trim & Vinyl Roof Waiver	V08
Paint-Special Order	V09
Full Vinyl Roof	V10
Full Vinyl Roof Gunmetal	V1A
Full Vinyl Roof Blue	V1B
Full Vinyl Roof Green	V1F
Full Vinyl Roof Paisley	V1J
Full Vinyl Roof Burgundy	V1M
Full Vinyl Roof Tan	V1T
Full Vinyl Roof White	V1W
Full Vinyl Roof Black	V1X
Full Vinyl Roof Gold	V1Y
Paint-Hood Performance	V21
Delete Sport Hood Treatment	V22
Paint-Hood Performance w/Eng. Callout	V24
Convertible Top	V30
Folding Sunroof	V30
Folding Sunroof White	V3W
Folding Sunroof Black	V3X
Folding Sunroof Special Order	V39

COLOR	CODE
Canopy Vinyl Roof	V40
Canopy Vinyl Roof Green	V4F
Canopy Vinyl Roof Parchment	V4L
Canopy Vinyl Roof White	V4W
Canopy Vinyl Roof Black	V4X
Canopy Vinyl Roof Gold	V4Y
Canopy Vinyl Roof Special Order	V49
Mouldings-Protective Vinyl Body Side	V50
Mouldings-Protective Vinyl Body Side Gunmetal	V5A
Mouldings-Protective Vinyl Body Side Blue	V5B
Mouldings-Protective Vinyl Body Side Green	V5F
Mouldings-Protective Vinyl Body Side Orange	V5K
Mouldings-Protective Vinyl Body Side Burgundy	V5M
Mouldings-Protective Vinyl Body Side Red	V5R
Mouldings-Protective Vinyl Body Side Tan	V5T
Mouldings-Protective Vinyl Body Side Black	V5X
Mouldings-Protective Vinyl Body Side Gold	V5Y
Sport Stripes Tape	V60
Sport Stripes Tape Blue	V6B
Sport Stripes Tape Green	V6F
Sport Stripes Tape Chartreuse	V6J
Sport Stripes Tape Red	V6R
Sport Stripes Tape Orange	V6V
Sport Stripes Tape White	V6W
Sport Stripes Tape Black	V6X
Sport Stripes Tape Gold	V6Y
Sport Stripes Tape Delete	V68
Accent Stripes Paint	V70
Accent Stripes Paint Blue	V7B
Accent Stripes Paint Green	V7F
Accent Stripes Paint Red	V7R
Accent Stripes Paint White	V7W
Accent Stripes Paint Black	V7X
Accent Stripes Paint Gold	V7Y
Accent Stripes Paint Delete	V78
Sport Stripes Tape	V80
Sport Stripes Tape Red	V8R
Sport Stripes Tape White	V8W
Sport Stripes Tape Black	V8X
Sport Stripes Tape Gold	V8Y
Sport Stripes Tape Delete	V88
Tape Stripe	V90
Tape Stripe White	V9W
Tape Stripe Black	V9X

ENGINE NUMBER

THE ENGINE IDENTIFICATION NUMBER for 6-cylinder engines is located at the right front of the block below the cylinder head.

ENGINE NUMBERS for 318, 340 and 360 CID V-8 engines are found at the left front of the block below the cylinder head. The engine number for 383 CID V-8 engines is located at the right side of the block adjacent to the distributor. The engine number for 440 engines is found on the left side of the block adjacent to the distributor. The engine number for 426 engines is located on the pan rail at the rear corner under the starter opening.

All high-performance engines will be painted orange.

The following identification will be included in the engine serial number:

THE FIRST TWO LETTERS will designate the manufacturing plant.

MANUFACTURING PLANT	CODE
Mound Road	PM
Trenton	PT

THE THREE NUMBERS following the plant identification indicate the cubic inch displacement: ie. 198 - 225 - 318 - 340 - 360 - 383 - 426 - 440.

THE FOUR NUMBERS following the model identification are the build date. This is a date code for manufacturing purposes.

THE FOUR NUMBERS following the build date are the engine production sequence number.

EXAMPLE
PT38332651234

In the example above:

PT	Trenton
383	Cubic Inch Displacement
3265	Build date code*
1234	Engine sequence number.

*1971 date codes run from 3260 thru 3624

VALIANT, DUSTER ENGINES

CID	NO. CYL.	HORSE-POWER	COMP. RATIO	CARB.
198	6	125	8.4:1	1 BC
225	6	145	8.4:1	1 BC
318	8	230	8.6:1	2 BC
340	8	275	10.3:1	4 BC

BARRACUDA ENGINES

CID	NO. CYL.	HORSE-POWER	COMP. RATIO	CARB.
198	6	125	8.4:1	1 BC
225	6	145	8.4:1	1 BC
318	8	230	8.6:1	2 BC
383	8	275	8.5:1	2 BC
383	8	300	8.5:1	4 BC

'CUDA ENGINES

CID	NO. CYL.	HORSE-POWER	COMP. RATIO	CARB.
340	8	275	10.3:1	4 BC
383	8	300	8.5:1	4 BC
426	8	425	10.2:1	2-4 BC
440	8	385	10.3:1	3-2 BC

FURY, SATELLITE ENGINES

CID	NO. CYL.	HORSE-POWER	COMP. RATIO	CARB.
225	6	145	8.4:1	1 BC
318	8	230	8.6:1	2 BC
340	8	275	10.3:1	4 BC
360	8	255	8.7:1	2 BC
383	8	275	8.5:1	2 BC
383	8	300	8.5:1	4 BC
440	8	335	8.51	4 BC
440	8	370	9.5:1	4 BC

GTX ENGINES

CID	NO. CYL.	HORSE-POWER	COMP. RATIO	CARB.
426	8	425	10.2:1	2-4 BC
440	8	370	9.5:1	4 BC
440	8	385	10.3:1	3-2 BC

ROAD RUNNER ENGIENS

CID	NO. CYL.	HORSE-POWER	COMP. RATIO	CARB.
383	8	300	8.5:1	4 BC
340	8	275	10.3:1	4 BC
426	8	425	10.2:1	2-4 BC
440	8	385	10.3:1	3-2 BC

1972 PLYMOUTH BARRACUDA

1972 PLYMOUTH VALIANT

1972 PLYMOUTH DUSTER

1972 PLYMOUTH FURY

1972 PLYMOUTH SATELLITE CUSTOM

1972 PLYMOUTH SATELLITE SEBRING

1972 PLYMOUTH SCAMP

VEHICLE IDENTIFICATION NUMBER

PLYMOUTH
VL29B2B123456

Located on a plate attached to the left side of the instrument panel, visible through the windshield.

FIRST DIGIT: Identifies the car make

MAKE	CODE
Valiant	V
Barracuda	B
Satellite	R
Fury	P

SECOND DIGIT: Identifies the price class

CLASS	CODE
Grand	G
High	H
Police	K
Low	L
Medium	M
Premium	P
Special	S
Taxi	T

THIRD & FOURTH DIGITS: Identify the body type

TYPE	CODE
2-Dr. Sedan	21
2-Dr. Hardtop	23
Convertible Coupe	27
2-Dr. Sports Hardtop	29
4-Dr. Sedan	41
4-Dr. Hardtop	43
2-Seat Wagon	45
3-Seat Wagon	46

FIFTH DIGIT: Identifies the engine

CID	CODE
198 CID 1 BC 6-Cyl.	B
225 CID 1 BC 6-Cyl.	C
Special Order 6-Cyl.	E
318 CID 2 BC 8-Cyl.	G
340 CID 4 BC Hi-Perf. 8-Cyl.	H
360 CID 2 BC 8-Cyl.	K
400 CID 2 BC 8-Cyl.	M
400 CID 4 BC Hi-Perf. 8-Cyl.	P
440 CID 4 BC 8-Cyl.	T
440 CID 4 BC 8-Cyl.	U
440 CID 3-2 BC Hi-Perf. 8-Cyl.	V
Special Order 8-Cyl.	Z

SIXTH DIGIT: Identifies the year
2 - 1972

SEVENTH DIGIT: Identifies the assembly plant

PLANT	CODE
Lynch Road, Detroit, MI	A
Hamtramck, MI	B
Jefferson Ave., Detroit, MI	C
Belvidere, IL	D
Newark, DE	F
St. Louis, MO	G
Windsor, Ontario, CAN	R

LAST SIX DIGITS: Identify the production sequence number starting at each plant with 100001

EXAMPLE

V	L	29	B	2	B	123456
Car Make	Price Class	Body Type	Engine	Model Year	Asm Plant	Production Sequence Number

BODY CODE PLATE

THE BODY CODE PLATE is located in the engine compartment on the left wheel housing, fender side shield or radiator yoke.

THE BODY CODE PLATE is read left to right, bottom to top. The information on the plate includes the car S.O. Number and the trim and paint codes.

CHRYSLER MOTORS
CORPORATION

				Line
XXX	XXX	XXX	XXX	6
XXX	XXX	XXX	XXX	5
XXX	XXX	XXX	XXX	4
XXX	XXX	XXX	XXX	3
XXX	XXX	XXX	XXX	2
XXX	XXX	XXX	XXX	1

LINE 1 - DIGITS 1, 2 & 3: Indicate engine codes

CID	CODE
198 CID 1 BC 6-Cyl.	E22
225 CID 1 BC 6-Cyl.	E24
225 CID 1 BC 6-Cyl.	E25
318 CID 2 BC 8-Cyl.	E44
340 CID 4 BC 8-Cyl.	E55
360 CID 2 BC 8-Cyl.	E57
400 CID 2 BC 8-Cyl.	E63
400 CID 4 BC Hi-Perf. 8-Cyl.	E68
440 CID 4 BC 8-Cyl.	E85
440 CID 4 BC Hi-Perf. 8-Cyl.	E86
440 CID 3-2 BC Hi-Perf. 8-Cyl.	E87
Special Order	E99

LINE 1 - DIGITS 4, 5 & 6: Indicate transmission codes

TRANSMISSION	CODE
3-Spd. Manual	D13
3-Spd. Manual	D14
3-Spd. Manual	D15
4-Spd. Manual	D21
3-Spd. Automatic	D34
3-Spd. Automatic	D35
H.D. Clutch 9 1/2"	D41
Special Order	D99

LINE 1 - DIGIT 7: Indicates car line

MAKE	CODE
Barracuda	B
Valiant	V
Satellite	R
Fury	P

LINE 1 - DIGIT 8: Indicates price class

CLASS	CODE
High	H
Police	K
Low	L
Medium	M
Premium	P
Sport	S
Taxi	T

LINE 1 - DIGITS 9 & 10: Indicate body type

TYPE	CODE
2-Dr. Sedan	21
2-Dr. Hardtop	23
2-Dr. Sports Hardtop	29
4-Dr. Sedan	41
4-Dr. Hardtop	43
2-Seat Wagon	45
3-Seat Wagon	46

LINE 1 - DIGIT 11: Indicates engine code

CID	CODE
198 CID 1 BC 6-Cyl.	B
225 CID 1 BC 6-Cyl.	C
Special Order 6-Cyl.	E
318 CID 2 BC 8-Cyl.	G
340 CID 4 BC Hi-Perf. 8-Cyl.	H
360 CID 2 BC 8-Cyl.	K
400 CID 2 BC 8-Cyl.	M
400 CID 4 BC Hi-Perf. 8-Cyl.	P
440 CID 4 BC 8-Cyl.	T
440 CID 4 BC Hi-Perf. 8-Cyl.	U
440 CID 3-2 BC Hi-Perf. 8-Cyl.	V
Special Order 8-Cyl.	Z

LINE 1 - DIGIT 12: Indicates model year
2 - 1972

LINE 1 - DIGIT 13: Indicates the assembly plant

PLANT	CODE
Lynch Road, Detroit, MI	A
Hamtramck, MI	B
Jefferson Ave., Detroit, MI	C
Belvidere, IL	D
Newark, DE	F
St. Louis, MO	G
Windsor, Ontario, CAN	R

LINE 1 - LAST SIX DIGITS: Indicate production sequence number

LINE 2 - DIGITS 1, 2 & 3: Indicate body paint color, or fleet or special order paint code

COLOR	CODE
Winchester Gray Metallic	GA4
Slate Gray Metallic	GA8
Charcoal Metallic	EA9
Blue Sky	HB1
Glacial Blue Metallic	GB2
Basin Street Blue	TB3
True Blue Metallic	GB5
Evening Blue Metallic	GB7
Midnight Blue Metallic	GB9
Rallye Red	FE5

COLOR	CODE
Burnished Red Metallic	GE7
Amber Sherwood Metallic	GF3
Sherwood Green Metallic	GF7
Sahara Beige	HL4
Coral Turquoise Metallic	FQ5
Mojave Tan Metallic	HT6
Chestnut Metallic	HT8
Tor-Red	EV2
Spinnaker White	EW1
Formal Black	TX9
Lemon Twist	FY1
Sun Fire Yellow	DY2
Honeydew	FY4
Gold Leaf Metallic	GY8
Tawny Gold Metallic	GY9
Special Order	999

LINE 2 - DIGITS 4, 5, 6 & 7: Indicate trim code

LINE 2 - DIGIT 4: Indicates price class

CLASS	CODE
High	H
Police	K
Low	L
Medium	M
Premium	P
Sport	S
Taxi	T

LINE 2 - DIGIT 5: Indicates seat and fabric type

SEAT	CODE
Cloth & Vinyl Bench	1
Vinyl Bench	2
Cloth & Leather Bench	A
Leather Bench	M
Cloth & Vinyl Bench Split Back	3
Vinyl Bench Split Back	4
Cloth & Leather Bench Split Back	B
Leather Bench Split Back	P
Cloth & Vinyl Bucket	5
Vinyl Bucket	6
Cloth & Leather	C
Leather Bucket	R
Cloth & Vinyl 50/50	7
Vinyl 50/50	8
Cloth & Leather 50/50	D
Leather 50/50	L
Cloth & Vinyl Special Design	9
Vinyl Special Design	H
Cloth & Leather Special Design	E
Leather Special Design	T

LINE 2 - DIGITS 6 & 7: Indicates interior color

FABRIC COLOR	CODE
Gray	A9
Medium Blue	B5
Dark Blue	B8
Green	F6
Green & White	FW
White & Green	G6
Parchment	L3
Light Tan	T5
Black	X9
Black & White	XW
Light Gold	Y3
Gold	Y5

LINE 2 - DIGITS 8, 9 & 10: Indicate upper door frame color, not listed

LINE 2 - DIGIT 11: Indicates the month of manufacture

MONTH	CODE
January	1
February	2
March	3
April	4
May	5
June	6
July	7
August	8
September	9
October	A
November	B
December	C

LINE 2 - DIGITS 12 & 13: Indicate the day of month of manufacture

LINE 2 - LAST SIX DIGITS: Indicate production sequence number

LINE 3 - DIGITS 1, 2 & 3: Indicate roof paint color, vinyl roof code or convertible top code

COLOR	CODE
Paint-Mono Tone	V01
Paint-Two Tone	V02
Paint, Trim & Vinyl Roof Waiver	V08
Paint-Special Order	V09
Full Vinyl Roof	V10
Full Vinyl Roof Gunmetal	V1A
Full Vinyl Roof Blue (Cancelled)	V1B
Full Vinyl Roof Green	V1F
Full Vinyl Roof Mock Turtle	V1G
Full Vinyl Roof Burgundy	V1M

COLOR	CODE
Full Vinyl Roof Walnut	V1T
Full Vinyl Roof White	V1W
Full Vinyl Roof Black	V1X
Full Vinyl Roof Gold	V1Y
Paint-Hood Performance	V21
Paint-Deck Performance	V25
Folding Sunroof	V30
Folding Sunroof White	V3W
Folding Sunroof Black	V3X
Canopy Vinyl Roof	V40
Canopy Vinyl Roof Green	V4F
Canopy Vinyl Roof Mock Turtle	V4G
Canopy Vinyl Roof White	V4W
Canopy Vinyl Roof Black	V4X
Canopy Vinyl Roof Gold	V4Y
Mouldings-Protective Vinyl Body Side	V50
Mouldings-Protective Vinyl Body Side Black	V5X
Sport Stripes	V60
Sport Stripes White	V6W
Sport Stripes Black	V6X
Sport Stripes Delete	V68
Accent Stripes Paint	V70
Accent Stripes Paint White	V7W
Accent Stripes Paint Black	V7X
Accent Stripes Paint Delete	V78
Sport Stripe Tape	V80
Sport Stripe Tape White	V8W
Sport Stripe Tape Black	V8X
Hood Stripes	V90
Hood Stripes White	V9W
Hood Stripes Black	V9A

ENGINE NUMBER

THE ENGINE IDENTIFICATION NUMBER for 6-cylinder engines is located at the right front of the block below the cylinder head.

ENGINE NUMBERS for 318, 340 and 360 CID V-8 engines are found at the left front of the block below the cylinder head. The engine number for 400 CID V-8 engines is located at the right side of the block adjacent to the distributor. The engine number for 440 engines is found on the left side of the block adjacent to the distributor.

All high-performance engines will be painted orange.

The following identification will be included in the engine serial number:

THE FIRST TWO LETTERS will designate the manufacturing plant.

MANUFACTURING PLANT	CODE
Mound Road ....PM	
Trenton ....PT	

THE THREE NUMBERS following the plant identification indicate the cubic inch displacement: ie. 198 - 225 - 318 - 340 - 360 - 400 - 440.

THE FOUR NUMBERS following the model identification are the build date. This is a date code for manufacturing purposes.

THE FOUR NUMBERS following the build date are the engine production sequence number.

EXAMPLE
PT38336451234

In the example above:

PT	Trenton
383	Cubic Inch Displacement
3645	Build date code*
1234	Engine sequence number

*1972 date codes run from 3625 thru 3990

BARRACUDA ENGINES

CID	NO. CYL.	HORSE-POWER	COMP. RATIO	CARB.
225	6	110	8.4:1	1 BC
318	8	150	8.6:1	2 BC
340	8	240	8.5:1	4 BC

DUSTER, VALIANT ENGINES

CID	NO. CYL.	HORSE-POWER	COMP. RATIO	CARB.
198	6	100	8.4:1	1 BC
225	6	110	8.4:1	1 BC
318	8	150	8.6:1	2 BC
340	8	240	8.5:1	4 BC

FURY ENGINES

CID	NO. CYL.	HORSE-POWER	COMP. RATIO	CARB.
318	8	150	8.6:1	2 BC
360	8	175	8.8:1	2 BC
400	8	190	8.2:1	2 BC
440	8	225	8.2:1	4 BC

SATELLITE ENGINES

CID	NO. CYL.	HORSE-POWER	COMP. RATIO	CARB.
225	6	110	8.4:1	1 BC
318	8	150	8.6:1	2 BC
400	8	190	8.2:1	2 BC
400	8	255	8.2:1	4 BC

ROAD RUNNER ENGINES

CID	NO. CYL.	HORSE-POWER	COMP. RATIO	CARB.
340	8	240	8.5:1	4 BC
400	8	255	8.2:1	4 BC
440	8	280	8.2:1	4 BC
440	8	330	10.3:1	3-2 BC

1973 PLYMOUTH BARRACUDA

1973 PLYMOUTH DUSTER

1973 PLYMOUTH FURY

1973 PLYMOUTH ROAD RUNNER

1973 PLYMOUTH SATELLITE SEBRING PLUS

1973 PLYMOUTH VALIANT

VEHICLE IDENTIFICATION NUMBER

PLYMOUTH
RL41G3A123456

Located on a plate attached to the left side of the instrument panel, visible through the windshield.

FIRST DIGIT: Identifies the car make

MAKE	CODE
Barracuda	B
Fury	P
Satellite/Sebring	R
Valiant/Duster	V

SECOND DIGIT: Identifies the price class

CLASS	MAKE
Police	K
Taxi	T
Low	L
Medium	M
High	H
Premium	P
Special	S
Taxi	G

THIRD & FOURTH DIGITS: Identify the body type

TYPE	CODE
2-Dr. Sedan Coupe	21
2-Dr. Hardtop	23
2-Dr. Sports Hardtop	29
4-Dr. Sedan	41
4-Dr. Hardtop	43
6-Pass. Wagon	45
9-Pass. Wagon	46

FIFTH DIGIT: Identifies the engine

CID	CODE
198 CID 1 BC 6-Cyl.	B
225 CID 1 BC 6-Cyl.	C
Special Order 6-Cyl.	E
318 CID 2 BC 8-Cyl.	G
340 CID 4 BC Hi-Perf. 8-Cyl.	H
360 CID 2 BC 8-Cyl.	K
400 CID 2 BC 8-Cyl.	M
400 CID 4 BC Hi-Perf. 8-Cyl.	P
440 CID 4 BC 8-Cyl.	T
440 CID 4 BC 8-Cyl.	U
Special Order 8-Cyl.	Z

SIXTH DIGIT: Identifies the year
3 - 1973

SEVENTH DIGIT: Identifies the assembly plant

PLANT	CODE
Lynch Road, Detroit, MI	A
Hamtramck, MI	B
Jefferson Ave., Detroit, MI	C
Belvidere, IL	D
Newark, DE	F
St. Louis, MO	G
Windsor, Ontario, CAN	R

LAST SIX DIGITS: Identify the production sequence number starting at each plant with 100001

EXAMPLE

R	L	41	G	3	A	123456
Car Make	Price Class	Body Type	Engine	Model Year	Asm Plant	Production Sequence Number

BODY CODE PLATE

THE BODY CODE PLATE is located in the engine compartment on the left wheel housing, fender side shield or radiator yoke.

THE BODY CODE PLATE is read left to right, bottom to top. The information on the plate includes the car S.O. Number and the trim and paint codes.

CHRYSLER MOTORS CORPORATION				Line
XXX	XXX	XXX	XXX	6
XXX	XXX	XXX	XXX	5
XXX	XXX	XXX	XXX	4
XXX	XXX	XXX	XXX	3
XXX	XXX	XXX	XXX	2
XXX	XXX	XXX	XXX	1

LINE 1 - DIGITS 1, 2 & 3: Indicate engine codes

CID	CODE
198 CID 1 BC 6-Cyl.	E22
225 CID 1 BC 6-Cyl.	E24
225 CID 1 BC 6-Cyl.	E25
318 CID 2 BC 8-Cyl.	E44
340 CID 4 BC 8-Cyl.	E55
360 CID 2 BC 8-Cyl.	E57
400 CID 2 BC 8-Cyl.	E63
400 CID 4 BC Hi-Perf. 8-Cyl.	E68
440 CID 4 BC 8-Cyl.	E85
440 CID 4 BC Hi-Perf. 8-Cyl.	E86
Special Order Engine	E99

LINE 1 - DIGITS 4, 5 & 6: Indicate transmission codes

TRANSMISSION	CODE
3-Spd. Manual	D13
3-Spd. Manual	D14
3-Spd. Manual	D15
4-Spd. Manual	D21
3-Spd. Automatic	D31
3-Spd. Automatic	D32
3-Spd. Automatic	D34
3-Spd. Automatic	D36
H.D. Clutch 9 1/2"	D41

LINE 1 - DIGIT 7: Indicates car line

MAKE	CODE
Barracuda	B
Fury	P
Satellite/Sebring	R
Valiant/Duster	V

LINE 1 - DIGIT 8: Indicates price class

CLASS	CODE
Low	L
Medium	M
High	H
Premium	P
Special	S
Police	K
Taxi	T
Taxi	G

LINE 1 - DIGITS 9 & 10: Indicate body type

TYPE	CODE
2-Dr. Sedan	21
2-Dr. Hardtop	23
2-Dr. Sports Hardtop	29
4-Dr. Sedan	41
4-Dr. Hardtop	43
2-Seat Wagon	45
3-Seat Wagon	46

LINE 1 - DIGIT 11: Indicates engine code

CID	CODE
198 CID 1 BC 6-Cyl.	B
225 CID 1 BC 6-Cyl.	C
Special Order 6-Cyl.	E
318 CID 2 BC 8-Cyl.	G
340 CID 4 BC Hi-Perf. 8-Cyl.	H
360 CID 2 BC 8-Cyl.	K
400 CID 2 BC 8-Cyl.	M
400 CID 4 BC Hi-Perf. 8-Cyl.	P
440 CID 4 BC 8-Cyl.	T
440 CID 4 BC Hi-Perf. 8-Cyl.	U
Special Order 8-Cyl.	Z

LINE 1 - DIGIT 12: Indicates model year
3 - 1973

LINE 1 - DIGIT 13: Indicates the assembly plant

PLANT	CODE
Lynch Road, Detroit, MI	A
Hamtramck, MI	B
Jefferson Ave., Detroit, MI	C
Belvidere, IL	D
Newark, DE	F
St. Louis, MO	G
Windsor, Ontario, CAN	R

LINE 1 - LAST SIX DIGITS: Indicate production sequence number

LINE 2 - DIGITS 1, 2 & 3: Indicate body paint color, or fleet or special order paint code

COLOR	CODE
Silver Frost Metallic	JA5
Blue Sky	HB1
Basin Street Blue	TB3
True Blue Metallic	GB5
Regal Blue Metallic	JB9
Rallye Red	FE5
Burnished Red Metallic	GE7
Mist Green	JF1
Amber Sherwood Metallic	GF3
Forest Green Metallic	JF8
Autumn Bronze Metallic	GK6
Sahara Beige	HL4
Coral Turquoise Metallic	FQ5
Mojave Tan Metallic	HT6
Chestnut Metallic	HT8
Spinnaker White	EW1
Formal Black	TX9
Lemon Twist	FY1
Sunfire Yellow	DY2
Honey Gold	JY3
Golden Haze Metallic	JMY6
Tahitian Gold Metallic	JY9
Special Order	999

LINE 2 - DIGITS 4, 5, 6 & 7: Indicate trim code

LINE 2 - DIGIT 4: Indicates price class

CLASS	CODE
A-Class	A
B-Class	B
Custom	C
Deluxe	D
Economy	E
F-Class	F
G-Class	G
High	H
J-Class	J
Police	K
Low	L
Medium	M
N-Class	N
Premium	P
Q-Class	Q
R-Class	R
Sport	S
Taxi	T
V-Class	V

LINE 2 - DIGIT 5: Indicates seat and fabric type

SEAT	CODE
Cloth & Vinyl Bench	1
Vinyl Bench	2
Cloth & Leather Bench	A
Leather Bench	M
Cloth & Vinyl Bench Split Back	3
Vinyl Bench Split Back	4
Cloth & Leather Bench Split Back	B
Leather Bench Split Back	P
Cloth & Vinyl Bucket	5
Vinyl Bucket	6
Cloth & Leather Bucket	C
Leather Bucket	R
Cloth & Vinyl 50/50	7
Vinyl 50/50	8
Cloth & Leather 50/50	D
Leather 50/50	L
Cloth & Vinyl Special Design	9
Vinyl Special Design	H
Cloth & Leather Special Design	E
Leather Special Design	T

LINE 2 - DIGITS 6 & 7: Indicates interior color

FABRIC COLOR	CODE
Gray	A9
Medium Blue	B5
Dark Blue	B8
Red-Black-White	EW
Green	F6
Copper-Black-White	KW
Parchment	L3
Light Tan	T5
Black	X9
Black & White	XW
Gold	Y4
Gold-Black-White	YW

LINE 2 - DIGITS 8, 9 & 10: Indicate upper door frame color, not listed

LINE 2 - DIGIT 11: Indicates the month of manufacture

MONTH	CODE
January	1
February	2
March	3
April	4
May	5
June	6
July	7
August	8
September	9
October	A
November	B
December	C

LINE 2 - DIGITS 12 & 13: Indicate the day of month of manufacture

LINE 2 - LAST SIX DIGITS: Indicate production sequence number

LINE 3 - DIGITS 1, 2 & 3: Indicate roof paint color, vinyl roof code or convertible top code

COLOR	CODE
Paint-Mono Tone	V01
Paint-Two Tone	V02
Paint, Trim & Vinyl Roof Waiver	V08
Paint-Special Order	V09
Full Vinyl Roof	V10
Full Vinyl Roof Blue	V1B
Full Vinyl Roof Green	V1F
Full Vinyl Roof White	V1W
Full Vinyl Roof Black	V2X
Full Vinyl Roof Gold	V1Y
Paint-Hood Performance	V21
Halo Style Vinyl Roof	V40
Halo Style Vinyl Roof Blue	V4B
Halo Style Vinyl Roof Green	V4F
Halo Style Vinyl Roof White	V4W
Halo Style Vinyl Roof Black	V4X
Halo Style Vinyl Roof Gold	V4Y
Mouldings-Protective Vinyl Body Side	V50
Mouldings-Protective Vinyl Body Side Black	V5X
Sport Stripes Tape	V60
Sport Stripes Tape White	V6W
Sport Stripes Tape Black	V6X
Accent Stripes Paint	V70
Accent Stripes Paint White	V7W
Accent Stripes Paint Black	V7X
Sport Stripe Tape	V80
Roof Strobe & Body Side (RM)	
Rear Deck (VL-S)	
Sport Stripe Tape White	V8W
Sport Stripe Tape Black	V8X
Hood Stripes	V90
Hood Stripes White	V9W
Hood Stripes Black	V9X

ENGINE NUMBER

THE ENGINE IDENTIFICATION NUMBER for 6-cylinder engines is located at the right front of the block below #1 spark plug.

ENGINE NUMBERS for 318, 340 and 360 CID V-8 engines are found at the left front of the block below the cylinder head. The engine number for 400 engines is found on the right side of the block adjacent to the distributor. The engine number for 440 engines is located on the left bank adjacent to the front tappet rail.

The following identification will be included in the engine serial number:

"A" ENGINE FAMILY

THE FIRST TWO LETTERS will designate the series and/or build plant.

THE THREE NUMBERS following the series and/or build plant are the cubic inch displacment: ie 198 - 225 - 318 - 340 - 360 - 400 - 440

THE LETTER following the model identification is the engine type.

THE FOUR NUMBERS following the engine type are the build date code.

THE FOUR NUMBERS following the build date code are the daily production sequence number.

"B" AND "G" ENGINE FAMILY

THE FIRST LETTER will designate the series.

THE THREE NUMBERS AND LETTER following the series are the cubic inch displacement and type.

THE THREE NUMBERS following the model identification and type are the build date.

THE NUMBER following the build date is the shift built.

ENGINE SERIAL NUMBER CODES DEFINED:

High Performance ....HP
Series (1973)...J
Low Compression LC
Mound Road Plant ....M
Premium Fuel Recommended ....P
Regular Fuel may be used ....R
Special Engine ....S
Windsor Plant ....W

EXAMPLE ("A" Engine Family)
JM318R42251234

In the example above:

J	Series (1973)
M	Mound Road Plant
318	Cubic Inch Displacement
R	Regular Fuel may be used
4225	Build date code*
1234	Daily engine sequence number

*1973 date codes run from 3991 thru 4355

EXAMPLE ("B" and "G" Engine Family)
J440R8-222

In the example above:

J	Series (1973)
440R	Cubic Inch Displacement and Type
8-22	Build date code
2	Shift built

BARRACUDA ENGINES

CID	NO. CYL.	HORSE-POWER	COMP. RATIO	CARB.
318	8	150	8.6:1	2 BC
340	8	240	8.5:1	4 BC

DUSTER, VALIANT ENGINES

CID	NO. CYL.	HORSE-POWER	COMP. RATIO	CARB.
198	6	95	8.4:1	1 BC
225	6	105	8.4:1	1 BC
318	8	150	8.6:1	2 BC
340	8	240	8.5:1	4 BC

FURY ENGINES

CID	NO. CYL.	HORSE-POWER	COMP. RATIO	CARB.
318	8	150	8.6:1	2 BC
360	8	170	8.4:1	2 BC
400	8	185	8.2:1	2 BC
440	8	220	8.2:1	4 BC

SATELLITE ENGINES

CID	NO. CYL.	HORSE-POWER	COMP. RATIO	CARB.
225	6	105	8.4:1	1 BC
318	8	150	8.6:1	2 BC
400	8	175	8.2:1	2 BC
400	8	260	8.2:1	4 BC

ROAD RUNNER ENGINES

CID	NO. CYL.	HORSE-POWER	COMP. RATIO	CARB.
318	8	170	8.6:1	2 BC
340	8	240	8.5:1	2 BC
440	8	280	8.2:1	4 BC

1974 PLYMOUTH VALIANT

1974 PLYMOUTH DUSTER

1974 PLYMOUTH FURY

1974 PLYMOUTH BARRACUDA

1974 PLYMOUTH SATELLITE SEBRING

1974 PLYMOUTH ROAD RUNNER

1974 PLYMOUTH 'CUDA

VEHICLE IDENTIFICATION NUMBER

PLYMOUTH
RL41G4A123456

Located on a plate attached to the left side of the instrument panel, visible through the windshield.

FIRST DIGIT: Identifies the car make

MAKE	CODE
Barracuda	B
Fury	P
Satellite/Sebring	R
Valiant	V

SECOND DIGIT: Identifies the price class

CLASS	CODE
Police	K
Taxi	T
Low	L
Medium	M
High	H
Premium	P
Special	S

THIRD & FOURTH DIGITS: Identify the body type

TYPE	CODE
2-Dr. Sedan Coupe	21
2-Dr. Hardtop	23
2-Dr. Sports Hardtop	29
4-Dr. Sedan	41
4-Dr. Hardtop	43
6-Pass Wagon	45
9-Pass. Wagon	46

FIFTH DIGIT: Identifies the engine

CID	CODE
198 CID 1 BC 6-Cyl.	B
225 CID 1 BC 6-Cyl.	C
Special Order 6-Cyl.	E
318 CID 2 BC 8-Cyl.	G
360 CID Hi-Perf. 8-Cyl.	H
360 CID 4 BC 8-Cyl.	J
360 CID 2 BC 8-Cyl.	K
360 CID Hi-Perf. 8-Cyl.	L
400 CID 2 BC 8-Cyl.	M
400 CID 4 BC 8-Cyl.	N
400 CID 4 BC Hi-Perf. 8-Cyl.	P
440 CID 4 BC 8-Cyl.	T
440 CID Hi-Perf. 8-Cyl.	U
Special Order 8-Cyl.	Z

SIXTH DIGIT: Identifies the year
4 - 1974

SEVENTH DIGIT: Identifies the assembly plant

PLANT	CODE
Lynch Road, Detroit, MI	A
Hamtramck, MI	B
Jefferson Ave., Detroit, MI	C
Belvidere, IL	D
Newark, DE	F
St. Louis, MO	G
Windsor, Ontario, CAN	R
Japan	5
Japan	9

LAST SIX DIGITS: Identify the production sequence number starting at each plant with 100001

EXAMPLE

R	L	41	G	4	A	123456
Car Make	Price Class	Body Type	Engine	Model Year	Asm Plant	Production Sequence Number

BODY CODE PLATE

THE BODY CODE PLATE is located in the engine compartment on the left wheel housing, fender side shield or radiator yoke.

THE BODY CODE PLATE is read left to right, bottom to top. The information on the plate includes the car S.O. Number and the trim and paint codes.

CHRYSLER MOTORS CORPORATION

				Line
XXX	XXX	XXX	XXX	6
XXX	XXX	XXX	XXX	5
XXX	XXX	XXX	XXX	4
XXX	XXX	XXX	XXX	3
XXX	XXX	XXX	XXX	2
XXX	XXX	XXX	XXX	1

LINE 1 - DIGITS 1, 2 & 3: Indicate engine codes

CID	CODE
198 CID	E22
225 CID	E24
225 CID	E25
318 CID	E44
360 CID 4 BC 8-Cyl.	E56
360 CID 2 BC 8-Cyl.	E57
360 4 BC 8-Cyl.	E58
400 CID 2 BC 8-Cyl.	E63
400 CID 4 BC 8-Cyl.	E64
400 CID 4 BC Hi-Perf. 8-Cyl.	E68
440 CID 8-Cyl.	E85
440 CID Hi-Perf. 8-Cyl.	E86
Special Order Engine	E99

LINE 1 - DIGITS 4, 5 & 6: Indicate transmission codes

TRANSMISSION	CODE
3-Spd. Manual Floor Shift	D13
3-Spd. Std. Manual Clm. Shift	D14
H.D. 3-Spd. Manual Clm. Shift	D15
4-Spd. Manual	D21
Standard Automatic	D34
H.D. Automatic	D35
H.D. Clutch	D41

LINE 1 - DIGIT 7: Indicates car line

MAKE	CODE
Barracuda	B
Fury	P
Satellite/Sebring	R
Valiant	V

LINE 1 - DIGIT 8: Indicates price class

CLASS	CODE
Police	K
Taxi	T
Low	L
Medium	M
High	H
Premium	P
Special	S

LINE 1 - DIGITS 9 & 10: Indicate body type

TYPE	CODE
2-Dr. Sedan Coupe	21
2-Dr. Hardtop	23
2-Dr. Sports Hardtop	29
4-Dr. Sedan	41
4-Dr. Hardtop	43
6-Pass. Wagon	45
9-Pass. Wagon	46

LINE 1 - DIGIT 11: Indicates engine code

CID	CODE
198 CID 1 BC 6-Cyl.	B
225 CID 1 BC 6-Cyl.	C
Special Order 6-Cyl.	E
318 CID 2 BC 8-Cyl.	G
360 CID Hi-Perf. 8-Cyl.	H
360 CID 4 BC 8-Cyl.	J
360 CID 2 BC 8-Cyl.	K
360 CID Hi-Perf. 8-Cyl.	L
400 CID 2 BC 8-Cyl.	M
400 CID 4 BC 8-Cyl.	N
400 CID 4 BC Hi-Perf. 8-Cyl.	P
440 CID 4 BC 8-Cyl.	T
440 CID Hi-Perf. 8-Cyl.	U
Special Order 8-Cyl.	Z

LINE 1 - DIGIT 12: Indicates model year
4 - 1974

LINE 1 - DIGIT 13: Indicates the assembly plant

PLANT	CODE
Lynch Road, Detroit, MI	A
Hamtramck, MI	B
Jefferson Ave., Detroit, MI	C
Belvidere, IL	D
Newark, DE	F
St. Louis, MO	G
Windsor, Ontario, CAN	R
Japan	5
Japan	9

LINE 1 - LAST SIX DIGITS: Indicate production sequence number

LINE 2 - DIGITS 1, 2 & 3: Indicate body paint color, or fleet or special order paint code

COLOR	CODE
Silver Frost Metallic	JA5
Powder Blue	KB1
Lucerne Blue Metallic	KB5
Starlight Blue Metallic	KB8
Rallye Red	FE5
Burnished Red Metallic	GE7
Frosty Green Metallic	KG2
Deep Sherwood Metallic	KG8
Avocado Gold Metallic	KJ6
Sahara Beige	HL4
Dark Moonstone Metallic	KL8
Sienna Metallic	KT5
Dark Chestnut Metallic	KT9
Spinnaker White	EW1
Formal Black	TX9
Sun Fire Yellow	DY2
Golden Fawn	KY4
Yellow Blaze	KY5
Golden Haze Metallic	JY6
Tahitian Gold Metallic	JY9
Special Order	999

LINE 2 - DIGITS 4, 5, 6 & 7: Indicate trim code

LINE 2 - DIGIT 4: Indicates price class

CLASS	CODE
Police	K
Taxi	T
Low	L
Medium	M
High	H
Premium	P
Special	S
Grand	G

LINE 2 - DIGIT 5: Indicates seat and fabric type

SEAT	CODE
Cloth & Vinyl Bench	1
Vinyl Bench	2
Cloth & Leather Bench	A
Leather Bench	M
Cloth & Vinyl Bench Split Back	3
Vinyl Bench Split Back	4
Cloth & Leather Bench Split Back	B
Leather Bench Split Back	P
Cloth & Vinyl Bucket	5
Vinyl Bucket	6
Cloth & Leather Bucket	C
Leather Bucket	R
Cloth & Vinyl 50/50	7
Vinyl 50/50	8
Cloth & Leather 50/50	D
Leather 50/50	L
Cloth & Vinyl Special Design	9
Vinyl Special Design	H
Cloth & Leather Special Design	E
Leather Special Design	T

LINE 2 - DIGITS 6 & 7: Indicates interior color

FABRIC COLOR	CODE
Gray	A9
Blue	B6
Wimbleton	EW
Green	G6
Parchment	L3
Tangier	LL
Chestnut	T7
Orange, Black & White	VW
Black	X9
Black & White	XW
Gold	Y3
White & Gold	YW

LINE 2 - DIGITS 8, 9 & 10: Indicate upper door frame color, not listed

LINE 2 - DIGIT 11: Indicates the month of manufacture

MONTH	CODE
January	1
February	2
March	3
April	4
May	5
June	6
July	7
August	8
September	9
October	A
November	B
December	C

LINE 2 - DIGITS 12 & 13: Indicate the day of month of manufacture

LINE 2 - LAST SIX DIGITS: Indicate production sequence number

LINE 3 - DIGITS 1, 2 & 3: Indicate roof paint color, vinyl roof code or convertible top code

COLOR	CODE
Paint-Mono Tone	V01
Paint-Two Tone	V02
Paint, Trim & Vinyl Roof Waiver	V08
Paint-Special Order	V09
Full Vinyl Roof	V10
Full Vinyl Roof Blue	V1B

COLOR	CODE
Full Vinyl Roof Green	V1G
Full Vinyl Roof Parchment	V1L
Full Vinyl Roof White	V1W
Full Vinyl Roof Black	V2X
Full Vinyl Roof Gold	V1Y
Paint-Hood Performance	V21
Decor Stripe PKG #2 (RH23)	V25
Delete "Dodge" Tape Block Letters	V38
Halo Style Vinyl Roof	V40
Halo Style Vinyl Roof White	V4W
Halo Style Vinyl Roof Black	V4X
Halo Style Vinyl Roof Gold Reptile Grain	V4Y
Mouldings-Protective Vinyl Body Side	V50
Mouldings-Protective Vinyl Body Side Black	V5X
Sport Stripes Tape	V60
Sport Stripes Tape Red	V6R
Sport Stripes Tape White	V6W
Sport Stripes Tape Black	V6X
Sport Stripes Tape Gold	V6Y
Sport Stripes Tape Delete	V68
Accent Stripes Paint	V70
Accent Stripes Paint Blue Green	V7B
Accent Stripes Paint Parchment	V7L
Accent Stripes Paint Red	V7R
Accent Stripes Paint White	V7W
Accent Stripes Paint Black	V7X
Accent Stripes Paint Gold	V7Y
Accent Stripes Paint Delete	V78
Sport Stripes Tape	V80
Sport Stripes Tape Parchment	V8L
Sport Stripes Tape Red	V8R
Sport Stripes Tape White	V8W
Sport Stripes Tape Black	V8X
Sport Stripes Tape Delete	V88
Sport Stripes-Body Side & Roof	V90
Sport Stripes-Body Side & Roof Red	V90
Sport Stripes-Body Side & Roof White	V9W
Sport Stripes-Body Side & Roof Black	V9X

ENGINE NUMBER

THE ENGINE IDENTIFICATION NUMBER for 6-cylinder engines is located at the right front of the block below #1 spark plug.

ENGINE NUMBERS for 318 and 360 CID V-8 engines are found at the left front of the block below the cylinder head. The engine number for 400 engines is found on the right side of the block adjacent to the distributor. The engine number for 440 engines is located on the left bank adjacent to the front tappet rail.

The following identification will be included in the engine serial number:

"A" ENGINE FAMILY

THE NUMBER AND LETTER will designate the model year and/or build plant.

THE THREE NUMBERS following the model year and/or build plant are the cubic inch displacement.

THE LETTER following the model identification is the engine type.

THE FOUR NUMBERS following the engine type are the build date code.

THE FOUR NUMBERS following the build date code are the daily sequence number (optional usage).

"B" AND "G" ENGINE FAMILY

THE NUMBER AND LETTER designate the model year and/or build plant.

THE THREE NUMBERS AND LETTER following the model year and/or build plant are the cubic inch displacement and type.

THE THREE NUMBERS following the model identification and type are the build date code.

THE NUMBER following the build date is the shift built.

ENGINE SERIAL NUMBER CODES DEFINED:

	CODE
High Performance	HP
Series (1974)	K
Low Compression	LC
Mound Road Plant	M
Premium Fuel Recommended	P
Regular Fuel may be used	R
Special Engine	S
Trenton Plant	T
Windsor Plant	W

NOTE: Series without "M" or "W" suffix indicates Trenton Engine Plant.

EXAMPLE ("A" Engine Family)
4M318R43201234

In the example above:

4	Model year
M	Mound Road Plant
318	Cubic Inch Displacement
R	Regular Fuel may be used
4320	Build date code
1234	Daily sequence number

EXAMPLE ("B" and "G" Engine Family)
4T440R8-222

In the example above:

4	Model year
T	Trenton Engine Plant
440R	Cubic Inch Displacement and Type
8-22	Build date code
2	Shift built

BARRACUDA ENGINES

CID	NO. CYL.	HORSE-POWER	COMP. RATIO	CARB.
318	8	150	8.6:1	2 BC
360	8	245	8.4:1	4 BC

DUSTER, VALIANT ENGINES

CID	NO. CYL.	HORSE-POWER	COMP. RATIO	CARB.
198	6	95	8.4:1	1 BC
225	6	105	8.4:1	1 BC
318	8	150	8.6:1	2 BC
360	8	245	8.4:1	4 BC

FURY ENGINES

CID	NO. CYL.	HORSE-POWER	COMP. RATIO	CARB.
360	8	180	8.4:1	2 BC
360	8	200	8.4:1	4 BC
400	8	185	8.2:1	2 BC
400	8	205	8.2:1	4 BC
440	8	230	8.2:1	4 BC

ROAD RUNNER ENGINES

CID	NO. CYL.	HORSE-POWER	COMP. RATIO	CARB.
318	8	170	8.6:1	2 BC
360	8	245	8.4:1	4 BC
400	8	250	8.2:1	4 BC
440	8	275	8.2:1	4 BC

SATELLITE ENGINES

CID	NO. CYL.	HORSE-POWER	COMP. RATIO	CARB.
225	6	105	8.4:1	1 BC
318	8	150	8.6:1	2 BC
360	8	200	8.4:1	4 BC
400	8	205	8.2:1	4 BC
400	8	250	8.2:1	4 BC

1975 PLYMOUTH DUSTER

1975 PLYMOUTH DUSTER

1975 PLYMOUTH GRAN FURY

1975 PLYMOUTH GRAN FURY

1975 PLYMOUTH GRAN FURY SPORT SUBURBAN WAGON

1975 PLYMOUTH FURY SPORT SUBURBAN WAGON

1975 PLYMOUTH SPORTS FURY

1975 PLYMOUTH SPORTS FURY

1975 PLYMOUTH VALIANT

1975 PLYMOUTH VALIANT

VEHICLE IDENTIFICATION NUMBER

PLYMOUTH
RL41G5A123456

Located on a plate attached to the left side of the instrument panel, visible through the windshield.

FIRST DIGIT: Identifies the car make

MAKE	CODE
Valiant	V
Fury	R
Gran Fury	P

SECOND DIGIT: Identifies the price class

CLASS	CODE
High	H
Police	K
Low	L
Medium	M
Premium	P
Special	S
Taxi	T

THIRD & FOURTH DIGITS: Identify the body type

TYPE	CODE
2-Dr. Sedan	21
2-Dr. Hardtop	23
2-Dr. Special	29
4-Dr. Sedan	41
2-Seat Station Wagon	45
3-Seat Station Wagon	46

FIFTH DIGIT: Identifies the engine

CID	CODE
225 CID 1 BC 6-Cyl.	C
Special Order 6-Cyl.	E
318 CID 2 BC 8-Cyl.	G
360 CID 4 BC 8-Cyl.*	J
360 CID 2 BC 8-Cyl.**	K
360 CID 4 BC Hi-Perf. 8-Cyl.*	L
400 CID 2 BC 8-Cyl.**	M
400 CID 4 BC 8-Cyl.	N
400 CID 4 BC Hi-Perf. 8-Cyl.**	P
440 CID 4 BC 8-Cyl.	T
440 CID Hi-Perf. 8-Cyl.	U
Special Order 8-Cyl.	Z

*With California emission package
**Not available with California emission package

SIXTH DIGIT: Identifies the year
5 - 1975

SEVENTH DIGIT: Identifies the assembly plant

PLANT	CODE
Lynch Road, Detroit, MI	A
Hamtramck, MI	B
Jefferson Ave., Detroit, MI	C
Belvidere, IL	D
Newark, DE	F
St. Louis, MO	G
Windsor, Ontario, CAN	R
Japan	5
Japan	9

LAST SIX DIGITS: Identify the production sequence number starting at 100001

EXAMPLE

R	L	41	G	5	A	123456
Car Make	Price Class	Body Type	Engine	Model Year	Asm Plant	Production Sequence Number

BODY CODE PLATE

THE BODY CODE PLATE is located on the left front fender side shield or wheel housing on Compact, Sport and Intermediate Models; and on the left side of the upper radiator support on Full Size Cars.

THE BODY CODE PLATE is read left to right, bottom to top. The information on the plate includes the car S.O. Number and the trim and paint codes.

```
          CHRYSLER MOTORS
             CORPORATION

                                    Line
  XXX   XXX   XXX   XXX              6
  XXX   XXX   XXX   XXX              5
  XXX   XXX   XXX   XXX              4
  XXX   XXX   XXX   XXX              3
  XXX   XXX   XXX   XXX              2
  XXX   XXX   XXX   XXX              1
```

LINE 1 - DIGITS 1, 2 & 3: Indicate engine codes

CID	CODE
225 CID 1 BC 6-Cyl.	E24
225 CID 1 BC 6-Cyl.	E25
318 CID 2 BC 8-Cyl.	E44
360 CID 4 BC 8-Cyl.*	E56
360 CID 2 BC 8-Cyl.**	E57
360 CID 4 BC Hi-Perf. 8-Cyl.*	E58
400 CID 2 BC 8-Cyl.**	E63
400 CID 4 BC 8-Cyl.	E64
400 CID 4 BC Hi-Perf. 8-Cyl.**	E68
440 CID 4 BC 8-Cyl.	E85
440 CID Hi-Perf. 8-Cyl.	E86
Special Order Engine	E99

*With California emission package
**Not available with California emission package

LINE 1 - DIGITS 4, 5 & 6: Indicate transmission codes

TRANSMISSION	CODE
3-Spd. Manual Floor Shift	D13
3-Spd. Standard Manual Clm. Shift	D14
3-Spd. H.D. Manual Clm. Shift	D15
4-Spd. Manual	D21
Standard Automatic	D34
H.D. Automatic	D35

LINE 1 - DIGIT 7: Indicates car line

1975 PLYMOUTH

MAKE	CODE
Valiant	V
Fury	R
Gran Fury	P

LINE 1 - DIGIT 8: Indicates price class

CLASS	CODE
High	H
Police	K
Low	L
Medium	M
Premium	P
Special	S
Taxi	T

LINE 1 - DIGITS 9 & 10: Indicate body type

TYPE	CODE
2-Dr. Sedan	21
2-Dr. Hardtop	23
2-Dr. Special	29
4-Dr. Sedan	41
2-Seat Station Wagon	45
3-Seat Station Wagon	46

LINE 1 - DIGIT 11: Indicates engine code

CID	CODE
225 CID 1 BC 6-Cyl.	C
Special Order 6-Cyl.	E
318 CID 2 BC 8-Cyl.	G
360 CID 4 BC 8-Cyl.*	J
360 CID 2 BC 8-Cyl.**	K
360 CID 4 BC Hi-Perf. 8-Cyl.*	L
400 CID 2 BC 8-Cyl.**	M
400 CID 4 BC 8-Cyl.	N
400 CID 4 BC Hi-Perf. 8-Cyl.**	P
440 CID 4 BC 8-Cyl.	T
440 CID Hi-Perf. 8-Cyl.	U
Special Order 8-Cyl.	Z

*With California emission package
**Not available with California emission package

LINE 1 - DIGIT 12: Indicates model year
5 - 1975

LINE 1 - DIGIT 13: Indicates the assembly plant

PLANT	CODE
Lynch Road, Detroit, MI	A
Hamtramck, MI	B
Jefferson Ave., Detroit, MI	C
Belvidere, IL	D
Newark, DE	F
St. Louis, MO	G
Windsor, Ontario, CAN	R
Japan	5
Japan	9

LINE 1 - LAST SIX DIGITS: Indicate production sequence number

LINE 2 - DIGITS 1, 2 & 3: Indicate body paint color, or fleet or special order paint code

COLOR	CODE
Silver Cloud Metallic	LA2
Powder Blue	KB1
Lucerne Blue Metallic	KB5
Starlight Blue Metallic	KB8
Rallye Red	FE5
Astral Blue Metallic	LB2
Vintage Red Metallic	LE9
Bittersweet Metallic	LK3
Frosty Green Metallic	KG2
Deep Sherwood Metallic	KG8
Avocado Gold Metallic	KJ6
Sahara Beige	HL4
Cinnamon Metallic	LT4
Moondust Metallic	LL5
Sienna Metallic	KT5
Dark Chestnut Metallic	KT9
Spinnaker White	EW1
Formal Black	TX9
Yellow Blaze	KY5
Golden Fawn	KY4
Inca Gold Metallic	LY6
Spanish Gold Metallic	LY9
Aztec Gold	JL6
Platinum Metallic	LJ2

LINE 2 - DIGITS 4, 5, 6 & 7: Indicate trim code

LINE 2 - DIGIT 4: Indicates price class

CLASS	CODE
Dodge Taxi	D
High	H
Police	K
Low	L
Medium	M
Premium	P
Special	S
Taxi	T

LINE 2 - DIGIT 5: Indicates seat and fabric type

SEAT	CODE
Cloth & Vinyl Bench	1
All Vinyl Bench	2
Cloth & Leather Bench	A
All Leather	M
Cloth & Vinyl Bench Split Back	3
All Vinyl Bench Split Back	4
Cloth & Leather Bench Split Back	B
All Leather Bench Split Back	P
Cloth & Vinyl Bucket	5
All Vinyl Bucket	6
Cloth & Leather Bucket	C
All Leather Bucket	R
Cloth & Vinyl 50/50	7
All Vinyl 50/50	8
Cloth & Leather 50/50	D
All Leather 50/50	L
Cloth & Vinyl Special Design	9
All Vinyl Special Design	H
Cloth & Leather Special Design	E
All Leather Special Design	T

LINE 2 - DIGITS 6 & 7: Indicates interior color

FABRIC COLOR	CODE
Medium Blue	B6
Blue & White	BW
Red	E7
Red	EE
Red, Black, White	EW
Green	G6
Green	GG
Green & White	GW
Copper, Black, White	KW
Parchment	L3
Parchment	LL
Chestnut	T7
Orange, Black, White	VW
Black	X9
Black & White	XW
Gold	Y3
Gold & White	Y4

LINE 2 - DIGITS 8, 9 & 10: Indicate upper door frame color, not listed

LINE 2 - DIGIT 11: Indicate the month of manufacture

MONTH	CODE
January	1
February	2
March	3
April	4
May	5
June	6
July	7
August	8
September	9
October	A
November	B
December	C

LINE 2 - DIGITS 12 & 13: Indicate the day of month of manufacture

LINE 2 - LAST SIX DIGITS: Indicate production sequence number

LINE 3 - DIGITS 1, 2 & 3: Indicate upper body color or vinyl roof codes

COLOR	CODE
Full Vinyl Roof White	V1W
Canopy Vinyl Roof White	V4W
Full Vinyl Roof Parchment	V1L
Canopy Vinyl Roof Parchment	V4L
Full vinyl Roof Black	V1X
Canopy Vinyl Roof Black	V4X
Full Vinyl Roof Gold	V1Y
Canopy Vinyl Roof Gold	V4Y
Full Vinyl Roof Green	V1G
Canopy Vinyl Roof Green	V4G
Canopy Vinyl Roof Gold-Reptile Grain	V4J
Full Vinyl Roof Red	V1E
Canopy Vinyl Roof Red	V4E

ENGINE NUMBER

THE ENGINE IDENTIFICATION NUMBER for 6-cylinder engines is located at the right front of the block below #1 spark plug.

ENGINE NUMBERS for 318 and 360 CID V-8 engines are found at the left front of the block below the cylinder head. The engine number for 400 engines is found on the right side of the block adjacent to the distributor. The engine number for 440 engines is located on the left bank adjacent to the front tappet rail.

The following identification will be included in the engine serial number:

"A" ENGINE FAMILY

THE NUMBER AND LETTER will designate the model year and/or build plant.

THE THREE NUMBERS following the model year and/or build plant are the cubic inch displacement.

THE LETTER following the model identification is the engine type.

THE FOUR LETTERS following the engine type are the build date code.

THE FOUR NUMBERS following the build date code are the daily sequence number (optional usage).

"B" AND "G" ENGINE FAMILY

THE NUMBER AND LETTER designate the model year and/or build plant.

THE THREE NUMBERS AND LETTER following the model year and/or build plant are the cubic inch displacment and type.

THE THREE NUMBERS following the model identification and type are the build date code.

THE NUMBER following the build date is the shift built.

NOTE: Series without "M" or "W" suffix indicates Trenton Engine Plant.

ENGINE SERIAL NUMBER & PARTS IDENTIFICATION CODES & SYMBOLS DEFINED:

	CODE
High Performance	HP
Series (1975)	L
Low Compression	LC
Mound Road Plant	M
Premium Fuel Recommended	P
Regular Fuel may be used	R
Special Engine	S
Trenton Plant	T
Windsor Plant	W

EXAMPLE ("A" Engine Family)
5M318R09101234

In the example above:

5M	Model Year and/or Build Plant
318	Cubic Inch Displacement
R	Regular Fuel may be used
0910	Build date code (0910 is September 10)
1234	Daily sequence number (optional usage)

EXAMPLE ("B" and "G" Engine Family)
5T440R8-222

In the example above:

5T	Model Year and/or Build Plant
440R	CID and type
8-22	Build date code
2	Shift built

VALIANT, DUSTER ENGINES

CID	NO. CYL.	HORSE-POWER	COMP. RATIO	CARB.
225	6	95	8.4:1	1 BC
318	8	145	8.5:1	2 BC
360	8	230	8.4:1	4 BC

FURY ENGINES

CID	NO. CYL.	HORSE-POWER	COMP. RATIO	CARB.
225	6	95	8.4:1	1 BC
318	8	150	8.5:1	2 BC
360	8	180	8.4:1	2 BC
400	8	165	8.2:1	2 BC
400	8	175	8.2:1	2 BC
400	8	190	8.2:1	4 BC
400	8	235	8.2:1	4 BC
440	8	215	8.2:1	4 BC

ROAD RUNNER ENGINES

CID	NO. CYL.	HORSE-POWER	COMP. RATIO	CARB.
318	8	150	8.5:1	2 BC
360	8	180	8.4:1	2 BC
400	8	165	8.2:1	2 BC
400	8	235	8.2:1	4 BC

1976 PLYMOUTH FURY

1976 PLYMOUTH FURY

1976 PLYMOUTH FURY STATION WAGON

1976 PLYMOUTH DUSTER

1976 PLYMOUTH GRAND FURY

1976 PLYMOUTH GRAND FURY

1976 PLYMOUTH VAILANT

1976 PLYMOUTH VOLARE

|

VEHICLE IDENTIFICATION NUMBER

PLYMOUTH
RL41G6A123456

Located on a plate attached to the left side of the instrument panel, visible through the windshield.

FIRST DIGIT: Identifies the car make

MAKE	CODE
Valiant	V
Fury	R
Volare	H
Gran Fury	P

SECOND DIGIT: Identifies the price class

CLASS	CODE
High	H
Police	K
Low	L
Medium	M
Premium	P
Special	S

THIRD & FOURTH DIGITS: Identify the body type

TYPE	CODE
2-Dr. Hardtop	23
2-Dr. Hatchback	24
2-Dr. Special	29
4-Dr. Sedan	41
2-Seat Station Wagon	45
3-Seat Station Wagon	46

FIFTH DIGIT: Identifies the engine

CID	CODE
225 CID 1 BC 6-Cyl.	C
Special Order 6-Cyl.	E
318 CID 2 BC 8-Cyl.	G
360 CID 4 BC 8-Cyl.*	J
360 CID 2 BC 8-Cyl.**	K
360 CID 4 BC Hi-Perf. 8-Cyl.*	L
400 CID 2 BC 8-Cyl.**	M
400 CID 4 BC 8-Cyl.	N
400 CID 4 BC Hi-Perf. 8-Cyl.**	P
440 CID 4 BC 8-Cyl.	T
440 CID 4 BC Hi-Perf. 8-Cyl.	U
Special Order 8-Cyl.	Z

*With California emission package
**Not available with California emission package

SIXTH DIGIT: Identifies the year
6 - 1976

SEVENTH DIGIT: Indicates the assembly plant.

PLANT	CODE
Lynch Road, Detroit, MI	A
Hamtramck, MI	B
Jefferson Ave., Detroit, MI	C
Belvidere, IL	D
Newark, DE	F
St. Louis, MO	G
Windsor, Ontario, CAN	R
Japan	5
Japan	9
Japan	7

LAST SIX DIGITS: Identify the production sequence number starting at each plant with 100001

EXAMPLE

R	L	41	G	6	A	123456
Car Make	Price Class	Body Type	Engine	Model Year	Asm Plant	Production Sequence Number

BODY CODE PLATE

THE BODY CODE PLATE is located in the engine compartment on the left wheel housing, fender side shield or radiator yoke.

THE BODY CODE PLATE is read left to right, bottom to top. The information on the plate includes the car S.O. Number and the trim and paint codes.

CHRYSLER MOTORS CORPORATION

				Line
XXX	XXX	XXX	XXX	6
XXX	XXX	XXX	XXX	5
XXX	XXX	XXX	XXX	4
XXX	XXX	XXX	XXX	3
XXX	XXX	XXX	XXX	2
XXX	XXX	XXX	XXX	1

LINE 1 - DIGITS 1, 2 & 3: Indicate engine codes

CID	CODE
225 CID 1-1 BC 6-Cyl.	E24
225 CID 1-1 BC 6-Cyl.	E25
318 CID 1-2 BC 8-Cyl.	E44
360 CID 1-4 BC 8-Cyl.*	E56
360 CID 1-2 BC 8-Cyl.**	E57
360 CID 1-4 BC Hi-Perf. 8-Cyl.*	E58
400 CID 1-2 BC 8-Cyl.**	E63
400 CID 1-4 BC 8-Cyl.	E64
400 CID 1-4 BC Hi-Perf. 8-Cyl.**	E68
440 CID 1-4 BC 8-Cyl.	E85
440 CID 1-4 BC Hi-Perf. 8-Cyl.	E86
Special Order Engine	E99

*With California emission package
**Not available with California emission package

LINE 1 - DIGITS 4, 5 & 6: Indicate transmission codes

TRANSMISSION	CODE
3-Spd. Manual Floor Shift	D13
3-Spd. Std. Manual Clm. Shift	D14
3-Spd. H.D. Manual Clm. Shift	D15
4-Spd. Standard	D21
4-Spd. O.D.	D24
Standard A904	D31
Standard A998	D32
Standard A999	D33
Standard Automatic	D34
H.D. A727	D35
Standard A727	D36
H.D. A904	D38

LINE 1 - DIGIT 7: Indicates car line

MAKE	CODE
Valiant	V
Fury	R
Volare	H
Gran Fury	P

LINE 1 - DIGIT 8: Indicates price class

CLASS	CODE
High	H
Police	K
Low	L
Medium	M
Premium	P
Special	S

LINE 1 - DIGIT 9 & 10: Indicate body type

TYPE	CODE
2-Dr. Hardtop	23
2-Dr. Hatchback	24
2-Dr. Special	29
4-Dr. Sedan	41
2-Seat Station Wagon	45
3-Seat Station Wagon	46

LINE 1 - DIGIT 11: Indicates engine code

CID	CODE
225 CID 1 BC 6-Cyl.	C
Special Order 6-Cyl.	E
318 CID 2 BC 8-Cyl.	G
360 CID 4 BC 8-Cyl.*	J
360 CID 2 BC 8-Cyl.**	K
360 CID 4 BC Hi-Perf. 8-Cyl.*	L
400 CID 2 BC 8-Cyl.**	M
400 CID 4 BC 8-Cyl.	N
400 CID 4 BC Hi-Perf. 8-Cyl.**	P
440 CID 4 BC 8-Cyl.	T
440 CID 4 BC Hi-Perf. 8-Cyl.	U
Special Order 8-Cyl.	Z

*With California emission package
**Not available with California emission package

LINE 1 - DIGIT 12: Indicates model year
6 - 1976

LINE 1 - DIGIT 13: Indicates the assembly plant

PLANT	CODE
Lynch Road, Detroit, MI	A
Hamtramck, MI	B
Jefferson Ave., Detroit, MI	C
Belvidere, IL	D
Newark, DE	F
St. Louis, MO	G
Windsor, Ontario, CAN	R
Japan	5
Japan	9
Japan	7

LINE 1 - LAST SIX DIGITS: Indicate production sequence number

LINE 2 - DIGITS 1, 2 & 3: Indicate body paint color, or fleet or special order paint code

COLOR	CODE
Silver Cloud Metallic	LA2
Powder Blue	KB1
Astral Blue Metallic	LB2
Big Sky Blue	MB4
Jamaican Blue Metallic	MB5
Starlight Blue Metallic	KB8
Rallye Red	FE5
Vintage Red Metallic	LE9
Jade Green Metallic	MF2
Deep Sherwood Metallic	KG8
Platinum Metallic	LJ2
Tropic Green Metallic	MJ5
Bittersweet Metallic	LK3
Moondust Metallic	LL5
Claret Red	MR6
Cinnamon Metallic	LT4
Dark Chestnut Metallic	KT9
Saddle Tan	MU2
Caramel Tan Metallic	MU3
Spitfire Orange	MV1
Spinnaker White	EW1
Formal Black	TX9
Golden Fawn	KY4
Yellow Blaze	KY5
Harvest Gold	MY3
Inca Gold Metallic	LY6
Spanish Gold Metallic	LY9

LINE 2 - DIGITS 4, 5, 6 & 7: Indicate trim code

LINE 2 - DIGIT 4: Indicates price class

CLASS	CODE
High	H
Police	K
Low	L
Medium	M
Premium	P
Special	S

LINE 2 - DIGIT 5: Indicates seat and fabric type

SEAT	CODE
Cloth & Vinyl Bench	1
All Vinyl Bench	2
Cloth & Leather Bench	A
All Leather Bench	M
Cloth & Vinyl Bench Split Back	3
All Vinyl Bench Split Back	4
Cloth & Leather Bench Split Back	B
All Leather Bench Split Back	P
Cloth & Vinyl Bucket	5
All Vinyl Bucket	6
Cloth & Leather Bucket	C
All Leather Bucket	R
Cloth & Vinyl 50/50	7
All Vinyl 50/50	8
Cloth & Leather 50/50	D
All Leather 50/50	L
Cloth & Vinyl Special Design	9
All Vinyl Special Design	H
Cloth & Leather Special Design	E
All Leather Special Design	T

LINE 2 - DIGITS 6 & 7: Indicates interior color

FABRIC COLOR	CODE
Medium Blue	B6
Blue & White	BW
Red	E7
Red	EE
Red & White	EW
Green	F6
Green	FF
Green & White	FW
Gold, Black, White	KW
Parchment	L3
Parchment	LL
Chestnut	T7
Tan	U5
Tan & White	UW
Black	X9
Black & White	XW
Gold	Y3
Gold & White	YW

LINE 2 - DIGITS 8, 9 & 10: Indicate upper door frame color, not listed

LINE 2 - DIGIT 11: Indicate the month of manufacture

MONTH	CODE
January	1
February	2
March	3
April	4
May	5
June	6
July	7
August	8
September	9
October	A
November	B
December	C

LINE 2 - DIGITS 12 & 13: Indicate the day of month of manufacture

LINE 2 - LAST SIX DIGITS: Indicate production sequence number

LINE 3 - DIGITS 1, 2 & 3: Indicate upper body color or vinyl roof codes

COLOR	CODE
Full Vinyl Roof Blue	V1B
Canopy Vinyl Roof Blue	V4B
Landau Vinyl Roof Blue	V3B
Full Vinyl Roof Green	V1F
Halo Vinyl Roof Green	V1F
Canopy Vinyl Roof Green	V4F
Canopy Vinyl Roof Green	V5F
Full Vinyl Roof Gold	V1Y
Halo Vinyl Roof Gold	V1Y
Canopy Vinyl Roof Gold	V4Y
Canopy Vinyl Roof Gold	V5Y
Full Vinyl Roof Parchment	V1L
Canopy Vinyl Roof Parchment	V4L
Landau Vinyl Roof Parchment	V3L
Full Vinyl Roof Red	V1E
Halo Vinyl Roof Red	V1E
Canopy Vinyl Roof Red	V4E
Canopy Vinyl Roof Red	V5E
Landau Vinyl Roof Red	V3E
Full Vinyl Roof Black	V1X
Halo Vinyl Roof Black	V1X
Canopy Vinyl Roof Black	V4X
Canopy Vinyl Roof Black	V5X
Landau Vinyl Roof Black	V3X
Full Vinyl Roof White	V1W
Halo Vinyl Roof White	V1W
Canopy Vinyl Roof White	V4W
Canopy Vinyl Roof White	V5W
Landau Vinyl Roof White	V3W
Full Vinyl Roof Tan	V1U
Landau Vinyl Roof Tan	V3U
Full Vinyl Roof Silver	V1A
Landau Vinyl Roof Silver	V3A
Canopy Vinyl Roof Silver	V4A
Full Vinyl Roof Gold	V1Y
Canopy Vinyl Roof Gold	V4Y

ENGINE NUMBER

THE ENGINE IDENTIFICATION NUMBER for 6-cylinder engines is located at the right front of the block below #1 spark plug.

ENGINE NUMBERS for 318 and 360 CID V-8 engines are found at the left front of the block below the cylinder head. The engine number for 400 engines is found on the right side of the block adjacent to the distributor. The engine number for 440 engines is located on the left bank adjacent to the front tappet rail.

The following identification will be included in the engine serial number:

"A" ENGINE FAMILY

THE NUMBER AND LETTER will designate the model year and/or build plant.

THE THREE NUMBERS following the model year and/or build plant are the cubic inch displacement.

THE LETTER following the model identification is the engine type.

THE FOUR LETTERS following the engine type are the build date code.

THE FOUR NUMBERS following the build date code are the daily sequence number (optional usage).

"B" AND "G" ENGINE FAMILY

THE NUMBER AND LETTER designate the model year and/or build plant.

THE THREE NUMBERS AND LETTER following the model year and/or build plant are the cubic inch displacement and type.

THE THREE NUMBERS following the model identification and type are the build date code.

THE NUMBER following the build date is the shift built.

NOTE: Series without "M" or "W" suffix indicates Trenton Engine Plant.

ENGINE SERIAL NUMBER & PARTS IDENTIFICATION CODES & SYMBOLS DEFINED:

	CODE
High Performance	HP
Series (1976)	
Low Compression	LC
Mound Road Plant	M
Premium Fuel Recommended	P
Regular Fuel may be used	R
Special Engine	S
Trenton Plant	T
Windsor Plant	W

EXAMPLE ("A" Engine Family)
6M318R09101234

In the example above:

6M	Model Year and/or Build Plant
318	Cubic Inch Displacement
R	Regular Fuel may be used
0910	Build date code (0910 is September 10)
1234	Daily sequence number (optional usage)

EXAMPLE ("B" and "G" Engine Family)
6T440R8-222

In the example above:

6T	Model Year and/or Build Plant
440R	CID and Type
8-22	Build date code
2	Shift built

FURY ENGINES

CID	NO. CYL.	HORSE-POWER	COMP. RATIO	CARB.
225	6	100	8.4:1	1 BC
318	8	150	8.5:1	2 BC
360	8	170	8.4:1	2 BC
360	8	175	8.2:1	4 BC
400	8	175	8.2:1	2 BC
400	8	210	8.2:1	4 BC
400	8	240	8.2:1	4 BC
440	8	205	8.0:1	4 BC

VALIANT, DUSTER ENGINES

CID	NO. CYL.	HORSE-POWER	COMP. RATIO	CARB.
225	6	100	8.4:1	1 BC
318	8	150	8.5:1	2 BC
360	8	220	8.4:1	4 BC

VOLARE ENGINES

CID	NO. CYL.	HORSE-POWER	COMP. RATIO	CARB.
225	6	100	8.4:1	1 BC
318	8	150	8.5:1	2 BC
360	8	170	8.4:1	2 BC

1977 PLYMOUTH FURY SALON

1977 PLYMOUTH FURY SALON

1977 PLYMOUTH FURY SPORT

1977 PLYMOUTH VOLARE

1977 PLYMOUTH GRAN FURY

1977 PLYMOUTH VOLARE STATION WAGON

1977 PLYMOUTH FURY STATION WAGON

1977 PLYMOUTH FURY STATION WAGON

VEHICLE IDENTIFICATION NUMBER

PLYMOUTH
RL41G7A123456

Located on a plate attached to the left side of the instrument panel, visible through the windshield.

FIRST DIGIT: Identifies the car make

MAKE	CODE
Volare	H
Fury	R
Gran Fury	P

SECOND DIGIT: Identifies the price class

CLASS	CODE
High	H
Police	K
Low	L
Medium	M
Premium	P
Special	S

THIRD & FOURTH DIGITS: Identify the body type

TYPE	CODE
2-Dr. Hardtop	23
2-Dr. Hatchback	24
4-Dr. Sedan	41
4-Dr. Hardtop	43
2-Seat Station Wagon	45
3-Seat Station Wagon	46

FIFTH DIGIT: Identifies the engine

CID	CODE
225 CID 1 BC 6-Cyl.	C
Special Order 6-Cyl.	E
318 CID 2 BC 8-Cyl.	G
360 CID 4 BC 8-Cyl.	J
360 CID 2 BC 8-Cyl.	K
360 CID Hi-Perf. 8-Cyl.	L
400 CID 4 BC Hi-Perf. 8-Cyl.	P
440 CID 4 BC 8-Cyl.	T
440 CID 4 BC Hi-Perf. 8-Cyl.	U
Special Order 8-Cyl.	Z

SIXTH DIGIT: Identifies the year
7 - 1977

SEVENTH DIGIT: Identifies the assembly plant

PLANT	CODE
Lynch Road, Detroit, MI	A
Hamtramck, MI	B
Jefferson Ave., Detroit, Mi	C
Belvidere, IL	D
Newark, DE	F
St. Louis, MO	G
Windsor, Ontario, CAN	R
Japan	5
Japan	7
Japan	8
Japan	9

LAST SIX DIGITS: Identify the production sequence number starting at each plant with 100001

EXAMPLE

R	L	41	G	7	A	123456
Car Make	Price Class	Body Type	Engine	Model Year	Asm Plant	Production Sequence Number

BODY CODE PLATE

THE BODY CODE PLATE is located in the engine compartment on the left wheel housing, fender side shield or radiator yoke.

THE BODY CODE PLATE is read left to right, bottom to top. The information on the plate includes the car S.O. Number and the trim and paint codes.

CHRYSLER MOTORS CORPORATION

				Line
XXX	XXX	XXX	XXX	6
XXX	XXX	XXX	XXX	5
XXX	XXX	XXX	XXX	4
XXX	XXX	XXX	XXX	3
XXX	XXX	XXX	XXX	2
XXX	XXX	XXX	XXX	1

LINE 1 - DIGITS 1, 2 & 3: Indicate engine codes

CID	CODE
225 CID 1 BC 6-Cyl.	E24
225 CID 1 BC 6-Cyl.	E25
225 CID 2 BC 6-Cyl.	E26
318 CID 2 BC 8-Cyl.	E44
360 CID 4 BC 8-Cyl.	E56
360 CID 2 BC 8-Cyl.	E57
360 CID 4 BC Hi-Perf. 8-Cyl.	E58
400 CID 4 BC 8-Cyl.	E64
400 CID 4 BC Hi-Perf. 8-Cyl.	E68
440 CID 4 BC 8-Cyl.	E85
440 CID 4 BC Hi-Perf. 8-Cyl.	E86
Special Order Engine	E99

LINE 1 - DIGITS 4, 5 & 6: Indicate transmission codes

TRANSMISSION	CODE
3-Spd. Manual Floor Shift	D13
3-Spd. Std. Manual Clm. Shift	D14
3-Spd. H.D. Manual Clm. Shift	D15
4-Spd. Standard	D21
4-Spd. O.D.	D24
Standard A904	D31
Standard A998	D32
Standard A999	D33
Standard Automatic	D34
H.D. A727	D35
Standard A727	D36
H.D. A904	D38

LINE 1 - DIGIT 7: Indicates car line

MAKE	CODE
Volare	H
Fury	R
Gran Fury	P

LINE 1 - DIGIT 8: Indicates price class

CLASS	CODE
High	H
Police	K
Low	L
Medium	M
Premium	P
Special	S

LINE 1 - DIGIT 9 & 10: Indicate body type

TYPE	CODE
2-Dr. Hardtop	23
2-Dr. Hatchback	24
4-Dr. Sedan	41
2-Seat Station Wagon	45
3-Seat Station Wagon	46

LINE 1 - DIGIT 11: Indicates engine code

CID	CODE
225 CID 1 BC 6-Cyl.	C
Special Order 6-Cyl.	E
318 CID 2 BC 8-Cyl.	G
360 CID 4 BC 8-Cyl.	J
360 CID 2 BC 8-Cyl.	K
360 CID Hi-Perf. 8-Cyl.	L
400 CID 4 BC Hi-Perf. 8-Cyl.	P
440 CID 4 BC 8-Cyl.	T
440 CID 4 BC Hi-Perf. 8-Cyl.	U
Special Order 8-Cyl.	Z

LINE 1 - DIGIT 12: Indicates model year
7 - 1977

LINE 1 - DIGIT 13: Indicates the assembly plant

PLANT	CODE
Lynch Road, Detroit, MI	A
Hamtramck, MI	B
Jefferson Ave., Detroit, Mi	C
Belvidere, IL	D
Newark, DE	F
St. Louis, MO	G
Windsor, Ontario, CAN	R
Japan	5
Japan	7
Japan	8
Japan	9

LINE 1 - LAST SIX DIGITS: Indicate production sequence number

LINE 2 - DIGITS 1, 2 & 3: Indicate body paint color, or fleet or special order paint code

COLOR	CODE
Silver Cloud Metallic	LA2
Wedgewood Blue	PB2
Cadet Blue Metallic	PB3
French Racing Blue	PB5
Regatta Blue Metallic (Volare Only)	PB6
Starlight Blue Sunfire Metallic	PB9
Rallye Red (Fury Only)	FE5
Vintage Red Sunfire Metallic	ME8
Jade Green Metallic	MF2
Forest Green Sunfire Metallic	PF7
Burnished Copper Metallic (N/A Volare)	PK6
Mojave Beige (N/A Fury)	PL3
Moondust Metallic (Fury & Gran Fury Only)	LL5
Russet Sunfire Metallic	PR8
Coffee Sunfire Metallic (N/A Volare)	PT7
Lt. Mocha Tan (Volare Only)	PT2
Caramel Tan Metallic (Volare Only)	MU3
Spitfire Orange (Volare Only)	MV1
Spinnaker White	EW1
Formal Black Sunfire Metallic	PX8
Jasmine Yellow (N/A Volare)	PY1
Golden Fawn (N/A Volare)	KY4
Yellow Blaze (Volare Only)	KY5
Inca Gold Metallic (N/A Volare)	LY6
Spanish Gold Metallic	LY9
Harvest Gold (Available Volare 2-Tone Only)	MY3

LINE 2 - DIGITS 4, 5, 6 & 7: Indicate trim code

LINE 2 - DIGIT 4: Indicates price class

CLASS	CODE
High	H
Police	K
Low	L
Medium	M
Premium	P
Special	S

LINE 2 - DIGIT 5: Indicates seat and fabric type

SEAT	CODE
Cloth & Vinyl Bench	1
All Vinyl Bench	2
Cloth & Leather Bench	A
All Leather Bench	M
Cloth & Vinyl Bench Split Back	3
All Vinyl Bench Split Back	4
Cloth & Leather Bench Split Back	B
All Leather Bench Split Back	P
Cloth & Vinyl Bucket	5
All Vinyl Bucket	6
Cloth & Leather Bucket	C
All Leather Bucket	R
Cloth & Vinyl 50/50	7
All Vinyl 50/50	8
Cloth & Leather 50/50	D
All Leather 50/50	L
Cloth & Vinyl Special Design	9
All Vinyl Special Design	H
Cloth & Leather Special Design	E
All Leather Special Design	T
Cloth 60/40	F
Cloth & Vinyl 60/40	W
All Vinyl 60/40	X
All Leather 60/40	Y

LINE 2 - DIGITS 6 & 7: Indicates interior color

FABRIC COLOR	CODE
Dove Silver	A3
Blue	B3
Medium Blue	B6
Blue & White	BW
Red	E7
Red & White	EW
Green	F6
Green	FF
Green & White	FW
Gold, Black, White	KW
Parchment	L3
Canyon Red	R4
Red & White	RW
Chestnut	T7
Tan	U5
Tan & White	UW
Black	X9
Black & White	XW
Gold	Y3
Gold & White	YW

LINE 2 - DIGITS 8, 9 & 10: Indicate upper door frame color, not listed

LINE 2 - DIGIT 11: Indicate the month of manufacture

MONTH	CODE
January	1
February	2
March	3
April	4
May	5
June	6
July	7
August	8
September	9
October	A
November	B
December	C

LINE 2 - DIGIT 12 & 13: Indicate the day of month of manufacture

LINE 2 - LAST SIX DIGITS: Indicate production sequence number

LINE 3 - DIGITS 1, 2 & 3: Indicate upper body color or vinyl roof codes

COLOR	CODE
Full Vinyl Roof Blue	V1B
Halo Vinyl Roof Blue	V2B
Landau Vinyl Roof Blue	V3B
Canopy Vinyl Roof Blue	V4B
Canopy Vinyl Roof w/Opera Window Blue	V5B
Full Vinyl Roof Green	V1F
Halo Vinyl Roof Green	V2F
Landau Vinyl Roof Green	V3F
Canopy Vinyl Roof Green	V4F
Canopy Vinyl Roof w/Opera Window Green	V5F
Full Vinyl Roof Red	V1R
Halo Vinyl Roof Red	V2R
Landau Vinyl Roof Red	V3R
Canopy Vinyl Roof Red	V4R
Canopy Vinyl Roof w/Opera Window Red	V5R
Full Vinyl Roof Red	V1E
Halo Vinyl Roof Red	V2E
Landau Vinyl Roof Red	V3E
Canopy Vinyl Roof Red	V4E
Canopy Vinyl Roof w/Opera Window Red	V5E
Full Vinyl Roof Black	V1X
Halo Vinyl Roof Black	V2X
Landau Vinyl Roof Black	V3X
Canopy Vinyl Roof Black	V4X
Canopy Vinyl Roof w/Opera Window Black	V5X
Full Vinyl Roof White	V1W
Halo Vinyl Roof White	V2W
Landau Vinyl Roof White	V3W
Canopy Vinyl Roof White	V4W
Canopy Vinyl Roof w/Opera Window Black White	V5W
Full Vinyl Roof Tan	V1U
Landau Vinyl Roof Tan	V3U
Full Vinyl Roof Silver	V1A
Halo Vinyl Roof Silver	V2A
Landau Vinyl Roof Silver	V3A
Canopy Vinyl Roof Silver	V4A
Canopy Vinyl Roof w/Opera Window Silver	V5A
Full Vinyl Roof Gold	V1Y
Halo Vinyl Roof Gold	V2Y
Canopy Vinyl Roof Gold	V4Y
Canopy Vinyl Roof w/Opera Window Gold	V5Y
Full Vinyl Roof Parchment	V1L
Landau Vinyl Roof Parchment	V3L
Canopy Vinyl Roof Parchment	V4L
Canopy Vinyl Roof w/Opera Window Parchment	V5L

ENGINE NUMBER

THE ENGINE IDENTIFICATION NUMBER for 6-cylinder engines is located at the right front of the block below #1 spark plug.

ENGINE NUMBERS for 318 and 360 CID V-8 engines are found at the left front of the block below the cylinder head. The engine number for 400 engines is found on the right side of the block adjacent to the distributor. The engine number for 440 engines is located on the left bank adjacent to the front tappet rail.

The following identification will be included in the engine serial number:

225 ENGINE
7225R21024A

THE FIRST DIGIT designates the model year and/or plant.

THE THREE NUMBERS following the model year and/or plant are the cubic inch displacement.

THE LETTER following the model identification is the engine usage code.

THE NUMBER following the engine usage is the shift built.

THE FOUR NUMBERS following the shift built are the date code.

THE LETTER following the date code is a parts identification code. These codes are explained below.

318 & 360 ENGINES
7M31810242579

THE NUMBER AND LETTER designate the model year and/or plant.

THE THREE NUMBERS following the model year and/or plant are the cubic inch displacement.

THE FOUR NUMBERS following the model identification are the date code.

THE FOUR NUMBERS following the date code are the daily sequence number (optional usage).

400 & 440 ENGINES
7T400H10242A

THE NUMBER AND LETTER designate the model year and/or plant.

THE THREE NUMBERS following the model year and/or plant are the cubic inch displacement.

THE LETTER following the model identification is the engine type.

THE FOUR NUMBERS following the engine type are the date code.

THE NUMBER following the date code is the shift built.

THE LETTER following the shift built is a parts identification code. These codes are explained below.

ENGINE SERIAL NUMBER & PARTS IDENTIFICATION CODES & SYMBOLS DEFINED:

	CODE
Oversize Cylinder Bore	A
Cast Crankshaft	E
Standard 4 BC	H
High Performance	HP
Toluca Engine Plant	K
Low Compression	LC
Mound Road Engine	M
Passenger Car Engine	R
Special Engine	S
Trenton Engine	T
Windsor Engine	W
O/S Valve Guide	X

EXAMPLE ("A" Engine Family)
7M318R09101234

In the example above:

7M	Model Year and/or Build Plant
318	Cubic Inch Displacement
R	Regular Fuel may be used
0910	Build date code (0910 is September 10)
1234	Daily sequence number (optional usage)

EXAMPLE ("B" and "G" Engine Family)
7T440R8-222

In the example above:

7T	Model Year and/or Build Plant
440R	CID and Type
8-22	Build date code
2	Shift built

VOLARE ENGINES

CID	NO. CYL.	HORSE-POWER	COMP. RATIO	CARB.
225	6	100	8.4:1	1 BC
225	6	110	8.4:1	2 BC
318	8	145	8.5:1	2 BC
360	8	155	8.4:1	2 BC
360	8	175	8.4:1	4 BC

PLYMOUTH ENGINES

CID	NO. CYL.	HORSE-POWER	COMP. RATIO	CARB.
225	6	110	8.4:1	2 BC
318	8	145	8.5:1	2 BC
318	8	145	8.5:1	2 BC
360	8	155	8.4:1	2 BC
400	8	190	8.2:1	4 BC
440	8	195	8.2:1	4 BC

1978 PLYMOUTH FURY WAGON

1978 PLYMOUTH FURY WAGON

1978 PLYMOUTH HORIZON

1978 PLYMOUTH HORIZON

1978 PLYMOUTH FURY

1978 PLYMOUTH FURY SALON

1978 PLYMOUTH VOLARE

1978 PLYMOUTH VOLARE WAGON

VEHICLE IDENTIFICATION NUMBER

PLYMOUTH
HL41G8B123456

Located on a plate attached to the left side of the instrument panel, visible through the windshield.

FIRST DIGIT: Identifies the car make

MAKE	CODE
Volare	H
Horizon	M
Fury	R
Caravelle	B

SECOND DIGIT: Identifies the price class

CLASS	CODE
High	H
Police	K
Low	L
Medium	M
Premium	P
Special	S

THIRD & FOURTH DIGITS: Identify the body type

TYPE	CODE
2-Dr. Hardtop	23
2-Dr. Hatchback	24
2-Dr. Coupe	29
4-Dr. Sedan	41
4-Dr. Hardtop	43
4-Dr. Hatchback	44
2-Seat Station Wagon	45
3-Seat Station Wagon	46

FIFTH DIGIT: Identifies the engine

CID	CODE
104.7 CID (1.7L) 2 BC 4-Cyl.	A
225 CID 1 BC 6-Cyl.	C
225 CID 2 BC 6-Cyl.	D
Special Order 6-Cyl.	E
318 CID 8-Cyl. 2 BC SD	G
360 CID 8-Cyl.	J
360 CID 2 BC 8-Cyl.	K
360 CID Hi-Perf. 8-Cyl.	L
400 CID 4 BC 8-Cyl.	N
Special Order 8-Cyl.	Z

SIXTH DIGIT: Identifies the year
8 - 1978

SEVENTH DIGIT: Identifies the assembly plant

PLANT	CODE
Jefferson Ave., Detroit, MI	C
Belvidere, IL	D
Newark, NJ	F
St. Louis, MO	G
Windsor, Ontario, CAN	R

LAST SIX DIGITS: Identify the production sequence nummber starting at each plant with 100001

EXAMPLE

H	L	41	G	8	B	123456
Car Make	Price Class	Body Type	Engine	Model Year	Asm Plant	Production Sequence Number

BODY CODE PLATE

THE BODY CODE PLATE is located in the engine compartment on the left wheel housing, fender side shield or radiator yoke.

THE BODY CODE PLATE is read left to right, bottom to top. The information on the plate includes the car S.O. Number and the trim and paint codes.

CHRYSLER MOTORS CORPORATION				Line
XXX	XXX	XXX	XXX	6
XXX	XXX	XXX	XXX	5
XXX	XXX	XXX	XXX	4
XXX	XXX	XXX	XXX	3
XXX	XXX	XXX	XXX	2
XXX	XXX	XXX	XXX	1

LINE 1 - DIGITS 1, 2 & 3: Indicate engine codes

CID	CODE
104.7 CID (1.7L) 2 BC 4-Cyl.	E12
225 CID 1 BC 6-Cyl.	E24
225 CID 2 BC 6-Cyl.	E26
Special Order 6-Cyl.	E99
318 CID 8-Cyl. 2 BC SD	E44
360 CID 8-Cyl.	E55
360 CID 2 BC 8-Cyl.	E57
360 CID Hi-Perf. 8-Cyl.	E58
400 CID 4 BC 8-Cyl.	E64
Special Order 8-Cyl.	E99

LINE 1 - DIGITS 4, 5 & 6: Indicate transmission codes

TRANSMISSION	CODE
3-Spd. Manual Floor Shift	D13
3-Spd. Std. Manual Clm. Shift	D14
3-Spd. H.D. Manual Clm. Shift	D15
4-Spd. Standard	D21
4-Spd. Manual Trans./Ax.	D22
4-Spd. O.D.	D24
Standard A904	D31
Standard A998	D32
Standard A999	D33
Standard Automatic	D34
H.D. A727	D35
Standard A727	D36
A404 Trans./Ax.	D37
H.D. A904	D38

LINE 1 - DIGIT 7: Indicates car line

MAKE	CODE
Volare	H
Horizon	M
Fury	R
Caravelle	B

LINE 1 - DIGIT 8: Indicates price class

CLASS	CODE
High	H
Police	K
Low	L
Medium	M
Premium	P
Special	S

LINE 1 - DIGIT 9 & 10: Indicate body type

TYPE	CODE
2-Dr. Hardtop	23
2-Dr. Hatchback	24
2-Dr. Coupe	29
4-Dr. Sedan	41
4-Dr. Hardtop	43
4-Dr. Hatchback	44
2-Seat Station Wagon	45
3-Seat Station Wagon	46

LINE 1- DIGIT 11: Indicates engine code

CID	CODE
104.7 CID (1.7L) 2 BC 4-Cyl.	A
225 CID 1 BC 6-Cyl.	C
225 CID 2 BC 6-Cyl.	D
Special Order 6-Cyl.	E
318 CID 8-Cyl. 2 BC SD	G
360 CID 8-Cyl.	J
360 CID 2 BC 8-Cyl.	K
360 CID Hi-Perf. 8-Cyl.	L
400 CID 4 BC 8-Cyl.	N
Special Order 8-Cyl.	Z

LINE 1 - DIGIT 12: Indicates model year
8 - 1978

LINE 1 - DIGIT 13: Indicates the assembly plant

PLANT	CODE
Jefferson Ave., Detroit, MI	C
Belvidere, IL	D
Newark, NJ	F
St. Louis, MO	G
Windsor, Ontario, CAN	R

LINE 1 - LAST SIX DIGITS: Indicate production sequence number

LINE 2 - DIGITS 1, 2 & 3: Indicate body paint color, or fleet or special order paint code

COLOR	CODE
Pewter Gray Metallic	RA2
Starlight Blue Sunfire Metallic	PB9
Cadet Blue Metallic	PB3
Wedgewood Blue	PB2
Mint Green Metallic	RF3
Augusta Green Sunfire Metallic	RF9
Citron Metallic	RJ3
Jasmine Yellow	PY1
Classic Cream	RY3
Spanish Gold Metallic	LY9
Golden Fawn	KY4
Caramel Tan Metallic	MU3
Light Mocha Tan	PT2
Spitfire Orange	MV1
Bright Canyon Red	RR4
Tapestry Red Sunfire Metallic	RR7
Spinnaker White	EW!
Formal Black	TX9
Crimson Red Sunfire Metallic	RR9
Dark Silver Metallic	JA5

LINE 2 - DIGITS 4, 5, 6 & 7: Indicate trim code

LINE 2 - DIGIT 4: Indicates price class

CLASS	CODE
High	H
Police	K
Low	L
Medium	M
Premium	P
Special	S

LINE 2 - DIGIT 5: Indicates seat and fabric type

SEAT	CODE
Cloth & Vinyl Straight Bench	1
Vinyl Straight Bench	2
Cloth & Leather Straight Bench	A
Leather & Vinyl Straight Bench	M
Cloth Straight Bench	N
Cloth & Vinyl Bench Split Back w/Center Arm Rest	3
Vinyl Bench Split Back w/Center Arm Rest	4
Cloth & Leather Bench Split Back w/Center Arm Rest	B
Leather & Vinyl Bench Split Back w/Center Arm Rest	P
Cloth Bench Split Back w/Center Arm Rest	G
Cloth & Vinyl Non-recline Bucket	5
Vinyl Non-recline Bucket	6
Cloth & Leather Non-recline Bucket	C
Leather & Vinyl Non-recline Bucket	R
Cloth Non-recline Bucket	J
Cloth & Vinyl 50/50 or Dual Recline Blucket	7
Vinyl 50/50 or Dual Recline Bucket	8
Cloth & Leather 50/50 or Dual Recline Bucket	D
Leather & Vinyl 50/50 or Dual Recline Bucket	L
Cloth 50/50 or Dual Recline Bucket	Z
Cloth & Vinyl Recline 60/40	W
Vinyl Recline 60/40	X
Cloth & Leather Recline 60/40	K
Leather & Vinyl Recline 60/40	Y
Cloth Recline 60/40	F
Cloth & Vinyl Non-recline 60/40	9
Vinyl Non Recline 60/40	H
Cloth & Leather Non-recline 60/40	E
Leather & Vinyl Non-recline 60/40	T
Cloth Non-recline 60/40	V

LINE 2 - DIGITS 6 & 7: Indicates interior color

FABRIC COLOR	CODE
Dove Silver	A3
Blue	B3
Blue & White	BW
Green	F6
Green & White	FW
Canyon Red	R4
Red & White	RW
Tan	U5
Tan & White	UW
Black	X9
Black & White	XW
Gold	Y3
Gold & White	YW

LINE 2 - DIGITS 8, 9 & 10: Indicate upper door frame color, not listed

LINE 2 - DIGIT 11: Indicates the month of manufacture

MONTH	CODE
January	1
February	2
March	3
April	4
May	5
June	6
July	7
August	8
September	9
October	A
November	B
December	C

LINE 2 - DIGITS 12 & 13: Indicate the day of month of manufacture

LINE 2 - LAST SIX DIGITS: Indicate production sequence number

LINE 3 - DIGITS 1, 2 & 3: Indicate upper body color or vinyl roof codes

COLOR	CODE
Full Vinyl Roof Blue	V1B
Halo Vinyl Roof Blue	V2B
Landau Vinyl Roof Blue	V3B
Canopy Vinyl Roof Blue	V4B
Canopy Vinyl Roof w/Opera Window Blue	V5B
Full Vinyl Roof Green	V1F
Halo Vinyl Roof Green	V2F
Landau Vinyl Roof Green	V3F
Canopy Vinyl Roof Green	V4F
Canopy Vinyl Roof w/Opera Window Green	V5F
Full Vinyl Roof Red	V1R
Halo Vinyl Roof Red	V2R
Landau Vinyl Roof Red	V3R
Canopy Vinyl Roof Red	V4R
Canopy Vinyl Roof w/Opera Window Red	V5R
Full Vinyl Roof Black	V1X
Halo Vinyl Roof Black	V2X
Landau Vinyl Roof Black	V3X
Canopy Vinyl Roof Black	V4X
Canopy Vinyl Roof w/Opera Window Black	V5X
Full Vinyl Roof White	V1W
Halo Vinyl Roof White	V2W
Landau Vinyl Roof White	V3W
Canopy Vinyl Roof White	V4W
Canopy Vinyl Roof w/Opera Window Black White	V5W
Full Vinyl Roof Tan	V1U
Landau Vinyl Roof Tan	V3U
Full Vinyl Roof Silver	V1A
Halo Vinyl Roof Silver	V2A
Landau Vinyl Roof Silver	V3A
Canopy Vinyl Roof Silver	V4A
Canopy Vinyl Roof w/Opera Window Silver	V5A
Full Vinyl Roof Gold	V1Y
Halo Vinyl Roof Gold	V2Y
Canopy Vinyl Roof Gold	V4Y
Canopy Vinyl Roof w/Opera Window Gold	V5Y

ENGINE NUMBER

THE ENGINE IDENTIFICATION NUMBER for 6-cylinder engines is located at the right front of the block below #1 spark plug.

ENGINE NUMBERS for 318 and 360 CID V-8 engines are found at the left front of the block below the cylinder head. The engine number for 400 engines is found on the right side of the block adjacent to the distributor.

The following identification will be included in the engine serial number:

225 ENGINE
8225R21024A

THE FIRST DIGIT designates the model year and/or plant.

THE THREE NUMBERS following the model year and/or plant are the cubic inch displacement.

THE LETTER following the model identification is the engine usage code.

THE NUMBER following the engine usage is the shift built.

THE FOUR NUMBERS following the shift built are the date code.

THE LETTER following the date code is a parts identification code. These codes are explained below.

318 & 360 ENGINES
8M31810241234

THE NUMBER AND LETTER designate the model year and/or plant.

THE THREE NUMBERS following the model year and/or plant are the cubic inch displacement.

THE FOUR NUMBERS following the model identification are the date code.

THE FOUR NUMBERS following the date code are the daily sequence number (optional usage).

400 ENGINES
8T400H10242A

THE NUMBER AND LETTER designate the model year and/or plant.

THE THREE NUMBERS following the model year and/or plant are the cubic inch displacement.

THE LETTER following the model identification is the engine type.

THE FOUR NUMBERS following the engine type are the date code.

THE NUMBER following the date code is the shift built.

THE LETTER following the shift built is a parts identification code. These codes are explained below.

ENGINE SERIAL NUMBER & PARTS IDENTIFICATION CODES & SYMBOLS DEFINED:

	CODE
Oversize Cylinder Bore	A
Cast Crankshaft	E
Standard 4 BC	H
High Performance	HP
Toluca Engine Plant	K
Low Compression	LC
Mound Road Engine	M
Passenger Car Engine	R
Special Engine	S
Trenton Engine	T
Windsor Engine	W
O/S Valve Guide	X

SPECIAL NOTE: 1978 F-Body info:

The Super Coupe Package	A-67
The Street Kit Car Package	A-43
Volare Sport Wagon Package	A-47

EXAMPLE ("A" Engine Family)
8M318R09101234

In the example above:

8M	Model Year and/or Build Plant
318	Cubic Inch Displacement
R	Regular Fuel may be used
0910	Build date code (0910 is September 10)
1234	Daily sequence number (optional usage)

EXAMPLE ("B" and "G" Engine Family)
8T400R8-222

In the example above:

8T	Model Year and/or Build Plant
400R	CID and Type
8-22	Build date code
2	Shift built

ENGINES

CID	NO. CYL.	HORSE-POWER	COMP. RATIO	CARB.
104.7 (1.7L)	4	50	8.2:1	2 BC
104.7 (1.7L)	4	55	8.2:1	2 BC
225	6	90	8.4:1	1 BC
225	6	100	8.4:1	1 BC
225	6	110	8.4:1	2 BC
318	8	140	8.5:1	2 BC
318	8	145	8.5:1	2 BC
318	8	155	8.5:1	4 BC
360	8	155	8.4:1	2 BC
360	8	175	8.4:1	4 BC
400	8	190	8.2:1	4 BC

1979 PLYMOUTH HORIZON HATCHBACK

1979 PLYMOUTH HORIZON HATCHBACK

1979 PLYMOUTH VOLARE WAGON

1979 PLYMOUTH VOLARE WAGON

1979 PLYMOUTH VOLARE

1979 PLYMOUTH VOLARE

VEHICLE IDENTIFICATION NUMBER

```
PLYMOUTH
HL41G9A123456
```

Located on a plate attached to the left side of the instrument panel, visible through the windshield.

FIRST DIGIT: Identifies the car make

MAKE	CODE
Volare	H
Caravelle	B
Horizon	M

SECOND DIGIT: Identifies the price class

CLASS	CODE
High	H
Police	K
Low	L
Medium	M
Premium	P
Special	S

THIRD & FOURTH DIGITS: Identify the body type

TYPE	CODE
2-Dr. Hardtop	22
2-Dr. Hatchback	24
2-Dr. Coupe	29
4-Dr. Sedan	41
4-Dr. Hatchback	44
2-Seat Station Wagon	45

FIFTH DIGIT: Identifies the engine

CID	CODE
104.7 CID (1.7L) 4-Cyl.	A
225 CID 1 BC 6-Cyl.	C
225 CID 2 BC 6-Cyl. H.D.	D
Special Order 6-Cyl.	E
318 CID 2 BC 8-Cyl. S.D.	G
360 CID 8-Cyl.	J
360 CID 2 BC 8-Cyl.	K
360 CID Hi-Perf. 8-Cyl.	L
Special Order 8-Cyl.	Z

SIXTH DIGIT: Identifies the year
9 - 1979

SEVENTH DIGIT: Identifies the assembly plant

PLANT	CODE
Lynch Road, Detroit, MI	A
Belvidere, IL	D
Newark, NJ	F
St. Louis, MO	G
Windsor, Ontario, CAN	R

LAST SIX DIGITS: Identify the production sequence number starting at each plant with 100001

EXAMPLE

H	L	41	G	9	A	123456
Car Make	Price Class	Body Type	Engine	Model Year	Asm Plant	Production Sequence Number

BODY CODE PLATE

THE BODY CODE PLATE is located in the engine compartment on the left wheel housing, fender side shield or radiator yoke.

THE BODY CODE PLATE is read left to right, bottom to top. The information on the plate includes the car S.O. Number and the trim and paint codes.

```
CHRYSLER MOTORS
CORPORATION

                                        Line
  XXX  XXX  XXX  XXX                      6
  XXX  XXX  XXX  XXX                      5
  XXX  XXX  XXX  XXX                      4
  XXX  XXX  XXX  XXX                      3
  XXX  XXX  XXX  XXX                      2
  XXX  XXX  XXX  XXX                      1
```

LINE 1 - DIGITS 1, 2 & 3: Indicate engine codes

CID	CODE
104.7 CID (1.7L) 4-Cyl.	E12
225 CID 1 BC 6-Cyl.	E24
225 CID 2 BC 6-Cyl. H.D.	E27
Special Order 6-Cyl.	E99
318 CID 2 BC 8-Cyl. S.D.	E44
360 CID 8-Cyl.	E53
360 CID 2 BC 8-Cyl.	E57
360 CID Hi-Perf. 8-Cyl.	E58
Special Order 8-Cyl.	E99

LINE 1 - DIGITS 4, 5 & 6: Indicates transmission code

TRANSMISSION	CODE
3-Spd. Manual Floor Shift	D13
3-Spd. Std. Manual Clm. Shift	D14
3-Spd. H.D. Manual Clm. Shift	D15
4-Spd. Standard	D21
4-Spd. Manual Trans./Ax.	D22
4-Spd. O.D.	D24
Standard A904	D31
Standard A998	D32
Standard A999	D33
Standard Automatic	D34
H.D. A727	D35
Standard A727	D36
A404 Trans./Ax.	D37
H.D. A904	D38

LINE 1 - DIGIT 7: Indicates car line

MAKE	CODE
Volare	H
Caravelle	B
Horizon & TC3	M

LINE 1 - DIGIT 8: Indicates price class

CLASS	CODE
High	H
Police	K
Low	L
Medium	M
Premium	P
Special	S

LINE 1 - DIGIT 9 & 10: Indicate body type

TYPE	CODE
2-Dr. Hardtop	22
2-Dr. Hatchback	24
2-Dr. Coupe	29
4-Dr. Sedan	41
4-Dr. Hatchback	44
2-Seat Station Wagon	45

LINE 1 - DIGIT 11: Indicates engine code

CID	CODE
104.7 CID (1.7L) 4-Cyl.	A
225 CID 1 BC 6-Cyl.	C
225 CID 2 BC 6-Cyl. H.D.	D
Special Order 6-Cyl.	E
318 CID 2 BC 8-Cyl. S.D.	G
360 CID 8-Cyl.	J
360 CID 2 BC 8-Cyl.	K
360 CID Hi-Perf. 8-Cyl.	L
Special Order 8-Cyl.	Z

LINE 1 - DIGIT 12: Indicates model year
9 - 1979

LINE 1 - DIGIT 13: Indicates the assembly plant

PLANT	CODE
Lynch Road, Detroit, MI	A
Belvidere, IL	D
Newark, NJ	F
St. Louis, MO	G
Windsor, Ontario, CAN	R

LINE 1 - LAST SIX DIGITS: Indicate production sequence number.

LINE 2 - DIGITS 1, 2 & 3: Indicate body paint color, or fleet or special order paint code

COLOR	CODE
Medium Cashmere Metallic	ST5
Bright Yellow	SY4
Yellow Flame	2602
Sunburst Orange	5233
Light Silver Metallic	1592
Garnet Red Sunfire Metallic	SR9
Teal Green Sunfire Metallic	SG8
Regent Red Sunfire Metallic	SR8
Light Yellow	SY2
Sable Tan Sunfire Metallic	RT9
Ensign Blue Metallic	SB7
Nightwatch Blue	SC9
Smoked Gray Metallic	SA5
Pewter Gray Metallic	RA2
Cadet Blue Metallic	PB3
Spinnaker White	EW1
Formal Black	TX9
Turquoise Metallic	SQ6
Teal Frost Metallic	SG4
Flat Black	DX9
Chianti Red	SR5
Flame Orange	SV3
Light Cashmere	ST1

LINE 2 - DIGITS 4, 5, 6 & 7: Indicate trim code

LINE 2 - DIGIT 4: Indicates price class

CLASS	CODE
High	H
Police	K
Low	L
Medium	M
Premium	P
Special	S

LINE 2 - DIGIT 5: Indicates seat and fabric type

SEAT	CODE
Cloth & Vinyl Straight Bench	1
Vinyl Straight Bench	2
Cloth & Leather Straight Bench	A
Leather & Vinyl Straight Bench	M
Cloth Straight Bench	N
Cloth & Vinyl Bench Split Back w/Center Arm Rest	3
Vinyl Bench Split Back w/Center Arm Rest	4
Cloth & Leather Bench Split Back w/Center Arm Rest	B
Leather & Vinyl Bench Split Back w/Center Arm Rest	P
Cloth Bench Split Back w/Center Arm Rest	G
Cloth & Vinyl Non-recline Bucket	5
Vinyl Non-recline Bucket	6
Cloth & Leather Non-recline Bucket	C
Leather & Vinyl Non-recline Bucket	R
Cloth Non-recline Bucket	J
Cloth & Vinyl 50/50 or Dual Recline Bucket	7
Vinyl 50/50 or Dual Recline Buckeet	8
Cloth & Leather 50/50 or Dual Recline Bucket	D
Leather & Vinyl 50/50 or Dual Recline Bucket	L
Cloth 50/50 or Dual Recline Bucket	Z
Cloth & Vinyl Recline 60/40	W
Vinyl Recline 60/40	X
Cloth & Leather Recline 60/40	K
Leather & Vinyl Recline 60/40	Y
Cloth Recline 60/40	F
Cloth & Vinyl Non-recline 60/40	9
Vinyl Non-recline 60/40	H
Cloth & Leather Non-recline 60/40	E
Leather & Vinyl Non-recline 60/40	T
Cloth Non-recline 60/40	V

LINE 2 - DIGITS 6 & 7: Indicates interior color

FABRIC COLOR	CODE
Blue	B3
Red	R4
Black	X9
Cashmere	T3
Teal Green	G5
Red	R4
Red/Black Plaid	VX
Yellow/Black Plaid	YX

LINE 2 - DIGITS 8, 9 & 10: Indicate upper door frame color, not listed

LINE 2 - DIGIT 11: Indicates the month of manufacture

MONTH	CODE
January	1
February	2
March	3
April	4
May	5
June	6
July	7
August	8
September	9
October	A
November	B
December	C

LINE 2 - DIGITS 12 & 13: Indicate the day of month of manufacture

LINE 2 - LAST SIX DIGITS: Indicate production sequence number

LINE 3 - DIGITS 1, 2 & 3: Indicate upper body color vinyl roof codes

COLOR	CODE
Full Vinyl Roof Silver	V1A
Halo Vinyl Roof Silver	V2A
Landau Vinyl Roof Silver	V3A
Full Vinyl Roof Blue	V1B
Halo Vinyl Roof Blue	V2B
Landau Vinyl Roof Blue	V3B
Full Vinyl Roof Green	V1G
Halo Vinyl Roof Green	V2G
Landau Vinyl Roof Green	V3G
Full Vinyl Roof Red	V1R
Halo Vinyl Roof Red	V2R
Landau Vinyl Roof Red	V3R
Full Vinyl Roof Tan	V1U
Halo Vinyl Roof Tan	V2U
Landau Vinyl Roof Tan	V3U
Full Vinyl Roof White	V1W
Halo Vinyl Roof White	V2W
Landau Vinyl Roof White	V3W
Full Vinyl Roof Cream	V1Y
Halo Vinyl Roof Cream	V2Y
Landau Vinyl Roof Cream	V3Y

ENGINE NUMBER

THE ENGINE IDENTIFICATION NUMBER for 6-cylinder engines is located at the right front of the block below #1 spark plug.

ENGINE NUMBERS FOR 318 and 360 CID V-8 engines are found at the left front of the block below the cylinder head.

The following identification will be included in the engine serial number:

225 ENGINE
9225R21024A

THE FIRST DIGIT designates the model year and/or plant.

THE THREE NUMBERS following the model year and/or plant are the cubic inch displacement.

THE LETTER following the model identification is the engine usage code.

THE NUMBER following the engine usage is the shift built.

THE FOUR NUMBERS following the shift built are the date code.

THE LETTER following the date code is a parts identification code. These codes are explained below.

318 & 360 ENGINES
9M31810241234

THE NUMBER AND LETTER designate the model year and/or plant.

THE THREE NUMBERS following the model year and/or plant are the cubic inch displacement.

THE FOUR NUMBERS following the model identification are the date code.

THE FOUR NUMBERS following the date code are the daily sequence number (optional usage).

ENGINE SERIAL NUMBER & PARTS IDENTIFICATION CODES & SYMBOLS DEFINED:

	CODE
Oversize Cylinder Bore	A
Cast Crankshaft	E
Standard 4 BC	H
High Performance	HP
Toluca Engine Plant	K
Low Compression	LC
Mound Road Engine	M
Passenger Car Engine	R
Special Engine	S
Trenton Engine	T
Windsor Engine	W
O/S Valve Guide	X

EXAMPLE ("A" Engine Family)
9M318R09101234

In the example above:
9M	Model Year and/or Build Plant
318	Cubic Inch Displacement
R	Regular Fuel may be used
0910	Build date code (0910 is September 10)
1234	Daily sequence number (optional usage)

ENGINES

CID	NO. CYL.	HORSE-POWER	COMP. RATIO	CARB.
104.7 (1.7L)	4	70	8.2:1	2 BC
104.7 (1.7L)	4	70	8.2:1	2 BC
225	6	100	8.4:1	1 BC
225	6	110	8.4:1	2 BC
318	8	135	8.5:1	2 BC
360	8	195	8.0:1	4 BC